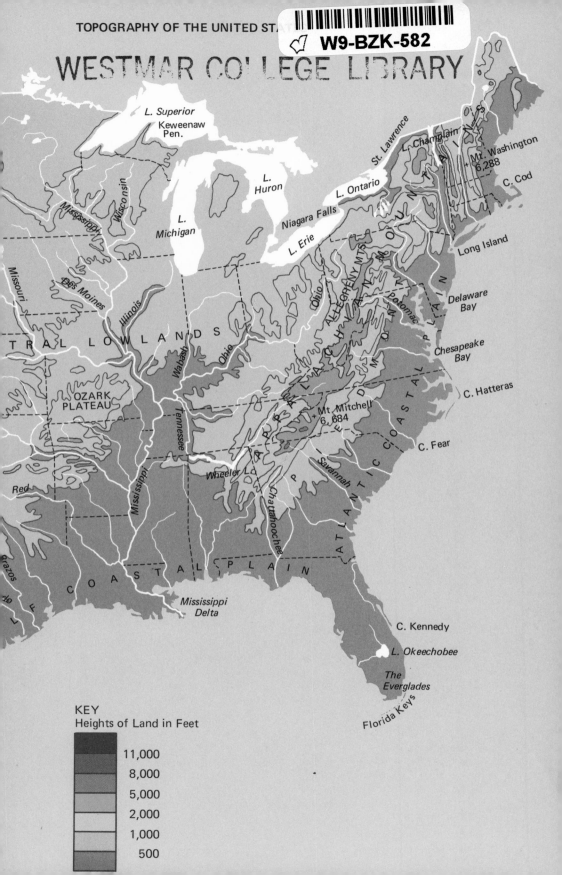

TOPOGRAPHY OF THE UNITED STATES

L. Superior
Keweenaw Pen.
L. Huron
L. Michigan
Mississippi
Wisconsin
St. Lawrence
L. Champlain
Mt. Washington 6,288
C. Cod
L. Ontario
Niagara Falls
L. Erie
Long Island
Missouri
Des Moines
Illinois
Ohio
ALLEGHENY MTS.
Potomac
Delaware Bay
TRAL LOWLANDS
Wabash
Ohio
Chesapeake Bay
OZARK PLATEAU
Tennessee
C. Hatteras
Mt. Mitchell 6,684
C. Fear
Red
Mississippi
Wheeler L.
Chattahoochee
Savannah
ATLANTIC COASTAL PLAIN
APPALACHIAN PIEDMONT
Brazos
GULF COASTAL PLAIN
Mississippi Delta
C. Kennedy
L. Okeechobee
The Everglades
Florida Keys

KEY
Heights of Land in Feet

11,000
8,000
5,000
2,000
1,000
500

AMERICAN
ECONOMIC
GROWTH
AN ECONOMIST'S
HISTORY OF THE
UNITED STATES

AMERICAN ECONOMIC GROWTH
AN ECONOMIST'S HISTORY OF THE UNITED STATES

By
LANCE E. DAVIS, California Institute of Technology
RICHARD A. EASTERLIN, University of Pennsylvania
WILLIAM N. PARKER, Yale University
DOROTHY S. BRADY, University of Pennsylvania
ALBERT FISHLOW, University of California, Berkeley
ROBERT E. GALLMAN, University of North Carolina
STANLEY LEBERGOTT, Wesleyan University
ROBERT E. LIPSEY, Queens College and NBER
DOUGLASS C. NORTH, University of Washington
NATHAN ROSENBERG, University of Wisconsin
EUGENE SMOLENSKY, University of Wisconsin
PETER TEMIN, Massachusetts Institute of Technology

Harper & Row, Publishers
New York, Evanston, San Francisco, London

Acknowledgments relating to individual chapters are given in the text. We wish here, however, to record our indebtedness to the publisher, Harper & Row. John W. Greenman was a model of patience and gentle encouragement throughout the long gestation period of the manuscript. And we are especially grateful for the tender, loving care of two remarkable editors, Sarah P. Cerny and Claire T. Rubin. The human as well as professional qualities which they brought to this job were deeply appreciated.

The inside back cover map is from the U.S. Bureau of the Census, *Census of Population: 1960, United States Summary* (Washington: U.S. Government Printing Office, 1963), p. S22, fig. 26.

AMERICAN ECONOMIC GROWTH:
AN ECONOMIST'S HISTORY OF THE UNITED STATES
Copyright © 1972 by Harper & Row

Standard Book Number: 06-041557-6

Library of Congress Catalog Card Number: 75-154879

CONTENTS

LIST OF TABLES

PREFACE

The growth of the American economy is a subject which still awaits its historian—or rather its economist. Many good books have been written describing its events. Much attention has been paid to its effects on the lives, society, and politics of Americans. Divergent judgments have been offered on the importance of one causal factor or another, and particularly on the role of business leaders in bringing the whole thing to pass, and on the morality of their activities as they did so. Yet a student of economics cannot make very much of all this. Even in accounts of individual episodes and institutions—the bank war, the slave plantations, the trusts—he often gains no real sense of the socioeconomic system which produced them and whose operation was affected by them. No comprehensive model has been clothed with the living materials of history, to show how the growth-inducing elements reacted on one another to propel and sustain this country's astonishing record.

The authors of this book do not claim that their efforts have filled this need. For reasons discussed in Chapter 1, we are not able to offer a comprehensive model of the growth process of the sort that would admit of mathematical expression or statistical testing. We do feel that our studies, knit loosely together according to a rough pattern, are a start—perhaps even a substantial one—in the direction of a better understanding. Each of us has done empirical research on one of the components of economic growth—resources, population, technology, transportation, and others. In doing so he has come to feel that he has hold of one of the pieces of the puzzle. Here we have laid these pieces together on the same table, in a design that may suggest something of the pattern.

As economists, we know that economic theory's powerful lens focuses clearly on small areas, distorts the periphery of the subject, and blacks out altogether certain parts of an historical scene. As research scholars, we are aware that some areas which our combined interests do not reach have been left untouched. As human beings who grew up in the same decades of American history, we assume that we have formed values and notions of relevance that have intruded themselves here. But as teachers, we have long wished for a book such as this which would help us transmit to our students some of the traditional materials mixed with new findings and dominated by new points of view. And, as Americans, we write in the hope of adding to our fellow citizens' understanding of the American growth record, to enable us all to see it—and the achievements and problems it has created for us—in a long perspective.

For us, writing this book has been an exciting and educating experience. When we first came together to discuss the project—on a snowbound weekend in Lafayette, Indiana, after a conference—we discovered many common attitudes toward both the use of economics in history and the important aspects of the growth process as exemplified in the United States. We also found out a fact that was surprising to us, though perhaps predictable by an outside observer—that when we pooled our interests they appeared to cover most of what we considered important. It was as if Adam Smith's invisible hand had been at work in the academic marketplace to call forth such specialization and complementarity. Our book has thus from the outset been conceived of as a common enterprise, and all of us share the responsibility for its sins. In each case a subject was assigned to the author who had made that topic the focus of his own research. The section on output growth was drafted by Robert Gallman, that on consumption by Dorothy Brady, those on resources and agriculture by William Parker, population by Richard Easterlin, labor by Stanley Lebergott, technology by Nathan Rosenberg, capital and finance by Lance Davis, manufacturing by Peter Temin, transportation by Albert Fishlow, international trade by Robert Lipsey, urbanization by Eugene Smolensky, and government by Douglass North.

The contributions exhibit individuality in style and approach and we have not tried to suppress these. But each of us read much of what the others wrote and we have been forthright in our criticisms of one another. It is our hope that the structure that joins our studies will prove strong enough to bear their weight, and that the unity we feel—deriving from common attitudes, common training, common concerns about American economic growth—will rise to the surface and make itself felt by the students, economists and historians alike, who choose (or are assigned) to read this text. Surely an economist's history may take its motto from the face of the coins of the United States. "The one out of the many" is a strength we would share with the economy and the nation whose growth we examine in these pages.

AMERICAN
ECONOMIC
GROWTH
AN ECONOMIST'S
HISTORY OF THE
UNITED STATES

1
INTRODUCTION

One hundred and fifty years ago, the United States was a growing country of great expectations. Its people, white and black, were already markedly different from their European or African stock, but they were not enormously richer. What white Americans had in abundance was hope—an image of a life vastly more cheerful than the life on an English estate, or in Dickens' London, or on a continental peasant holding. Black Americans were slaves, and the worst feature of their slavery was that it denied by law that hope, that opportunity for improvement, on which the ambitions of free men fed. Between 1840 and 1920 the American hope was shared by over 25 million immigrants, and for many of them, or for their children, it was realized. A glimmer of it was even seen after the Civil War by the freedmen, imprisoned in the cast-off shell of southern slavery, and it impelled them in time to break out in massive waves of migration northward.

By the start of the twentieth century, Americans began consciously to feel themselves a rich nation, and potentially a powerful one. Subsequent events, including two world wars, more than bore out this feeling. Following World War II, however, American wealth and power began to unsettle the rest of the world, and in the 1960s it began to trouble Americans themselves. Recently the strength of this country has seemed almost to overwhelm both the world order and the rather frail domestic social basis on which it had been balanced. In the world at large, the United States has come to be looked on somewhat as a spaceship, equipped with death-dealing rays and inhabited by creatures from another planet. To alarmists at home, it has begun to seem that the massive growth of the American economy must be controlled before it destroys the natural basis of life on the continent and drains the entire planet of resources. These guilty nightmares are not relieved by the knowledge that similar growth has occurred elsewhere—notably in Europe and Japan—and that the efforts of a large segment of mankind are directed to initiating it in countries now oppressed by poverty.

Whether for good or ill—and more likely for a bit of both—American history has provided the modern world with its most conspicuous example of this sweeping transformation we call economic growth. With the growth in volume of output have come changes in the ratio of capital to output, a changing mix of material inputs, alterations in labor skills, a shifting composition of the final product, and a sharp shift in the distribution of productive resources among industries and regions. As conditions for this growth over 150 years, the labor force and capital stock have increased, the market has moved out across the continent, technologies for production and distribution have appeared and been replaced, and demand patterns have been adapted to new possibilities and new constraints. The growing economy has made increasing use of money and credit instruments in ever more sophisticated forms and has created complex organizations for amassing capital and controlling human effort.

These economic changes have been accompanied by equally dramatic changes in American society. Birth rates and death rates have fallen; family size has changed; men have moved their places of residence; schools, churches, political organizations, and the state have undergone changes in their social functions and sometimes in their sustaining ideals. The influence of the growing economy has penetrated into the intimate depths of Americans' daily experience, altering its quality. The attitudes, aspirations, and experience of individuals have been shattered and reshaped by the realities of income growth and the impact of massive affluence.

In this book, we deal with the history of this growth and of the changing conditions behind it, using categories and theories that economists have developed for such study. The present chapter first examines the book's choice of topics and their arrangement. Then it looks at the methods and materials employed to shape and add substance to these topics, and at the attitude toward historical study which the book reveals. Finally, this chapter attempts a candid assessment of the value and extent of the study on which we have embarked.

THE FRAMEWORK OF THE STUDY

First, consider the American economy as a great machine, devouring every year the inputs of resources, labor, and capital and producing a great quantity of goods for final use: the gross national product. Part I of our book exhibits the record of this economic machine's output and discusses what that output has meant in terms of human wants and needs. Chapter 2 examines the size and shape of the American economy, as it was transformed from the separate economies of farm households and artisan shops of the early nineteenth century to the great structure of independent firms and industries of the present day. The familiar series of national income and product provide the basic framework for this chapter. Insofar as possible, growth rates are computed and the composition of the flows of inputs and output is measured. Something is even said about that most intimate of economic matters, the distribution of income among social and economic groups. Chapter 3 narrows the focus to consumer goods and examines how consumers have spent their increasing incomes over the past 150 years. Part I thus presents our object of study: the material result of American economic growth. The remainder of the book is devoted largely to examining the elements that combined to cause this growth in size and efficiency.

Increases in the supply of basic inputs—resources and labor—are examined first in Part II. Chapter 4 brings onstage America's expanse of land and the resources it contains. These resources first came within the sphere of European culture, to be exploited by modern technology, as a result of the burst of European expansion following the Renaissance. The resources in the area east of the Mississippi River came under England's influence during her great political and commercial expansion in the seventeenth and eighteenth centuries. These resources became American through the wars and treaties of 1776–1848 and were welded together politically and socially by the explorations, trade, and settlement of that era. But the fulfillment of three conditions was required to convert them into raw materials for the American economic machine. First, they had to be "discovered." Information about their physical characteristics had to be transmitted to the farmers, miners, and lumbermen who would exploit them. Second, they had to be brought within the economic reach of markets, and techniques for exploiting and shipping them had to be devised. Third, the gains from resource discovery and exploitation had to be related through a system of ownership rights to the risks and costs incurred. As these conditions were met, the resources could be rapidly utilized to form the material foundation of a growing economy.

The second basic resource—a relatively skilled labor force—also depended for its growth upon a variety of socioeconomic developments, and ultimately upon the process of population growth, examined in Chapter 5. Since people, like ideas and materials, come from both importation and natural growth, migration and natural increase are both considered. The natural increase of a population depends on birth and death rates; their movement, their underlying causes, and their net effect on the course of economic growth are the principal parts of the story. Consideration is given, too, to qualitative improvements in the population—its longevity, health, and schooling. But the human urge to migrate toward a freer and richer environment also finds expression in American history, in the movement of Europeans to the Western hemisphere and of Europeans and their descendants from east to west within North America. Similar motives impelled a surplus rural population to move, first from farms in the East to textile mills, and later from Midwest farms to the towns and urban centers of new industrial districts. This native flow was augmented by streams from the rural areas and ghettos of Europe, from Ireland, and from Southern and Eastern Europe to the cities along the Atlantic Coast and the Great Lakes. The rural–urban movement continued in recent decades as blacks and poor whites have left farms in the South for northern cities. These two types of rural exodus—the movement to new land and the crowding into urban centers—are discussed not only in Chapter 5 but elsewhere in this book, as part of the agricultural and urban expansion.

From the increasing population a labor force for farms and industries was formed in the nineteenth century. This labor force has grown in skills and organization. In Chapter 6 the human sources of this growth are surveyed, and the shifting distribution of the stream among occupations and industries is measured. The growth in productivity of the labor force is seen to reflect the changes in the whole American environment—the resource discoveries, the transportation improvements, the technical changes, and the accumulation of capital. The more traditional subjects of labor history are also treated here— the shift from slavery to wage and tenant labor in the South, the workers' loss of independence with industrial growth, and the growth of unionism's "countervailing power" against employees' and employers' combinations.

Part II, then, exhibits the histories of the resource and labor inputs into the economic machine. Part III looks at the machine itself. Chapter 7 presents the technical basis of the drastic and dynamic changes in the economy's productive processes and equipment, and explores the intellectual and social bases of these developments. In doing so, it takes us into a stream of history uniquely modern. Populations have grown, new lands have been discovered, trade has flourished in many places and periods in history. Even the characteristic institutions of capitalism—the use of money, banks, and credit and the organization of trade for private gain—found footholds earlier and elsewhere. But the outpouring of new inventions, processes, and materials that began in Europe during the Renaissance, that drew on the unfolding natural science in the seventeenth and early eighteenth centuries and has expanded since 1800 into an irresistible flood of gathering force—this phenomenon marks off the modern world from the rest of human history. Chapter 7 is concerned both with the peculiarly American features of the ideas that came to fruition in the United States, and with the mixture of economic, intellectual, and purely random elements that controlled the direction of this great movement.

In Chapters 8, 9, and 10 on capital formation and financing, we move into the last of the supply variables in our description of the physical sources of the growth of total output. *Capital* is the economist's term for the stock of applied techniques embodied in the fixed plant, equipment, construction, and land improvements of the producing sectors—and that stock is an important determinant of the pace and direction of economic growth. It is through the renewal of society's capital stock that new technological developments become a part of the productive process; the more rapidly this stock expands, the more quickly will new techniques be diffused. But if the capital stock is to grow, two conditions must be met. First, income receivers (firms or individuals) must decide (either willingly or as the result of financial pressure) to retain in some form a portion of the income they receive. Second, producers wishing to increase their capital stock must be able to finance such an increase by spending out of or beyond their current incomes. In both respects there are a psychological and an institutional side to the savings–investment process, and both sides are examined in these chapters. The special features of the capitalistic system by which some controls over this process are taken from the hands of savers and put into those of borrowers and financiers responsible for the money supply are also developed here.

In Figure 1.1 the elements that we feel are important for the study of a growing economy are shown. Roman numerals refer to the parts of the book in which these[1] elements are treated. Parts II and III provide the history of those activities that produced the opportunity for economic growth—the growth whose measurement was the subject of Part I. Part III also describes the response of savers, investors, and financiers to the growth of real wealth, as reflected in their decisions to accumulate tangible assets for investment puposes. Part II and a portion of Part III, then, are devoted in large measure to describing and analyzing social activities that are partly but not wholly economic in character and motivation—activities that developed out of the whole political, social, intellectual, and economic history of the nation. The

FIGURE 1.1
The framework of a growing capitalistic economy [foreign sector (14) omitted]

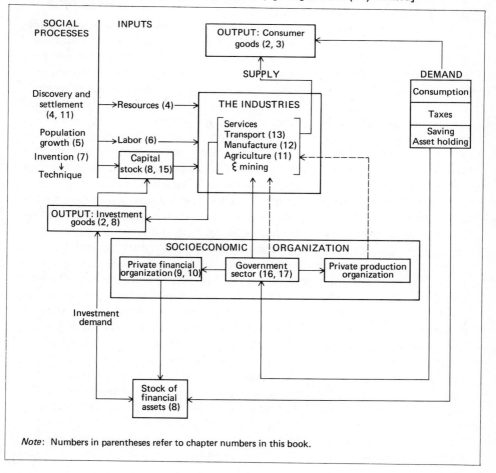

Note: Numbers in parentheses refer to chapter numbers in this book.

[1] For purposes of simplicity, the foreign sector (exports, imports, and capital flows) is omitted from this figure. This body of economic relationships, which should in fact be divided among Parts II (imported resources), III (net capital flows), and IV (export demand), is treated as a single unit in Chapter 14.

economic analysis of costs and benefits can help explain these phenomena, but economic motivations do not wholly govern them and on their histories economics alone cannot have the last word. In the institutions of finance and investment, treated in Part III, economic considerations do play a dominant role. Finance may be viewed, indeed, like the producing industries discussed in Part IV, with costs, profits, small firms, and large concentrations. It is an industry with the possibility of calculating the gain from decisions more closely than can be done in most branches of production.

From Parts II and III, we move in Part IV to the center of the diagram, to the output-producing activities themselves. There a production organization combines materials, labor, technique, and equipment (the produced means of production) into a product in the expectation of selling it at a price that exceeds the cost. Here is the home of the price system, where purposive activity transforms objects and labor power into market values, and flows of costs and benefits are measured in money terms.

In Part IV the industries and productive activities are broken down into their traditional branches—agriculture, manufacturing, transportation, and trade.[2] This traditional sectoral division of the industries rests on the relatively low degree of substitutability among—and the relatively high degree within—the sectors as defined. Thus, if one views our economic machine as an immense sausage maker, one set of activities is devoted to producing the meat and spices that will go into the machine, one set to moving them to the machine, a third to making the sausage, and a fourth to overseeing its distribution to the consumers. All four steps are necessary and, since they must occur in sequence, one cannot be substituted for another. A railroad may replace a canal, but it cannot be substituted for a farm or factory.

If complete data were available, it would be possible for us to show in great detail the movement of goods through the processes of production as value is added, through the contributions of labor and capital, to the semi-finished product at each stage. Our treatment of the great industrial sectors does not do this in any exact way. Instead, each sector is considered in terms of its own history. Agriculture (Chapter 11) is a basic industry, formed as soil and men came together in the eighteenth and nineteenth centuries, incorporating a certain family structure in its farms, responding to markets and to the progress of technical knowledge. Its economic result was to contribute food and fiber without sharp rises in their relative costs to a growing industrial–urban economy, to send an army of laborers from the farms to villages and city factories, and in return to take America's manufactures in abundance. In the discussion of manufacturing (Chapter 12), the growth of two major industries—textiles and ferrous metals—is detailed through the phases of their 150-year history. These developments are set in the framework of a manufacturing sector responding to the growth of demand, the changes in factor supplies, and the rapid obsolescence of its productive techniques in a

[2] These chapters do not examine the entire corpus of productive activity. Mining, a rather small but important industry, and services, a major and growing sector, are missing, as is domestic trade. We hope to treat these activities in later editions of the book.

sensitive and successful way. In the chapter on internal transport (Chapter 13), the vital but peculiar features of this economic activity are made manifest. The struggle of rail and canal in the mid-nineteenth century is replaced by the struggle of rail and truck in the twentieth, and the widely ramifying effects of the continuous reduction in transport costs are made evident. Chapter 14 is devoted to foreign trade, a sector which presents to the economist many of his most interesting problems, and is of particular significance to the student of underdeveloped economies today.

The spatial arrangement of economic activity and the laboring population is part of the productive process. Hence, Chapter 15 on industrial location has been placed in Part IV along with the industry studies. As one reads Chapter 15, it may be useful to review Chapter 3, in which the patterns of consumption are detailed. The spatial agglomeration of populations in urban masses imposes special technological constraints on demand patterns. As a result, there exists an "urban consumption package" that is demanded in ever-increasing quantities as the nation's population becomes more urbanized. These demand patterns, taken in conjunction with the level of total income, the distribution of that income, and the conditions of supply, determine the composition of the economy's final output.

Two aspects of the subject of economic organization are treated in the two chapters (16 and 17) that form Part V. These are (a) the problems engendered by the spatial aspects of economic growth and (b) the legal constraints on economic organization—the rules that set limits on human behavior and that channel and routinize responses to economic changes. Chapter 16 considers a major aspect of the organizational problem imposed by modern economic growth: the problems of living in and governing cities. Chapter 17 attempts to link a theory of political organization with the historical facts of economic change in order to provide an explanation for the changing organizational structure of the economy. With these organizational questions our book comes to a close.[3]

METHOD AND METHODOLOGY

Since the authors of this book are economists, they have tended to use the methods and methodology of the economist in studying history. There are, as a result, many similarities in the authors' individual attitudes toward method. However, there are some differences as well, and the reader should be aware of both.

First, it is apparent that the authors agree that chopping history into topics aids exposition and analysis. They know, as well as anyone, that this is not the way history was lived. The individual forms the central focus of all his interpersonal activities—social, political, economic, religious, criminal,

[3] The subject of industrial organization, which would form a proper topic for Part V, is treated to some extent in the chapters on capital, agriculture, and transportation. Clearly there are sufficient similarities between the forms of organization in all these industries that they deserve to be treated separately, but we have not done so here.

sportive, or educational—but economic processes may nevertheless have histories of their own. Men's economic activities exhibit discernible regularities in one generation after another and appear to have strong, internal causal connections over time. The growth of labor unions in the 1930s, for example, was partly a response to the economic and political environment of that decade; but it also depended on union activity in the 1920s and even the 1890s. It is thus both possible and useful to write the history of labor-union development as a repetitive response to an evolving environment of industrialism.

Our chapters are, with a few exceptions, attempts to get at the inner nature of these linkages over time in aspects of American economic life. As economists we have been trained to examine elements in a situation separately and to combine such elements in models following behavioral rules and exhibiting interactions found in the real world. The heart of the economist's method is a set of simplifying assumptions, and it is toward analysis based on such assumptions, rather than toward a complete description of the moving reality, that our work is directed. We offer, then, an economist's history of the United States. Our picture has validity if we have chosen the right questions to ask and examined the right elements to answer them.

In the treatment of each subject there is a blending of abstractions with concrete detail. The treatment and the proportions in the blend vary according to the author's taste and training and the subject at hand. Models are more fully specified in some chapters than in others. In Chapter 10, on the commercial banks, one of the most difficult expository problems—the relationship among banks, the price level, and the volume of savings—is handled by the elaboration of a formal model with symbols whose simple manipulation permits the author to trace the connections. With the model in mind the reader can more easily order the facts about the banking system's institutional development and gain some appreciation of their effect on the rate of capital formation and growth and the phenomenon of cyclic instability. In Chapter 15, on industrial location, a similarly specified model is used. However, these explanations are meaningful only to the extent that the models have some relation to the reality they purport to explain. In other chapters, the authors have used a looser structure. In almost every case, they have assumed that the reader has some acquaintance with the main features of the model of the competitive economy presented in elementary economics courses. Thus, for example, the chapters on agriculture, manufacturing, and transportation depend on the application of the concepts of supply and demand. These concepts permit the authors to examine the developments in those sectors in a novel manner and to draw some conclusions about American growth which are at variance with traditional teachings. In the study of manufacturing, for example, the model is used to explore the relative contributions of various cost and market factors to the expansion of textile output in the early decades of the nineteenth century. In the chapter on transportation a model is used to help explain the westward expansion of the railroad network, the replacement of canals by railroads, and the productivity increases in transportation between 1870 and 1900.

The authors are also concerned in varying degrees with problems that are not strictly economic—in particular with the development of the legal and industrial structure within which economic activity has taken place. In the chapter on government (Chapter 17), an effort is made to base on certain economic considerations a model of the process of institutional change and to utilize that model in explaining the development of the federal government's economic powers and activities. Suggestions are made in other chapters—those on agriculture and manufacturing, for example—as to how the numbers, composition, scale, and internal structure of the production units have changed in response to changes in the economic environment. Since economics contains no dynamic theory of political or institutional change, these efforts cannot be systematically pursued. They show, however, how useful such a theory would be and provide a number of partial, but suggestive, hypotheses.

In much of what we have written here, we are not speaking as economists at all, but simply as scholars of a subject with—we hope—an educated instinct for its important dimensions. We have not endeavored to utilize mathematical formulations or econometric tests or to employ a full-blown growth model in a precise and comprehensive way. We have applied here to history writing only the economist's habits of thought: separating, structuring, analyzing, counting. Underlying much of our interpretation, too, is the economist's assumption of rational, profit-maximizing behavior. Given this assumption, we feel, much of American economic history makes sense. Its use reveals also, by contrast, how "noneconomic" behavior—based on ignorance, market power, government interference for social (or nonsocial) purposes— can produce "noise" and modifications in the system's operation. Even many of these irrationalities, we suspect, however, may turn out to be rational when subjected to the scrutiny of an ingenious logic and a sympathetic insight into the actual conditions under which they occurred. Engaging in this exercise of finding rational patterns in history is, we confess, a source of endless delight to us. It is for those who read the book to judge whether our efforts add to their understanding of historical change.

WHY STUDY AMERICAN HISTORY?

Is the historical record simply a laboratory for testing economists' theories about markets and human psychology—the playroom of agile and naive minds? Does the analysis of history, like that of nature, help us predict and influence the course of future events? On the answer to these questions, social scientists are in some disagreement.

Those economists who spend time and thought in constructing formal models of an economy hope to capture the main lines of economic progress in their formulations. Prediction in this sense means that if human beings within a specified environment continue to behave in the future in certain specified ways, then a certain economic result—for example, a certain growth rate—will be achieved. But no one supposes that social scientists can foresee the whole future even a few years ahead, much less over long spans of time.

Those who fail to share even a limited faith in formal scientific procedures take a slightly different point of view of the value of historical study. They argue that while history is indeed unpredictable, still the exposure of a mind to the record of the past, ordered and described as best one can do it, has an important educational effect. The value of studying history, they argue, lies in the way that it stimulates the intellect. Thus, for them, history would become a bore if it could be stripped completely bare and reduced to a formal model.

Whatever their view of history, both groups agree that a familiarity with past experience helps to educate men who would mold public policy. Political leaders survive through their understanding—whether conscious or instinctive —of the nation as a system of human interrelationships—political, social, economic—moving through time. This awareness of the range, variety, and intricacy of human social life takes a little of the surprise from tomorrow's events. History, like foreign travel or like life fully lived, is, in this view, a sophisticating experience.

These reasons have particular force for the uniquely modern events surveyed in the history of economic growth. Here, where we have little evidence to go on, even an ounce of wisdom distilled from historical records should not be passed by. No one supposes that developmental planners in India or Colombia can (or would want to) reproduce American history in such different natural, technical, and social settings. Some of the American experience —for example, the development of an agricultural experiment and extension system—is of value; some—such as banking history—may show what to avoid. But much of American history should show to Americans what a unique and lucky affair it has been, and lead us to approach the experiences of other people with a measure of sympathy and self-consciousness.

The authors of this book believe that much of history can be known and presented in a form that communicates some portion of truth to others. The selection of economic growth as their central topic derives from their feeling that this growth has been an important element in the modern world. The study of economic history did not always have this emphasis, and may not always keep it. From 50 to 100 years ago, in England and on the continent of Europe, economic historians—who were just then becoming a recognized species of scholar—were concerned less with growth than with the organization of economies; less with the production of wealth than with its distribution. An impulse made itself felt at that time to reexamine the forms of a competitive, laissez-faire economy and to investigate alternative forms for organizing economic life. In Germany, leading economic historians examined the relation between a booming economy and the strength of the national state. And everywhere, Marxian socialists expected and encouraged the class system based on the private ownership of capital to destroy itself as a result of falling profit rates and the exploitation of the proletariat.

American economists' interest in the dynamic questions of economic history was strengthened by the recovery from the depression of the 1930s and the emergence of the problems of the "underdeveloped" world, which at last began to impinge upon Americans' picture of the future. The continued growth in wealth and power of the capitalist or semicapitalist West, at odds with Marxist prophecy, set at rest for a while the question of economic institutions and organization. Assuming the mixed public and private economic organization that had characterized the West, what—American economists asked in the 1950s—were the growth processes which had led in the United States, and might lead everywhere, to the increase in wealth?

History in the 1960s made Americans and American economists more cautious about the prospects for their own society and the chances that the world could become wealthy by American aid and the direct imitation of American experience. Whether the main questions of the 1970s concern growth, poverty, environmental management, national dissolution, or national expansion, their solution will be helped, we believe, by attention to some of the lessons that the study of economic history can teach. The problems of the future will demand some understanding of how they arose out of the American past—out of the very abundance of success Americans have had in conquering a continent and creating a productive economy. And they will continue to require the reasoned analysis and trained habits of thought which are acquired through practice in thinking about historical experience.

American economic history is a unique but meaningful accomplishment of a national society. The men, the resources, the techniques, the patterns of saving and demand, the institutional and legal forms discussed here are of the past. All were changing, evolving, destroying, and renewing themselves while economic growth was going on, and partly as a result of it. What we have chronicled and analyzed here will never recur in exactly the same atmosphere of natural, technical, and market opportunity. Knowledge of one portion of the historical experience of a few tens of millions of people, on a rich but small fraction of the globe, over a few centuries of life, is but a little knowledge. Modern economic growth originated in Europe and has continued to occur in different forms of society, in settings partly similar, partly dissimilar, to our own. Without some knowledge of those histories one cannot appreciate fully the uniqueness and character of the American experience. And, since the American future will almost certainly not resemble the American past, it is only from foreign histories that we can guess what our own society may encounter. The study of history is a beginning, but not the end, of an understanding of how men react in society with one another. Without an educated instinct for those reactions, social reformers—radical or reactionary—cannot shape or affect them, however pure their passions, however earnest their intent, however violent their methods. Without a knowledge of history men become victims, rather than masters, of their environment.

part I
THE RECORD
OF AMERICAN
ECONOMIC
GROWTH

2
THE PACE AND PATTERN OF AMERICAN ECONOMIC GROWTH

This chapter is concerned with long-term changes in the size, performance, and composition of the American economy. It looks at the broad sweep of American growth and provides a general background for the subsequent chapters. The discussion is organized around the concept of the *national product.* Perhaps the less specific term "social product" is more appropriate, since during roughly one third of the period dealt with in this chapter the American people were part of the British Empire, not an independent national entity. But we will use the more familiar term "national product."

The national product is a measure of the total output of a society and it is therefore a useful device for describing the size of an economy—more useful than the alternatives that spring to mind, such as geographical area or population. In fact, it is a uniquely appropriate measure of size, since the economic life of a society, by definition, revolves around the production and distribution of commodities and services.

Size and performance do not necessarily go together. A small economy may perform well; a large one, poorly. The performance of an economy must be judged by the level of material well-being enjoyed by the members of the society it serves. As a first approximation, an economy serves well if it produces a large volume of commodities and services relative to the number of people in the society; that is, if national product per capita is high. Of course, the specific wants met within a society will depend upon the way in which output is divided among its members. While there are no generally accepted criteria by which one distribution may be judged superior or inferior to another, the discussion of the performance of an economy should encompass not only the level of output per capita, but also the way in which it is distributed. Both topics are dealt with in this chapter.

A growing economy does not expand at the same pace along all fronts. The relative importance of different regions, industries, and classes of goods typically changes. These broad shifts in the makeup of the economy are revealed in measurements of the composition of the national product.

Time series of the national product, product per capita, distribution of income, and composition of output provide a useful summary of the growth experience of a society. Economic historians, however, are interested not only in what happened, but also in how and why it happened. Such questions can be approached by way of economic theory. A large part of this book is devoted to the analysis—as distinct from the description—of change. The analysis begins in this chapter with an attempt to isolate the sources of long-term economic growth and the factors responsible for compositional changes.

Economists usually approach the question of long-term growth from the supply side. They begin with the concept of a production function, which describes how factors of production (land, labor, capital) are combined in the process of production.[1] Growth in output (or output per capita) can be accounted for in terms of growth in factor inputs (or inputs per capita) and improvements in factor productivity. The analysis is carried this far in the present chapter, while subsequent chapters are devoted to the forces responsible for the historical increases in the supplies of land, labor, and capital and the improvement in factor productivity.

The core of economic theory (price theory, distribution theory, production theory) describes how resources are allocated among competing uses. While the body of this theory has been developed in a static context, it nonetheless provides an approach to the question of the changing composition of the economy during the process of growth. Elements of the theory are used for this purpose in this as well as in subsequent chapters.

The measurement and analysis of economic growth along the lines described in the preceding paragraphs call for a very large volume of data. Before 1840 no regular and reasonably complete census of economic activities was carried out in the United States, however. The available estimates of the level and composition of national product and of the supplies of factor inputs before 1840 are few and incomplete, and they rest on insecure empirical bases. The account of American growth given in this chapter is therefore necessarily divided into two fairly distinct parts. The first part treats the 240-odd years from earliest colonial times to 1840. The purpose of this section is to establish the broad path of long-term economic change. The section is descriptive, the results are by no means conclusive, and a good deal of attention is necessarily given to supporting the judgments offered, since they rest on a store of evidence that has not received wide scholarly attention. The second section is more quantitative and the analysis is somewhat more complete and detailed. Less attention is devoted to the justification of the conclusions reached, since the data on which they rest have had the benefit of fairly wide discussion among economic historians. Both sections, of course, are directed to the same basic issues; both deal with long-term changes in the size, performance, and composition of the American economy.

---

[1] This concept is discussed further later in this chapter and also in Chapter 7.

AMERICAN GROWTH BEFORE 1840

Colonizing North America

In May of 1609, Sir Thomas Gates left England with a fleet of eight supply ships, bound for the settlement at Jamestown, Virginia, which he hoped to reach by late summer. It was a year before Gates set foot in Jamestown, however. A storm cost him his flagship and forced him to lay up in Bermuda until early May of 1610. By the time he arrived in Virginia, more than half the colonists were dead of starvation or disease and the rest were physically debilitated and emotionally spent. One man had been convicted of cannibalism.

> This was the "Starving Time" for Virginia, just as there were to be starving times for Bermuda, Plymouth, and Barbados, when men suffered and died, because they had not yet learned the art of colonization, and had come to America inadequately supplied and equipped and unfamiliar with the method of wresting a living from the wilderness.[2]

The settlers in the New World were projected into an environment which was in many ways unfamiliar to them. The experiences of Roanoke, Jamestown, Saghadoc, and Plymouth all showed that the colonists could not depend upon an unbroken contact with the Old World as an element in the solution of their fundamental problems. They had to provide themselves very quickly with shelter, protection, clothing, and food, and they had to use the resources of the new and strange environment to these ends. In some measure, however, productive activities could be guided by experience gained in the Old World. Among the later immigrants, the Palatinate Germans became successful farmers when they found limestone soils of the kind they had cultivated at home, while the Scotch–Irish, who brought with them a distrust of such soils, were able to choose successfully among the options open to them in the Alleghenies (which resembled the land they had farmed in Europe), although their principle of selection would have cost them good locations elsewhere. The characteristics of the soil could be judged by its color and by the type and development of the vegetation found on it. But these guides were sometimes disastrously misleading. In coastal Virginia wheat ran to stalk, and in New England decades passed before success was achieved with the crop, although the land seemed to be satisfactory wheat land. Vegetation was in some respects new and the settlers had to learn and relearn to read the signs correctly. "The nut-bearing trees were excellent guides to good land; there were, however, disappointing 'hickories' such as pignut. . . . In the East, oak soil bore an excellent reputation but to the westward, scrub willow and post oak thrived on anything but rich soil."[3]

The first settlers selected farming sites under serious constraints, of course. Land clearing was an arduous task. It took a family several weeks to clear an acre of forest and, given the uncertainties of the supply line to Europe, the

---

[2] Charles M. Andrews, *The Colonial Period of American History*, vol. 1 (New Haven: Yale University Press, 1934), pp. 110–111.

[3] Archer Butler Hulbert, *Soil, Its Influence on the History of the United States* (New Haven: Yale University Press, 1930), pp. 72–73; see also chap. 8, *passim*.

first settlers could not afford the investment required to carve farms out of the woods. They planted where land was already relatively clear—on river meadows, woods openings, or the abandoned fields of the Indians.[4] Where it was necessary to bring forest land under cultivation, they did not clear away the trees. They killed them and planted between them. Stumps might be left standing for years. This procedure limited the effectiveness with which animal power could be applied to agriculture, but the early settlers had few work animals. None were native to North America and few were brought over in the early decades. The chief natural forage crops—rye grass and broom straw—were poor for wintering animals, and it was not until European grasses were introduced in the mid-1660s that work animals could be wintered with good results. The Pilgrims had not a single plow for their first dozen years at Plymouth.[5]

It took time to learn to grow European crops in American soils. There were also new crops and techniques to be mastered. The Indians grew corn, beans, and pumpkins together in hills, the corn providing a framework on which the bean plants could climb; the pumpkins, a species of mulch to keep out the weeds. The technique was designed by cultivators who had no work animals, and it minimized the input of human labor required. Corn and pumpkins were entirely new crops for the Europeans, but with a little care and a lot of rain, the Indian techniques produced very large yields. Pilgrim diet for many years depended heavily on these foods, and corn has remained one of the chief American grain crops, an element in human diet and the principal animal feed.[6]

The soil, plants, and climate of North America posed problems for the colonists. So did the human inhabitants. The Indians naturally resisted foreign occupation and it is only surprising that their resistance was not more continuous and violent. The colonists also had frequent brushes with the Spanish in the South and the French in the North and West. Peckham lists military engagements in 15 of the 25 years between the beginning of the Glorious Revolution (1688) and the end of Queen Anne's War (1713), including the capture or destruction of Schenectady, Oyster Bay, Fort William Henry, Deerfield, and Port Royal and attacks on York, Wells, Fort Nelson, St. Augustine, Pensacola, Montreal (twice), and Quebec (twice).[7] In addition, there were persistent political and social struggles within and among the colonies.

---

[4] "Famine and pestilence had left eastern Massachusetts comparatively bare of inhabitants at the time of the settlement of Plymouth; the vacant corn-fields of the dead Indian cultivators were taken and planted by the weak and emaciated Plymouth men, who never could have cleared new fields." Alice Morse Earle, *Home Life in Colonial Days* (New York: Macmillan, 1913), pp. 129–130.

[5] William C. Langdon, *Everyday Things in American Life, 1607–1776* (New York: Scribner's, 1937), pp. 281–282, 297. The lack of work animals also meant that the colonists were denied an important source of fertilizer. It is sometimes said that the settlers were not much concerned with maintaining the fertility of the soil, since land was abundant. But while it was abundant, it was by no means cheap, in view of the heavy investment required to clear it. The Indians used fish as fertilizer and apparently the settlers at Plymouth followed their example. See Earle, *op. cit.*, p. 130.

[6] Pumpkins had many uses. They were cooked like squash, dried and used in powder form as a sweetener, and fermented to make a type of wine. This last use suggests desperation. Learning to drink water was a trial for the Pilgrims, who had formerly regarded it as an aid in cooking and a medium for washing, but by no means something to be drunk liberally. Pumpkin wine may have changed their minds. See Earle, *op cit.*, pp. 142, 143, 147, 148.

[7] Howard H. Peckham, *The Colonial Wars, 1689–1762* (Chicago: University of Chicago Press, 1964), pp. 222–225.

Nonetheless, workable solutions were found to the problems of production, and the political and military conflicts did not prevent economic growth. Population increased, and by the early eighteenth century control had been obtained over a narrow belt of coastal land running from Maine to what is now Charleston. By that time, the colonists numbered well over 300,000, roughly the current population of Wichita, Kansas. In the context of the period, this population was by no means small. One should recall that all of England and Wales contained only about 5.5 million persons at the turn of the century. More to the point, the colonists were far more numerous than their French and Spanish enemies in Canada and Florida and probably more numerous than the Indian tribes east of the Mississippi. And they had begun to feel crowded in their coastal strip of territory.

The Peace of Utrecht, which ended Queen Anne's War in 1713, began a fairly long period of relative peace (Peckham's table lists only three battles over the next 25 years, quite widely separated in time and space, and only five more over the following 15 years). This date represents a reasonable place to take stock of colonial economic achievements and to consider both the structure of the American economy and the ways in which the proceeds of economic activity were distributed. By 1713 the colonies had not only outgrown their origins as outposts of specific business enterprises, but had also assumed a shape which made them independent, in important ways, of the empire of which they formed a part. They were perhaps not viable as independent units, nor capable of political union among themselves. But a system native to the New World had begun to develop, and one can begin to see in it something much more than an Old World enclave.

The American Economy at the Beginning
of the Eighteenth Century

By the time of the Peace of Utrecht the days of starvation were long since past. The southern and middle colonies were self-sufficient in basic foods. New England probably was not self-sufficient, but this fact reflects not a failure of the economy of that region, but rather the specialization of the American colonies and the significance of colonial and international markets. New England bought food from the middle colonies and paid for it out of earnings made in the carrying trade and from the sale of fish and lumber products, ships, and rum. New Englanders specialized in the production of things for which their pattern of resources gave them a trading advantage. And so did the settlers in the other colonies. South Carolina exported rice; Virginia and Maryland, tobacco, deerskins, and bar iron; the middle colonies, grains, animal products, and pelts. In the early eighteenth century, the value of colonial exports to England alone ran about £1 per head per year, and total trade, including intercolonial trade, must have been considerably larger. At a time when national income per capita, even in the relatively rich countries of the world, ran probably no more than £8 or £9, this volume of trade is very impressive. It suggests that the colonies were exploiting their natural advantages and were developing a complex and productive organization.

There is other evidence of economic improvement. The graceful brick public buildings and dwellings of colonial America date from the eighteenth century. The seventeenth century built with timber, a cheaper material that also saves labor in construction. Eighteenth-century house furnishings and dress were also more expensive and elaborate than their seventeenth-century counterparts. However, the evidence that has come down to us on these matters tends to reflect the position of the well-to-do. We all know what Monticello and Mount Vernon look like and have some feeling for the material side of the life of their inhabitants. There weren't many families so rich, and it is of some importance to know how the generality of men lived and how far the improved level of economic performance was reflected in their experience. On these matters we have much less evidence.[8]

There appears to be fairly general agreement among scholars that the English level of life at the beginning of the eighteenth century was high by contemporary standards. It is also generally agreed that the real wages of workers were better in colonial America than in England. The suggestion is that the American standard of life was abundant. But men working for wages composed only a very small fraction of the American labor force—perhaps 5 percent. Fully one quarter of American workers were bound laborers, and at least half of that group were bound for life. For these people, the wages obtained by free workers had little immediate relevance. Most of the rest of the work force, perhaps 60 percent, were small farmers and fishermen whose well-being depended upon their investment, skill, and luck. Their success, or lack thereof, surely had an impact on wage rates, since they were occasional hirers of labor. The level of the wage for labor also established a floor below which incomes from farming were not likely to fall for extended periods, since farmers had the option of hiring out. However, the relationship between the average farming income and the income from wages cannot be specified quantitatively, and the "floor" established by the wage rate was not so high that one can exclude the possibility that the per capita income of free Americans might have been well below the English level.

A basis for a more general comparison can be obtained from the work of George Taylor.[9] According to Taylor, income per capita came to about $45 in the American colonies around 1710–1720, the valuation being in prices of 1840. Expressed in prices of 1720, the figure would be roughly $28, or £5 to £6. Thus, according to Taylor's figure, American per capita income was somewhat below the level achieved in England around the turn of the century (£8 to £9). However, Taylor's estimate may very well be too low. It implies that *total* income per capita was about equal in real terms to the per capita level of *food and fuel consumption* of the United States in the mid-nineteenth century. Since we know that colonial income was not devoted exclusively to food and fuel, the inference one must draw from Taylor's work is that per

[8] According to Charles M. Andrews [*Colonial Folkways* (New Haven: Yale University Press, 1921), p. 72] improvement in dress was fairly general by the middle of the eighteenth century. Earle's account (*op. cit.*, chap. 12) tends to support this view. But Earle's evidence is drawn chiefly from New England and both Earle and Andrews concentrate on the experience of free men.

[9] George Rogers Taylor, "American Economic Growth Before 1840: An Exploratory Essay," *Journal of Economic History*, vol. 24, no. 4 (December 1964), pp. 427–444.

capita food and fuel consumption must have risen quite markedly after 1720. But since that is a very doubtful proposition, it is best to regard Taylor's estimate as a lower limit, a minimum value. The upper limit should probably be set at the level of English per capita income, or about $60 in prices of 1840. That is, the best guess one can now make is that per capita income was lower in America than in England, but not much lower.

In other relevant respects, Americans may have been generally in a somewhat better position than Englishmen. Despite the fact that the average American was subject to debilitating endemic diseases and catastrophic epidemics, he was probably healthier than the typical Englishman and he probably lost fewer of his number by epidemic. For free men and perhaps even for indentured servants, the chances for economic and social improvement were better in the New World than in the Old. One should not make too much of these advantages, of course. By modern standards, death rates were high and the incidence of death, capricious. For a child of, say, 12 or 14, kidnapped and carried to the New World to work under indenture until 21, the prospects for improvement were remote in time and the probability of living to see freedom, well below one. The plantation system had a firm grip on southern agriculture and perhaps 30 percent of the southern population were in perpetual slavery. Africans transported to America may or may not have had fuller stomachs and better health than their relatives at home. But their prospects for freedom and human dignity were negligible.

In summary, by 1713 the colonists had secured a fairly firm grip on the coast from Maine to Charleston. They were a numerous people and they had begun to exploit successfully the advantages of their new environment and of their numbers. Perhaps 85 to 90 percent of them lived from farming, forest activities, and fishing, but mining and manufacturing employed significant numbers. By the standards of the times, their level of economic performance was impressive. The distribution of the proceeds of economic activity was probably somewhat more egalitarian than in Europe, and social and economic mobility was high. But there were already pronounced inequalities. A few planting and mercantile families were rich, while one quarter of the population did not possess even personal freedom.

Economic Growth, 1710–1840

If it is correct to suppose that per capita output in 1710 ran between $45 and $60 (prices of 1840), then aggregate product must have been about $15 to $20 million. At the time of the first reliable economic census, in 1840, the figure was approximately $1530 million, which means that over the intervening 130 years real national product had increased seventy-five to a hundredfold (see Table 2.1). That is, for every dollar's worth of output in 1710, there was between $75 and $100 worth in 1840. These comparisons relate to *real* output; the effects of price-level changes have been eliminated.

As will appear in subsequent sections of this chapter, the rate of growth experienced by the American economy was one of the highest in recorded history. But while the size of the economy expanded at an unusually rapid pace, the improvement in the performance of the economy was not extraordinary. Real national product per capita did rise, probably by between 50 and 100 percent over the full 130-year period (see Table 2.1). Against the background of the European experience of the preceding thousand or so years, the gain realized by the American economy was by no means a negligible accomplishment. But, as we will see, compared with nineteenth- and twentieth-century growth in Europe and America, the improvement between 1710 and 1840 was quite modest—an average gain of only .3 to .5 percent per year. Rates five times these levels have been common in modern times.

So much for the long-term average pace of change. What can be said about deviations from the average? Were there any major shifts in the speed with which the size and/or the performance of the American economy changed? The period was replete with important events and developments to which historians have been willing to assign prominent economic consequences.

The long period of peace after 1713 was broken sharply by the French and Indian War (1755–1759), which disturbed trade in some measure and curbed colonial westward expansion. But the interruption was relatively brief, and in other respects the years between the Peace of Utrecht and the Revolution are regarded as generally good ones for the American economy. Population increased very rapidly (see Table 2.2) and occupied a large new territory. The colonists advanced westward from the coastal plain. By 1775 they had populated the Piedmont and the eastern valleys of the Appalachians and had sent parties of explorers and pioneers through the mountain passes and into the Mississippi Valley. The colony of Georgia had been founded in the South, and

TABLE 2.1
Estimates of population, real net national product,
real net national product per capita, and average annual rates of change, 1710–1840

	1710 (1)	1840 (2)	Rate of Change 1710–1840 (3)
(a) Population (thousand)	332	17,120	3.1%
(b) Real NNP (million)	$15–$20	$1,530	3.4–3.6%
(c) Real NNP per capita	$45–$60	$90	.3–.5%

SOURCES

Row (a), *Columns (1) and (2):* U.S. Bureau of the Census, *Historical Statistics of the United States, Colonial Times to 1957,* Series A-2 and Z-1 (Washington: U.S. Government Printing Office, 1960).
Rows (b) and (c), *Column (1):* See text. Values are in prices of 1840.
Row (b), *Column (2):* See Table 2.9 for the source and method of estimation. Values are in prices of 1840.
Row (c), *Column (2):* Row (b) divided by Row (a).
  Column (3): Computed from Columns (1) and (2), using the compound interest rate formula:

$$Q_{1840} = Q_{1710}(1+r)^{130}$$

where the Qs refer to the variables (population, NNP, and NNP per capita), the subscripts to the years 1710 and 1840, and the superscript to the number of years of compounding.
  For example, the equation for calculating the average annual rate of change of population is

$$17,120 = 332(1+r)^{130}$$

TABLE 2.2

Average annual rates of change of population, selected periods between 1710 and 1840

1710–1770	3.2%
1770–1780	2.6
1780–1793	3.5
1793–1807	3.1
1807–1820	2.9
1820–1840	2.9
1710–1840	3.1

SOURCES: Adapted from U.S. Bureau of the Census, *Historical Statistics of the United States, Colonial Times to 1957*, Series A-2 and Z-1 (Washington: U.S. Government Printing Office, 1960). See also Table 2.1, source note to Column (3).

the large gaps in settled territory that had lain between Virginia and Charleston in 1713 had been partly filled.

If output had grown no faster than population, real product would have increased almost sevenfold, or at an annual rate of 3.2 percent, a respectable rate. But it is generally believed that growth proceeded more rapidly than this and that product per capita increased. There are those who believe that per capita output improved at an average rate as high as 1 percent per year and that the level of performance achieved just before the Revolution was roughly equal to the level reached in 1840. But this seems at once too favorable an interpretation of the prewar experience and too unfavorable a view of the subsequent decades.

The performance of an economy depends upon the volume of factors of production (land, labor, and capital) available per member of the population and upon the productivity of the factors. That is, if the labor force, land supply, and capital stock are all large relative to the population, if the factors are of good quality and if they are used both intensively and effectively, then the level of output per capita will be high, and vice versa. Now, we have no measures of factor productivity in 1774, but we do have some information on factor supplies at that date and in 1805 and 1840. The figures in Table 2.3 rest on this information. The first three columns of the table contain index numbers of the volume of total factor inputs (land, labor, and capital) and of the volume of total factor inputs per member of the population. (The source notes to the table tell how the index numbers were computed, and the section in this chapter on the growth of national product after 1840 explains the economic rationale for the computational procedure.) According to these data, factor supplies increased a good deal faster than population, and by 1840 the volume of factors available per person was 22 percent greater than in 1774. This means that if factor productivity had been the same at the two dates, real national product per capita would have been 22 percent greater in 1840 than in 1774. But we can be virtually certain that productivity was actually higher at the later date than at the earlier one. Even if we assume only a very limited advance in productivity, the total improvement in performance between the two dates

TABLE 2.3
Index numbers and rates of growth of factor inputs
and factor inputs per capita, 1774, 1805, 1840

	Index Numbers Base 1774			Average Annual Rates of Change		
	1774 (1)	1805 (2)	1840 (3)	1774–1805 (4)	1805–1840 (5)	1774–1840 (6)
(a) Supply of factors	100	291	846	3.6%	3.1%	3.5%
(b) Supply of factors per capita	100	114	122	.4%	.2%	.3%

SOURCES

Estimated from data in, or underlying :
    U.S. Bureau of the Census, *Historical Statistics of the United States, Colonial Times to 1957*, Series A-2 and Z-1 (Washington : U.S. Government Printing Office, 1960).
    Stanley Lebergott, "Labor Force and Employment, 1800-1960," in *Output, Employment, and Productivity in the United States After 1800*, Dorothy S. Brady (ed.), Studies in Income and Wealth, vol. 30 (New York : National Bureau of Economic Research, 1966), p. 117.
    Robert E. Gallman and Edward S. Howle, "Fixed Reproducible Capital in the United States, 1840–1900," mimeographed.
    Robert E. Gallman, "The Social Distribution of Wealth in the United States of America," Third International Conference of Economic History, Mouton, 1965.
    Raymond W. Goldsmith, "The Growth of Reproducible Wealth of the United States of America from 1805 to 1950," in International Association for Research in Income and Wealth, *Income and Wealth of the United States : Trends and Structure* (Income and Wealth, Series 2) (Cambridge, England : Bowes & Bowes, 1952), pp. 307, 310.
    Robert E. Gallman, "Changes in Total U.S. Agricultural Factor Productivity in the Nineteenth Century," in *Agricultural History* (forthcoming).
    Alice Jones, "Wealth Estimates for the American Middle Colonies," *Economic Development and Cultural Change*, vol. 18, no. 4 (July 1970), pp. 127, 134.

The estimates rest on the following assumptions :
    The labor force participation rate (ratio of labor force to population) was the same in 1774 and 1805 as in 1810.
    The average annual population growth rates from 1774 to 1805 and 1774 to 1840 were the same as the population growth rates from 1770 to 1805 and 1770 to 1840, respectively.
    Per capita wealth in the American colonies in 1774 was equal to per capita wealth in the Middle colonies. (This assumption may bias the computed growth rates in a *downward* direction.)
    The elasticity of output with respect to labor was .68 ; with respect to property, .32. (See the section below on the growth of national product after 1840.)

is unlikely to have been much less than 35 or 40 percent, which would place the level of per capita product between $60 and $70 in 1774. While the data on which Table 2.3 rests are imperfect, we can nonetheless say with some assurance that the level of performance before the Revolution was well below the 1840 level. The long-term gains in per capita product in the six and one-half decades before the Revolution were probably quite modest, perhaps less impressive than the advance over the next six and one-half decades.

While these appear to be reasonable conclusions, they should not be understood to imply that the decades after 1774 were entirely prosperous. Roughly 30 of the next 66 years fell within periods which have been regarded as poor ones for the American economy. To begin with, the Revolution (1775–1783) temporarily put an end to the conditions favorable to the rapid growth of total output and may have led to a retrogression in per capita product. The war curtailed immigration, which is an important source of labor, since immigrants are heavily concentrated in the working ages. The war also drew off manpower and destroyed some capital, while the emigration of Tories diminished the labor force and the pool of entrepreneurs. (The relatively slow growth of population over the decade 1770–1780, shown by Table 2.2, probably reflects these phenomena.) The immediate effects of the war on factor supplies (and factor supplies per capita) were thus unfavorable.

The war also probably diminished the effectiveness with which factors were used. Trade was disturbed and the financial expedients of the Congress produced inflation and disarranged the pricing system, probably with adverse effects on the allocation of resources. War demands may have stimulated certain areas of production, but there is no good reason to suppose that the *net* effect was strongly positive. On the other hand, one should not overestimate the disturbances to the economy. The economy was not a closely integrated, modern system and the war, while prolonged, did not at any time engage a large fraction of American resources. (The Continentals never put an army larger than 25,000 into the field, and Washington's troops often came to only a few thousand; this at a time when the labor force must have been at least three quarters of a million.) While the effects of military activities were thus unfavorable, they were not catastrophic.

Population growth picked up sharply in the decade after the war, as the data in Table 2.2 suggest. But there may have been no pronounced improvement in per capita product. The Americans were now outside the British Empire and no longer had favorable access to imperial markets. Nor were they welcomed in the ports of the other main European powers. Barriers of every sort stood in their way. While these matters might not trouble self-sufficient frontier farmers nor even drive their more market-oriented countrymen to penury, they were nonetheless matters of moment. Before the war exports probably accounted for 15 percent of American income. Adjustments to less favorable trading circumstances must have forced the adoption of various second-best allocations of resources, with a consequent loss of potential income.

The situation changed dramatically after 1793. As a consequence of persistent European conflicts, the carrying trade moved into American hands and American ports became centers of trade. The value of goods brought into the country for reexport increased thirtyfold between 1793 and 1807 and the freight earnings of American ships quadrupled, reaching a value equal to about $7 for every man, woman, and child in the United States. In the context of the per capita national product levels we have been discussing, this is an enormous value.

The period of American commercial prominence came to a close with the Embargo of 1807. Manufacturing, still of the mill-shop-domestic variety, briefly flourished in the protected market. But the War of 1812, and even more important, the end of European hostilities in 1814, which signaled the return of the former belligerents to full participation in world trade, damaged American manufacturing and provided no recompense in the form of importantly expanded commercial opportunities. The American economy appears to have experienced a decade of near stagnation. But a corner was turned in the mid-1820s and there followed an extended period of pronounced growth.

In summary, then, the years from 1774 to 1840 were mixed. There were long periods in which events unfavorable to growth had an important influence and also long periods when the economy seems to have moved forward vigorously. On balance, the favorable elements were dominant. Factor supplies increased almost eightfold and we have already seen that the volume of factors per capita was substantially higher at the end of the period than at the beginning. To complete the picture we should know the pattern of productivity change, a subject on which we have only limited, if suggestive, information.

Table 2.4 shows that the level of labor income per worker in 1840 varied quite widely among the three industrial sectors distinguished—agriculture, manufacturing, and all other. Since in competition each factor is paid the value of its marginal product, the data suggest that labor productivity differed from one sector to the next. The first explanation that springs to mind is that factor proportions were different in the three sectors. Other things being equal, one would expect that the marginal product of labor would be highest in the sector in which the ratio of land and capital to labor is the highest. But an examination of the underlying data shows that the figures in Table 2.4 are not to be explained in these terms. Factor proportions were quite similar in the three sectors and, indeed, it was in agriculture, not manufacturing, that the highest ratio of property to labor appeared.

Of the remaining potential sources of productivity difference, two were probably of paramount importance. First, the average skill level—that is, the quality—of labor was probably highest in manufacturing and lowest in agriculture. Second, the economy of 1840 was surely not in equilibrium and therefore the data in Table 2.4 probably reflect a malallocation of resources. That is, there were too few resources in manufacturing and too many in agriculture,

TABLE 2.4
Labor income per worker, by industrial sectors, 1840 (dollars)

Sector	Labor Income per Worker
(1) Agriculture	$140
(2) Nonagricultural sectors	267
(a) Manufacturing	450
(b) All other	212

SOURCES

Sectoral labor income: (a) Labor income is defined as gross income less gross property income. Property income was estimated at 10 percent of the value of the land and fixed reproducible capital employed in each sector. The estimates of property employed are from Gallman and Howle, *op. cit.* (b) Gross agricultural income is the adjusted value ($608 million) appearing in Robert E. Gallman, "Gross National Product in the United States, 1834–1909," in *Output, Employment, and Productivity in the United States After 1800*, Dorothy S. Brady (ed.), Studies in Income and Wealth, vol. 30 (New York: National Bureau of Economic Research, 1966), p. 56, plus the value of firewood consumed (p. 47, $121 million). (c) Manufacturing gross income is $250 million (see Gallman, *op. cit.*, p. 47, and the sources cited therein). (d) Gross income in all other sectors is GNP ($1540 million, see Gallman, *op. cit.*, p. 26) minus agricultural and manufacturing gross income and also minus the shelter value of residences (an output produced exclusively by property). The shelter value of residences was taken from worksheets underlying Gallman, *op. cit.* pp. 19, 27. Of course residential property was deducted from the property employed in the "all other" sector before the gross property income of the sector was computed.

Labor force: Lebergott, *op. cit.*, p. 117.

given the existing pattern of demand and productivity levels. That this was true is suggested by the fact that the agricultural work force was expanding more slowly than the nonagricultural work force. The composition of the labor supply was changing in response to differential income opportunities (see Table 2.5).

Whether these explanations are correct or not, the facts remain that there were disparities among sectoral labor productivity levels and that in 1840 a larger fraction of the work force was attached to the high-productivity sectors than was true in 1810. That being the case, there is good reason for believing that average skill level and average labor productivity were higher at the later date. Row (1) of Table 2.6 represents an effort to judge the general importance that one should attach to these facts. The number appearing in Row (1) does not represent a measurement of an historical event. Rather, it represents what *would have happened* if sectoral labor productivity levels had remained unchanging in the face of the historical shifts in the composition of the work force. Under these (partly hypothetical) circumstances, labor productivity would have gone up and real national product per member of the population would have risen by about $9. Since total national product per capita in 1840 was only about $90, the gain from the upgrading of the labor force would have been quite substantial.

Row (1) of Table 2.6 treats only one source of productivity advance—the improvement in the labor force that is reflected in the changing sectoral distribution of labor. Is it likely that the measure captures an important fraction of the actual improvement in performance due to the advance of factor productivity? The answer is that it probably does. A similar calculation for the period 1840–1900 yields a value equal to more than half of the per capita income gain arising out of productivity increase. In the years before 1840, when the labor-force estimates show an unusually marked compositional change, the measurement probably accounts for an even larger fraction of the performance gain rooted in productivity advance.

The measurements indicate that after 1810 the gain in labor productivity associated with the changing sectoral composition of the labor force was an important source of improvement to the performance of the economy. Can the same be said about the decades before 1810? Probably not. Table 2.5 shows

TABLE 2.5
Industrial distribution of the labor force, 1810–1840 (percent)

Sector	1810	1820	1830	1840
(1) Agriculture	80.9	78.8	68.8	63.1
(2) Nonagricultural sectors	19.1	21.2	31.2	36.9
(a) Manufacturing	3.2	—	—	8.8
(b) All others	15.9	—	—	28.1
(3) Totals	100.0	100.0	100.0	100.0

SOURCE: Lebergott, *op. cit.*, p. 117.

TABLE 2.6
Increases in real national product per capita associated
with changes in the allocation of labor, 1810–1840

	1810–1840
(1) Industrial allocation of the total labor force	$9
(2) Regional allocation of agricultural labor	$2
(3) Total	$11

SOURCES

Row (1): The calculations underlying Table 2.4 yielded total labor income in 1840. Dividing through by the total labor force (Lebergott, *op cit.*, p. 117) gave average labor income for the whole economy, $187.

The sectoral estimates of labor income per worker in 1840 were then multiplied by the sectoral labor-force figures in 1810 (Lebergott, *op. cit.*, p. 117). The results measure the level of (real) labor income that would have been achieved in each sector in 1810 if labor in each sector had been as productive at that date as it was in 1840. The sectoral figures were then added up and divided by the total labor force in 1810 to yield average labor income for the whole economy, $160.

The difference between the two values computed above—$187 and $160—measures the gain in labor productivity that would have occurred if sectoral levels of productivity had remained constant, but the historical changes in the composition of the labor force had taken place. The computed gain is $27.

About one third of the population was in the labor force in 1840. Consequently, the computed gain per person is equal to the computed gain per worker ($27) divided by 3, or $9.

Row (2): The calculations rest on work by Easterlin reported in a paper by Paul David ["The Growth of Real Product in the United States Before 1840: New Evidence and Controlled Conjectures," *Journal of Economic History*, vol. 27, no. 2 (June 1967), pp. 178, 179]. According to Easterlin's calculations, the effect of the regional redistribution of agricultural labor between 1810 and 1840 would have raised real agricultural output per worker by just under 6 percent, or about $10 per worker. In 1840 roughly one fifth of the population worked in agriculture. Therefore, the gain per member of the total population would have been $10 divided by 5, or $2. [See also William N. Parker, "Sources of Agricultural Productivity in the Nineteenth Century," *Journal of Farm Economics*, vol. 49, no. 5 (December 1967), pp. 1455–1468.]

Row (3): Row (1) plus Row (2).

that in 1810 roughly 80 percent of the work force was in agriculture and only about 3 percent was in manufacturing. The share in manufacturing is unlikely to have been much lower at any earlier date and the fraction in agriculture was probably never over 90 percent after, say, 1710. The scope for structural shifts of the kind that took place after 1810 was simply very limited before that date. This is not to say that labor productivity did not rise before then, but only that improvement is not likely to have shown itself in major changes in the sectoral —or skill—distribution of the work force. These considerations also suggest that the long-term pace of productivity improvement was probably more limited before 1810 than afterward, although there were no doubt episodes of marked advance, as when the Americans took over the carrying trade after 1793.

The calculations underlying Row (1) of Table 2.6 capture only one dimension of the shifting composition of the economy. The figure in Row (2) is the result of an effort to deal with a second. In the decades before 1840 the American economy was expanding westward. We know that the movement had prominent direct effects on agricultural productivity. For example, southern farmers were in the process of adopting cotton as their chief cash crop, and by 1840 cotton accounted for 10 percent of American agricultural output and two thirds of the value of American exports. The great westward surge of the 1830s brought the crop to Alabama and Mississippi, where land yields (and thus labor productivity) were higher than in the East. The chief source of the productivity gains in cotton during the three decades before 1840 was the westward movement of cotton cultivation.

Row (2) of Table 2.6 is the result of an effort to appraise the impact of the regional redistribution of agriculture on per capita income. It was computed in much the same way as Row (1), the only difference being that the underlying productivity measure incorporates total income, rather than only labor income. The table shows that per capita income (total population) would have risen about $2 had regional labor productivities remained at their 1840 levels as the westward movement took place. Presumably the advance would have been largely a consequence of the improved average quality of agricultural land arising out of the exploitation of the western territories.

In summary, the two measures yield a total advance of $11 in per capita real national product, a value larger than the gain attributable to the increase in the supply of factors of production per capita between 1805 and 1840. The suggestion is that per capita product probably rose by $20 or more in the 30-odd years before 1840, which means that the annual rate of advance was probably a good deal higher than the estimated rate of growth for the full period, 1710–1840, and probably higher than the rate for either of the two long periods previously discussed, 1710–1774 and 1774–1805. That is, the performance of the American economy, as measured by per capita product, was probably increasing at a rising rate.

We are left with the question of how the proceeds of growth were distributed among the American people. Was growth associated with increasing equality, or were the disparities among income groups widening? This is a subject that has been receiving increasing attention in recent years and all the returns are not yet in. There are some indications that inequalities were widening. For one thing, 12 percent of Americans remained in slavery in 1840 and they probably did not share substantially in the improved material conditions of life. For another, the notable fortunes appear to have increased in size very rapidly, inviting the inference that wealth was becoming more closely held. It is said that the richest man in eighteenth-century America held property worth $1 million, while the first few decades of the nineteenth century produced several multimillionaires, the wealthiest of whom, John Jacob Astor, probably left in excess of $20 million at his death in 1848. But these are inadequate bases for firm judgments concerning trends.

Table 2.7 provides some information on the structure of wealth holdings before the Civil War. Each figure records the fraction of wealth owned by a given fraction of the population of families (including in families single individuals living alone). For example, the figure in Column (1), Row (a) says that the richest 1 percent of the families in the United States in 1860 are estimated to have held 24 percent of all the wealth. Rows (b) through (e) show wealth holding within various divisions of the United States. The figures are not altogether trustworthy, but the main contrasts that appear in the table surely reflect reality.

TABLE 2.7
Estimates of the size distribution of wealth in the United States in 1860

	Percent of Wealth Held by the Richest		
	1 Percent of Families (1)	5 Percent of Families (2)	10 Percent of Families (3)
(a) United States	24	53	72
(b) Cotton-growing South	30	58	79
(c) Rural Louisiana	50	84	96
(d) Rural Maryland	16	45	65
(e) Three large cities	45	73	85

Note: The table treats slaves as wealth holders. Wealth excludes the value of slaves.

SOURCE: Robert E. Gallman, "Trends in the Size Distribution of Wealth in the Nineteenth Century: Some Speculations," in *Six Papers on the Size Distribution of Wealth and Income,* Lee Soltow (ed.), Studies in Income and Wealth, vol. 33 (New York: National Bureau of Economic Research, 1969), pp. 6, 7, 22, 23.

The data show very great concentration within the two sections of the plantation South appearing in the table—rural Louisiana, which was dominated by sugar and cotton planting, and the cotton-growing South. Notice the contrast between the figures for these regions and the figures for rural Maryland, which was no longer a plantation state. If data were available for the rural sections of a northern state, the contrast would be even more striking.

The concentrated wealth holding in the South reflects the slave system, of course. Most slaves were permitted to hold little property and in any case had few opportunities to accumulate wealth. The bottom of the wealth pyramid was therefore distended by a very large group of propertyless families. Slavery was also associated with the plantation system of agriculture. While most southern farmers owned no slaves or possessed only one or two and cultivated modest acreages, a few operated very large plantations. The range of individual land holdings was thus probably wider in the South than in the North; and the distribution of property among free men, more unequal. This was certainly true in the sugar regions of Louisiana and the rice territories of South Carolina; less certainly in the cotton regions.

A second notable feature of the table is that it shows a very unequal wealth distribution within the cities. The cities were commercial and manufacturing centers, heavily populated with young workers who lived in rented quarters and worked with capital owned by others. These workers were the urban equivalent of landless northern farm workers, but they were more numerous in their environment than were the farm workers in theirs. The typical northern farming unit was still the family farm, drawing most of its capital and labor from the family. But northern commercial and manufacturing firms, while small by current standards, were outgrowing the small family operation, and many workers were no longer applying their skill through their own tools within their own workshops. Their situation, however, was better than that of the farm worker. As pointed out previously, skill levels and income levels were higher on average outside agriculture than within it. The urban worker possessed a form of wealth not measured in the census returns—his skill—and therefore the wealth distributions in Table 2.7 tend to overstate the wealth concentration in cities. Furthermore, the urban distribution was skewed by the presence in cities of disproportionately large numbers of young workers (see Chapter 3)—workers who were in the early stages of their careers and therefore had not yet accumulated much wealth. Thus, the data in the table exaggerate the magnitude of *persistent* wealth differences among economic classes.

The 1860 census data permit one to take a closer look at the characteristics of rich and poor. Few of the data have been gathered together and analyzed, and therefore this discussion must be restricted to the urban situation, looking at evidence for one city, Charleston. Charleston cannot be regarded as an entirely typical American city of 1860, but the main features of the distribution of wealth—which are all that we are interested in here—are probably broadly representative of the urban situation in the United States at that time. The following observations rest on a sample of free families. The sample was drawn from the original schedules of the census enumerators and includes data on all free families with wealth of $50,000 or more and 5 percent of all other free families.

Rich families in Charleston are to be distinguished by the age of the household head. Of 80 families with wealth of $50,000 or more, 70 were headed by persons over 44 years of age, while in less than a quarter of the households with no wealth was the family head this old. Across the entire wealth distribution, wealth and the age of the family head are directly related. *This is exactly what one should expect to find at all times and all places.* Wealth, after all, is accumulated by saving and inheritance, and both forms of accumulation favor older persons over younger ones.

A second distinguishing feature of the wealthy families is that they were typically headed by native Americans. At least 75 of the 80 richest household heads were American, and as one scans the wealth distribution from top to bottom, the proportion of native family heads falls until it reaches a level of roughly 60 percent in the families with no wealth. No doubt age and nativity are related factors. Most of the foreign-born in Charleston were Irish and Germans, groups that had come into the country in large numbers beginning in the late 1840s. Immigrants were disproportionately young adults of limited means, and consequently the heavy immigration distended those classes in the society that held little or no wealth. More generally, the marked wealth inequalities in the cities, and even in the rural North, may reflect in some measure the changing composition of families due to the pronounced immigration of the 1850s, rather than a deterioration of the position of the poor.

Among native free Americans, white families were richer than nonwhite. Probably none of the latter in Charleston (which were numerous, incidentally) owned as much as $10,000. Most had a recent personal or family history of slavery, had received little wealth by inheritance, and had earned what they owned themselves. In this respect they were similar to the immigrants ; indeed, they seem to have been better off than the Irish, although not so well situated as the Germans.

The employed heads of rich households typically followed high-paying occupations—they were planters, merchants, bankers, lawyers, doctors, or high government officials. While among those with no wealth, one fifth listed no occupation and another fifth held jobs in personal service—they were washerwomen, seamstresses, servants, housekeepers, and so on. Other occupations appearing frequently were laborer, clerk, bookkeeper, seaman, stevedore, policeman, midwife, nurse, and drayman, all of which received relatively little pay. The groups between these extremes contained large numbers of mechanics and other skilled artisans; that is, workers whose rates of pay lay toward the top of the range for manual laborers. Few family heads in these groups reported that they had no occupation.

The association between wealth holding and occupation was probably two-sided. Doctors are found near the top of the wealth distribution because they received large incomes and thus were able to accumulate wealth. But those trained in medicine were probably disproportionately drawn from the ranks of the wealthy, since the wealthy were better able to finance the necessary training and more likely to have the necessary motivation. Doctors were both rich because they were doctors and doctors because they were rich.

Finally, families headed by males were generally better off than families headed by females, just as they are today. The importance of inheritance and occupation come through very clearly in these data. Females who headed rich families were generally native whites who listed their occupation as "lady" or "at home"; presumably they were the relicts or maiden daughters of wealthy men. Females who headed poor families were disproportionately Irish or nonwhite; that is, members of groups in which inherited wealth of any magnitude was unusual. Females who headed poor families typically held low-paying jobs in personal service. Presumably women were restricted in their training for, and selection of, jobs by the role they were conceived to play in society. Social constraints probably applied to other groups as well, namely the Irish and the blacks. Such constraints would have affected the identity of the poor; that is, females, the Irish, and the blacks would have been forced into low-paying jobs and therefore disproportionate numbers of them would appear among the heads of poor families. These constraints could also have affected the relative amounts of labor supplied to given occupations and industries and therefore influenced relative productivities. For example, if women were restricted chiefly to jobs in personal service, the supply of labor to the industry might have been (and probably was) larger than it would have been under free market conditions. Therefore, the wage rates in this industry would have been depressed, contributing to economic inequality.

The characteristics of rich and poor described above have an enduring quality. Most of them would reappear in an account of American urban wealth holding in 1770 or 1900 or 1970. But the questions of how wealth holding affected the income distribution and how both distributions changed over time remain to be treated. Both are taken up in the next section.

AMERICAN GROWTH SINCE 1840

Level of National Product in 1840

In 1840 American net national product (NNP) ran something over $1.5 billion. In isolation this figure doesn't mean very much. Is an economy that produces $1.5 billion worth of goods large or small? The answer depends upon the standard of comparison used, of course. The American economy of 1840 was at least 75 times the size it had been in 1710, as we have already seen. But on the other hand it was only about as large as the economy of Iowa is today. Looked at from the vantage point of 1710, the level of output in 1840 is enormous, while viewed from the present, it appears very modest indeed.

More to the point, how large was the American economy in the context of the world of 1840? Unfortunately, the statistical records of other countries are even thinner than U.S. records and we do not have even reliable population figures for the large Asiatic countries (China, India, and Russia), let alone national product estimates. For the European countries there is a little more information. We know that by 1850 the U.S. population was equal to or greater than the population of every European country except France and the states that ultimately composed Germany, and was very much larger than that of most countries. Data on national product are virtually restricted to France and Great Britain—two economies that must have been among the largest in Europe, since both were populous and well developed in terms of the standards of the day. Great Britain had already experienced some 80 years of industrialization and without doubt had the most modern economy in the world. France was well behind Britain in degree of modernization, but was more heavily populated and produced as large a volume of goods. In 1840 U.S. NNP was roughly two thirds the size of NNP in either France or Britain (see Table 2.8). The disparities in size among the three economies were thus quite modest. Against the standards of the mid-nineteenth century, then, the American economy must be regarded as large.

Growth of National Product After 1840

Tables 2.9 and 2.10 show that in the 120-odd years following 1840, U.S. national product increased about sixtyfold, an average annual rate of increase

TABLE 2.8
Comparisons of British, French,
and American national products, c. 1840 and 1950

American National Product as a Percent of	1840	1950
(1) British national product	66–77	454–555
(2) French national product	64	666–833

SOURCE: Derived from Gallman, "Gross National Product . . .," *op. cit.*, p. 5, Table 1, Rows (1A), (1B), and (3). The figures for 1840 refer to national income in prices of 1840; the figures for 1950, to GNP in prices of 1950. The comparisons in Row (1) refer to Great Britain in 1840 and the United Kingdom in 1950.

TABLE 2.9
Indexes of labor, land, capital, and net national product,
United States, 1840–1960 (1840 = 100)

Year	Labor	Land	Capital	Net National Product[f]
1840	100	100	100	100
1850	146	135	181	161
1860	196	208	357	253
1870	228	240	512	324
1880	313	307	785	520
1890	412	415	1,559	765
1900	514	566	2,343	1,037
1910	662	761[a]	3,683[a]	1,573
1920	735	844[b]	4,942[b]	2,000
1930	863	1,085[c]	6,575[c]	2,952
1940	994	1,003[d]	6,204[d]	3,115
1950	1,142	1,008	8,088	4,566
1960	1,308	1,165[e]	10,531[e]	5,994

[a] 1912.
[b] 1922.
[c] 1929.
[d] 1939.
[e] 1958.
[f] Decade averages (e.g., 1840 = 1834–1843), except for 1860, 1870, and 1960, which refer respectively to 1859, 1869, and 1957.

SOURCES

Labor: Computed from labor-force data in Lebergott, *op. cit.*, p. 117.

Land
1840–1900: Tables underlying Gallman and Howle, *op. cit.* The chief component estimates were made by weighting physical volumes (e.g., crop land, forest land, pasture, railroad land, etc.) by 1860 prices. The rest were deflated by the implicit price index of the chief components. The series excludes public land.
1912–1958: The 1900 estimate described above was extrapolated to subsequent years on estimates in Raymond W. Goldsmith, *The National Wealth of the United States in the Postwar Period* (New York: National Bureau of Economic Research, 1962), p. 120, Table A-6 (private and public land, expressed in 1947–1949 prices).

Capital
1840–1900: Depreciable Capital: Gallman and Howle, *op. cit.* The estimates are expressed in prices of 1860. Inventories: Procedures and sources are described in Robert E. Gallman, "The Social Distribution of Wealth in the United States of America," Third International Conference of Economic History, Mouton, 1965, p. 331. One change in procedure was made: The calculations for this table were carried out with deflated series. The underlying source provides series deflated on the base 1879. The base was shifted to 1860, without reweighting.
1912–1958: The estimate for 1900 was extrapolated to subsequent years on estimates in Goldsmith, *op. cit.*, p. 119, of total net stock, excluding military, and minus land (see above), consumer durables (p. 120), and monetary metals (p. 120). The Goldsmith series is expressed in prices of 1947–1949.

Net national product
1840–1900: GNP in prices of 1860, less inventory changes, from Gallman, "Gross National Product...," *op. cit.*, adjusted as follows:
(1) The mean annual change in inventories was calculated from inventory data described above and was added to GNP. (Mean change, 1840–1850, added to GNP, 1834–1843; mean change, 1840–1860, added to GNP, 1844–1853; mean change, 1850–1860, added to GNP, 1859; etc.)
(2) Capital consumption was computed from the depreciable capital stock estimates and was subtracted from GNP. (See Lance Davis and Robert E. Gallman, "The Share of Savings and Investment in Gross National Product During the 19th Century, United States of America," Fourth International Conference of Economic History, Indiana University Press, forthcoming.)
1910–1950: The 1900 estimate (1894–1903) described above was extrapolated to subsequent years on estimates in Simon Kuznets, *Capital in the American Economy* (New York: National Bureau of Economic Research, 1961), p. 521, net national product, variant III, valued in prices of 1929.
1957: Estimate of 1950 (1944–1953) was extrapolated to 1957 on estimates in John W. Kendrick, *Productivity Trends in the United States* (New York: National Bureau of Economic Research, 1961), p. 292, net national product valued in prices of 1929.

TABLE 2.10
Average annual rates of change of real net
national product and factor inputs, 1840–1960 (percent)

	1840–1960	1840–1900	1900–1960
(1) Net national product	3.56	3.98	3.12
(2) Labor force	2.17	2.77	1.58
(3) Land supply	2.08	2.93	1.25
(4) Capital stock	4.03	5.40	2.63

SOURCE: Computed from data underlying Table 2.9, by use of the compound interest formula (see Table 2.1).

of just under 3.6 percent. These measurements refer to the volume of output, since price-level changes have been eliminated from the underlying data. They are therefore similar to the figures in Table 2.1. A comparison of the growth-rate estimates in Tables 2.1 and 2.10 shows that the long-term pace of growth was about the same in the 130 years before 1840 as in the 120 years after that date.

Judged against the records of other countries, American growth was extraordinarily rapid. This is suggested by the data in Table 2.8. In 1840 the American economy was smaller than either the British or the French economy, while 110 years later it was four or five times as large as the British economy and seven or eight times as large as the French. Bear in mind that during this period both the British and French economies were growing at long-term rates that were very high by the standards of previous history and the modern experience of most other countries.

Sources of U.S. Growth

A very large part of this book is devoted to explaining the extraordinary American growth record. In this chapter we begin the explanation by identifying the major sources of growth and indicating roughly how important each was. A previous section of this chapter distinguished between the effects of growth in factor inputs and growth in factor productivity, and some measures of the former were assembled. In effect it was argued that a 1 percent rise in factor inputs, other things being equal, should result in a 1 percent increase in output. If it calls forth a larger or smaller increase in output, then "other things" are not equal; factor productivity has changed. Notice that under these rules of reasoning, economies and diseconomies of scale are treated as components of productivity change.

As long as all factor inputs increase at the same rate, there is no difficulty in computing the effects of changes in aggregate inputs and productivity. For example, if output has been growing at an annual rate of 4 percent and factor inputs have grown at an annual rate of 3 percent, then productivity must have been going up 1 percent per year (4 percent − 3 percent), and therefore it accounted for one quarter of the growth of output (1 percent ÷ 4 percent). Conceptual and computational difficulties arise because factor supplies rarely increase at the same rate. For example, Table 2.9 shows that between 1840 and 1960 the labor force increased thirteenfold, the supply of land, just under twelvefold, the supply of capital, 105-fold. If these diverse patterns are to be summarized, we need some system for weighting them. Furthermore, the diversity shown in Table 2.9 suggests the desirability of distinguishing the effects of the growth of each factor individually.

The effect of an increment to a factor supply can be thought of as a function of both the size of the increment and the relative importance of the factor in question. Of course, each factor is all-important, in the sense that there is no output unless all three factors are present. What we are examining here, however, is the relative importance of a small change in a given factor. The notion of elasticity is useful in this connection. The elasticity of output with respect to any input is the percentage increase in output that takes place with a 1 percent increase in the given input. For example, if the increase in output associated with a 1 percent rise in the labor supply is .7 percent, then the elasticity of output with respect to labor is said to be .7. If we had proper elasticity measures, then the data in Table 2.10 could be used to estimate the effect of the growth of each factor on output. For example, if the elasticity of output with respect to labor had been .7 for the period of 1840–1960, then for each percentage point of the average annual growth rate of labor, the associated output growth would have been .7 percent. We could then multiply the average growth rate of labor [2.17 percent (see Table 2.10)] by .7 to obtain the impact of the growth of the labor supply on net national product (2.17 percent $\times .7 = 1.52$ percent = the rate of growth of NNP associated with the growth in the labor supply). The question is: How do we obtain elasticity measures?

The increase in output associated with a small increment in any factor is called the *marginal product* of the factor. Evidence relating to marginal productivity could be used to compute elasticities. Now we know that in competition each factor is paid the value of its marginal product. While the American economy has at no time been in a perfectly competitive equilibrium, the assumption that actual factor payments roughly approximate factor marginal productivities is one that economists have nonetheless been prepared to make. On this assumption we can accept factor incomes as measures of factor productivities. Furthermore, we can adopt the *share* of the factor in national income as an appropriate measure of the elasticity of output with respect to an increase in the factor. Bear in mind that national income and net national product are two sides of the same coin. The net national product measures the net output of the economy, while the national income measures the income generated in the production process. In the system of social accounts used in this chapter, the national income is exactly equal to the net national product. The share of a factor in the national income is the part of the total output that the factor receives for the role it plays in production. If labor receives 70 percent of the national income, for example, we can then assume that (other things being equal) a 1 percent increase in the supply of labor would be associated with a .7 percent increase in output. That is, we can assume an elasticity of .7. Notice that on these rules of measurement the sum of the elasticities of all factors must be equal to one, since the factor shares in national income exhaust total national income. This also means that a 1 percent increase in all factor supplies, other things being equal, is associated with a 1 percent increase in output; and we are back where we began, except that we now have a more manageable problem to deal with.

We need measurements that fit the economic concepts of factor incomes. Unfortunately, records are not kept in the form we need. For example, a farmer earns income from the operation of his farm. Part of the income is attributable to his labor, part to his entrepreneurial activities, part to his land, part to the capital he has invested. But it is a rare farmer who attempts to distinguish these components of his income, and a rarer farmer still who records the necessary information. Consequently the available figures on the factor distribution of national income are partly estimated, and no two estimators achieve exactly the same results. Fortunately the disparities among the various estimates are not inordinately great, and the end results of the computations to be described here are not very sensitive to modest changes in the elasticities used. The first two columns of Table 2.11 show two sets of estimates of the share of property income in national income, each made in quite a different way. The figures in the first column rest on direct estimates of property income, whereas those in the second depend upon figures derived as residuals—that is, by subtraction of labor income from national income. While the two series differ at particular dates, the general picture emerging from them is gratifyingly consistent. The estimated levels for the full period, 1850–1910, are quite close, and both series show that while the share changed from one date to the next, there was no marked tendency for the share to rise or fall.

The figures in Table 2.11 have some analytical interest. The data in Table 2.9 show that factor supplies increased at very different rates and this finding leads one to ask how the distribution of national income was affected. Two forces were at work to change the distribution. First, the supply of property (land and capital) grew much faster than the supply of labor. If relative factor productivities had remained unchanged, the share of property in total income would have gone up. But with changing factor proportions one would expect that relative factor productivities would have shifted (unless technical change was biased in just the correct way), the productivity of labor rising relative to the productivity of capital. The data suggest that these two forces just offset each other during the nineteenth century, so that factor shares remained unchanged; while in the twentieth century, the latter had greater weight, so that the fraction of income flowing to property declined somewhat.

To return to the main point, the estimates of income shares yield the elasticity figures we need. Table 2.12 records the contributions of the growth of factor inputs and productivity to the growth of output, calculated in the way described above. Panel 2 shows these contributions in percentile form. It shows that during the period 1840–1960 about four tenths of the growth of output was associated with the growth of the labor force, less than 6 percent with the growth in the land supply, just under one fourth with the increase in the capital stock, and just over one fourth with the rise in factor productivity.

The contribution of productivity advance to aggregate output growth is

TABLE 2.11
Estimated shares of property income in national income, 1840–1958 (percent)

Periods	Interest-Rate Method (1)	Budd (2)	Denison (3)
1840	29.6	—	—
1850	32.7	31.7	—
1860	35.1	34.9	—
1870	—	37.0	—
1880	29.6	37.0	—
1890	33.9	30.5	—
1900	32.5	36.8	—
1910	30.8	37.6	30.5[a]
1850–1910	32.8	35.1	—
1909–1929	—	—	31.1
1929–1958	—	—	27.0

[a] 1909–1913.

SOURCES

Column (1): Implicit rates of return to property were computed from Denison's property share estimates for 1914–1923, 1924–1933, 1934–1943, 1944–1953 (see below) and the underlying national income and wealth figures. The rates of return to land and capital did not differ materially. Therefore, only the aggregate rate of return for all property was used. The computed rate of return was roughly extrapolated to the nineteenth-century dates on the interest rate data in Sidney Homer, *A History of Interest Rates* (New Brunswick, N. J.: Rutgers University Press, 1963), pp. 287, 288, 341, 351, 360. The extrapolated rates were used with the nineteenth-century property estimates (current prices) to estimate income to property at each date. Property income was divided by net national product (current prices) to yield the estimates in the table. The assumed rates of return to property were:

1840	10.0%	1880	8.5%
1850	10.0	1890	7.0
1860	9.5	1900	6.5
1870	11.0	1910	8.0

The rates computed from Denison's work were:

1922	8.4%	1939	7.6%
1929	6.0	1950	5.9

Column (2): Edward C. Budd, "Factor Shares, 1850–1910," in *Trends in the American Economy in the Nineteenth Century*, William N. Parker (ed.), Studies in Income and Wealth, vol. 24 (New York: National Bureau of Economic Research, 1960), p. 382.
Column (3): Edward F. Denison, *The Sources of Economic Growth in the United States* (New York: Committee for Economic Development, 1962), p. 30.

impressive. Far more impressive, however, is the role of productivity growth in the improvement of the level of performance of the economy. In the nineteenth century, almost 50 percent of the rise in real per capita income was due to factor productivity gains, while in the twentieth century the comparable figure has been 80 percent. It should be clear, then, that modern improvements in material well-being rest very prominently on gains in productivity and that the search for reasons for the success of the American economy must be pursued with special vigor in this quarter.

The table also shows that the pattern of growth changed quite markedly over time. First of all, there is a strong suggestion that growth has slowed down. The rate of change of output was a good deal higher in the nineteenth century than in the twentieth. Second, the relative importance of the sources of growth shifted. The rates of increase of all three factor inputs dropped very prominently

TABLE 2.12
Contributions of factor inputs and productivity
to the growth of net national product, 1840–1960

Contributions of	1840–1960	1840–1900	1900–1960
Panel 1 : Average Annual Rates of Growth			
(1) Labor force	1.52%	1.88%	1.12%
(2) Land supply	.21	.38	.08
(3) Capital stock	.81	1.03	.60
(4) Productivity	1.02	.69	1.32
(5) Totals (growth of NNP)	3.56%	3.98%	3.12%
Panel 2 : Percentage Distributions			
(1) Labor force	42.7%	47.2%	34.8%
(2) Land supply	5.9	9.6	2.5
(3) Capital stock	22.8	25.9	18.6
(4) Productivity	28.6	17.3	44.1
(5) Totals	100.0%	100.0%	100.0%

SOURCES

Panel 1 : Rates of growth of factor inputs (see Table 2.10) were multiplied by factor shares in national income. The factor shares used were :

	1840–1960	1840–1900	1900–1960
Labor	.70	.68	.71
Land	.10	.13	.06
Capital	.20	.19	.23

See Table 2.11.
The results were summed and subtracted from the rate of growth of net national product (see Table 2.10), to yield the contribution of productivity advance. See the text.
Panel 2 : The data in Panel 1, expressed as percentage distributions. See the text.

(see Table 2.10), much more prominently than the rate of change of output. At the same time, the contribution of productivity advance increased dramatically. The data suggest that in the period 1840–1900 the rise in factor productivity accounted for less than 20 percent of output growth, while the figure rose to well over 40 percent in the years 1900–1960.

The subsequent chapters of this book treat the forces underlying the growth of factor supplies and productivity and the long-term changes in the patterns of growth, matters that are not part of the subject of this chapter. However, it may be useful at this point to notice one characteristic of the concept of productivity advance as developed in this chapter. The concept is a catch-all. Although this matter was touched on previously, it is desirable to go into it a little further here.

The measures of factor supplies used are stocks of factors available to the economy. In the estimation of these supplies no allowance was made for changes in the intensity of the use of factors, such as changes in the level of unemployment, in the length of the workday, week, or year, or in the system of work shifts. Insofar as such changes affected the growth of output, their impacts are contained in the productivity measure, not in the measures of factor supplies.

The measurements of factor supplies also treat factor inputs as though they were homogeneous at each moment in time and across time. Changes in the quality of factors across time—improvements in the skill level of workers, the depletion of crop land, the discovery of new mineral resources, etc.—are recorded in productivity change insofar as they affected output. They are not incorporated in the factor supply estimates. Output changes due to improvements in the allocation of resources or to economies or diseconomies of scale are similarly captured in the productivity measure, as are the effects of technical changes. The point is that the forces underlying productivity change as defined here are numerous and complex. Two appear to have been of particular importance—the improvement in the skill level of labor and technical change, both of which are treated in detail in subsequent chapters.

Performance of the Economy

Levels and rates of change of per capita product.   Early in this chapter it was suggested that by 1710 American income per capita was high by the standards of the day. The situation in 1840 was similar. Great Britain remained perhaps the richest country in the world and per capita income in the United States lay somewhat below the British level (see Table 2.13). The disparity between British and American performance was modest and American product per head probably compared favorably with experience in the rest of Europe. For example, the existing records suggest that income per person was higher in the United States than in France, and France at that date was by no means one of the less developed economies in Europe. The performance of the American economy was therefore impressive, by contemporary standards.

In the 120-odd years following 1840, per capita product increased roughly sixfold, or at an average annual rate of over 1.5 percent. Should this be regarded as a high rate of change? Table 2.14 is designed to help answer this question. The table contains estimated rates of growth of per capita product, expressed in a form different from any yet used in this chapter. The table should be interpreted in the following way. Row (1b) says that if the average annual rate of growth in the United States over the period 1834–1843 to 1894–1903 had

TABLE 2.13
Comparison of per capita national product in Britain,
France, and the United States, c. 1840

American National Product per Capita as a Percent of	
(1) British national product per capita	71–83%
(2) French national product per capita	128%

SOURCE: See Table 2.8.

TABLE 2.14
Growth of per capita product, selected countries, long periods

	Coefficient of Multiplication in a Century
(1) United States	
(a) 1710 to 1840	1.4–1.7
(b) 1834–1843 to 1894–1903	4.1
(c) 1894–1903 to 1957	5.2
(d) 1834–1843 to 1957	4.6
(2) England and Wales, United Kingdom	
(a) 1700 to 1780	1.2
(b) 1780 to 1881	3.5
(c) 1855–1859 to 1957–1959	3.7
(3) France, 1841–1850 to 1960–1962	5.2
(4) West Germany, 1871–1875 to 1960–1962	5.2
(5) Netherlands, 1900–1904 to 1960–1962	3.5
(6) Switzerland, 1890–1899 to 1957–1959	4.4
(7) Denmark, 1870–1874 to 1960–1962	5.9
(8) Norway, 1865–1874 to 1960–1962	5.7
(9) Sweden, 1861–1865 to 1960–1962	12.1
(10) Italy, 1898–1902 to 1960–1962	5.6
(11) Canada, 1870–1874 to 1960–1962	5.3
(12) Australia, 1861–1865 to 1959/60–1961/62	2.2
(13) Japan, 1879–1881 to 1958–1961	10.4
(14) European Russia, U.S.S.R., 1913 to 1958	11.4

SOURCES

Row (1) : See text.

Rows (2)–(14) : Simon Kuznets, *Modern Economic Growth* (New Haven : Yale University Press, 1966), pp. 64, 65.

persisted for 100 years, the value at the end of the 100-year period would have been 4.1 times as large as the value at the beginning. The comparisons permitted by the table are of exactly the same type as the comparisons permitted by average annual growth rates ; that is, all growth experiences are expressed in common time units. The reason that average *centennial* rates have been used in the table, rather than average *annual* rates, is that they give one a clearer notion of the significance of differences in growth rates. For example, we know that per capita product grew at a rate of between .3 and .5 percent per year over the years 1710–1840 and at a rate of about 1.4 percent between 1840 and 1900 (1834–1843 to 1894–1903). The former rates are smaller than the latter, but how significant is the difference ? According to Table 2.14, per capita product would have increased between 40 and 70 percent had the former rates prevailed for a century, and over 300 percent had the latter persisted for a century. Neither comparison is easy to come to grips with, but the figures in Table 2.14 are a little more meaningful than are the average annual rates.

What does Table 2.14 show ? First of all, it shows that the American growth rate has increased over time, as the preceding paragraph pointed out. A similar finding emerges from the data relating to Britain. The timing of the acceleration of the British rate coincides with the British Industrial Revolution, while the acceleration of the American rate is associated with the diffusion of that revolution to the United States. The phrase "Industrial Revolution," however, has unfortunate connotations. It invites one to envision an abrupt transition—a "takeoff," as W. W. Rostow has termed it—while the data underlying the calculations suggest that the increase in the rate of growth took place over an extended period. Second, the phrase centers attention on industrial growth, whereas the changes associated with the accelerations and with the modern high rates of growth were by no means confined to the industrial sectors, as the subsequent chapters of this book will show. The important point to notice at this stage, however, is that modern growth has proceeded at extraordinarily high rates, compared with what went before.

The second thing to notice about the table is that only 14 countries are represented in it. While the table could be expanded somewhat with enough effort, it does include most of the existing long-term product per capita series. Since record keeping tends to go hand-in-hand with economic growth, the statistics in Table 2.14 are therefore a biased collection. They represent economies in which rapid growth took place over an extended period, but do not represent those which were not growing or were growing slowly. Most of the world's population lives in countries not represented in the table. Thus the table suggests that only a minority of the world's population has been experiencing the very pronounced improvements in material well-being that have been one of the consequences of modern economic growth. The disparities between the levels of life of the minority and the majority have been growing apace.

The next point to notice is that the modern American rate of growth in product per capita (e.g., 1834–1843 to 1957) falls toward the middle of the distribution in the table—higher than the rates experienced by the United Kingdom, the Netherlands, and Australia; much lower than the Japanese, Swedish, and Russian rates (which, however, are for a shorter period); and roughly the same as the French, German, Swiss, Danish, Norwegian, Italian, and Canadian rates. This finding is in pronounced contrast to that discussed in the previous section, where it was pointed out that the rate of increase in the *size* of the American economy was unusually high.

Finally, as noted previously, the American level of performance was high by contemporary standards as early as 1840, and probably a good deal earlier. Rapid rates of growth have been evident in the American record from the early decades of the nineteenth century. Modern growth began in the United States from an unusually favorable base and at a very early date. Thus, despite the fact that the American growth rate has not been extraordinarily high by the standards of experience in other developing countries, the level of performance in the United States has been persistently above the level of performance in most of the countries of the world, including those listed in Table 2.14.

Real content of per capita product.   In the preceding sections national product per capita has been used as an index of material well-being. The choice seems reasonable enough, since national product is intended to measure the total output of a society; and one would suppose that, other things being equal, the material condition of a people might be judged by the value of output of the society compared with the number of persons who live in it. However, it is now time to take a closer look at the concept and the actual measurements of national product that have been made, in order to obtain a clearer idea of the meaning of the comparisons contained in the preceding pages. (This topic will be discussed in more detail in Chapter 3.)

The national product estimates of a country are based on the records kept by the people of the country. The volume and quality of the economic records people keep depend upon the importance they attach to material things and to the degree of development of the economy in which they live. For example, a farmer who produces crops only for his own consumption and that of his family is less likely to keep detailed records than one who is producing for a market. The records collected by social institutions also depend upon the level of economic development. For example, the United States conducted a complete population census as early as 1790 for political reasons but did not attempt an industrial census before 1810 and did not carry out a reasonably complete census of economic activities until 1840.

As a consequence, national product estimates relating to the early years of a country's history generally rest on a more limited empirical base than do the estimates relating to recent years. Similarly, national product figures for developed countries are usually more reliable than those for underdeveloped countries. To simplify the discussion, in the rest of this section the term "underdeveloped country" will be used to refer both to modern underdeveloped countries and to the early history of countries that are currently developed.

In general, if national product estimates are in error because records are incomplete or inaccurate, one would suppose that the error would be in the direction of *under*stating the true level of national product. The term "bias" will be used to describe such a situation. That is, national product estimates are *biased downward*, insofar as basic records are incomplete. Since the records of developed countries are better than those of underdeveloped countries, one would suppose that the relative size of the error would be smaller in the first case than in the second. This means that the measurements of per capita product probably *over*state the disparities among countries in levels of economic performance at any given time and probably exaggerate the rate of growth experienced across time (i.e., estimated growth rates have an *upward* bias). But while this is true in a general way, it is not necessarily a serious source of error. There are two reasons for this. First, the economies of underdeveloped countries are relatively simple, and primary production—especially agricultural production—figures prominently in total output (see the next section). Therefore, to obtain a fair idea of the level of performance does not require the enormously complex records necessary to measure the output of a developed economy. The fact that underdeveloped countries do not have complete records is not a serious barrier to national product estimation, so long as primary output can be estimated with some accuracy.

Second, national income estimates do not arise naturally and automatically out of the records. Records must be processed by economists, who generally fill in gaps by inferences from indirect evidence. There is no reason to suppose that these inferences generally understate actual output. For example, so far as the U.S. national product series is concerned, there is no good reason to suppose that the recorded rates of change are biased upward because of errors in the estimates for early years. If anything, the bias runs in the other direction.

In several places above, the national product has been referred to as a measure of total output. But in fact the measurements actually made have a narrower scope than this. For practical reasons, national product is restricted to output produced for a market, with two important exceptions. All primary products—for example, all farm products—are counted as part of national product, whether or not they are produced for a market. The same is true of the rental value of houses. The national product includes an estimate of the value of the shelter produced by houses occupied by their owners. With these exceptions, however, the national product consists of marketed goods, which means that whenever a man marries his housekeeper the national product declines, as textbook authors are fond of pointing out. When the lady is drawing a salary for her services, she contributes to measured national product, but when the salary stops, her output is no longer counted—a peculiar convention.

Obviously, the course of change of national product is not going to be affected much by marriages between housekeepers and their employers, and the matter would be unimportant if that were all there were to it. But there is more to it than that. We know that during the process of economic growth specialization has increased and economic self-sufficiency has diminished. Many of the manufactured goods purchased in markets today—baked goods, canned goods, preserved meats, soap, clothing, furniture, and so forth—were typically produced in the home for home consumption 150 years ago. Even investment goods were "home produced." Farmers cleared and fenced their own land and built houses, sheds, and barns with their own hands using materials taken from their farms. The conventional measures of national product exclude these goods and therefore understate the total volume of output of any economy. Since home production is more important in underdeveloped countries than in developed economies, the conventional measures tend to exaggerate disparities in levels of material well-being between developed and underdeveloped economies. For the same reason, long-term rates of growth of per capita real national product tend to exaggerate the improvement in material well-being within a given country.

It would be useful to know how important this type of bias is. For obvious reasons the information we have on the subject is incomplete, but we do have some evidence relating to U.S. experience from 1840 to 1900. Estimates have been made of the real value of the investments carried out by farmers and of certain important types of home manufacturing—the production of baked goods, preserved meats, textiles, and clothing. With these estimates, one can compute the rate of growth of per capita real national product, inclusive of the main elements of home manufacturing.[10] The more inclusive measure yields an annual rate of growth of 1.15 percent, or about .3 percent less than the

[10] See Robert E. Gallman, "Gross National Product in the United States, 1834–1909," in *Output, Employment, and Productivity in the United States After 1800*, Dorothy S. Brady (ed.), Studies in Income and Wealth, vol. 30 (New York: National Bureau of Economic Research, 1966), p. 35.

figure obtained from the conventional national product estimates. To put the matter the other way around, the rate of change of real national product per capita, measured conventionally, appears to exaggerate the rate of advance of material well-being by less than .3 percent per year in the years 1840–1900. The bias is not negligible, but neither is it of overwhelming importance.

In the years since 1900, the bias in measured rates of growth arising from this source has probably been a good deal less important than it was for the nineteenth century. The transfer of economic activities from the home to the marketplace has probably proceeded at a more limited pace in this century than in the last. After all, by 1900 the process had already gone far, leaving relatively limited opportunities for further transfers. Furthermore, in this century the process has actually been reversed in certain areas, most prominently in the provision of services. For example, in the nineteenth century, domestic servants were relatively numerous, while today they are not. In part, domestic servants have been replaced by commercial laundries and cleaning establishments, carry-out food services, and so forth. But in part they have been replaced by members of the household, working with improved household equipment—modern kitchen stoves, washing machines, dish washers, vacuum cleaners, and so on. The transfer of these activities from the marketplace to the home introduces a *downward* bias in the computed twentieth-century rate of growth, which tends to offset any biases produced by the transfer of manufacturing from the home to the marketplace. On balance, then, the measured twentieth-century rate of growth may reflect no net bias from this source.

At a more general level, one of the things Americans have bought with their increased productive capacity is more leisure time—that is, more time away from recognized economic activity. Some of this time is used to produce goods and services formerly purchased in markets, as just indicated, and some is spent in activities (such as education) that ultimately result in higher productivity. But whether the increased leisure is used purposively or not, it has value, as witnessed by the fact that we have chosen it in preference to the additional goods we could have had by working longer hours. One could make a compelling case that leisure should be counted as part of the value of output of our economy and that such an adjustment of NNP would be a major one. Simon Kuznets has made two calculations of the value of leisure.[11] According to the Kuznets figures, proper adjustment of the NNP to account for the value of leisure would raise the rate of growth of per capita product by between one fifth and two fifths. The estimates are rough, but they do suggest the importance of this aspect of our long-term growth.

In *The Road to Wigan Pier* George Orwell describes the end of Karel Capek's play, *R.U.R.*, ". . . when the Robots, having slaughtered the last human being, announce their intention to 'build many houses' (just for the sake of building houses, you see)."[12] The idea is grotesque precisely because economic activity

[11] Simon Kuznets, "Long-Term Changes in the National Product of the United States of America Since 1870," in International Association for Research in Income and Wealth, *Income and Wealth of the United States: Trends and Structure* (Income and Wealth, Series 2) (Cambridge, England: Bowes & Bowes, 1952), p. 68.
[12] (New York: Berkley, 1961), p. 158.

is *human* activity directed toward *human* ends and the robot society has no fundamental human dimension. The concept of the national product is equally grotesque unless it is informed by human ends. But notice that the identification of "human ends" involves a philosophical position concerning the nature of man. The existing national product measures were developed against an individualistic background, which helps explain why per capita national product has been a crucial measure of performance. But this conception of man has not been accepted at all times or in all places. For example, Mercantilist writers tended to think of the nation, not the individual, as the fundamental social unit and to judge the performance of the economy in terms of the military power it afforded the nation.

The individualistic foundation of the modern national accounts—the notion that the individual is the end of the system, not a means to some other end— should be clearly borne in mind. At the same time, one should recognize that this idea has been imperfectly translated into empirical statements, a point that will be elaborated in the following paragraphs.

The "net national product" is supposed to consist of the volume of goods and services that can be consumed by humans without diminishing the capacity of the economy to produce. It is not always easy, however, to make the ideal measurement. For example, imagine a very simple society consisting of one family producing one product, corn. In the first year the family harvests 100 bushels of corn. Is this the *net national product* of the society? Of course not, since the family has to put away, say, 5 bushels to serve as seed for next year and 35 bushels to feed the mule that they use for plowing, cultivating, and harvesting. The net national product is therefore only 60 bushels.

So far so good. But suppose the children in the family have been riding the mule for pleasure. Now the economy has two products, not one: corn and "mule riding." One way to take into account the value of the second product would be to attribute part of the mule's consumption of corn to "final output." That is, if the mule works 600 hours a year and he is ridden by the children for 100 hours, then we might count one seventh of the mule's corn consumption as part of final product, on the ground that the corn "produced" the output, "mule riding," and represents the best measure we can make of the value of mule riding.

Every economy has characteristics of the kind described above and they produce special problems for the measurement of national product. In the simple case described, the problem is easily solved. But in real economies, it is not so simple. Our hypothetical mule has an analogy in the modern automobile. On one hand, cars are used to commute to work and to ride to shopping centers, just as the mule is used to work in the cornfield. But cars are also used for pleasure, as the mule is ridden by the children. If we had adequate records, we could allocate expenditures on cars between "intermediate" (work) and "final" (pleasure) categories and in this way obtain an accurate measurement of net national product. But we don't have adequate records, and therefore we include all expenditures on private automobiles as part of final product. That is, we *overstate* the value of net national product. Similar problems are posed by government expenditures, many of which are "intermediate" in nature. For example, expenditures on police are largely intermediate, since the police are intended to maintain the system—or set of rules—within which output is produced, rather than directly adding to final output. The Department of Commerce estimates, which treat government expenditures as "community consumption," involve substantial double-counting, while the estimates of Simon Kuznets and the National Bureau of Economic Research—which are used in this chapter—are less open to this criticism.

The automobile produces problems of another kind. Expenditures by private persons for gasoline are counted as part of the national product. The burning of gasoline in cars produces smog. Smog exacerbates respiratory ailments. People with respiratory ailments go to doctors for cures. The doctors' services count as part of the national product. Some patients die anyway. They enter the national product in the form of a fee to a mortician, which gives the national product an odd look. Thus events which can only be regarded as unfavorable produce results that lead to *increases* in measured national product.

The point is that the net national product is supposed to be a *net* measure of the goods and services serving human wants and needs. In fact, the measures made are *gross*, not net, since they include some "intermediate" goods (equivalent to the corn fed to the mule) and they fail to account for losses involved in the methods of production we use (such as smog). How much too large our actual measurements are, we do not know. We can be sure, however, that the measures that we have for the United States 100 years ago are more nearly net than those we have for the United States today. The increasing complexity of the economy nearly guarantees that there is more "double-counting" today than formerly, while the scale and form of resource exploitation have increased the relative magnitude of the costs that are left unaccounted for. These factors tend to bias the measured rates of growth in an upward direction.

Thus far we have been talking about the identification of items of output to be counted as part of the net national product. But outputs consist of dissimilar things, and in order to sum them into a total, one must measure them against a common scale. The scale used is value, and relative values are established by market prices. The intellectual warrant for this procedure is that prices reflect a society's demand patterns (referring back to the notion of the individual as the end of the system) and technical capacities (embodied in supply schedules). Obviously, the empirical problems of implementing such a scheme are formidable. But such problems are not central to the interpretive issues with which we are concerned. This chapter is concerned with comparisons across time and space and therefore we will concentrate on comparative problems.

To begin with, imagine a very simple economy that produces just two final goods, good *a* and good *b*. We have data for two periods in the history of the economy, period 1 and period 40, and we want to measure the relative change in output between these two periods. The data are as shown on p. 48, where Q is defined as output and P is defined as price.

The data show that the national product quadrupled over this period. But

	Period 1			Period 40		
	Q	P	$Q \times P$	Q	P	$Q \times P$
Good a	50	$2	$100	100	$4	$400
Good b	100	$1	$100	200	$2	$400
NNP (ΣQP)			$200			$800
Index, base period 1			100			400

part of the increase was due to a doubling of prices, explicable, let us say, in terms of simple quantity theory reasoning—that is, the supply of money increased faster than output. Obviously the rise in prices, in itself, represents no real gain in material well-being. Therefore, we must take out the price change. We can do this by expressing output in *both* periods in the prices that existed in *one* of them—that is, by deflation. In this example it doesn't matter which price base is used. The *relative* gain is 100 percent, whether all values are expressed in prices of period 1 or in prices of period 40. This is evident since the output of each final good doubled between period 1 and period 40.

A little thought will show that the selection of the price base for deflation will not affect the measured *rate* of change, so long as *either*: (a) both outputs change at the same *rate*, or (b) both prices change at the same *rate*. But in a growing and complex economy, outputs and prices do not change at the same rates; relative outputs and relative prices constantly shift.[13] Under these circumstances, the choice of the deflation base will affect the computed rate of growth, as the following example shows.

Data:

	Period 1		Period 40	
	Q	P	Q	P
Good a	50	$2	200	$1
Good b	100	$1	200	$1

NNP Expressed in Prices of Period 1 :

	Period 1	Period 40
Good a	$100	$400
Good b	$100	$200
NNP (ΣQP)	$200	$600
Index, on base 1	100	300

NNP Expressed in Prices of Period 40 :

	Period 1	Period 40
Good a	$ 50	$200
Good b	$100	$200
NNP (ΣQP)	$150	$400
Index, on base 1	100	267

[13] The rest of this discussion is also relevant to international comparisons of national product and national product per capita.

Expressed in prices of period 1, real NNP increased by 200 percent in this example; expressed in prices of period 40, it increased by only 167 percent. Thus, the computed rate of growth depends upon the deflation base selected.

How should one interpret these results? In effect, the first measure says: "If you appraise the output of the economy in terms of the *pattern of demands and productive capabilities* of period 1, then NNP was three times as large in period 40 as in period 1"; while the second measure says: "If you appraise the output of the economy in terms of the *pattern of demands and productive capacities* of period 40, then NNP was 2.67 times as large in period 40 as in period 1." This seems sensible enough. After all, the national product is an evaluative concept. It is certainly reasonable to suppose that the rate of growth will depend upon the relative importance (prices) attached to the various items of output and that the relative importance of items of output will change over time with shifts in tastes, income, the distribution of income, and supply conditions. The question is whether there are any general rules that describe how the selection of a particular price base will affect the computed rate of growth. It turns out that there is a useful guide of this kind.

Empirical tests show that in a growing economy, long-term relative changes in output are inversely related to long-term relative changes in prices. That is, if the output of a good increases rapidly compared with the outputs of other goods, its price will fall relative to the prices of other goods. The empirical results make sense in terms of the theory of demand. Furthermore, a little thought will show that, given this relationship, selection of an early year price base for deflation will result in *higher* rates of growth than selection of a late year price base. Given the base for deflation, one can generally tell the direction of the change in the measured rate of growth that would be produced by selection of an alternative base. For example, the prices used in this chapter to deflate the national product of 1840–1900 are 1860 prices. We can be fairly sure that had 1840 prices been selected, the computed rate of growth for the period would have been somewhat higher; had 1900 prices been chosen, the growth rate would have been lower. Indeed, the 1860 price base was selected for the nineteenth-century series and the 1929 price base for the twentieth-century series precisely in order to produce growth rates that lie toward the middle of the range of possible results. Additionally, of course, the selection of price bases that have a *common* temporal location (each toward the middle of the relevant time period) simplifies the comparison and interpretation of nineteenth- and twentieth-century growth experiences.

The preceding remarks lead to a conclusion of some interest. Relative prices can change because supply relationships shift and/or because the structure of demand changes. The empirical generalization described above suggests that changes proceeding from the supply side have been more important, over the long run, than changes proceeding from the demand side. To put the matter another way, the structure of demand has been a lot more stable during growth than the structure of supply.

In summary, rates of change in real per capita national product are imperfect measures of changes in material well-being. Per capita national product estimates summarize a vast range of the most relevant data and represent the best place to begin a study of economic growth. However, they are subject to various biases which, while they tend to offset, are surely not fully compensatory. There are also problems of interpretation related to the price base that must not be forgotten. One should also bear in mind, of course, that these measures relate to the material aspects of life and guard against the temptation to treat them as though they had a wider relevance. Finally, the level of per capita product reflects the capacity of an economy to administer to the wants and needs of its members. But the way in which these wants and needs are met depends upon the way in which income is distributed and the kinds of goods produced. These subjects are dealt with in the next section and, more fully, in subsequent chapters.

Trends in the size distribution of income.   We have seen that per capita national product was high as early as 1840. But Americans did not share equally in the abundance. We do not have conclusive evidence concerning the distribution of income by size for 1840, but we do have one estimate of wealth holdings for 1860 (see Table 2.7). According to this estimate, 5 percent of the families owned about 50 percent of the private wealth of the United States. Now we know that income from wealth accounted for about 30 percent of national income before the Civil War (see Table 2.11). If we assume that all types of property received the same rate of return, we can infer that the rich families received about half of the property income earned in the United States, which would give them about 15 percent of the national income. But of course rich families also earned "service" income—that is, income from work of one kind or another, including the management of plantations and other business firms. According to evidence relating to the twentieth century, the rich have typically earned between half and two thirds of their total income from service. Assuming the same was true before the Civil War and assuming that the top wealth holders were also the top income recipients, then the richest 5 percent of families received between 30 and 45 percent of the total national income—15 percent in the form of property income and 15 to 30 percent in the form of service income. The estimating procedure almost certainly *overstates* the degree of income concentration, but an estimate by Seaman for 1867 suggests that the lower of the two values may be in the correct neighborhood.[14] To be on the safe side we can adopt a wide range and say that the richest 5 percent of families probably received between 25 and 35 percent of the national income.

Notice what this implies. The rich families received average incomes six to ten times as large as the average incomes of the remaining 95 percent of families. In terms of our previous discussion, the disparity between the rich 5 percent and the remaining 95 percent was as great as (and perhaps greater than) the disparity between average American per capita income in 1957 and in 1840. To put the point another way, the difference was equal to the proceeds of at least 117 years of growth, at the rate experienced by the United States in the period 1840 to 1957.

[14] Ezra C. Seaman, *The American System of Government* (New York: Scribner's, 1870), p. 242.

American income distribution before the Civil War was strikingly unequal, then, but presumably this situation exists in all large societies. The question is how antebellum America compared with other countries and other times. Evidence relating to this point is scanty and treacherous, indeed, but it is worth some attention. Table 2.15 gathers together information on the share of income received by the richest 5 percent of families in various European countries in the nineteenth and twentieth centuries and in the United States in the twentieth century. The data are not fully comparable, and therefore modest differences cannot be regarded as evidence of real disparities. Still, two points of considerable interest emerge from the table. First, the degree of concentration suggested by the U.S. data before the Civil War does not appear to be markedly different from the degree of concentration exhibited by the European data that refer to the nineteenth and early twentieth centuries. Second, the evidence shows that, in all of the countries for which we have data, including the United States, the degree of concentration diminished in the years since the 1930s and, in one or two cases, in the years since World War I. Consequently, the degree of concentration exhibited in the 1950s is a good deal less pronounced than that of the antebellum United States.[15]

We know that inequality has diminished somewhat in this century. What

TABLE 2.15
Share in national income received by the richest 5 percent of tax or consuming units, various countries, nineteenth and twentieth centuries (percent)

	1870s 1880s	1890s 1900s	1912 1913	1925	1928 1929	1935 1936	1938 1939	1942– 1949	1950s	1962
(1) United States	—	—	—	—	30	27	26	21	21	20
(2) United Kingdom	48	—	43	—	33	—	31	24	18	—
(3) Prussia	26	27	30	—	26	—	—	—	—	—
(4) Saxony	34	36	33	—	28	—	—	—	—	—
(5) West Germany	—	—	—	—	—	—	—	—	18	—
(6) Netherlands	—	—	—	—	—	—	19	17	13	—
(7) Denmark	37	28	—	26	—	—	25	19	18	—
(8) Norway	—	27	—	—	—	—	20	14	—	—
(9) Sweden	—	—	—	—	—	28	—	22	17	—

Note: Not all the country series are continuous. Specifically, in the case of the United Kingdom the first two figures are drawn from one study, the third from another, the fourth and fifth from another, and the sixth from still another; in the cases of Prussia and Saxony, the first three figures are from one study, the fourth from another; in the case of Denmark, three studies each contributed two figures.

SOURCES

Row (1): Selma F. Goldsmith, "Changes in the Size Distribution of Income," in *Inequality and Poverty*, Edward C. Budd (ed.) (New York: Norton, 1967), p. 66.
Rows (2)–(9): Kuznets, *Modern Economic Growth, op. cit.*, pp. 208–210.

[15] The measure of concentration used in these paragraphs was adopted out of necessity, since we have no good indications of other facets of the antebellum American distribution. However, the assertion that concentration diminished in the United States during several decades of the present century is based not only on a measured decline in the share of income received by the rich, but also on modest increases in the share received by those at the base of the income pyramid. (See the sources cited in Table 2.15.) In the last two decades, however, there has been very little change in the distribution. The middle-income groups have gained at the expense of both the rich and the poor, but gains and losses have been very limited. See Edward C. Budd, "Postwar Changes in the Size Distribution of Income in the U.S.," *American Economic Review*, vol. 60, no. 2 (May 1970), p. 260.

can we say of trends in the nineteenth century? Unfortunately, very little. We know that the degree of inequality before the Civil War depended in some measure on the institution of slavery. Part of the earnings of slaves was expropriated by slave owners and, since slave holdings were concentrated, this meant a direct transfer of income from the poor to the rich. The Civil War destroyed the institution, and while freedmen after the war were in fact imperfectly free, nonetheless their economic position *vis-à-vis* the other members of southern society—and in particular the former planters—was no doubt improved. But the war also killed an extraordinarily large fraction of the southern work force, destroyed southern capital—land improvements, buildings, railroads, and so on—and forced a reorganization of southern productive methods. As a result, southern income per capita fell sharply, both in absolute terms and relative to the rest of the country (see Table 2.16). Thus, while the war may have diminished inequalities within the South, it widened the income gap between North and South, and it is difficult to know whether the net result was to increase or decrease income concentration for the country as a whole.

In the decades after the war there is no very clear indication of a marked trend in the distribution of income. Regional income inequalities did not diminish appreciably before the turn of the century (Table 2.16), nor did sectoral differences in income per worker (Table 2.17). Neither of these sets of measures bears directly on the size distribution of income. Nonetheless, regional and sectoral income differences contribute to inequality, and a marked narrowing or widening of them, other things being equal, would be reflected in changes in the size distribution of income for the nation. For example, in the twentieth century we find a diminution in both regional and sectoral income disparities coinciding with a reduction in the degree of income concentration (Tables 2.15, 2.16, 2.17).

There is also no indication of a marked shift in the functional distribution of income in the nineteenth century (Table 2.11). The shares of property and labor in total income changed from one decade to the next, but no long-term trend emerged. Property income is much more heavily concentrated than is

TABLE 2.16
Personal income per capita in each region as a percentage
of U.S. average per capita income, 1840–1950

Regions	1840	1860	1880	1900	1920[a]	1930[a]	1940[a]	1950[a]
United States	100	100	100	100	100	100	100	100
Northeast	135	139	141	137	132	138	124	115
North Central	68	68	98	103	100	101	103	106
South	76	72	51	51	62	55	65	73
West	—	—	190	163	122	115	125	114

[a] Cycle averages: 1920 = 1919–1921, 1930 = 1927–1932, 1940 = 1937–1944, 1950 = 1948–1953.

SOURCE: Richard A. Easterlin, "Regional Income Trends, 1840–1950," in *American Economic History*, Seymour E. Harris (ed.) (New York: McGraw-Hill, 1961), p. 528.

TABLE 2.17
Income per worker in agriculture, manufacturing and mining, and all other sectors
as percentages of national income per worker, 1939–1955

Sectors	1839–1859	1869–1879	1889–1899	1919–1940	1950–1955
United States	100	100	100	100	100
Agriculture	45	42	37	47	76
Manufacturing and mining	113	93	128	120	123
All other	200	220	160	120	100

SOURCE: Robert E. Gallman and Edward S. Howle, "Trends in the Structure of the American Economy Since 1840," in *The Reinterpretation of American Economic History*, Robert William Fogel and Stanley L. Engerman (eds.) (New York: Harper & Row, 1971), data underlying pp. 26, 27, and 28, Tables 1, 2, and 3.

labor income, and therefore a change in the functional distribution, other things being equal, would find expression in a change in the size distribution of income. A development of this kind occurred in the twentieth century, as an examination of Tables 2.11 and 2.15 will show. The diminution in income concentration coincides in time with a rise in the fraction of national income received by labor. Furthermore, in the twentieth century there has been a tendency for the concentration of private wealth holdings to diminish (Table 2.18). Other things being equal, this development would tend to reduce inequalities in the distribution of wealth income and therefore work in the direction of a more egalitarian aggregate income distribution. The sketchy evidence we have relating to the wealth distribution in the nineteenth century, however, does not suggest that there was any marked reduction in concentration over the last several decades of that century.

Most of the indirect indicators that we have, therefore, do not testify to a dramatic shift in the size distribution of income in the last two or three decades

TABLE 2.18
Share of personal sector wealth (equity) held by top wealth holders,
selected years, 1922–1956

Year	Top 1 Percent of Adults	Top .5 Percent of All Persons	Top 2 Percent of Families
1922	32	30	33
1929	36	32	—
1933	28	25	—
1939	31	28	—
1945	23	21	—
1949	21	19	—
1953	24	23	29
1956	26	25	—

SOURCE: Robert J. Lampman, *The Share of Top Wealth-holders in National Wealth, 1922–56* (New York: National Bureau of Economic Research, 1962), p. 24. Reprinted by permission of the publisher.

of the nineteenth century. However, there is one bit of evidence which suggests that there may have been a narrowing in inequalities. Lee Soltow has measured income concentration among the rich, using tax data, and he concludes that inequalities within this group were somewhat larger in the late 1860s and early 1870s than just before World War I. The movement between the two periods is not pronounced, compared with the drift toward greater equality that he records across the years 1914 to 1965, but it is noticeable.[16]

Thus there may have been a modest reduction in inequality between the years just after the Civil War and the years just before World War I. Between World War I and the 1950s there was a more pronounced reduction associated with a narrowing of regional and sectoral income differences, a rise in labor's share of national income, and a diminution in the concentration of wealth holdings. Since then, the distribution has been fundamentally stable, although the share of income received by the middle-income groups has risen slightly, while the shares of the very rich and the poor have declined modestly.

Composition of the American Economy

The preceding sections of this chapter describe changes in the size and performance of the American economy. They recount a record of very rapid long-term growth, and while they emphasize increases in the aggregate volume of output (and output per capita), they suggest that the composition of the economy has also changed. This section amplifies the account of this compositional change.

The previous section pointed out that per capita (per worker) income levels in 1840 differed markedly among regions and industrial sectors. If differential per capita income levels can be taken to represent differential economic opportunities, then one would expect to find that factors of production would be drawn toward those regions and industrial sectors in which incomes were relatively high. The fraction of each factor supply located in these regions (sectors) would tend to grow over time, as would the fraction of total output produced in them.

The data in Tables 2.19 and 2.20 suggest that, on the whole, the developments that might have been predicted from the 1840 data did, in fact, occur. The agricultural shares of the work force and income declined, while the shares of the other two sectors in labor force increased, as did the share of manufacturing and mining in income. The fraction of the total population in the low-income South fell from almost four tenths in 1840 to less than three tenths in the twentieth century, while the South's share in income dropped from very nearly 30 percent to about 20 percent. The high-income West, which appears in the table for the first time in 1860 with 2 percent of the population and 4 percent of the income, had roughly one seventh of both total population and aggregate income by 1950 (Table 2.19). The North Central and Northeast regions pose something of a puzzle, since the former was

---

[16] Lee Soltow, "Evidence on Income Inequality in the United States, 1866–1965," *Journal of Economic History*, vol. 29, no. 2 (June 1969), pp. 279–286.

TABLE 2.19
Percentage distribution of national income and the labor force,
by industrial sector, 1839–1955

	1839– 1859	1869– 1879	1889– 1899	1919– 1940	1950– 1955
Panel A: Labor Force					
Agriculture	56.9	51.9	41.5	21.5	10.5
Manufacturing and mining	14.1	20.7	21.8	24.7	24.4
All other	29.0	27.4	36.7	53.8	65.1
Totals	100.0	100.0	100.0	100.0	100.0
Panel B: National Income					
Agriculture	25.8	21.6	15.2	10.4	8.8
Manufacturing and mining	14.0	17.5	24.7	26.2	29.5
All other	60.2	60.9	60.1	63.4	61.7
Totals	100.0	100.0	100.0	100.0	100.0

SOURCE: Gallman and Howle, "Trends ...," *op. cit.*, data underlying pp. 26, 27, and 28, Tables 1, 2, and 3.

TABLE 2.20
Percentage distribution of population and personal income, by region, 1840–1950

Regions	1840	1860	1880	1900	1920	1930	1940	1950
Panel A: Population								
United States	100	100	100	100	100	100	100	100
Northeast	43	36	31	30	30	30	29	28
North Central	20	29	35	35	32	32	30	30
South	37	33	31	30	29	29	30	29
West	—	2	4	5	9	10	11	13
Panel B: Personal Income								
United States	100	100	100	100	100	100	100	100
Northeast	58	50	44	41	39	41	36	32
North Central	13	20	34	36	32	32	31	32
South	29	26	15	15	18	16	20	21
West	—	4	7	8	10	11	14	15

SOURCE: Easterlin, "Regional Income Trends . . . ," *op. cit.*, p. 535.

gaining in share of population and income before 1880 and the latter losing, while the data in Table 2.16 suggest that the economic situation in the Northeast was the more favorable. Presumably migrants into the North Central area were attracted by the prospects of this new region, rather than by the current income levels. These expectations seem to have borne fruit, since per capita income in the region was at the national average by 1880. Furthermore, the data underlying the table show that at that date income per worker in both agriculture and the nonagricultural sectors was at least as high in the North Central area as it was in the Northeast.[17]

The account of compositional change offered above is by no means a complete one. It unfolds from a static model of the economy in which factors are reallocated in response to a given set of economic opportunities. If the economy had, in fact, been static, the per capita income differentials of 1840 would have been erased in a relatively short time, given the pronounced factor movements suggested by Tables 2.19 and 2.20. But the previous section shows that these differentials actually widened over part of the nineteenth century and that they began to narrow at a rapid pace only in the twentieth. Clearly other factors were at work that had a bearing on relative economic opportunities and, therefore, on the allocation of factors of production and the composition of output. We shall now consider several of these factors.

The widening of regional and sectoral income differentials in the nineteenth century is attributable in large measure to the Civil War, the bloodiest conflict in which this nation has ever engaged. Over half a million soldiers died— 100,000 more than American losses in World War II and about twice as many Americans as have died in all other wars taken together, including Vietnam. The number killed came to almost 5 percent of the work force of 1860, and the number under arms, between 25 and 35 percent.

While the destruction of the war fell with special force on the South, the North was also severely damaged. Almost 70 percent of the soldiers who died came from northern units, and the diminution of immigration during the war reduced growth not in the South, which did not receive a substantial part of nineteenth-century immigration, but in the North. Contrary to popular belief, northern industry did not, on balance, benefit from the stimulation of war demand. The war was fought with muskets and rifles, and Wacht has shown that all the small arms used by the Union could have been produced from roughly 1 percent of United States iron production.[18] After small arms, the largest war demand placed on heavy industry may well have been the demand for horseshoes, and, according to Uselding, one firm supplied all of the horseshoes for the Union army.[19] The point is that in terms of the arms and equipment used, the Civil War was not a modern war and did not result in a marked increase in the productive capacity of heavy industry, nor did it speed the adoption of new techniques of production. Across the entire decade of the 1860s heavy industry grew at a rate well below that experienced before the war. Light industry was dealt a severe blow by the reduction in supply of perhaps its most important raw material, cotton. As late as 1870 the structure of industry still showed the distorting effects of the war. Textile output was only modestly larger than in 1860. Thus the widely held notion that the North experienced large immediate and direct economic gains from the war is mistaken.

---

[17] *Per capita total* income in the former region remained lower chiefly because it was less industrialized.
[18] Richard F. Wacht, "A Note on the Cochran Thesis and the Small Arms Industry in the Civil War," *Explorations in Entrepreneurial History*, Series 2, vol. 4, no. 1 (Fall 1966), pp. 57–62.
[19] Paul J. Uselding, "Henry Burden and the Question of Anglo-American Technological Transfer in the 19th Century," *Journal of Economic History*, vol. 30, no. 2 (June 1970), p. 331.

While the North suffered from the war, southern losses were even greater. As late as 1870, the level of real income per head was only about 60 percent of the prewar level, and it was not until 1880 that prewar economic performance was once again attained in the South. The heavy and enduring impact of the war on the South was an important factor in the widening of regional income differences after 1860 and, since the South was predominantly agricultural, in the failure of the sectoral income differentials to diminish materially before the twentieth century.

The economic effects of subsequent wars have been quite different. They have not been fought across American soil and they have killed fewer Americans. They have increased the demand for American output and have put pressure on the economy, which has tended to accelerate the reallocation of resources. On the whole, the reallocations have been in the directions established by long-term forces and therefore have tended to narrow income differences.

A second factor that affected relative income levels was the emergence of new opportunities due to the discovery of new resources and the development of technological knowledge. Between 1840 and the Civil War the territory of the continental United States increased by over two thirds, rising from 1.8 million square miles to 3.0 million square miles. As each new block of territory was brought in, the regional and sectoral stakes were changed. For example, Table 2.16 shows that in the territories of the Mountain and Pacific states, which were added to the United States after 1840, the level of income per head was almost twice the national average in 1880. There were also resource discoveries in the old states—copper and iron in Michigan in the 1850s, petroleum in Pennsylvania in 1860—while technical innovations, such as the internal combustion engine, drastically altered the value of existing resources. Such discoveries can operate either to narrow or to widen regional and sectoral income differences, of course, and no comprehensive measure is available to show their net effects in American history.

Finally, shifts in the structure of demand affected relative income levels and the allocation of resources. The concept of the income elasticity of demand—the sensitivity of demand to changes in income—is a useful one in this connection. The income elasticity of demand for a good is the percentage change in the quantity demanded that is associated with a 1 percent change in income. If elasticity is greater than one, demand rises (or falls) faster than income and there is a tendency for the share of the good in total output to rise (fall). The reverse is true for elasticities less than one, and when a good has an elasticity equal to one, the demand for it will rise (fall) in step with income.

Budget studies show that the income elasticities of food and fuel items tend to be less than one; those for items of clothing, close to one; those for consumer durables, greater than one; for housing, slightly less than one; for medical, educational, and entertainment items, greater than one. These cross-section studies would lead one to expect that during a period of advancing income per capita, such as the United States has experienced in the last century and a half or so, the structure of consumer demand would shift.

TABLE 2.21
Percentage distribution of the output of consumer goods, by types of goods, 1839–1953

Periods	Perishables	Semidurables	Durables	Services	Total
1839–1859	52	16	5	27	100
1869–1898	49	17	7	27	100
1899–1918	45	16	8	31	100
1919–1938	39	16	10	35	100
1939–1953	44	16	10	30	100

SOURCE: Based on Gallman and Howle, "Trends . . . ," *op. cit.,* p. 33, Table 9.

Perishable items, such as food and fuel, would comprise an ever-smaller fraction of total output. The share of durables and certain services in output would rise, while the share of semidurables (clothing) would remain constant and the share of shelter would decline modestly. Also, technical change has been especially fruitful in the development of new consumer durables, which constitutes a second reason for expecting that, across time, the share of durables in expenditures might increase. The evidence we have on the composition of the output of final consumer goods conforms with these expectations, as an inspection of Table 2.21 will show.

The shift in the structure of demand has tended to perpetuate sectoral income differences. The agricultural sector, in which income per worker was initially low, produces chiefly food and textile fibers. Demand for agricultural output has therefore grown less than proportionately with income. The importance of this point is even greater than the data in the table suggest. In the pre–Civil War years, perishables composed roughly half of the value of output of consumer goods. Since perishable goods consisted chiefly of unprocessed farm goods (e.g., milk and vegetables) or lightly processed ones (e.g., flour, meats), a large part of the expenditures on them flowed to farmers. In the mid-twentieth century, the share of perishables had fallen to something over 40 percent of all consumer goods. Furthermore, the perishables involved were much more heavily processed and had passed through more hands on the way from the farmer to the consumer. The fraction of expenditures on perishables that flowed to farmers was therefore much smaller in the mid-twentieth century than in the mid-nineteenth.

The shift in the structure of demand therefore operated to maintain sectoral income differences and to accelerate the shift of resources away from agriculture and toward the other two sectors.

SUMMARY

It has been estimated that in the late 1950s, while the United States accounted for only about 6 percent of the world's population, it produced roughly one third of the world's output. The preeminent position of the U.S. economy at that time was the legacy of some 300 years of extraordinary growth. In the mid-seventeenth century, the American economy was a scattering of settlements on the eastern seaboard. Two hundred years later it rivaled most European economies in size, and another hundred years later it was far and away the most productive economy in the world.

American growth before the nineteenth century flowed chiefly from an increase in the factors of production—land, labor, and capital. The supplies of all these continued to grow apace in the nineteenth century while factor productivity also advanced, accounting for perhaps one fifth of total growth. Rates of change in factor supplies have slowed down in the present century, but the growth of productivity has accelerated. Roughly two fifths of the increase in real national product in this century is attributable to productivity advance. The role of productivity advance in the rise of material well-being has been even more remarkable. Almost half the gain in per capita product in the nineteenth century and roughly 80 percent in the twentieth century was due to the improvement in factor productivity. Subsequent chapters of this book deal with the forces responsible for the growth of factor supplies and productivity.

The first decades of colonization were a period of trial and sacrifice. But by the early eighteenth century Americans enjoyed a rude plenty. At that time, income per capita probably fell not far short of the British level. The performance of the American economy probably improved modestly before the Revolution. What happened between that time and the early nineteenth century is difficult to discern, but there was probably a further modest advance, most of it concentrated in the years 1793–1807, the heyday of the American merchant marine. The pace of change picked up in the early decades of the nineteenth century, and in the years between 1840 and 1960 income per capita increased about sixfold. The average rate of gain of per capita product during this period was rapid when compared with the experience of most countries during most historical periods, but about average when compared with rates of growth in other developed countries during the last century. However, the acceleration of the rate of change in the early nineteenth century came when the United States level of performance was already high and it came at an early date, so that the United States has had a longer experience with modern high rates of growth than have most other countries. Consequently, the level of per capita income in the United States is today the highest in the world.

In mid-nineteenth-century America the distribution of income and wealth was unequal, although not unusually so by the standards of the European economies of the day. Whether inequalities had widened or narrowed over the preceding centuries, we cannot presently say. We can say, however, that both the income and the wealth distribution have grown more egalitarian since that time, the development being concentrated chiefly in the two or three decades before the 1950s. The distribution of income appears to have been roughly stable since that time.

The structure of the American economy has changed drastically during the process of growth. Factor proportions have shifted, since the supply of capital has increased much faster than the supply of labor. Wage rates have gone up relative to the interest rate and labor's share of the national product has increased.

Factors of production have been reallocated from one region and from one sector of the economy to another, in response to differential economic opportunities. The center of gravity of the American economy has shifted westward, while at the same time the fraction of output accounted for by agriculture has declined and the fraction accounted for by industry has increased. The shift in the sectoral allocation of resources has been under way since the beginning of the nineteenth century and it has been formed in part by changes in the structure of final demand associated with the long-term increase in per capita income. The shifts in the structure of the economy have therefore been a fundamental part of American long-term economic growth.

SUGGESTED READING

Abramovitz, Moses. "Economic Growth in the United States." *American Economic Review,* vol. 52 (September 1962).

Aptheker, Herbert. *The Colonial Era.* 2nd ed. New York: International Publishers, 1966.

Conference on Research in Income and Wealth, Studies in Income and Wealth, vols. 24 and 30 (also essays in vols. 3, 11, 33, 34). New York: National Bureau of Economic Research.

Craven, Wesley Frank. *The Colonies in Transition : 1660–1713.* New York: Harper & Row, 1968.

David, Paul. "The Growth of Real Product in the United States Before 1840: New Evidence and Controlled Conjectures." *Journal of Economic History,* vol. 27, no. 2 (June 1967).

Denison, Edward F. *The Sources of Economic Growth in the United States.* New York: Committee for Economic Development, 1962.

Duffy, John. *Epidemics in Colonial America.* Baton Rouge: Louisiana State University, 1953.

Gallman, Robert E. "Fundamental Concepts of Statistical Studies as Applied to History." In *Approaches to Economic History,* edited by George Rogers Taylor. Greenville, Del.: Eleutherian Mills-Hagley Foundation, forthcoming.

Kuznets, Simon. "Long-Term Changes in the National Product of the United States of America Since 1870." In International Association for Research in Income and Wealth, *Income and Wealth of the United States: Trends and Structure* (Income and Wealth, Series 2). Cambridge, England: Bowes & Bowes, 1952.

Morris, Richard B. *Government and Labor in Early America.* New York: Octagon Books, 1965.

North, Douglass C. "Early National Income Estimates of the U.S." *Economic Development and Cultural Change,* vol. 9, no. 3 (April 1961).

Taylor, George Rogers. "American Economic Growth Before 1840: An Exploratory Essay." *Journal of Economic History,* vol. 24, no. 4 (December 1964).

U.S. Bureau of the Census. *Historical Statistics of the United States, Colonial Times to 1957.* Washington: U.S. Government Printing Office, 1960.

3
CONSUMPTION AND THE STYLE OF LIFE

Great increases in an aggregate like real national product per capita, while impressive, are difficult to relate to individual experience. Some feeling for what these changes have meant in everyday life can be obtained by looking in detail at the changing pattern of consumption during the course of American economic growth. This chapter relies principally on a comparison between the 1830s and the 1930s, periods for which the available data are relatively abundant. The population is considered in three segments, those residing on farms, those in villages, and those in cities, since there are important differences among these groups. After indicating the relative importance of these groups in the national market, the chapter focuses on individual components of living levels—how well people ate, the nature of their housing, their attire, and so on. It then goes on to a more aggregative discussion of expenditure trends and differences. Finally, the chapter concludes with an overall appraisal of the trend in the level of living.

THE SIZE OF RURAL AND URBAN MARKETS

Economic activity is concerned with the production of the various kinds of food, housing, clothing, and other goods and services that are used by consumers. The kinds of goods and services used vary widely over the scale of wealth and income, and as a consequence the numerical importance of the different classes—the poor, the middle classes, and the rich—affects the allocation of production among different end uses. The minimal needs of the poor for shelter, clothing, and other essentials confine their diets to staples and the cheaper qualities of other goods. The rich are provided with the finest the arts and crafts can produce, whereas the middle classes are satisfied with moderate qualities in the goods and services they consume.

When the poor are numerous, inferior foods plus the luxuries of the rich account for the largest part of the final output of the economy. When the middle classes become numerically important, production is directed toward superior foods and moderate qualities in other goods and services. In America, the large middle class of farmers and craftsmen in eighteenth- and nineteenth-century rural communities gave rural households the largest share in aggregate consumption. Moreover, since they produced their own housing and fuel and most of their food, their share in the consumption of other goods must have exceeded their share in aggregate income.

The share in aggregate expenditures of different groups in the population in the nineteenth century and earlier can be estimated only roughly, for want of statistical information representative of all sections of the country. Even a crude statistical picture, however, can indicate how important rural households were in the market for manufactured goods and services. In the 1830s, about 66 percent of all households were on farms, 23 percent in villages, and 11 percent in cities. On the supposition that farm families on the average were able to spend $100, village families $200, and city families $300 over and above their outlays for housing and fuel, rural families (farm and village) would have accounted for 76 percent of all such expenditures. According to our assumptions and estimates, the shares in such expenditures by type would have been somewhat as shown in Table 3.1. The large share of the rural population in expenditures for the various classes of commodities offers an explanation of the American stress on low-priced articles that could be accommodated within moderate or low budgets. When most rural families were spending less than $25 on house furnishings in a year, that sum placed an upper bound on the prices families were willing or able to pay for particular pieces of furniture. Serviceable furniture, simply designed, was a legacy of the colonial period. In the 1830s, laborers' families were buying bedsteads for as little as $1.50 to $3, bureaus for $10 to $20, clocks for $5 to $10, and chairs for 50 cents to $1.50.

For a number of commodities, the rural market was even more important to American producers than our estimates suggest. The wealthy in the cities and on the plantations imported from abroad their furniture, glass, china, silverware, musical instruments, carriages—in fact, everything that did not have to be fitted to the person. As a consequence the urban market for American manu-

TABLE 3.1
Share in expenditures, by type, of population
in specified place of residence, 1830s (percent)

Items	Farms	Villages	Cities
Purchased foods	36	37	27
Clothing	58	26	16
House furnishings	53	23	24
Transportation	45	31	24
Reading and recreation	50	26	24
All purchases	45	31	24

factures was, in general, limited to households with much less than $500 to spend on goods and services other than housing and fuel. Thus urban and rural families with limited or modest means stimulated the evolution of fabricated goods designed for mass consumption.

Households with limited resources usually are willing to accept uniformity in the design of the articles they buy. Though rural communities were scattered, the flow of goods designed and manufactured in other places worked against the development of local tastes and preferences fixed by tradition. Different nationality groups did bring their customs with them into the New World, but in their adaptation, blending, and borrowing, the forms of things, like the people, became Americanized. The functional designs in furniture, tableware, clocks, family wagons, and stoves which were spreading through the rural communities in the first half of the nineteenth century prepared the way for industrialization in the manufacture of consumer durable goods.

With the growth in urban communities the shares of rural households in the aggregate expenditures for various products declined, but throughout the nineteenth century these households almost certainly still accounted for a large fraction of all consumer purchases. If by 1900 the share in expenditures of rural communities had been reduced in proportion to the decrease in their share in the population, it would still have represented half of the market for clothing and house furnishings and more than half for passenger vehicles. Rural households, in a real sense, were dominant in the market for consumer goods until the twentieth century. The founding of Montgomery Ward and Sears Roebuck just before the turn of the century testifies to their importance.

By the 1930s, rural households numbered less than half (42 percent) of the total number of households, with 23 percent on farms and 19 percent in the villages. Farm families spent, on the average, $566, village families $884, and city families $1169 on goods and services other than housing, fuel, light, and refrigeration. Urban communities had become dominant in the market (Table 3.2), and goods and services were designed for urban households with the money to spend on new models and new varieties of things. Model T automobiles and small radios were perhaps the last products that reflected principally the influence of rural consumers with modest incomes on the

TABLE 3.2
Share in consumption expenditures, by type, of population
in specified place of residence, 1930s (percent)

Item	Farms	Villages	Cities
Purchased foods	11	17	72
Clothing	17	17	66
House furnishings	15	18	67
Transportation	17	18	65
Reading and recreation	11	17	72
All purchases	13	18	72

kinds of goods and services produced. The 25 million Model Ts produced before 1929 effected the diffusion of the automobile ; in the 1930s, the age of the used car was already well along its way.

City water systems and electric power plants brought facilities and conveniences into twentieth-century homes that farm households generally could acquire only by installing home power plants. A home plant powerful enough to pump water was expensive, and small plants did not provide many lights or much power. Thus farm households had much less than a proportionate share in the rising aggregate of electrical equipment produced for the home. In the 1930s, the great majority of farm homes, except in the Pacific region, lacked running water and electricity for lighting and other uses. After the extension of rural electrification systems in the 1940s, prosperous farmers provided their families with all the modern facilities and conveniences, but where small-scale farming is the rule, farm dwellings have generally not been modernized even today.

HOUSING AND HOUSEHOLD GOODS

As we have seen in the rural communities, where most of the population lived before the twentieth century, a sizable middle class exerted a strong influence on the kinds of consumer goods and services produced in America. In the colonial period and until well into the nineteenth century, the farmers, craftsmen, and merchants who made up this middle class filled the needs of the community for a wide variety of goods : building materials, the foods that could be produced in the locality, firewood, furniture and household equipment, wagons, shoes and other articles of leather, and the fibers that were used in the manufacture of textiles. Men assisted one another in the construction of houses, churches, and schoolhouses under the guidance of a carpenter and helped their neighbors operate their farms. Women's work in the home included food processing, spinning, and much weaving, sewing, and knitting. Through such production in the homes and in the community, households attained a comfortable level of living even though their incomes were very modest in modern terms.

Housing

The housing built by farmers, craftsmen, and others in the rural communities of the eighteenth century were substantial in construction but simple in design. One-story log houses and frame houses with one or two rooms and an attic under the rafters were the most common types. Cellars and basements were practically unknown and frequently there was no flooring except the hard earth. The fireplace with a chimney that provided heating and cooking, and a few windows with shutters were the only conveniences found in these dwellings. Country residents had their wells, privies, bake ovens, smokehouses, and food storage areas outside their dwellings. There were sheds for doing the laundry and there was space in the barn for the loom. Since all these appointments were outside, farm households were more comfortable than those of the workingmen and craftsmen in the cities.

The water supply in cities was a communal affair. Before the nineteenth century, public wells were maintained to serve the needs of the population. Only the well-to-do living in the outskirts had their own wells. Establishments known as wash-houses were located by the rivers and canals. There, for a fee, housewives or their servants could take care of the laundry—much as they do in cities in today's less developed countries. Under these circumstances rural life had distinct advantages.

A log or frame house with one or two rooms cost less than $200 to build in the early decades of the nineteenth century, and rooms could be added when household resources permitted. By the 1830s, four-room houses, some with two stories, had replaced one- and two-room homes in rural communities. With larger houses, rural families with moderate incomes purchased more furniture than their colonial predecessors.

In Table 3.3 the size of dwelling is related to the level of expenditures for goods and services other than shelter. Houses were larger in successively higher expenditure brackets, and farmhouses were larger than houses in the cities and in the villages. Most farm households in the 1830s probably did not spend more than $200; houses of three to five rooms were the most prevalent. In the 1930s, the average farm family's expenditures were somewhat over $500 and the average family's house had six or seven rooms. It is clear that even with rising incomes the work of keeping house placed limits on the size of the dwelling, as did declining family size.

The emergence early in the nineteenth century of the millwork and the hardware industries brought farmers and other rural residents the means for improving the interior arrangements in their homes. Prefabricated doors, window frames, shutters and sashes, butts, hinges, and other hardware encouraged farmers to invest more in their dwellings. The balloon frame, an American innovation in construction introduced in the 1830s, reduced the cost of construction on the site and, along with prefabricated components, greatly changed the architecture of country dwellings. Two-story dwellings with varied outlines became more and more numerous and their designs became

TABLE 3.3
Average number of rooms per dwelling, by place of residence and level of household expenditure, 1830s and 1930s

Total Household Expenditures Excluding Shelter	1830s			1930s		
	Farms	Villages	Cities	Farms	Villages	Cities
Under $200	4	4	2	4	—	—
$200–$500	5	4	3	6	5	4
$500–$1000	8	5	4	7	6	5
$1000–$2000	12	8	6	8	7	5
$2000–$3000	12	10	9	9	7	6

more ornate. Farmers were no less willing than the residents of villages, cities, and suburbs to have a choice among many different plans for their houses.

Before the Civil War, architects, builders, and contractors were already exploiting individual preferences in the selection of parts—windows, sashes, doors, hardware, plumbing—and in the arrangement of the dwelling space. Instead of becoming cheaper, as they did initially, the components of houses became more varied and more expensive. Prospective owners in rural communities and in the new residential sections of cities and the suburbs were encouraged by the industry to contract for individual designs, with the result that the complex operation of assembly permitted no gains in productivity. Instead, house building became an important example of the increasing costs of production associated with individuation in the product.

Household Equipment

The activities of the rural farm communities demanded house furnishings at moderate prices (see Table 3.13 at the end of this chapter), equipment for operating a home with comparatively few domestic services (outside of the South), and the convenience of private transportation equipment. Manufacturing, in the course of time, moved out of the household and away from the rural community, but economic development and technical change did not alter the basic tastes and preferences of these communities. Households on farms and in the villages were receptive to innovations that helped the housewife maintain a comfortable home, and these households gave the possession of household equipment its prominence in the American standard of living.

Colonial craftsmen in rural communities produced sturdy, serviceable, durable goods that farm households could afford. They used less costly materials and simple designs in the manufacture of furniture, pots, kettles, pans, utensils, jars, bottles, pails, buckets, dishes, tableware, and other equipment. Local woods were used in the construction of furniture; in the beginning, wood was used extensively for articles such as pails, buckets, bowls, plates, mugs, forks, and spoons. Iron was used in place of copper for pots and kettles, and earthenware was used instead of glass for jars, jugs, and bottles.

By the end of the colonial period, stoneware, tin, and Britannia ware (an alloy of tin, antimony, and copper) were replacing wood for the production of dishes, forks, and spoons. House furnishings and other consumer goods were flowing through the channels of trade, and apt designs in a product, wherever they originated, were widely adopted. Goods produced in rural communities were transported to the cities to help serve the needs of growing populations, and artisans in the cities were led to concentrate on the kinds of goods persons of moderate means could afford.

Men's activities in the agricultural communities of the nineteenth century centered on farming, construction, and the services such as blacksmithing and wagon repair that were necessary in every vicinity. Women's activities in the home were as diverse as they had been in the eighteenth century. However, women were aided in various ways that made their work easier and more productive.

The chief developments in household equipment during the early part of the nineteenth century had to do with cooking. Cook stoves with ovens were perfected and the varieties of pots, pans, and kettles for special uses multiplied. Some mechanical equipment—grinders, presses, and the like—came into the home, but only the coffee grinder was widely used. There were few commercial bakers in rural communities, and the kitchen stove with assorted ovenware supported household baking—an industry that did not wane in importance until the twentieth century.

Canning, the first modern process of food preservation, was brought into the household with the invention of the Mason jar in the late 1850s. The plentiful supply of foods produced on farms for home consumption and the well-equipped kitchens in rural homes channeled canning activities into the home; as a result the commercial canning industry grew slowly in America. All kinds of equipment used in preparing foods for cooking and canning were perfected in the second half of the nineteenth century, and the forms of grinders, mixers, pitters, and presses remained essentially unchanged for generations. Home canning was still an important industry in the 1940s, and its claim on strategic materials was given a high priority during World War II.

The sewing machine, perfected later in the nineteenth century, affected the manner of living more than any other labor-saving device available for household use. Apparel and household textiles had to be regarded as durable goods when a needle and a length of thread provided the only means of fastening two pieces of fabric together. Tailors, dressmakers, and seamstresses manufactured apparel for the well-to-do, but in the majority of rural households women produced all their own clothing and their children's clothing and some menswear. Itinerant tailors came into homes to manufacture men's coats, breeches, and capes, while the women made the shirts, vests, and knitted underwear and hose. Women sewed the trousers worn by seamen and laborers, and when trousers replaced breeches in male attire early in the nineteenth century, rural housewives took up their manufacture. Mending and repairing clothing was an important activity, for changes in styles were not frequent and articles of clothing were not discarded until they could no longer be repaired.

The consumption of textiles was limited by the labor required to turn them into articles of clothing and mattresses, pillows, sheets, pillowcases, quilts, and comforters. Without the sewing machine, the factory production of textiles might not have expanded as greatly as it did after it displaced home spinning and weaving. The sewing machine gave an impetus to the production of men's clothing in factories and the manufacture of clothing for women and children in the home. Home sewing added to women's wardrobes and to their supplies of household textiles and altered the practices of discard and retention. Repairing became less important and laundering began to claim more time. Articles of clothing and bedding were replaced before the material was so worn that it could not be salvaged for other uses. As replacement became more frequent, rural households began to be increasingly affected by changes in style and fashion.

Rural residence placed a premium on individual ownership of the equipment needed for production in the household, for possession of such equipment was the precondition for best utilizing the diverse activities of the housewife. Urban households also adopted equipment that could be accommodated in the dwellings, and both the arrangement of dwellings and their location were affected by the requirements for home production. Urban families with moderate means sought homes where the women could engage in home production on a rural scale. Their preferences favored the evolution of the single-family home with ample space for household operations and the storage of preserved foods. Thus the need for production in the home influenced house building, and urban households reinforced the rural demand for the necessary equipment.

Interior Decoration

Furniture before the modern era was of two kinds : the simple stools, benches, chests, and box beds that most men built for their families, and the handsome chairs, tables, bureaus, and bedsteads that cabinet makers produced for the wealthy. Colonial wheelwrights, woodturners, and cabinet makers also designed inexpensive furniture for persons with modest means ; their chairs, beds, and tables were among the array of household goods that peddlers brought into rural communities. As households acquired furniture that was more or less standardized in design, individuality in the interior of the house was expressed more and more in the selection of different combinations of the kinds of things that were produced for the market. Textiles, bedding, curtains, and later floor coverings were used extensively in small homes to create some uniqueness in decorative effect. Later the multiplication of lamps, pottery, glass, and ceramics made the possible combinations of things so numerous that every home could look different in some respect.

In houses of one or two rooms, the bed was the prominent piece of furniture, and bed coverings and curtains were made decorative in many ways by the professional weaver or by the housewife's skill with the needle. As larger houses became the rule and even the children and servants slept in beds, box beds with or without wooden slats were replaced by beds with springs made of woven rope. However fast or slowly bedsteads came into common use, bedding—in particular, featherbeds and mattresses—spread rapidly when cotton textiles, ticking, and sheeting came on the market. The women in rural communities made featherbeds, pillows, and mattresses, and most often quilts and coverlets. When we consider a shift from straw mats and blankets to pillows, mattresses, sheets, pillowcases, and quilts (as well as blankets), the rapid rise in the cotton textile industry is not hard to explain. Pillows and mattresses were a significant part of the more comfortable image that drew immigrants across the Atlantic.

The mattresses women sewed were not thick or tufted, and the process of making beds every day included flattening the mattresses with a wooden paddle. As they were able to acquire them, households put more mattresses on their beds and piled them high with the quilts (and possibly coverlets) that provided the decorative note in their furnishings. Ticking by the yard was, by the 1830s, cheaper than tow cloth ; a housewife could make a full-length mattress for an outlay of $1.70. Homemade mattresses and quilts served the needs of rural households until late in the nineteenth century.

City families were able to buy leather, hair, and fleck bolsters, mattresses, and pillows from the cabinet makers and upholsterers who manufactured these articles before the sewing machine brought them into factory production. But a ready-made mattress was expensive before the 1860s, and city families of modest means, like rural families, relied on home manufacture. They had to buy not only the ticking, but also the filling, which was usually feathers before the cotton industries brought padding on the market. Padding was expensive at first and probably not too satisfactory except for pillows, and city families bought feathers by the bushel when they could afford an ample supply of bedding.

Bedsprings, made of cones of iron wire fastened together, were not unknown in the 1830s, but they apparently did not come into widespread use until after the Civil War had fostered the development of many kinds of lightweight camp beds. In the 1870s, a family could buy a simple metal bed equipped with springs for as little as $5. Farm families buying bedsteads in the 1930s spent $11 or less on their purchases (see Table 3.14 at the end of this chapter).

The appearance of other furniture in even the smallest of homes and the eventual use of glass in windows gave housewives even more opportunities to use textiles for color and decoration. From bed curtains they progressed to window curtains, ruffles and flounces for their beds and chairs, and cloths for their tables. Textiles were used as lavishly as possible in nineteenth-century households plagued with dust and dirt that came first from open fireplaces and later from coal- and wood-burning stoves and furnaces.

Early in American history clocks and other items once considered luxuries were being produced for less privileged families. Gaily stenciled articles of tin and looking glasses were among the temptations offered by peddlers to colonial families.

The poor in rural England in the seventeenth century had wall hangings of painted cloth instead of the fine tapestries and oil paintings found in the homes of the wealthy. Before 1730, wallpaper, no doubt in imitation of European fashions, had become the style among the well-to-do in the colonies. Substitutes for wallpaper in the form of cheap engravings and woodcuts must have been widely available to rural residents before the Revolution.

Prints, like other ephemera, were not systematically collected and conserved, so that the historical record of their distribution will always be spotty and blurred. According to contemporary accounts, engravers and later lithographers were established wherever there was printing and publishing above a modest scale. They produced inexpensive prints to sell separately, as well as illustrations for the printers' papers and books. The Currier and Ives slogan "prints for the people" was not a new idea, but the surviving volume of their work indicates both a large operation for the time and a highly competitive quality for their price.

Prints for 10 to 25 cents were carried by peddlers into rural communities, but there is no way to estimate the extent of their geographic distribution. The illustrated weeklies and monthlies already common before 1860 may have been more widely distributed, providing more households with interesting and decorative items to pin up on their walls before the daguerrotype and the camera brought the possibility of family portraits into the homes of farmers and workingmen.

Private Transportation Equipment

The wagon and the carriage offer the best illustrations of the search for low-cost serviceable designs in the goods produced for farmers and other rural residents. Colonial farmers able to buy four-wheeled wagons made them serve a dual purpose by converting them into passenger vehicles for transporting their families to church observances and other social occasions. Demountable seats suspended on wooden springs were set in the box and a hooped frame with a cover could also be added.

Early in the nineteenth century, a lightweight family wagon that could be drawn by one horse made its appearance in rural communities and the farm wagon was relegated to transporting farm products to market. The cost of the family wagon was very low compared with prices paid by the wealthy for their carriages. By the 1840s, the frame cover and seats were fixed, and with the addition of springs and cushions in the next two decades the family wagon became transformed into the American buggy.

The buggy was the prototype of the Model T automobile, and its widespread diffusion in rural communities gave the carriage industry a broad base in mass consumption. The universal need for wagons to transport goods fostered the wheel-making industry in the eighteenth century. The evolution of the buggy and other types of carriage depended chiefly on the development of wheels that were light, strong, and durable. It is not clear just when American wainwrights began to use the straight grain of the wood for the rims of wheels, but their invention of steaming and bending the wood to the desired shape was in wide use by the 1860s, and machinery for performing the various operations in wheel making had already been developed. The light wheel with many spokes made the one-horse carriage a reality, and mechanization in its manufacture allowed for the production of comparatively inexpensive vehicles.

It was the rural communities in the first decades of the twentieth century that adopted the automobile for private use. Various forms of public transportation served the transportation needs of city dwellers before the 1920s, and residents of the largest cities did not acquire great numbers of automobiles before the 1940s. The automobile greatly strengthened the concept of rural residence as the ideal in the American standard of living. The growth of suburbs before the twentieth century was governed by the location of public transportation—boats and ferries, horsecars, railroads, and then electric streetcars. The widened spread of the suburbs was the inevitable consequence of the automobile (see Chapter 5).

Heating and Cooking Needs

Most farmers produced their own firewood for heating and cooking until other fuels were brought into the market of country towns. Indeed, firewood was the chief fuel in rural communities until World War II, although fuel oil for heating and kerosene, gasoline, and bottled gas for cooking were coming into use.

Fuel was a costly element in the city workers' budgets, especially when inefficient fireplaces were the only means for heating and cooking. The search for more efficient cooking and heating equipment suitable for the dwellings in the growing cities of the eighteenth and early nineteenth centuries led to many innovations in the design of stoves on both sides of the Atlantic. The use of stoves on ships and later in railroad cars added stimulus to the search for simple, efficient, compact designs. American stove makers adapted and developed Benjamin Franklin's fireplace and Count Rumford's oven into various types of small stove that came into widespread use near the beginning of the nineteenth century. The diffusion of stoves made its contribution to low-cost housing simply by eliminating the masonry in the fireplace.

Stoves and other household articles were an important part of the output of the iron foundries. The small stoves of the early nineteenth century weighed between 200 and 300 pounds. If every household had acquired a new stove in a given year, the purchases would have exceeded iron output many times. Annual purchase rates were, of course, quite low. Then, as now, the innovation automatically became a part of new housing, while it was only gradually introduced into older housing. It is impossible to guess how fast stoves moved into the farmhouses in the older sections of the country, but they did become almost universal except in sharecroppers' houses before the 1870s.

The qualitative evidence on the geographical diffusion of stoves is familiar. They moved with the pioneers into the sod-house frontier in the almost treeless plains beyond the Mississippi and north into the Dakotas after the Civil War, and around the Horn into California after the discovery of gold. The cabin furnishings shown in TV westerns give an authentic picture of the goods that increasingly traveled, overland or by water, into the newly settled regions.

Although kerosene for lighting became almost universal in the 1860s and 1870s, kerosene or gasoline plates, ranges, and stoves were not produced in quantity until the 1920s. Gas for cooking had taken over in most cities by the third decade of the twentieth century, but the farmers' woodlots continued to serve most of their needs for heating and cooking until the 1950s.

Lighting

When the first settlers came to New England and Virginia, window glass, candlelight, and lamps had just begun to appear in the homes of the lesser freeholders and farmers in the mother country. Glassworks entailed a heavy capital investment, and the industry developed very slowly in America before the middle of the nineteenth century. Since imported glass was expensive, farmhouses generally did not have glass panes in their windows. Curiously enough, it was the paper industry, stimulated by the American emphasis on books and other printed matter, that supplied the substitute for glass. Oiled paper served as panes to admit light when the shutters were open.

Daylight and artificial light were important in the diverse activities of households and in the enjoyment of the books and other reading matter that came into their possession. Candles, which households could produce for themselves, added to the list of goods families in rural communities could consume with only a small money outlay for equipment and utensils. Most of the urban population bought their candles ; even unskilled laborers' families could afford some use of candlelight.

Among Benjamin Franklin's inventions was a lamp for street lighting that was adapted for households as a lantern which became a common article in farmhouses by the early decades of the nineteenth century. It seems plausible that farmers bought glass for their lanterns before they installed glass panes in their windows. Oil lamps, suited to reading and fine work such as sewing, were expensive, and although supplies of whale oil increased until the 1850s, these lamps probably satisfied only the demand of the upper-income groups. The lantern with its candle remained the supplement to the firelight for the winter evening's activities in the homes of farmers before the Civil War.

The great whaling industry was already on the decline before a substitute for whale oil was brought onto the national market. Whaling voyages grew longer and longer in the first half of the nineteenth century, eventually extending up to five years, with the result that the price of lamp oil increased more or less steadily with the cost of production. The rapid growth of the petroleum industry needed no promotion other than the development of inexpensive Argand lamps, and the whaling industry was kept alive after the 1860s much more by corset stays than by candles, wax, and oil. Farm families used kerosene for lighting until electric power was extended into rural areas. Even by 1941, more than half of the farm families and about one third of other rural families had only kerosene lamps for light.

SUNDRIES

The importance of goods and services other than shelter, food, clothing, and domestic service at all levels of expenditure indicates that they represent essentials to well-being that are varied in cost to suit the purchasing power of the consumer. Table 3.4 shows the distribution of these expenditures among the component categories for levels of living that were higher than the averages in the 1830s but lower than the averages in the 1930s. Expenditures on furnishings were lower in the 1930s than in the 1830s, although this category includes the many new kinds of equipment that were being adopted. The larger expenditures of the 1830s reflect the needs of growing populations in newly settled communities where new housing represented a large part of the existing inventories.

The expansion of the areas of settlement also infuenced the expenditures for churches ; church buildings, like homes, called for a considerable volume

TABLE 3.4
Sundry purchases, by place of residence and level of household expenditure,
1830s and 1930s (dollars)

Item	Farms		Villages		Cities	
	1830s	1930s	1830s	1930s	1830s	1930s
Total household expenditures excluding shelter	200	200	500	500	1000	1000
Sundry purchases	66	75	130	178	230	380
Furnishings	16	9	30	20	67	50
House operation	3	6	15	21	23	44
Medical care	5	14	13	34	24	60
Transportation	9	21	24	36	41	99
Reading, recreation	4	6	9	20	18	49
Personal care	6	5	8	15	18	28
Tobacco	5	7	8	15	8	27
Church, charity	18	7	23	17	31	23

of new construction. By the 1930s, much of the manmade environment was inherited, and the majority of families in the older sections of the country lived in dwellings that had been built from 10 to 50 (or more) years earlier and had been equipped in various ways by their previous occupants.

Expenditures on the other categories of goods and services were generally higher in the 1930s than 100 years before. The increases were the greatest in the cities. The increased expenditures for household operation reflect the multiplication of preparations for laundering, house cleaning, and dishwashing and the consumption of much more soap. Toilet soap was a large item in personal care, as were shaving cream and various other creams and lotions. Although soap making as a household activity had not disappeared from low-income rural areas, large-scale production had long since displaced the local chandler.

The expenditures on reading and recreation in the 1830s were mainly for almanacs and school books in rural communities and for school books and newspapers in the cities. The American farmers' almanacs combined a calendar with weather records, advice on farming operations, travelers' guides, wit and humor, and general information. Almanacs published in the cities, like *Poor Richard's Almanac* and *The Old Farmer's Almanac*, were widely distributed in rural communities, but the surviving examples in libraries and museums indicate that the output of widely dispersed country printers must also have been considerable. Although farm journals and newspapers eventually grew in importance, the country almanac continued to offer its varied entertainment and local advertising throughout the nineteenth century.

Traveling shows, panoramas, animal exhibits, and the like journeyed through the rural communities when roads permitted; such entertainment as exhibits, curiosities, museums, and balloon shows was generally available in the cities.

Circuses and other traveling shows multiplied during the nineteenth century, not losing their importance as popular entertainment until the introduction of motion pictures in the early decades of the twentieth century. Farming communities since colonial times had provided their own means of recreation in the country fairs with their exhibits of livestock and other products of agriculture, handicrafts, implements, and machines. In time the circuses and traveling shows came to be standard features of the country fair, as did manufacturers' exhibits of new equipment for the farm and the home. The almanac and the general store, along with the country fair, kept the farming community informed about every sort of new development.

The motion picture, more than any other item, accounts for the rise in expenditures for reading and recreation between the 1830s and the 1930s. Whereas fairs and circuses were annual affairs only, motion pictures provided a regular arrangement for paid entertainment. Phonographs and radios made their contribution to these expenditures, although the inexpensive radio did not come on the market until the decade before World War I. Newspapers and magazines became relatively inexpensive, and families generally brought more and more such reading matter into their homes.

The rise in expenditures for transportation and for recreation illuminates the incongruities in economic development which affected family life in rural communities and in poorer urban neighborhoods. Owning an automobile and going to the movies do not depend on the facilities and equipment in the home, and such innovations could be widely diffused before dwellings generally were equipped with running water, bathrooms, electric lights, and modern household equipment. Only with increases in income could households enjoy most of the innovations that characterize modern living.

REFINEMENTS IN THE MANNER OF LIVING

Human wants are expanded by the introduction of more diversity in available goods and services. As the supply of different kinds of goods increases, men come to want variety in their diets and in their recreation ; they strive for distinction in their homes and in their apparel ; they want to harmonize uniformity and diversity in experience.

Variety in the Diet

Variety in the diet depends on the kinds of foods produced and on the diversity of ways of combining them in cooking and serving. The colonists in America had, by 1700, orchards bearing apples, cherries, peaches, pears, plums, and quinces. Their herds of cattle and swine and their flocks of sheep and poultry afforded a large quantity of the meats that Europeans favor over fish and game. Over the course of a year, the markets in the cities were stocked with essentially the same fresh foods that are used today, but the foods on hand were determined by the season. The only out-of-season substitutes for fresh meats, vegetables, and fruits were cured meats and fish, and dried or pickled vegetables, and fruits. Change in dietary patterns had to wait until the seasonal variation in supplies was reduced by the introduction of canning, which provided other substitutes for fresh foods than those produced by the ancient techniques of preservation and refrigeration.

Given seasonal limits on the choice of ingredients, most of the variations in meals came through the cooking, particularly in the breads and pastries. The first settlers in the colonies brought with them a taste for fresh breads of all kinds; ovens for baking and other equipment for cooking hot breads were symbols of good living. Ovens in rural communities were frequently built out of doors, covered or in a little shelter; in cities they were built at the side or at the back of the fireplace. Although colonial homes are usually described as having ovens, it is likely that most dwellings lacked this convenience until cast iron stoves had displaced the fireplace.

Some forms of equipment for cooking quick breads were probably widely used in the homes of small farmers and workingmen in the colonial period. There is no way of guessing how early the frying pans, griddles, Dutch ovens, Scandinavian waffle irons, and reflector ovens found their way into rural communities, but the frequent purchases of such articles by U.S. arsenals and armories in the first years of the nineteenth century suggest that their diffusion came fairly early in the eighteenth century, if not before. At any rate, the hotcakes, griddle cakes, biscuits, shortbreads, tarts, and pies that loomed large in American diets in 1776 were no less important in 1876, when French cartoons of the Exhibition in Philadelphia scoffed at the American's lack of appreciation of gastronomy.

Cereals in the form of porridge or bread, and meats, potatoes, and dried pulses (peas, beans, lentils, etc.) provided the bulk in American diets before the twentieth century. Poor or rich, a man's weekly fare was around 15 pounds of concentrated foods; and a woman's, 12 or 13 pounds. The habitual use of stimulating beverages, common since ancient times and even before, may be connected in part with the nature of man's diet as well as with the inadequacies of supplies of safe drinking water. Three new beverages from Asia, the Near East, and America became popular in the eighteenth century—tea, coffee, and chocolate. They were all used with sweetening agents, and in combination with the taste for hot breads they account for what must have been a substantial increase in the consumption of sugars before the middle of the eighteenth century. Plentiful supplies of sugar from West Indian plantations converted sweets from a luxury into a necessity, first in the form of molasses and small amounts of crystallized sugar and later as inexpensive white sugar.

To the diverse kinds of alcoholic beverages used by Europeans—beers, wines, and spirits—the cultivation of sugar cane added rum. Much of early American history is connected with the colonial appetite for sugars and stimulating beverages. Whiskey and gin could be produced in most farming communities once they were supplied with copper boilers and pewter worms, which were available for less than $50 in the 1790s, and farmers could and did add distilling to their varied activities. Nevertheless, rum held its own in consumption along the eastern seaboard until the 1840s.

The importance of salts, spices, sugars, and beverages is exhibited in Table 3.5. Farmers able to spend $200 on their households in the 1830s spent $27 on such goods, most of which were imported from the West Indies, South America, or Europe. The expenditure was apparently quite typical. Farm households that produced their own supplies of cereals, meats, and whiskey or gin needed about $23 worth of preservatives and flavors to provide variation in their diets. (For representative prices, see Table 3.11 at the end of this chapter.)

White flour was added to the essentials—among salts, spices, and flavorings—before the 1830s, and it became the principal cereal used wherever and whenever the general stores were well stocked with provisions. The white flour produced in the merchant mills for consumption in the cities eventually became the staple in the diets of most farm families. The consumption of bakery products followed a similar dispersion pattern, beginning with barrels of crackers shipped into rural communities. By the 1930s, the average farm household was using bakery bread and many kinds of packaged foods. Even those with only a $200 a year to spend bought some bakery products.

TABLE 3.5
Purchases of food, by place of residence and level
of household expenditure, 1830s and 1930s (dollars)

Item	Farms		Villages		Cities	
	1830s	1930s	1830s	1930s	1830s	1930s
Total household expenditures excluding shelter	200	200	500	500	1000	1000
Food purchases	78	82	245	253	436	483
Fresh meats, poultry, eggs	0	2	39	47	125	86
Fresh fruits, vegetables	2	2	6	36	36	73
Flour, cereals	22	33	49	15	42	16
Cured meats, fish	25	8	87	13	34	27
Fats	—	—	5	5	15	16
Dried fruits, vegetables	—	—	—	3	6	3
Salt, saltpeter, spices	5	1	4	1	4	2
Sugars, syrups	9	15	25	14	63	22
Coffee, tea, chocolate	9	8	20	11	26	16
Alcoholic beverages	4	3	5	5	10	17
Dairy products	2	4	5	31	53	68
Baked goods	0	3	0	21	14	46
Canned goods	0	1	0	34	0	44
Soft drinks	0	a	0	11	6	17
Eating out	0	2	a	6	2	30

a Less than 50 cents.

Distinctive Costumes

The use of dyes and pigments to vary the appearance of materials and of persons, like the preserving and cooking of foods, goes back to the earliest written records of history. Dyes—as essential to dress as salt is to the diet—and the berries, plants, and barks which yielded the different colors were important articles of trade and commerce before the rise of the chemical industries. The colonists and pioneers found native sources for their dyestuffs, but imports of the superior barks and indigos were not long in finding their way into established rural communities. The homespuns of rural weavers and the linens woven by women were decorated with many-colored threads. Even the leather jackets worn by men were adorned with fringes of colored threads.

Buttons and buckles in many designs were essential in European costumes, but information on developments in their manufacture in the United States is scanty. Stamping machines had mechanized the production of brass buttons before 1800, but other kinds of buttons and buckles were probably made by hand until much later. Nevertheless, general stores in the 1830s were selling many kinds of buttons—bone, pearl, gret, Yankee—and buttons were traded by peddlers for rags and potash. As cloth from textile factories came into rural communities, a profusion of other decorative items went along. Colored silks for embroidery, tapes, ribbons, edgings and laces, and lengths of velvet for the front of men's vests were part of the array of goods offered the farmer and his wife.

Sewing by women in the home, and on occasion by itinerant tailors, provided families with most of their clothes, but fur hats, leather caps, belts and suspenders, and, above all, shoes were articles that Americans sought in their markets. The New England shoe industries date back to 1750, and their women's shoes were shipped all over the colonies. Hat making and shoe making were important activities in the cities. The widespread use of hats and well-made shoes, noted in many travelers' accounts in the early years of the nineteenth century, was without any doubt the contribution of colonial industry.

Farmers in the 1830s able to spend $66 or even much less for clothing were buying hats for $3.50 and shoes for $1 to $3 (Table 3.12). Women's shoes, with uppers of prunella cloth, cost $1.50. Table 3.6 shows that shoes, hats, and accessories were important among the purchases of rural as well as urban households in the 1830s.

PATTERNS OF EXPENDITURE

The way consumers spend a given amount of money depends on the kinds of goods and services they produce for their own use. City families buy almost all the goods they need, whereas in some rural communities families produce almost all their own food, fuel, and building materials. A considerable fraction of the total expenditures of city families goes for food and shelter, including fuel, while rural households with the same total outlay are able to buy much more in the way of other goods and services.

TABLE 3.6
Purchases of clothing, by place of residence and level
of household expenditure, 1830s and 1930s (dollars)

Item	Farms		Villages		Cities	
	1830s	1930s	1830s	1930s	1830s	1930s
Total household expenditures excluding shelter	$200	$200	$500	$500	$1000	$1000
Clothing purchases	54	36	100	63	200	138
Hats, caps, bonnets	4	2	4	3	10	7
Boots, shoes, slippers	4	9	7	14	10	25
Hosiery	1	3	4	5	12	13
Belts, suspenders, cravats, ties	1	1	3	1	3	1
Gloves, mittens	1	1	4	2	6	3
Coats, clocks, shawls	—	4	2	7	6	20
Women's dresses, suits	—	4	0	8	8	18
Men's suits, separates	1	5	2	9	30	20
Underwear, nightwear	—	5	—	6	—	18
Shirts	—	1	—	3	—	5
Handkerchiefs	1	a	4	1	5	1
Umbrellas, parasols	—	—	a	a	5	1
Cloth, leather, notions	38	a	63	2	70	2
Services	3	a	7	2	35	4

a Less than 50 cents.

Table 3.7 shows strikingly how the production of food for home consumption affected expenditures for other goods and services in the 1830s and 1930s and how the allocation of expenditures to the various purposes changed over time.

The contrast between the expenditures of households on farms and those in the cities is quite clear. At every level of expenditure farm households spent less on food and therefore more on clothing and on sundry goods and services. Village families with little to spend were more like urban families, while those with more to spend were in the 1830s like farmers and in the 1930s like city dwellers. The suburbs accounted for only a small fraction of this rural nonfarm (village) population in the 1830s, but they were becoming dominant by the 1930s.

All studies of family living expenditures have confirmed Engels' law: Outlays for food decline proportionately and outlays for other goods and services rise as the level of total expenditure increases (Table 3.7, top panel). The decrease in food expenditure is offset mainly by an increase in the proportion for sundries. Over time, food expenditures at a given income level increase somewhat, along with those for sundries, while expenditures for clothing and domestic service decrease.

TABLE 3.7
Patterns of consumer expenditures, by place of residence
and level of household expenditure, 1830s and 1930s

Total Household Expenditures Excluding Shelter	1830s			1930s		
	Farms	Villages	Cities	Farms	Villages	Cities
Purchases of Food, Percentage of the Total:						
Under $200	40	65	65	45	—	—
$200–$500	34	54	61	38	54	60
$500–$1000	27	40	48	30	42	52
$1000–$2000	21	25	38	26	38	41
$2000–$3000	19	17	30	21	28	35
Purchases of Clothing, Percentage of the Total:						
Under $200	27	16	15	18	—	—
$200–$500	27	19	15	18	12	10
$500–$1000	26	21	19	18	13	13
$1000–$2000	26	20	21	18	14	14
$2000–$3000	25	21	21	19	17	15
Outlays for Servants, Percentage of the Total:						
Under $200	1	4	a	1	—	—
$200–$500	3	4	2	1	1	a
$500–$1000	6	6	10	2	1	a
$1000–$2000	7	8	18	3	3	2
$2000–$3000	8	9	20	4	4	5
Sundry Purchases, Percentage of the Total:						
Under $200	32	19	20	36	—	—
$200–$500	36	23	22	43	33	30
$500–$1000	41	33	23	50	44	35
$1000–$2000	46	47	23	53	45	43
$2000–$3000	48	53	29	56	51	45

a Less than .5 percent.

Some simple comparisons based on Table 3.7 summarize the influence on expenditures of level of income, place of residence, and technological changes. In Table 3.8, the income effect is suggested by a comparison of Columns (1) and (2); the place-of-residence effect, by comparison of Columns (2) and (3); and the effect of technological progress by comparison of Columns (3) and (4). The income effect shown in the expenditures of farm households with $1500 compared with those spending only $100 [Columns (2) and (1)] is very great. It represents the contrast between the large houses maintained with servants and the compact homes where the women tended to the housework and spinning, weaving, and knitting. In the large houses, servants, under the supervision of the housewife, did the cooking, baking, preserving, house cleaning, and laundry—also the sewing in localities with no dressmakers or

TABLE 3.8
Farm and city household expenditures,
excluding shelter, 1830s and 1930s (dollars)

	Farms		Cities	
Item	1830s (1)	1830s (2)	1830s (3)	1930s (4)
Total	100	1500	1500	1500
Food	40	315	570	615
Clothing	27	390	315	210
Servants	1	105	270	30
Sundries	32	690	345	645

milliners. Higher incomes were manifested by larger houses; more household service; fine qualities in clothing, furnishings, and carriages; more education for children; and a greater association with the world outside the local community.

The effect of residence location shown by the comparison of farm and city households in the 1830s [Columns (2) and (3)] indicates how the production of food for home consumption provided a higher level of living on the farm. Farm households must have had as many servants as city families, if not more; but having their own food supplies, the farmers' money outlays for food were lower. Since expenditures for food and servants were lower on the farms, expenditures on the sundry goods and services were much higher than in the cities.

By the 1930s, many disadvantages of urban living had been overcome—largely by the extension of city water and electric power systems, and by the introduction of an array of electrical equipment. Burdensome housekeeping tasks like carrying in water and fuel and carrying out wastes were eliminated. Ways had been found to secure all the comforts found in wealthy establishments without the problems associated with servants. The comparison of city families' spending in the 1830s and the 1930s [Columns (3) and (4)] thus shows a secular increase in expenditures on food and sundries, and a decrease in expenditures on clothing and servants. In the 1930s, city families at the expenditure levels studied were spending almost as much as the farm families at corresponding levels on the sundry goods and services which reflect the refinements connected with rising incomes.

Housing expenditures were treated in various ways in the different sources of information on family living expenditures. There is a lack of precision in comparisons, since the exact amount of total expenditures for all goods and services except shelter as given by family accounts and surveys requires adjustments for these variations in definition and classification. The cost-of-living estimates can be adjusted for the omission of some types of goods and services by the proportions given in the more complete sources. A few observations about total expenditures including housing may, however, be made.

Among city families of a given size, the outlays for food and shelter at a given level of total expenditure seem to have remained more or less steady over time (Table 3.9). In the 1930s, expenditures by rural families for food and shelter amounted to about eight tenths of those made by city families who spent the same total amount for all goods and services. It cost much less to construct a spacious house on the farm than in the city, and, in whatever way such farm expenses as taxes, insurance, and mortgage payments might be allocated between the farm and the home, the farmer's expenditures on housing were much lower than the city dweller's. Farm families, with their housing costs reckoned as the rental value of their dwellings, did not differ in the 1930s from residents in villages (rural nonfarm families). During and after World

TABLE 3.9
Expenditures for food and shelter, by level of household expenditure, urban families of three sizes, c. 1800–1960 (dollars)

Size of Family and Year	Approximate Level of Total Expenditures				
	$200	$500	$1200	$2000	$4000
Three persons					
1816–1817	—	—	—	1001	—
1830s	—	—	671	—	—
1859	—	321	—	—	—
1874	—	—	—	1112	—
1901	142	340	687	—	—
1918	—	—	—	1066	—
1935–1936	—	357	685	1015	1702
1941	—	—	723	1019	1737
1944	—	—	732	1191	—
1950	—	—	—	1148	1758
1960–1961	—	—	—	1116	1884
Four persons					
1780	137	—	—	—	—
1830s	132	364	—	—	—
1874	149	362	750	—	—
1901	130	352	—	—	—
1909	—	320	—	—	—
1918	—	—	744	979	—
1935–1936	—	—	704	1050	1823
1941	—	—	738	1110	1856
1944	—	—	—	—	1802
1950	—	—	—	1162	1880
1960–1961	—	—	—	1069	1872
Six persons or more					
1792–1798	—	—	—	—	1905
1874	—	374	780	1407	—
1901	170	358	760	—	—
1909	—	359	758	—	—
1918	—	—	793	1162	—
1935–1936	—	—	823	1285	2037
1941	—	379	799	1237	1870
1950	—	—	—	1211	2032
1960–1961	—	—	—	—	2067

War II, however, outlays for food and shelter among rural nonfarm families with expenditures over $3000 increased to the levels characteristic of city families. The expenditures of farm families for food and shelter continued to be lower by about 20 percent than the expenditures of city families of the same size who spent as much as their farm counterparts on all goods and services.

The fairly stable division of the family budget seems to support the observation that whenever or wherever housing expenditures were comparatively low, food expenditures were higher. Rents and the payments of homeowners are contractual and are not quickly adjusted when incomes and prices rise over a short period of time. In wartime and in postwar years, the outlays for shelter were lower than in other years among city families spending the same amount for family living. Food expenditures were correspondingly higher. Expenditures for shelter rose in the interwar years to an apparent balance with expenditures for food and for all other goods and services.

The tables in this section indicate considerable stability in the bounds that govern consumers' outlays for food, shelter, and other goods and services. They suggest little of the dramatic changes detailed elsewhere in this chapter in the kinds of goods and services produced for the uses of consumers, or of the shifts in emphasis within the broad categories of consumption. Goods and services have to be itemized in quite fine detail in order to exhibit adequately the historical changes in the pattern of consumption. The underlying nature of the changes, however, can be at least suggested by a small number of groups in the summary of consumers' expenditures. Comparison of a budget estimate for 1792–1798 with the recent information on spending shown in Table 3.10 reveals the most pervasive underlying tendencies in the types of goods and services used by consumers. The expenditure for household operation in 1792–1798 was almost entirely for four servants, their wages, their food, and some clothing. Household operation in 1960–1961 covered laundry and cleaning supplies, telephone service, and a very small outlay of $40 for

TABLE 3.10
Household spending, 1792–1798 and 1960–1961

Item	Expenditures		
	1792–1798	1960–1961	1960–1961
Number of persons	6	5	7
Housing	$ 600	$ 645	$ 644
Fuel	200	214	268
Food at home	1105	1114	1282
Clothing Personal care Medical care	960	1050	937
Household operation	1032	282	285
Transportation	267	623	644
Total	$4164	$3928	$4060

domestic service. Transportation costs in 1792–1798 represented the cost of keeping horses, while in 1960–1961 they related mainly to the automobile. Some fraction of the expenditures for servants should have been allocated to transportation in the estimates for 1792–1798, but how much is hard to guess. At any rate, the comparison manifests the shift from household production on the part of housewives and servants to materials and supplies used with labor-saving equipment.

THE RISE IN THE LEVEL OF LIVING

By the end of the nineteenth century, the upper middle class already repre-sented a significant segment of the market for consumers' goods and services, and their share in aggregate consumption increased with the growth of popu-lation and income in the urban communities of the twentieth century. Long before the urban population outnumbered the rural, households with incomes above the average were able to combine the benefits of rural residence with the advantages of city life. The expansion of cities into outlying districts and the spread of their populations over the city boundaries into the suburbs were supported by each new development in transportation, and an ever-increasing part of economic activity went into the provision of commodious single-family homes in pleasant surroundings for the prosperous middle class.

As the middle class moved out of the cities, the older residential districts were given over to lower-income groups. As the culmination of this process, housing in districts that were once relatively high-income neighborhoods was converted for use by the poor. Urban households with low incomes did gain some of the conveniences of modern living by inheriting the housing of more affluent families, but converted housing did not fully provide for the rapidly growing populations of the largest cities.

The refinements that households with modest means were introducing into their homes in the 1830s and earlier became, before 1900, available to the poor. By the 1870s, such articles as beds, bedding, chairs, tables, dishes, knives, and forks were considered indispensable. Even the addition of a few accessories—clocks, mirrors, and floor coverings—did not, in the estimation of observers, bring the household above the constantly rising minimum standard. Most of the households living at or below the levels described in Tables 3.11 through 3.14 were included in the third of the nation described by President Roosevelt in the 1930s as "ill-fed, ill-housed, ill-clothed."

Not all rural communities participated in the growth of income, and in some communities in the twentieth century families continued to live much as their forefathers had. In the Appalachian and central highlands, in the Great Lakes cutover region, and in the cotton-growing areas of the South, there are still large populations that have shared very little in the benefits of modern living. The out-migration from regions that were left stranded by economic develop-ment intensified the social problems of the cities (see Chapters 5 and 16). In an atmosphere of economic growth, men who are unable to provide their families with more than their fathers and grandfathers provided do not share in

TABLE 3.11
Prices paid for specified foods, by place of residence
and level of household expenditure on food, 1830s and 1930s

Item	Farms		Villages		Cities	
	1830s	1930s	1830s	1930s	1830s	1930s
Food expenditure	$78	$82	$245	$253	$450	$485
Price per Pound (cents):						
Beef for stew	5	13	8	15	8	16
Potatoes	2	3	2	3	3	3
White flour	2	3	2	4	3	4
Pork						
Salt side	10	16	10	17	10	18
Strip bacon	10	17	10	25	10	30
Salt	2	6	2	7	3	7
Pepper	40	—	40	—	22	—
Ginger	40	—	40	—	26	—
Sugar	13	4	13	5	15	5
Molasses	8	7	8	8	18	8
Coffee	17	20	27	27	15	30
Tea	72	42	87	53	125	50
Chocolate	20	20	20	22	25	25
Butter	—	33	17	35	20	35
Cheese	12	22	13	25	10	27

the benefits of industrial development. The things that were new in rural communities in the 1930s compared to the 1880s—movies, automobiles, and radios—served only to heighten the disparities between what had once represented the achievement of a higher standard and what now indicated an ever-increasing lag behind the prevailing norms.

Today, the great majority of American families live on a scale that compares well with the way wealthy families lived 200 years ago. Of the essentials, food and clothing have become less important in the aggregate, but housing and household operation, with all the array of modern facilities and equipment, have become a more important element in the total. The purchase and operation of automobiles represent a larger fraction of aggregate spending than did outlays for clothing in the past. Of the other kinds of goods and services, equipment for recreation and public entertainment has increased considerably, and direct and indirect expenditures for education have grown dramatically. In the past only the well-to-do provided tutors for their sons and sent them to private academies, colleges, and universities. By the middle of the twentieth century, the development of educational institutions provided for secondary and higher education on a very broad scale. Literacy was a part of the American standard of living from the earliest times, and a rising standard of literacy can be considered a concomitant of economic development (see Chapter 5).

TABLE 3.12
Prices paid for specified articles of clothing, by place of residence
and level of household expenditure on clothing, 1830s and 1930s (dollars)

Items	Farms		Villages		Cities	
	1830s	1930s	1830s	1930s	1830s	1930s
Clothing expenditures	54	36	100	63	200	138
Price per Article:						
Men's apparel						
Overcoats	—	9	28	15	39	28
Suits						
Wool	—	18	28	18	37	28
Cotton, linen	—	—	—	10	30	11
Hats, fur, wool	3	2	4	2	6	3
Trousers, pantaloons	—	3	6	4	—	5
Vests	2	—	4	—	6	—
Shirts	—	1	—	1	—	2
Hose, wool	a	a	a	1	2	1
Boots, leather	3	5	4	7	5	8
Shoes, leather	1	3	2	4	3	5
Gloves, leather	1	1	1	1	2	2
Suspenders	a	—	a	—	1	—
Ties, cravats	1	1	1	1	2	1
Umbrellas	—	—	—	—	5	2
Women's apparel						
Cloaks, coats	—	13	—	15	32	22
Bonnets, hoods, hats	—	1	2	2	3	3
Shoes	1	3	1	3	2	4
Gloves	—	1	1	1	2	2
Parasols, umbrellas	—	1	—	2	3	a
Handkerchiefs	a	a	a	a	2	2

a Less than 50 cents.

Widespread diffusion of material well-being in combination with a high
level of health and educational attainment is an achievement that is unique in
history. Western civilization, particularly in the United States, has demonstrated that advances in technology and industrial development can provide
the greater part of the population with the goods and services that represent
high levels of consumption. Events in the 1960s bring the hope that means
will be found also to provide the populations living in decaying neighborhoods,
urban and rural, with comfortable homes in pleasant surroundings and with
more and better education for their children.

"All progress is based upon the universal innate desire on the part of every
organism to live beyond its means."[1] Consumption in America was governed
by the determination of large numbers in the population to achieve a higher
standard of living through their own efforts.

[1] Samuel Butler, *Notebooks*; selections arranged and edited by H. F. Jones (New York: Dulton, 1921),
pp. xvi, 437.

TABLE 3.13
Prices paid for specified articles of household equipment, by place of residence and level of household expenditure on equipment, 1830s and 1930s (dollars)

Items	Farms		Villages		Cities	
	1830s	1930s	1830s	1930s	1830s	1930s
Furnishings and equipment expenditures	16	9	30	20	67	50
Price per Article:						
Home manufacture						
Spinning wheel	4	—	5	—	5	—
Loom	12	—	18	—	25	—
Coffee mill	1	—	1	—	1	—
Sewing machine						
Treadle	—	15	—	25	—	40
Electric	—	—	—	65	—	80
Kitchen stoves						
Wood, coal	12	35	25	43	50	48
Kerosene, gas	—	—	—	51	—	56
Electric	—	—	—	100	—	100
Washing machines						
No power	10	10	10	—	10	—
Kerosene, gasoline	—	56	—	80	—	—
Electric	—	65	—	64	—	64
Irons						
Flat	—	1		1		1
Electric	—	4	—	6	—	6
Vacuum cleaners						
Hand	—	3	—	4	—	5
Electric	—	40	—	48	—	48
Refrigerators						
Ice-box or house		10		25		29
Kerosene, gas	—	35	—	54	—	150
Electric	—	110	—	130	—	145

POSTSCRIPT ON SOURCES

The tables in this chapter represent the best estimates that can be derived from the records and other information consulted of the division of the family budget in the 1830s. The data for the 1930s come from the national survey and are as accurate as interview surveys can yield. Detailed comparisons of expenditures in the twentieth century with those in the nineteenth for income brackets above $3000 cannot be made until more records and accounts are summarized and published. It is hoped that such source material will appear in America, as it has recently in Europe. The statistical picture of changes in expenditures on particular goods and services must currently be drawn chiefly from information for 1930–1936, when the larger part of the population was still spending less than $3000 on family living.

TABLE 3.14
Prices paid for specified articles of furnishings, by place of residence
and level of household expenditure on furnishings, 1830s and 1930s (dollars)

Items	Farms		Villages		Cities	
	1830s	1930s	1830s	1930s	1830s	1930s
Furnishings and equipment expenditures	16	9	30	20	67	50
Price per Article:						
Bureaus, chests	5	9	8	11	20	16
Bedsteads	4	11	5	9	28	15
Cradles, cribs	2	8	3	8	4	8
Cupboards, sideboards	—	9	10	8	25	21
Chairs	1	2	1	3	2	3
Tables	—	4		5	29	6
Clocks	10	2	10	2	45	3
Looking-glasses, mirrors	1	1	1	2	2	3
Music boxes	—	—	—	—	50	—
Pianos	—	—	—	—	225	—
Fiddles	—	—	20	n.a.	—	—
Flutes	—	—	15	n.a.	—	—
Phonographs	—	—	—	—	—	—
Radios	—	—	—	—	—	—

Information on family expenditures comes from three kinds of sources: account books, estimates of the "cost of living" by informed observers or consumers, and surveys of income and outlays. The information available from account books is a haphazard collection of material that has been summarized and published. Typically it is never clear what expenditures were omitted from the accounting records or how outlays made by home owners—such as taxes, interest, and repairs—were treated. Estimates of the cost of living vary in their coverage. Generally, purchases that were not recurrent or that were related to activities outside the home were omitted. Observers did not include furniture, medical care, contributions to church and charity, or expenditures for excursions and vacations in their estimates. Investigators who brought questionnaires to families via the mails or through interviews did not ask for reports on such expenditures. The cost of food served to boarders and servants was not separated from expenditures for family consumption—in family account books, in estimates of the cost of living, or even in the early surveys that purported to give a comprehensive account of consumer expenditures. In Table 3.9 the data for 1918 and earlier periods were adjusted to correspond to the coverage and classifications used in the surveys conducted in 1935–1936 and later, to the extent that the available information permitted.

The estimates presented in Table 3.9 for 1874 and later years were derived by summary tables from statistical investigations in which the families were generally classified by income. Surveys of family expenditures before the 1930s did not extend to the higher-income groups. The later surveys, which included all income groups, showed that cross-sectional relationships are continuous and the association, say, between food outlays and total expenditures excluding shelter, can be extrapolated upward over a moderate range. Extrapolation of the data from the surveys in 1950 and later cannot be justified. With prices and income at higher levels than ever before, the number of families living on $1000 a year or less is so small that their expenditures do not influence the averages in the lowest income brackets. Also, families in the lowest income brackets spend considerably more than their money receipts on current consumption.

In addition to the sources listed in the extensive bibliography *Family Living in the United States and Other Countries* (U.S. Department of Agriculture, Miscellaneous Publication 223) and the sources cited in *Historical Statistics of the United States from Colonial Times to the Present* and its *Continuation* (U.S. Bureau of the Census), accounts and budgets can be found in family histories and various other sources. In J. Oberholtzer's *Philadelphia, a History of the City and Its People,* a budget for a "genteel family" in 1789–1791 and 1792–1798 was attributed to the U.S. recorder, but the original source has not been located. In the congressional documents for later years a number of budgets and accounts are cited to show increases in the cost of living that call for higher government salaries. The Massachusetts Bureau of Statistics of Labor, in its annual report for 1870, reconstructed a worker's budget for 1780 from the list of articles put under price control by the Massachusetts legislature.

Budgets have been estimated frequently for comparison with wage levels. Matthew Carey, in *An Appeal to the Wealthy of the Land,* presented a budget for a laborer's family to show how much a man should earn to support a family of four in 1833. The various state bureaus of labor statistics presented budgets as well as records of expenditures for various dates after 1870.

Storekeepers' records in company towns have been summarized in such histories as *Hopewell Village, A Social and Economic History in an Iron-Making Community* by Joseph E. Walker. Such records were also summarized in " Prices Paid by Vermont Farmers for Goods and Services . . . 1790–1940 " by T. M. Adams.

Family accounts appear in such histories as *With Hammer in Hand, the Dominy Craftsmen of East Hampton, New York* by Charles F. Hummel, and *How a Family Lived in the 1850s* by Paul D. Converse, a publication of the University of Illinois Bureau of Economic and Business Research.

At various points in this chapter, reference has been made to the prices paid by consumers for various types of goods. The tables appended here bring together price data for a number of major items of consumption.

SUGGESTED READING

Adams, T. M. "Prices Paid by Vermont Farmers for Goods and Services and Received by Them for Farm Products 1790–1940: Wages of Vermont Farm Labor, 1780 – 1940 " Bulletin 507. Burlington: Vermont Agricultural Experiment Station, 1944.

Beecher, Catherine E., and Harriet Beecher Stowe. *The American Woman's Home.* New York: 1869.

Carman, Harry J. (ed.). *American Husbandry.* New York: Columbia University Press, 1939.

Coolidge, John P. *Mill and Mansion, A Study of Architecture and Society in Lowell, Mass., 1820–1865. 2nd. ed. Hicksville, N.Y.: Russell Publishing Company, 1967.*

De Crèvecoeur, St. John. *Sketches of Eighteenth Century America,* edited by Henri L. Bourdin, Ralph H. Gabriel, and Stanley T. Williams. New Haven: Yale University Press, 1925.

Downing, A. J. *The Architecture of Country Houses.* New York: Appleton-Century-Crofts, 1850.

Ellis, Mrs. Sarah. *House Keeping Made Easy.* New York: Harper & Row, 1858–1860.

Giedion, Siegfried. *Mechanization Takes Command.* New York: Oxford University Press, 1948.

Giedion, Siegfried. *Space, Time and Architecture,* 5th ed. Cambridge, Mass.: Harvard University Press, 1967.

Great Britain. *View of the United States of America, Forming a Complete Emigrants' Directory.* London: Edwards and Knobb, 1820.

Great Britain. *The British Mechanics and Labourers Handbook and True Guide to the United States.* 1840.

Iverson, Marion. *The American Chair, 1630–1890.* New York: Hastings, 1957.

Jackson, Joseph. *Development of American Architecture, 1783–1830.* Philadelphia: David McKay, 1926.

Johnson, Lawrence A. *Country Store Keeping in America, 1620–1920.* Rutland, Vt.: Charles E. Tuttle, 1961.

Kimball, Fiske. *American Architecture.* Indianapolis: Bobbs-Merrill, 1928.

Kouwenhoven, John A. *Made in America: The Arts in Modern Civilization.* Garden City, N.Y.: Doubleday, 1948.

Langdon, William Chauncy. *Everyday Things in American Life, 1776–1876.* New York: Scribner's, 1941.

Ormsbee, Thomas Hamilton. *Early American Furniture Makers: A Social and Biographical Study.* New York: Tudor, 1937.

Tryon, Rolla Milton. *Household Manufacture in the United States, 1640–1860.* Chicago: University of Chicago Press, 1917.

Tryon, Warren S. (ed.). *A Mirror for Americans: Life and Manners in the United States 1790–1870 as Recorded by American Travellers.* Chicago: University of Chicago Press, 1952.

U.S. Bureau of Labor Statistics. *How American Buying Habits Change.* Washington: U.S. Government Printing Office, 1959.

Wade, Richard C. *The Urban Frontier: The Rise of Western Cities, 1790–1830.* Cambridge, Mass.: Harvard University Press, 1959.

Walker, Joseph E. *Hopewell Village: A Social and Economic History of an Iron Making Community.* Philadelphia: University of Pennsylvania Press, 1966.

Wheeler, Gervase. *Homes for The People.* New York: G. E. Woodward, 1867.

Young, Edward. *Labor in Europe and America.* Philadelphia: S. A. George, 1875.

part II
RESOURCES, NATURAL AND HUMAN

4
THE LAND, MINERALS, WATER, AND FORESTS

The economic history of American natural resources can be divided into four phases: (*a*) exploration, (*b*) appropriation, (*c*) exploitation, and (*d*) conservation. As the American society spread out over the continent, these phases were reenacted successively in new regions and over new subsoil mineral deposits. This chapter is concerned with the first two and the fourth of these phases. Exploration may be defined as the collection of socioeconomic processes by which knowledge of the quality and extent of resources was acquired and incorporated into the body of knowledge useful to the economy. Appropriation is the process by which the legal right to exploitation was transferred from the Indians through the American government to the settlers and mining enterprises which finally exercised it. These two processes are not strictly economic in motivation; that is, they were not directed by clearly calculable prospects of financial gain. This is clearly the case with geographical exploration; the knowledge of the land gained was in no wise capturable by the explorers for profit. Much knowledge of minerals deposits came to light as the accidental by-product of other activities; even the conscious mineral exploration of prospectors involved an uncertainty so great as hardly to qualify as an economic activity much above the level of a sweepstake. As knowledge of the probabilities of discovery in an area rose, the exploration phase gave way to exploitation under conditions of risk.

The activities of exploration form part of American social and political history, although their economic consequences were very great. The human pursuits and passions which we observe in those activities set the boundaries of knowledge and material opportunities within which the settled economic activities of mining and agriculture took place. The third phase—exploitation —is more properly a part of the history of mining and agriculture, covered in part in later chapters of this book. Conservation—treated here briefly—also belongs to the general subject of social organization and government intervention examined more fully in Chapter 17.

EXPLORATION

Geographical Exploration

Knowledge about American economic geography was gained in the eighteenth and nineteenth centuries both from expeditions sent out for military or scientific purposes and from unorganized forays by thousands of individuals and small bands operating on their own account.

In the orderly exploration of its domain, the American government had a surprisingly good record in view of the loose methods by which that domain was to be disposed of. The great expedition of Lewis and Clark (1804–1806) set the model in organization, technique, and scope for the less extensive, but sometimes more sensational, expeditions of Zebulon Pike, the Army engineers, and John C. Frémont before the Civil War. These expeditions were similar to one another in many respects. They were of a paramilitary character and organization, and in each, political, military, and scientific purposes were commingled. Military officers led them and the men were drawn from the social groups that composed the army—often directly from its ranks. Thanks in part to a tradition originating in Jefferson's luminous intelligence, they carried along scientific observers and produced notes, sketches, and diaries in abundance. The impulse of an expanding nation to define its perimeter and to probe for weakness along it was prominent, though generally unvoiced. The expedition of Lewis and Clark, for example, was not only an exploration of the Louisiana Purchase but also a thrust into the Oregon territory, and the explorations to the southwest were rightly viewed by the Spanish and Mexican authorities as preludes to an invasion. Investigations among the Indians were pursued to test their disposition and strength as well as to observe their habits and customs. The stated purpose of the expeditions was often narrow indeed—to measure and fix a boundary, to investigate (in the 1850s) the best route for a transcontinental railway, to observe and collect botanical and zoological specimens, to produce an accurate geological map. But whatever the stated purpose, the expeditions were an outlet for restless ambition and curiosity and they yielded a rich harvest of geographical information about the American continent.

Supplementing the information gathered by the expeditions was the mass of informal gossip acquired by private individuals and by small bands organized for some private purpose. Hunters, missionaries, scientists, thrill-seekers all went through the West and many left written records of their adventures and observations. By far the most ubiquitous of these individuals were the fur traders and trappers. Even in the eighteenth century they were numerous, fanning out from Montreal in the vanguard of the French exploration and settlement. By 1800 several thousand of them were working either on their own account or in small companies. St. Louis became the main gathering point for expeditions into the West, and trappers often went into the mountains for several years, meeting the boat from St. Louis once or twice a year in a prearranged rendezvous to exchange furs for provisions. These "mountain men" became indeed a "tribe of white Indians," adapted thoroughly to the country, and in many cases not very interested in a return to civilization.

The fur trade thus illustrates an important point in what might be called "communications theory" as applied to social systems. The mountain men and the French fur trappers were known for their complete immersion in the life of the wilderness. They acquired an intimate knowledge of the country. At the same time, they became cut off from their "civilized" origins so that the knowledge they gained was not readily available to settlers in the East and investors in Europe. Those who penetrated the western country in organized expeditions—the manner in which the British customarily organized the fur trade—learned somewhat less, but captured more for the generations that were to come. Somewhere between the extremes of intimacy and remoteness lay the ideal attitude and organization for acquiring and transmitting knowledge of new country to the inhabitants "back home."[1]

As a furnisher of information about American geography, it is interesting to note, the beaver—the main quarry of the fur trade—was a particularly significant animal. The great buffalo hunts of the mid-nineteenth century provided more sensational examples of slaughter; the grizzly bear was a more dangerous enemy; elk and deer offered more thrilling sport. But the beaver, whose fur was demanded in the hat trade, was—relative to his size and abundance—more highly prized. At $5 to $10 a pelt, beavers lived by the thousands along the western streams. To gather this harvest was not the work of an occasional foray into the mountains. Two visits were needed to each beaver's lodge or bank—one to set the trap and another to collect the victim. As lower streams became trapped out, the little animal lured the trappers deeper into the wilderness. A force of men was drawn steadily inland from the Mississippi and Missouri along all their tributaries. No investigations add so much to the early knowledge of a region's geography as those which furnish information about its drainage system. That knowledge, thanks to the aquatic habits of the beaver, was the trapper's stock in trade, and the increase of that knowledge was—thanks to his greed—the condition of his subsistence.

The American penetration into the interior provided, then, a great spectrum of modes of communication and a great body of information of varied content and reliability. Well-written, half-poetic books like Frémont's and Pike's, and works of real literary art like Parkman's *Oregon Trail*, Dana's *Two Years Before the Mast*, and Washington Irving's *Astoria* and *Captain Bonneville* were widely circulated and helped create a consciousness of the West. The semi-official reports of Lewis and Clark (after an unfortunate publication history), the various army reports, and the enormous report on the route for a transcontinental railroad became solid reference works. The personal narratives of

[1] The economics of the fur trade is itself a most absorbing chapter in American economic history. Profit margins were high, a year's catch might bring several thousand dollars, and with the profits of a few year's work, a trapper might return to set up a small trading business and be "fixed for life." In this respect it was a prelude to the activity of gold prospecting, and very like it in many ways. As time went on and the risks became known, it became profitable for larger capitalists to enter the field. By clever trading, boldness mixed with caution, and methods that fell between the astute and the unscrupulous, John Jacob Astor and his American Fur Company organized the trade after 1830 in much the same way John D. Rockefeller organized the petroleum industry later in the century. Astor was able to acquire the foundation for the first vast American fortune before the economic basis of his enterprise was destroyed by a decline in the demand for beaver (through a shift in taste to silk hats) and by the trapping out of the small animals over much of the West.

Dunbar, Pattie, Gregg, the German nobleman Maximiliam Wied von Neuwied, and many others had their narrower circles of influence.

The reports and books turned up miscellaneous information about trees, ferns, Indians, rocks, mountains, river systems, weather, and terrain—information of economic value, some of it correct, some of it misleading. Much of it related to the general physical character of the new lands and their suitability as places of human habitation, although without tests or experience the travelers and explorers could not predict just what sort of settlement would be best in a given region or what crops the soils and climate would sustain.[2]

As railroads and land speculators became involved in the western movement, specially written guides to immigrants put the whole process of information dissemination on a semicommercial basis. And, as in all such movements, the most important was the intimate information diffused in small circles by word of mouth from the tales of hunters, trappers, and the members of expeditions themselves. It is not possible to recapture now this floating mass of rumor and it would never have been too wise to try to assess its veracity. Perhaps more men were excited about the West through the lies of trappers than through the scientific facts published in government reports. After the Civil War and the opening of the transcontinental railroads much of the mystery of the interior of the continent disappeared. The orderly mapping of the terrain was carried on in several special surveys until 1789, when it was made a continuing function of the newly formed U.S. Geological Survey. Still, every period has its heroes, and the lifework of John Wesley Powell stands high in the annals of geographical exploration. It was he who, as a government engineer, had the vision to perceive the true value of the arid lands of the West. He made a series of explorations between 1867 and 1876, and his *Report of the Lands of the Arid Regions of the United States* (1878), compiled in Washington with several collaborators, set the objectives for the use and management of these lands for decades. With Powell, the heroic period of western exploration came to an end.

Minerals Exploration

Underneath the American soil in 1800, and generally unnoticed by the first explorers, lay the rich and varied mineral deposits on which much of American industrial strength was to be based. Perhaps in no other element in its growth has the sheer luckiness of the American economy been more evident. No doubt over such a wide area one would have expected that supplies of minerals of some sort would have been found. Yet the explorations into South America, Africa, and the Asian interior in the nineteenth century failed to uncover reserves of so many different minerals, particularly of the fuels and metals

---

[2] In at least one famous case where the observer went beyond mere observation to interject judgment, a mistake was made which impeded the settlement of the grasslands for perhaps a decade. Discouraged by the outcome of his expedition to the lands around the Platte River, Major Long wrote that the country was "almost wholly unfit for cultivation, and of course uninhabitable by a people dependent upon agriculture for their subsistence." His companion, James, expressed the wish that the region "might forever remain the unmolested haunt of the native hunter, the bison, and the jackal." *James's Account of S. H. Long's Expedition, 1819–1820.* Part 1 in Early Western Travels, 1748–1846, Reuben Gold Thwaites (ed.) (Glendale, Calif.: Arthur H. Clark, 1905), p. 20.

appropriate to nineteenth-century industrial techniques. Observing the procession of discoveries in the United States one ponders the fate that made discovery of a mineral come in such close proximity to the development of its important industrial use. The technology of steam and iron on which the English Industrial Revolution was based depended on supplies of coal; indeed, the abundance of coal in England and Northern Europe was no doubt a factor in shaping that technology and in limiting its transferability to other parts of the world. How then did it happen that as settlement went westward during the late eighteenth century, coal began to be turned up under the Pennsylvania soil? The steel-making inventions of the mid-eighteenth century required massive ore deposits and, almost simultaneously with these inventions, such deposits were uncovered around Lake Superior close to water transport and at the other end of a lake system from the coal. Finally, as the gasoline engine began to draw upon petroleum reserves, the vast fields in mid-continent and in Texas and California were opened up. It is hard to believe that the course of technology in the nineteenth century was shaped by the availability of minerals in the United States. Nevertheless, as industrial technology called for materials, the American subsoil deposits appeared to answer the demand from domestic sources. Mixed with some interaction between industrial technology and demand and the discovery of supplies, there must have been some colossal good fortune. This luck, in land booms, in the politics of territorial expansion, and most of all in minerals discovery, gave the nineteenth-century development the atmosphere of a carnival, directed by that unseen Magician whose name was well known and readily invoked by the orators of a religious age.

Nevertheless, despite its spectacular episodes, the process of minerals discovery in the United States followed in each region and in each deposit a path with discernible regularities. In a first stage, which may be called "observation," explorers, hunters, Indians, and even early settlers passing over the terrain took note of the external evidences of the mineral deposit. The nature of these observations depended greatly upon the physical characteristics of the mineral and of its deposition. In Pennsylvania a hunter putting out his campfire in the late eighteenth century observed that the fire continued to smoulder under the ground; another, picking up a stone to throw at a woodchuck, saw below it the black glint of coal. In Michigan copper in a pure state had been known and used by the Indians and observations of the rock were made by early travelers. In Minnesota iron deposits deflected the compass needles of land surveyors and the fact was duly noted. Oil seepages in water wells, gas explosions from underground sources, outcrops and the glint of metal on hillsides—such incidents were reported concerning nearly every deposit in the decades preceding its true "discovery." Their frequency depended upon a number of factors, notably: (a) the number of such outcrops or other telltale clues, (b) the density of settlement and movement over the area, and (c) the level of "mineral-mindedness" of the population—its ability to recognize minerals and its interest in recording their observation. The easier the mineral was to discover by common-sense techniques, the denser the settlement in the region; or the more interested the population in minerals discovery, the greater were the number of observations reported. What distinguishes such observations from true discovery is the failure of those observing the minerals or hearing about them to follow up their find. The knowledge gained was not incorporated into the body of information available for utilization by prospectors, miners, and industry at large. It remained buried in diaries or vanished from the lips of the teller. A minerals *discovery*, then, requires that an observation be made by, or transmitted to, someone with the knowledge and capacity to initiate a more thorough, planned exploration and exploitation, and at a time when such an effort appears to be feasible and profitable. The analogy might be made to a match and a fuse. Many matches may be struck, flicker, and die out, or light the fuse for only a short sputter. But under just the right conditions the right match will make a firecracker explode. A minerals discovery, like a geographical or technological discovery, implies an economy and a society in which it can be incorporated and eventually utilized. The timing of discoveries, then, depends loosely upon the surrounding possibilities of exploitation, and more exactly upon the frequency of the observations made in such a favorable setting.

American history is full of minerals discoveries. Gold in Georgia and North Carolina in the early 1830s provided an early sensational incident. Lead in Illinois, copper in Michigan, iron in Minnesota, and the most famous, the gold discovery on the American River in California in 1848, followed the same pattern. In each case the act of discovery was followed rather rapidly by the extraordinary phenomenon of the minerals "rush," a wholly uncoordinated effort on the part of prospectors to seek out the full extent of the deposit and to stake claims on it. Figure 4.1 is an effort to show the chronological procession of these discoveries. The California Gold Rush of 1848–1850, however, was so different in degree as to be different in kind from all the others. It was a major social movement which, in the space of two years, drew tens of thousands of men into the California hills. Two consequences followed from it—first, for the California economy, a general stimulus through the demands of the miners and the gold supplies used by them to buy commodities; second, for minerals exploration itself, the formation of a floating body of prospectors, perhaps 100,000 strong, ready to fan up the coast and back to the East at the slightest rumor of gold. So a succession of gold rushes, each with its particular incidents, became characteristic of the second half of the century. Nor were the rushes all for gold; sometimes incidentally, even more valuable deposits of silver, copper, lead, and zinc were turned up. First in coal, where the seams were charted even before 1850, then much later and more slowly in the metals, scientific techniques of exploration came to replace the wild and feverish activities of the private prospectors. The history of oil discovery followed a path similar to that of gold. A rush occurred into western Pennsylvania following the drilling of Colonel Drake's famous well, and across the great fields in the mid-South, Oklahoma, Texas, and California. The random activity of prospectors, working on small evidences—outcrops, seepages, gas holes—and on hunches about the shape of the terrain, produced the first strikes, followed by colossal rushes and accompanied by vast waste.

FIGURE 4.1
Time pattern of discoveries and exploitation
of mineral deposits, by regions, 1800–1930

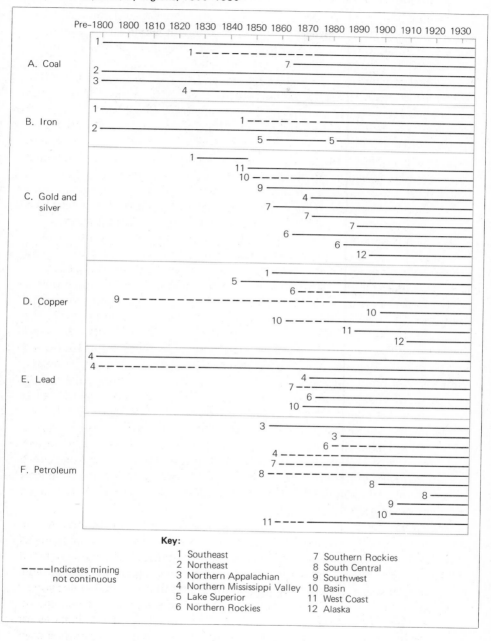

APPROPRIATION

Land Acquisition by the Federal Government

The information-gathering activities of explorers, trappers, and minerals prospectors revealed the extent of the American continent and most of its intimate secrets. The map on the inside of the front cover shows in summary form the well-known topography of the United States—the great river valleys, the grassy plains, the arid and mountainous regions, and the fertile areas most easily reached from the Pacific. Even before settlers arrived to fight the Indians for the land, however, another potentially formidable obstacle lay in the way of American expansion—the claims of other nations to the area. Much of the speed and exhilaration of the American expansion of the nineteenth century — particularly of the 1840s and 1850s—was due to the fact that these nominal barriers to the spread of American political institutions tumbled over like the little pig's house of straw before the huffing and puffing of American politicians, the threats of American military force, and the restlessness of ranchers and fortune hunters on the extreme of the frontier. The astonishing suddenness with which Napoleon offered in 1803 to dispose of the entire Louisiana territory has been seen in retrospect as a maneuver designed to keep it from falling into English hands. But it attests to the fact that, given the deployment of forces in Europe, the United States even at this early time was the national power best able, and most strongly motivated, to control by force the territory on this continent. The speed with which Jefferson and his representatives snapped the offer up shows that there were Americans conscious of this "Manifest Destiny"—40 years before the phrase was coined.[3] In Texas in the 1830s and in California a decade later, the sequence was slightly different. In Texas, Yankees overthrew the weak Mexican rule, in advance of their government, and secured annexation to the United States in 1845. A dispute over the Texas boundary in 1846 led to the War of 1846–1848 with Mexico, by which California and the Southwest were taken into the federal union. In these cases, the ambitions of leaders in Washington and on the frontier, backed by the power and presence of a relatively strong national government, placed huge areas west of the Mississippi River under the nominal sovereignty of the American government, and gave the United States a title to the land and its resources that was recognized by other nations.

The Indian tribes were the second obstacle which lay in the way of the absolute power of the American federal government to dispose of the lands as it pleased. From the earliest settlements in Massachusetts it was recognized either by the European governments or by the early settlers that some legal title to the land was vested in the Indian tribes and that a formal extinction of such right (if not of the Indians themselves) was desirable prior to settlement. Such a theory was required as protection not so much for the Indians as for the white men's governments as they tried to retain sovereignty over their own settlers. In the sixteenth and seventeenth centuries, the European crowns

---

[3] Curtis M. Geer, *The Louisiana Purchase and the Westward Movement,* vol. 8 in The History of North America, Guy Carleton Lee (ed.) (Philadelphia: George Barrie & Sons, 1904), chap. xii.

claimed overlordship to the land "discovered" by their citizens. Indians were accorded rights of occupancy in the lands, and in some colonies a special effort was made to acquire title transfer from the Indians to the colonial government. Nowhere was private acquisition of land from the Indians permitted without some state intervention.[4] The United States government was similarly impelled to go through the formality, at least, of recognizing an Indian interest in the land and then formally securing it by treaty and purchase, even within much of the areas already purchased from France or taken by revolution and treaty from Mexico.

It is common knowledge that Indians everywhere were relentlessly pursued, tricked, and forced from the lands guaranteed by these treaties, and that their resistance was put down by military expeditions extending through the 1880s. By an act of 1871, the whole pretense of recognizing the Indian tribes as sovereign nations was abandoned; the Indians were treated like a conquered people, marked for early assimilation or for extinction. Under the Dawes General Allotment Act from 1887 to 1934, a ridiculously misguided effort was made to turn the Indians into family farmers on 160-acre plots, and much reservation land (mostly too poor to farm) was allotted for this purpose. A recent authority writes:

> Under the Dawes Act, conditions on reservations eventually became scandalous. Indian life was marked by poverty, squalor, disease, and hopelessness. In general, Indians received little or no education and were still treated as wards, incapable of self-government or making decisions for themselves. Whatever revenues the tribes received from land sales were dissipated, with virtually none of them going to assist the Indians to create sound foundations for the development of the human and economic resources of the reservation.[5]

Defeated in the field and corrupted and socially undermined by life on reservations, the Indian nations have experienced some revival of their independence only since the Indian Reorganization Act of 1934. In a series of law suits in the 1960s, some Indian groups won substantial damages for underpayment for their tribal lands taken in the nineteenth century. The whole story is the tragic one of the clash of two mutually unassimilable civilizations—a story repeated in history from the days of the conquests of the Egyptian pharaohs. That it was conducted under the shadow of legality with lip service paid to legal doctrines of property rights only added Victorian hypocrisy to the cruelty of the inevitable destruction of the weak by the strong. Like the rash injustices that a man may commit in his youth, the experience may not have been without its effect on the American character and the American self-image.

Land Disposal Before the Homestead Act

To acquire lands from remote or weak foreign governments and to wrest them from thin and wandering bands of neolithic aborigines were not difficult tasks for a central government endowed with gunpowder and enthusiasm. Far more

[4] Marshall Harris, *Origin of the Land Tenure System in the United States* (Ames: Iowa State University Press, 1953), pp. 155–178.
[5] Alvin M. Josephy, Jr., *The Indian Heritage of America* (New York: Knopf, 1968), p. 351.

difficult was the task of protecting the national domain from the nation's citizens, particularly since a large and active body of those citizens believed that they, as individuals, had a God-given right to its unrestricted use.

Fortunately, before the great impulses to land- and minerals-grabbing in the West began to be felt, the national government had been able to establish the skeleton of an orderly procedure for land disposal. The individual states of the Confederation—within whose own domains land-grabbing and speculation had been rife—ceded to the central government in 1785 their claims, derived from colonial charters, to the lands north and west of the Ohio River; and these cessions were extended to cover the Alabama and Mississippi land claims of Georgia in 1802. The western lands of North Carolina and Virginia south of the Ohio, being quite thoroughly disposed of, particularly through warrants to veterans of the colonial militias, were readily formed into the states of Kentucky and Tennessee. The lands subject to federal disposal, then, comprised most of the areas of the present states of Alabama, Florida, and Mississippi, and the Northwest Territory, as established under the Confederation, plus the lands west of the Mississippi as they were acquired, with the exception of Texas, whose republican status gave its state government control over its unsold lands (about three fourths of its area) at the time it entered the Union. Recognition of Spanish and Mexican claims and grants in Louisiana, New Mexico, and California, and in very small amounts in Arizona and Colorado, removed a small fraction (7 percent) of the lands in those states from the national domain.

Over most of this great area, a uniform system of survey and subdivision was enforced from 1785 onward, along a plan suggested by Jefferson, possibly derived from Dutch and Roman precedent.[6] It was a typical product of that doctrinaire rationalism to which the world owes the codified legal reforms introduced in England by the utilitarian philosophers, in France by Napoleon, and in India by (among others) Macaulay and James Mill. There was far less central planning in the colonizing of the Eurasian interior under the dukes and czars of Muskovy and Russia than in the land disposals of Indiana, Iowa, and Illinois.

By this system of rectangular survey established in the Ordinance of 1785, the land was to be mapped and measured into townships of 36 sections of 1 square mile each. The auction was established as the mode of sale for land and the size of the parcels was initially set at 1 section (640 acres) at a minimum price of $1 per acre. Thus orderly deeds to land could be drawn up and boundary disputes minimized. The job of lawyers and courts was made great enough to be lucrative but not so complex as to be impossible.

Before the system of disposal at public auctions had been fully established by the Land Act of 1796, the Congress, in need of quick money, had made sales to land companies and grants to satisfy the claims of veterans to back pay. The large grants to the Ohio and Scioto Companies and the confused and corrupt

---

[6] William D. Pattison, *Beginnings of the American Rectangular Land Survey System, 1784–1800,* University of Chicago Department of Geography Research Paper no. 50 (Chicago: University of Chicago Press, 1957), pp. 57–66.

grants to the Yazoo Companies in Alabama and Mississippi were based on colonial precedent, but the theory behind them became untenable under the pressure of frontier democracy. Grants to the states of school lands (Section 16 of every township)[7] were continued as first established under the Northwest Ordinance (1787). Grants of land for transportation—roads and canals—included both rights-of-way and land to be sold to raise funds. Such grants culminated in the antebellum period in the grant of 2,500,000 acres to the Illinois Central Railroad in 1850. In this and later railroad grants the companies received alternate sections of land in a checkerboard pattern on a strip extending from 12 to 80 miles on either side of their track through the public lands. The minimum price for the land retained by the government in these strips was doubled to maintain sales proceeds, but much of it was eventually sold at lower prices.

The land companies, state agencies, and railroads disposed of their granted lands at private sales through land offices, or sometimes through auctions. Prices on these markets, however, were presumably regulated by the rate and terms of disposal of the federally held lands. Between 1796 and 1863 when the Homestead Act provided for free land to registered claimants on the public domain, the federal lands were disposed of at auctions, held first in Philadelphia, Cincinnati, and Pittsburgh, and then after 1800 at many points in the newly opened territories, just within the line of settlement. The customary events in a new area, then, were: first, the survey, running several hundred miles beyond the settlements; next, the announcement of the lands offered; and finally, the auction. The land laws, whose changing course is summarized in Table 4.1, set a minimum price for the bidding and a minimum size of tract—two dimensions of the sale which settled to $1.25 an acre after 1820 and 40 acres after 1832. Credit sales were initially allowed, then suspended in 1820; and the rights of previous occupants on the land (squatters) were the subject of continuing controversy, threats, and violence. An act in 1841 ensured the right of an occupant to bid on 160 acres at the minimum price, and so set the stage for the Homestead Act and free land. Lands that were not disposed of at the auctions remained on sale; the Graduation Act of 1854 provided that the price of such lands should be reduced until their final disposal.

The land system—with its surveys, land offices, and public auctions—was both a folk institution and an instrument of high state policy. In a frontier region, the location of the office and the auction were important decisions on which the whole business life of a region might hang. The speed of surveying—which depended on the generosity of congressional appropriations for the purpose—set the rate at which lands could be opened up, the prices that they would command, and the whole level of land values in a region. The patronage which gave surveyors and auctioneers their jobs also gave them access to information about the lands that was often of considerable value. The little cadre of small businessmen—lawyers, bankers, land agents, and loan sharks—that formed around the land office were the advance agents of commercial

[7] After 1848; also Section 36.

TABLE 4.1
Major public land laws

Year	Price (per acre)	Size (acres)	Conditions
1785	$1 minimum	640 or more	Cash sale; amended in 1787 to provide for payment of one third in cash, the remainder in three months
1796	$2 minimum	640 or more	One half of purchase price paid within 30 days, the remainder within one year
1800	$2 minimum	320 or more	One fourth of purchase price paid within 30 days, then annual installments of one fourth for three years, at 6 percent interest
1804	$2 minimum ($1.64 for cash)	160 or more	Credit as in act of 1800; discount to $1.64 per acre for cash payment
1820	$1.25 minimum	80 or more	End of credit system; cash payment only
1830	$1.25 minimum	160 maximum	Squatters on public domain land allowed to purchase their tracts at the minimum price (preemption); temporary act, had to be renewed biennially
1832	$1.25 minimum	40 or more; 160 limit on preemption	Cash purchase only; right of preemption reaffirmed
1841	$1.25 minimum	40 or more; 160 limit on preemption	Cash purchase only; established right of preemption, doing away with necessity of renewing legislation
1854 (Graduation Act)	12.5 cents minimum	40 or more	Reduction of the sale price of land in proportion to the length of time it had been on the market; price ranged from $1 for land unsold for ten years to 12.5 cents for land unsold for thirty years
1862 (Homestead Act)	Free	160 or less	Payment of an entry fee and five years continuous residence; land could be preempted after six months' residence for $1.25 per acre cash
1873 (Timber Culture Act)	Free	160	Cultivation of trees on one quarter of a 160-acre plot gave the settler title to the whole 160 acres; amended in 1878 to require the cultivation of trees on only one sixteenth of the plot

TABLE 4.1 (continued)

Year	Price (per acre)	Size (acres)	Conditions
1878 (Timber and Stone Act)	$2.50	160 or less	Sale of lands chiefly valuable for timber or stone resources to bona fide settlers and mining interests
1877 (Desert Land Act)	$1.25	640; reduced to 320 maximum in 1890	Sale of a section of land to a settler on condition that it be irrigated within three years; amended in 1891 to increase the amount of improvements required, with one eighth of the land to be under cultivation; payment to be 25 cents at time of entry, $1 at the time of making proof of compliance with the law
1909 (Enlarged Homestead Act)	Free	320 acres	Five years' residence with continuous cultivation; designed for semiarid lands that were nonirrigable and had no minerals or merchantable timber
1916 (Stock-Raising Homestead Act)	Free	640 acres	Designed for land useful only for grazing; conditions similar to previous Homestead laws

SOURCES: Benjamin H. Hibbard, *A History of the Public Land Policies* (Madison: University of Wisconsin Press, 1965), *passim;* and Roy M. Robbins, *Our Landed Heritage: The Public Domain, 1776–1936,* (Lincoln: University of Nebraska Press, 1962). *passim.*

capitalism. The settler–speculators, interested in opening lands or in holding them off the market, exercised strong pressures. And the squatters, with families, shotguns, and a strong sense of moral right, combined with local settlers to form a brooding, even a menacing presence as the bidding proceeded.[8]

As a matter of state policy, the federal sales opened a free market for private ownership of the land in fee simple at the pound of an auctioneer's gavel. It was this fact which constituted the land system's most important contribution to the economy at large. Strong controversies continued until passage of the Homestead Act on the terms of the government's sales in all the dimensions outlined above, and small local squalls centered on the rate of opening of the lands, the choice of surveyors, and the location of the offices, on charges of corruption and favoritism and local monopoly enforced by threats and pressures at the auctions. By and large, these controversies were resolved in favor

[8] Allan G. Bogue, "The Iowa Claim Clubs: Symbol and Substance," *Mississippi Valley Historical Review,* vol. 45 (1958), pp. 231–253.

of easy terms and cheap land. The supplies offered were consistently so large that the auction price rarely rose above the minimum, and credit supplies were adequate to get the land into the hands of actual cultivators—who might still be interested in resale of their holdings—after one or two resales at most. The land system was run, not to maximize federal revenues, but to minimize political pressures, and this was done largely by keeping land in abundant supply.[9] But more important than these details was the fact that a commercial market for land existed in the frontier regions from the very outset. Land—the ancient source of political power and social authority, the object of a religious veneration by every agricultural society in the world—was made, through the federal land system, an asset like any other, put under the auctioneer's hammer to be sold in fee-simple ownership to the highest bidder. No more striking proof can be found of the utter freedom of American capitalism from the feudal restrictions and scruples that still hung heavy on the European economies in the early nineteenth century. American agriculture and small-town business was born in the presence of a free market in land. What had taken capitalism, even in England, four centuries to achieve, and was achieved then only with many qualifications and encumbrances, was handed to the farmers, speculators, and small businessmen of nineteenth-century America as a natural right.

Land Distribution in the West

With the purchase of Alaska in 1867, the United States completed its territorial expansion on the North American continent. Under the famous Homestead Act of 1862, land at last became available to settlers without cost. The culmination of a policy which had grown increasingly liberal since 1785, the act required only that a settler reside five years on his claim and cultivate it. To complete his patent, the General Land Office required that the settler erect a house on the holding and make it his continuous place of residence. The required time of residence, however, could be commuted to six months (later raised to fourteen months) upon cash payment of $1.25 an acre.[10]

In strict terms, the Homestead Act, like much other legislation and legal practice originating in the East, was not well adapted to economic conditions in the new lands in the Missouri Valley, the Rocky Mountains, and the arid Southwest. The unit, a quarter section (160 acres), was derived from practice in the humid and forested areas; it represented the maximum size for a farm where trees had to be cleared, mixed farming or dairying carried on, and family labor utilized. The adaptation of farming to the geography beyond the 98th meridian involved many changes in plant and animal stock, in implements and practices, in home construction and fencing, in transportation and power-generating techniques. These adaptations, described in W. P. Webb's fine book, *The Great Plains,* are an outstanding instance of human ingenuity. Equal ingenuity was applied in modifying the rigidities of the Homestead Act. One

---

[9] Peter Passell, "Essays in the Economics of Nineteenth Century American Land Policy" (Ph.D. dissertation, Yale University, 1970), chap. 2.
[10] In the original act, both husband and wife could file for a claim, and so receive 320 acres. This provision—evidently an oversight—was later rescinded.

of the most prevalent means of adaptation was fraud. Absentee claims were supported by false testimony of nominal residence. Houses were sworn to be 12×14 without specifying that the unit was inches instead of feet, and at least one house in Nebraska was put on wheels and moved from claim to claim.[11] These frauds were not all caused by the inappropriateness of the Homestead Act, to be sure, nor did they represent simply the blind impulse of economic rationality breaking through doctrinaire legal restraints. But their effect was to permit larger holdings and faster appropriation of the land than the law had contemplated.

Another source of flexibility in western land disposal were the large grants made to the railroads and to the states in the West. The federal government in the 1860s, continuing the precedent of the Illinois Central grant of 1850, endowed two major transcontinental railroad projects and a number of other lines with grants of alternate sections of land in a checkerboard pattern for distances ranging from 6 to 40 miles on either side of their tracts through the public domain. In all a total of 223 million acres was granted by the federal government and the states in this way. The lands so allotted became the source of revenues through sales or the pledge of the mortgage bonds of the roads as construction proceeded. Ideally such lands were to be bought up by settlers whose steady economic activities in the new areas would both raise the value of the squares of the checkerboard remaining in government hands, and bring traffic and revenues to the railroad. They were available on purchase without limit, and so permitted the development of large wheat farms and ranches, as well as timber and grazing areas. Their effectiveness as a means of orderly encouragement of the economy of the western states has never been carefully explored. Certainly the land-grabbing and land-jobbing activities of the railroads resulted in some large fortunes for speculators and manipulators. Much of the land was unsuitable for any productive purpose and a portion (about 20 percent) reverted to the federal government unsold and became again part of the public domain. Still the railroad lands actually sold, added to the school lands and other large grants made to the western states for sales, accounted for about 30 percent of the lands disposed of west of the Mississippi.[12]

In addition to the large amounts of land thus thrown on the market, the restrictive effects of the Homestead Act were further relieved by later laws. The Desert Land Act of 1877 provided for sales of blocks of land of 640 acres at \$1.25 an acre in the arid regions, provided that irrigation was carried out by the purchaser within three years. This act was modified in 1890 to allow 320-acre blocks, with a requirement of irrigation on one quarter of the area. Under the Timber Culture Act, between 1871 and 1891, claims of 160 acres in addition to a homestead might be made if a portion (one fourth in the original act, reduced to one sixteenth in 1878) was planted in trees a specified distance apart. The Land Commissioner reported in 1887 that not one claim in one

[11] Fred A. Shannon, *The Farmer's Last Frontier* (New York: Holt, Rinehart & Winston, 1945), pp. 56–59.
[12] Interestingly, the percentage is similar for the eastern United States, primarily because of the large federal grants (25 million acres) to the state of Florida.

TABLE 4.2
Federal land disposal, by sale and type of grant

Method of Disposition	Percent of Total	Millions of Acres
Cash entries and miscellaneous disposals	29.1	300
Homesteads	27.6	285
Grants to states	21.8	225
Military bounties and private land claims	9.2	95
Grants to railroad corporations	8.8	91
Timber and stone, timber culture, and desert land entries	3.4	35
Total	99.9	1031

SOURCE: Marion Clawson, *Uncle Sam's Acres* (New York: Dodd, Mead, 1951), p. 93. Reprinted with author's permission.

hundred under this act was made in good faith by a bona fide settler.[13] In the 1890s, efforts to promote irrigation led to the Carey Act (1894) which gave states in the arid region one million acres each, provided that the proceeds of their sales be used to furnish irrigation works for the lands so disposed of. The National Reclamation Act of 1902 involved the federal government in irrigation projects, providing for the use of the proceeds of federal land sales in certain arid districts for the construction of irrigation works. The Enlarged Homestead Act of 1909 expanded the standard homestead tract to 320 acres in regions suitable for dry farming. In 1916, the Stock-Raising Homestead Act allowed claims up to 640 acres of land declared suitable only for grazing. To these changes in the restrictions on homesteading should be added the encouragement given by the Timber Cutting Act mentioned below. The acts that helped to promote irrigated agriculture were based in part on fanciful expectations for the irrigation possibilities in the West and proved to be of minor quantitative importance.[14] But all in all, in the areas marked off for homesteading, the whole system centered on the Homestead Act was not ineffective in encouraging rapid settlement. Altogether, 1,346,163 final entries were patented under the acts up to 1923, and 21,3867,601 acres—about 20 percent of the total public lands disposed of—were thus taken into cultivation in family-sized farms. About one quarter of this lay east of the Great Plains; the rest was largely in the Plains states or in California. The pattern of federal land disposal is shown in Table 4.2.

Sales and grants had disposed of most of the arable land in the West by 1920—and more besides. Still a major part of the area of a number of western states was neither homesteaded nor granted away; it was retained by the federal government, which held in 1970 about 50 percent of the surface area of the states west of the Plains, excluding Alaska, and 99 percent of Alaska.

[13] U.S. General Land Office, *Annual Report of the Commissioner, 1887* (Washington: U.S. Government Printing Office, 1887), p. 68.
[14] Roy M. Robbins, *Our Landed Heritage: The Public Domain, 1776–1936* (Lincoln: University of Nebraska Press, 1962), Part IV, *passim*.

Today national forests, parks, and grassland leased for grazing cover much of the area. With the stabilization of the federal holdings about 1920, the era of land disposal came to an end, except in Alaska. Already the era of conservation had begun, and the public domain began to be looked at not as an incubus to be gotten rid of, but as a social resource whose rational administration and management were proper functions of the federal government.

Trees, Metals, Water, and Oil

A tangle of laws tried to sort out the rights to all the resources with which the trans-Mississippi West was richly (or with respect to water, poorly) endowed. Their history derives not from the conflict between the social and the private interests in property, but from the effort to separate property in different kinds of resources present on and under the soil. English law, largely followed in the eastern states, commonly attached the ownership of timber, water use, and minerals to the ownership of the soil itself. Where the lord of the land had always been also the basic unit of local government, and agriculture had been the universal use of the land, such a doctrine seemed simple and natural, and raised few difficulties. But to Americans, set in a lawless wilderness, resources seemed to belong to those who used them; there was no instinctive acknowledgement of the right of the landowner—particularly of a remote central government—to the minerals, forests, water, or oil which others might discover or use on the land. This sentiment found its expression in the behavior of the timber companies, ranchers, and miners who cut, grazed, and dug on the public domain.

Before 1891, when the first forest reserves were set aside, trees were treated—like Indians and buffalo—as obstacles to settlement, and those who cut them performed a public service. Federal policy, if it could be called such, was directed only to ensuring that settlers had adequate supplies, particularly in timber-scarce areas. The Timber Cutting Act of 1878 legalized the practice of settlers and miners of cutting from the public lands without charge for construction purposes. The Timber and Stone Act of that year put up timber lands for sale in parcels of 160 acres or less, for individual use by the purchaser, at a minimum price of $2.50 an acre.[15] Until 1897 orderly and regular harvesting of timber from the public domain was not contemplated by the law. Timber companies could obtain timber legally only by buying and holding large tracts of land, by purchasing timber from settlers as they cleared their holdings, or by stealing it from the public domain. Economic historians have not been able to quantify the relative contributions of these various sources to the national production.

Minerals differed from forest resources in several respects. They were obviously great prizes to the discoverer and could be searched out on a small scale by individual prospectors armed only with a pan, a pick, and enthusiasm. Some legal precedent existed for the separation of the rights of ownership of

---

[15] The act provided that timber not bid on at such an auction might be disposed of to commercial buyers. Collusion at the sales was common, and about 13.5 million acres of timber lands were sold off under this act.

subsoil deposits from the rights even of private owners of the soil. In England, in the rich Cornish tin district, miners had long had the right to follow an underground vein for a certain distance on either side of the point of discovery. This right, originating in local custom, enforced by miners' courts elected and supported by the mining communities themselves, had achieved the status of common law. In Prussia, too, the Free Mining Law of 1865 gave prospectors the right, on fulfillment of certain legal formalities, to search for minerals and to extract them, even under the private lands of a peasant. By and large, the federal courts, appalled at the complexity of adjudicating disputes over sub-terranean property, tried to follow the simple rule of recognizing claims to the soil and the veins beneath it. On the lands which fell into private hands before minerals were discovered, it was thus generally possible for the owners to sustain their subsoil rights. But before 1866 the disposition of mineral rights in the public domain fell under the administrative control of the War Depart-ment, policy was uncertain, and miners acquired customary claims to minerals —and to the water necessary to wash them out—which could not be dis-lodged when the federal government came to assert its ownership of the soil.

The most interesting bit of legal history in this connection occurred in the succession of mining districts from California to Colorado which sprang up on the former Mexican territory between 1848 and 1866. The gold discovery at Sutter's Mill occurred almost simultaneously with the acquisition of California from Mexico. And by sheer accident the discovery came just when federal policy toward minerals discoveries on the public domain had been thrown into chaos. Before the copper strikes in northern Michigan in the mid-1840s, the system had been a simple one of leasing deposits to the finder, in return for a royalty, amounting in the case of the Illinois lead deposits to a modest 6 percent. This system, applied at first also in Michigan, had collapsed under the rush of prospectors and the impossibility of collecting royalties from them. Before the Mining Act of 1866, the country had no national mining law; and after about 1847, there was no tried technique for granting or adjudicating claims on the public domain. It was a simple matter for the military governor of California in 1848 to void all the mineral rights conceded by the Mexican government, but a tour of the mining districts, swarming with prospectors and their retinues, convinced him of the utter impracticability of imposing from the outside any alternative system of legal control. The choice in the mining districts lay between total anarchy, with accompanying violence, and the development of local customs, locally enforced.

One stands here in the presence of law at its most primitive origins, arising from the requirements of social existence. The miners, however, were not wholly without access to social precedent. They developed rules governing the following of claims on a vein, the length of a claim on a vein, precedence in the case of counterclaims, and the election of miners' courts to settle claims —all remarkably similar to the rules that had been formulated centuries before in the mining districts of Cornwall and sustained for those districts as part of the common law of the region. The carrier of the culture was probably the Cornish miners who had come west, perhaps by way of the lead districts of

Wisconsin and Illinois, where they had formed a large colony.[16] In the absence of statutory law, this local law was confirmed by the U.S. Supreme Court as the law of the land throughout the public domain.

The first effective federal mining act (1866) was an effort to codify this law, and endeavored to give miners a claim to a shaft and the veins leading out of it without "bounding planes" from any other surface points. But the courts found it impossible in practice to implement the law and reverted to a simpler policy of acknowledging surface claims with underground rights attached.[17] The law of 1870 defining sales of land containing placer deposits allowed land to be sold at $2.50 an acre on claims between 10 and 160 acres. By this time most placer deposits had been exhausted, but the law continued to govern oil deposits on federal lands.

The western mining industry also shaped the law governing water rights. Miners, particularly in placer deposits, needed water to wash the soil away from the ore, and they took water freely on the public domain for this purpose. Later, ranchers and farmers on irrigated lands had similar industrial water requirements, wholly different in kind and volume from the simple household needs of a settler's family. Water law, as formulated in the East and in England by 1850, was based on the doctrine of "riparian rights" appropriate perhaps to the needs of farmers in humid regions. By this doctrine, the owner of a stream bank or lake front had an inherent right in the use of the water. He might divert some of it for domestic purposes, but he might not appreciably diminish its quantity or quality to the disadvantage of other riparian owners downstream. After 1850, this whole doctrine became seriously compromised in the East under a series of state laws and court decisions made to accommodate industrial users of water. In the mining districts in the West, the doctrine was replaced by a contrary doctrine of "prior appropriation." In its extreme form, this latter doctrine was adhered to only in the arid states between the Great Plains and California, where ordinary farming interests were early subordinated to mining, ranching, or irrigated agriculture. Property in water was quite separated from property in land and became the subject of special legal treatment. This so-called Colorado doctrine was derived from a less extreme version which was adopted in California and in the tier of states from North Dakota to Texas.

The speedy appropriation of America's vast oil reserves required a similar special interpretation of the law of property. Oddly enough, neither in Pennsylvania nor in Texas did the disposal of oil come under federal law. In Pennsylvania in the 1850s, the oil lands were bid away from private hands by prospectors and drillers; in Texas, the public domain was state property; and even in Oklahoma, the reservation of the land to the Indians until 1891, and the rapid rush of settlers after that date, soon put the oil discoveries on private lands under

---

[16] Arthur Cecil Todd, *The Cornish Miner in America* (Glendale, Calif.: Arthur H. Clark, 1967); Curtis H. Lindley, *A Treatise on the American Law Relating to Mines and Mineral Lands*, vol. 1 (San Francisco: Bancroft-Whitney, 1914), p. 9.

[17] For example, the law provided that, in the case of conflicting claims, the claimant controlling the peak or apex of a vein should control the deposit in both directions. Where a vein "peaked" several times, this rule produced claims almost impossible to untangle.

state laws. Even on private property, however, oil as a resource presented a peculiar legal problem. To extract coal or metallic minerals from under the surface of another man's land required the physical invasion of his subsoil area by the miner. But oil, which lay in pools in the ground, could be sucked off by the first drill to reach the deposit. The cheapest way to get oil was not to pump it, but to reach the deposit first and allow the oil to be propelled through the drill pipe by the pressure of the natural gas imprisoned in the bed. Once this gas was dissipated, the cost of obtaining the oil rose greatly. To cope with oil's natural characteristics, the Pennsylvania Supreme Court in 1889 devised the rule of capture. While admitting that the analogy was somewhat fanciful, the court likened oil—for want of a better simile—to a wild animal; it was *ferae naturae*. Like an antelope, it might pass from one property to another, and it belonged to the man who caught it.

The attitude of the states toward oil was also influenced by the facts and logic of industrial organization. In Pennsylvania, law was further shaped by the needs and peculiarities of the coal industry, an industry of many small producers supplying a competitive resource product. It was clearly not in the interests of the coal owners either to conserve the state's oil deposits or to furnish the world a notable example of public regulation. This intense individualism was picked up by the small producers of oil who dominated the industry in its early decades in the mid-continent field. But two differences from coal gave to oil a unique, and much more troubled, legal history. First, its natural characteristics—referred to above—cried out for some joint effort, even in the interests of the producers sharing a pool. Second, unlike the coal industry, oil production, because of the possibility of achieving large economies of scale in pipeline transporting and refining, became subject to oligopolistic organization early in its history. For a time this control did not push backward to the producing fields, but by 1928 roughly half of the oil produced was in the hands of the Standard Oil group and five other major independent companies.[18] There came then a strong impulse to regulate production, not only explicitly to conserve the resource, but also to maintain the price.

The history of oil discovery and production in the 1920s and 1930s is a history of efforts at group regulation, by agreements among producers or by public bodies in the oil-producing states—efforts thwarted in the courts by federal law and in practice by the many small producers whose uncontrolled drilling turned up new fields. In Texas in 1927, for example, a voluntary agreement to limit production was broken up by the smaller producers. A similar effort, under the authority of the Texas Railroad Commission, charged with preventing wasteful practices in the fields, was made in August 1930. It fell to pieces almost immediately under the weight of gigantic discoveries in East Texas. By August 1931, the East Texas field alone was producing one third of the total U.S. requirements of oil and the price per barrel had dropped from $1.23 to 24 cents.[19] At this point the Governor of Texas declared a state of insurrection in the East Texas field and sent in the National Guard to

[18] Myron W. Watkins, *Oil: Stabilization or Conservation* (New York: Harper & Row, 1937), p. 26.
[19] *Ibid.*, p. 49.

close down the wells. Orders of the federal courts were ignored and the quotas set by the Railroad Commission were enforced by the state troops. Similar control efforts in Oklahoma had an almost identical history. A statewide scheme to regulate drilling and transport was wrecked by the discovery of the field in Oklahoma City in December 1928, and martial law was declared in these fields about the same time that it was in Texas. Not until 1935 did an interstate compact in oil take effect and gain the tolerance of the federal courts, and not until 1941 did Pennsylvania join it. By this time the process of exploration was well shared between the large producers and the small operators and prospectors. Since then, exploration and exploitation of the reserves have gone hand in hand with the encouragement of practices less wasteful than those of an earlier era.

CONSERVATION AND MANAGEMENT

By the 1880s, the legal channels for placing mineral resources in private hands had become fixed. In the decades from 1890 to 1910, a forest management and disposal policy was developed. By 1920, the national domain of agricultural land was nearly wholly disposed of, and by the early 1940s, discoveries of new, cheap oil fields under the continental United States did not recur in all this period. The main thrust of American policy had been directed—with the notable exception of forests—toward the transfer of all these resources and the problems of their managements from the public domain to private ownership.

Like all human actions, this policy may be viewed from a cynical or an idealistic point of view. To the cynic and to the naturalist, the policy has seemed one of ruthless spoliation of the gifts of God—an extermination of many species of wildlife; a waste of soil, forests, and natural oil and gas; a reckless disregard for the order of nature by which all life must ultimately be maintained. From such a view, no social purpose in the policy is evident; the political and legal structure which produced the privatization of the national heritage appears simply a corruption of democratic government in the interests of human greediness. The economist, however, looks for an "invisible hand" directing human actions to a social purpose, and he is not content until he has found one.

Nineteenth-Century Exploitation

The distribution of even irreplaceable natural resources to private hands may be looked on as a policy of deep social wisdom, designed to achieve a rapid rate of exploration and discovery and a rapid development of the resource base in a situation of great uncertainty. Under nineteenth-century conditions —with growing supplies of population and capital, a production organization of growing efficiency, and a technology directed toward saving labor—the economy of the capitalist West was under heavy pressure to discover natural materials and to bring them into economic utilization. At the same time, the knowledge of where these materials lay, how they might be recognized, and what dangers might attend their discovery was extremely limited. The strategy of nineteenth-century capitalism in such a situation was to give many small risk takers the chance of an immense reward—the reward of ownership—for successful discoveries, and to let the failures go to the wall. This "buckshot approach" to exploration, described in the earlier sections of this chapter, was characteristics of innovation in all lines in the nineteenth century—not only in resource discovery but also in technological change, and even in the less risky processes of agricultural and manufacturing production. The strength of the competitive small-scale organization of economic life lay in the fact that, with active-enough competitive activity and enough prizes in the game to lure the adventurers on, new resources, new inventions, and new products were constantly turned up, and their results taken up by the economy and diffused and routinized in the orderly processes of production. When the risk of failure was high, these activities of discovery could not be successfully organized on a large scale or directed by the cumbersome and timid apparatus of a state bureaucracy. In the United States, the competitive organization was attempted even where large capital was required and large economies of scale were present, as in the case of railroads, and where extraordinary resource wastage occurred, as in oil discovery and production. Everywhere the emphasis was not on the conservation, or even the ideal allocation, of resources, but on the rate of new discovery. As long as uncertainty was high and rich new finds continued to turn up, this organization of the activity of discovery and development contributed to the rapid rate of economic growth.

Policies of Conservation

Even during the nineteenth century, at the height of the opening and appropriation of the continent's lands, forests, water, wildlife, and minerals, a few voices were raised in favor of a policy of conservation. The early conservationists were an odd mixture of many impulses and motivations. Some—naturalists like Charles R. Marsh and John Muir—had a simple love of wild nature and of the aesthetic and spiritual experiences it evoked. Some were doubtless moved as much by a loathing of man as by a love for the divine creation. Still others, like Carl Schurz, in the tradition of socialist thought, looked on the resource heritage as the property of the whole society, to be suitably administered by the state.[20] Finally, there were European observers and even a few Americans who looked ahead to the time when soils would be eroded, forests cut and burned away, and minerals exhausted. However, so long as these sentiments were based on wholly different values from those of the mass of the population, or on a different pattern of time preference in the use of resource products, there could be little expectation of an effective conservation policy.

[20] U.S. Department of the Interior, *Annual Report of the Secretary, 1877* (Washington: U.S. Government Printing Office, 1877), pp. xv–xx.

In the twentieth century, rich resource discoveries have been rarer and the techniques of locating minerals have become more efficient. At the same time, the corporate income tax has affected the value of the prizes in the game.

As early as the 1920s, the oil and mining industry appeared to find it no longer profitable to carry on exploration without the assurance of a sizable tax subsidy from the government for its efforts. Such a policy constituted in a sense a move from wholly free enterprise in minerals discovery, with ownership or ruin as the reward, to an orderly, planned continuous search for minerals under partial government subsidy. Tax subsidies have appeared in two forms: (a) the charging of exploration costs as an operating expense against current receipts from sales instead of as a capital cost to be depreciated, and (b) the so-called percentage depletion allowance, which permits a substantial credit against income to allow for the depletion of a deposit resulting from its exploitation each year. Whether the principles behind these two allowances are consistent with one another and whether the allowed rates are excessive have been matters of much controversy.

To maintain supplies of resources—soil chemicals and land contours, forests, wildlife, water, and ultimately air—the cooperation of public authorities and private owners has become increasingly important. Much conservation work has been carried on piecemeal—confined to one area or one aspect of an area's resource problem—soil erosion, deforestation, aridity, floods. But by the 1930s, the relation among forests and other soil cover, water conservation, and soil erosion had become evident. The policy toward the forests was established in the 1890s when reserves were first set aside from the public domain and provision made for their management and for controlled cutting and sale of the timber. Theodore Roosevelt's enthusiasm for creating national forests led to a requirement of congressional approval for the creation of further such reserves. The Weeks Act of 1911 empowered the President to buy forest lands in the East at the headwaters of navigable streams and to add to the national forests. Closer study of the role of forests in land management was promoted by the setting up of forest experiment stations after 1928; finally, in the 1930s, under the New Deal, the federal government assumed positive responsibility for improving and reforesting lands, for example, in the cutover areas of the Great Lakes region and parts of New England and the southern Appalachians. The Taylor Act of 1934 made somewhat similar provisions for the nonforested grazing lands still in the public domain, permitting grazing by payment of fees and giving the government power to develop water-power sources and to control erosion on such lands. The integration of soil, water, and forest management with the governments agricultural programs was accomplished by the establishment of the Soil Erosion Service in the 1930s and by the Soil Conservation and Domestic Allotment Act of 1938, which placed agricultural production controls on the legal basis of soil conservation. This act was partly a legal device to circumvent the Supreme Court's objections to the production control program under the Agricultural Adjustment Act. But by it, together with the creation of a "soil bank" in the 1950s and the encouragement given to the planting of trees and creation of artificial ponds on farms, resource management was brought down to the "grass roots" level in the settled agricultural areas.

The basic character of federal responsibility for flood control was fixed in the Flood Control Act of 1936, in which national flood-control policy, already in existence for the Mississippi River and a few others since 1917, was integrated under the Corps of Engineers and the Department of Agriculture in a program of watershed improvement and soil conservation. In 1928 Boulder Dam on the Colorado River—the first federal multipurpose dam, furnishing water, power, and flood control to the Southwest—was authorized. Its construction, begun in 1931, represented the triumph of Herbert Hoover, the great social and mining engineer, over the prejudices of President Hoover, the theorist and moralist of free enterprise. With the creation of the Tennessee Valley Authority in 1933, an integrated attack was made on the resource problem of an entire river basin. As with many great projects, the idea did not spring full-blown from the basis of some high social purpose. The original dam (Wilson Dam at Muscle Shoals on the Tennessee River in northern Alabama) was begun in 1918 to furnish electric power for nitrates production during World War I. The war ended before the dam was completed, and through the 1920s it remained, like a huge half-finished white stone elephant, among the government's stock of assets. Private interests were able to prevent its completion for power production, but could not acquire it from the government at a bargain. Efforts to turn it to private use, even those made by Henry Ford in 1921–1924, were to no avail. Public use remained a gleam in the eye of George W. Norris and a few other Progressive senators. Following the model of a state project on the Miami River in Ohio, this half-forgotten plan was taken up in the 1930s in the Tennessee Valley Authority. The Authority's goals were conceived along grand lines—to control floods, prevent erosion, promote reforestation, and furnish power and rural electrification over an area now covering nearly all of Tennessee and an appreciable portion of the surrounding states. The careful use of the resources of the area was to attract industry, improve agriculture, and raise the standard of life of this portion of the central South.[21] In the Northwest the great dam at Grand Coulee on the Columbia River was finished in 1941. In a period when government planning no longer seemed like a dirty word, these projects were public and private cooperative efforts that set a standard for resource management.

Emerging Resource Problems

In its policy toward agricultural land and forest and grassland resources, the United States by 1940 had managed to achieve a considerable turnaround from the nineteenth-century policy of unrestricted use, with its high rate of discount of the future and its disregard for long-run damage. But in the 1960s a new package of resource problems appeared, with a spectacular deterioration of the urban environment. Appropriation of water and air by private persons and municipalities, without regard for external costs of such usage, had pro-

[21] Frank E. Smith, *The Politics of Conservation* (New York: Random House, 1966), pp. 178–239.

duced polluted water and poisonous air for all to use and breathe. Only slowly have nineteenth-century attitudes toward resources been overcome. Public action has moved with great hesitation, long lags, and timid measures. The reasons for the ineffectiveness of resource consumers in enforcing simple guarantees of their own health and comfort are considered more fully in the last chapter of this book.

In the case of the depletable resources—minerals and fuels—the record is a bit different. Since the main use of gold is to be returned to the ground in vaults as reserve for the international banking system, rapid depletion of gold mines is a matter of little consequence—except perhaps to the world price level. However, the increasing exploitation of other metals in the past 100 years forced the American economy to depend on lower-grade deposits, made usable by new techniques of beneficiation; on more careful recycling of scrap; and on imports from areas in Canada, Latin America, and Africa, where the nineteenth-century processes of exploration and discovery are still in progress. In certain minerals, notably tin, American deposits have always been negligible; access to the still-ample overseas deposits depends on international political and market conditions. In the important case of iron, improvements in processing techniques have brought large reserves of lower-grade ores into economic use. In 1955 the U.S. Geological Survey estimated ore reserves, raised to a commercial level of 60 percent iron by beneficiation techniques, at 5.5 billion tons, yielding 3 billion tons of iron—a 50-years' supply at consumption levels of the 1960s, but less if allowance is made for the growth in demand. Even now, imports from Canada, Latin America, and West Africa account for two thirds of U.S. ore consumption, by iron content. In the case of copper, lead, zinc, and possibly aluminum, the U.S. reserves position is more unfavorable. At the 1970 level of consumption, proven reserves at current cost levels are only a few years ahead of demand. In all these metals, exploration of the U.S. and foreign subsoil is far from exhustive. However, the best estimates are that at current rates of growth of American and foreign consumption, world reserves—including probable new finds—should not cover demand at current, or slightly rising, levels of cost for more than three to six decades.[22]

In the case of the mineral fuels, the situation is brighter. Known oil reserves in the United States are never more than 10 to 15 years ahead of supply, but the steady process of subsidized exploration has kept them there since the large-scale utilization of oil began. In the 1960s, some rise in the ratio of production to proven reserves was observed. The recovery of deposits under the ocean, the application of better—and somewhat more expensive—recovery techniques from present wells, and eventually the use of oil in shale in vast quantities promises some price rises but no exhaustion in the foreseeable future. The abandonment of an import quota restriction policy which in effect forces over three quarters of domestic consumption to be drawn from domestic resources would significantly reduce oil prices. If the American

[22] Based on estimates by the U.S. Bureau of Mines published in *Minerals, Facts and Figures, 1970* (Washington: U.S. Government Printing Office, 1971).

market were opened to the world's huge oil reserves, the American oil industry would shrink in size and domestic deposits would be conserved, although the rate of discovery of new deposits also would slow down. In the case of coal, even known reserves are still enormous relative to present rates of utilization. An authoritative study in the early 1960s estimated U.S. coal reserves at over 200 billion tons, a 500-years' supply at consumption rates and extraction costs of 1960.[23]

In all these cases, economists tend to be less concerned about resource problems than many laymen because of their faith—justified so far by modern history—in the ingenuity of technology as the ultimate resource. The achievements of recent decades lie all around us—the development of aluminum and plastics to replace iron in many uses, the development of synthetic rubber and synthetic textile fibers, the amazing discovery of atomic energy as a source of fuel and light. None of these technological solutions to resource problems is as simple as it first appears. As with wonder drugs, unexpected "side effects" make themselves felt. The difficulties of disposing of the radioactive wastes from atomic power plants, for example, raise serious problems. Nevertheless, the possibility that chemistry and atomic physics may achieve the medieval alchemist's goal of transmuting one element into another gives hope that resource problems are solvable. The fundamental question is this: Will scientific technology be as kind to the American economy in the twenty-first century as nature was to it in the nineteenth? Certainly as long as economic nationalism is a major fact in the world, a heavy dependence on imports is a risky business. Still, in the end, however high the domestic or foreign resource supplies and discovery rates may be, ultimate reliance must be placed on the savings and substitutions permitted by new technology.

A resource policy for the next hundred years, then, must rest on expectations very different from those of the past hundred years. In renewable resources, emphasis must be placed on the management of the total natural environment so as to preserve the ecological balance not only of the countryside and the drainage basins, but of the city as well. This may produce further retreat from the unlimited freedom of resource discovery and use that attended this country's nineteenth-century expansion. In the use of the depletable resources, reliance on medium-grade domestic deposits and imports is at best a temporary stopgap, though one that may last in many lines another half-century, assuming international political conditions that favor foreign trade in resource products. As the users of resources continue to increase their demands around the world, mankind's ultimate resource must be a chemical and physical technology of fantastic ingenuity. As in the use of the renewable resources, there can be little question here that the social sponsorship and direction of such research is a necessity of national—and of human—survival. Can the American society devise institutions and ways of behavior that will permit it to survive in a world where expansion and appropriation of the simple and obvious gifts of nature are no longer the answer to the dissatisfaction of every

---

[23] Hans H. Landsberg *et al.*, *Resources in America's Future* (Baltimore: Johns Hopkins, 1963), p. 414.

group in our society? The American experience with the shifting role of government in the economy gives rise to a moderate optimism (see Chapter 17). But only history will tell whether such optimism is warranted.

SUGGESTED READING

Billington, Ray Allen. *The Far Western Frontier, 1830–1860.* New York: Harper & Row, 1956.

Billington, Ray Allen. "The Origin of the Land Speculator as a Frontier Type." *Agricultural History,* vol. 19, no. 4 (October 1945), pp. 204–212.

Carstensen, Vernon (ed.). *The Public Lands: Studies in the History of the Public Domain.* Madison: University of Wisconsin Press, 1963.

Chittenden, Hiram Martin. *A History of the American Fur Trade of the Far West.* Two vols. New York: 1902. Reprint. Stanford, Calif.: Academic Reprints, 1954.

Gates, Paul Wallace. *History of Public Land Law Development.* Washington: U.S. Government Printing Office, 1968.

Gates, Paul Wallace. "The Homestead Law in an Incongruous Land System." *American Historical Review,* vol. 41, no. 4 (July 1936), pp. 652–681. Reprint. Vernon Carstensen, (ed.). *The Public Lands: Studies in the History of the Public Domain.* Madison: University of Wisconsin Press, 1963.

Gates, William. *Michigan Copper and Boston Dollars: An Economic History of the Michigan Copper Mining Industry.* Cambridge, Mass.: Harvard University Press, 1951.

Goodwin, Cardinal. *The Trans-Mississippi West: A History of Its Acquisition and Settlement, 1803–1852.* New York: Appleton-Century-Crofts, 1922.

Green, Fletcher M. "Georgia's Forgotten Industry: Gold Mining." *Georgia Historical Quarterly,* vol. 19, no. 2 (June 1935), pp. 93–111; and vol. 19, no. 3 (September 1935), pp. 210–228.

Green, Fletcher M. "Gold Mining: A Forgotten Industry of Ante-Bellum North Carolina." *North Carolina Historical Review,* vol. 14, no. 1 (January 1937), pp. 1–19; and vol. 14, no. 2 (April 1937), pp. 135–155.

Gregg, Josiah. *Commerce of the Prairies; or, The Journal of a Santa Fe Trader During Eight Expeditions Across the Great Western Prairies, and a Residence of Nearly Nine Years in Northern Mexico.* New York: 1844. Reprint. Norman: University of Oklahoma Press, 1958.

Hibbard, Benjamin Horace. *A History of the Public Land Policies.* New York: 1924. Reprint. Madison: University of Wisconsin Press, 1965.

Hill, Forest G. *Roads, Rails and Waterways: The Army Engineers and Early Transportation.* Norman: University of Oklahoma Press, 1957.

Ise, John. *The United States Forest Policy.* New Haven: Yale University Press, 1920.

Josephy, Alvin M., Jr. *The Indian Heritage of America.* New York: Knopf, 1968.

Landsberg, Hans H., Leonard L. Fischman, and Joseph L. Fisher. *Resources in America's Future: Patterns of Requirements and Availabilities, 1960–2000.* Baltimore: Johns Hopkins, 1963.

Nash, Gerald D. *United States Oil Policy, 1890–1964.* Pittsburgh: University of Pittsburgh Press, 1968.

Parkman, Francis. *The Oregon Trail.* Boston: 1849. Reprint. Madison: University of Wisconsin Press, 1969.

Paul, Rodman. *California Gold: The Beginning of Mining in the Far West.* Cambridge, Mass.: Harvard University Press, 1947. Reprint. Lincoln: University of Nebraska Press, 1967.

Pickard, T. A. *A History of American Mining*. New York: 1932. Reprint. New York: Johnson Reprint, 1966.

Robbins, Roy M. *Our Landed Heritage; The Public Domain, 1776–1936*. Princeton: 1942. Reprint. Lincoln: University of Nebraska Press, 1962.

Russel, Robert R. *Improvement of Communication with the Pacific Coast as an Issue in American Politics, 1783–1864*. Cedar Rapids, Iowa: Torch Press, 1948.

Semple, Ellen Churchill. *American History and Its Geographic Conditions*. Boston: Houghton Mifflin, 1903.

Shinn, Charles H. *Mining Camps: A Study in American Frontier Government*. New York: 1885. Reprint. New York: Knopf, 1948.

Webb, Walter Prescott. *The Great Plains*. Boston: 1931. Reprint. New York: Grossett & Dunlap, n.d.

5

THE AMERICAN POPULATION

In the 1960s the term "population explosion" became common parlance. The fears conjured up by this term, the graphic projections of a planet inundated with human bodies, have aroused widespread public concern. But rapid population growth is not a wholly new phenomenon in the history of mankind. The United States is itself a case in point, for it has had a remarkably high rate of population growth throughout much of its history.

Unfortunately, it is not easy to distill with confidence the lessons of history in this area, for population has been a long-neglected subject in economic history. A glance at standard economic history texts will show that the topic is often treated only cursorily and is sometimes wholly omitted. Rarely is a full chapter devoted to population. In recent years growing attention has been given to the subject, but much remains to be done. Even the historical facts are not fully established. For example, such a basic matter as the trend in the American death rate in the nineteenth century remains uncertain.

In view of this situation, this chapter is necessarily somewhat speculative. An attempt has been made first to set down some of the available facts of American population growth. How fast did the population grow? What were the relative roles of fertility, mortality, and immigration? In the case of immigration, where did the people come from? How did the location of the population change over time, and what relation, if any, did this movement have to the process of economic growth? Did native-born whites, immigrants, and nonwhites play different roles in the geographic and economic changes that were going on?

These questions relate to quantitative aspects of population growth and distribution. But there are also qualitative features which bear importantly on the process of economic growth. How young was the population at a

The research for this chapter was supported in part by National Science Foundation grant GS-1563. The comments of the following readers are gratefully acknowledged: Glen G. Cain, John D. Durand, Stanley Engerman, Henry A. Gemery, John R. Hanson, Simon Kuznets, William H. Newell, and Mark Perlman.

given time, and what was the trend in average age ? How did the health of the American population compare with that elsewhere ? What about its level of education ? Was the United States relatively advanced in schooling or was it a laggard ?

The first part of this chapter will be devoted to such questions concerning the nature of American population. Where possible, an attempt will be made to note similarities and differences between the American experience and those of other developed countries.

With the facts established, it becomes possible to focus on the causes and effects of population growth. In the second part, we turn to the determinants of American population growth. How can one explain the exceedingly high rate of growth ? Perhaps even more challenging, how can one explain the rather early decline in the rate of natural increase, given the seemingly limitless economic opportunities ? Some writers have likened human population growth to the multiplication of fruit flies in a jar. The aptness of this analogy is called into question by American experience, and there is need to know why.

The final part of this chapter takes up the effect of population growth on the rate of economic growth. What role did population growth play in the increase of total and per capita product ? Was high population growth an obstacle to economic development, as is said to be the case with regard to today's less developed countries ? Or was it an important stimulus ? Is the American case in some way unique ? While no claim is made that the answers to these questions are given here, an attempt is made to indicate some of the relevant considerations and to arrive at a tentative judgment of their relative weight, speculative though it must be.

THE NATURE OF AMERICAN POPULATION GROWTH[1]

Growth and Origins

The single most distinctive feature of American population history is the unusually high rate of growth. This growth was accomplished partly through immigration and importation of slaves and partly through high natural increase among the foreign-born and their descendants. In the course of time, a variety of races and nationalities came to be represented in America's "melting pot." Nevertheless, throughout American history, the vast majority of the population continued to be of northwestern European, and especially United Kingdom, descent.

Rate of total increase.   In 1790 the U.S. population was less than that of present-day Norway, around 3.2 million persons. Today its population total of over 200 million places the United States fourth among the nations of the world in terms of size. Despite this immense increase, the population density remains relatively low, about 55 persons per square mile compared with a world average of 65.

---

[1] To avoid repeated interruption in the text, citations in this part have been kept to a minimum. The principal sources underlying the discussion appear in the Suggested Reading list at the end of the chapter. Of special value were the works by Thompson and Whelpton ; the Taeubers ; Grabill, Kiser, and Whelpton ; Hutchinson ; Folger and Nam ; and the U.S. Census Bureau publications.

The rapidity of American population growth can be appreciated by comparing it with current world experience. The concern today over the world's "population explosion" relates to a rate of total increase of the world population of around 2 percent per year, a figure that results in a doubling of numbers every 35 years. From 1790 through 1860, and for a century or more before 1790, the American population growth rate averaged close to 3 percent per year, a figure that doubles population in only 23 years (see Table 5.1). In

TABLE 5.1
Average growth rate of population, by component of change,
1790–1968 (per thousand per year)

Period	Total Increase	Birth Rate	Death Rate	Net Migration Rate[a]
1790–1800	29.9	—	—	—
1800–1810	30.8	—	—	1.0
1810–1820	28.4	—	—	.8
1820–1830	28.7	—	—	1.1
1830–1840	28.1	—	—	3.3
1840–1850	30.4	—	—	7.1
1850–1860	30.2	—	—	9.4
1860–1870	23.5	—	—	5.8
1870–1875	25.5	40.8	21.8	6.7
1875–1880	18.3	38.8	23.8	3.4
1880–1885	25.4	36.9	21.0	10.1
1885–1890	19.9	35.3	20.6	5.8
1890–1895	20.1	34.3	19.5	4.5
1895–1900	16.3	31.6	18.8	2.8
1900–1905	18.5	30.0	17.6	6.0
1905–1910	19.8	29.6	16.6	6.9
1910–1915	17.5	27.5	14.7	5.3
1915–1920	10.5	26.1	16.2	1.1
1920–1925	16.9	25.0	11.3	3.6
1925–1930	12.5	21.5	10.6	2.0
1930–1935	7.0	18.3	11.0	−.4
1935–1940	7.2	18.3	11.3	.2
1940–1945	10.6	21.2	10.9	.5
1945–1950	15.6	24.5	9.9	1.3
1950–1955	17.2	24.8	9.5	1.8
1955–1960	17.0	24.6	9.4	1.8
1960–1964	15.3	22.7	9.4	2.0
1965–1968	11.1	18.3	9.5	2.2

[a] For period prior to 1870, migration of white population only divided by mid-decade average of total population. For 1870–1955, the sum of the components does not exactly equal total increase, because net migration refers to alien arrivals less departures and thus includes some nonmigratory movements.

SOURCES

Through 1870: Warren S. Thompson and P. K. Whelpton, *Population Trends in the United States* (New York: McGraw-Hill, 1933), pp. 1, 303.

For 1870–1964: Richard A. Easterlin, *Population, Labor Force, and Long Swings in Economic Growth: The American Experience* (New York: Columbia University Press, 1968), p. 189.

For 1965–1968: U.S. Bureau of the Census, *Statistical Abstract of the United States, 1969* (Washington: U.S. Government Printing Office, 1969), p. 6.

Europe, throughout the period since 1800, there has been no country with a growth rate even half as high for as much as two consecutive decades.

After 1860 the rate of population growth in the United States started to decline. The decade of the 1930s registered the lowest increase on record, about .7 percent per year. An upsurge associated with the post World War II baby boom raised the rate to 1.7 percent per year by the mid-1950s. Since then the growth rate has again moved downward. From 1967 to 1970 it was about 1 percent per year, not far from the all-time low. In an international comparison this rate places the United States still somewhat above the current rates in most European countries, but considerably below the rates in the less developed parts of the world.

The rise and subsequent decline in the rate of population growth since World War II comprise the most recent of rather similar waves in the rate of population growth. Most of these swings have been around 15 to 25 years in length. The evidence on the existence of the swings is clearest for the period since 1820, but there are indications that they may have occurred in the colonial period also. To a substantial extent they have been due to waves of immigration, though as noted, the most recent movement was caused by a swing in the birth rate. In this chapter, the principal focus is on long-term trends rather than on these swings, but some attention will be given to the fluctuations here and also in Chapter 15, since they are intimately related to urban development.

Components of population change.   How was the high rate of U.S. population growth since 1790 accomplished? The usual response is immigration. (Importation of slaves was abolished by Congress in 1808.) But this is only part of the story. Persons born abroad never accounted for more than 15 percent of the population; most of the people, white and nonwhite, were born here. This was true even as early as 1790.

The other element accounting for America's high population growth, along with immigration, was a very high rate of natural increase. This reflected both a very high birth rate and a relatively low death rate. At the start of the nineteenth century, the crude birth rate was on the order of 45 to 50 per thousand, a rate considerably above that in northwestern Europe at the time and comparable to if not higher than the rates in many of today's less developed nations. The crude death rate was perhaps on the order of 20 per thousand, placing the United States among the most favorably situated countries of the world with regard to mortality conditions at that time.

After 1800 fertility moved downward, exerting a depressing effect on the rate of total increase. But for some time this was offset by a rising rate of immigration. After 1860 the depressing effect of the fertility decline began to dominate the rate of total increase; and eventually, with World War I and subsequent immigration restriction, declining immigration also contributed to a lower rate of total increase. Over the period as a whole it was basically the persistent reduction in fertility which lowered the rate of population growth.

Origins of the population.   The era of independence started with a white population predominantly of British descent, most of whom were born and raised in America, and a black slave population, also largely native-born, concentrated in the South. The proportion of whites to blacks in the nation as a whole was about four to one, though in the South it was two to one. The fact that the great bulk of the population—perhaps as much as nine tenths—was born in America was due to the very high rate of natural increase, which, as mentioned above, dwarfed the contribution of immigration and importation of slaves to population growth. Among whites, those of British origin accounted for almost four persons in five. The remainder was nearly all from northwestern Europe, chiefly Germany and Holland (Table 5.2).

The history of the next half-century was almost entirely that of this population and its descendants. Immigration was free, but the flow before 1840 remained low, though it was rising. The late 1840s mark the initiation of the first major influx of the nineteenth century. Similar great waves of immigration were to recur at about 15- to 25-year intervals until World War I.

Initially, as in the colonial period, northwestern Europe was the principal area from which the migrants came. However, the proportion of migrants

TABLE 5.2
White population, by area of origin, 1790 and 1920

Origin	1790	1920
Number, millions	3.2	94.8
All countries, percent	100.0%	100.0%
Europe[a]	97.7	94.4
North and west	89.9	63.1
Great Britain and Northern Ireland	77.0	41.4
Eire	4.4	11.2
France	1.9	1.9
Netherlands	3.3	2.0
Scandinavia and Finland	.9	4.7
Belgium and Switzerland	2.4	1.9
East and central	7.5	26.7
Germany	7.4	16.3
Poland	—	4.1
Austria-Hungary, Czechoslovakia	.1	3.3
Russia	—	2.3
Rumania, Bulgaria, Yugoslavia	—	.7
Southern and other	.2	4.7
Italy	—	3.6
Spain, Portugal, Greece	.2	.7
Turkey, Syria, Lebanon	—	.2
Other	—	.2
America	2.3	5.6
North America	1.6	4.4
Latin America and West Indies	.7	1.3

[a] Includes a small number from the Middle East.

SOURCE: Thompson and Whelpton, op. cit., p. 91, assuming the 1790 population was distributed by origin in the same proportions as the 1920 colonial stock.

from the United Kingdom was substantially less, and among them there was a much larger representation from Ireland. Toward the end of the century, a major change in the origins of the flow developed, with southern and eastern European nations predominating (Table 5.3). This phenomenon, characterized by contemporaries as the "New Immigration," was a central target of the restrictive legislation with national origins quotas that was passed in the 1920s. Earlier, incipient flows from Asia to the Pacific Coast had been substantially terminated by legislation and treaties which sought to stem the "Yellow Peril." In absolute numbers, the net inflow of about 24 million persons between 1840 and World War I is unmatched in the history of the world. Compared with other nations, the United States was indeed something of a "melting pot," though it appears that the ingredients considered appropriate for the pot were rather narrowly defined from a world-wide and even European point of view.

The vast immigration contributed to the expansion of the American population not only directly, but also through the ensuing generations of native-born offspring to which it gave rise. When one takes account of this factor, there can be little doubt that nineteenth-century immigration greatly increased the size of the American population. Let us assume that in the absence of immigration natural increase of the colonial stock would have been the same as it was in the presence of immigration. (As we shall see later in this chapter, this is probably a reasonable guess.) On this assumption, between 1790 and 1920 immigrants and their descendants contributed just as much to population growth as did the multiplication of the original colonial stock, white and nonwhite combined. In other words, the actual 1920 population was double that which would have resulted from multiplication of the colonial stock alone. By region, however, there were important variations. Little of the post-colonial immigration flow went to the South, and even in 1920 the population of this area was composed very largely of descendants of the colonial population.

TABLE 5.3
Reported immigration, by area of origin, 1821–1890 and 1891–1920 (percent)

Origin	1821–1890	1891–1920
Number, thousands[a]	15.4	18.2
Total, percent[b]	100%	100%
Europe	90	89
North and west	82	25
East and central	5	39
South	3	25
America	8	8
Asia	2	3

[a] Includes a small number of immigrants of unspecified origin plus a small number from Oceania and Africa.
[b] For those with area of origin shown.

SOURCE: Conrad Taeuber and Irene B. Taeuber, *The Changing Population of the United States* (New York: Wiley, 1958), pp. 53, 57.

This post-colonial immigration was responsible for the decline in the share of the nonwhite population from one in five to one in ten. The 1920 black population, which accounted for all but 4 percent of nonwhites, was very largely descended from the black population in the United States at the start of the nineteenth century. (It included also a small number of black immigrants, chiefly from the West Indies, and their descendants, plus the descendants of an unknown but probably relatively small number of slaves illegally imported before 1860.) The natural increase of the black population from 1790 to 1920 appears, over the period as a whole, to have been remarkably like that of the colonial white stock, averaging around 25 percent per decade. Consequently the proportion between whites and nonwhites descended from the colonial period was about the same in 1920 as it was in 1790.

The remainder of the nonwhite population, numbering around .4 million persons in 1920, comprised chiefly Indians, Chinese, and Japanese. There is no good record of the trend in the American Indian population, but it was probably downward for most of the nation's history. According to a very rough estimate, the indigenous population in 1492 was probably around 1 million persons. Though the census figures since 1920 show some increase, even by 1960 the Indian population numbered only about half a million.

As has been noted, the national origins of the nineteenth-century immigration flow differed increasingly in the course of time from those of the colonial white stock. As a result, the predominantly British origin of the white population was progressively reduced. But even as of 1920, over half the white population was of United Kingdom descent (Table 5.2). Moreover, in terms of positions of political, social, and economic importance, the representation of this group was substantially greater than its numerical importance in the population. In terms of cultural values and heritage, the United States remained largely British in nature, as it was at the time of independence.

The basic makeup of the American population was fixed by 1920—the racial mix and national origins of the population today remain much as they were then. Before 1920, massive immigration from increasingly diverse European sources was the principal factor altering the composition of the population. The drastic restrictions passed in the 1920s on the volume and national composition of immigration had their intended result of effectively fixing the makeup of the nation's population. Also, because of immigration restriction, the American population today is a much more home-grown population than it was half a century ago, and its ties with its foreign origins are correspondingly diminished. In 1910 two persons in five in the white population were either foreign-born or had at least one foreign-born parent; today, the proportion has fallen to one in five, and only one person in twenty was born abroad.[2]

[2] The Immigration Act of 1965 abolished the national origins quota system and the special immigration restrictions relating to Asians. The new law sets ceilings on immigration from both Western hemisphere and non-Western hemisphere countries. (The former were previously not subject to the quota.) It assigns preferences with a view to facilitating reunion of families and to supplying labor for specific types of occupations in which there is a shortage.

Spatial Distribution

The aspect of American population distribution which has typically captured most attention is the great wave of western settlement. In time, this brought under control an area stretching from the Atlantic to the Pacific, over three times that held at independence. From the viewpoint of American economic growth, this settlement process is fundamental to understanding the development of the resource base of the American economy. It is also one of the features that differentiates American economic development from European experience. In most European countries the process of settlement was largely or wholly completed before modern economic growth occurred. In the United States settlement and modern economic growth for the most part took place concurrently.

The irony is that, having brought this vast area under its sway, the American population is in the process of abandoning much of it. This is because of an even more fundamental spatial aspect of modern economic growth—the trend toward population concentration in urban, and, more recently, suburban areas. During much of the nineteenth century, the changing location of the American population was a composite of the two tendencies toward westward expansion and urban concentration. In the twentieth century, urbanization and its variant, suburbanization, have emerged as the dominant forces in spatial redistribution. Indeed, the settlement process is now, in effect, being reversed as people increasingly abandon the countryside for towns and cities. This phenomenon of rural depopulation, the reverse of urbanization, is also characteristic of European experience.

Partly because of the concurrence of modern economic growth and settlement of the nation, the spatial mobility of the population in the United States has been much higher than it has in the economic development of European nations. Indeed, it appears that urbanization in the United States occurred more rapidly than in many other developed nations. However, because the United States was initially so much more rural than many of these countries, its current degree of urbanization is still not the highest in the world.

Settlement.   The process of settlement can be conveniently summarized by taking four north–south sections of the country. The first comprises the three East Coast divisions shown in Figure 5.1; the second, the two East Central, from the Appalachians to the Mississippi; the third, the two West Central divisions, comprising chiefly the vast plains areas; and the fourth, the two western divisions. As shown in Table 5.4, in 1790 virtually the entire population was in the three East Coast divisions. Subsequently, the share of this region fell sharply, and by 1910 it accounted for only around two persons in five. Since then, the share of this region has leveled off.

The East Central and West Central regions show patterns of change that are similar to each other, though different in timing. In both regions, there is a phase of rapidly increasing share in the total population followed by one of decline. The East Central region leads in the process, reaching its peak around 1860, about a half-century before the peak for the West Central. It appears that in the most recent half-century the population share of the

FIGURE 5.1
Regions and geographic divisions of the United States

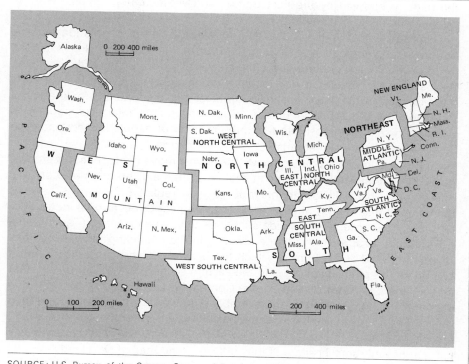

SOURCE: U.S. Bureau of the Census, *Census of Population: 1960, United States Summary* (Washington:
U.S. Government Printing Office, 1963), p. S2, fig. 2.

TABLE 5.4
Distribution of population, by geographic region, 1790–1960 (percent)

Region	1790	1860	1910	1960
East Coast	97	51	41	40
East Central	3	35	29	27
West Central	—	12	22	18
West	—	2	8	15
United States	100	100	100	100

SOURCE: U.S. Bureau of the Census, *Census of Population: 1960, United States Summary* (Washington:
U.S. Government Printing Office, 1963), p. 1-19.

East Central region may be stabilizing, like that of the East Coast region. In contrast, the western region, the area settled latest, is still in the first phase of the pattern followed by the East Central and West Central regions, with its population share still growing.

Considering the United States as a whole, the rate of population redistribution among regions has slowed markedly in this century. For example, in the seven decades before 1860, the area with a declining population share, the East Coast, lost about half of the total. In the most recent half-century, the reduction in the share of the losing areas has amounted to only about a fourteenth of the total population. Such statements relate, of course, to population *shares*. In absolute terms the number of people has continued to increase in all the main regions.

From the economic point of view, these vast movements reflect a process of population redistribution more in keeping with the distribution of economic opportunity. This is illustrated in a rough way in Table 5.5. Column (5) shows the regional distribution of land suitable for regular or occasional cultivation, according to a recent nationwide survey of soil characteristics. (The regional classification is approximately the same as in the preceding table, but differs slightly because of the form in which the basic data were presented.) About one quarter of cultivable land is in the eastern section of the country, another third in the East Central, and so on. Comparing Columns (5) and (6), one sees that some regions are more favorably endowed with cultivable land than others. For example, the East Central has about a third of the cultivable land but only a fifth of the total land area of the country; in contrast, the West has a noticeably smaller share of the cultivable land than of total land.

Table 5.5 shows that the trend in the regional distribution of the agricultural labor force was toward greater correspondence with the regional distribution of cultivable land. Thus, the East Coast, which initially contained all of the agricultural labor force, showed a steady decline. On the other hand, the West

TABLE 5.5
Distribution by region of agricultural labor force,
1790–1950, and of cultivable and total land, 1960 (percent)

Region	Agricultural Labor Force				Cultivable Land (5)	Total Land (6)
	1790 (1)	1840 (2)	1900 (3)	1950 (4)		
East Coast	100	75	43	36	24	19
East Central	—	25	39	37	34	20
West Central	—	—	13	16	29	21
West	—	—	4	11	14	40
United States	100	100	100	100	100	100

SOURCE: U.S. Department of Agriculture, *Basic Statistics of the National Inventory of Soil and Water Conservation Needs* (Washington: U.S. Government Printing Office, 1962); and Alvin Tostlebe, *Capital in Agriculture* (Princeton: Princeton University Press, 1957), underlying worksheets.

Central and western regions showed rising shares. These changes were accomplished by migration, both international and internal; regional differences in natural increase did not in general play a significant role.

In this century as economic opportunity has increasingly centered in cities, urbanization, rather than settlement, has come to dominate the process of spatial redistribution of population. Hence the regional shares of *total* population tend increasingly to reflect the influence of urbanization. For example, it is urban opportunities that explain the leveling off of the share of the East Coast in *total* population shown in Table 5.4, as compared with the continuing decline in the East Coast's share of agricultural labor force shown in Table 5.5.

Urbanization. Because urbanization is the central subject of Chapters 15 and 16, only a few principal features will be noted here. The trend may be brought out most simply by considering the proportion of population residing in communities of 2500 persons or more (Table 5.6). In 1790 the population was overwhelmingly rural—nineteen persons out of twenty were living in places with less than 2500 population. By 1960 the balance had shifted drastically in the other direction; only one person in three was rural. More refined attempts to distinguish rural from urban, such as the concept of "metropolitanized area" used in Chapter 15, yield a current rural proportion as low as one person in ten.

This increase in urban population involved growth both in the number of urban places and in their average size. In 1790 there were only 24 urban places, and none exceeded 50,000 in population. By 1950 the number of urban places had grown to 4741, of which 232 had populations exceeding 50,000. Thus today about one American in three lives in a city greater in size than any that existed at the time of the nation's founding. The growth of urban places by size has revealed a strikingly stable pattern, shown in Chapter 15, Figure 15.7. This phenomenon has characterized other developed nations as well and has given rise to the concept of a "system of cities."

The trend toward urbanization shows an interesting contrast with that toward westward settlement. Initially, the redistribution of population by region proceeded very rapidly. However, after 1860 it started to slow down,

TABLE 5.6
Distribution of population, by rural–urban residence, 1790–1960 (percent)

Date	Total	Rural	Urban
1790	100	95	5
1840	100	89	11
1880	100	72	28
1920	100	49	51
1960	100	37	63

SOURCE: U.S. Bureau of the Census, *Census of Population: 1960, United States Summary, op. cit.,* p. 1-29.

and by the end of the century it had largely run its course. On the other hand, although the percentage growth rate of the urban sector was quite high from 1790 to 1840, the share of population which it absorbed rose only slowly. After 1840 the situation changed noticeably, and by the end of the century urban areas were the principal destination of population movements. Thus, initially population redistribution consisted of a more widespread dispersion over the land, but for over a century it has increasingly become a process of concentration in urban areas.

In any society of considerable size, the mass of the population before the era of modern economic growth was necessarily concentrated in rural areas and engaged chiefly in agricultural production. The massive concentration of a nation's population in urban centers is a new phenomenon on the world scene. At bottom, it is due to the nature of modern technology which underlies economic growth. This technology has brought major economies of scale in a number of lines of nonagricultural production and has drastically reduced transportation costs. The resulting concentration of nonagricultural production has been reinforced by what are known as "agglomeration economies" and the shift in consumption patterns toward a smaller proportion of food as per capita incomes rise. The details of this process are elaborated in Chapter 15.

Suburbanization.   While the flow toward urban centers has continued in this century with little real evidence of significant abatement, an important variation has emerged: the phenomenon of suburbanization. Urban growth always involved a gradual extension into and eventual incorporation of surrounding areas, but in the nineteenth century the central city remained the hub of activity. In recent decades, however, suburban growth has been taking place partly at the expense of central cities. Some notable examples have occurred of absolute declines in the central-city population despite continued growth in the urban conglomerate of which it forms the center. This has been true, for example, of Boston, New York, Philadelphia, Washington, Chicago, and San Francisco. Typically, some new urban migrants have continued to move into the central-city area, but this movement has been more than offset by a larger outflow to the environs by former central-city residents.

This development is partly a reflection of consumer preferences as incomes rise and single-family houses on private plots of land are increasingly sought. It is partly a reflection of changing locational decisions by business firms. Fundamental to both of these have been technological developments—an electric power transmission system and, most important of all, the development of motor-vehicle transportation and an associated road and highway system. The latter has drastically altered the configuration of transport costs compared with those under the previous railroad and horse-and-wagon systems. As a result, single urban centers are tending to be replaced by clusters of centers, and a tendency toward "megalopolis" has emerged—a vast urban sprawl such as is now becoming manifest in the corridor stretching from New York City to Washington, D.C.

Depopulation of rural areas.   The widespread movement toward the periphery of urban areas has created an impression among some observers that population in the United States is becoming more dispersed. In fact, the opposite is the case. The suburban movement is but a counter-ripple on a general tide toward increased population concentration. This becomes clear when one turns to the countryside and notes the growing tendency toward depopulation, a development which the United States shares with other developed nations, and for similar reasons.

The phenomenon of rural depopulation was attracting attention as early as 1900. At that time the Bureau of the Census pointed out that almost half of the 292 counties enumerated in 1790 had passed their peak population prior to 1900 and were in a phase of population decline. (Ten counties actually had smaller populations than in 1790.) The trend was linked to the shifting course of economic opportunity.

> The agricultural prosperity of the original area of the United States reached its highest point about 1880; after that date the competition of the West in agricultural products became rapidly greater, thus increasing the problems of the eastern farmer, and offering added inducements for removal to more favored sections or for migration to cities.[3]

This development in the East was the harbinger of a more general trend. In 1900, the rural farm population of the United States as a whole was still increasing, though at a declining rate. After 1940, a sharp absolute decline set in, and with it population declines became common in many parts of the country. At the present time there are over 3100 counties in the United States. Of these, more than half have lost population in each of the last two inter-censal decades (see the map on the inside of the back cover). This movement has involved not only a flow toward urban areas, but a tendency toward an emptying out of population from large areas in the interior of the nation and increasing concentration on the coasts (including the Great Lakes as a coastal area). Even in areas as large as states, a significant leveling off of population and even in some cases absolute declines have appeared— examples are the Dakotas and Nebraska, West Virginia, Mississippi, Arkansas, Oklahoma, and (since 1960) Wyoming.

Before 1960, such absolute declines in population were almost entirely the product of out-migration which more than offset natural increase. Protracted out-migration of young adults tends eventually, however, to reduce the number of couples of childbearing age remaining in an area to the point where there are not enough births to offset the deaths occurring to the larger older population. This phenomenon of natural population decrease has quite recently started to appear in a number of counties, and it has been estimated that it might characterize about a sixth of all the counties in the nation by 1970.

Rural depopulation is dramatic testimony to the crucial role of the market system in reallocating resources. The primary cause, as suggested by the Census Bureau's discussion of the 1900 scene, is the progressive relative

[3] U.S. Bureau of the Census, *A Century of Population Growth from the First Census of the United States to the Twelfth, 1790–1900* (Washington: U.S. Government Printing Office, 1909), p. 71.

decline in agriculture as a source of economic opportunity. In some places other factors have played a role as well; the impact on Appalachia of the declining relative importance of coal in the economy is an example.

Implications.   This discussion provides some useful perspective on current urban problems. Frequently pollution and congestion are charged to excessive population growth. Especially among laymen it is thought that the solution to such problems is to stop the "population explosion". As the foregoing suggests, however, dense urban concentrations of population have arisen not from *growth* of the American population, but from growing concentration in a limited number of centers of a once widely dispersed population. This has occurred to such an extent that wide areas of the country are now showing declining population density while a few areas are soaring to unprecedented levels. If the increase in population from around 4 to 151 million between 1790 and 1950 had been distributed evenly over the 1950 land area, the 1950 density of population would have been a little over 50 persons per square mile, about the same as that of the states of New Hampshire and Vermont. But one fourth of the increase has been concentrated in only 28 counties which together account for little more than .5 percent of the nation's entire land area. For this group of counties the average population density in 1950 was 2170 persons per square mile. Within this group, New York County (Manhattan) had the highest density—almost 90,000 persons per square mile. At the other extreme one fourth of the population increase was diffused over 2305 counties, accounting for almost seven tenths of the total land area. The average density in this group was 18 persons per square mile.

As additional evidence that it was economic growth, and particularly the adoption of modern technology, that was responsible for urban concentration, consider the following: Between 1880 and 1940, the U.S. population grew by about 80 million persons, while the urban percentage rose from 28 to 56 percent. In the same period, the population of prepartition India increased by around 130 million on a land area less than half that of the United States. But the urban percentage in India rose from only 9.3 percent to 12.8 percent. If the United States had wished to prevent urbanization, it could have done so by avoiding, not population growth, but economic growth. This is not to suggest that the ills due to urban concentration are an unavoidable consequence of economic development. It is, rather, to point out that the solution to such problems must lie in trying to modify, not the decisions of households regarding family size and migration, but those of business firms and nonprofit organizations regarding the location of their economic activities, decisions which heretofore have clearly disregarded the social costs of increasing geographic concentration. When one sees how the changing course of economic opportunity has pulled the American population first westward and then even more strongly cityward, to such an extent that numerous areas begin to empty not long after they are filled, it is ironic indeed to find that population increase rather than economic development is charged for urbanization and its problems.

The Roles of Different Population Groups

In the nineteenth century, native whites, immigrants, and nonwhites participated differently in the economic growth and spatial redistribution of the population. Westward expansion was accomplished primarily by native whites. But in urban growth after 1840, especially the growth of large cities, immigrants and their descendants played a disproportionate part (though native whites dominated the more influential urban occupations). Blacks remained concentrated in southern agriculture and participated in its westward expansion. In the twentieth century, as urban concentration emerged as the dominant spatial process, there was a growing tendency towards greater similarity in the economic function and location of the three population groups, though important differences continued between whites and nonwhites.

As long as agriculture remained important and settlement was a major spatial process, contacts among population groups of different origin remained limited. But as urbanization increasingly came to the fore, problems of integration became more pressing. In the nineteenth century, the problem took the form of assimilation of those of foreign stock; in this century, of nonwhites. Thus urbanization, itself a product of economic growth, helped in turn to precipitate problems of social integration.

Settlement and urbanization. The trends may be most meaningfully shown if the white population is divided into those of native and of foreign "stock." The foreign stock includes immigrants plus the first generation of their descendants—that is, native-born persons of foreign or mixed parentage. Native stock is defined as native-born persons of native parentage, and includes the grandchildren and subsequent descendants of immigrants. By these definitions, 55 percent of the American population in 1890 was native white stock; 33 percent, foreign white stock; and 12 percent, nonwhite.

The extent to which these groups participated in agricultural settlement is roughly indicated by the composition of the rural population toward the end of the nineteenth century in the areas settled subsequent to independence. As of 1890 in the North Central and western regions, 62 percent of the rural population was native white stock; 37 percent, foreign white stock; and 1 percent, nonwhite. In the South Central region, 67 percent was native white stock; 2 percent, foreign white stock; and 31 percent, nonwhite. Thus in both areas the native white stock was disproportionately represented. But there is an interesting contrast between North and South in the roles of foreign white stock and nonwhites. Outside the South, the foreign white stock accounts for almost all of the remaining rural population; within the South, the nonwhites do.

The above figures reflect the results of the entire century of settlement after 1790. Immigration became much more important quantitatively from the 1840s onward, and settlement in the period after 1840 shows a larger role for the foreign white stock than settlement in the period as a whole. The foreign white stock contributed 46 percent of the *increase* in the rural population of the North Central and western regions between 1840 and 1890, while the native white stock contributed 53 percent and the nonwhite, 1 percent. Still, the native white stock had a majority share. Moreover, these figures are the most favorable for the showing of the foreign white stock, since the South is omitted.

It is when one turns to the figures on urban population that the role of the foreign stock stands out. Although the foreign stock accounted for only a third of the nation's population in 1890, it made up 53 percent of the urban population. The native white stock accounted for 40 percent of the urban population; and nonwhites, 7 percent. Again, as in the case of the rural population, there was a striking difference between the South and the rest of the country in the roles of foreign stock and nonwhites. Nonwhites accounted for only 2 percent of the urban population outside the South, but for 33 percent within the South. The role of the foreign white stock in urban areas in the South was correspondingly reduced, though it accounted for almost a quarter of the urban population in that region.

Because of the varying roles the three population groups played in spatial redistribution of the population, they exhibited important differences in location as of 1890, differences which were germane to the development of their attitudes and subsequent behavior. The native white stock was still an essentially rural and small-town group both inside and outside the South. Three out of four people in this group lived in rural areas, and only 8 percent were in cities of 100,000 or more. In contrast, the foreign white stock was predominantly urban (58 percent), and a substantial share—one person in three—was in large cities. As of 1890, nine out of ten blacks remained in the South, and four out of five were in rural areas.

The twentieth century has seen a major revolution in these patterns as settlement ended and urban concentration became the dominant force shaping population distribution. The result has been a dramatic change in the distribution of both the native white stock and the nonwhites. By 1960, almost two persons out of three of native white stock were in urban areas. For nonwhites the proportion was a little higher. Even in the South, the concentration in urban areas was not much less—among both whites and nonwhites in this region almost six tenths were in urban areas.

In addition, in the case of nonwhites a major redistribution by region took place. Between 1890 and 1960, the percentage of nonwhites in the South dropped from 90 to 56. This shift is one facet of the cityward flow of blacks, which involved not only a movement within the South from farm to city, but also a major shift from the South to large northern centers.

The foregoing figures imply that the native white stock and nonwhites were principally involved in rural depopulation. But even today close to a third of these two groups remains rural, though the rural population is now chiefly occupied in nonfarm rather than farm activities.

As is brought out in Chapter 16, the growing urban concentration of the population has vastly multiplied the contacts among groups from different backgrounds. In the nineteenth century the problem of assimilation of immigrants, especially those from southern and eastern Europe, began to be felt with increasing urgency. Cutting off the supply of immigrants, through legislation discriminating on the basis of national origin, made the problem more manageable. At the same time, as we shall see, education of the children of immigrants made it possible for them to move up the occupational scale, and fostered their assimilation. But the curtailment of the immigrant labor supply had domestic repercussions. In the figures already quoted in this section there is an indication that immigrants and nonwhites were to some extent substitute sources of labor—where one group was large, the other was typically small. With the foreign labor supply largely cut off, periods of high labor demand in the North began increasingly to generate large movements of blacks out of the South. World War I and the 1920s were the first of these periods. After an interruption during the depression of the 1930s, this process was resumed during World War II and the following years. With this shift in the sources of labor supply, the problem of assimilating immigrants was transformed into that of integrating blacks.

Thus the urban concentration of population which goes with modern economic growth has, along with other factors, precipitated some of the major issues of integration, issues which were less pressing as long as locations of the various race and nativity groups remained so disparate. In this, as in so many other aspects of its growth, the United States has been undergoing an experience similar to those in other developed nations. Although the form varies depending on circumstances, the issue of social integration has been so pervasive in the history of economic growth that an historian of the process has identified it as a special phase of the process of modernization. Writing of the period he calls "the integration of society," Cyril Black says:

> The central problem ... is that individuals ... are torn from their relatively autonomous communities and are brought into contact in the urban context with a wide variety of unfamiliar people. Many problems of human relations that at an earlier stage were avoided or compromised on some local basis now have to be met frontally. The institutions of advanced societies are not yet fully understood, and the means of controlling them in the interest of social stability are still being formulated.[4]

Black specifically cites the racial problem in American as "an example, although a particularly acute one, of the crises the integration of society provokes."[5]

Occupational characteristics.   The differences among the major population groups in their trends in spatial distribution were due to an important extent to differences in their participation in agricultural and nonagricultural activity. The question naturally follows whether within the nonagricultural sector the various groups played different roles in filling the emerging occupational requirements of industrialization. To throw light on this, Table 5.7 presents the number of workers in each major occupational group in 1910 (the earliest date for which such data are readily available) and, for each such group, the

[4] Cyril Black, *Dynamics of Modernization* (New York: Harper & Row, 1966), p. 86.
[5] *Ibid.*, p. 87.

TABLE 5.7
Distribution of labor force in major occupational groups,
by nativity, parentage, and color, 1910 (percent)

Occupational Group	Number (millions)	Native White of Native Parentage	Foreign Stock			Nonwhite	All Classes
			Native White of Foreign or Mixed Parentage	Foreign-Born White	Total		
Farm	11.5	61	12	9	21	18	100
Nonfarm	25.8	42	22	26	48	10	100
White collar	8.0	56	27	17	44	1	100
Manual							
Craftsmen and operatives	9.8	40	24	30	54	6	100
Laborers	4.5	33	14	37	51	17	100
Service workers							
Other than private household workers	1.7	35	19	26	45	20	100
Private household workers	1.9	23	13	21	34	43	100
All occupations	37.3	48	19	21	40	12	100

SOURCES: D. L. Kaplan and M. C. Casey, *Occupational Trends in the United States, 1900 to 1950*, U.S. Bureau of the Census Working Paper no. 5 (Washington: U.S. Government Printing Office, 1958); and E. P. Hutchinson, *Immigrants and Their Children, 1850–1950* (New York: John Wiley, 1956), underlying worksheets.

distribution by color, nativity, and parentage. The table shows that while each population group was represented in each occupational class, the native white stock was the predominant group filling white-collar jobs; the foreign stock, manual jobs; and the nonwhite, domestic service (labeled in the table, "private household workers"). In general, the native white stock predominated in higher-status occupations, the foreign stock occupied an intermediate position, and the nonwhites were at the bottom of the ladder. There is also an interesting difference between the first and second generations of the foreign white stock. Although the two generations were about equal in size in 1910, the children of immigrants had a noticeably larger share than the immigrants themselves in white-collar occupations and a noticeably lower share in the other, lower-status occupations.

The predominance of the native white stock in the higher-level occupations suggests that this group, despite its numerical inferiority in the cities, may have exerted disproportionate influence in decisions shaping the expansion of urban economic activity in the nineteenth century. That this is so is dramatically supported by studies of business leaders in the 1870s and from 1900 to 1910.[6] The study for the latter period, for example, covered 190 persons in what is called the "business elite"—men who were either presidents or chairmen of the largest American corporations in manufacturing and mining, railroads, public utilities, and finance, or partners in the leading investment-banking houses. Although in nonfarm occupations as a whole, only four persons in

[6] See the articles by Miller and by Gregory and Neu in the Suggested Reading list at the end of this chapter.

ten were of native white stock, among the business elite, eight out of ten were of native white stock. These men (there were no women in the group) were almost all from old American families and of British descent. The largest proportion came from the New England and Middle Atlantic states, and they hailed from business family backgrounds. The poor immigrant or poor farm boy who rose "from rags to riches" was, as far as this group goes, a rare exception—only six persons in the entire group fit this description. Thus, the descendants of the colonial white stock played a leading role not only in agricultural settlement, but also in decisions underlying urban development. Although the foreign stock were the majority in urban areas, their function was typically to fill the manual occupations necessary for industrial growth.

As a result of their differing economic roles, there were substantial differences among the several population groups in their occupational distribution and hence in their economic and social status. Table 5.8 shows that, as of 1910, both the native white stock and nonwhites were distributed about evenly between farm and nonfarm occupations. However, in nonfarm occupations, two fifths of the native whites were in white-collar occupations and only one fifth were in the three lowest-status categories (laborers and service occupations). In contrast, only 2 percent of nonwhites were white-collar workers and 76 percent were in the lowest-status groups. Within farm occupations the same type of pattern appears. Four out of ten white farm workers were owners or part owners ; among nonwhites this was true of only about one in ten.

In contrast to the other two groups, the overwhelming majority of the foreign stock were in nonfarm occupations, with manual jobs predominating.

TABLE 5.8
Distribution of labor force of specified nativity, parentage,
and color, by major occupational group, 1910 (percent)

| Occupational Group | Native White of Native Parentage | Foreign Stock | | | Nonwhite | All Classes |
		Native White of Foreign or Mixed Parentage	Foreign-Born White	Total		
Farm	49	19	13	16	46	31
Nonfarm	51	81	87	84	54	69
Total, all occupations	100	100	100	100	100	100
White collar	41	38	20	28	2	31
Craftsmen and operatives	36	41	43	43	22	38
Laborers	13	11	24	18	30	17
Other than private household workers	5	6	7	6	14	7
Private household workers	4	4	6	5	32	7
Total, nonfarm occupations	100	100	100	100	100	100

SOURCES : Kaplan and Casey, op. cit. ; and Hutchinson, op. cit., underlying worksheets.

While the occupational distribution for this group was not as favorable as it was for the native white stock, it was markedly superior to that for nonwhites. Moreover, comparing the first and second generations within this group, there is a noticeable indication of upward mobility from one generation to the next. Indeed, the distribution for native whites of foreign or mixed parentage is strikingly like that for those of native parentage. While the rags to riches story is a gross exaggeration, significant improvement was possible for those of foreign origin. The process typically required a generation or more, however.

In this century, with the decreasing role of immigration as a source of labor supply and the growing movement of the native white stock out of rural areas, the occupational disparities between native and foreign white stocks have virtually disappeared. In 1950, the native stock had slightly more persons in farm work; and the foreign stock, in crafts and operative occupations. Aside from this, the occupational distributions of the two groups were almost identical. At the same time, the share of the foreign white stock in the white labor force as a whole fell between 1910 and 1950 from close to a half to under a third. The effect of these two developments was to make the white working population as a whole increasingly homogeneous in the course of this century.

The nonwhite population also participated in the trend to urban areas, as well as in the rise within the urban sector in white-collar occupations. Nevertheless, even by 1965, nonwhites remained highly concentrated in lower-status occupations. The proportion in white-collar occupations was one person in five, a noticeable improvement over the situation half a century earlier. But over half of nonwhites were still laborers, service workers, or farm workers. The figures for whites were almost the reverse—almost half were in white-collar jobs and only about one quarter were in the four lower-status classifications. Thus, while within the white population major differences in socioeconomic status between groups were substantially eliminated, this was not the case between whites and nonwhites.

Although, in comparison with whites, nonwhites were concentrated in lower-status occupations. this does not mean that they filled the bulk of such jobs in 1965. Because whites outnumber nonwhites by almost nine to one in the labor force as a whole, the major proportion of even low-status jobs were filled by whites. Thus, in the lower-status occupations other than domestic service, nonwhite workers accounted for only one out of four or five workers. Domestic service, where nonwhites came close to accounting for half of the work force, was the notable exception.

Age

Successful economic growth is often linked to qualitative features of the population, to the ability and capacity of a population to learn new ways of doing things. Compared with other nations, the U.S. population has shown a rare combination of youth, health, and schooling. This section and the two sections following summarize these characteristics and note their possible relevance to modern economic growth. Differences among groups within the population are also briefly touched on.

Comparative level and trend.   The comparative youth of the American population is shown in Table 5.9. In the middle of the nineteenth century, half of the American population was less than 19 years of age. In contrast, of the 14 European nations listed in the table, there is none with a median age as low as 21 years and most are clustered in a range around 23 to 25 years. In comparison with the European situation, the United States was clearly in a class by itself, though perhaps other areas of overseas settlement such as Latin America, Canada, and Oceania were in a similar situation. Viewed in terms of the present world situation, the American age structure around 1850 was similar to that of populations in the less developed areas of southern and eastern Asia today.

In discussing the effect of age structure on economic growth, the view is frequently advanced that a very youthful population involves a high burden of child dependency on working adults. As a result, the possibility of saving and capital formation is said to be impeded. Any judgment based on the usual measures of dependency burden (e.g., the proportion of those under 20 and over 65 to those 20 to 64) would lead to the conclusion that the American population in the nineteenth century was particularly handicapped in this respect, though, as will appear subsequently, it was less so as the century wore on. Perhaps the successful growth performance of the American economy simply reflects the influence of other positive factors outweighing

TABLE 5.9
Median age of population, United States and European countries, c. 1850

United States	18.9
Great Britain	22.5
France	28.5
Germany[a]	23.0
Belgium	24.8
Netherlands	24.1
Switzerland	26.0
Norway	23.6
Sweden	24.1
Denmark	24.7
Austria[b]	24.0
Italy	23.8
Portugal[c]	24.5
Spain[d]	25.2
Greece	21.5

[a] 1880.
[b] 1869.
[c] 1864.
[d] 1877.

SOURCES: U.S. Bureau of the Census, *Historical Statistics of the United States, Colonial Times to 1957*, Series A-86 (Washington: U.S. Government Printing Office, 1960); Department of Economic and Social Affairs, *The Aging of Population and Its Economic and Social Implications* (New York: United Nations, 1956), Table III.

this negative one. Or, conceivably, the positive contribution of child labor in a predominantly agricultural situation may have been unusually important in the United States. Perhaps too, as some writers have suggested, a younger population may more readily take up new forms and types of work and be more willing to move to new locations, as economic growth often requires. Examples of the leading role of youth in new economic opportunities are abundant. Consider the following figures: The share of young adults aged 20 to 29 in the U.S. population as a whole was a little over 18 percent in 1840 and 1850. Notice the much larger proportion of young adults in the large cities and areas of new settlement than in the population as a whole:

1840:	Cities of 100,000–500,000	25.1
	Cities of 25,000–100,000	25.3
1850:	West (Mountain and Pacific)	36.4

These figures reflect the substantial movement of young persons to the emerging centers of new economic opportunity.

Causes of changes in age distribution.   Recent advances in demography have shown that fertility plays a much more important role than mortality in determining the age distribution of the population. Thus, the youthfulness of the American population was a reflection chiefly of its unusually high birth rate. As the birth rate moved downward during the nineteenth century, the median age of the population gradually rose, though it was not until 1910 that the white population reached the position prevailing in many European countries 60 years earlier (see Table 5.10). For whites this rise in average age was accelerated by the influx of immigrants in the nineteenth century. Immigration contributed relatively little to the group under 15 years of age, and over two thirds of it was concentrated between the ages of 15 and 40. Indeed, because of the special age structure of this migration, it served to maintain a highly stable proportion of young adults aged 20 to 29 in the population right down to World War I, despite the substantial shift that was

TABLE 5.10
Median age of population, by color, 1790–1960

Year	White	Nonwhite
1790	15.9[a]	—
1820	16.5	17.2
1850	19.2	17.4
1880	21.4	18.0
1910	24.5	21.1
1950	30.8	26.1
1960	30.3	23.5

[a] Males only.

SOURCES: U.S. Bureau of the Census, *Historical Statistics of the United States, Colonial Times to 1957,* Series A-89, A-92 (Washington: U.S. Government Printing Office, 1960); and U.S. Bureau of the Census, *Statistical Abstract of the United States, 1965* (Washington: U.S. Government Printing Office, 1965), p. 23.

taking place in average age. Through 1950, the trend toward an older popula-tion accelerated, but the post-World War II swing in the birth rate has more recently interrupted this trend.

Differentials.   The white population was slightly younger than the non-white in the early nineteenth century (see Table 5.10). This relation was reversed in the course of time, and for almost a century there has been a sizable excess in the average age of whites over nonwhites. The differential impact of immigration in raising the age of the white population may partly explain this. Note how the differential developed chiefly in the years when immigration was rising in proportion to population growth.

Health

Comparative level and trend.   Health has many facets, and a variety of measures are necessary to obtain a comprehensive picture. For a summary impression, expectation of life at birth is generally accepted as the best single indicator.[7] While comprehensive data are lacking for much of American history, reliance has typically been placed on the limited data available, chiefly for the state of Massachusetts. Table 5.11 presents these figures together with those for various other countries at about half-century intervals to 1950.

These data indicate that since 1800 health in the United States has generally been similar to that in northwestern Europe, especially in England and Wales, from which such a sizable share of the population derived. This places the United States among the leaders with regard to health, for northwestern Europe has led the rest of the world in terms of life expectation. On the other hand, at present and for some time in the past, conditions have been even better in the Scandinavian countries than in the United States. Around 1960, the life expectancy of males at birth in Scandinavia was about four years greater than that of the white male population in the United States.

The trend suggested by the table is one of mild improvement in the United States in the first half of the nineteenth century, a more rapid advance in the second half, and an even sharper rise in the twentieth century. With regard to developments after 1850, the United States appears generally to fit the pattern of northwestern Europe.

Unfortunately, these statements regarding American conditions in the nineteenth century rely very heavily on evidence for one state, Massachusetts, at two widely separated dates, 1789 and 1855. For the first year, the data are of uncertain reliability; for the second, their representativeness is question-able, since Massachusetts was already relatively urbanized and had recently experienced heavy immigration, especially from Ireland. A recent examination of evidence on child mortality found that in the mid-nineteenth century, mortality was above average in the urbanized states of the Northeast.[8]

---

[7] Statistical Commission, *International Definition and Measurement of Levels of Living: An Interim Guide* (New York: United Nations, 1961), p. 5.
[8] Yasukichi Yasuba, *Birth Rates of the White Population in the United States, 1800–1860: An Economic Study* (Baltimore: Johns Hopkins, 1962), p. 100.

TABLE 5.11
Expectation of life at birth, various countries, 1789–1950

Country	1789	c. 1850	c. 1900	c. 1950
United States				
Death registration states	—	—	49.2	68.1
Massachusetts	35.5	39.4	47.8	—
England and Wales	—	40.9	50.5	70.8
France	—	40.0	47.0	68.1
Germany	—	37.0[a]	46.6	66.5
Belgium	—	—	47.1	64.7
Netherlands	—	36.8	52.2	72.5
Switzerland	—	—	50.7	68.6
Norway	—	46.4	56.3	72.9
Sweden	36.1[b]	43.0	55.7	72.0
Denmark	—	42.2	54.6	71.2
Austria	—	31.7[c]	40.1	64.4
Hungary	—	—	37.5	66.9
Czechoslovakia	—	—	40.3	69.1
Italy	—	35.2[d]	44.5	67.9
Spain	—	—	34.8	61.1
U.S.S.R.	—	—	32.0	68.0
Mexico	—	—	33.3[e]	49.7
Chile	—	—	40.7[e]	51.9
Australia	—	—	57.0	68.4
New Zealand	—	—	59.3	70.4

[a] 1871/2–1880/1.
[b] 1776–1795.
[c] 1866–1875.
[d] 1876–1887.
[e] 1930.

SOURCES
Massachusetts: Thompson and Whelpton, *op. cit.,* p. 240.
Death registration states: Taeuber and Taeuber, *op. cit.,* p. 273.
Europe, first two dates: R. R. Kuczynski, *The Measurement of Population Growth* (New York: Oxford University Press, 1936), pp. 184–186.
All countries except the United States, last two dates: United Nations, *The Situation and Recent Trends of Mortality in the World* (New York: United Nations, 1962), pp. 22–23, 28, 31, 35.

It is possible that health conditions in the United States may actually have been superior to those in northwestern Europe throughout much of the nineteenth century. Several recent studies of local areas in the colonial period suggest that in the eighteenth century, health and mortality conditions were better here than in England.[9] For 1850, indicators of inhabitants per dwelling and food supply per head show a better position for the United States than for England.[10] Also, since in both countries conditions were worse in urban areas, the more rural character of the United States compared with England would lead one to expect a better average health situation.

[9] See the studies by Grant, Greven, Lockridge, and Potter in the Suggested Reading list at the end of this chapter.
[10] See also Wilson. H. Grabill, C. V. Kiser, and P. K. Whelpton, *The Fertility of American Women* (New York: Wiley, 1958), pp. 2, 10, 11.

The Taeubers, in their recent monograph, state that "there is no conclusive evidence of substantial declines in mortality in the first half of the nineteenth century."[11] They express the view that "mortality was declining through- out the last half of the nineteenth century," but the basis for this is primarily the evidence for Massachusetts plus " known advances in medicine and public health."[12] Yasuba suggests that "the death rate may have increased somewhat . . . during the few decades preceding the Civil War."[13] The possibility that health conditions in American cities deteriorated throughout a good part of the nineteenth century is noted in Chapter 16.

These observations suggest as a more defensible generalization that American health conditions in the first part of the nineteenth century were at least as good as and perhaps better than those in northwestern Europe. If they were indeed better, then in the United States as a whole there may have been little improvement for a good part of the nineteenth century. This implies that the similarity of mortality conditions in the United States and northwestern Europe at the end of the nineteenth century may reflect a catching up of the European nations with the United States.

Causes of death.   Although the United States was among the leaders with regard to health conditions, conditions were far from ideal in the early part of our history. Defective as the data on causes of death are, they attest to the prevalence of epidemic and infectious diseases in the last half of the nineteenth century.

> Measles, diphtheria, and whooping cough were prevalent; scarlet fever and cholera were recurrent; typhus was reported occasionally. The percentages of reported deaths due to contagious diseases were 28 in 1850, 21 in 1860, and 19 in 1870. The major killer was " consumption " with 10 per cent of all deaths in 1850, 12 in 1860, and 14 per cent in 1870. Croup and pneumonia ranked second. . . .
>
> In 1900, influenza, pneumonia, and tuberculosis were responsible for almost a fourth of all deaths. The infectious diseases of childhood were major hazards to survival, as was the diarrhea that threatened infants in the second summer. Typhoid epidemics were frequent in the cities.[14]

In contrast, the principal causes of death today are cancer, cardiovascular diseases, and traffic accidents. The shift during the past century in causes of death in the United States is also characteristic of other countries, and reflects principally the operation of major advances in public health and medicine.[15]

A study of economic growth necessarily focuses on the material components of living standards. But note should at least be made of the immense contribu- tion to human welfare represented by the substantial or complete elimination from common experience of most of the dread diseases enumerated above. To be freed from the burden of the sudden and arbitrary incidence of such

[11] Conrad Taeuber and Irene B. Taeuber, *The Changing Population of the United States* (New York: Wiley, 1958), p. 269.

[12] *Ibid.*, p. 271.

[13] Yasuba, *op. cit.*, p. 101.

[14] Taeuber and Taeuber, *op. cit.*, pp. 272–273.

[15] George J. Stolnitz, "A Century of International Mortality Trends," *Population Studies*, vol. 9, no. 1 (July 1955), pp. 24–25.

killers must be reckoned as one of the major advances of all times in well-being. At the same time the improvement in vigor and vitality that goes with this change has undoubtedly contributed to more effective economic performance and thereby to economic growth.[16]

Differentials in expectation of life. The biggest advances in reducing mortality have been in the youngest ages, particularly childhood. Life expectation at birth has increased in the last century and a half by over 30 years, but at age 20, it has risen by only about half this amount, and at age 60, the advance has been hardly discernible. In welfare terms, this has meant that the unhappiness attendant upon loss of a child or baby has been vastly reduced. In economic terms, the wastage of mothers' lives in bearing and raising children who never survive to adulthood is now dramatically less. Writing of this trend in England, R. M. Titmuss has observed:

> The typical working class mother of the 1890's, married in her teens or early twenties and experiencing ten pregnancies, spent about fifteen years in a state of pregnancy and in nursing a child for the first years of its life. She was tied, for this period of time, to the wheel of childbearing. Today, for the typical mother, the time so spent would be about four years. A reduction of such magnitude in only two generations in the time devoted to childbearing represents nothing less than a revolutionary enlargment of freedom for women....[17]

As for differentials by sex, there does not seem to have been any major difference between males and females in life expectation at ages 20 and 60 until the beginning of this century. Since then, however, a substantial gap has emerged in favor of females. In 1948–1951, males aged 20 could expect, on the average, to live to 68.9 years; females, to 73.7 years. This implies that, whereas in the past there was a fairly equal probability of the husband or wife dying first, at present, the husband is much more likely to die first, leaving the wife to face a substantial period of widowhood.

Sometimes a low expectation of life at birth is construed as implying that individuals will have short time horizons. But even when expectation at birth was relatively low, those who survived to the start of adulthood had a reasonable span of years left before them. For example, the Massachusetts data for 1855 indicate that although expectation at birth was only around 40 years, males who survived to age 20 could expect, on the average, to live to 60 years of age. By 1949–1951, this prospect had been lengthened to about 69 years. There is little in these figures to suggest that in 1850 decision making at the start of adulthood would be substantially different from that in 1950 because of differences in life prospects.

Throughout American history, there have been important differences in mortality experience among various parts of the population. Perhaps the greatest difference has been that between whites and nonwhites. Around 1900, life expectation at birth for nonwhites was 33.8 years—16 years less than

---

[16] For a pioneering exploration which suggests the importance of health in economic development, see Wilfred Malenbaum, "Health and Productivity in Poor Areas," in *Empirical Studies in Health Economics*, H. E. Klarman (ed.) (Baltimore: Johns Hopkins, 1970), pp. 31–54.

[17] Richard M. Titmuss, *Essays on "The Welfare State"* (New Haven: Yale University Press 1959), p. 91.

that of whites at that time, and even less than that of whites a century earlier. By 1950, the life expectation of nonwhites had increased dramatically to over 60 years. The differential had been noticeably reduced, though it was still substantial, about 8 years.

The evidence on life expectation for the foreign-born versus native-born whites suggests a somewhat better situation for the native-born. At the beginning of the twentieth century, the native-born had an edge in terms of life expectation at age 20 of around 2.5 years. This compares with an advantage of whites over nonwhites at that time of around 7 years. By 1940, the differential between the native- and foreign-born white populations had virtually disappeared.

Until very recent times, mortality almost everywhere in the world has been higher in urban places than in rural, reflecting crowded living conditions, lack of sanitation, and the absence of protection against infectious diseases. As brought out in Chapter 16, the United States was no exception in this respect. Estimates for the beginning of the twentieth century place expectation of life at birth in rural areas 10 years above that in urban, though reporting biases may exaggerate the differential. By the middle of the century, however, this differential appears largely to have disappeared, a development in keeping with experience in many other places of the world.

Education

Comparative situation.   In exposure to formal education, the American population appears to have been among the highest, if not the highest, of the nations of the world from at least the early nineteenth century onward. The figures in Table 5.12 are subject to many biases, but they provide an approximate idea of the relative development of schooling in different parts of the world since 1830. The figures cover enrollments in primary, secondary, higher, and technical schools, though occasionally data for nursery and adult schools are also included. Among the comparability problems are the occasional use of attendance rather than enrollment data (the former tend to be somewhat lower); variations in the time of year for which enrollment data are reported; differences in the length of the school day and school year; and differences in the proportion of school age to total population. The last results in a downward bias in the twentieth-century data for a number of developed countries in which a decline in the ratio of school-age to total population followed a decline in the birth rate. Similarly, at a given date it biases downward the figure for more developed countries compared with less developed ones.[18]

The high rank held by the United States from the very beginning is evident in the table. In only a few countries of northwestern Europe are values comparable to those in the United States to be found. It is possible that the relative youth of the American population may result in some upward bias

[18] For useful discussions of various educational measures, not only enrollment, but attendance, illiteracy, attainment, and so on, see the Folger and Nam volume in the Suggested Reading list at the end of this chapter.

TABLE 5.12
School enrollment as percentage of population of all ages, various countries, 1830–1928

	1830	1887	1928
United States	15	22	24
United Kingdom	9	16	17
France	7	15	11
Germany	17	18	17
Netherlands	12	14	19
Switzerland	13	18	—
Norway	—	13	17
Sweden	14[a]	15	13
Denmark	—	12	16
Austria	5[b]	13	14
Hungary	—	12	16
Italy	3	11	11
Spain	4	11	11
U.S.S.R.	—	11	11
Argentina	—	7	14
Brazil	—	3	9[c]
Mexico	—	5	9
Chile	—	4	15[c]
Japan	—	7	13
India	—	2	4
Turkey	2	3	4
Egypt	—	3	6
Nigeria	—	—	1[c]
Australia	6	14	16

[a] Includes Norway.
[b] Includes Hungary.
[c] 1938.

SOURCE: C. Arnold Anderson and Mary J. Bowman (eds.), *Education and Economic Development* (Chicago: Aldine, 1965), pp. 426–429.

in these data, but not enough to alter this basic conclusion. The leading student of trends in American education, Albert Fishlow, writing in reference to the first half of the nineteenth century, has expressed the view that "the United States probably was the most literate and education conscious country in the world."[19]

Trend of education.   The educational situation at the time of the founding of the nation has been described as follows:

In all of the Northern states, laws were in force in 1790 which provided for the education of children in the rudiments of knowledge. In New England nearly everyone possessed a common school education, and a person of mature years who could not read and write was rarely to be found. . . .

In the Middle states there were fewer state laws relating to compulsory education, but public schools were common. There were very few freeborn illiterates in these states. . . .

[19] Albert Fishlow, "The Common School Revival: Fact or Fancy?" in *Industrialization in Two Systems*, Henry Rosovsky (ed.) (New York: Wiley, 1966), pp. 40–67.

In the Southern states there were but a few free public schools, because of the dispersed situation of the inhabitants; and in the larger towns there were but few academies. Education was confined largely to the wealthier classes. Wealthy men were accustomed to send their sons to the colleges in the Northern states or to Europe to complete their education. In the thinly settled western sections a large proportion of the people were illiterate. Among the slaves, illiteracy was almost the universal condition.[20]

Although these conditions were better than those prevailing in most other countries, by modern standards the situation left much to be desired. The length of the school year was probably less than two months and attendance, in a largely rural society, was haphazard. Fishlow estimates that the generation attending school in 1800 received on the average a *life* total of 210 days of education.[21]

The extent of progress during the nineteenth century is indicated by the fact that this statistic more than doubled between 1800 and 1850, and more than doubled again between 1850 and 1900. By the end of the century, the average life total of days of education had been raised fivefold—to 1050 days.[22] Much of this progress took the form of raising the average level of education of the population to that of elementary-school graduation (see Chapter 6).

In the twentieth century, and particularly since 1920, the uptrend has continued, moving the population toward a situation in which high-school graduation is typical. In 1920, the average degree of schooling of young adults, those aged 25 to 34, was 8.4 years, only slightly more than a primary-school education. A figure not much less than this would probably be representative of the situation at the end of the nineteenth century as well. By 1960, the median years of schooling had risen to 12.2 years, indicating that more than half of those aged 25 to 34 had completed high school. The present projection to 1980, 12.6 years, implies a notable slowing in the rate of advance, reflecting an assumption that the movement toward college education as a general condition will not proceed (and is not proceeding) as fast as the movement toward universal secondary education.

Differentials in education. There is a well-established association between educational attainment and occupational status, higher levels in each being positively correlated. Because education is both an avenue of opportunity and a vehicle for economic and social stratification, the subject of educational differentials among groups in the population is of special interest.

By far the most dramatic differential is that between whites and nonwhites. In 1870, over four fifths of the nonwhite population was illiterate; for the white population, in contrast, the proportion was only about one person in ten. In the ensuing decades, illiteracy among nonwhites declined steadily and the differential was markedly reduced, though not eliminated. The illiteracy figures, however, overstate the reduction in the white–nonwhite educa-

[20] U.S. Bureau of the Census, *A Century of Population Growth* ...., *op. cit.*, pp. 31–32.
[21] Fishlow, *op. cit.*, p. 65.
[22] *Ibid.*

tional differential. Data on median years of school completed by those aged 25 to 29 show that between 1920 and 1940 the educational advantage of whites over nonwhites actually increased, from 3.1 to 3.7 years. By 1960, however, the advantage had dropped sharply, to 1.5 years.

While illiteracy was higher among the white immigrant population than among native whites, the differential was not very great. Throughout the period after 1870 (when data first became available), almost nine tenths of the foreign-born were literate, though not always in English. Moreover, data for 1910 show that illiteracy among the children of immigrants was actually slightly less than among those of native white stock. It is clear that within the white population the educational gap among different nativity and parentage groups was nowhere near as important as the gap between whites, taken as a whole, and nonwhites.

With regard to geographic differentials, the South lagged noticeably behind the rest of the country. Fishlow's estimates for white persons in 1850 show enrollment rates in the South to be around six tenths or less of those elsewhere in the country.[23] This differential has persisted down to the present, though in lesser magnitude. Also, schooling in urban areas has been significantly ahead of that in rural; that is, data relating to literacy rates and educational attainment consistently show urban levels higher than rural.

These areal differences in educational development may in part account for the large extent to which the nineteenth-century influx of European immigrants was assimilated within a couple of generations. As has been noted, this group was much more concentrated in urban areas and outside the South than was the population of colonial stock. Consequently, immigrants' children, though not the immigrants themselves, generally acquired superior schooling to that available to the colonial stock, an asset which offset some of the liabilities of foreign background.

By comparison with white immigrants, the blacks' geographical distribution, being both rural and southern, meant a double handicap in terms of access to schooling. This handicap was quite aside from any racial differential in the quality of facilities provided, an important factor in itself. The question is sometimes raised: If European immigrants "made it" in American society "on their own," why haven't blacks? But even by 1940, three quarters of a century after emancipation, the percentage of blacks in urban areas outside the South was only 19 percent. In contrast, as early as 1890, 54 percent of the foreign stock were located in urban areas outside the South. Given the importance of education as an avenue of upward mobility, these geographical factors gave the foreign white stock an advantage relative to the native white population which the black population has not started to match even today.

Even if all classes of the population and all parts of the country participated equally in education, there would remain one important differential. Steady educational progress over time means that young persons will be better educated than their seniors—in short, there will be a generation gap. When

---

[23] *Ibid.*, p. 49.

there is a rapid advance in the diffusion of education, such as the movement toward universal secondary schooling in the United States in the first half of this century, the gap between successive generations can become dramatic. The following figures compare sons with fathers in terms of the percentage graduating from high school.[24] In all periods, the percentage of sons graduating from high school substantially exceeds that of fathers. In the period of rapid expansion of secondary schooling, however, the gap widened markedly. Thus almost two thirds of the sons reaching 18 in the period 1946–1955 graduated from high school, but only one fourth of the fathers of this group had. In time this differential will decline, as the sons who benefited from this rapid expansion in turn become fathers. But the figures provide a striking illustration of the manner in which progress gives rise to differences between generations.

Percent Graduating	Period in Which Sons Reached Eighteenth Birthday			
	1916–1925	1926–1935	1936–1945	1946–1955
Sons	30	44	54	65
Fathers	14	17	19	25
Difference	16	27	35	40

Nor are such differences confined to the realm of education. A secular growth rate of real per capita income of 15 percent per decade implies that on the average the standard of living enjoyed by sons at age 25 would be 40 percent higher than that of their fathers when they were 25 years old. It is no wonder that grumbling about "kids having it so good" is commonplace. Much more attention needs to be given to the welfare implications of the intergeneration differences produced by rapid social and economic development.

Causes of educational development. In very broad terms, it is possible to identify some of the influences underlying the emphasis on education in America. In the colonial period, religious considerations appear to have played a significant part. The importance of religion in the establishment of the colonies, particularly those in New England, led to an early emphasis on ability to read the Bible. Political factors, too, played a part, especially with the growing extension of suffrage in the nineteenth century. For proper participation in a democracy, education of the common man was increasingly recognized as essential. Another argument stressed the economic importance of education. Thus, to Horace Mann, one of the leaders of the free-school movement of the nineteenth century, education was "the grand agent for the development or augmentation of national resources; more powerful in the production and gainful employment of the total wealth of a country than all

[24] John K. Folger and Charles B. Nam, *Education of the American Population* (Washington: U.S. Government Printing Office, 1967), p. 139.

the other things mentioned in the books of the political economists."[25] But a systematic inquiry into the specific causal factors shaping educational development from one time to another and the growing public commitment of resources to this purpose has yet to be done. Indeed, such inquiry is only now becoming possible as a result of recent efforts to establish the quantitative record of the growth of education.

Effect of education.   The effect of education on economic growth has received considerable attention in recent years. Differences in wages among workers of different educational levels have been used to estimate the marginal productivity of additional years of schooling. For example, one admittedly crude, but widely quoted estimate noted in Chapter 6 concludes that 23 percent of the growth of national product from 1929 to 1957 could be attributed to education. Estimates of this type, however, have been questioned on various grounds. One important problem arises from the observed positive association between education and ability. Because of this correlation, it is uncertain to what extent wage differentials may be taken as indicative of the influence of education rather than ability. Another problem lies in the relation of education to technological change. Typically the contribution imputed to education is calculated at the expense of that made by technological change. In one study, in fact, the contribution of technological change is reduced to zero. As a glance at Chapters 6 and 7 will show, this makes no sense in terms of historical experience. While education is undeniably important in the development process, there is need for deeper research into the content of education and the channels through which it influences economic growth.

Some of the specific ways in which education may operate can be indicated. First, even if it does not in itself alter individual capacities, education may make for a more efficient use of society's human resources by improving the selection and recruitment of talent.[26] In a society characterized by a normal distribution of human abilities, it seems likely that more able persons will be used more effectively if there is a formal education system than if there is not. The educational process provides a relatively objective (though not perfect) means for screening persons according to ability and enhances the likelihood of better utilization of persons, as compared with a situation in which, for example, social class or kinship are the prevailing criteria for selection.

Second, education affects individual capacities directly. It may do this in part by providing specialized training for particular jobs. The importance of this type of education is sometimes questioned on the grounds that the kind of work done by the vast bulk of the labor force can be learned fairly quickly. For example, on-the-job training has prevailed formally or informally in agriculture and industry throughout history. Perhaps more important are the general skills provided by education in such subjects as reading, writing,

---

[25] As quoted in Fishlow, *op. cit.*, pp. 40–41.
[26] See also David Landes, "Technological Change and Development in Western Europe, 1750–1914," in *The Cambridge Economic History of Europe*, H. J. Habakkuk and M. Postan (eds.), vol. 6 (Cambridge, England: Cambridge University Press, 1965), Part I, pp. 567, 594.

and mathematics. At a minimum, these affect the ability to comprehend and follow instructions. Even more, they facilitate learning new ways of doing things, they enhance the ability to take on new jobs, and they add spatial mobility by reducing some of the obstacles to moving. Awareness of new opportunities is increased by the ability to make better use of the information provided by books, papers, and so on. Beyond this, education, through its approach to problem solving and the tools it provides, promotes the development of new ways of doing things, ranging from minor variations in the performance of a given task all the way to major inventions and scientific discoveries. The latter, though they do not immediately affect economic productivity, may ultimately be of overriding consequence.

Finally, education affects a society's attitudes. It fosters a view that problems may be solved by rational analysis and that it is possible to obtain control over one's environment. A recent survey in Pakistan found, for example, that literate persons were significantly different from illiterate ones in their willingness to consider innovation in agriculture and in their belief that men would some day understand the causes of floods, droughts, and epidemics.[27] Education thus affects people's goals and aspirations. It may raise the vision of economic and social betterment as a credible alternative to the traditional style of life.

That a variety of influences of the type described above were at work in the United States even at a fairly early date is evidenced by the reports of careful observers. Let us take two examples, both from around 1850 (see also Chapter 6).

By the mid-nineteenth century, American progress in manufacturing had been so marked as to arouse the curiosity and concern of the British. A commission sent to investigate the causes of American success was much impressed by the role of education. The following is an excerpt from the report:

> The compulsory educational clauses adopted in the laws of most of the States, and especially those of New England, by which some three months of every year must be spent at school by the young factory operative under 14 or 15 years of age, secures every child from the cupidity of the parent, or the neglect of the manufacturer; since to profit by the child's labour during *three-fourths* of the year, he or she must be regularly in attendance in some public or private school conducted by some authorized teacher during the other fourth.
>
> This lays the foundation for that wide-spread intelligence which prevails amongst the factory operatives of the United States, and though at first sight the manufacturer may appear to be restricted in the free use of the labour offered to him, the system re-acts to the permanent advantage of both employer and employed.
>
> The skill of hand which comes of experience is, notwithstanding present defects, rapidly following the perceptive power so keenly awakened by early intellectual training. Quickly learning from the skilful European artizans thrown amongst them by emigration, or imported as instructors, with minds, as already stated, prepared by sound practical

[27] Howard Schuman, Alex Inkeles, and David H. Smith, "Some Social-Psychological Effects and Noneffects of Literacy in a New Nation," *Economic Development and Cultural Change*, vol. 16, no. 1 (October 1967), pp. 1–14.

education, the Americans have laid the foundation of a wide-spread system of manufacturing operations, the influence of which cannot be calculated upon, and are daily improving upon the lessons obtained from their older and more experienced compeers of Europe.[28]

A complementary observation relating to the public press is contained in a study by George Tucker, a professor at the University of Virginia in the mid-nineteenth century:

> There is yet another source of popular instruction—the periodical press. . . . It keeps every part of the country informed of all that has occurred in every other which is likely to touch men's interests or their sympathies. Nor, in attending to the vast, does it overlook the minute. Every discovery in science or art, every improvement in husbandry or household economy, in medicine or cosmetics, real or supposed, is immediately proclaimed. Scarcely can an overgrown ox or hog make its appearance on a farm, or even an extraordinary apple or turnip, but their fame is heralded through the land. Here we learn every legislative measure, from that which establishes a tariff to that which gives a pension; every election or appointment, from a president to a postmaster; the state of the market, the crops, and the weather. Not a snow is suffered to fall, or a very hot or very cold day to appear, without being recorded. We may here learn what every man in every city pays for his loaf or his beefsteak, and what he gives, in fact, for almost all he eats, drinks, and wears. . . .
>
> According to the census of 1840, there were then in the United States 130 daily newspapers, 1142 issued weekly, and 125 twice or thrice a week, besides 237 other periodical publications. Such a diffusion of intelligence and information has never existed in any other country or age.[29]

Tucker's statement suggests especially the importance of the communications media in the diffusion of knowledge. Moreover, the frequent references in it to agriculture make clear that farmers as well as manufacturers were commercially oriented and interested in new ways of doing things.

Perhaps the most pervasive features of modern economic growth are the variety and magnitude of the changes in economic life which it entails. First and foremost, modern economic growth requires major changes in technology. Education contributes both to the learning of new methods of production and to the development of still-newer methods. Beyond this, economic growth entails the development and spread of new practices of business organization and management. For workers, there is the question of adapting to new working conditions and to the requirements of a much-heightened geographical, industrial, and occupational mobility; for consumers, new channels for the disposition of funds; for investors, new financial outlets; for governments, new problems of law and administration. In these and other ways, economic development means a transformation to a vastly different way of life. Education plays an important role in this transformation because it enhances both the capacity and desire of a society for change.

To say this, however, is not to deny that the state of knowledge concerning

---

[28] Report of the Committee on the Machinery of the U.S.A., quoted in *The American System of Manufactures,* Nathan Rosenberg (ed.) (Edinburgh: Edinburgh University Press, 1969), pp. 305–306.

[29] George Tucker, *Progress of the United States in Population and Wealth in Fifty Years* (Press of the Hunt's Merchants' Magazine, 1843), pp. 148–149.

the effect of education on economic growth is still far from adequate. Much more work is needed, not only on the quantity, but on the content of education —the subjects taught, the materials used, the time devoted to each subject, how it is taught, by whom it is taught—and on the relative importance of the various possible channels through which education impinges on economic growth.

Aside from economic growth, it is important in closing to recognize that the improvement in education, as in health, itself represented a major contribution to human welfare. Even if there had been no significant effect on economic progress, education opened the minds of growing numbers of people. It provided increasing access to the stock of knowledge and culture embodied in printed works that would otherwise have remained beyond reach. No one would argue that the educational process has been ideal; but neither would anyone argue for a return to a general condition of illiteracy. Indeed, it is because of the general welfare contributions which health and education make that modernization is an irreversible process. No society which has had the benefit of such gains would be willing to return to a state of illiteracy and low life expectancy.

DETERMINANTS OF AMERICAN POPULATION GROWTH

In seeking to understand the causes of American population growth since 1790, we will focus on the factors governing fertility and immigration trends. While the long-term record of these two factors is somewhat clearer than the record for mortality, their causes are less certain. As far as the future course of American population growth is concerned, the outlook for fertility is the major unknown. In what follows, the discussion takes up first immigration and then fertility, identifying the major problems with regard to each, noting relevant theoretical considerations, and suggesting possible answers. In the light of this, attention is then turned to the rate of total increase, including consideration of possible interdependence among fertility, immigration, and mortality.

In the case of mortality, the trend for much of the nineteenth century remains uncertain. The dramatic decline since that time was very largely due, as noted, to major advances in public health and medicine. The fact that expectation of life in the United States is not as great as it is in several other countries indicates that there is room for further improvement. and this is especially true with respect to minority groups. But as the Taeubers point out, "even the total elimination of death from birth to age 45 would not produce future reductions in mortality comparable to those that have occurred in the last half century of almost miraculous decline."[30] Moreover, in the absence of major breakthroughs in research on malignancies and the major cardiovascular–renal diseases of older age, it is unlikely that the death rate will play a major part in future changes in the rate of population growth,

[30] Taeuber and Taeuber, *op. cit.*, p. 287.

In official projections of American population growth to 1990, for example. the projected death rate is very close to its current level.

While the discussion that follows is consistent with the rather general evidence available, this subject is one on which much more research is needed.[31] The conclusions suggested here are highly tentative and are advanced partly in the hope of stimulating further inquiry.

Immigration

According to economic theory, if adequate information is available, migration is caused by differences between two areas in lifetime income-earning opportunities, allowance being made for transfer costs and nonpecuniary considerations such as cultural ties. Various types of data—such as comparative wage rates—make clear that opportunities in the United States were generally superior to those in Europe.[32] But while this situation accounts for the direction of the flow, it is not sufficient to explain the noticeable variations in migration over time and by area of origin, which are the central problems in this subject (see Tables 5.1 and 5.3). Why is it that toward the middle of the nineteenth century a pronounced uptrend occurred in the movement of Europeans to the United States? Why did this movement take a wavelike form? Why did the origins of the migrants shift increasingly in the course of time from northern and western Europe to southern and eastern Europe?

In general, migration variations in time or space arise from changes in one or more of the basic determining conditions. Thus, changes may occur in income-earning opportunities at the origin or destination, in the availability of information, in transfer costs, or in nonpecuniary factors. The explanation of changes in observed migration behavior thus becomes a matter of identifying which of the basic determining conditions changed. This analytical point needs underscoring. All demand and supply conditions enter into the determination of prices and quantities at all times. But if one's interest is in explaining the *change* between two dates in, say, the price of a good, then attention should be focused on which demand and/or supply conditions changed. This is the approach adopted here. The suggestion that a change in the volume of migration was due to the change in factor x does not mean that other factors played no part in the determination of migration, but only that they did not vary in a way that would account for the observed change in behavior.

Let us consider first the secular uptrend in European emigration during the nineteenth century. Two developments seem principally responsible. One was the industrialization process in the United States and the demands that it generated for manual labor in factories and construction work. Although industrial growth was taking place as early as the 1820s and 1830s, it was not until toward the middle of the century that it reached a magnitude involving

---

[31] For further discussion of some of the issues covered in this part see the works by Easterlin, Jerome, Kuznets, and Yasuba in the Suggested Reading list at the end of this chapter.

[32] Stanley Lebergott, *Manpower in Economic Growth: The American Record Since 1800* (New York: McGraw-Hill, 1964). p. 40.

labor demands of substantial size. Confronted with the cost of native labor, which was being drained away by western agricultural opportunities, employers sought to recruit cheaper foreign labor by publicizing opportunities in the United States and by other means.

The other principal factor in the uptrend of migration was the surge in population growth in Europe associated with the onset of modernization. When population is stable and sons can succeed to their fathers' positions, the inclination to move may be low, especially in traditional societies. But under conditions of accelerating population growth, the opportunities becoming available by virtue of the death or retirement of fathers are necessarily less than the number of individuals seeking them. The result is a growing number of people forced to seek new opportunities, including opportunities abroad. The population upsurge in nineteenth-century Europe placed increasing numbers in this position and thereby made for an uptrend in emigration. To some extent a decline in overseas transportation costs during the course of the century strengthened this tendency.

Another possible causal factor in the uptrend of European emigration was the occurrence of catastrophic events such as famines, wars, revolutions, epidemics, pogroms, and so on. From the viewpoint of economic theory, such events imply in part changes in income-earning prospects, in part changes in the nonpecuniary advantages or disadvantages of a particular location. But it is doubtful that catastrophic events could explain the secular rise in emigration. To do so, one would need to establish that on the average the frequency or severity of such events increased in the course of the nineteenth century. But such events have persisted throughout the history of Europe. On the average, famines and epidemics diminished during the nineteenth century. Indeed, this trend was in part responsible for the acceleration of population growth. This is not to say that such events exerted no direct causal influence. European emigration in the nineteenth century would certainly have been less and its origins different if there had been no such dislocations. But the uptrend in the general level of emigration does not seem explicable in terms of these events.

To turn from the trend to the swings in U.S. immigration, these appear to be due to major surges and relapses in American economic conditions and thus in the growth of the demand for labor. In principle, simultaneous wavelike movements in the European countries—in population growth or catastrophic events, for example—could have caused the surges in migration to the United States. But such does not seem to have been the case. For example, while there were fluctuations in population growth in the European countries, and these influenced the migration pattern for any one country, the timing differed among countries and a common pattern that would have produced the observed emigration surges did not exist. Similarly, study of the timing of catastrophic events in Europe reveals that as many or more such events occurred in periods of low emigration to the United States as in periods of high emigration. On the other hand, when the United States experienced a major economic boom or relapse it tended to generate the same type of response in all of the European countries. Thus the waves in migration were primarily the product of variations in labor demand conditions in the United States. A tight American labor market offered the prospect of jobs at relatively attractive wage rates; a slack labor market meant great uncertainty about obtaining employment, whatever the wage rate.

But while American conditions were chiefly responsible for immigration fluctuations over time, European conditions were responsible for variations in space—that is, in the origins of the migrants. Thus, given labor demand conditions in the United States, those countries which were experiencing more intense population pressure or catastrophic events would typically respond most sensitively to that demand. The Irish exodus during the mid-nineteenth-century potato famine is a case in point. Similarly, the shift in the origins of migration from northern and western to southern and eastern Europe appears to be due to the shifting incidence of modern economic development with its attendant surge in population growth and associated dislocations. This process started in northern and western Europe and proceeded across the face of the continent in the course of the nineteenth century. Toward the end of the century, as the incidence of population pressure grew in southern and eastern Europe, this area's role in the overseas flow rose correspondingly.

To sum up, the secular uptrend in European emigration was caused principally by two developments—the labor demands in the United States generated by the onset of the industrialization process and the wave of population growth and dislocations in Europe attendant upon the emergence and spread of economic development there. The decline in migration following World War I is clearly the result of a change in American policy. Immigration to the United States followed a wavelike pattern as a result of swings in American labor demand conditions. Within Europe, shifts over time in the relative importance of the countries of origin occurred chiefly as a result of the shifting incidence through time of the process of modernization and the differential occurrence of catastrophic events.

Fertility

The central question with regard to American fertility concerns the causes of the long-term decline, which antedated the declines in most other developed nations. There is also the question of the post-World War II upsurge and the more recent downturn in fertility (see Table 5.1). The factors responsible for these developments are the central concern of this section. First, however, it is necessary to set out briefly the economic theory of fertility, since this is not ordinarily included in standard textbooks.

Theory of fertility.   The point of departure for this analysis is the theory of consumer choice. Suppose that households view children as a type of consumption good, yielding satisfaction like economic goods in general. Household desires for children can then be conceived in terms of an indifference map with number of children on one axis and commodities on the other. Any given point on the map expresses the degree of satisfaction attaching to that particular combination of children and commodities. One can think too of a price tag attaching to children. This consists of the dis-counted cost of the various expense items required to have and raise children, due allowance being made for their prospective contribution, if any, to family income. Together with product prices and household income, this cost establishes a budget-line constraint. The interaction of this externally determined constraint with the subjectively determined indifference map de-termines the combination of children and goods which will yield most satis-faction under given conditions of tastes, prices, and income. If the relative price of children were higher, perhaps because the prices of child-care items rose more than the average price of goods in general, the optimal combination would shift toward more goods and fewer children. If the subjective attractive-ness of commodities rose relative to that of children, a similar shift would occur. Finally, if the level of household income were higher, the optimal combination would include both more children and more goods, though the increase would not necessarily be proportionate. Thus, in equilibrium, the number of children people have would vary directly with household income and with the price of goods relative to children, and inversely with the strength of desires for goods relative to children.

Admittedly, it seems unrealistic to view household decisions about having children as such a highly rational process. But several considerations suggest a certain plausibility to the approach. First, if one takes commodity purchases proper, to which the theory of consumer choice is ordinarily applied, economic theory does not claim that households actually go through precise calculations. Rather, the argument is that purchase decisions involve a rough weighing of preferences against constraints of the type spelled out rigorously in the formal theory. More importantly, if the constraints or preferences change, behavior will change in a way predicted by the theory. Thus, confronted with higher prices for certain goods, a typical household will tend to substitute other goods. Again, if the household's income rises, it will feel freer to expand its purchases generally. While typically there are no actual calculations—indeed, reactions may be in a sense automatic rather than the product of conscious deliberation—behavior does change in a way that implies the type of sub-jective balancing of preferences against constraints envisaged by the theory. The situation is similar with regard to fertility decisions. Children, like com-modities, are a source of satisfaction. Indeed, just as one observes that one household differs from another in the intensity of its desire for a given good—say, a vacation trip abroad—so, too, we detect differences in the strength of desires or tastes for children. Moreover, children, like commodities generally, are not costless. From prenatal medical expenses through college education, a child involves a long succession of outlays, of which the typical household is painfully aware. Finally, just as different commodities compete with one another for the household's dollar, so, too, do children compete with goods. Having another child this year may mean sacrificing a new car or a long-awaited month at the shore. Desires, costs, income—these do enter people's thinking about having children. And if this is so, then there is some plausibility to supposing that decisions about having children involve a rough balancing of preferences and constraints, maybe largely subconscious, of the type described in the economic theory of household commodity purchases.

For the explanation of actual fertility, however, the theory of consumer choice is not sufficient in itself. For one thing, fertility as usually measured relates to births, whereas the consumption good represented on an indifference map is surviving children, for this is what parents really want. This means that the state of infant and child mortality needs to be added to the analysis as a determining factor. For households to achieve a given number of surviving children, the necessary number of births is higher, the higher the level of infant and child mortality.

Further, in the case of children, unlike most goods, households are producers as well as consumers. Since coition is itself a satisfaction-yielding activity, there is a tendency for the number of children produced to exceed the optimal number. Production and consumption can be brought into line by resort to various methods of fertility limitation. Practices of this sort range from those governing the formation and dissolution of unions during the reproductive period; through time-honored methods of fertility limitation such as abstinence, withdrawal, and induced abortion, legal or illegal; to modern contraceptives such as the IUD and oral pill. Observed fertility behavior therefore depends in part upon attitudes toward and the extent of information about fertility-control practices as well as the supply conditions of such practices. If there were a variety of commonly known and costless fertility-control practices, and no taboos on the use of such practices, then the actual number of births would tend to conform to the optimal number. But, in fact, fertility-control practices at any given time are limited in number, and they are not costless. Moreover, knowledge about such practices is imperfect, and different methods have varying degrees of social acceptance. As a result, in any actual situation, the use of fertility control will be less than perfect, and actual births will exceed the optimal number. The greater the supply of methods of fertility control and the lower their cost, the wider the diffusion of information about them, and the fewer the taboos on their adoption, the more nearly will actual fertility approach the optimal level.

To sum up this brief discussion of the theory of fertility, the following causal view is suggested. Tastes, prices, and income determine the optimal number of children. The latter, together with infant and child mortality conditions, determines the optimal number of births. Finally, actual births exceed optimal births to an extent that depends upon the attitudes toward and the extent of information about fertility-control practices, and the supply conditions of such practices. (A fuller model would need to allow also for the extent of uncertainty in households' evaluations of the determining factors.)

To apply this framework to the interpretation of actual fertility experience, it is necessary first to expand the discussion of tastes to include the factors shaping preferences for children and goods. While people's attitudes or tastes are doubtless influenced in part by current conditions, it seems reasonable to suppose that an even more important part is played by their prior experience. Where they were born and brought up, the kind of religion and education they had, how well off their parents were—these are all circumstances which go into the formation of attitudes regarding desirable life styles. These aspirations as to life style embrace among other things preferences with regard to number of children and level or standard of living.

Although a wide variety of factors enter into the formation of attitudes toward goods and children, we are especially interested here in those whose influence might change over time, since the object of our explanation is to analyze temporal variations in fertility. There is a parallel here with the analysis of immigration, in which the desire to explain variations in migration led to a focus on those causal factors whose influence was changing. Three aspects of the process of economic development stand out as altering the intensity of desires for goods versus children. One of these is the growth of per capita income itself and the consequent secular uptrend in the level of living. The others are the progress of education and the introduction and diffusion of new goods. All of these tend to alter tastes in a manner adverse to fertility because they create or strengthen consumption outlets which compete with children as a source of satisfaction. Consider, for example, the secular growth in income. This trend means that young adults typically come from more prosperous family backgrounds than those of the preceding generation and that their views on the material attributes of the "good life" are correspondingly enhanced. Goods which to one generation of young adults may have been luxuries become necessities to the next—the automobile is a case in point. Similarly, education creates awareness of and opens access to new modes of enjoyment. Thus, while children are a recognized source of welfare to all, it is usually only those of higher educational status who consider foreign travel as a serious consumption alternative. The progress of education during economic development means that a growing number of households experience such a widening of consumption alternatives. And clearly, the development of new goods such as those described in Chapters 3 and 7 directly widens the range of items in competition with children.

With this view of taste formation added to our framework for fertility analysis, we are ready now to turn to the interpretation of actual experience. The next section takes up the recent swing in fertility, while the following one considers the secular trend.

The recent swing in fertility.   We are concerned here with the post-World War II baby boom and the subsequent decline in fertility. It is useful to start by considering how a secular uptrend in per capita income during economic development might be expected to influence fertility. The usual argument, based on economic theory, is that since income growth implies an outward shift in the budget constraint, people will have more children as economic growth occurs, other things being equal. It is true that income growth does imply an outward movement in the budget line, making it possible for a later generation to enjoy a larger volume of consumption goods—including more children—than an earlier generation. But our previous discussion has suggested that other things cannot be assumed to be equal from one generation to the next. This is because the secular growth in income exerts an influence on behavior, not only through the budget line, but also through changes in tastes. The later generation, which comes from more prosperous parental households, acquires a greater taste for goods relative to children. Thus, while on the one hand income growth operating through the budget constraint makes it possible for a later generation to have more children, on the other income growth operating through the formation of desires for goods versus children encourages having fewer children. When this latter influence is recognized, the usual argument that secular income growth leads to higher fertility becomes questionable. For example, if the taste influence of income growth were to outweigh the budget-line effect, then income growth would tend to cause a secular decline in fertility. We do not know which influence is likely to predominate. Indeed, it is possible that the two influences may cancel, and that secular income growth may leave fertility unchanged.

Even if income had little effect on the trend in fertility, however, it might still be a significant factor in fertility fluctuations. For while the two influences through which income growth works might cancel secularly, they would not necessarily cancel over shorter intervals. This, in fact, seems to be part of the explanation of the recent swing in fertility. Briefly, the argument is as follows.

The tastes of young adults in the 1930s were a heritage largely of the prosperous 1920s. But normal income growth for this cohort was sharply interrupted by the Depression. As a result, they cut back severely on the number of children they had. In contrast, young adults of the post-World War II period were in an unusually favorable position to fill their goods aspirations. This was not only because the income situation of young adults improved drastically during and after the war. It was also because the consumption desires of the postwar cohort were shaped by the economic stagnation of the 1930s and the austerity conditions of World War II, and hence advanced little over those of their predecessors. Sudden affluence without the customary secular advance in goods aspirations—just the reverse of their predecessor's situation—resulted in a sharp increase in the number of children born to the postwar generation of young adults.

The 1960s represent to some degree a return to conditions for young adults more like those of the 1930s, though not nearly so drastic. On the one hand, the growth of income among young persons slowed down markedly in this period. On the other, consumption aspirations were noticeably higher than those of the post-World War II cohorts. This was due to the influence on the most recent generation's tastes of the material affluence produced by the long postwar economic boom during which it was brought up. The consequent diminution in relative affluence of young adults during the 1960s led in turn to a reduction in their fertility.

We have seen that fluctuations in the rate of population growth are not a new phenomenon in our history. Previously, however, it was swings in immigration which were responsible for them. The shift in the source of these movements from immigration to fertility raises a question whether the recent swing bears any logical connection to its predecessors. The answer to this is yes. As long as free immigration was permitted, the rise and fall of immigration in response to swings in American labor demand acted as a buffer to moderate the impact of this demand on the native white population. With the restriction of immigration, however, this buffer was removed, and the movement in labor demand came to result chiefly in a swing in the income of young adults, rather than in their number as it had in the past, with a consequent impact on fertility.

This discussion has implications for the future of fertility change. The relative prosperity of young adults appears to depend not only on the state of the economy generally, but also on their number—the smaller the relative number of young adults, the better off they are. Thus, in the post-World War II period young workers were in relatively short supply as compared with the situations in both the 1930s and the 1960s. We have seen previously in this chapter that changes in age distribution arise chiefly from changes in fertility, and this is also true of the recent shifts in the relative number of young persons. For example, the surfeit of young workers in the 1960s is itself a result of the postwar baby boom. By the same token, the fertility decline of the 1960s portends a relative scarcity of young workers emerging in the latter part of the 1970s. This, in turn, raises the possibility of improvement in the relative affluence of young adults and the development of a new baby boom. We do not know whether this will in fact happen, but one implication is clear. In thinking of the future of United States fertility, it would be unwise to assume that the fertility rate is likely to level off at some constant value. Rather, it is possible that continued fluctuation of the type experienced in recent decades (though not necessarily of the same amplitude) may characterize future experience as well.

Before leaving the subject of swings in fertility, consideration should be given to the possible role of changes in the supply of and information about contraceptive methods. It is natural to suppose that the fertility decline of the 1960s was due to the growing use of the oral contraceptive pill, and there is probably some validity in this view. Such an explanation would still be consistent with the theoretical framework developed earlier, which recognizes the possible causal role of contraceptive developments. But it would be unwise to place undue weight on this factor alone. For one thing, the decline in fertility dates from 1957, while the earliest date at which the pill could have had a detectable influence was 1962. An expert assessment concludes that as of 1965 "even if a generous allowance were made for the amount of the overall decline that might be attributed solely to the use of the pill, it would probably not exceed half of the decline that has taken place."[33] Moreover, shifts in contraceptive practice clearly cannot explain the post-World War II upsurge in fertility. On the contrary this upsurge occurred despite a major advance in contraceptive knowledge made during the war when indoctrination in birth-control methods was widely provided for those in the

---

[33] National Center for Health Statistics, *Natality Statistics Analysis: United States—1963 and 1964* (Washington: U.S. Government Printing Office, 1966), p. 12.

armed forces. It would seem, therefore, that both the rise and fall of fertility since World War II must be due to factors other than the contraceptive situation alone.

The secular fertility decline.   In analyzing the secular trend in fertility, it is useful to subdivide the population into several component groups, each subject to rather different conditions. For the present discussion, attention will be focused on a classification in terms of location—frontier areas, settled agricultural areas, new urban areas, and old urban areas. The argument is that the basic fertility determinants vary among these locations in such a way that fertility tends to be progressively lower as one moves from the first to the fourth of these situations. Since the course of American economic growth involved exactly such a shift in the location of the population, the result was a continuing secular pressure toward fertility reduction.

Whereas the analysis of the recent swing in fertility was built primarily on the influence of income change on fertility behavior—through both changing tastes and the budget constraint—the present analysis will largely bypass income, on the grounds, previously suggested, that secularly the net balance of the two influences arising from income growth is uncertain. Instead, emphasis will be placed on the cost of children, fertility-control practices, and factors (other than income change) influencing tastes—all of which exert a differential effect by location.

To take up first the matter of tastes, reference has already been made to the manner in which education tends to alter attitudes by broadening the consumption alternatives to children. Typically education was more advanced, and hence this influence was stronger, in older rural areas than on the frontier, in urban areas than in rural, and in older urban areas than in newer urban areas.

Much the same type of argument may be made concerning the situation with regard to new goods. The availability of new products was typically greater in older rural areas than on the frontier because the marketing system was more advanced. Similarly, people in urban areas were more exposed to new goods than those in rural areas by virtue of the greater market potential offered by the higher-density population, with those in older urban areas being more exposed than those in newer.

As for costs of childbearing, both the outlays on and returns from children tended to create cost differentials among areas which had an effect on fertility similar to that of tastes. On the frontier, with its demands for breaking and clearing new land, the potential labor contribution of children was greater than it was in established agricultural areas. Also, where land was relatively abundant, the problem of establishing mature children on farms of their own was less serious. Nevertheless, even on the family farms in the established agricultural areas, the labor contribution of children was higher than it was in cities where work possibilities were more restricted. At the same time the costs of childbearing were higher in the cities, since food and housing were typically more expensive than in rural areas. Thus, taking account of both costs and returns, children were increasingly expensive as the situation changed from frontier to settled agricultural areas to an urban location.

Finally, consider the situation with regard to methods of fertility limitation. In general, knowledge and availability of a variety of practices are likely to be greater in urban areas than in rural. Similarly these conditions are likely to be better in settled agricultural areas than on the frontier, which is at the periphery of the communications network.

Putting these influences together leads one to expect the following ordering of areas by fertility level from high to low at any given time: frontier, settled agricultural areas, new urban areas, old urban areas. Also, since frontier areas gradually became transformed into settled agricultural areas and new urban areas into old, one would expect that over time fertility would decline as new areas "age." Moreover, since "new" and "old" are matters of degree, not of kind, one might expect that even in settled agricultural areas and older urban areas, fertility would continue to decline, at least for some time, as "aging" continues. In urban areas this process is reinforced by the trend in the composition of the population by origin. Initially, the populations in urban areas are dominated by migrants from rural areas or abroad who bring with them a high-fertility heritage. In the course of time, these first-generation urbanites are gradually replaced by second and later generations born and raised in urban areas, and with consequently lower fertility "tastes." Even today fertility differences are observed between new rural migrants to urban areas and those who originate in urban areas.[34] Thus to the pattern of cross-section differences by location noted above, one can add an expectation of fertility declines through time in all four locations.

These expectations are in fact supported by the available evidence. Table 5.13 presents data bearing on fertility trends and differences by rural and urban residence and region from 1800 to 1840 and, for comparison, for 1950. The data are ratios of children under 5 to females aged 20 to 44. The figures are for the white population; brief reference will be made later to the patterns for nonwhites. Although such ratios are imperfect measures of fertility, they provide a reasonably reliable basis for the inferences drawn here. Unfortunately, these data are not available for the period when the Mountain and Pacific divisions were being settled, though one would expect these areas to be somewhat different from the others because of the importance of mining rather than agriculture in their early development.

Consider first the differentials by location in the early part of the nineteenth century. Among rural areas, fertility was lower in the older settled areas in the East than in those undergoing settlement, the areas west of the Appalachians. This is true in both the North and the South. Even the seemingly partial exception, the West South Central division, is not really one because the figures are dominated by Louisiana, an area which was settled early. The same differential between newer and older regions also holds for urban areas. Finally, within every division, urban fertility is lower than rural fertility. This can be quickly seen from the fact that at each date almost all urban ratios are below the U.S. average, and almost all rural ratios are above. Thus, there is a

[34] See Otis Dudley Duncan, "Farm Background and Differential Fertility," *Demography*, vol. 2 (1965), and the citations of earlier works by Goldberg and Freedman given therein.

TABLE 5.13
Number of children under 5 years old per 1000 white women 20 to 44 years old,
rural and urban, by division, 1800–1840 and 1950

Area	1800	1810	1820	1830	1840	1950
Rural						
West South Central	—	1557	1522	1463	1495	703
West North Central	—	1810	1685	1703	1481	702
East South Central	1799	1701	1635	1529	1424	720
East North Central	1840	1706	1616	1484	1291	679
South Atlantic	1365	1347	1310	1209	1185	677
Middle Atlantic	1339	1344	1235	1100	1006	596
New England	1126	1079	952	851	800	612
All divisions	1319	1329	1276	1189	1134	673
Urban						
West South Central	—	727	866	877	846	542
West North Central	—	—	—	1181	705	514
East South Central	—	1348	1089	863	859	494
East North Central	—	1256	1059	910	841	491
South Atlantic	861	936	881	767	770	450
Middle Atlantic	852	924	842	722	711	432
New England	827	845	764	614	592	486
All divisions	845	900	831	708	701	479
United States	1281	1290	1236	1134	1070	551

SOURCE: Wilson H. Grabill, C. V. Kiser, and P. K. Whelpton, *The Fertility of American Women* (New York: Wiley, 1958), p. 17.

clear and consistent pattern of fertility in frontier areas exceeding that in older established areas, and of rural fertility generally exceeding urban.

In terms of trends, the United States ratio declines from 1810 on, and this pattern is seen to occur in both rural and urban sections of all geographic divisions. Frontier areas become progressively settled and new urban areas are transformed into old, while within the older rural and urban areas the process of aging continues.

This evidence is consistent with the interpretation advanced here, but it is at best suggestive. For the period 1800–1860, however, Yasuba has done an intensive analysis of the fertility ratios of states.[35] His results, which bear particularly on rural fertility patterns, are consistent with the present interpretation. He finds that the most important factor associated with fertility differences and trends was population density—the higher the density, the lower the fertility ratio. Yasuba interprets population density as a measure of the availability of land, and argues that:

> [I]n a community where the supply of land is limited, the value of children as earning assets is low and hence the demand for children may not be so great as where there is plenty of open land nearby. The increased cost of setting up children as independent farmers and fear of the fragmentation of family farms may further encourage the restriction of family-size in densely populated areas.[36]

[35] Yasuba, *op. cit.*
[36] *Ibid.*, p. 159.

More recently, Forster and Tucker have extended Yasuba's analysis, strengthening and refining the basic finding of inverse association between density and fertility.[37]

Mention should be made of another possible influence on the secular fertility decline: the improvement of infant and child mortality. The figures in the table fail for the most part to reflect this influence, since they relate not to births but to surviving children as of the census date. As had been noted, the trend in mortality for much of the nineteenth century is uncertain. But it is clear that from the late nineteenth century onward, there was a substantial improvement in infant and child mortality, and this probably strengthened the tendency toward fertility decline.

The outlook for the secular trend of fertility in the future remains uncertain. The analysis creates some presumption of a negative trend associated with continued progress in education, the introduction of new goods, and advances in methods and knowledge of fertility limitation. But the effect of some of the other factors mentioned above has been largely exhausted. This is substantially true, for example, of the one just noted, infant and child mortality, since the scope for further reductions in this area is quite limited. Similarly, the United States is not far from being in a situation in which almost all of the population is born and raised in urban areas, and thus the negative effect of a declining proportion of persons coming from a high-fertility rural heritage has largely run its course. Moreover, the discussion has heretofore set aside the secular influence of income growth. But the possibility cannot be ruled out that even when the taste effect is included, the net effect of income growth is to raise fertility. The sizable fertility swing of recent decades has taught many experts the hazards of generalizing about the long-term course of fertility, and it seems wisest at this stage of knowledge simply to admit that we do not know.

It is worth noting that the fertility declines of the past were accomplished entirely by voluntary action on the part of the population. To some extent marriage was deferred.[38] But also there were declines in fertility within marriage. These developments took place in a situation where not only was there no public policy to help those interested in fertility limitation, but attitudes and even laws in many states were hostile to the practice or even discussion of contraception or other fertility-control practices. To emphasize the voluntary nature of this development, however, is not to suggest that there was no need for family planning policies then or, for that matter, today. Historical experience shows a voluntary decline in fertility, but this is not necessarily the optimal rate of decline from the point of view of social welfare. One can only conjecture how many houshoulds suffered the miseries of unwanted children because of the hostile public environment. Today the evidence on this matter is straightforward and the need for intelligent public policy is evident.[39]

---

[37] Colin Forster and G. S. L. Tucker, *Economic Opportunity and American Fertility Ratios, 1800–1860* (New Haven: Yale University Press, forthcoming).

[38] Taeuber and Taeuber, *op. cit.*, pp. 147–152; and Yasuba, *op. cit.*, chap. 4.

[39] See, for example, Ronald Freedman, P. K. Whelpton, and Arthur A. Campbell, *Family Planning, Sterility, and Population Growth* (New York: McGraw-Hill, 1959).

In the literature on the demographic transition, the secular fertility decline is typically linked to the processes of urbanization and industrialization. But the American experience suggests an additional dimension associated with the transformation of a rural area from frontier area to settled agricultural area. Nor is this pattern peculiar to the United States. Canada seems to show a similar one, while in Europe the association of high fertility and settlement has been noted with regard to parts of Scandinavia, Finland, and Russia in the nineteenth century.[40] Thus, seen very broadly, the American fertility decline reflects not only the processes of urbanization and industrialization but that of settlement as well. It is of great interest to know more about this aspect because of its implications for today's less developed countries. The traditional view of secular fertility decline has led to emphasis on the necessity for industrialization in these areas before a decline is likely to occur. The American experience raises the possibility that, as population increasingly presses against land resources, fertility declines may set in within the rural sector itself.

In closing, it needs to be emphasized that this interpretation of American fertility, while it has some support in the evidence, is nevertheless largely speculative. Moreover, there are additional dimensions to the fertility decline that need to be incorporated in any interpretation. For nonwhites, fertility trends are less clear, partly because they have been studied less and partly because the data are poorer. It appears, however, that in the antebellum period fertility was high and may have shown little trend. As has been often pointed out, there was an obvious financial incentive for slave owners to encourage maximum fertility. Between the end of the Civil War and the early twentieth century, however, there was a substantial decline in nonwhite fertility. At the same time the decline in white fertility in the South appears to have noticeably slowed—indeed, it was at this time that the South gradually emerged as the high-fertility section of the country. These contrasting fertility changes in the South had the effect of reversing the usual differential—by 1910 fertility ratios for nonwhites were actually lower than those for whites. Could these developments have been connected with the drastic organizational changes in southern agriculture after the Civil War? With the new patterns of migration which developed? We do not know, but clearly any attempt to explain the national trend needs to be able to incorporate such striking developments.

Rate of Total Increase

We have already seen that the United States had perhaps the highest sustained rate of population growth in the world. To Adam Smith, Thomas Malthus, and other observers around the end of the eighteenth century, American

---

[40] See Per Goran Ohlin, " The Positive and Preventive Check: A Study of the Rate of Growth of Pre-industrial Population" (Ph.D. dissertation, Harvard University, 1956), pp. 398–404; and Gustaf Utterstrom, " Two Essays on Population in Eighteenth-Century Scandinavia," in *Population in History,* D. V. Glass and D. E. C. Eversley (eds.) (London: Edward Arnold, 1965), p. 528.

conditions seemed unusually favorable for population expansion. In the light of the foregoing discussion, it is time now to ask whether this was in fact the case, and if so, what were the principal conditions that favored unusually high population growth? Can the eventual decline in the rate of population growth be ascribed to changes in these basic conditions? The foregoing analysis of the components of population change provides a basis for investigating these issues.

Consider first the unusually high rate of growth. Five factors seem principally responsible:

1. The relatively plentiful supply of good land resources
2. Unusually favorable health conditions
3. Early and rapid economic development
4. The onset of economic development in Europe and especially the surge in population growth to which it gave rise
5. A policy of free immigration for most of the period

Almost any reasonable assumption about alternative states of these determinants leads to the conclusion that American population growth would have been less in other circumstances. Let us consider each in turn.

A plentiful supply of good land resources contributed to rapid population growth by providing economic opportunities in a frontier environment, one conducive to high fertility. These opportunities also attracted immigrants, though they were of less importance than urban opportunities. If the terrain of the United States from the Appalachians to the Rockies had been a vast wasteland, unsuitable for settlement, the pressures for fertility reduction would have been greater and opportunities for immigration less. In fact, the territory brought under American sovereignty proved to be surprisingly hospitable for settlement, though as shown in Chapter 4 the prospects were uncertain at the beginning of the nineteenth century. Moreover, while firm evidence is not available, it seems that the United States was unusually well endowed compared with other areas of new settlement. The interior of Australia was, in fact, a wasteland. The Canadian Shield made a large section of Canada unsuitable for settlement. In Brazil, there were tropical jungle conditions. American population growth might have been even higher if a vast fertile plain had stretched from Atlantic to Pacific, but the actual situation, though short of this, appears to have been quite favorable on a comparative basis. This was doubtless an important factor in the sustained high growth rate.

With regard to health conditions, the high ranking of the United States at an early date has already been noted. If health had been poorer and mortality correspondingly higher, population growth would have been less. To this it might be objected that if mortality had been higher, fertility too would have been higher and population growth consequently unaffected. A direct association between fertility and mortality is, in fact, often observed, and, as we have seen, it has a plausible rationale. If parents want a specific number of surviving children, then the higher the level of infant and child mortality, the greater the number of births they will need to have. However, American fertility at the start of the nineteenth century was already extremely high. According to Coale and Zelnik, the birth rate at this time "was markedly higher than that ever recorded for any European country and is equalled in reliably recorded data only by such unusually fertile populations as the Hutterites and the inhabitants of the Cocos—Keeling Islands."[41] Given this very high birth rate, it seems reasonable to conclude that if American mortality had been substantially higher, higher fertility rates would not have compensated for it, and population growth would have been lower.

The reasoning with regard to early and rapid economic development as a factor promoting high population growth is similar to that regarding the role of land resources. Economic development meant the provision of new opportunities for supporting households. It thus stimulated population growth through immigration, particularly by providing urban job openings. Similarly, it provided additional opportunities for native persons to establish families, though the urban context, as noted, was less conducive to raising large families than the rural. In the absence of economic development, opportunities for support of new population would have been confined largely to agriculture. Immigration would have been less and the pressures for fertility reduction would have mounted more rapidly, since opportunities would have been largely confined to those possible with the existing land resources cultivated under premodern technology. Indeed, it is likely that not only population growth but also the extent of settlement would have been less, since some of the land actually brought under cultivation was contingent upon technological innovation associated with economic growth (see Chapters 4 and 11).

The way in which high American population growth was promoted by the surge in European population growth can be most readily seen by assuming the opposite conditions in Europe. Suppose population there had been stationary, with breadwinners of the second generation able to succeed to openings created by deaths among the first generation. Even though economic opportunities in the United States were favorable, it seems likely that fewer Europeans would have been willing to undertake the perils of a long journey to a new land. In actuality, however, the wave of European population growth associated with the onset of modern economic development there fostered emigration and the rapid growth of American population.

Correspondingly, it seems obvious that the free immigration policy of the United States increased total population growth by permitting demand and supply forces to exert their full impact. However, with regard to this and all the factors said to have promoted population growth via immigration, there remains an important question to be faced: Did immigration merely take the place of native population growth which would otherwise have occurred? It has been argued that the competition of immigrants exerted a depressing

---

[41] Ansley J. Coale and Melvin Zelnik, *New Estimates of Fertility and Population in the United States* (Princeton: Princeton University Press, 1963), p. 35.

effect on the fertility of the native population, and that in the absence of immigration, native fertility would have been higher and population growth the same.[42] Note that formally there is a similarity here to the argument about the effect of health conditions. In each case, the issue turns on the extent to which different components of population change may be related— in particular, on the extent to which the birth rate may be a function of the death rate and/or immigration rate.

The argument that immigration led to lower fertility is suspect, however, because declines in American fertility are observed in times and places, not only where immigration was high, but also where immigration offered little or no competition. As has been noted, fertility turned down early in the nineteenth century, before any substantial influx of immigrants occurred. Recent studies in colonial demography suggest that in parts of New England such declines may have occurred even in the eighteenth century. Moreover, fertility declines occurred not only in the areas of immigration but in others as well, notably the American South. What seems to be a common feature of many areas where fertility declines set in is not that they were experiencing competition from foreign immigrants, but that the land supply had been largely exhausted and the process of settlement completed.

At issue here is the likely course of the American birth rate if there had been no immigration. If one follows the line of reasoning suggested previously, one must consider the type of economic activity that the native population would have followed. In the absence of a foreign labor supply in the nineteenth century, it seems plausible to suppose that the workers for American industrial expansion would have been drawn more from rural areas than was actually the case. The rate of settlement would therefore have been slowed. When nonagricultural labor demands were being supplied by an influx of foreign laborers, a demand for agricultural expansion to feed the new workers was generated. If the nonagricultural labor demand had been wholly supplied by a transfer of labor from rural to urban areas, no new food demands would have been generated. There would have been, of course, the problem of maintaining the agricultural output these workers would otherwise have produced, but it is quite unlikely that, with rural areas losing labor, this problem would have been solved by expanding settlement. This conclusion implies that over time, the native-born population would have been less involved in new settlement and more engaged in urban activities—that is, more exposed to a low- than a high-fertility environment. The suggestion is that if there had been no immigration, not only is it doubtful that fertility would have been higher than that actually observed, but it might possibly have been lower.

In sum, it is doubtful that American population growth would have been unaltered if immigration had been prevented. In the absence of immigration, American population growth would probably have been lower in the nineteenth century. The immigration component of population growth would

---

[42] See the summary of Francis A. Walker's arguments in Warren S. Thompson and P. K. Whelpton, *Population Trends in the United States* (New York: McGraw-Hill, 1933), pp. 304–305.

have been eliminated, and the birth rate, rather than increasing to compensate for this, might itself have been lower.

Thus America's land resources, health conditions, economic growth, and immigration policy all favored high population growth. Can the early decline in fertility, leading eventually to a declining population growth rate, be reconciled with this conclusion? The answer has already been suggested. The point is that American conditions favored, not the maximum growth rate biologically possible, but growth higher than that which would have occurred under plausible assumptions regarding alternative conditions. As the basic conditions themselves changed—partly as a result of high initial population growth—they exerted influences moderating the population growth process. Stated quite simply, as long as economic opportunities were largely of the frontier settlement type, extremely high fertility and high population growth rates were favored. But this high population growth itself made for a growing proportion of population situated in conditions of settled agriculture, conditions less favorable to continued high fertility. In addition, the process of modern economic growth shifted the population increasingly into urban centers, into an environment even less favorable to high fertility and rapid population growth. Actual population growth was higher than that which would have occurred if modern economic growth had not taken place at all and economic opportunities had been confined essentially to those offered by premodern agriculture. But it was less than it would have been if economic opportunities had continued to be only frontier agriculture. This last contingency of "continued" frontier agriculture is impossible, however, since the population growth responding to such conditions necessarily eliminates them. Inevitably, then, conditions favoring such extremely high population growth rates do not persist, and as the environment of economic opportunities is altered, population growth moves downward. The American experience shows, on one hand, a configuration of economic opportunities over time that could hardly be more favorable to population growth. On the other hand, as this configuration became less favorable to population increase —as it had to by virtue of the growth of population itself—population growth voluntarily adapted to these changed conditions. We need to know more about the specifics of this process, but it seems clear that in broad outline this is one of the main lessons to be drawn from America's population experience.

Many of those who view population growth as a great threat to future welfare see human populations as breeding independently of environmental constraints, and therefore feel justified in projecting current population growth rates unchanged into the future. But an alternative possibility is that human populations do respond to environmental factors and adjust their growth accordingly. The long-term historical experience of the American population suggests just such an adjustment. While we cannot predict with certainty the outlook for the secular growth rate of population, it seems reasonable to suppose that the same process of adjustment to the environment that has occurred in the past will continue in the future.

EFFECTS OF POPULATION GROWTH ON ECONOMIC GROWTH

What about the effect of population growth on the rate of economic growth? In current discussions of less developed nations, high population growth is often viewed as an obstacle to modern economic growth. On the other hand, in the case of the United States the view is sometimes advanced that high population growth was an important stimulus to development. What can be said on this issue?

The answer, as in the case of the causes of population growth, is that we do not know for sure. The argument that will be developed here is that high population growth contributed to high growth in *total* GNP and more rapid and extensive settlement of the country. The growth of GNP *per capita*, however, might have been much the same even if population growth had been considerably less—say, half of that which actually occurred. It should be emphasized that this conclusion is speculative and that there is need for deeper research. The analytical framework will be the standard production-function approach of economic theory, employed in Chapter 2 and elsewhere in this volume.

Aggregate GNP

The distinction between aggregate and per capita GNP is fundamental. With regard to total GNP, the argument is straightforward. If population growth had been substantially less, labor-force growth would have been less rapid and land would have come under cultivation more slowly. With fewer savers, capital accumulation would have been less.[43] The slower growth in factor inputs would in turn have implied a slower growth in aggregate output. Over the last century or so, the actual trends in the United States have been roughly consonant with this argument. A secular decline in the growth rate of population has been accompanied by a secular decline in the growth rate of national product (Table 2.10, p. 35).

Per Capita GNP

It is when one considers per capita output that the problem becomes most challenging. In analyzing this question, it is desirable to distinguish between immigration and natural increase components of population growth. We have seen that between 1790 and 1840, immigration remained low, though it was rising. In the late 1840s, however, a major influx was initiated which, taking into account descendants as well as immigrants, is estimated to have doubled the American population by 1920. Suppose that population growth had been kept much lower by immigration restrictions. What, then, would have been the course of per capita output?

---

[43] The possibility that a slower population growth rate would have raised per capita savings was noted earlier in this chapter. This would tend to offset in some degree the effect on capital accumulation of a slower growth in the number of savers. But it is highly unlikely that such an effect, if it did occur, would have been sufficient to maintain capital accumulation at the rate actually observed, let alone raise it enough to compensate for the slower growth in land and labor inputs.

The conclusion suggested here is that per capita output growth would not have been substantially different. This conclusion rests chiefly on theoretical considerations, but it is pertinent first to look at the temporal patterns of change in the growth of per capita output and population. Is there any evidence of an association between the long-term trends in the two magnitudes? The answer is no. Prior to 1860, the secular growth rate of population remained very high. As shown in Chapter 2, however, the long-term trend in the growth rate of per capita output appears to have moved upward (see especially p. 24). The per capita growth rate of GNP from 1805 to 1840, before immigration became substantial, appears to have been higher than in the two prior periods, 1710–1774 and 1774–1805. By this time the rate of per capita output growth was approaching and perhaps had already reached a magnitude characteristic of modern developed nations. In the two decades before 1860, it was clearly at such a level.[44]

Before 1860, therefore, persistently high population growth was accompanied by a secularly increasing growth rate of GNP per capita. After 1860, the pattern shifts. The growth rate of GNP per capita remains high, with little evidence of a secular trend, but the growth rate of population moves downward. Thus each magnitude shows a long period of secular stability during which the other changes markedly. There is little in this to suggest that the two variables were causally associated to any significant extent. But since the comparison does not allow for the many other factors that were changing at the same time, one cannot rely on this evidence alone.

Let us turn, therefore, to the theoretical analysis. In theory, there are various ways in which high population growth through immigration may have advanced or retarded per capita output growth. To summarize the analysis which follows, high immigration probably promoted higher per capita output growth by speeding up the expansion of settlement to more fertile western lands and through producing a more productive age distribution in the population. There may also have been a favorable effect arising from economies of scale. On the other hand, high immigration probably slowed the rate of improvement in the education and health of the population and to that extent retarded per capita output growth. However, probably none of these influences was very sizable, and they probably tended to be offsetting.

The major impetus to American growth was rapid innovation and the adoption of modern technology, plus associated capital formation. These developments were fostered by a young, vigorous, relatively educated population with strong economic motivation operating under institutions which favored the pursuit of personal gain. All of these conditions existed before the vast nineteenth-century immigration, and would have continued to operate even in the absence of that immigration. This suggests that transformation of the American economy to a modern technological base and the accompanying growth of per capita income would have occurred at about

---

[44] Robert E. Gallman, "Gross National Product in the United States, 1834–1909," in *Output, Employment, and Productivity in the United States After 1800*, Dorothy S. Brady (ed.), Studies in Income and Wealth, vol. 30 (New York: National Bureau of Economic Research, 1966).

the same pace even if immigration had been restricted and population growth much slower.

Land quality. Consider first the expansion of settlement. The typical Malthusian argument sees population growth as forcing the extension of cultivation to poorer lands, with a consequent diminution in productivity. In the United States, however, this does not generally seem to have been the case. Yields per acre were typically somewhat higher on western lands, and as settlement proceeded westward average productivity tended to rise, though only to a limited extent (see Chapters 2 and 11). If immigration had been lower, this positive effect on per capita income growth would have been correspondingly less.

Labor-force growth and quality. It has already been noted that immigration altered the age distribution of the population. Of interest here is the fact that it tended to raise the proportion of the working-age population to total population and, within the working-age population, tended to keep the proportion aged 20 to 29 higher than it would otherwise have been. Both effects are considered favorable—the first because it raises the proportion of workers to dependents and the second because it increases the proportion of more vigorous, younger workers within the working group. But an estimate of the quantitative effect on per capita product of these age-distribution changes would show them to be small in relation to the observed growth in per capita product. Moreover, these influences comprise a one-time change associated with the shift from low to high immigration. Once the conditions of high immigration were established the contribution of this effect would be exhausted. An analogous situation is the contribution to per capita product growth achieved by reducing the unemployment rate. Once the economy stabilizes at a new lower rate, this source of growth is ended.

Offsetting these positive effects is the effect of immigration on the general level of health and education of the labor force. As indicated earlier, the foreign-born had higher illiteracy rates and lower life expectancy than the native-born. It can be argued, therefore, that in the absence of immigration, the average health and education of the labor force would have shown more rapid improvement, and, correspondingly, per capita product would have grown more rapidly. But again, the quantitative size of this effect would not be very great. For example, the difference in illiteracy rates by nativity in 1910 was less than 10 percentage points.

Did immigration add special skills or entrepreneurial abilities to the labor force? Certainly there were immigrants who succeeded as entrepreneurs and others who had special labor skills. As we have seen, however, the foreign-born are actually underrepresented among the industrial leaders of the nineteenth century; the great bulk of the "captains of industry" were native-born. The mass of immigrants filled manual jobs which could have been done by native workers.

What about economic motivation? Did immigration provide a group in the population with an exceptional urge to get ahead? This seems dubious. The interest in material gain runs back to the very founding of this country.

It was manifest in both towns and rural areas in the seventeenth century and was the despair of some early religious leaders. The story of land speculation seems much the same whether one is looking at Puritans in seventeenth-century New England or their descendants in the nineteenth-century Midwest.[45]

Economies of scale.   In certain industries, it is usually argued, technology is such that at very large scales of operation great economies can be achieved. Only if there is a large potential mass market is it profitable to undertake such businesses. The growth of the American population to such substantial size is seen as a stimulus to the establishment of such industries.

There may be some merit in this argument, though the meaning and importance of scale economies require a good deal more empirical study than they have received. However, even very large-scale industries in the United States today, such as the automobile industry, are able to support several firms and a much larger number of plants. There is continuing debate among experts in industrial organization whether a still larger number of firms might not be economically justifiable. Also, it must be remembered that even without nineteenth-century immigration, the U.S. population would still have been fairly sizable. As of 1920, descendants of the 1790 colonial stock numbered around 52 million, about half the actual population. Given even this population at that time, the United States would have exceeded in population size every European nation except Germany and Russia. Furthermore, some of the smaller European nations, most notably Sweden, have achieved higher per capita product growth rates than the United States. A smaller United States might have been more involved in international trade in the latter part of the nineteenth century. This would have required only a continuation of earlier trends—after all, in the mid-nineteenth century, the American clipper-ship fleet was preeminent in the world.

Capital formation.   Because capital formation and technological change are so intertwined, the issues considered in this section overlap those in the next.

It is sometimes argued that by promoting a high rate of population growth, immigration served to create an aura of expanding market opportunities and thereby stimulated investment. This view was particularly stressed by Alvin Hansen in the late 1930s.[46] Subsequent attempts to test empirically the connection between population growth rates and capital formation were inconclusive. Scholars interested in less developed nations today tend to question the relevance of the argument to those countries, even where land resources are extensive, as they were in the nineteenth-century United States.

Another possible argument is that immigrants had a higher propensity

[45] Charles S. Grant, *Democracy in the Connecticut Frontier Town of Kent* (New York: Columbia University Press, 1961); Sumner Chilton Powell, *Puritan Village* (Middletown, Conn.: Wesleyan University Press, 1963); Darrett B. Rutman, *Winthrop's Boston* (Chapel Hill: University of North Carolina Press, 1965); Merle Curti, *The Making of an American Community* (Stanford: Stanford University Press, 1959); Allan G. Bogue, *From Prairie to Corn Belt: Farming on the Illinois and Iowa Prairies in the Nineteenth Century* (Chicago: University of Chicago Press, 1963); and Robert P. Swierenga, *Pioneers and Profits: Land Speculation on the Iowa Frontier* (Ames: Iowa State University Press, 1968).
[46] Alvin H. Hansen, *Fiscal Policy and Business Cycles* (New York: Norton, 1941).

to save than native Americans and thereby furthered more rapid capital accumulation. While there is no evidence on savings rates by nativity group, it does seem that the rate of capital formation in the nineteenth-century United States moved up around the same time that immigration became important. On the other hand, the rate of capital accumulation was already fairly high in the first half of the nineteenth century (see Chapter 8). Moreover, in Canada and Australia toward the end of the nineteenth century, the shares of gross national capital formation in GNP were relatively low.[47] Both of these countries were also experiencing high immigration and high population growth. One would have thought that if immigration promoted saving and investment, these countries too would show high rates of capital formation.

The question naturally arises: If the role of population growth is discounted as a major factor in stimulating capital accumulation, what then did provide the stimulus? The answer is that in both low and high population-growth countries, the principal stimulus to investment was the profit opportunities offered by the burgeoning developments in modern technology. This observation leads, in turn, to the central issue of this discussion. Would the growth and spread of modern technology have occurred as rapidly in the United States in the absence of substantial nineteenth-century immigration?

Innovation and technological change. To answer this question it is relevant to consider what was happening in the first half of the century. As has been noted, this was a period in which immigration played a small role in population growth, and its economic history is essentially that of the colonial stock and its descendants. The growth rate of per capita income in this period rose toward modern levels, and the rate of capital accumulation was high. The progress of technology was such that it provoked from Commissioner of Patents Henry L. Ellsworth the statement in 1843 that "[t]he advancement of the arts, from year to year, taxes our credulity, and seems to presage the arrival of that period when human improvement must end."[48] As shown in Chapter 7, it was during this period that the American system of manufacturing came into being, a system so distinctive that the world's leading industrial nation, Great Britain, sent a special commission to study it. Most of the leaders in the development of the American machine-tool industry were native Americans. Eli Whitney, for example, "came from that best school of mechanics, the New England hill farm. Most of the early American mechanics, like him, came from the country and had the same training of hard work with simple implements, and learned to turn their hand to nearly everything, and to work with few and rough tools."[49] As we have seen, even in the period of high immigration, America's industrial leaders were not poor immigrants, but native Americans, typically of colonial stock, from urban and business backgrounds.

---

[47] Simon Kuznets, *Modern Economic Growth: Rate, Structure, and Spread* (New Haven: Yale University Press, 1966), p. 238.

[48] *Annual Report of the Commissioner of Patents*, Senate Document no. 150, 28th Congress, 1st Session (1844), p. 6.

[49] Joseph Wickham Roe, *English and American Tool Builders* (New Haven: Yale University Press, 1916), p. 146. See also the interesting genealogies of firms compiled by Roe.

These observations add up to the impression that even before immigration rose markedly in the nineteenth century, the United States was well started on the transformation of its economy to modern technology. Nor should this conclusion come as a surprise when one recognizes the principal characteristics of white Americans. They shared a common cultural heritage with the leaders in the process of modern economic growth, the English, and were in close touch with developments in that country; they were strongly oriented toward material gain; they were perhaps the healthiest and best-educated population in the world; and they were operating within a framework of institutions that favored economic mobility. Indeed, from the viewpoint of prospective economic growth, the American population was an especially favorable selection from the English population. In England, Nonconformist groups provided entrepreneurs for the Industrial Revolution far out of proportion to their numbers. For example, Hagen examined the backgrounds of 92 British innovators in the period 1760–1830. He found that while English Nonconformists accounted for only 7 percent of the population of England and Wales, they contributed 41 percent of the English and Welsh entrepreneurs whose religion was known.[50] In the United States, the much higher representation of English Nonconformists in the population provided an unusually favorable basis for modern economic growth.

In the latter part of the nineteenth century, immigration contributed importantly to the industrial labor force. In the absence of immigration, labor costs would probably have been higher. Would this fact have substantially impeded the adoption of modern technology? Perhaps so, but Habakkuk has argued that American technology progressed more rapidly than English technology in the first half of the nineteenth century, and that the reason was the scarcity of labor, a condition which immigration restriction would have helped perpetuate.[51] Moreover, it is likely that in the absence of heavy immigration, domestic reserves of labor would have been more fully tapped. It has already been suggested that the rural native white population would have been pulled more rapidly into urban centers and that agricultural settlement would have been correspondingly slower. It is possible, too, that women would have participated more in the industrial labor force. It is pertinent to note that females helped fill labor needs in the textile mills in the first half of the nineteenth century when immigration was low. Also, the nonwhite population might have been brought more rapidly into urban employment. Note that the first great movement of nonwhites to northern cities occurred during World War I when labor demand was high and immigration cut off.

Finally, it should be noted that in Europe, and especially northwestern Europe, high emigration did not prevent the development and adoption of modern technology. Table 2.14, p. 41, shows that while in the United States between 1840 and 1957 the coefficient of multiplication per century of real per capita product was 4.6, in the major European countries it was as follows:

[50] Everett E. Hagen, *On the Theory of Social Change* (Homewood, Ill.: Dorsey, 1962), p. 297.
[51] H. J. Habakkuk, *American and British Technology in the Nineteenth Century* (New York: Cambridge University Press, 1962).

United Kingdom, 1850s–1950s	3.7
West Germany, 1870s–1960s	5.2
France, 1840s–1960s	5.2

Is it likely that in the absence of heavy immigration the relative standing of the United States would have been significantly reduced? Or is it more plausible to suppose that the same processes which raised per capita product so markedly in the European countries would also have operated in the United States?

The experience of northwestern Europe should make it clear that heavy immigration was not critical to the transfer of modern technology. To some extent the new technological developments were available to anyone who was interested in books and periodicals, in the growing technical literature. Also foreign visitors in England observed the new techniques and in some cases copied them or stole blueprints. English artisans and mechanics with special know-how and skills were induced to go abroad and set up factories or workshops employing more modern methods. Means such as this for obtaining the new technology were successfully employed by the French and Germans, and by Americans as well.[52]

Lower population growth due to natural increase.   The foregoing reasoning, if accepted, applies with little essential change to the case of lower population growth due to reduced natural increase of the colonial stock. Suppose that as a result of, say, a government family-planning program, fertility had fallen more rapidly in the nineteenth century as families avoided unwanted children. Would the consequent reduction in the rate of population growth have altered significantly the growth of per capita product? To answer this, one could retrace the foregoing argument—the effects on the quantity and quality of other factor inputs, on scale, on innovation and technical change—with perhaps some variations in emphasis one way or the other. But if one continues to stress the critical role of the characteristics of the American population at independence—its values, capacities, and heritage—and the favorable institutional environment for adopting and developing modern technology, it is hard to imagine any great alteration in the rate of growth of per capita product.

A smaller America?   Perhaps a few additional words are necessary to avoid misunderstanding. We have asked about the probable consequences for economic growth of a substantially lower rate of population growth in the period since 1790. Necessarily, the discussion centered on the effect of substantially reduced immigration, since this would have been the surest way of lowering population growth. The answer suggested was that the economy would have grown less in aggregate size but that per capita product growth might not have been much different. In reaching this conclusion, no judgment is implied on the desirability of lower population growth and the

---

[52] See W. O. Henderson, *Britain and Industrial Europe, 1750–1870*, 2nd ed. (Leicester: Leicester University Press, 1965); and Jonathan Hughes, *Industrialization and Economic History: Theses and Conjectures* (New York: McGraw-Hill, 1970), chap. 5.

restriction of immigration. In a number of respects other than aggregate GNP the United States would have been much different in the absence of nine-teenth-century mass immigration. It is true that with the same per capita product growth based on modern technology, many of the structural changes in the economy would still have occurred. For example, the proportion of urban concentration, the change in occupational structure, and the shifts in consumption patterns would probably have been quite similar. But there would have been differences in industrial structure too, in part related to greater involvement in world trade. As for geographic expansion, it seems likely that some areas now being depopulated might never have been settled. Correspondingly, the reduction of the indigenous Indian population might not have been so drastic. Without nineteenth-century immigration, the American population would exhibit much less cultural variety than it does today. Con-ceivably, the role of women and of nonwhites would have been different. Economic assimilation of nonwhites might have proceeded more rapidly and problems of racial integration might have been posed sooner. Inter-nationally, a smaller United States more dependent on world trade would have been a less dominant voice in world politics.

These remarks should suffice to suggest that lower population growth might have had dramatic consequences of various kinds. In suggesting that per capita product growth might not have been drastically different, there is no intention to deny the possibility of other important effects.

A capsule view. In the preceding section we considered the causes of American population growth. In this section, we examined its effects on the rate of growth of total and per capita product. Can the two analyses be merged to present a composite view of the growth of per capita product, population, and total product since 1790? Because the variety of causal factors and possible interconnections is large, the picture is potentially complex. But the previous discussion, which views population growth as essentially a product of certain environmental conditions and as not exerting a major effect on the rate of per capita product growth, leads to a quite simple picture. The critical features can be distilled by noting that America's growth rate of per capita product was of the same order of magnitude as that of the major countries of northwestern Europe, but its population and total product growth rates were much larger. Why was this the case?

With regard to per capita product growth, the United States was participat-ing in essentially the same process as the other countries: the growth and spread of modern technology associated with the onset of modernization. As noted, the characteristics and capacities of the American population and the associated institutional environment were favorable to this process and this perhaps accounts for America's early start. But basically all of the countries were involved in the same transition.

In the United States, however, this process was accompanied by high population and high total output growth, which was not the case in Europe. Why? When all is said and done, the critical factor seems to have been America's vast extent of good land resources. With regard to other factors favoring population growth, such as health conditions and economic develop-ment, the situation of the United States was not so strikingly different from that of northwestern Europe. But with regard to land resources, it was a world apart. If the territory of the United States had remained confined to that of the original 13 colonies, per capita output growth would probably have been much the same, but population and total output growth would have been more like those in the European countries. Thus it is modern economic growth occurring in the context of abundant land resources which accounts for America's distinctive population and output growth.

SUGGESTED READING

Bernard, William S. (ed.). *American Immigration Policy.* New York: Harper & Row, 1950.

Bogue, Donald. *The Population of the United States.* Glencoe, Ill.: Free Press. 1959.

Coale, Ansley J., and Melvin Zelnik. *New Estimates of Fertility and Population in the United States.* Princeton: Princeton University Press, 1963.

Easterlin, Richard A. "Influences in European Overseas Emigration before World War I." *Economic Development and Cultural Change,* vol. 9, no. 3 (April 1961), pp. 331–351.

Easterlin, Richard A. *Population, Labor Force, and Long Swings in Economic Growth: The American Experience.* New York: Columbia University Press, 1968.

Easterlin, Richard A. "Towards a Socio-Economic Theory of Fertility: A Survey of Recent Research on Economic Factors in American Fertility." In *Fertility and Family Planning: A World View,* edited by S. J. Behrman *et al.* Ann Arbor: University of Michigan Press, 1969.

Fishlow, Albert. "The Common School Revival: Fact or Fancy?" In *Industrialization in Two Systems,* edited by Henry Rosovsky. New York: Wiley, 1966, pp. 40–67.

Folger, John, K., and Charles B. Nam. *Education of the American Population.* Washington: U.S. Government Printing Office, 1967.

Freedman, Ronald, P. K. Whelpton, and Arthur A. Campbell. *Family Planning, Sterility, and Population Growth.* New York: McGraw-Hill, 1959.

Gilboy, Elizabeth W., and Edgar M. Hoover. "Population and Immigration." In *American Economic History,* edited by Seymour Harris. New York: McGraw-Hill, 1961, pp. 247–280.

Glass, D. V., and E. Grebenik. "World Population." In *The Cambridge Economic History of Europe,* edited by H. J. Habakkuk and M. Postan, vol. 6. Cambridge, England: Cambridge University Press, 1965, pp. 56–90.

Grabill, Wilson H., C. V. Kiser, and P. K. Whelpton. *The Fertility of American Women.* New York: Wiley, 1958.

Grant, Charles S. *Democracy in the Connecticut Frontier Town of Kent.* New York: Columbia University Press, 1961.

Gregory, F. W., and I. D. Neu. "The American Industrial Elite in the 1870's." In *Men in Business,* edited by William Miller. Cambridge, Mass.: Harvard University Press, 1952, pp. 193–211.

Greven, Philip J., Jr. *Four Generations: Population, Land, and Family in Colonial Andover, Massachusetts.* Ithaca, N.Y.: Cornell University Press, 1970.

Hall, Charles E. *Negroes in the United States, 1920–32.* Washington: U.S. Bureau of the Census, 1935.

Hansen, Marcus Lee. *The Atlantic Migration, 1607–1860.* Cambridge, Mass.: Harvard University Press, 1940.

Hutchinson, E. P. *Immigrants and Their Children, 1850–1950.* New York: Wiley, 1956.

Jerome, Harry. *Migration and Business Cycles,* New York: National Bureau of Economic Research, 1926.

Kaplan, D. L., and M. C. Casey. *Occupational Trends in the United States, 1900 to 1950.* U.S. Bureau of the Census Working Paper no. 5. Washington: U.S. Government Printing Office, 1958.

Kiser, Clyde V., Wilson H. Grabill, and Arthur A. Campbell. *Trends and Variations in Fertility in the United States,* Cambridge, Mass.: Harvard University Press, 1968.

Kuznets, Simon. "Long Swings in the Growth of Population and in Related Economic Variables," *Proceedings of the American Philosophical Society* (February 1958), pp. 25–52.

Kuznets, Simon, and E. Rubin. *Immigration and the Foreign Born,* Occasional Paper 46. New York: National Bureau of Economic Research, 1954.

Kuznets, Simon, et al. *Population Redistribution and Economic Growth, United States, 1870–1950.* Three vols. Philadelphia: American Philosophical Society, 1957–1964.

Lockridge, Kenneth. "Land, Population, and the Evolution of New England Society, 1630–1790." *Past and Present,* no. 39 (April 1968), pp. 62–80.

Miller, William. "American Historians and the Business Elite." *Journal of Economic History,* vol. 9 (1949), pp. 184–208.

Okun, Bernard. *Trends in Birth Rates in the United States Since 1870.* Baltimore: Johns Hopkins, 1958.

Potter, J. "The Growth of Population in America, 1700–1860." In *Population in History,* edited by D. V. Glass and D. E. C. Eversley. London: Edward Arnold, 1965, pp. 631–688.

Spengler, Joseph J. *The Fecundity of Native and Foreign-Born Women in New England.* Washington: Brookings Institution, 1930.

Taeuber, Conrad, and Irene B. Taeuber. *The Changing Population of the United States.* New York: Wiley, 1958.

Thompson, Warren S., and P. K. Whelpton. *Population Trends in the United States.* New York: McGraw-Hill, 1933.

Thornthwaite, Warren C. *Internal Migration in the United States.* Philadelphia: University of Pennsylvania Press, 1934.

Tucker, George. *Progress of the United States in Population and Wealth in Fifty Years.* Press of the Hunt's Merchants' Magazine, 1843.

United Nations. Department of Social Affairs. *The Determinants and Consequences of Population Trends.* New York: United Nations, 1953.

U.S. Bureau of the Census. *Census of Population: 1960, United States Summary.* Washington: U.S. Government Printing Office, 1963.

U.S. Bureau of the Census. *A Century of Population Growth from the First Cenuss of the United States to the Twelfth, 1790–1900.* Washington: U.S. Government Printing Office, 1909.

U.S. Bureau of the Census. *Comparative Occupation Statistics for the United States, 1870 to 1940.* Washington: U.S. Government Printing Office, 1943.

U.S. Bureau of the Census. *Historical Statistics of the United States, Colonial Times to 1957.* Washington: U.S. Government Printing Office, 1960.

U.S. Bureau of the Census. *Historical Statistics of the United States, Continuation to 1962 and Revisions.* Washington: U.S. Government Printing Office, 1965.

U.S. Bureau of the Census. *Negro Population, 1790–1915.* Washington: U.S. Government Printing Office, 1918.

U.S. Bureau of the Census. *Statistical Abstract of the United States, 1969.* Washington: U.S. Government Printing Office, 1969.

U.S. Bureau of the Census. *Statistical View of the United States: Being a Compendium of the Seventh Census.* Washington: U.S. Government Printing Office, 1854.

U.S. National Resources Committee. *The Problems of a Changing Population.* Washington: U.S. Government Printing Office, 1938.

Yasuba, Yasukichi. *Birth Rates of the White Population in the United States, 1800–1860: An Economic Study.* Baltimore: Johns Hopkins, 1962.

6
THE AMERICAN LABOR FORCE

Who would commend the history of Europe's colonies as cheerful reading, or soothing? What multiplied miseries existed in the Spanish colonies, from Mexico to Costa Rica to Bolivia; what bloody revolts in the French, from Santo Domingo to Martinique; what desolation in the Portuguese. Even the history of most British colonies alternates between dullness and despair: this is surely the case of Ireland and India. Why does the record for the United States generally seem so much more sanguine? The imperial breadth and scope of the new nation was certainly a factor. But was Canada any less imperial? Its mineral wealth also contributed. But the typical centers of rising riches in the United States included Nantucket (its wealth acquired by chasing whales in the South Pacific) and Charleston and Newport (theirs from trading in African slaves). Hence no sufficient explanation is to be found in mere minerals. One key must be the character of the labor force and the skill with which that force was productively deployed.

The following pages review the experience of Americans as workers, focusing on these major topics: how demand shaped the industrial pattern of employment, 1800–1860 and 1865 ff; labor force trends; control and allocation of labor, with attention to the decline in self-employment and the rise of the working class; productivity and real income trends; the geographic redistribution of labor; and a review of the growth and impact of unions.

Before looking at the experience of the American people as laborers and producers of wealth, however, we will do well to remember their role as consumers. For a certain competent greediness for material objects is needed if economies are to "go." The American Indian consumed less than $10 per person in trade goods as late as the 1830s. He showed little willingness to shift to the new American mode of existence—a shift so necessary if more and ever more goods were to be acquired. It was not that the noble savage possessed a set of values that differed totally from those of the white, yellow, and black men who replaced him. (He evinced little less zest for hatred and for war than "civilized" man. And he valued the products of the distillery and the armory no less than his successors.) But he showed little interest in material accumulation, and hence failed to use his energies in ways that induced output increases, that created measured economic growth.

The men who have dominated the United States since the red men suffered under no such disability. Symbolic, surely, is the still-revered Christopher Columbus, who carefully explained that "Gold is excellent. Gold is Treasure, and he who possesses it does whatever he wishes in this life, and succeeds in helping souls into Paradise."[1] Columbus, Pizarro, and a dozen other Spanish emissaries racked the New World for gold. Raleigh even persuaded James I to release him from prison to make one last try for American gold. Centuries of ardent, greedy exploration followed. These eventually (and incorrectly) made it clear that neither apes and ivory nor gold and silver were to be found in North America.

After these generations of single-minded treasure seekers, new and greater contingents of immigrants followed: Those who saw a prospect of earning income by the most pedestrian types of labor. The United States began to attract those who cherished the bright hope of working from dawn to dusk to achieve their own land and a higher income. Here was "every allurement to emigration, and the means of subsistence so easy as to produce a rapid increase in population" (in 1812); surely (in 1824), every resident of Ireland should "work or beg his passage over," "quit that den of wretchedness . . . (and) become superior beings," and (in 1859), "every necessary of life is sluttishly plentiful . . . it is not possible to find a man hungry."[2] Beyond a man's own prospects were those for his children. All the inconveniences of immigration—"a new but good word"—were justified to give "my children a career of enterprise" (1814); for in the United States "a father can settle his children about him. They need not be hewers of wood and drawers of water" (1826).[3]

These incentives varied in strength over the years. But they never ceased to attract migrants. Even in depression years—1837, 1857, or 1873—when distress permeated our cities, men continued to come. Some starved to death. Others regretted that their misfortunes lacked this terminus. But in no year from 1837 until mass immigration was blocked did less than 25,000 immigrants enter the United States. In nations where primogeniture forced second and third sons to look beyond the family farm (e.g., France), the prospects in the United States were mildly preferred to those offered by the great cities at home. In other nations (e.g., Ireland), the high odds for landlessness and starvation harshly emphasized the attractions of the United States, as a fecund people provided a ghastly version of the Malthusian model.[4]

---

[1] Quoted by Carl Becker, *Progress and Power* (New York: Knopf, 1949), p. 79.

[2] Festus Foster, *An Oration* (Springfield, Mass.: Merriam, 1812), p. 1; William Newnham Blane, *An Excursion Through the United States* . . . (London: 1824), pp. 169–170; James Caird, *Prairie Farming* (London: Longmans, Green, 1859), p. 94.

[3] Morris Birkbeck, *Notes on a Journey in America* (London: 1819), pp. 9, 98; Timothy Flint, *Recollections* (1826), p. 250.

[4] However miserable conditions in Ireland, of course, no one would have migrated unless he expected that he —or his children—would be less miserable in some other land.

What was the focus of the economy to which these migrants headed?[5] The overwhelming fact during its first half-century, from 1789 to 1839, was that it was a peasant economy, as were the economies of Europe and Asia. Three fourths of its labor force in 1800, and still no less than 60 percent in 1840, engaged in farming. The goods sent back to England by those who signed the Mayflower Compact were forest and farm products. Two centuries later, American manufacturing (in its widest definition) still encompassed no more than 3 percent of the labor force.

These farms were not, of course, on landed estates, such as the feudal domains that pockmarked Poland and Hungary. Typically the Americans worked on small farms hacked out of the wilderness and run by families with rarely more than one hired laborer. As peasants around the world, they planted mostly subsistence crops, worked from first light to dark, used the labor of father as well as mother and as many children as she provided. (One family in 1846 had "26 strong healthy boys," such number clearly affecting "the amount of help."[6]) Unlike many other peasants, however, Americans had prospects of buying their own land.

The attractions that drew immigrants over these two centuries turned largely on factors associated with the yeoman's way of life. Land hunger is an ancient and endemic human disease. Rarely before in history had an opportunity been provided for satisfying that hunger so tangibly, so cheaply. Farms in the most populous American states in 1800 averaged about 150 acres. The contrasting data for Europe suggest how extravagantly grand this prospect was.

The strangeness of the terrain, the lurking Indians, the dangers of the ocean voyage, and the costs of breaking forested land to farm use—all these deterred many a faint heart and many a rational maximizer. But the advantages of the yeoman's life drew millions. These people, and their descendants, constituted the American labor force.

Were they all committed to the land? Surely not. Our very first official immigration report, for 1821, records the arrival of a falconer, a dancing master, even a rope dancer.[7] And many a migrant never ventured beyond the ports of New York, Boston, or Charleston. But the 1800–1840 totals given in Table 6.1 emphasize the attractions of the land as opposed to city work, the possibilities of import substitution, and so on.

In addition to the free migrant stream, millions of future Americans were bought from the native chiefs of Africa. Virtually all these migrants also farmed, growing food, tobacco, or cotton on territories wrested from the Cherokee, the Seminole, the Mexican.

Prior to 1820, the American economy focused on subsistence: Farming was the task of men; child-rearing and home crafts, that of the women.

But once the barrier of independence had been crossed, comparative

---

[5] The U.S. economy at this time was itself not made up largely of new migrants, but of the children and grandchildren of former migrants. See Chapter 5 for a discussion of the ratio of migrant increase to natural increase.

[6] U.S. Department of Agriculture, *Wages of Farm Labor in the United States* (Washington: U.S. Government Printing Office, 1892).

[7] Peter Force, *The National Calendar for MDCCCXXI* (1821), p. 237.

Table 6.1
The labor force, 1800–1960[a] (thousands)

	Labor Force (Age 10 and older)			Agriculture (10 and older)	Fishing	Mining	Construction	Manufacturing			Trade	Transport		Service	
												Ocean Vessels	Railway		
Year	Total	Free	Slave					Total Persons Engaged	Cotton Textile Wage Earners	Primary Iron and Steel Wage Earners				Teachers	Domestics
1800	1,900	1,370	530	1,400	5	10	—	—	1	1	—	40	—	5	40
1810	2,330	1,590	740	1,950	6	11	—	75	10	5	—	60	—	12	70
1820	3,135	2,185	950	2,470	14	13	—	—	12	5	—	50	—	20	110
1830	4,200	3,020	1,180	2,965	15	22	—	—	55	20	—	70	—	30	160
1840	5,660	4,180	1,480	3,570	24	32	290	500	72	24	350	95	7	45	240
1850	8,250	6,280	1,970	4,520	30	102	410	1,200	92	35	530	135	20	80	350
1860	11,110	8,770	2,340	5,880	31	176	520	1,530	122	43	890	145	80	115	600
1870	12,930	—	—	6,790	28	180	780	2,470	135	78	1,310	135	160	170	1,000
1880	17,390	—	—	8,920	41	280	900	3,290	175	130	1,930	125	416	230	1,130
1890	23,320	—	—	9,960	60	440	1,510	4,390	222	149	2,960	120	750	350	1,580
1900	29,070	—	—	11,680	69	637	1,665	5,895	303	222	3,970	105	1,040	436	1,800
1910	37,480	—	—	11,770	68	1,068	1,949	8,332	370	306	5,320	150	1,855	595	2,090
1920	41,610	—	—	10,790	53	1,180	1,233	11,190	450	460	5,845	205	2,236	752	1,660
1930	48,830	—	—	10,560	73	1,009	1,988	9,884	372	375	8,122	160	1,659	1,044	2,270
1940	56,290	—	—	9,575	60	925	1,876	11,309	400	485	9,328	150	1,160	1,086	2,300
1950	65,470	—	—	7,870	77	901	3,029	15,648	(350)	(550)	12,152	130	1,373	1,270	1,995
1960	74,060	—	—	5,970	45	709	3,640	17,145	(300)	(530)	14,051	135	883	1,850	2,489

Employment[a]

[a] Persons engaged (employees, self-employed, and unpaid family workers), except as specified. Age 10 and over.

SOURCE: Stanley Lebergott, *Manpower in Economic Growth: The American Record Since 1800* (New York: McGraw-Hill, 1964), p. 510.

advantage was never far behind. The gradual accretion began. American production slowly replaced imports; subsistence agricultural production was reduced in favor of production for a world market; home manufactures were replaced first by the workshop and then by the manufacturing establishment. The rugged simplicity of the self-contained life gave way to specialization. Even the "Mayflower" families had shipped some lumber to London. Later residents found greater markets—exporting to customers who ranged from the Hanseatic League to the Barbary pirates. The commitment to agriculture indicated by the labor-force figures really masks a major shift in product mix. Farming was farming still, but one must imagine behind these totals a growing concentration on particular export crops as labor was reallocated from subsistence to a specialized, export focus. The importance of this shift lies in the margin of advantage it provided and in its forecast of trends that developed later in the nineteenth century. (The employment possibilities in farm exports were numerically trivial prior to the Civil War.[8])

Beyond the roughly 70 percent of the labor force engaged in farming only one other group of numerical consequence existed in 1800. That consisted of a trebly talented set of small craftsmen—who made their own products, often carried them to markets, and usually sold them to the final consumer as well. They were shoemakers, hat makers, barrel makers, men who made flour scoops, men who made candles, and the ubiquitous local blacksmiths. The largest group of such craftsmen were the millers—of wheat, oil, or lumber.

Other occupations make a far more modest numerical showing than the vivacity of their appearance in this historic record would suggest. The immortal dramas of the Mountain Men, of Bridger, Sublette, and Ashley and Jed Smith, were played out—even in the peak years, the 1830s—by somewhat fewer than 500 American trappers wandering through the Rockies.[9] The mystic and perilous enterprise celebrated by *Moby Dick* involved no more than 10,000 whalers at its peak. These enterprises offered critical contributions to growth, for they searched out new investment possibilities, developed labor skills, and trained entrepreneurs. But as employers, their importance was negligible.

DEMAND AND THE INDUSTRIAL PATTERN OF EMPLOYMENT

If we are to understand the remarkable changes in the pattern of employment by industry that have occurred since 1800 we must begin with the choices made by American entrepreneurs. Their decisions can hardly be ignored in short-run analysis; for understanding secular change they are central.

---

[8] Douglass North has stated that "direct income from the cotton trade was probably no more than 6 percent of any plausible estimate of national income which we might employ" for the period to 1860. He notes that accounting for the income generated in financing and distributing cotton would add significantly. Douglass North, *The Economic Growth of the United States, 1790–1860* (New York: Norton, 1961), p. 69. However, a review of transfer costs suggests that growing and distributing U.S. farm exports could account for no more than one tenth of U.S. employment, and probably less.

[9] Stanley Lebergott, *Manpower in Economic Growth: The American Record Since 1800* (New York: McGraw-Hill, 1964), p. 8.

An overwhelming fact about the first century of the American economy is that most of its entrepreneurs were not busy maximizing current incomes by producing for the market. They were, instead, primarily investors, intent on building up equities (in farms and handicraft enterprises) to yield independence and future income for themselves and their children. As long as they accepted current incomes below those available as wages in the market, and as long as they had funds to dissipate in current consumption, they could persist in attempting to create an independent and remunerative economic base for their families. They were not isolated from the discipline of the market so much as insulated from it for a time. How long a time depended on the current and expected gap between actual and alternative incomes and the inevitably personal, perhaps idiosyncratic, choice of discount factors. Without recognizing this orientation it would be difficult to understand the prolonged concentration on farming and the hand trades evident in Table 6.1. Such expectations, refreshed by each new wave of migrants and complemented by national policies that persistently kept down the cost of farm land, worked to retain a large share of the free population in farming for many decades. Moreover, the high return in cotton production (plus the belief that the returns from using slave labor were highest in agriculture) intensified the concentration of the slave-labor force in agriculture.

Meanwhile other entrepreneurs, dominated by shorter vision and bolder competence, were more consistently consulting the possibilities of comparative advantage.[10] Of course, the economically relevant factor endowment of a developing nation may change drastically from time to time—together with its comparative advantage. The U.S. endowment of labor, for example, varied markedly, as did the political and social attractiveness of the United States versus that of Ireland. And its endowment of coal and gold, though fixed by nature, could not become economically relevant without mineral discovery—a process with many a stochastic element. Comparative advantage dictated how output would be concentrated in one set of industries rather than another. But having said so much, have we necessarily expounded the pattern in Table 6.1 ? Hardly. For the demand for labor is another matter. That has been fixed by two interacting factors: (a) the ratio of total U.S. costs (production plus distribution; labor plus capital plus resources) to those of other nations for each industry and (b) the proportion of labor costs to total costs in any given industry's production function. Total costs might indicate that the United States had a "comparative advantage" in growing wheat. But "excessive" labor costs in wheat growing could lead to production functions that used hardly any labor. Hence the share of wheat growers in the U.S. labor force could be tiny.[11] It is with this contingent qualification that we turn to the actual change in employment.

---

[10] Those who accepted below-market incomes for themselves but anticipated high incomes for their children were still adapting to America's comparative advantage. But we may usefully distinguish them from those with a higher rate of time discount, who sought to maximize their own incomes in the near term on the basis of prices and expected prices in that period.

[11] Fortunately cost pressures propagate, input substitution takes place, and we find that, in the large, the distribution of output by industry and that of manpower by industry are similar.

Employment Change, 1800–1860

What were the major employment gains from 1800 to the Civil War? Roughly half of the 9 million labor-force increase went into agriculture, as men swarmed into new areas. New crops were attempted—mulberry trees (for silkworm culture) in Michigan, sugar beets in Ohio. But for the most part, old crops were tried on newly broken land—wheat in Kansas and Missouri, cotton in Alabama and Texas, tobacco in Ohio and Kansas. Most of the remaining employment gains were in retail trade or construction, and in such skilled handcrafts as coopering, blacksmithing, and carriage making.[12]

But suppose one emphasizes the rate of increase. Which sectors grew at rates sharply greater than average? Mining is one sector that obviously qualifies. A succession of mineral discoveries increased mining employment nearly eighteenfold. Gold in Virginia, then in Georgia, ultimately in California; iron in Connecticut, then in Missouri, ultimately in Michigan and Minnesota; copper, silver, petroleum, borax—the list of minerals is long, their discoveries striking, and the sudden rush of emigrants they brought to the new regions vital in searching out the nation, in speeding settlement.

Manufacturing is another high-growth sector. A significant index of the rise of the United States to economic eminence was the steady gain in factory employment. That gain testifies primarily to (a) the decline in home manufactures and (b) a rising level of income, which generated ever-greater demands for consumer goods.

Between 1810 and 1840, factory employment rose almost sevenfold—more than the gain reported for any other sector shown in Table 6.1. (The exuberant gain in factory employment from 1800 to 1840 probably outpaced that for the other sectors as well.) And from 1840 to the eve of the Civil War factories again grew at a faster rate than other sectors. This was the nascent period of industrialization in the United States. Several aspects of this change require our attention.

First, much of this employment growth marks the transition from older methods of production to newer ones. It does not measure the growth in commodity output. The factories were taking over activities from the home and the plantation. Men surely ate bread before there was a baking industry and wore clothes before a textile industry had been established. Some of these activities are masked in the table—for example, women whose primary activity was plantation farming also made clothes for slaves. Other production does not appear at all—that of home-baked bread, for example—since housewives are not included in the labor force.

Hence the rise in factory production and employment does not imply a proportionate rise in the production and consumption of goods. But it does mean that a significant volume of manpower and capital resources were freed from handicraft work to be used more efficiently in factories and retail stores.

Even as the factory system developed, it began to change. Some of the

---

[12] These crafts are not separately estimated in Table 6.1, but are included in the labor-force total.

increasing number employed in cotton textiles from 1800 to 1840, though not an enormous number, were busy making textile machinery. As time went on, specialization proceeded further. Such activities began to concentrate in firms in the machinery industry. Eventually, of course, textile mills ceased producing their own power and began to buy electric power from the newly developing utility industry (Chapter 12). Farmers who once made their own cedar shakes and did their own blacksmithing became customers of the newly expanding lumber, carriage, and machinery factories.

Variations in export markets brought differential growth by sector—with a gaining demand in England for American wheat, in China for American textiles, in the West Indies for American barrels, in Norway for American printing machinery. But even " King Cotton " accounted for little more than 5 percent of U.S. employment at any point, while—as noted above—exports as a whole probably never accounted for over 10 percent. Hence the variations in Table 6.1 trace back chiefly to variations in American demand.

Engel's law, stipulating that when consumers advance their incomes at a given rate they increase their food expenditures at a slower rate, was strictly enforced in the United States during the nineteenth century. In contrast, consumer spending for housing and clothing probably rose more swiftly than spending for food, and that for durables (e.g., sewing machines) and services rose perhaps even more swiftly. Thanks to productivity advances, however, it is not likely that the pattern of employment increases was quite the same.

Employment Changes Since 1865

For the century following the Civil War, we have a morass of data on employment change. Even the least of these figures tells us much about national values and purpose. (For example, the fact that from 1900 to 1960 the number of clergymen rose by 100,000, while the count of hairdressers rose by 300,000, tells us something about changing market demands for various kinds of consolation and ministration.) We shall single out for comment only five of the major shifts in industrial composition. (Data are from Table 6.2 and from the somewhat noncomparable Table 6.1.)

Farming. The cresting of farm employment around 1910 is one of the great landmarks in our economic history, marking the apogee for an industry and a way of life that had developed over centuries only to decline abruptly in the next few decades. Not unreasonably in the 1930s Congress perpetuated the memory of this halcyon period for farmers by pegging farm prices to a 1910–1914 benchmark. Directly after the World War I expansion of 1915–1920 farm prices began to erode, then the flow of inputs to farming fell, followed finally by the level of employment in farming. By the end of the 1960s, this giant ex-king of industries commanded no more personnel than did finance. Not unrelated to this collapse was the set of associated social changes during and after World War II in which, among other events, sharecroppers abandoned the South in vast numbers and the Supreme Court handed down its one man—one vote ruling.

TABLE 6.2
Employees in nonfarm establishments, by industry, 1900–1969 (in thousands)

Year	Total	Mining	Contract Construction	Manufacturing	Transport and Utilities	Trade	Finance	Service	Civilian Government Employment				
									Total	Federal Civilian	Public Education	State Nonschool	Local Nonschool
1900	15,178	637	1,147	5,468	2,282	2,502	308	1,740	1,094	239	487	95	273
1901	16,294	703	1,274	5,817	2,404	2,765	322	1,880	1,129	239	499	101	290
1902	17,395	685	1,393	6,305	2,754	2,827	337	1,903	1,191	264	512	107	308
1903	17,858	834	1,290	6,527	2,666	2,979	351	1,982	1,229	270	521	114	324
1904	17,640	801	1,257	6,199	2,743	2,992	369	2,002	1,277	287	529	120	341
1905	18,707	889	1,208	6,739	2,905	3,170	385	2,076	1,335	312	538	126	359
1906	20,069	894	1,391	7,226	3,110	3,442	405	2,215	1,386	328	546	132	380
1907	20,523	1,051	1,436	7,322	3,114	3,486	423	2,243	1,448	344	566	138	400
1908	19,259	900	1,308	6,570	3,069	3,299	442	2,164	1,507	357	584	145	421
1909	21,203	998	1,376	7,661	3,229	3,585	464	2,326	1,564	372	600	151	441
1910	21,697	1,068	1,342	7,828	3,366	3,570	483	2,410	1,630	389	622	157	462
1911	22,093	1,052	1,249	7,870	3,426	3,813	520	2,491	1,672	396	635	162	479
1912	23,191	1,083	1,337	8,322	3,552	4,073	568	2,539	1,717	400	654	167	496
1913	24,143	1,182	1,412	8,751	3,570	4,232	613	2,626	1,757	396	677	172	512
1914	23,190	1,027	1,267	8,210	3,445	4,128	657	2,647	1,809	402	696	177	534
1915	23,149	1,022	1,195	8,210	3,439	4,091	694	2,637	1,861	395	727	182	557
1916	25,510	1,168	1,208	9,629	3,579	4,476	738	2,796	1,916	399	751	186	580
1917	25,802	1,267	1,027	9,872	3,722	4,320	771	2,783	2,000	438	769	191	602
1918	26,432	1,311	928	10,167	3,877	4,110	809	2,769	2,461	854	787	196	624
1919	27,270	1,067	1,011	10,702	4,055	4,213	868	2,905	2,449	794	807	201	647
1920	27,434	1,180	850	10,702	4,317	4,012	902	3,100	2,371	655	835	211	670
1921	24,542	906	1,035	8,262	3,929	3,960	968	3,085	2,397	561	879	215	742
1922	26,616	880	1,315	9,129	3,897	4,708	1,081	3,151	2,455	544	917	236	758
1923	29,231	1,181	1,408	10,317	4,185	5,194	1,175	3,247	2,524	537	941	239	807
1924	28,577	1,091	1,556	9,675	4,063	5,047	1,211	3,298	2,636	543	971	244	878
1925	29,751	1,065	1,680	9,942	4,018	5,717	1,264	3,300	2,765	553	1,010	263	939
1926	30,599	1,168	1,756	10,156	4,077	5,864	1,328	3,397	2,853	549	1,047	270	987
1927	30,481	1,100	1,761	9,996	3,997	5,942	1,380	3,360	2,945	547	1,070	292	1,036
1928	30,539	1,038	1,704	9,942	3,886	6,047	1,484	3,399	3,093	561	1,099	299	1,080
1929	31,339	1,087	1,497	10,702	3,916	6,123	1,509	3,440	3,065	533	1,143	1,389	
1930	29,424	1,009	1,372	9,562	3,685	5,797	1,475	3,376	3,148	536	1,173	1,449	

Year												
1931	1,520	1,184	560	3,264	3,183	1,407	5,284	3,254	8,170	1,214	873	26,649
1932	1,495	1,171	559	3,225	2,931	1,341	4,683	2,816	6,931	970	731	23,628
1933	1,457	1,144	565	3,166	2,873	1,295	4,755	2,672	7,397	809	744	23,711
1934	1,502	1,145	652	3,299	3,058	1,319	5,281	2,750	8,501	862	883	25,953
1935	1,554	1,174	753	3,481	3,142	1,335	5,431	2,786	9,069	912	897	27,053
1936	1,644	1,198	826	3,668	3,326	1,388	5,809	2,973	9,827	1,145	946	29,082
1937	1,692	1,231	833	3,756	3,518	1,432	6,265	3,134	10,794	1,112	1,015	31,026
1938	1,789	1,265	829	3,883	3,473	1,425	6,179	2,863	9,440	1,055	891	29,209
1939	1,797	1,293	905	3,995	3,517	1,462	6,426	2,936	10,278	1,150	854	30,618
1940	1,879	1,327	996	4,202	3,681	1,502	6,750	3,038	10,985	1,294	925	32,376
1941	1,928	1,392	1,340	4,660	3,921	1,549	7,210	3,274	13,192	1,790	957	36,554
1942	1,859	1,411	2,213	5,483	4,084	1,538	7,118	3,460	15,280	2,170	992	40,125
1943	1,786	1,388	2,905	6,080	4,148	1,502	6,982	3,647	17,602	1,567	925	42,452
1944	1,738	1,378	2,928	6,043	4,163	1,476	7,058	3,829	17,328	1,094	892	41,883
1945	1,757	1,380	2,808	5,944	4,241	1,497	7,314	3,906	15,524	1,132	836	40,394
1946	1,926	1,415	2,254	5,595	4,719	1,697	8,376	4,061	14,703	1,661	862	41,674
1947	2,083	1,499	1,892	5,474	5,050	1,754	8,955	4,166	15,545	1,982	955	43,881
1948	2,237	1,550	1,863	5,650	5,206	1,829	9,272	4,189	15,582	2,169	994	44,891
1949	2,328	1,620	1,908	5,856	5,264	1,857	9,264	4,001	14,441	2,165	930	43,778
1950	2,418	1,680	1,928	6,026	5,382	1,919	9,386	4,034	15,241	2,333	901	45,222
1951	2,375	1,712	2,302	6,389	5,576	1,991	9,742	4,226	16,393	2,603	929	47,849
1952	2,402	1,787	2,420	6,609	5,730	2,069	10,004	4,248	16,632	2,634	898	48,825
1953	2,447	1,893	2,305	6,645	5,867	2,146	10,247	4,290	17,549	2,623	866	50,232
1954	2,558	2,005	2,188	6,751	6,002	2,234	10,235	4,084	16,314	2,612	791	49,022
1955	4,727		2,187	6,914	6,274	2,335	10,535	4,141	16,882	2,802	792	50,675
1956	5,069		2,209	7,278	6,536	2,429	10,858	4,244	17,243	2,999	822	52,408
1957	5,399		2,217	7,616	6,749	2,477	10,886	4,241	17,174	2,923	828	52,894
1958	5,648		2,191	7,839	6,806	2,519	10,750	3,976	15,945	2,778	751	51,363
1959	5,850		2,233	8,083	7,130	2,594	11,127	4,011	16,675	2,960	732	53,313
1960	6,083		2,270	8,353	7,423	2,669	11,391	4,004	16,796	2,885	712	54,234
1961	6,315		2,279	8,594	7,664	2,731	11,337	3,903	16,326	2,816	672	54,042
1962	6,550		2,340	8,890	8,028	2,800	11,566	3,903	16,853	2,902	650	55,596
1963	6,868		2,358	9,226	8,325	2,877	11,778	3,951	16,995	2,963	635	56,702
1964	7,248		2,348	9,596	8,709	2,957	12,160	4,036	17,274	3,050	634	58,331
1965	7,696		2,378	10,074	9,087	3,023	12,716	4,151	18,062	3,186	632	60,815
1966	8,227		2,564	10,791	9,551	3,100	13,245	4,261	19,214	3,275	627	63,955
1967	8,679		2,719	11,398	10,099	3,225	13,606	4,313	19,447	3,208	613	65,857
1968	9,109		2,737	11,846	10,592	3,383	14,081	4,449	19,768	3,267	610	67,860
1969	9,471		2,756	12,227	11,102	3,558	14,644		20,121	3,410	628	70,139

SOURCES

1900–1954: Lebergott, *Manpower . . . , op. cit.*, p. 514.
1955–1969: *Economic Report of the President, 1970*, Table C-27.

Government. The rise of the public sector is perhaps the next most obvious, most massive change. Through the slow expansion of worldly concern, we moved from the deployment of a handful of soldiers in Asia against Aguinaldo in 1900, to the employment of many more in Asia against Ho Chi Minh in 1965. And since the military destruction function became much more capital-intensive, the rate of growth for employment in the procurement of military hardware rose even more speedily. The bulk of the remaining public-sector growth was associated with state construction of roads and local school expenditures.

Manufacturing. A bewilderingly large proportion of current factory output goes for goods unknown to our grandfathers. (For example, a Bureau of Labor Statistics city worker's budget, often referred to in discussions of poverty, includes, as essential, expenditures for air-freshener spray, autos, electric toasters, fryers, washing machines, radios, air conditioners, and other items unknown before recent decades.) Rising incomes expanded the markets for wines, bowling shoes, and underground newspapers. Changing tastes led to more capital-intensive methods of preventing birth, giving birth, destroying bodies, and interring them. Most important of the new goods markets, however, was probably that for automobiles, with their inputs (gasoline, oil, tires) and complements (roads, traffic courts, ambulances, advertising circulars). Automobiles had originally served to break the local monopolies enjoyed by railroads, assemblers of farm products, doctors, grocers, saloon keepers. But in time they became an essential complement of almost any significant American activity. How else, for example, could demonstrators be efficiently assembled at the scene of a demonstration together with policemen and TV cameras? How else could chamber music lovers, rock festival participants, or rotary club members meet economically in out-of-the-way locales?

Trade. As the home declined from its prominence as a center of production, and as incomes rose, a vast distribution network developed. Purveying silverware, salt, and wines as in colonial times, it also added such former home products as pork chops and applesauce, soap and whiskey, women's dresses and other spring tonics. A significant expansion in trade employment was needed to distribute the new products.

Services. The vast gains in service employment were generated by a hodge-podge of different, and often unrelated, forces. One was a demand shift associated with changes in the perceived role of the Deity, accompanied by mild rises in the count of nuns, ministers, and priests. Another was a supply shift associated with changes in the perceived status of domestic servants, with the increases stemming from the vast immigration flows of 1900–1913 being eventually succeeded by sharp declines in the 1960s after the civil rights movement gathered momentum. Pressures exerted through the political process brought the greatest gains—those linked to more schools, standing armies, deductible business lunches, wider access to hospitals. Finally, changing tastes and rising incomes worked to expand, almost without halt, the employment of specialists in Baez and Zimmerman, in the arts of Vince Lombardi and Andy Warhol, in the repair of Chevrolets and Frigidaires.

A further factor may be suggested, although we have remarkably little evidence of its existence. Productivity advances in the service industries were probably more sluggish than those in manufacturing, mining, and agriculture.[13] If so, a given dollar increase in service demand would generate more employment than an equal increase in the demand for factory or farm goods. Is it likely that today's lawyer, teacher, librarian, and milliner handle more "customers" than their predecessors in 1800? The increasing share of employment in services that we see in Table 6.2 probably reflects both (a) a consumer shift toward services and (b) relatively greater advances in the efficiency of commodities production, resulting in price declines and increased income available for services.

Labor-Force Trends

The course of the American labor force since 1800 is summarized rather simply in the first column of Table 6.1. Inevitably the trend largely repeats the trend of population—until recent decades. Consider the two components of the labor force: male and female. In ours, as in other male-dominated societies, it has been customary for the men to enter the labor force early in life and work until death. And from 1850 (the date of our first reasonably reliable census report on the subject) until today, something like 90 percent of the men in the prime age groups have been in the labor force year in and year out. Two forces, however, have increasingly shortened their years in the labor force. One was the advancing presence of formal education, which has kept youngsters in school year after unremitting year, delaying their entrance to the labor force. (This secular trend began with the Ordinance of 1787, when the federal government began to shower financial blessings on education. It was modified markedly after World War II, as many youngsters made work and school complementary activities.) A second force is that happy combination of affluence and legislation since 1936 which has caused the laborer to retire even earlier from the labor force—to delight, to inanity, or to distress, as the case may be.

Of the trend for women, more may be said. Working at household chores and raising children, women in the nineteenth century were not part of the market economy and hence not often members of the labor force. As Table 6.3 indicates, even as late as 1900, when the United States possessed a large and flourishing urban industry, few women with family responsibilities worked. As the nation urbanized from 1900 to 1960, the U.S. averages changed. Those for single women (plus widows and divorcees) in 1960 came to resemble those for single women (etc.) in cities in 1900. Not so for married women— whose participation rates rose to a startling degree.[14] That rise represents in

---

[13] What little evidence we have relates to more recent periods. See Victor Fuchs, "A Statistical Analysis of Productivity in Selected Service Industries in the United States, 1939–63," *Review of Income and Wealth* Series 12 (September 1966); also William Baumol and William Bowen, *The Performing Arts* (Cambridge, Mass.: M.I.T. Press, 1968), chap. 7.

[14] For a more extended discussion of causes see the chapter by Stanley Lebergott in *The Brookings Quarterly Econometric Model of the United States*, J. S. Duesenberry *et al.* (eds.) (Washington: Brookings Institution, 1965); Clarence Long, *The Labor Force Under Changing Income and Employment* (Princeton: Princeton University Press, 1958); and John D. Durand, *The Labor Force in the United States, 1890–1960* (New York: Gordon and Breach, 1968).

TABLE 6.3
Percent of women in the labor force[a]

	1900			1967
	In Cities of 50,000 and Over	In Smaller Cities and Country	United States	United States
Total	26.0	16.6	18.8	39.7
Single	46.6[b]	26.2[b]	31.3	50.7
Married	5.8	5.5	5.6	37.8
Widowed	28.7	32.6	31.5	27.0
Divorced	59.0	54.3	55.3	71.2

[a] Percent of all women in given status and area group—for example, of all single women in 1967, 50.7 percent were in the labor force.
[b] Includes women of unknown marital status.

SOURCES: U.S. Bureau of the Census, *Census of Population: 1900, Supplementary Analysis and Derivative Tables* (Washington: U.S. Government Printing Office, 1906), pp. 441, 466; U.S. Bureau of Labor Statistics, *Marital and Family Characteristics of Workers, March 1967* (Washington: U.S. Government Printing Office, 1968), Table A.

part a shift in employer preferences as they reacted to rising male wage rates by substituting less expensive female labor. It also results from a shift in supply: The tangible attractions that an extra paycheck permitted (a washing machine, TV, new furniture) drew women into the labor force. The decline in the size of the family and the displacement of the population toward urban areas were also obviously facilitative. Table 6.4 reports the resultant figure for the 1960s. It is in the same league as those for Western Europe, but considerably below those for the more tightly organized labor markets of the lower-income Iron Curtain countries.

TABLE 6.4
Percent of married women employed, 1960s

Country	Percent Employed
West Germany	28
Belgium	35
U.S. urban	36
French urban	39
Torun, Poland	61
Olomuc, Czechoslovakia	78
Kazoulik, Bulgaria	86
Pskov, U.S.S.R.	93

SOURCE: Data from Phillip Converse, "Gross Similarities and Differences in Time Allocation," Sixth International Sociology Conference, Evian, France, September 1966.

CONTROL AND ALLOCATION OF LABOR

Every society has its modes for allocating labor to the dull tasks of existence, and to the delightful ones. Perhaps most ancient are those in which family heads guide the labor of their relatives and those in which owners direct the labor of their slaves. Both were prominent in Greece and Rome, in sub-Saharan Africa, in all of Asia. Both also appeared in North America. (Tiny theocracies such as Plymouth also existed, and military encampments such as Jamestown. But they were numerically trivial.)

When the nineteenth century began, about half our labor force was busy in family enterprise—growing wheat and corn, making houses, whiskey, clothes, and other goods for the family itself. About one quarter was enslaved. (Every state but Massachusetts and Vermont had its slaves.) And about one quarter consisted of employees and independent craftsmen—blacksmiths, coopers, cigar makers.[15]

What are the broad changes by status that have occurred since 1800? There were primarily two: the ending of slavery and the decline in the role of the independent entrepreneur.

When Edward Ruffin fired on Fort Sumter, he initiated the most dramatic change of the entire period—the transformation of slaves into employees. The sharecropper status assumed by most ex-slaves meant that they began sharing the risks of boll weevils and crop failure, risks normally assumed not by employees but by entrepreneurs. What evidence we have on the ending of slavery suggests that the system in the South did not end because it was un-profitable to slaveholders. In fact a pioneering systematic study, and one of the most extensive to date, suggests a current monetary rate of return from slave-holding fully equal to that of alternative investments of equal risk.[16] And since, its calculus omits the capital gains accruing from the stock of slaves over any decade from 1789 to 1859, the private monetary gains were even greater.[17]

The transformation of slaves into employees was hardly a straightforward one, despite the assistance of the Freedman's Bureau in setting wages and conditions of employment. A significant number of female slaves withdrew from the labor force altogether, preferring to keep house rather than labor in the fields. Cotton planters reported, "The women and children have ceased to work; women seldom now work in the fields; they all ambition 'keeping house'; one third of the hands [before the war] were women who now do not work at all."[18] The proportion of nonwhite females in the labor force fell from perhaps 90 percent under slavery to 22 percent in the years after the war.[19]

---

[15] Needless to add, our measures of labor input relate to marketed labor and labor in family businesses. They do not include labor in child-rearing or housekeeping. The latter (not being within ready reach of market valuation, or any very accurate measurement in hours of input) is excluded from our current measures of employment, as its results are excluded from our measures of GNP. Table 6.1 follows this convention. (Since slave labor was bought and sold, it is included. The empirical effects of such inclusion may be trivial in some instances, however: In 1800 there were fewer than 1500 slaves in New England.)

[16] Alfred Conrad and John Meyer, *The Economics of Slavery* (Chicago: Aldine, 1964), chap. 3.

[17] This omission offsets a variety of upward biases that have been objected to in the Conrad–Meyer estimates.

[18] F. W. Loring and C. F. Atkinson, *Cotton Culture and the South* (Boston: A. Williams, 1869), pp. 14, 15, 20, 106, 109.

[19] See the estimates for 1830 and 1890 by Stanley Lebergott in *Demographic and Economic Change in Developed Countries* (New York: National Bureau of Economic Research, 1960), p. 391.

After 1800 the ratio of the entrepreneurial group to the labor force began its long decline, while the working class rose correspondingly. The latter, of course, encompasses within its broad reaches both the executives and the janitorial staffs of General Motors, dutiful museum attendants, frenetic gogo dancers, and resplendent airline pilots.

Why the long decline in the self-employed ratio? Basically the shift was due to price, and hence production-function, changes. Land tended to rise in price as population density increased and—after 1862—because the federal government ceased keeping land prices down as it had done by issuing Mexican War warrants and passing such legislation as the Graduation Act (1854) and the Homestead Act (1862). (See Chapter 4.) The rise of land prices pushed up capital requirements in agriculture. Moreover, the rising price of labor tended increasingly to bring about the substitution of machinery and land for labor, thus further increasing investment requirements for entrepreneurs. As farming (and nonfarm enterprise as well) became more capital-intensive, the ease with which employees could transform themselves into entrepreneurs declined.[20]

As a rough indication of the rise in capital costs we may make the estimates shown in Table 6.5. The young man enamored of hard labor, and ready to save for a farm, had to work over twice as long in 1960 as in 1830 to finance a typical farm. The rising real wage level that had induced increasing capital

TABLE 6.5
Farm self-employment, 1830–1960, changing capital and labor requirements

	1830	1960
Capital per farm	$600	$60,000
Average farm wage per month	$8.85	$198
Average interest rate	10%	6%
Months farm laborer had to work to service first year of capital investment	6.8	18.1

SOURCES

Capital: An 80-acre farm at the government minimum of $1.25 per acre plus $500 for 40 acres of timber, a log cabin, and so on. J. M. Peck, *A Guide for Emigrants* (1831), p. 186, gives $642 for Illinois in 1831, including 80 acres for wood and pasture as well as 80 for cultivation. Solon Robinson's figures indicate that an 80-acre farm in Indiana in 1842 plus 400 acres in timber came to $575. [Herbert Kellar (ed.), *Solon Robinson*, vol. 1 (Indianapolis: Indiana Historical Society, 1936), pp. 327, 346.] Clarence Danhof, "Farm Making Costs and the Safety Valve," *Journal of Political Economy*, vol. 49 (June 1941), estimates higher figures—but these were for larger farms. For 1960 we take the average value of land and buildings for commercial farms [U.S. Bureau of the Census *Census of Agriculture: 1959*, vol. 2 (Washington: U.S. Government Printing Office, 1959), p. 1212] and adjust it upward by data from the *Balance Sheet of Agriculture* for value of livestock, machinery and crop inventories. [U.S. Bureau of the Census, *Statistical Abstract of the United States, 1967* (Washington: U.S. Government Printing Office, 1967), p. 616].
Farm wage: Lebergott, *Manpower . . . op. cit.,* Table A-23, p. 539, and U.S. Bureau of the Census, *Census of Agriculture: 1959*, vol. 2, *op. cit.,* p. 312.
Interest rate: For Champaign, Ill. in 1835–1837, R. F. Severson *et al.*, "Mortgage Borrowing as a Frontier Developed," *Journal of Economic History*, vol. 26 (June 1966), pp. 147–168.

[20] Farmers increasingly had to resort to the capital markets, where lenders could hardly have the same optimistic view of their prospects as they did.

intensity on farms (and hence an increasing scale of farm investment) also drove down the proportion of self-employment—for it made employee status ever more attractive. The attraction of self-employment was unable to stand up against the rising entry cost on the one hand and the advancing attractions of employee status on the other.

The erosion of the farm base for the self-employed, however, did not become obvious until after 1900. In that year, as Table 6.6 reports, about 13 million persons still worked in family businesses and another 13 million worked as employees. With this one-to-one ratio between the independent and the hired worker groups, the United States could still retain the self-image of an open society. Its workers could still, not unreasonably, seek to become entrepreneurs. Such hopes, no less than the power of court injunctions and employer actions, explain why less than 4 percent of the labor force was unionized in 1900.[21]

Self-employment reached its peak—perhaps not surprisingly—in the Coolidge years, 1926–1927. From then on it declined absolutely, as it had been falling relatively since McKinley's day. Although nonfarm enterprise added 33 million employees from 1926 to 1968, less than a million additional entrepreneurs sufficed to guide their work.[22] In fact, of course, even these new entrepreneurs directed few workers. The additions came almost wholly in trade and service, where they typically supervised relatives plus a few clerks who might have come out of *The Merchant of Yonkers*, or, more fashionably, *Hello, Dolly!*

TABLE 6.6
Labor force and employment, 1900–1968 (millions)

	1900	1941	1960	1968
Civilian labor force	28.4	55.9	70.6	78.7
Self-employed and unpaid	12.7	12.8	10.9	8.1
Unpaid family workers	3.0	2.0	1.7	1.0
Self-employed	9.7	10.8	9.2	7.1
Farm	5.8	5.2	2.8	2.0
Service	1.1	1.6	2.2	—
Trade	1.3	2.3	2.4	—
Construction	.5	.5	.8	—
Manufacturing	.4	.3	.4	—
Other	.4	.9	.6	—
Employees	12.5	35.5	53.4	—
Domestic service	1.8	2.1	2.5	1.9
Unemployed	1.4	5.6	3.9	2.8
Armed forces	.1	1.6	2.5	3.5

SOURCES

1900–1960: Lebergott, *Manpower ....*, op. cit., Tables A-3, A-4, A-7; pp. 512, 513, 516.
1968: Data for persons over age 16 from *Manpower Report of the President* (January 1969), *Supplement*, pp. 1, 12.

[21] H. G. Lewis, *Unionism and Relative Wages in the United States* (Chicago: University of Chicago Press, 1963), p. 244.
[22] 1900: Lebergott, *Manpower . . . .*, op. cit., p. 513. 1968: *Manpower Report of the President* (January 1969), *Supplement*, pp. 1, 12.

The final fading of independent entrepreneurship synchronized with two events : the deadly accumulation of unemployment in the 1930s, and the swift rise in the organized proportion of the labor force, from 8 percent in the beginning of the Roosevelt–Truman era (1932) to 26 percent at its end (in 1952). By 1967, as a result of declines in farm employment, the total self-employed group had dwindled to about 12 percent, few of whom were employers.[23] (That percentage may not even exceed the corresponding rate for the Union of Soviet Socialist Republics.) Most of the 71-million-member labor force now took their orders from other employees—corporate officers, foremen, and others. These all possessed power, but hardly the power (nor the perspective) of the classic independent entrepreneur. The "employing class" was on its way to extinction.

Supervision of Labor

Increases in the size of the employee class forced other changes. When the self-employed had been relatively numerous, most employees were directly supervised by them. With the rise of the corporation, other methods of directing labor became necessary.

One ancient method which was widely used was self-direction via piece rates. Iowa lead miners were paid by the pound, Virginia coal miners by the bushel. Those who fished for cod off Massachuetts or oysters off Maryland were also paid on a piece rate. The greater the value of the catch, the larger their return. Early iron workers were paid per bushel of charcoal made and per ton of pig iron poured. And the fur trappers, of course, received so much per skin. Piece rates enabled the entrepreneur to share his risk with the worker : The fewer whales sighted, the less the wages to pay, and the end of a coal vein brought a corresponding drop in the wage bill.

We have little basis for judging the extent to which manufacturing relied on piece rates before the end of the nineteenth century. True, the first textile-mill spinners and weavers were paid by the piece, sometimes working at home, sometimes on company premises. Early iron factories paid puddlers by the ton, hat factories paid hatters by the hat, and so on. But by the 1840s domestic manufacturing and the putting-out system had fairly well ended ; manufacturers appear to have ceased relying primarily on such techniques for creating industrial discipline.

Our first reliable data are for 1890. Table 6.7 compares them with data for 1958. For the great initiatory industries of the Industrial Revolution—cotton textiles and iron—the 1890 data report only relatively tiny proportions working at piece rates. Similarly small ratios appear for food, lumber, stone, clay, and glass. Neither the age of an industry nor its rate of technological advance appears to explain which industries extended the use of incentive schemes most swiftly over the next half-century. The proportion for all factories rose from 18 to 27 percent, with increases for nine of the ten industries which were

[23] U.S. Bureau of Labor Statistics, *Labor Force and Employment in 1965*, Special Labor Force Report no. 69 (Washington : U.S. Government Printing Office, 1965), Table C-4.

TABLE 6.7
Percentage of factory workers on piece work (1890) or incentive pay (1958)

	1890	1958
All manufacturing	17.9	27.0
Tobacco	64.1	30.9
Furniture	54.2	25.0
Apparel	51.3	59.3
Leather	44.0	63.2
Paper boxes[a]	45.3	20.0
Printing	14.6	3.8
Textiles	13.4	39.7
Food	10.4	11.5
Chemicals	5.6	8.8
Lumber	4.1	6.3
Instruments	45.2	29.2
Toys, sporting goods[a]	24.5	24.0
Nonelectrical machinery	21.2	25.9
Fabricated metals	18.6	23.1
Electrical machinery	15.6	40.3
Primary metals	10.1	46.4
Jewelry, silverware[a]	10.0	35.0
Transport equipment	4.6	10.4
Stone, clay, and glass	8.4	25.1

[a] The U.S. Bureau of Labor Statistics coverage is too limited to permit showing two-digit totals for paper or miscellaneous.

SOURCES

1890: Computed from data in U.S. Bureau of the Census, *Census of Population: 1890, Manufactures* (Washington: U.S. Government Printing Office, 1895), Part 1, Table 4.

1958: L. E. Lewis, "Extent of Incentive Pay in Manufacturing," *Monthly Labor Review*, vol. 83 (May 1960), p. 461.

below average in 1890. A corresponding regression to the mean occurred for some industries which in 1890 were most startlingly above average—tobacco, furniture, paper boxes. But many above-average industries did not fall. The surest characterizations of the general trends would appear to be these: First, a wider reliance on incentive schemes as a mechanical method of cost control by industries that had not tested them much before 1890; and second, generous and continued use of such schemes by industries noted for sluggish productivity advances and for their persistent demands for tariff protection (leather, apparel, knitting, steel, glass).

An ancient and somewhat fatuous adage appears in antebellum discussions on cotton farming: "The footsteps of the master fertilize the furrows." In small factories, as well as on farms, it was customary for the owner–entrepreneur to be conspicuously present, closely supervising his employees. But as firms increased in size, such control of effort became increasingly unsatisfactory. The entrepreneur's comparative advantage now lay in general coordination: He could no longer afford to concentrate on supervision. The hired supervisor first appeared, then became increasingly characteristic, and finally was all but ubiquitous (Table 6.8). The mild rise in the foreman ratio from 1910 to 1940 must be put alongside the concurrent mild decline of self-employment in

TABLE 6.8
Employment status of workers in manufacturing, 1910, 1940, and 1960 (thousands)

Status	1910	1940	1960
(a) Self-employed	504.00	324.00	383.00
(b) Foremen	175.00	293.00	742.00
(c) Employees	7,280.00	10,601.00	17,530.00
(d) Foremen per 100 employees	2.40	2.76	4.23

SOURCES

Row (a): Lebergott, *Manpower . . . , op. cit.,* Table A-7.

Rows (b)–(d)
  Employees
    1910: Gladys Palmer and Ann Ratner, *Industrial and Occupational Trends in National Employment* (Philadelphia: University of Pennsylvania Press, 1949), app. III. These data are based on the population census, and hence comparable with the other data shown here.
  Foremen, Employees
    1910: U.S. Bureau of the Census, *Census of Occupations: 1910* (Washington: U.S. Government Printing Office, 1912), p. 91.
    1940: U.S. Bureau of the Census, *Census of Occupation Characteristics: 1940* (Washington: U.S. Government Printing Office, 1942–1943), Table 9.
    1960: U.S. Bureau of the Census, *Census of Occupation by Industry: 1960* (Washington: U.S. Government Printing Office, 1964), pp. 17, 19.

manufacturing. The dramatic 1940–1960 increase in the ratio is another matter. Presumably spiraling wage rates accounted for most of that rise. Perhaps spreading unionization in the 1940s accounted for the rest. Increases in the number of foremen mark the attempt to tighten up on labor costs, as does the growth of in-plant courses on foremanship, foremen's institutes, and other such developments.

Beyond self-pacing (via incentive schemes) and human pacing (via foremen) was labor control by machine. As flour poured out of the bolting chest in Oliver Evans' first mill, the miller had to see to its sacking. And the melt from the more primitive blast furnaces required the founder to pour it out into sows and pigs to cool. But machine pacing became far more widespread. Trolleys conveyor belts, and machine lines began to link workers in every kind of factory. When animal carcasses were shoved along the first packing-plant conveyor line (in the 1850s), and when the first Fords came racketing down the assembly lines (in 1913), workers had to adjust to the speed of the line— unless, in Chaplinesque fashion, they were prepared to halt the entire factory. As the years passed assembly-line techniques and continuous processing methods for controlling payrolls were adopted ever more widely. That only 3 percent of cigarette workers and only 13 percent of motor-vehicle workers worked under incentive schemes by 1958 emphasizes how mechanical methods of controlling labor cost had taken over from controls by foremen and by piece rate.

Allocation of Labor: Macro Aspects

Every person in the national labor supply could be evaluated by every employer in the economy for every job to be filled—if only information were complete and costless, and resources were transferable without cost. Most human societies have precluded the development of any such unmitigated complexity. Ancient systems of caste and inheritance have usually provided fairly full information to bound the area of competition—for example, this person comes from caste X, and caste X works only on leather.

The open, boisterous society that characterized the United States during its formative first century, however, adopted no such system. How could it? People arrived daily from different societies with differing status rules. Every "species of trade, commerce, and profession and manufacture is equally open to all without requiring any regular apprenticeship, admission or license," wrote Albert Gallatin, Secretary of the Treasury in the 1820s. "Every man who finds business unprofitable, or employment scarce may change his residence until he finds himself suited, without incurring the risk of being sent back to his parish, as would be the case in England" wrote Henry Carey in the 1830s.[24]

Moreover, the new arrivals were likely to have been the more deviant, obstreperous members of whatever system it was they left. Hence uniform U.S. caste and class regulations were not feasible. The labor market did develop some institutions for guaranteeing labor quality. The indenture system sought to provide assurances as effective as those in finance (in which banks interposed their name by way of guaranteeing the quality of commercial paper). But it had largely died out by the 1820s: Enforcing service against men who fled to the western wilderness was an expensively hopeless task. The padrone system for Italian migrants, and the Tongs for the Chinese, did provide some such certification later on. But these schemes were rare, and their absence for the main Irish and German migrant streams indicates how unimportant they were in the total allocation process. Moreover, even these infrequent contract-labor schemes were outlawed by Congress in the Contract Labor Act of 1882.[25]

Even the internationally common modes of restricting entry to the professions had difficulty establishing themselves in America. There were requirements, quite casual, that lawyers train in law offices; but many a new state passed legislation during the 1840s to permit any person to serve as a lawyer.

Two consequences followed from the failure to structure the labor market by occupational caste rules. One was that labor moved relatively promptly to those activities in which it could command the highest returns. Higher rates offered by a new firm, a new industry, would freely beckon labor away from older activities. Operatives in industries with rising employment and wage rates could not prevent entry. The honest American workman could riot against foreign immigrants. He could form Know-nothing parties led by men as bearded and romantic as Frémont. But neither course did much to restrict entry. At most, congressional representatives from the East could slow down the throwing open of western lands at lower and lower prices. But as wages

---

[24] Henry Carey, *Essay on the Rate of Wages* (Philadelphia: Carey, Lea and Blanchard, 1835), pp. 130, 132.
[25] M. W. Jernegan, *Laboring and Dependent Classes in Colonial America* (New York: Ungar, 1931); and Charlotte Erickson, *American Industry and the European Immigrant 1860–1885* (Cambridge, Mass.: Harvard University Press, 1957), discuss attempts to import indentured and contract labor. As a continuing supplier of labor, the contractor had to supply both the specified quantity and minimal quality of labor in order to get repeat orders and a useful reputation.

in the East tended to rise, the real price of western land dropped—and so did the possibility of escape to the West. Such reallocation brought ever more effective utilization of labor.[26] That increasingly effective utilization reports its presence in the data on productivity, output per manhour, and real wages.

Withdrawing workers from older areas and industries forced corresponding and important impacts on the sectors which they left. Thus the growth of the factory system in New England shifted the potential workers from New England's major activity: Operatives "were taken chiefly from the agricultural class, and when they were withdrawn wages rose."[27] When workers left New England for the Midwest in the 1830s, as when they left the Midwest for the Mountain states in the 1870s, similar pressure on wages tended to develop.

Employers inevitably fought such cost pressures. Their attempts took three forms. The first was to support open immigration. A persistent flow of workers with lower wage horizons than those of American workers helped keep down wages in the East. But results were not guaranteed. The immigrants themselves joined the westward migration. And although employers were better off than they would have been without foreign immigration, they still confronted rising wage rates and labor costs. The second way in which employers attempted to fight cost pressures was to recruit foreign workers for particular jobs. In so doing they inevitably fell afoul of the alternative opportunities for new Americans. Frequently their investment in hiring and transport costs went up in smoke. "Don't let them stay" in the city long, "as the railroad construction may get hold of them" wrote a Missouri entrepreneur to an agent who was importing German hands for his works.[28] And an historian records the typical experience of a company importing emigrants to work in the Chicopee and the Slater mills of Massachusetts: "A very large proportion" of the migrants "left for higher wages" in other firms.[29] The inability of employers in the older firms and areas to stop this constant pressure of rising costs meant that to survive as producers they had to improve their productivity. This was their third alternative.[30] For many, the passage of time and the experience of producing more and more goods made possible just such improvements. For others, we may presume that the threat of failure, or even diminished market share, stimulated them to greater efforts. (The classic, if absurd, story is that of Henry Ford improving not merely the partial productivity of labor but that of his firm by removing desks and chairs so that the headquarters staff had to be cut.) In some cases firms and farms simply went out of business. These associated responses to cost pressures help explain the spectacular American experience with productivity advance.

---

[26] A lengthy, detailed, and irrelevant literature discusses how many native workmen went west. But, except to nativists, the migration of both recent immigrants and natives affected wage rates. After all, the threat of leaving can affect an employer's behavior as well as a lover's.

[27] Representative Hudson of Massachusetts, *Congressional Globe* (1842), p. 60.

[28] James Norris, *Frontier Iron* (Madison, Wis.: Society Press, 1964), p. 57.

[29] Erickson, *op. cit.*, p. 46.

[30] The creation of monopolies (e.g., by product differentiation) or cartels was a less feasible alternative.

PRODUCTIVITY AND REAL INCOME TRENDS

The ebullient, persistent advance in output per worker decade after passing decade has been a loud testimonial to one achievement of the American economy. Of the existence of that advance there is little question (cf. Chapter 2). Tables 6.9 and 6.10 report massive declines in major industries and point to impressive cuts of employment requirements in every decade for which we have data.

But what were the causes of this advance? And what were its results in real income: Did they generate income rises or were they simply distributed away in the purchase of additional inputs (most probably capital)? Let us consider first some causes.

The x Factor

Perhaps the first disturbing, fascinating, statistically based report was that in which Abramovitz noted: (a) that man-hours (per capita) hardly changed from the decade of the 1870s to 1944–1953 and (b) that a combined index of

TABLE 6.9
Employment requirements per unit of output (index, 1889 = 100)

Year	Total Output[a] (1)	Iron Ore (2)	Copper (3)	Petro-leum (4)	Bitumin-ous Coal (5)	Cotton Textiles (6)	Rail-roads (7)
1859	—	131	752	—	—	—	—
1860	153	—	—	—	102	148	218.0
1869	—	189	427	—	—	—	—
1870	131	—	—	—	125	173	167.0
1879	—	168	267	—	—	—	—
1880	102	—	—	189	148	118	132.0
1889	—	100	100	100	—	—	—
1890	100	—	—	—	100	100	100.0
1899	—	—	—	61	—	85	—
1900	89	—	—	—	83	—	75.0
1902	—	55	96	—	—	—	—
1904	—	—	—	82	—	86	—
1909	—	46	111	38	—	83	74.0
1910	82	—	—	—	77	—	—
1914	—	—	—	41	—	77	—
1918	—	—	—	—	61	—	—
1919	—	—	—	—	—	—	80.7

[a] Employment divided by GNP.

SOURCES

Column (1): GNP data from unpublished estimates of Robert E. Gallman. Employment trend estimated as labor-force trend, unemployment changes for these years being relatively slight. Labor-force data from Lebergott, Manpower... op. cit., p. 510. GNP data are for 1859, 1869, and so on, while employment is for 1860, 1870, and so on.

Columns (2)–(5), (7): Computed from estimates of Herfindahl, Williamson, Eliasberg, Fishlow in Output, Employment, and Productivity in the United States After 1800, Dorothy S. Brady (ed.), Studies in Income and Wealth, vol. 30 (New York: National Bureau of Economic Research, 1966), pp. 308, 378, 428, 626.

Column (6): T. Y. Shen, "Job Analysis and Historical Productivities in the American Cotton Textile Industry: A Study in Methodology," Review of Economics and Statistics, vol. 40 (May 1958), p. 156.

TABLE 6.10
Farm productivity trends, 1800–1960

	Man-hours per				
	100 bu.	100 bu.	1 bale	cwt.	cwt.
Period	Wheat	Corn	Cotton	Hogs	Turkeys
1800	373	344	601	—	—
1840	233	276	439	—	—
1880	152	180	304	—	—
1900	108	147	283	—	—
1910–1914	106	135	276	3.6	31.4
1930–1934	70	123	252	3.2	26.7
1960–1963	12	11	49	2.2	3.0

SOURCES: U.S. Department of Agriculture, *Labor Used to Produce Field Crops*, Statistical Bulletin 346 (Washington: U.S. Government Printing Office, 1964), Tables 1 and 2; and U.S. Department of Agriculture, *Labor Used to Produce Livestock*, Statistical Bulletin 336 (Washington: U.S. Government Printing Office, 1963), Table 1.

man-hours and capital inputs rose by a trivial 14 percent—while output soared 248 percent. Productivity, in other words, accounted for virtually the entire growth in output per head. But since productivity is merely a name to cover the statistical measure of the relationship between inputs and outputs, this striking result "may be taken to be some sort of measure of our ignorance about the causes of economic growth in the United States."[31]

A later study by Denison drove toward a similar conclusion. He attempted to dissect the 2.89 percent annual rate of gain in aggregate real output over the period 1909–1957 (that portion of the longer time span for which our data are most reliable). And he found that 1.67 percent, or over half the growth, was attributable to productivity, to "the residual," to *x*, to "the measure of our ignorance." But in a fascinating endeavor he then went on to speculate as to what might have contributed to *x*, the unknown. His judgments are shown in Table 6.11. The dominance of productivity differences was accentuated when Denison made an even more immense, and pioneering, study of European growth rates. For he found that income per person in northwest Europe in 1960 averaged only 41 percent of that in the United States—and he attributed over four fifths of that income gap to *x* differences.[32]

Causes of Productivity Advance

The significant contribution made by education is inferred largely from the higher rate of wages paid to more highly educated persons. Because of the complicated interrelationship between formal education on the one hand and,

[31] Moses Abramovitz, *Resource and Output Trends in the United States Since 1870* (New York: National Bureau of Economic Research, 1956), pp. 8, 11.
[32] Edward Denison, *Why Growth Rates Differ* (Washington: Brookings Institution, 1967), p. 332. Some 29.7 points are attributed to "output per unit of input," but one must also add to this his items for (a) efficiency from shorter hours, and (b) education, to arrive at the usual measure of x.

TABLE 6.11
Sources of real income growth in two periods (percent)

	1909–1929	1929–1957
Real national income	100	100
Increase in land, labor, capital	57	31
Increase in x	43	69
In education	12	23
In effectiveness of work because of shorter hours	8	11
In economies of scale	10	11
In advance of knowledge and other x items	13	24

SOURCE: Data computed and adapted from Edward Denison, *Sources of Economic Growth in the United States and the Alternatives Before Us* (New York: Committee for Economic Development, 1962), pp. 148, 266.

on the other, "native" ability, family background, social position, contacts, and richness of informal learning experience, it is not yet clear that it is formal education per se that contributes so magnificently to economic growth. But there is no question of the richness and acuteness of the literature that emphasizes the critical role of investment in human capital (cf. Chapter 5). If we look to the contribution of education over time in this country, we must at least distinguish between the period up to, say, the 1890s, when the high-school movement expanded, and the period thereafter. As late as 1870, the average child raised in the North attended school less than three months out of a year.[33] Adult immigrants to the United States could be assumed to have had only a trivial amount of schooling. And public schools hardly existed in the South until after the Civil War. Hence, during the burgeoning period of economic advance up to the Civil War, the usual adult probably averaged less than two months of schooling over six to eight years. Albert Fishlow has costed the expenditures for education in the United States. He found that direct expenditures for schools, teachers, and so on took about 1 percent of our GNP (or less) before the Civil War. The percent did not exceed that for the class-restricted education system of Great Britain before the Conservative party reforms of the 1870s.[34] Reckoning in the further costs in wages that students did *not* earn because they were in school would raise that ratio to not quite 2 percent.[35]

The median years of schooling ultimately completed by persons born since 1890 has been estimated as follows by Beverly Duncan:[36]

[33] Cf. the comments by Stanley Lebergott in *Output, Employment, and Productivity in the United States After 1800*, Dorothy S. Brady (ed.), Studies in Income and Wealth, vol. 30 (New York: National Bureau of Economic Research 1966), p. 126.
[34] Albert Fishlow, "Levels of Nineteenth-Century American Investment in Education," *Journal of Economic History*, vol. 26 (December 1966), pp. 430, 432. [See also Lewis Solmon, "Capital Formation by Expenditures on Formal Education, 1880 and 1890," *Journal of Economic History*, vol. 29 (March 1969), p. 167.]
[35] Fishlow, *op. cit.*, p. 230.
[36] Beverly Duncan, "Trends in Output and Distribution of Schooling," in *Indicators of Social Change*, Eleanor Sheldon and Wilbert Moore (eds.) (New York: Russell Sage, 1968), p. 611.

Denison's data show that the proportion of growth attributable to education almost doubled between 1909–1929 and 1929–1957. The data below on

Year of Birth	Median Schooling (years)
1890	7.0
1900	7.9
1910	9.7
1920	10.1
1930	11.5
1940	11.7
1950	12.9

the years of schooling to which adults had been exposed show that the rise was from grade-school completion for the typical labor-force member in 1909–1929 to high-school completion in the later period. Does this finding imply that each year of education given to children of the Great Depression contributed more powerfully to economic growth than each year given their forebears? (The marginal contribution to economic growth might still be greater from those years when reading, writing, and simple ciphering were learned than from those in which, between lassitude and rebellion, students read *Evangeline, Macbeth,* or *The Scarlet Letter.*)[37]

What of those other forces that brought productivity advances? Central to them was a society with an unusual zest for adopting new methods of production. That willingness came out of the open qualities of American society —which, of course reinforced them. Immigrants flooding in from nations around the world brought an immense conflict of production ideas and alternatives. And since no established American system had been reinforced over the centuries, many of these alternatives were considered and tested. "The mechanics, artisans and laborers of this country are remarkable for a disposition to learn," wrote Charles Ingersoll in 1823. "A mechanic in Europe is apt to consider it almost irreverent . . . to suppose that anything can be done better than as he was taught . . . by his father or master." Hence Americans are not afflicted by that "habitual repugnance to improvement so common to all mankind, especially the least informed classes."[38]

Had the barriers to entry in the various occupations and industries been as tough and inelastic as they were in various European and Asian countries, the immigrants would have been blocked from intemperately trying out new techniques of production. As it was, established customs, guilds, and municipal regulations were lacking. New production techniques were attempted widely and had their chance to prove themselves. Some of these techniques involved different methods of organizing labor. Systematic management techniques may not have developed until the end of the nineteenth century, when Frederick

[37] Conceivably Denison overestimates the contribution of schooling in this period. [See David Schwartzman, "The Contribution of Education to the Quality of Labor, 1929–1963," *American Economic Review,* vol. 58 (June 1968).] If so the role of *x* ingredients, already huge, becomes greater still.
[38] Robert E. Spiller, *The American Literary Revolution, 1783–1837* (New York: New York University Press, 1967), p. 255.

Taylor developed "the science of shoveling," and the "laws" that determined how a laborer carries a pig of cast iron most efficiently from one place to another.[39] But George Washington's instructions for his plantation overseers, and early farm journals full of reports on crop-rotation schemes, show that the history of efforts to utilize labor efficiently in the firm was a long one. Beyond the techniques embodied in better management and in skills taught to workers, were those embedded in new machinery per se. American history is, of course, replete with examples, from the improved plow developed by Thomas Jefferson and the mechanized flour mill created by Oliver Evans before the Constitution was even adopted, to the electronic amplifiers essential to the well-being of the young in later decades.

Changes in Labor Requirements

The effect of these technical advances on the requirements for labor can be documented for some critical periods. For the major transition from hand to machine methods in manufacturing, an enormous study made by the Commissioner of Labor in 1898 enables us to compute a striking pair of figures (Table 6.12). Of every 100 workers required by the older hand methods, 82 became superfluous when the machines came. Of course the "hand methods" in this survey often required tools, and even some primitive machines, while the "machine methods" of 1900 were hardly the last word in technology. Nonetheless, the advance was so staggering as to cast aside virtually all of the older types of organization.

The machine technology referred to above stood for "best practice" about 1900. But best-practice technology was initially adopted by only a handful of firms. Older equipment (and older buildings suited only to the older equipment) still continued profitably competing with the newer.[40] Even when that was impossible, entrepreneurs were often reluctant, or unable, to adopt new technologies. The long process of capital wastage takes time. So does the reluctant withdrawal of entrepreneurs from positions that they no longer grace. Hence the actual output per worker does not advance as rapidly as a new technology permits.

TABLE 6.12
Man-hours required per unit of output in manufacturing

Hand methods	100
Machine methods	18

SOURCES: Ratios of hand- to machine-labor hours computed for several hundred factory products from U.S. Commissioner of Labor, *Thirteenth Annual Report, 1898*, vol. 1 (Washington: U.S. Government Printing Office, 1899), pp. 24–76, units 28–653. The ratios were weighted together using relevant data on value added by industry as given in U.S. Bureau of the Census, *Census of Population: 1870, The Statistics of Wealth and Industry* (Washington, U.S. Government Printing Office, 1872), pp. 339–405.

[39] Frederick W. Taylor, *The Principles of Scientific Management* (New York: Norton, 1916), pp. 41, 65.
[40] This is possible because a capital loss in the value of old equipment occurs when the better comes on the market. Once this is written down, however, the equipment may then be competitive and warrant further use. The relevant considerations are reviewed in the fine study by W. E. G. Salter, *Productivity and Technical Change* (New York: Cambridge University Press, 1960), chaps. 4 and 5.

If we surmise that the hand–machine transition took place between the end of the Civil War and the turn of the century, we can contrast the actual decline in labor requirements with the potential decline noted above. The actual 1870–1900 decline in workers required per man-hour was 31 percent[41] —compared with a potential decline of 82 percent had the hand–machine transition been made wholly in this period. Since we cannot date when hand methods were replaced by machines, the comparison is hardly precise; nor do machine methods used in the late 1890s necessarily define the ones potentially available in 1870. But the comparison probably does indicate that the transition from hand to machine labor took considerably longer than the availability of a new technology would indicate.

For the more recent period, we can say something more about the contribution of various factors to the overall decline in manpower requirements. The condition of such a decline required, of course, some substitution of capital (chiefly in the form of plant and equipment). And as one would expect, productivity advances were also taking place in the output of plant and equipment, with significant reductions in their (relative) price. A major study by David and Van De Klundert has concluded that for the private economy as a whole the "efficiency of labor increased by roughly 54 percent more than the efficiency of capital" between 1900 and 1960.[42] The substitution of capital for labor that these efficiency advances encouraged was marked. It was also, judged by the changing aspect of factories, substantial. Morishima and Saito report a 1.1 percent annual rate of change in the capital/labor ratio, which they attribute to the causes shown in Table 6.13.

The 1.1 percent rate of change over the half-century is the same in the two subperiods. Its components are not. The cost of capital rose significantly relative to that of labor in the first period, and reversed in the second; as a result it had little net effect over the half-century. According to these results,

TABLE 6.13
Annual percent change in capital/labor ratio

| Period | Total Effect | From Inventions | | From Farm–Nonfarm Shift | Price Effect |
		Induced	Autonomous		
1902–1955	1.1	−.2	−.5	1.6	.2
1902–1929	1.1	.1	−.5	2.6	−1.1
1929–1955	1.1	−.6	−.6	.3	2.0

SOURCES: Michio Morishima and Mitsho Saito, "An Economic Test of Sir John Hick's Theory of Biased Induced Inventions," in Value, Capital and Growth, J. R. Wolfe (ed.) (Chicago: Aldine, 1968), p. 439. See also Murray Brown, On the Theory and Measurement of Technological Change (New York: Cambridge University Press, 1966), p. 158. Brown analyzes only the nonfarm economy, and as a result avoids the serious conceptual problems involved in vivisecting the entrepreneur between his capital and labor contributions.

[41] Estimate of John Kendrick from U.S. Bureau of the Census, Long-Term Economic Growth, 1860–1965 (Washington: U.S. Government Printing Office, 1966), p. 190.
[42] Paul David and T. Van De Klundert, " Biased Efficiency Growth and Capital-Labor Substitution in the U.S., 1899–1960," American Economic Review, vol. 55 (June 1965), p. 381.

therefore, the major factor in cutting labor intensity was the shift away from farming, with the 1902–1929 shift being largely responsible. (Since the massive advances in farm productivity took place after the 1930s, this finding of a trivial 1929–1955 contribution is somewhat puzzling, albeit not actually inconsistent.) The data suggest a steady contribution of autonomous inventions (made and adopted under general impulses to do better) making for capital intensity as much in the early as the later period. But those inventions induced by the changing relative prices of capital and labor were another matter. For these were most potent in the governmental-stimulated, social security-underpinned, union-growth, nonimmigration period after 1929. (Those various adjectives, intended partly to suggest causes, are primarily to caution against any single explanation of why labor-saving inventions were adopted. Relative price changes in turn reflected a variety of major forces.)

The most meaningful general view of the results of American productivity advance appears in the data on real GNP, and hence in the per capita figures appearing in Chapter 2. However, Tables 6.14 and 6.15 show the joint contribution of fuller employment, lower prices, and rising money wages as they affected a major component of the American labor force—namely, nonfarm workers.[43]

These estimates report no real income advance from 1860 to the mid-1880s, and slow gains to World War I. Somewhat more marked rates of advance appear during the 1920s, all of them partially neutralized by the prolonged misery of the 1930s. It is the performance during and since World War II that really stands out, for it is spectacular by any prior standard. Gains made during this mere 20-year period proved to be greater (in both dollar and percentage terms) than those made in prior periods of half a century or more (Table 6.15). It is hard to doubt that a major contributor has been the pressure on capacity created by government demands for war production. The failure of the savings rate to increase, particularly during postwar periods of price stability, suggests that the results of real wage increases were avidly taken in the form of ever more goods and services. Fortunately it is not within the province of economics to decide whether corollary advances in happiness followed.

GEOGRAPHIC REDISTRIBUTION OF LABOR

The most explosive, divisive issue ever to appear in American politics concerned the allocation of labor. For it was explicitly over the right to move its slaves to new territories and states that the South broke up the Union. (One may choose to view that right as a mere proxy for political control of the national legislature. But if so, what was the goal of such control?) Addressing the U.S. Senate in January 1861, that distinguished southern leader, Robert Toombs, listed "my own demands." His first demand was "that the people of the United States shall have an equal right to emigrate and settle in the present or any future acquired territory with whatever property they possess, including

---

[43] Of course, the problems of valuing the major items of income in kind for farm workers—food and housing—do not arise if we restrict our attention to this significant group. Note, however, that the trend in overall GNP per person in the labor force will be affected by the changing farm–nonfarm employment mix.

TABLE 6.14
Earnings of nonfarm employees, 1860–1900

| Year | Daily Earnings | Annual Earnings[a] | | Consumer Price Index (1914 = 100) |
		Money	Real (1914 dollars)	
1860	$1.09	$363	$457	79.5
1861	1.11	370	439	84.3
1862	1.15	383	398	96.2
1863	1.38	459	382	120.1
1864	1.52	506	421	150.3
1865	1.54	512	328	155.9
1866	1.47	489	322	151.9
1867	1.44	479	338	141.6
1868	1.50	499	367	136.0
1869	1.49	496	380	130.4
1870	1.47	489	375	124.9
1871	1.45	482	386	116.9
1872	1.46	486	416	116.9
1873	1.40	466	407	114.5
1874	1.32	439	403	109.0
1875	1.27	423	403	105.0
1876	1.21	403	393	102.6
1877	1.17	389	388	100.2
1878	1.14	379	397	95.4
1879	1.12	373	391	95.4
1880	1.16	386	395	97.8
1881	—	409	415	98.6
1882	—	428	431	99.4
1883	—	438	459	95.4
1884	—	441	478	92.3
1885	—	446	492	90.7
1886	—	453	499	90.7
1887	—	462	509	90.7
1888	—	466	505	92.3
1889	—	471	510	92.3
1890	—	475	519	91.5
1891	—	480	525	91.5
1892	—	482	527	91.5
1893	—	458	505	90.7
1894	—	420	484	86.7
1895	—	438	520	84.3
1896	—	439	521	84.3
1897	—	442	529	83.5
1898	—	440	527	83.5
1899	—	470	563	83.5
1900	—	483	573	84.3

[a] Full-time equivalent; does not allow for unemployment.

SOURCE: Lebergott, *Manpower ..., op cit.*, pp. 524–528.

TABLE 6.15

Nonfarm employees, annual earnings, 1900–1960[a]

	Money Earnings				Real Earnings (1914 dollars)	
Year	After Deduction for Unemployment	When Employed	Income Loss from Unemployment	Consumer Price Index (1914 = 100)	After Deduction for Unemployment	When Employed
1900	$ 441	$ 483	$ 42	84.3	$ 523	$ 573
1901	466	497	31	85.4	546	582
1902	503	528	25	86.3	583	612
1903	506	534	28	88.0	575	607
1904	493	538	45	88.8	555	606
1905	515	550	35	88.5	582	621
1906	557	566	12	90.2	618	627
1907	575	592	23	93.8	613	631
1908	499	577	75	91.5	545	631
1909	551	600	38	91.3	604	657
1910	576	634	58	94.7	608	669
1911	583	644	67	95.2	612	676
1912	602	657	47	97.2	619	676
1913	642	687	45	98.9	649	695
1914	613	696	65	100.0	613	696
1915	597	692	93	101.1	591	684
1916	706	760	59	108.7	649	699
1917	805	866	76	127.7	631	678
1918	1041	1063	25	150.0	694	709
1919	1174	1215	26	172.5	681	704
1920	1343	1426	104	199.7	672	714
1921	1105	1330	230	178.1	620	747
1922	1148	1289	129	166.9	688	772
1923	1313	1376	44	169.7	774	811
1924	1284	1396	98	170.3	754	820
1925	1336	1420	61	174.8	764	812
1926	1411	1452	33	176.2	801	824
1927	1399	1487	64	172.8	810	861
1928	1394	1490	80	170.9	816	872
1929	1462	1534	74	170.9	855	898
1930	1294	1494	194	166.4	778	898
1931	1068	1406	328	151.5	705	928
1932	807	1244	423	136.1	593	914
1933	722	1136	401	128.8	561	882
1934	789	1146	351	133.3	592	860
1935	851	1195	339	136.7	623	874
1936	932	1226	293	138.1	675	888
1937	1072	1341	268	143.1	749	937
1938	956	1303	357	140.6	680	927
1939	1029	1346	320	138.4	743	973
1940	1113	1392	280	139.5	798	998
1941	1332	1561	212	146.5	909	1066
1942	1740	1858	119	162.5	1071	1143
1943	2125	2181	57	172.5	1232	1264
1944	2323	2360	38	175.3	1325	1346
1945	2364	2424	61	179.3	1318	1352
1946	2394	2529	134	194.4	1231	1301
1947	2532	2657	125	222.7	1137	1193
1948	2867	2999	132	239.5	1197	1252
1949	2855	3075	214	237.2	1204	1296
1950	3047	3255	208	239.5	1272	1359
1951	3392	3526	134	258.5	1312	1364
1952	3607	3732	123	264.4	1364	1411
1953	3804	3927	122	266.7	1426	1472
1954	3781	4033	250	267.5	1413	1508
1955	4106	4224	211	266.9	1538	1583
1956	4236	4445	209	270.9	1564	1641
1957	4410	4657	247	280.3	1574	1663
1958	4413	4818	405	287.9	1533	1673
1959	4728	5069	341	290.5	1626	1748
1960	4908	5260	352	294.9	1665	1785

[a] Excludes armed forces.

SOURCE: Lebergott, *Manpower ..., op. cit.,* p. 524.

slaves." And he concluded: The North sought "to outlaw $4,000,000,000 of property of our people in the Territories of the United States. Is not that a cause of war?"[44] If one considers the sequence of climactic compromises—1820, 1850, and the rejected offers of 1861—as well as the endeavors to include Texas in the Union, one returns again to the critical importance slave owners attached to their freedom to deploy labor for maximum return.

Labor reallocation did not always awaken such a sense of outrage and urgency. But reallocation was a critical process from the onset of American history. For exploration in a new land inevitably turned up even better sites for commercial endeavor. (Indeed Henry Carey thought he had discovered a fallacy in the Ricardian rent doctrine—basing his idea on the evident fact that the worst land in the United States was cultivated first and the best land, in the central and western states, was cultivated only later on.) Western New York in the 1820s offered richer land than did Connecticut. Illinois in the 1840s offered richer land than New York did. And California in the 1880s superseded Illinois. The iron deposits first worked in New Jersey and Connecticut proved serviceable in the Revolutionary War. But in the 1830s, they could not remotely compete with those later discovered in Pennsylvania. Nor, in turn, could those contest with the Marquette Range discoveries of the 1850s. Each discovery, in sum, tended to shift the locus of demand for labor. In turn, as population accumulated in these new areas, they generated demands for more specialized talents. In Mark Twain's celebrated description of civilization, first came the jail and the liquor dispenser—and later on the church. And, one may add, the market for still other specialized skills. Cincinnati, which had no inhabitants in 1820, was a commercial mart by 1840, supplying work for half a dozen portrait painters.

In a relatively land-rich country—as the United States surely was into the twentieth century—the substitution of better land for expensive labor may have dominated the substitution of machinery for labor. Hence the forces that we now associate with the substitution of machinery for labor were, in the nineteenth century, linked with the shift to newer, better lands.

Producer incentives were expressed in the most direct fashion. "Dr Sir," began one 1832 letter to a leading North Carolina Whig Congressman: "I expect to start . . . next month a number of Slaves either to Mississippi or Louisiana, to make an establishment for my son James M. Wright, who sets out on Wednesday week to select a spot for permanent residence. . . . What can you tell me about the advantages of each?"[45] An equivalent inquiry in later years, when the price of land had risen so much more than the price of machinery, would query the county agent on the preferences in the latest choices in milk coolers or manure spreaders.

Causes of Labor Redistribution

The supply side of labor reallocation is somewhat more complex. One may presume that over the past century of free labor, 1865–1965, workers moved

[44] *Congressional Globe* (January 7, 1861), pp. 270–271.
[45] Quoted in Henry Shanks (ed.), *The Papers of Willie Person Mangum*, vol. 1 (Raleigh, N. C.: State Department of Archives and History, 1950), p. 577.

to areas of higher expected returns, as did capital. But what is one to encompass under "expected returns"? As a single simple generalization we can do reasonably well in asserting that labor moved to those states and regions that offered the highest wage rates. Data for 1830–1950 show that within the broad regions of major migration—North Central and South—population moved toward the states with highest wage rates and away from those with the lowest rates.[46] The relationships are clear. In most instances they are significant. Where they are not, shortcomings in the measurement seem to be involved.[47] But even where the data are fairly precise—as in Figure 6.1, where migration rates for blacks in 1940–1950 are related to personal income figures for 1946—the presence of other explanatory factors exists.

Before the Civil War, and possibly up to World War I, most labor in the United States was supplied in family enterprises. Its geographic allocation was decided by the extent to which the head of the family was suffused by optimism and enlightened by information. The family expectations encompassed nonmonetary as well as financial goals. There is therefore no reason to assume that family decisions to initiate farm or business operations tracked the

FIGURE 6.1
Black migration rate, 1940–1950

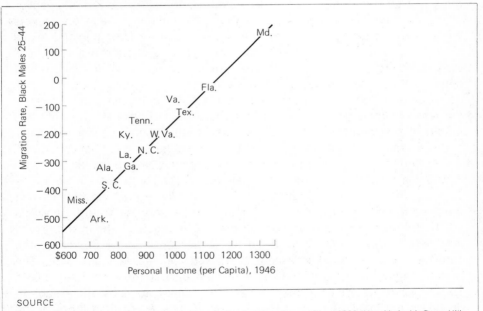

SOURCE

Stanley Lebergott, *Manpower in Economic Growth: The American Record Since 1800* (New York: McGraw-Hill, 1964), p. 99.

[46] See also Lebergott, *Manpower . . . , op. cit.,* pp. 74–99.
[47] Data for some of the early years are particularly subject to qualification. The review cited above simply relates wage rates at the beginning of the decade to population growth or migration over the subsequent decade. But in so doing it ignores possible changes in wage differentials during the decade—no mean omission.

course that market wages and prices would have signaled. (Indeed, the mortality rate among small businesses in later years suggests the contrary.) If so, the inadequacies of many a family farm probably had to be compensated for by extra work and by lowered consumption on the part of family members. The goods thrown upon the market by family enterprise would have tended to keep down prices, including the price of labor. The widespread complaints concerning the "scarcity" of hired labor on the frontier may therefore reflect the low level to which family labor had driven real wages in those areas. Real wage levels in eastern and southern cities proved more attractive.

The movement of labor, however dominated by prospective financial returns (rudely evident in the wage-rate data), was also motivated by other forces. One was the expectation of greater freedom—a factor without which the migration of rural blacks both to southern cities and to the North could not be fathomed. Only the prospect of fewer restraints can explain the persistent movement of this group out of the rural South to locations where their housing was not much better, their real incomes were more irregular, and the way of life was strange and disturbing.

Of growing importance were the attractions of cities. Urban population rose far more swiftly than total population. The movement into cities proved as significant in the reallocation of labor as movement between the states. A vital force making for this flow—we cannot surely say "the" vital force—was the wider choice among employers offered by the city. The job alternatives facing rural workers before the Civil War were defined by the few farmers within walking distance. (Indeed, when the first major New England textile mills were founded in the 1830s, they had to send out the black "slavers' wagons" to recruit and transport girls to the new mills.) As one measure of density we can estimate that in 1960 a Chicago worker who spent 25 cents on bus fare or gas could choose among 100,000 employers—but workers in the rest of Illinois, with the same 25 cents, could choose among only one fiftieth of that number.[48] Moreover, workers who offered specialized skills, and were therefore still more restricted in the number of potential employers, would find an even greater margin of advantage in going to the city.

The reallocation from initial to preferred locus could explain some reshuffling of labor. But it cannot explain the immense tidal movements that occurred in the American past. The central explanatory factor in these was a southern birth rate persistently above the U.S. average. Births in the rest of the United States would have failed to fill the opportunities offered by the industries of other regions, except at markedly increased wage rates. The South, the great American breeding area, helped stock those other regions.[49] The high birth rate meant more workers competing for jobs, more sons to divide up the family farm, and hence opportunities worse than those of the

[48] This estimate is derived in "Tomorrow's Workers," in *Planning for a Nation of Cities*, Sam B. Warner (ed.) (Cambridge, Mass.: M.I.T. Press, 1966), p. 125.

[49] Conrad Taeuber and Irene B. Taeuber, *The Changing Population of the United States* (New York: Wiley, 1958), p. 251, present data for whites showing each of the three southern divisions to be above the U.S. average in every census, 1800 to 1950. The U.S. average for blacks, most of whom lived in the South, was also in excess for the periods reported. Before 1880, this excess was equally true in the two North Central regions for whites.

older generation. In a sufficiently dynamic economy a concurrent shift in the southern agricultural or industrial production function would have neutralized the consequences of its population production function. But in fact migration proved the readier choice. Thus the South for more than a century, by producing, educating, and training more children than chose to remain in it, has filled jobs throughout the rest of the nation.

Beyond individual choice in labor reallocation, however, lies the looming shadow of the state. For throughout our history, a series of governmental actions have shaped the incentives to move. On balance, the state has slowed down the geographic reallocation of labor. Thus, in 1830–1860, states and cities gave bountifully for the construction of roads, canals, and railroads. These facilities made it possible for the areas involved to expand output—and successfully compete in distant markets. By increasing job opportunities within the individual city or state these transport improvements reduced the incentives for their labor to migrate.[50] A century later, tax exemptions offered to new enterprise by the individual states worked in the same direction.[51] Major federal internal improvement programs, notably the TVA and farm parity program in the 1930s, the Housing Acts of the 1940s and 1950s, and the Economic Development Act of the 1960s, worked in the same direction.

A series of irregular local actions may have been quantitatively more decisive in slowing the reallocation of labor—but we have mostly anecdotal materials concerning them. These actions involved municipal and county assistance to peonage systems supported by some individual employers. For centuries, English legislation forbade workmen to cross parish boundaries in search of better jobs, vagrants "and idle men" being taken up by the authorities and put into the workhouse. The tradition, fading in England throughout the nineteenth century, did not take root in the United States before the Civil War. After the war, however, southern employers found their workers to be less obedient and manageable than previously. The ex-slaves failed to treat their new-found freedom as an incidental event: "Hundreds of Negroes in their new freedom were loafing about towns, refusing to work, and when they did work, only staying on any job long enough to get a few dollars ahead. This was most annoying to farmers."[52] Or, as another southern scholar has put it, "The first efforts of employers to obtain adequate results with free labor were most discouraging. Negroes everywhere seemed bent on testing the physical reality of their emancipation. . . . Harassed planters resorted to all sorts of devices to stimulate exertion from their sable charges, but with little avail."[53] To handle these "annoying" and "most discouraging" reactions planters found the discipline of the market insufficient, as was to be expected. "Most of the Southern states passed laws requiring all contracts with Negroes to be put in writing"; the worker who quit before the end of that contract " became

---

[50] A lesser, partially offsetting force, of course, was the reduced cost of a one-way ticket out of the state.
[51] See John Moes, *Local Subsidies to Industry* (Chapel Hill: University of North Carolina Press, 1962).
[52] W. D. Weatherford, *The Negro from Africa to America* (New York: George H. Doran, 1924), p. 345.
[53] Bell I. Wiley, "Salient Changes in Southern Agriculture Since the Civil War," *Agricultural History*, vol. 13 (1939), p. 65.

a vagrant, he forfeited his salary for the whole year, he could be arrested and taken back to his place of work, and in case of necessity could be handled by the county court as a criminal."[54] Although the presence of federal troops in the South after the Civil War was construed as an outrage and insult by political and social leaders of the area, the troops apparently helped prevent a truly free labor market from developing. For the Freedman's Bureau provided military enforcement of the sharecropping contracts signed by the freedman. Higher wages offered by farm operators in Mississippi and Arkansas after the war had tended to draw labor from Georgia and South Carolina. By enforcing contracts, the Freedman's Bureau helped reduce such migration to better jobs and slowed the market adjustment process.[55]

Toward a National Labor Market

The allocation and reallocation of labor among the regions of the nation were, of course, mediated by wage-rate changes. An effectively functioning market would have forced down interarea wage differentials—given unchanged supply and demand schedules. Psychological and financial transfer costs would, of course, prevent differentials being forced down to zero.[56] Moreover, attractions of climate, opportunity, etc., could compensate for reported wage differences. Nonetheless, if a well-functioning, interrelated system of labor markets were moving labor about, one would expect to see reductions in wage differentials. Such reduction did in fact take place in the United States. We can follow its course in data for farm labor, a large group in the market to whose wage rates most others could be linked. Decade after decade, the coefficient of variation for farm-labor wage rates declined.[57]

The two exceptions to this broad trend are important—and informative. In the wake of both the Civil War and the two world wars, the coefficient rose. Its recent rise testifies to the effects of substantial plant expansion in the New England and North Central regions, the bidding up of wage rates to attract labor to new jobs and new plants. Increased variance in the weary aftermath of the Civil War reflected actual wage-rate declines in many southern states in the face of large, sometimes violent, increases in the North. Such declines derive in no small measure from the decline of cotton production in the Old South. This decline was due to the rise of Texas and Arkansas as cotton producers, and to the wartime substitution of Indian cotton and American wool for cotton grown in the Old South.

A closer inspection of what was happening within the regions emphasizes the tendency toward convergence. But it also focuses on those sudden departures that did occur whenever production-function changes forced comprehensive shifts in the demand curves—as when textile factories bur-

---

[54] Weatherford, *op. cit.*, p. 345.

[55] Charles W. Ramsdell, in "Presidential Reconstruction in Texas," *Texas Historical Association Quarterly* (January 1909), pp. 214, quotes General Kiddo, Assistant Commissioner of the Freedman's Bureau for Texas. His Circular Order 14 "forbid the enticing of contract laborers from one employer to another." The unruliness of some employees is indicated by a published order listing "freedmen who had left their employers, also named, and notifying other employers not to hire them." Parallel orders exist for Georgia.

[56] This statement is untrue given certain—unlikely—supply conditions.

[57] Lebergott, *Manpower . . . , op. cit.*, p. 135.

geoned in Massachusetts and Connecticut from 1830 to 1850, when home-steading and railroads brought thousands of new farmers into the North Central region from 1870 to 1880, and so on.

As mentioned above, one single grand measure, proportionately limited in meaning, is the coefficient of variation for wages of farm laborers by state. Its long-term decline from 1818 to 1940 succinctly emphasizes the formation of a national labor market. It is almost inconceivable that rates for any state could now, as in 1800, be double the national average.[58] As the population became homogenized, as producers perfected their ability to substitute one type of labor (or machinery) for another, wage rates inevitably drew together.

UNIONIZATION

To those cognizant of the history of European labor movements, how remark-ably tame the history of the American labor movement must seem. How few were its charismatic leaders, its intense followers, its intermittent revolutions. How temperately ardent was the political involvement of unions. Was the union impact on employment, wages, and working conditions equally mild? Let us begin with Table 6.16, which casts a backward glance at the trend in union membership. How miniscule the labor movement was during the first century and a half of our national life, from 1783 to 1933. It is perhaps otiose to speculate why the American labor movement was (probably) so much smaller and (perhaps) so much less effective than European labor movements, for we lack any systematic analysis of how effectively the latter transformed their conditions of work. Nonetheless, there seems to be widespread belief that the impact of these labor movements differed as widely as did their character.

If the size and economic impact of the American and European labor move-ments differed, and not merely their style and noisiness, what characteristics seem to have been involved? One characteristic is surely the continuous (and greater) rate of flow of U.S. workers from old to new industries, jobs, and regions. It was apparent to employers at an early date that the option of moving west—Connecticut workers to western New York, New York workers to Ohio, Ohio workers to Nebraska, and so on—would be determinative in setting wages and working conditions. Our first available migration figures report that approximately 25 percent of the 1850 population who had been born in New England had moved along to other states, many to forested lands in western New York, perhaps 10 percent to what was "the West"—largely across the Mississippi.[59] Of course the leverage of workers in wage negotia-tions required only that the threat that some would quit and move on be credible; that credibility would be produced if a sufficient number of persons

[58] Charles Gayarre, *History of Louisiana*, vol. 3 (New York: Redfield, 1855), p. 438, quotes Pantollio's memo to Napoleon: Louisiana rates "are twice as high as in the United States." Our first systematic data, for 1860, show Louisiana less than 20 percent above the U.S. average.
[59] U.S. Bureau of the Census, *Census of Population: 1850* (Washington: U.S. Government Printing Office, 1853), p. xxxvi.

TABLE 6.16
Union membership, 1830–1960

	Union Membership (thousands)	U.S. Labor Force (thousands)	Percent Organized
1830	26	4,200	.6
1860	5	11,110	.1
1870	300	12,930	2.3
1880	50	17,390	.3
1883	210	—	—
1886	1,010	—	—
1890	325	23,320	1.4
1900	791	29,070	2.7
1910	2,116	37,480	5.6
1920	5,034	41,610	12.1
1930	3,632	48,830	7.4
1935	8,728	52,600	16.6
1940	8,944	56,290	15.9
1945	14,796	65,600	22.6
1950	15,000	65,470	22.9
1960	18,117	74,060	24.5

SOURCES

Membership
   1830–1883: Based on data from John R. Commons *et al., History of Labour in the United States,* vol. 2 (New York: Kelley, 1921), pp. 9, 47, 177, 314, 381; and Carroll Wright in *One Hundred Years of American Commerce,* C. dePew (ed.) (New York: D. O. Haynes, 1895), p. 15.
   1886: See Leo Wolman, *Growth of American Trade Unions, 1880–1923* (New York: National Bureau of Economic Research, 1924). The 1883–1886 increases shown in Wolman for the AF of L, Knights of Labor, and three railway unions were added to the 1883 figure used above.
   1890: Wolman, *op. cit.,* p. 32, Table 1.
   1900–1960: U.S. Bureau of the Census, *Historical Statistics of the United States* (Washington: U.S. Government Printing Office, 1965), pp. 97–98.
Labor Force: Lebergott, *Manpower . . . , op. cit.,* pp. 510–512. Data are for persons aged 10 and over.

did move on from time to time. However, vigorous potential union leaders were drawn off to their own farms or businesses or to the West. A second characteristic of the labor movement was that American labor leadership was more politically abstemious than European, certainly prior to the 1930s. Possibly its experience with the labor injunction was determinative; but American unions opposed federal minimum wages and laws limiting work by women in mines at a time when their European counterparts were hotly urging more and more government regulation of conditions of work. As far as political alliances go it is noteworthy how split the labor movement was as late as the 1930s: Of the handful of top leaders, such dominant figures as Lewis and Hutcheson supported the Republicans, and Murray and Dubinsky supported the Democracts.

The Early History

The American union movement hardly existed prior to 1860. Can we date its beginning? Did its first stimulus come when the first indentured servant fled to the distant West before finishing out his indenture? When the first group of workers in a shop quit to enforce their demand for a higher wage? Or when (in 1806) the law fined striking Philadelphia shoemakers a week's pay because of their (successful) attempts to keep scabs from working?[60] Perhaps the most useful date to pick as the start of the union movement per se is 1830. It was in 1828 that an entrepreneur first speculated on there being enough potential subscribers to warrant starting a workingman's newspaper. In 1833 Ely Moore became the first union man elected to Congress.[61] In 1834, the female workers of probably the largest company in the nation "turned out" on strike because of a pay cut.[62] And in 1834 there were something over 26,000 union members.[63]

But it is well to note the aspect of these union members. Cordwainers, saddlers, bakers, tailors, coopers, they were primarily small businessmen. Their affiliation with a union meant no more nor less than that of barbers and plumbers in our own day: Technically union members, they used their membership largely to assist price fixing in their business transactions. Such success as these first unions of small businessmen and skilled workers enjoyed reflected the difficulty employers had in finding ready substitutes for craftsmen. In that handicraft economy, skill was needed, but labor markets lacked the close information links and cheap transport that came only after the Civil War.

Following the Civil War the area of product competition widened substantially—with corresponding impact on the derived demand for labor, and thereby on the U.S. labor movement. A very crude indication of widening competition is given if we compute tons of products moved per dollar of GNP (Table 6.17). The greater the volume of goods exported from a city or a country, or the further the penetration of distant markets, the larger the shipping ratio grows.[64] From 1859 to 1879 it advanced spectacularly.

A second indicator of widening markets was the increase in the number of traveling salesmen. That rise was hampered by ordinances—for example, in 1868 Baltimore decided that only permanent residents of Maryland were competent to sell goods in that city.[65] The numbers of traveling salesmen nonetheless jumped:

1860	1,000
1870	7,000
1880	28,000

Nearly every wandering "drummer" sold goods in one region which were made in another—perhaps enough of them to pay his salary and travel expense.

[60] Data in John R. Commons (ed.), *A Documentary History of American Industrial Society*, vol. 3 (New York: Russell and Russell, 1910), pp. 28, 106, 123, and 236, indicate that fines of $8 and a week's pay averaged about as much.

[61] John R. Commons et al., *History of Labour in the United States*, vol. 1 (New York: Kelley, 1921), p. 461.

[62] George Wadleigh, *Notable Events in the History of Dover, New Hampshire* (Dover, N.H.: 1913).

[63] *Working Man's Advocate* (June 21, 1834), quoted in John R. Commons (ed.) *A Documentary History of American Industrial Society*, vol. 6 (New York: Russell and Russell, 1910), p. 191.

[64] Mere transfer from nonrail to rail modes also, and unsatisfactorily, tends to make this ratio rise. The latter bias, however, is not likely to obscure its use for our present purposes.

[65] Gerald Carson, *The Old Country Store* (New York: Dutton, 1965), pp. 163–165.

TABLE 6.17
Widening markets, 1855–1899

Year	GNP (millions of 1860 dollars) (1)	Tons Shipped by Rail (millions) (2)	Ratio (2) ÷ (1) (3)
1855	$ 3.6	23	7
1859	4.1	37	9
1869	5.4	129	25
1879	8.4	297	42
1889	12.4	615	50
1899	17.5	976	50

SOURCES
GNP: Figures of Robert E. Gallman.
Tonnage: Edwin Frickey, *Production in the United States 1860–1914* (Cambridge, Mass.: Harvard University Press, 1947), p. 100. Were we to include wagon and water shipment, the rise in the ratio would probably be greater and its timing different.

A third crude indicator is the development of fast freight lines. First came Kasson's Dispatch in 1855–1856, and then (in 1866–1868) the Red and Blue Lines in the North and the Green Line in the South.[66] The success of such enterprises was founded on a rising demand for prompt shipment of an increasing volume of goods across state borders.

But if output flows were expanding, harsher competition among the laborers who manufactured those goods was inevitable. Local shoemakers suddenly began to find themselves in active competition with shoemakers from Lynn, Massachusetts. Local cigar makers found themselves in direct competition with craftsmen in Louisville and Jersey City.

Labor responded to these pressures, creating national unions. If a national level of wages could be established then "labor would be removed from competition"—or, more realistically, northern labor would not be in quite as much competition. As Lloyd Ulman has put it, "The need for national unionism arose in part as the output of producing units in widely scattered areas" entered the same markets. And that need was enhanced because of labor's geographic mobility, "which often paralleled the national markets for products."[67] Union membership jumped to 300,000 by 1870, from a trivial 5000 in 1860. In the 1860s some 19 national unions were founded, plus 10 more in 1870–1873, an extraordinary expansion by prior standards.[68] That expansion was wholly limited to the unions of skilled workers, however. It may have been speeded along by the Reconstruction statute preventing criminal action

[66] George Taylor and Irene Neu, *The American Railroad Network, 1861–1890* (Cambridge, Mass.: Harvard University Press, 1956), pp. 69–81.
[67] Lloyd Ulman, *The Rise of the National Trade Union*, 2nd ed. (Cambridge, Mass.: Harvard University Press 1966), p. 43. See also John R. Commons, *History of Labour in the United States*, vol. 2 (New York: Kelley, 1921), p. 358.
[68] Computed from data in Commons, *History of Labour ...*, *op. cit.*, vol. 2, pp. 46–47, 176.

against workers who broke contracts of employment.[69] But while this law strengthened the position of both skilled and unskilled workers, the supersession of planters by ex-slaves as the suppliers of unskilled farm labor probably nullified any effects it might have had in tending to keep up wages for unskilled labor.

The expanding unionization of skilled groups stopped abruptly in 1872. From 1872 to 1879, wage rates fell by almost 25 percent—a decline without precedent and without successor even during the long, dark 1930s.[70] Is it surprising that few new national unions were founded during this period? That the numbers of old ones fell abruptly from 30 to 8? Or that membership in unions fell perhaps 80 percent?

It was probably not before the 1880s that a durable U.S. labor movement was created. The expansion of industry across the land, the introduction of new technologies, the heightened flow of immigration, the increased density of population, the feeling that the frontier had ended—all these factors contributed to its growth.

The Established Movement

The clearest indication that a new labor movement had really been created was the law it helped force through Congress forbidding Chinese immigration. The first really national convention of labor unions—mostly white—met in August 1869 and adopted a plank favoring the exclusion of Chinese labor. The first national convention of black labor unions met four months later and also adopted a plank favoring the exclusion of Chinese contract labor.[71] Spirited agitation followed, spearheaded by earlier immigrants—Kearney, an immigrant from Cork, Day from Canada, Welloc from England, and others. Their opposition took form in a League of Deliverance, achieving in 1882 a congressional enactment that cut off Chinese immigration.[72] As an expression of xenophobia, this achievement may have been remarkably satisfying to the very newest immigrants—for it promised to protect them from those who otherwise would have followed them. But as an attempt to raise wages by restricting supply, it failed. For the Chinese were simply replaced by a stream of other low-paid migrants—Japanese, Italian, Hungarian. In 1885 the first law forbidding the import of contract labor was passed[73] with somewhat more effect, but still subject to wide evasion.

The second proof that the labor movement had come of age—or at least, of an age—was its wild expansion in the 1880s. That expansion was only in small measure a growth of the traditional craft unions, banded together in the American Federation of Labor. It was far more surely the swift surge of unskilled and semiskilled labor to the mystic banners of the Knights of Labor.

---

[69] Frederick Meyers, *Ownership of Jobs* (Berkeley: University of California Press, 1964), p. 19. The statute permitted only civil suits for damage. Meyers points out that imprisonment for debt had fairly well ended by 1850—a necessary complement.

[70] Data from Lebergott, *Manpower ...*, *op. cit.*, p. 528. Obviously factors other than the cycle came into play in determining union success.

[71] Commons, *History of Labour ...*, *op. cit.*, vol. 2, p. 137.

[72] *Ibid.*, pp. 252–268.

[73] U.S. Immigration Commission, *Reports*, vol. 2 (Washington: U.S. Government Printing Office, 1911), pp. 569–577.

For the Knights had, unbelievably, won a strike against the railway system of the great financial mogul of the age, Jay Gould—the man so powerful that Mark Twain accused him of single-handedly having taught the American people to worship money. Because of the intricacies of the financial structure that Gould was then creating, the system yielded on layoffs that had been made by one of its component railroads.[74] That the strike failed to cancel the wage cut that was originally at issue was, perhaps, taken for granted. But the fact that the Wabash Railway agreed to take strikers back without prejudice was considered by many unskilled workers as a dramatic proof of major union advance. Within a single year, over 600,000 people joined new lodges of the Knights of Labor, open as they were to skilled and unskilled alike. In part they were drawn by this palpable success in tilting with employers. In part they came because they construed the Knights' support of an eight-hour day as implying ten hours' pay for eight hours' work. The Knights, however, lacked the strong central leadership of the regular unions. They were unable to control an eruption of wildcat strikes by the new lodges. The overwhelming failure of these strikes was perhaps inevitable: Funds to feed thousands of strikers for extended periods did not exist. Nor could a host of largely un-skilled workers[75] prevent their replacement by scabs, native or immigrant, or by simple machinery. Moreover, a shift in employer resistance curves took place. A bomb explosion in 1887 in Chicago's Haymarket—in which a police sergeant was killed—exacerbated employer opposition and soon deflated the movement.[76] The Knights, having gone up like a rocket, came down like a stick.

Whatever durable union growth there was by 1900 was achieved by the slow organizing of skilled workers into craft unions, mostly those affiliated with the AF of L. The philosophy that attracted their members had been defined with charming simplicity by Adolph Strasser, an early AF of L leader. Asked about the union's "ultimate ends" he replied:

> We have no ultimate ends. We are going on from day to day. We are fighting only for immediate objects.... We want to dress better and to live better, and to become better citizens generally.... We are opposed to theorists.... We are all practical men.[77]

Having "no ultimate ends" can be taken very simply to mean that the craftsmen in AF of L unions knew themselves to be incapable of restricting the supply of skilled labor to U.S. industry in general, and capable of holding on with great difficulty even in the industries where they were relatively strong. Subject to replacement by immigrants, by women, by machines, their strength usually rested on only a thin stratum of nuisance value in the form of substitution costs.

Such costs were critical for certain firms. But they were hardly potent in the larger economy. For there, thousands of new firms were being founded. New

---

[74] Commons, *History of Labour....*, *op. cit.*, vol. 2, pp. 368–370.
[75] *Ibid.*, p. 407.
[76] Robert Ozanne, *A Century of Labor-Management Relations at McCormick and International Harvester* (Madison· University of Wisconsin Press, 1967).
[77] Adolph Strasser in 1883, quoted in Commons, *History of Labour . . . ., op. cit.*, p. 309.

industries were continuously being established. And new technologies were being steadily adopted. The footholds for union organization were therefore few and often crumbling. In 1870 the bulk of membership in trade unions (not including the amorphous "city locals") was in the Knights of St. Crispin (50,000 shoemakers), plus another 50,000 miners, typographical workers, iron founders, and cigar makers.[78] When the St. Crispins sought to exercise their influence, the Goodyear sewing machine and a host of other machines were introduced. So promptly and widely were their skills replaced that by 1900 less than 2 percent[79] of shoe workers were organized. As the International Typographical Union grew, so did attempts to develop typesetting machines. After vast expenditures by Mark Twain and others searching for great wealth, the Mergenthaler machine was developed and began replacing union members. As the Glass Bottle Blowers' Union grew in strength, so did attempts to develop a blowing machine—and eventually Owens proved one out. As the skilled steel workers advanced in power, Andrew Carnegie, Frick, and U.S. Steel began substituting even more highly skilled chemists plus mechanical controls, driving the Union from the mild eminence it held in the early 1890s to virtual nonexistence from 1900 to 1938.[80] Indeed only the railway craft unions survived in strength, presumably because of the support provided by the intricate web of oligopoly and federal regulation.

Two corollary factors also made for union failure. One was the feasibility of monopsonistic cartels, with employers agreeing not to employ (i.e., to "blacklist") workers who were "troublemakers." Probably blacklisting was most effective where there were only a few companies in the same industry and area—as in several steel companies[81]—or where information could readily be transmitted between oligopsonists—as in the Pullman strike of 1893.[82] A second factor was the utilization of government facilities to restrict strike activity. Labor injunctions halted coercive union endeavors—those intended to keep other workers from replacing those on strike, as well as those aimed at keeping consumers from buying and suppliers from providing materials. The injunction seems to have served effectively both to limit the vigor of such activities and to break strikes.[83]

[78] *Ibid.*, p. 47. We included the numerically trivial group of cigar makers because it included nearly one quarter of the workers in that industry.

[79] Leo Wolman, *Ebb and Flow of Trade Unionism* (New York: Macmillan, 1936), p. 198.

[80] Shortly after U.S. Steel was formed, its executive committee adopted a resolution "That we are unalterably opposed to any extension of union labor and advise subsidiary companies to take firm position when these questions come up and say that they are not going to recognize it, that is, any extension of unions in mills where they do not now exist; that great care should be used to prevent trouble and that they promptly report and confer with this corporation." David Brody, *Steelworkers in America* (New York: Russell and Russell, 1960), p. 62. It is perhaps significant of the role of steel in our economy that, as U.S. Steel started the twentieth century with withdrawal of union recognition, it was also U.S. Steel that dramatically broke ranks in the late 1930s in recognizing the SWOC and thereby the CIO.

[81] See the letters printed in Commission in Inquiry, Interchurch World Movement, *Report on the Steel Strike of 1919* (New York: Harcourt, Brace & Howe, 1920), p. 219. A rebuttal volume distributed by the U.S. Steel Company does not comment on this portion of the report.

[82] An employee's successful court suit against a blacklist sponsored by the Chicago and Northwestern Railway is reported in U.S. Industrial Commission, *Reports*, vol. 4 (Washington: U.S. Government Printing Office, 1900), pp. 508–509.

[83] See Felix Frankfurter and Nathan Greene, *The Labor Injunction* (Gloucester, Mass.: Peter Smith, 1930), pp. 101, 102, 268. Such consequences followed despite, or because of, forbidden acts such as singing "Stand Up for Jesus" and "The Victory May Depend on You," "in a threatening or hostile manner"; or because of court requirements in an area where virtually all the miners were foreign-born, that union pickets "shall be able to speak the English language."

The absolute number of union members rose mildly until World War I. The wartime increase was viewed as the wonderful (or outrageous) result of a bargain in which unions agreed to a nonstrike pledge in return for lessened opposition to union organization. But Table 6.16 points to only the mildest of gains by 1920.

Unionism After the 1930s

A great divide in the history of the American labor movement was created by the 1930s, for two reasons. The first was the government's conscious adoption of a policy favoring the free organization of unions. Only in the 1930s did it become a matter of congressional objurgation that an employer's secret agent, operating as the union secretary, would turn membership lists over to his employer.[84] Company representatives beat up Walter Reuther and others trying to organize Ford workers in 1937, and company representatives and police shot striking Republic steel workers in 1937, but these were the last vestiges of tactics that had been accepted, if not acceptable, under the old order.[85] The high drama of subornation, threats, maiming, and killing as techniques for stopping labor organization disappeared after the late 1930s, to be replaced by general acceptance—at least outside of agriculture and outside the South. The generation of management and labor leaders who have flourished since the 1940s replaced these often wild adventures in sadism and illicit relationships by dull but serviceable agreements to work together till retirement.

The second factor making the 1930s a critical decade for labor was the massive rise in unemployment from 1929 to 1932. Craft unions had dominated the union movement from its inception. But it was industrial unionism that brought the vast rise in membership from 1933 to 1939, as the union movement began substantial recruitment of semiskilled and unskilled workers.

Recent studies of union growth have established models to explain the year-to-year changes in membership from 1904 to 1960.[86] They indicate that one major force present throughout the period was a quickening of demand: The more employment increased, and the more persistent that increase was over time, the more union membership grew. (Prospective union members and union organizers apparently both recognized that joining was safer, and more remunerative, when the demand for labor was strengthening.) These studies found as well that high levels of unemployment were stimuli to worker dissidence and hence to membership.[87] And they found that the tides of social acceptance and rejection, of support and revolt, brought parallel response in

---

[84] Lewis Silverberg, The Wagner Act After Ten Years (Washington: U.S. Bureau of National Affairs, 1945), p. 80.

[85] Fortune (November 1937). A measure of the change is the perceptive comment by Henry Ford II ("Bargaining and Economic Growth," a speech made on June 22, 1964) that "the atmosphere of militancy and crisis that surrounds the negotiation of a new agreement ... is a dangerous anachronism, an obsolete carryover from the bitter labor-management conflicts of a generation and more ago."

[86] O. Ashenfelter and J. H. Penceval, "American Trade Union Growth: 1900–1960," Quarterly Journal of Economics, vol. 83 (August 1969); Irving Bernstein, "The Growth of American Unions," American Economic Review, vol. 44 (June 1954).

[87] Employment increases bring unionism because of shifts in the demand schedule. High levels of unemployment also help unionism—by moves along the demand schedule.

the Congress (via legislation and via its changing membership and investiga-tions) that indicated growing social acceptance of unions and facilitated increasing membership, or the converse. The vast pressure of government in stoking the market for teachers, for medical care, for public services, can go far toward explaining rising union membership in the late 1960s, after years of numerical membership stability.

UNION IMPACT

The results of these many decades of unionism are difficult to determine. Three kinds of impact on workers may be noted. First, as direct owner super-vision dwindled, the opportunities afforded foremen and other supervisors for indulging their personal choice and satisfactions increased greatly. One highly significant force making for union growth, then, was the workers' desire to reduce arbitrariness in the hiring and firing of workers and harsh treatment by supervisory personnel. Of course, personal contact with the owner did not guarantee happy understanding : The years of the Kohler strike alone offer flat disproof of that possibility. But some supervisors were paid partly in opportunities for psychological advantage and petty extortion—neither particularly benefiting the employer. Second, other benefits to workers from union organization (directly and as tactics to head off unionization) included costly actions to install fire escapes, washrooms, inside toilets, cafe-terias, paid holidays, compensation for death on the job, occupational illness, and so on. We have no systematic measure of the extent of total union impact inclusive of such advances. (It may be a fair inference that these benefits grew along with wages : For example, higher wages in auto plants in the 1960s were not achieved by shortening the lunch period.)

However, we do have an indicator of a third category of union impact—the impact on wages. This indicator is biased because it omits the above elements, but it is surely relevant and suggestive. For this purpose we utilize a recent series of investigations reviewed and reworked by H. G. Lewis.[88]

As one would expect, union ability to raise wages has varied greatly among industries. For unskilled workers in recent decades, as well as for common labor in building construction, Lewis puts the wage-rate advantage of union over nonunion labor at less than 5 percent. At the other extreme, the advantage for bituminous coal miners is put at from 40 percent (in 1909–1913) to 50 percent (in 1956–1957). Lewis surmises that on the whole, union wage rates exceeded nonunion rates as follows :[89]

1923–1929	15–20 percent
1931–1933	Over 25 percent
1939–1941	10–20 percent
1945–1949	0–5 percent
1957–1958	10–15 percent

[88] H. G. Lewis, *Unionism and Relative Wages in the United States* (Chicago: University of Chicago Press, 1963).
[89] *Ibid.,* p. 193.

From these data Albert Rees has estimated that in recent years unions raised wages of their members by something like 10 to 15 percent.[90]

Such a ratio of advantage is surely nothing like the wild proportions sometimes urged. How significant is it? Considering the mere percentage tells us nothing: It is less than 100 percent and more than zero, but is it significant? Perhaps the simplest way of testing its significance is to define union dues as an investment in securing higher wages. We can then compute the rate of return on that investment. (In so doing, of course, we understate the true rate of return, for we value improved working conditions and fringe benefits at zero.)

Suppose that we take the average wage for those industries in which most union members were employed in 1958, the most recent year covered by Lewis' study.[91] Multiplying that wage by 12 percent—midway in Rees' 10 to 15 percent range—gives roughly $600 as the annual return from union membership. Now during this period, union dues have been averaging about $50 a year.[92] If $600 is the annual return on a $50 investment in union dues, the member's rate of return is well over 1000 percent.[93] Such a rate compares most favorably with alternative investments available to small investors.

When unions first developed in any industry, their impact on wages and working conditions may well have been more powerful than subsequently. And their prowess has surely been greater in some industries—mining, trucking, steel—than in others. Unions that have been able to organize an entire industry could reduce entrepreneurial profits, could slice the returns to specialized capital locked into that industry.

Union impact on wages should in turn have helped stimulate the substitution of competing products and firms for those made by union industry as well as the substitution of machinery for labor.[94] The direction of these efforts is highly likely, but their historic magnitudes are unknown. For the competition of products and the substitution of capital for labor were taking place long before unions appeared, and continue in sectors where union members are no more common than aardvarks. We could not measure these magnitudes without an adequate econometric model, and even with one, the dynamics involved in the long historic process we are noting might well prevent a clear-cut conclusion.

---

[90] Albert Rees, *The Economics of Trade Unions* (Chicago: University of Chicago Press, 1962), p. 79.

[91] U.S. Department of Commerce, *The National Income and Product Accounts of the United States, 1929–1965* (Washington: U.S. Government Printing Office, 1966), Tables 6.1–6.3. We include mining, construction, manufacturing, transport, and communication.

[92] Richard Lester, *Economics of Labor* (New York: Macmillan, 1964), p. 176.

[93] From the $600 figure one must really deduct the difference between the average days' wages lost in strikes by (a) union members and (b) nonunion workers. But any such adjustment is a trivial affair: Even if we assumed that nonunion workers lost no time in strikes, we still have less than two days a year work lost in strikes by union members. [See the data in the U.S. Department of Labor, *Handbook of Labor Statistics* (Washington: U.S. Government Printing Office, 1968), pp. 300–301.]

[94] We say "should ... have helped" since, on comparative–static assumptions, employers could be expected to substitute away from union labor toward other inputs—either on their own or as an involuntary consequence of consumer reactions to the higher prices of union-made products. But whether this theoretical proposition involved one day's work less for union labor or 1 million man-years less has yet to be established, despite heroic work by H. G. Lewis and some others.

SUGGESTED READING

Ashenfelter, O., and J. H. Penceval. "American Trade Union Growth : 1900–1960." *Quarterly Journal of Economics*, vol. 83 (August 1969).

Bancroft, Gertrude. *The American Labor Force*. New York: Wiley, 1958.

Becker, Gary. *Human Capital*. New York: National Bureau of Economic Research, 1964.

Bowen, W. G., and T. A. Finegan. *The Economics of Labor Force Participation*. Princeton: Princeton University Press, 1969.

Brissenden, P. F. *The I.W.W.* New York: Russell and Russell, 1919.

Commons, John R. (ed.). *A Documentary History of American Industrial Society*. New York: Russell and Russell, 1910–1911.

Durand, John D. *The Labor Force in the United States, 1890–1960*. New York: Gordon and Breach, 1968.

Franklin, J. H. *From Slavery to Freedom*. New York: Knopf, 1960.

Galenson, W. *The CIO Challenge to the AFL*. Cambridge, Mass.: Harvard University Press, 1960.

Jernegan, M. W. *Laboring and Dependent Classes in Colonial America*. New York: Ungar, 1931.

Levinson, E. *Labor on the March*. New York: Harper & Row, 1938.

Marshall, F. R. *Labor in the South*. Cambridge, Mass.: Harvard University Press, 1967.

Morris, R. B. *Government and Labor in Early America*. New York: Columbia University Press, 1946.

Schultz, Theodore. "Capital Formation by Education." *Journal of Political Economy*, vol. 68 (December 1960).

Slichter, S. H. *Union Policies and Industrial Management*. Westport, Conn.: Greenwood, 1941.

Slichter, S. H., J. Healy, and E. R. Livernash. *The Impact of Collective Bargaining on Management*. Washington: Brookings Institution, 1960.

Spero, S., and A. Harris. *The Black Worker*. New York: Atheneum, 1931.

Taft, P. *Organized Labor in American History*. New York: Harper & Row, 1964.

Twentieth Century Fund. *How Collective Bargaining Works*. New York: The Fund, 1942.

Ulman, Loyd. *The Rise of the National Trade Union*. 2nd. ed. Cambridge, Mass.: Harvard University Press, 1966.

U.S. Industrial Commission. *Reports*. Vols. 2, 12, 14, 17. Washington: U.S. Government Printing Office, 1900–1901.

Ware, N. J. *The Labor Movement in the U.S., 1860–1895*. New York: Random House, 1929.

Yellen, S. *American Labor Struggles*. New York: Arno, 1936.

part III
TECHNOLOGY AND CAPITAL FORMATION

7
TECHNOLOGICAL CHANGE

This chapter first looks at the general nature of inventive activity and the social, intellectual, and economic factors that influence the demand for and supply of inventions. It then examines in more detail the record of inventive activity in the United States since 1800 and the changing forces that have shaped the course of American technological progress.

Let us, as a first approximation, think of technological progress as consisting of changes in production methods which allow more output to be produced from a given volume of labor and resources, or allow a given output to be produced with a smaller volume of labor and resources. If we consider the input—output relation to be represented by a mathematical function, shown by a line or curve on a graph, such a change represents a shift of the whole function. It is important that such a shift be distinguished from other ways of increasing the output of an economic system. An economy (or factory or farm) obviously increases its output simply by using more inputs. People may work longer hours, or a larger proportion of the population may enter the labor force, or a larger proportion of incomes may be saved and used to accumulate more capital. Economies may exist when production occurs on a larger scale, so that a given percentage increase in inputs results in a greater percentage increase in output. A serious understanding of the process of economic growth requires that we sort out the relative importance of these separate means of increasing output. This is much easier to do conceptually than to do empirically, partly because many new techniques must be embodied in new kinds of capital equipment and skills before they can become economically significant. Moreover, some of the most interesting and subtle aspects of the process of economic change concern the *interrelationship* among the various sources of such change, the

The research for this chapter was supported by the Harvard University Program on Technology and Society under a long-term grant from the International Business Machines Corporation.

FIGURE 7.1

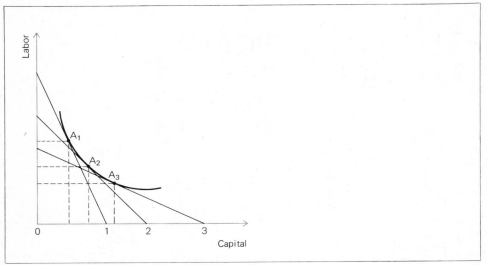

dependence of the behavior of one variable upon the simultaneous behavior of one or more of the other variables.

We may begin by assuming that, at a given moment in time, there exists a spectrum of known ways in which resources may be combined to produce a given volume of final output. Which of these technically feasible combinations will be selected—which one will minimize costs—will depend upon the relative prices of the various inputs. The optimum input combination will change as price relationships among inputs change (Figure 7.1). Thus, if the supply of capital is increasing more rapidly than the supply of labor and if, as a result, labor becomes relatively more expensive than capital, we would expect a shift to more capital-intensive methods—A_1 to A_2 to A_3.

On the other hand, the optimum input combination will also change as a result of the introduction of a new and superior technique. In Figure 7.2 this is represented by an inward shift of the isoquant from 1 to 2—that is, it becomes possible to produce the same volume of output with a smaller volume of inputs. This case, in contrast to the first one, represents an improvement in total resource productivity and its pervasive importance in the long run is a main reason for our interest in the role of technological change in the growth of the American economy.

In examining the historical role of technological change, it is helpful to visualize the American economy in the year 1800. In that year the economy was overwhelmingly agricultural; production was mostly for local markets; only the most rudimentary forms of land transportation were available; productive activity typically centered upon the family unit. Now assume that such an economy experienced growth in population and capital stock, with

FIGURE 7.2

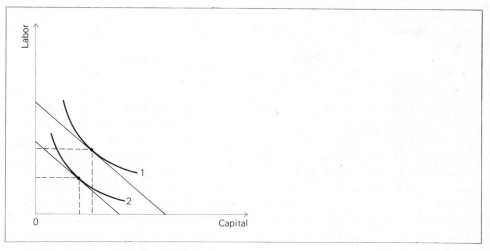

no changes in production techniques. What would this economy look like if it grew by adding to its stock of capital more and more of the tools, equipment, and transport forms of 1800, if its population and labor force continued to grow, and if it gradually expanded extensively to exploit the resources of the American continent? The social system conjured up by these suppositions might have gratified Thomas Jefferson, with his vision of a broadly based, egalitarian economy of prosperous small farmers. But without the major improvements in productivity created by technological change, the existing late twentieth-century American economy would be completely inconceivable.

Our exercise could usefully be carried one step further by dropping the assumption of unlimited resources. It is a matter of simple arithmetic that continued population growth within any finite land area means a continued reduction in resources per capita. Eventually this reduction in resource inputs per capita will restrict the society's capacity to increase its output per capita. Eventually, when all the available land is already being intensively cultivated and population is continuing to grow at a rapid pace, the prospects for the future become dim indeed.

We have, in fact, sketched out the essential features of the world seen by the early nineteenth-century English political economists, notably Malthus and Ricardo. It was precisely in considering the future prospects for such a society that the classical economists first discovered and examined the historical implications of the law of diminishing returns. Their dreary forecasts were the product of their reflections over the long-run prospects for a society experiencing (a) an unalterable land constraint, (b) continuing population growth, and therefore (c) a declining rate of growth of total output. Within the framework of their reasoning, a stationary state, characterized by low or zero profits, no capital accumulation, and a maximum attainable population size barely surviving at subsistence-level incomes, seemed alarmingly probable and not very far distant.

THE ROLE OF TECHNOLOGY IN AMERICAN ECONOMIC GROWTH

If we compare the world of the 1970s with the world of 1800 and with the dreary conclusions of the futurologists of that generation, it is clear that, in the industrialized countries, a major reason for the differences lies in the effects of technological change and the complete failure of the forecasters to anticipate them. Economists in the past decade have been busily at work attempting to repair this neglect. When they have addressed themselves to the question posed earlier, of the relative importance to economic growth of using more inputs as against using inputs more efficiently, they have found that the latter source seems to be overwhelmingly the more important. Quantitative studies for the United States have suggested that no more than 15 percent of the observed rise in per capita incomes could be accounted for by growth in the (qualitatively unchanged) stock of capital per worker. These studies were very crude in their methods, and much effort is now being devoted to developing more refined measures. But it now seems clear that technological change has made a massive contribution to the growth of the American economy.

The productivity-increasing impact of technological change has had major effects on the structure and organization of our modern economic system. Many of the differences between the American economy in 1800 and in 1970 can be traced to an increasing reliance upon a technology possessing certain characteristics, requiring economic activity to be organized in different and specific ways. Moreover, the rising levels of income over the past 150 years have been associated with those changes in the composition of demand and thus of final output sketched out in Chapter 3. The most spectacular and far-reaching change is the decline in the relative importance of the agricultural sector as the percentage of consumer budgets spent on food has declined; closely associated with this trend is the rising importance of the service sector, a sector which, it should be noted, includes the growing activities of government. The impact of technology, then, lies not only behind the changing productivity of economic inputs but also behind the drastic changes in the *composition* of output and the shifting composition and allocation of inputs (e.g., changes in the industrial and occupational composition of the labor force). The long-term downward decline in the length of the workweek and the corresponding increase in leisure-time activities have been the result of growing productivity, combined with a set of tastes which has treated leisure time as a "superior good" increasingly demanded with rising income. The imperatives of technological change have generated spatial shifts in the location of industry and produced a whole complex of phenomena associated with urbanization. These phenomena are explored in Chapters 15 and 16.

The relationship between technological change and long-term growth can be seen by examining the productivity-increasing aspects of such change. But this is far from the whole story. American society in the 1970s is vastly different from the world of 1800, not just because technological change makes it possible to produce more output per unit of input, but because it has also provided an expanded array of new commodities and services. Our lives have been profoundly transformed by these new goods and services: instant means of communication, high-speed travel, modern electronics, chemistry, synthetic materials, the medical technologies of birth prevention and death postponement, and the instruments of a potentially apocalyptic military capacity. We cannot hope to arrive at a mature understanding of the long-term impact of technological change without recognizing explicitly its effect on the composition as well as the volume of the economy's final output.

In Chapter 3 we glimpsed how technology has altered the operation of an ordinary American household. The protracted drudgery of food preparation has been substantially reduced by a long series of innovations which have located food preparation and processing in commercial firms and have permitted households to store prepared foods for prolonged periods of time. These techniques have made possible a much more interesting, varied, and nutritious diet (the evidence of TV dinners to the contrary notwithstanding). Canning techniques, which originated from military requirements during the Napoleonic Wars, became widespread in the United States after 1840. The rise of meat-packing firms and commercial bakeries and the development of efficient ice-boxes, refrigerators,[1] and freezers compressed the time devoted to food processing and preparation in the household. The sewing machine, which made its commercial appearance in the 1850s, was rapidly introduced into homes in subsequent decades, and drastically reduced the time used in making clothing for family members. American manufacturers sold 1.5 million sewing machines between 1856 and 1869 and 4.8 million from 1869 to 1879. With electrification of the home came an impressive collection of household appliances: the vacuum cleaner, water heater, washing machine and drier, and dishwasher. Cooking has been much simplified by electric and gas stoves, but it should also be remembered that the cast iron stove, which these typically replaced, was one of the most important domestic innovations in the first half of the nineteenth century. In the heating of homes, wood fires were replaced by coal, and later oil and gas were introduced into the central heating unit. When these units were subjected to thermostatic control the heating of homes became completely automated.

The sources of lighting in the American household have passed through a series of improvements from candles and oil lamps in the early nineteenth century to the predominance of kerosene lamps after 1860 and some use of gas lighting in the 1890s and after. All this was swept away by electric lighting in the early decades of the twentieth century—a transition which was accelerated in the 1930s by the establishment of the Rural Electrification

[1] The development of the refrigerated railroad car had been instrumental in delivering the meat from meat-packing plants to households.

Commission, which subsidized the extension of electrification into rural America.

Another collection of inventions placed the individual household in touch with the outside world and exposed the family to a series of outside ties and influences which have had far-reaching social and cultural consequences. The telephone, patented in 1876, made possible instantaneous communication with other telephone subscribers. The phonograph, developed in the last quarter of the nineteenth century, brought durable recordings of music and the human voice into the living room.[2] Commercial radio broadcasting began in the 1920s and commercial television broadcasting began after World War II. This "plugging-in" of the household to the outside world brought with it new and pervasive cultural influences and led to dramatic alterations in the pattern of leisure-time activities.

Members of the household who ventured some distance from their homes would have required, on land, either a horse or some form of horse-drawn transport at the beginning of the nineteenth century. Canals became an important alternative after the opening of the highly successful Erie Canal in 1825. Then, starting in the 1830s, the country began to be progressively linked by a railroad network, moving individuals at previously unheard-of speeds. In the first decade of the twentieth century, the automobile, providing its owner with a private form of transportation, began its remarkable growth, and the country's network of surfaced roads expanded in response to the automobile's needs. (The automobile had been preceded—and assisted—by the bicycle craze of the 1890s, but this ingenious device was used largely for recreational purposes.) Commercial aviation, which was initiated in the 1930s (production of the highly reliable DC-3 was begun in 1935), was held up by World War II and experienced a mushrooming growth in the postwar years. With the advent of the jet plane it became possible to span a continent—or an ocean—in less than six hours.

One important effect of these innovations upon the conduct of the household and the family in general, which should not go unnoticed, is the rise in the female labor-force participation rate—especially among married women.[3] Several technological forces, including the increasing effectiveness and wider diffusion of birth-control technology, worked in this direction. The transfer of traditional household functions outside the household and the availability of a growing range of household appliances reduced the time required for the performance of household tasks. At the same time, the availability of the increasingly numerous consumer durables—both those which facilitated the performance of housework and those desired for recreational purposes—created an inducement to enter the labor force in order to earn the incomes with which to purchase them. Finally, those inventions which lowered the cost of office work—the typewriter, telephone, and other new office equip-

---

[2] It is an interesting commentary on the limited vision and social imagination of even the most versatile inventor that Thomas Edison is said to have thought that the phonograph would be useful principally to record the last wishes of old men on their deathbeds.

[3] The labor-force participation rate for females rose from 18.2 percent in 1890 to 29.0 percent in 1950.

ment—increased employment opportunities of a kind which were readily undertaken by females.

Aside from the major new products which we have considered so far, technological change has also been responsible for innumerable product alterations and quality changes, some of which are indistinguishable from product innovation itself. Is the ball-point pen "just" a modification of the fountain pen and the modern washer-drier "merely" a modernized version of the old-fashioned wringer washing machines? Perhaps. But—to use a different example—the effectiveness of antibiotics in the treatment of infectious disease suggests strongly that some qualitative improvements should be recognized as differences in kind—the difference in this case between life and death. Surely many pharmaceutical innovations, from the ubiquitous aspirin and vitamins to more recent antihistamines, tranquilizers, and contraceptive pills, have brought more effective release from pain, disease control, freedom from discomfort and stress, and a degree of control over the reproductive consequences of sexual relations—changes of truly massive significance to the human condition, although most difficult to express in quantitative terms.

Technology has generated product changes of all sorts, from discrete changes without closely identifiable antecedents to much more numerous, smaller modifications whose cumulative effects are now very large. The American landscape is littered with artifacts of a now obsolete or nearly obsolete technology—not only fountain pens and wringer washing machines, but also shaving mugs, milk bottles, 78 rpm records, inner tubes, automobile seat covers, trolley cars, Mason jars, and newsreels. Each of these once widely used products has now been largely or entirely superseded.

TECHNOLOGY AND RESOURCE ENDOWMENT

Technological knowledge ought to be understood as the sort of information which improves man's capacity to control and to manipulate the natural environment in the fulfillment of human goals, and to make that environment more responsive to human needs.[4] The intimate relationship between technology and environment becomes apparent as soon as one asks the question: What constitutes a natural resource? The answer is not a simple one, but the best way to begin is by saying: It all depends. If we define resources in terms of mineral deposits or acres of potentially arable land, qualifications spring to

[4] This definition of technology is in conformity with the classic "man v. natural environment" conceptualization which received an early philosophical formulation in the work of John Locke, and is essentially the modern view. Talcott Parsons, for example, states that ". . . technology is the socially organized capacity for actively controlling and altering objects of the physical environment in the interest of some human want or need." [Talcott Parsons, *Societies* (Englewood Cliffs, N.J.: Prentice-Hall, 1966), p. 15.] This view represents a useful and legitimate abstraction and is the one adopted here. It should be understood, however, that the view excludes much of importance to a broader understanding of the social impact of technology. Specifically, a considerable amount of technology has as at least one of its uses the manipulation of people themselves. Commercial advertising on TV and other communication media is an obvious example. The Winchester repeating rifle improved man's capacities as a hunter of game but also brought about important changes in power relationships between human groups, such as the westward-moving American settlers and the Plains Indians. To define technology solely in terms of the capacity it provides for the exploitation of the natural environment is to overlook some of its critical social functions.

mind. The Plains Indian did not cultivate the soil; neither coal, oil, nor bauxite constituted a resource to the Indian population nor, for that matter, to the earliest European settlers in North America. It was only when technological knowledge had advanced to a certain point that such mineral deposits became potentially usable for human purposes. A further economic question turns, in part, upon accessibility and cost of extraction. Improvements in oil-drilling technology (as well as changing demand conditions) make it feasible to extract oil today from depths which would have been technically impossible 50 years ago and prohibitively expensive 20 years ago. Similarly, low-grade taconite iron ores are being routinely exploited today, although they would have been ignored earlier in the century when the higher-quality ores of the Mesabi Range were available in abundance. The rich and plentiful agricultural resources of the Midwest were of limited economic importance until the development of a canal network, beginning in the 1820s with the completion of the Erie Canal, and later a railroad system which made possible the transportation of bulky farm products to eastern urban centers at low cost. Natural resources, in other words, cannot be cataloged in geographic or geological terms alone. Their economic usefulness is subject to continual redefinition as a result of both economic changes and alterations in the stock of technological knowledge.

These observations are highly relevant to the central interests of this chapter. We have seen that, from a more abstract point of view, a growth in the stock of technological knowledge may be reduced either to (a) a shift in the production function—an increase in output obtainable from a given quantity of inputs; or (b) the creation of a new production function—the introduction of a new product or service. But from the perspective of the economic historian surveying the historical experience in the wealth, and poverty, of nations, the production and use of technological knowledge must be seen against the backdrop of specific societies with different cultural heritages and values, different human capital and intellectual equipment, and an environment with a very specific collection of resources. The emphasis on the specificity of resources is important because resources establish the particular framework of problems, of constraints and opportunities, to which technological change is the (occasional) human response. Although we may usefully *conceive* of technological change for analytical purposes and for purposes of quantification in an abstract way as an alteration in the relationship between inputs and outputs, it does not *occur* in the abstract, but rather in very specific historical contexts. It occurs, that is, as a successful solution to a particular problem thrown up in a particular resource context. For example, the cutting off of an accustomed source of supply during wartime has often been an important stimulus for the development of new techniques. France's early commercial leadership in the production of synthetic alkalis (utilizing the Leblanc process) was, in large measure, a result of losing her access to her traditional supplies of Spanish barilla during the Napoleonic Wars. The Haber nitrogen-fixation process was developed by the Germans during World War I when the British blockade deprived them of their imports of Chilean nitrates. The loss of

Malayan natural rubber as a result of Japanese occupation in World War II played a critical role in the rapid emergence of the American synthetic-rubber industry. On the other hand, the fact that the British led the world in the development of a coal-using technology was hardly surprising in view of the abundance and easy accessibility of her coal deposits and the growing scarcity of her wood-fuel supplies, which increasingly constrained the expansion of her industries in the seventeenth and eighteenth centuries. Indeed, the steam engine itself originated as a pump for solving the problem of rising water levels which impeded extractive activity in British mines for coal as well as other minerals. It seems equally fitting and proper that the British are currently performing the pioneering work in the development of techniques for the instrument landing of airplanes in dense fog; and conditions of the natural environment make it appropriate for the Israelis to be devoting much effort to cheap desalination techniques, the Dutch to the development of salt-resistant crop varieties, and the students at California Institute of Technology to perfecting an electric motor for use in automobiles. In all these cases, technological exploration is intimately linked up with patterns of resource availability or conditions of the natural environment in particular locations.

The distinction between innovation and adaptation (or between a shift in a production function and movement along an existing production function) is frequently much overstated. It is a common practice (especially among textbook writers) to draw smooth continuous curves (as we have done) to represent the spectrum of techniques available at a given time. Frequently, however, only a very limited number of points among such possibilities are actually known. It is often also the case that a product can be created under carefully controlled laboratory conditions but cannot be produced in commercial quantities without a great deal of further research and engineering. Under these circumstances, the exploratory activity induced by changes in factor prices is of a sort requiring high levels of skill and insight fully comparable to what is ordinarily described as innovation. To call such extensions of the production function, in response to changing factor prices, "adaptations" or "adjustments" but not "innovation" is to understate the effort, the creative skills, and the economic importance which such activities frequently involve.

In the United States, perhaps the most enduring and pervasive influence shaping the contours of technological development has been the very high land/labor ratio, the general abundance of natural resources relative to a small population. A distinctive feature of much American innovation, therefore, was that it was directed toward making possible the exploitation of a large quantity of such resources with relatively little labor or that it substituted units of the abundant input (natural resources) for units of the scarce input (labor, and, to a lesser extent, capital). For example, in the area of agriculture, a major thrust of agricultural innovation in the second half of the nineteenth century was to increase the acreage which could be cultivated by a single farmer, in large measure by substituting animal power for manpower. In Chapter 11, in a study of cereal production (wheat, corn, and oats), it is demonstrated that output per worker in the United States more than tripled between 1840 and

1911. Some 60 percent of this increase is attributed to mechanization, a process which raised the feasible acreage/worker ratio. Virtually all of the growth in productivity can be explained by the combination of mechanization with the westward expansion of agriculture. The major improvements came in the harvesting and post-harvesting operations—previously highly labor-intensive activities. In fact, it is found that 70 percent of the total gain from mechanization was attributable to only two innovations, the reaper and the thresher. In corn production, the replacement of the hoe by the cultivator in the middle decades of the nineteenth century and the introduction of the corn picker in the 1890s were responsible for major reductions in labor requirements. In the South, the cotton gin attacked the highly labor-intensive activity of the manual removal of the seeds from the cotton boll after the cotton had been picked, and thus eliminated a basic constraint upon the westward spread of cotton cultivation in the southern states. Before the development of the cotton gin, production had been confined to seacoast areas where it was possible to grow the long-stranded sea-island cotton. The cotton gin, by sharply reducing the cost of seed removal, made it economically feasible to raise the short-staple upland cotton. With this innovation, cotton culture could be extended far beyond its earlier area. Later in the nineteenth century the introduction of cheap barbed-wire fencing in the West—an area with few natural materials for fences—made practicable the highly land-intensive techniques of live-stock raising which became so characteristic of the region.

In order to exploit the vast forest resources of the country, the United States in the first half of the nineteenth century brought to an advanced stage of perfection a whole range of woodworking machines for sawing, planing, mortising, tenoning, shaping, and boring, in addition to innumerable more specialized machines (and in addition to important improvements in the design of that much more venerable instrument, the axe). If manufacturing sectors are ranked by value added by manufacture, the lumber industry in 1860 was, according to the U.S. census of that year, the second largest industry in the United States, after cotton goods. In the western and southern states it was the most important manufacturing industry. During this same period, per capita lumber consumption in the United States may have been as much as five times as high as in England and Wales.

By the 1850s, American woodworking machinery was generally acknowledged by Europeans to be the most sophisticated and ingenious in the world. The relatively limited degree to which these machines were adopted in Europe, however, seems to have reflected the fact that they were, in many ways, wasteful of wood—a consideration much less important in the United States than in Great Britain in the first half of the nineteenth century. American circular saws, for example, while very fast, had thicker blades, with their teeth spaced widely apart, and converted a distressingly large portion of the log into sawdust. They also generally used more power and required less care and maintenance—characteristics well adapted to American resource endowment but ill adapted to conditions in the British Isles. Indeed, an observer writing in the early 1870s, who was familiar with British and American woodworking methods, stated categorically that: "Lumber manufacture, from the log to the finished state, is, in America, characterized by a waste that can truly be called criminal. . . ."[5] This characterization might have been reasonable if American techniques had been employed in Britain. Given the relative factor scarcities in the United States, however, these techniques, by substituting cheap wood for expensive labor, may well have been optimal. In England, by contrast, handicraft technology, which amounted to the substitution of (relatively) cheap labor for (relatively) expensive wood, continued to prevail.

SOME FACTORS UNDERLYING INNOVATIVE ACTIVITY

Technological change, as we have seen, can be examined as an adaptive, problem-solving activity whereby techniques are developed which enable a society to exploit the opportunities and to overcome the constraints implicit in its environment. Economic growth reflects the success which a country has had in mobilizing its resources to achieve technological breakthroughs. Why do some societies have a much greater apparent *capacity* than others to generate the appropriate inventions? Why are some societies much more receptive to the introduction of inventions made elsewhere? Questions of this sort go far beyond conventional economics and involve human skills, motivation, and the efficiency of social and economic institutions. The two questions are quite distinct, since requirements for successful inventive activity may be very different from the requirements for rapid *adoption* of inventions, once made. It has been observed often that the French had great inventive talent but were weak in the application of new inventions, whereas the Japanese, on the other hand, have not been responsible for many major inventions but have had a remarkable capacity for putting foreign inventions to their own uses.

In the United States in the nineteenth century, the rapid rate of technological change reflected both a high level of inventive activity and a rapid rate of adoption. The United States possessed an advantage common to all latecomers in industrialization: It was able to borrow and to modify a technology which had been developed by others. Immigrants to the United States brought European technology with them and continued to draw heavily upon it. The intense energy and single-mindedness with which Americans pursued economic goals were notorious.[6] The strong utilitarian bent in American society was described as follows in an article, "Forty Days in a Western Hotel," which appeared in *Putnam's Magazine* in December 1854, as follows.

[5] J. Richards, *A Treatise on the Construction and Operation of Wood-Working Machines* (London 1872), p. 141.

[6] Perhaps the large flow of immigrants into American society added to the strong economic orientation of the American population. The Europeans who migrated to the United States probably did not constitute a random sample of the European population; they must have been a self-selected group including many who were especially responsive to economic incentives and prepared to experience privation and uncertainties and to endure the strangeness of a new culture and environment if it held out the prospect of eventual economic improvement.

The genius of this new country is necessarily mechanical. Our greatest thinkers are not in the library, nor the capitol, but in the machine shop. The American people is intent on studying, not the hieroglyphic monuments of ancient genius, but how best to subdue and till the soil of its boundless territories; how to build roads and ships; how to apply the powers of nature to the work of manufacturing its rich materials into forms of utility and enjoyment. The youth of this country are learning the sciences, not as theories, but with reference to their application to the arts. Our education is no genial culture of letters, but simply learning the use of tools.[7]

These comments well express certain attitudes and values behind the high rate of technological change in the nineteenth century. These positive social values, as well as the absence of the inhibiting institutions prevalent in Europe, cooperated to direct much of the creative energy of the American population into pursuits which often resulted in the development of new and superior techniques.

Not only did American society devote a large proportion of its resources to inventive activities, it also equipped the American people through formal education with skills which helped make them successful both as inventors and as successful borrowers and modifiers of technologies developed elsewhere. As early as 1830, the United States was second only to Germany in the proportion of the total population enrolled in school. If slaves, for whom no education was provided, are excluded, the (white) American population of 1830 probably ranked first in the world by this admittedly crude measure. In 1850 the American figures for school enrollment were certainly the highest in the world and, by that date, the white American population was among the best educated of the world's masses. The figures for New England, where much of the inventive activity was concentrated, were substantially above the average. This commitment to education was a major conditioning factor, of far-reaching significance in its effects upon invention and diffusion.[8]

It is difficult to say a great deal in purely economic terms about national differences in inventiveness and the capacity for "creative response." But economic reasoning helps to answer more modest questions about these subjects. The search for new techniques in a country is strongly influenced by its factor endowment, which poses specific constraints and provides specific opportunities for participants. Inventive activity involves the use of scarce and valuable resources; like other economic activities, it is responsive to market forces and prospects of financial gain. These prospects occur as the net result of conditions of demand and of supply. Inventive activity, then, receives its changing direction over time from the changing perceptions of the future profits (profit expectations) to be derived from the solution of specific technical problems. Since the activity is rooted in the perception of profit possibilities, it will be influenced by any forces which (a) alter the revenue flow which the use of the invention is expected to generate, or (b) alter the expected cost of making the invention.

[7] The article, by J. Milton Mackie, was published anonymously but reprinted later in Mackie's book, *From Cape Cod to Dixie and the Tropics* (New York: 1864). The quotation is from pages 200–201 of the book.

[8] For the data upon which this paragraph is based, see Richard A. Easterlin, "A Note on the Evidence of History," in *Education and Economic Development*, C. Arnold Anderson and Mary Jean Bowman (eds.) (Chicago: Aldine, 1965), pp. 426–427.

The Role of Demand

The demand conditions of an invention are influenced by any increase in revenue flows or any reduction in expenditure flows associated with the employment of the invention. The expected returns will be affected by any forces which alter the demand for the final product to which the invention may be related. Such forces may include changes in per capita income, changes in family size and age composition of the population, and urbanization. Schmookler has shown that variations in demand forces are a major determinant of variations in the allocation of inventive effort to specific industries.[9] For over a century, he found in the data close correspondence between variations in the purchase of railroad equipment and components, and variations in patenting activity (see Figure 7.3). Reductions in the purchase of railroad equipment were followed by a lagged decline in the number of patents issued in this industry. The lag, Schmookler argued, means that variations in the sale of equipment induce the variations in numbers of patents. Schmookler found similar relationships in petroleum refining and building, although the long-term data on these industries are less comprehensive. In cross-sectional data for a large number of industries in the years before and after World War II, Schmookler also found a very high correlation between inventions of capital goods in an industry and the volume of sales of capital goods to that industry. Schmookler's empirical data, therefore, strongly support the view that inventors perceive the growth in the purchase of equipment by an industry as signaling an expansion of profit prospects in that industry, and direct their talents accordingly. Similarly, Griliches has shown that the entry of hybrid corn-seed producers into different portions of the national market was closely related to expected demand, as measured by each region's market density.[10]

The demand for, and the profitability of, specific kinds of inventions may change in response to numerous forces, including economic growth itself. The much higher levels of per capita incomes today as compared to the early nineteenth century, and the differences in the composition of expenditures associated with higher levels of per capita income (Engel's law), are surely related to the shift from the inventions in food preparation and processing of 150 years ago to the inventions oriented toward leisure-time activities today. Specific features of the natural environment also decisively and differentially affect the profitability of different inventions, as we have mentioned. For example, America led the world in the commercial exploitation of the steamboat, a development which antedated the application of steam power to railways. It was hardly an accident that in the United States the conditions of geography, especially the vast system of natural inland waterways flowing into the Mississippi Valley, made the steamboat superior to alternative means of transport by a wide margin. In Great Britain and Western Europe, coastal waterways and canals were highly efficient and substantially reduced the relative attractiveness of the steamboat. (See Chapter 13.)

---

[9] Jacob Schmookler, *Invention and Economic Growth* (Cambridge, Mass.: Harvard University Press, 1966)
[10] Zvi Griliches, "Hybrid Corn: An Exploration in the Economics of Technological Change," *Econometrical*, vol. 25 (October 1957).

FIGURE 7.3
Capital formation and patents in the railroad industry, 1840–1950

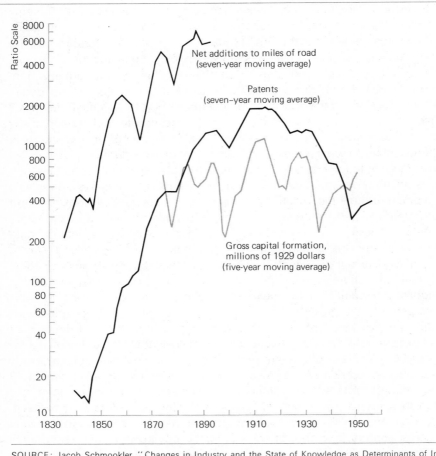

SOURCE: Jacob Schmookler, "Changes in Industry and the State of Knowledge as Determinants of Industrial Invention," in *The Rate and Direction of Inventive Activity* (New York: National Bureau of Economic Research, 1962), p. 200. Reprinted by permission of the publisher. Net additions to miles of roads are used as representative of capital formation for the early years when a more direct measure is not available.

Frequently, demand for a particular invention is generated or increased by the introduction of another invention, if the performance of one depends upon that of the other. The interdependence among component parts of a complex technology generates internal imbalances and pressures which push exploratory activity in specific directions. Thus, improvements in automobile engine design, permitting operation at higher speeds, led to the invention of improved braking systems and stronger and more reliable tires. Important innovations in the design and construction of bridges in the United States came largely with the expansion of the railroad system, which required large numbers of bridges of high performance specification. And George Westinghouse's important invention of the air brake occurred after people became seriously concerned over the difficulty of stopping long trains carrying heavy goods at high speeds. Improvements in weaving operations in textiles in eighteenth-century England increased the profitability of inventions in spinning by increasing the demand for spun yarn. In the machine-tool industry just after the turn of the twentieth century, a new alloy dramatically increased the speed at which machine tools could cut metal. This innovation generated numerous changes in the other component parts of the machine tool—the structural, transmission, and control elements—without which the high-speed steel tools could not have been fully utilized. The cone pulley, a primitive device for altering the speed of the machine tool in accordance with the requirements of the work in hand, was replaced by sophisticated gear-change devices which operated by shifting a lever. Similar sequences of shifting profitability have occurred in recent years with the introduction of cemented carbide and ceramic tools. Interdependence in the components of the lathe could be duplicated in the relationship between milling cutters and milling machines or grinding wheels and grinding machines. Examples of this sort could be multiplied endlessly.

Growth in final demand and the malleability of consumers' tastes add another demand influence on the course of technological change. The public's willingness to accept a homogeneous final product was indispensable in the transition from a labor-intensive handicraft technology to highly specialized machines. Across a whole range of commodities British consumers imposed their tastes on the producer in a manner which seriously constrained his exploitation of machine technology. English observers in the mid-nineteenth century often noted with no small astonishment that American products were designed to accommodate not the consumer, but the machine. One author notes of the American cutlery trade, for example, that "where mechanical devices cannot be adjusted to the production of the traditional product, the product must be modified to the demands of the machine. Hence, the standard American table-knife is a rigid, metal shape, handle and blade forged in one piece, the whole being finished by electroplating—an implement eminently suited to factory production."[11] Even with respect to an object as ostensibly utilitarian as a gun, the British civilian market was long dominated by peculiarities of taste which precluded machine techniques. Similarly, America's early leadership in mechanizing the production of men's clothing reflected a great willingness on the American side to accept a "ready-made" suit.

A close relationship has existed, then, between the composition of demand and homogeneity of product, on the one hand, and the range of technological possibilities open to society, on the other. In order to be suitable for mass-production techniques, the producer must be able to design his product with some minimum degree of freedom, and it seems apparent that, in this respect, the American producer was much less constrained by consumer tastes than was his English counterpart. This difference had a great deal to do with the origin of mass-production technology in the United States rather than in Eng-

[11] G. I. H. Lloyd, *The Cutlery Trades* (London: Longmans, Green, 1913), pp. 394–395.

land and with early American leadership in products which were particularly well suited to such techniques. The distinctive nature of American goods, as they were exhibited at the London Crystal Palace Exhibition in 1851, was perceptively noted by British observers in the official catalog:

> The absence in the United States of those vast accumulations of wealth which favour the expenditure of large sums on articles of mere luxury, and the general distribution of the means of procuring the more substantial conveniences of life, impart to the productions of American industry a character distinct from that of many other countries. The expenditure of months or years of labour upon a single article, not to increase its intrinsic value, but solely to augment its cost or its estimation as an object of *virtu*, is not common in the United States. On the contrary, both manual and mechanical labour are applied with direct reference to increasing the number of the quantity of articles suited to the wants of a whole people, and adapted to promote the enjoyment of that moderate competency which prevails among them. [12]

The Role of Supply

So far our discussion of the determinants of the direction of inventive activity has been confined to demand forces. But clearly these forces alone can no more explain the allocation of inventive resources than they can, alone, provide an explanation for the determination of the price of a commodity. For such an explanation we must consider, also, the role of supply phenomena. The basic argument is that, at any time, demand and supply considerations interact to provide, for the whole range of inventive possibilities, a configuration of profit expectations which, in turn, shapes the allocation of inventive resources. Furthermore, changes in the allocation of such resources over time may result from changes in the structure of demand, changes in the conditions of supply, or both. Economic growth requires, in the long run, a general relaxation of supply constraints; nevertheless, constraints must be known if one is to explain the specific direction of inventive activity at any given time. People possessing technical skills inevitably work on problems which their knowledge and training render interesting, potentially soluble, and potentially rewarding. Such people devote their attention to only a small subset of all those inventions which would, if successfully developed, prove rewarding. They choose those which fall somehow within their line of vision and which seem to have a good chance of solution. Supply considerations, broadly considered, determine the repertoire of responses to demand forces available to the inventors in a society at any given time.

What can now be said about the nature of these supply constraints? Clearly, the prospective cost of an invention will depend upon the supply of all the factors involved in inventive activity. Such costs reflect the relative scarcity of these factors and their specific qualities, which may be relevant to an inventive process. The essence of inventive activity is the capacity to solve

---

[12] *Official Description and Illustrated Catalogue of the Great Exhibition of the Works of Industry of All Nations,* vol. 3 (London: 1851), p. 1431. See also Chapter 3 for a detailed treatment of the relationship between the socioeconomic characteristics of the American population and the nature of the demand for consumer goods.

certain problems, and this depends upon the supply of inventive skills, sharpened by on-the-job training or by formal education, and the organized technological and scientific knowledge available to the people who possess those skills.

Changes in these human and nonhuman inputs over time are responsible for differential shifts in the production functions for different categories of human wants, or for different ways of satisfying the same want or the same category of wants. Improvements in the appropriate skills, talents, and knowledge combine to lower the expected cost and therefore to raise the expected profitability of a particular inventive effort.

At this point, the discussion must be shifted from the abstract and general to the particular and specific. For technological change is not something which has emerged in a random way from all sectors of the economy. It is, rather, the result of certain acquired problem-solving skills which, in our history, have been heavily concentrated in some specific sectors of the economy. Throughout the nineteenth century, although with decreasing emphasis after 1870, these skills were heavily concentrated in metallurgy, machine tools, steam power, and engineering. The invention of new machines or machine-made products—the cotton gin, reaper, thresher, cultivator, typewriter, barbed wire, revolver, sewing machine, bicycle, automobile—involved the solution of problems which required mechanical skill, ingenuity, and versatility but not, typically, a recourse to scientific knowledge or experimental methods. In related areas where such knowledge would have been highly relevant—for example, in guiding metallurgical practice—it was virtually nonexistent. Metallurgy was an area dominated by a crude empiricism of trial-and-error techniques which, however, were highly successful in solving the simple problems in the early stages of the development of the art. Until roughly the last third of the nineteenth century, modern metallurgical science, involving a serious study of the structure and chemical composition of material, was quite unknown.

As late as 1869, when Mendelejeff published his periodic table of the elements, not a single journal specializing in the science of chemistry was published in the United States. The major publication outlet for American chemistry was the *American Journal of Science*, founded by Benjamin Silliman, Sr., in 1818, to cater to the whole range of scientific interests.

Increasingly in the last century, in large part as a result of advances in science, the focus has shifted to techniques and processes based on chemistry, electrical engineering and electronics and, more recently, the biological sciences. With the dramatic growth of these science-based industries in the twentieth century, technological change has become increasingly dependent upon the exploitation of scientific knowledge—often knowledge of recent acquisition. The development of hybrid corn in the 1930s required a sophisticated knowledge of genetic processes ; the post-World War II development of the transistor was made possible by quantum mechanics as it emerged in the 1920s ; and the spectacular growth in synthetic materials was built upon an advanced understanding of molecular chemistry. This growing intimacy between scientific and techno-logical advances in certain industries is a very recent phenomenon, and has been associated with drastic organizational and institutional changes on the supply side in recent decades : an increasing dependence upon an educational establishment for skilled personnel and a massive commitment of federal funds to higher education and research since World War II. In the early growth of our industrial society, enormous strides were made on the basis of mechanical ingenuity and crude empiricism, producing a growing mastery of metal-making and metal-using techniques, but with very limited access to scientific know-ledge. Now progress in many areas is thrust closely against the constraints im-posed by the knowledge frontier. We will return to this subject shortly.

Price-Induced Adaptations

We have discussed so far the ways in which demand and supply forces affect the allocation of inventive resources. But the effect of market forces upon the broader process of technological change is much more general and pervasive than has been explicitly recognized.

First, the price mechanism is critical to the *selection* of a technology. Given the range of available productive techniques of differing factor intensities, and given also the existing prices of the factors of production, the appropriate least-cost technique can be determined. Relative price differences, therefore, provide an important explanation for observable differences between regions or countries in the techniques employed. The use of wood in nineteenth-century America in places where the British had employed masonry, brick, or metals, is a case in point. Furthermore, *changes* in relative factor prices will account, over time, for decisions to adopt techniques of differing factor in-tensities from those previously employed.

Secondly, the relative prices of factors may influence not only the selection among existing techniques, but the *direction* of technological change as well. Under strictly competitive conditions an inventor will not be concerned with the relative factor-saving bias of a potential invention. Cost reduction will be sought in any and all directions ; whether a particular invention will have a labor-saving, resource-saving, or capital-saving bias is of no particular interest. As Salter has put it, speaking of Hicks' theory of induced inventions :

> If . . . the theory implies that dearer labour stimulates the search for new knowledge aimed specifically at saving labour, then it is open to serious objections. The entrepreneur is interested in reducing costs in total, not particular costs such as labour costs or capital costs. When labour costs rise any advance that reduces total cost is welcome, and whether this is achieved by saving labour or capital is irrelevant. There is no reason to assume that attention should be concentrated on labour-saving techniques. . . .[13]

On the other hand, if there are firmly held expectations about the *future* path of relative price changes, the payoff function to invention will be influenced

---

[13] W. E. G. Salter, *Productivity and Technical Change* (New York : Cambridge University Press, 1960), pp. 43–44.

by these expectations. If, for example, businessmen infer that in the past there has been an historical trend, associated with a high rate of capital accumulation, for the capital/labor ratio to rise and if, in the absence of contrary evidence, they extrapolate this trend into the future, their expectations will be that labor costs will rise relative to the cost of capital. It will therefore pay to attempt invention in directions which will economize upon the factor of production whose relative price is expected to rise. Such expectations appear to have played a major role in the widely observed and much commented upon tendency for Americans to *invent as well as adopt labor-saving machinery*. It was not the high level of wages as such, but rather the persistent pressures on the labor market, the numerous opportunities for labor in a resource-abundant environment, and the high degree of labor mobility that conditioned entrepreneurs to expect further future increases in the cost of labor relative to other inputs, and gave them a strong bias toward the development of labor-saving techniques. It should be noted, however, that the motivation is perfectly general. Firmly held expectations about the future rise in the relative price of *any* input can be expected to induce exploratory activity to economize on the use of that particular input.

Finally, it must be emphasized that the contribution of an invention to economic growth depended not on the timing of the invention itself but on the rate of its adoption and diffusion. Our earlier discussion would lead us to expect that the relative attractiveness of any invention would vary in different economic environments. In fact, relative profitability serves as a powerful variable in explaining the timing of major inventions and the rate at which they have been adopted in the past.

TECHNOLOGICAL ADVANCES IN THE UNITED STATES

The earlier sections of this chapter have been devoted to an examination of the factors—social, intellectual, and economic—influencing the demand and supply of inventions and the general course, character, and organization of inventive activity. It is possible now to examine more closely the actual history of inventions in the United States since 1800.

A description of all the technological changes which occurred in this period would quickly bog down in a morass of tedious detail and add little to our perspective or understanding. The treatment therefore has been divided into three parts, showing the history in relation to certain important problems. First, we will concentrate on some distinctive features in the forward thrust of American production methods in the nineteenth century. In the next section we will examine distinctive—and more complex—characteristics of twentieth-century technological change as it emerged out of nineteenth-century origins. This separation by centuries is for expository convenience only, and will not—in fact, cannot—be adhered to strictly. Finally, in the history of energy utilization, we observe an area so strong in long-term continuities that it is reserved for treatment in a separate section.

TABLE 7.1
Sector shares in commodity output, 1839–1899 (percent)

Year	Agriculture	Mining	Manufacturing	Construction
1839	72	1	17	10
1849	60	1	30	10
1859	56	1	32	11
1869	53	2	33	12
1879	49	3	37	11
1889	37	4	48	11
1899	33	5	53	9

SOURCE: Robert E. Gallman, "Commodity Output, 1839–1899," in *Trends in the American Economy in the 19th Century*, William Parker (ed.) (New York: National Bureau of Economic Research, 1960), p. 26. Reprinted by permission of the publisher.

The Nineteenth Century

Much of the technology introduced into the U.S. economy in the nineteenth century was in no way peculiar to America. For the major components of industrial change—the substitution of machinery for handicraft skills (as in textiles), the widespread application of new power sources (particularly the steam engine) to industry and transportation, and the massive utilization of cheap iron (and, later, steel)—the United States was drawing upon a stock of innovations which had been previously developed and employed in Great Britain. (A discussion of many of the manufacturing techniques used is contained in Chapter 12.) However, in the nineteenth century, America also developed an industrial technology possessing certain features which distinguished it from the technology which had been developed earlier in Great Britain. These features were so special that, by the first half of the 1850s, they were beginning to be admired and borrowed without reservation by Great Britain.

The manufacturing sector was relatively small early in the nineteenth century, but grew at a striking rate and was easily the largest sector by the end of the century. This growth is apparent in Table 7.1. Within the manufacturing sector, more and more resources were devoted to supplying critical machinery inputs which were responsible for the growth in productivity in other sectors of the economy. Successful economic development in the nineteenth century was accompanied by a compositional shift in the stock of capital in favor of machinery.[14]

Technological change in the nineteenth century, then, was generated and eventually institutionalized in a very special way. It emerged in large measure as an accumulation of solutions to a range of technical problems facing a group of specialized manufacturing firms. These firms were the producers of capital goods—machinery and equipment used as inputs in other sectors of the economy. The growing skill exhibited by these firms in solving problems of

[14] Gallman's figures show a sharp rise in manufactured producers' durables as a proportion of the total output of capital goods (i.e., manufactured producers' durables plus total construction). This ratio rose from 10 percent in 1839 to 15 percent in 1859, to 20 percent in 1879, and stood at 31 percent in 1899. See Robert E. Gallman, "Commodity Output, 1839–1899," in *Trends in the American Economy in the 19th Century*, William Parker (ed.) (New York: National Bureau of Economic Research, 1960), p. 36.

specialized machine production ought to be regarded as the basic learning process underlying nineteenth-century industrialization. In saying this we are by no means neglecting other sectors, such as transportation, for we are looking at the sector of the economy which produced rolling stock and locomotives for the railroads; nor are we neglecting mining, for the increasingly sophisticated tools and machinery of mining originated here; nor are we neglecting agriculture, for in the nineteenth century, productivity growth in agriculture was largely a process of mechanization. (Indeed, the nineteenth-century mechanization of agriculture took place with little change in its power sources, since the new machines—the reaper, steel plow, cultivator, etc.—utilized that traditional power source, the horse.)[15]

The American system.   Europe became spectacularly aware of the existence of a special sort of technology in the United States at the great Crystal Palace Exhibition in London in 1851. What most impressed observers at that time was the technology of complex mechanisms utilizing interchangeable parts. That is to say, they were impressed by a method of producing mechanisms possessing closely fitting and interacting components in such a way that a given component of any one of the mechanisms would fit and perform equally well, *with no adjustments*, in any of the other mechanisms. The phrase coined at this period by the British, "the American system of manufacturing," referred specifically to this characteristic. Appropriately enough, the British public first observed this interchangeability in a display of American firearms at the Crystal Palace. A parliamentary committee sent to observe American techniques of firearms manufacture paid the ultimate compliment to American skill: It arranged for the purchase of a large quantity of the machinery for making firearms and installed this machinery in a gun-making arsenal in England.[16]

In a report on its visit to the U.S. armory at Springfield, the committee stated:

With regard to the interchange of parts between the machine-made muskets of the United States' Government, which has caused so much discussion, the Committee particularly interested themselves; and with the view of testing this as fully as possible selected with Colonel Ripley's permission ten muskets, each made in a different year, viz., from 1844 to 1853 inclusive, from the principal arsenal at Springfield, which they caused to be taken to pieces in their presence, and the parts placed in a row of boxes, mixed up together. They then requested the workman, whose duty it is to "assemble" the arms, to put them together, which he did—the Committee handing him the parts, taken at hazard—with the use of a turnscrew only, and as quickly as though they had been English muskets, whose parts had carefully been kept separate.[17]

[15] Mechanization did encourage the breeding of mules and involved a large-scale substitution of horses and mules for oxen, since the latter did not move swiftly enough to serve as efficient sources of motive power for the new machinery. Thus, whereas in the state of Illinois in 1850 there were about 3.5 horses for each ox, by 1870 this ratio had risen to about 43 horses for each ox. Charles H. Fitch, "Report on the Manufactures of Interchangeable Mechanism," in U.S. Bureau of the Census, *Census of Population: 1880*, vol. 2, *Manufactures* (Washington: U. S. Government Printing Office, 1883), p. 78.
[16] In the next 15 or 20 years, similar American gun-making machinery was shipped to Russia, Prussia, Spain, Turkey, Sweden, Denmark, Egypt, and other countries (Fitch, *op. cit.*, p. 4).
[17] "Report of the Committee on the Machinery of the U.S.A." in *The American System of Manufactures*, Nathan Rosenberg (ed.) (Edinburgh: Edinburgh University Press, 1969), pp. 121–122.

Interchangeability was worked out first in firearms partly because it vastly simplified the repair of the product. On the battlefield easy repair was important and it was possible even to reconstruct a damaged weapon if the parts were interchangeable. An army equipped with such weapons eliminated the dependence upon skilled armorers. But the feature is important for all products. One need only imagine the problems of repair and maintenance of complex products such as automobiles, bicycles, television sets, and typewriters in the absence of the high degree of standardization and precision manufacture of component parts. Interchangeability was essential also in the new and dramatically different technique of manufacture which came to dominate the light metal-working industries. It was in these industries that American technology developed unique features—of which interchangeability was one—which spread to a progressively wider range of products in the course of the nineteenth and twentieth centuries.

To appreciate the true significance of the new technology, we must consider the system which it replaced, one relying upon the developed skills of individual handicraftsmen. In gun making, the lock, stock, and barrel were each the work of a separate group of craftsmen. The locks, which were particularly intricate mechanisms, were produced by methods which involved the forging of component parts on an anvil, extensive filing to fit individual parts together, and finishing by polishing and hardening. In all this the file was the indispensable instrument which made fine adjustments, assuring that separate parts would interact easily. The gunstock was one of the most serious bottlenecks in firearms production as long as handicraft methods were employed. Its highly irregular shape seemed to defy the development of effective machine techniques, and the hand shaping of the stock, employing whittling knife, chisel, and file, was an extremely tedious and costly operation. Indeed, one authority stated that, before the introduction of woodworking machinery, a skilled man was capable of producing only one or two stocks a day.[18]

A major feature of the new American technology may now be simply stated: It eliminated or at least substantially reduced the very costly fitting activities which were an inseparable aspect of the older handicraft system. The new machines saved labor by eliminating the need for the highly labor-intensive fitting operations. A crucial difference between the old and new techniques is the difference between fitting and assembling. The parliamentary committee quoted earlier was so amazed at this feature that it enclosed the word "assemble" in quotation marks throughout its report.

> The workman whose business it is to "assemble" or set up the arms, takes the different parts promiscuously from a row of boxes, and uses nothing but the turnscrew to put the musket together, excepting on the slott, which contains the band-springs, which have to be squared out at one end with a small chisel. He receives four cents per musket, and has put together as many as 100 in a day and 530 in a week, but his usual day's work is from 50 to 60.
> The time is $3\frac{1}{2}$ minutes.[19]

[18] Fitch, *op. cit.*, p. 14.
[19] "Report of the Committee on the Machinery of the U.S.A.," in *The American System of Manufactures,* Nathan Rosenberg (ed.) (Edinburgh: Edinburgh University Press, 1969), pp. 142–143.

The fundamental revolution in productive techniques implied by a system under which fitting was abolished and a workman could assemble a musket using "nothing but the turnscrew" has been insufficiently appreciated. We are now so far removed in time from a society where craft skills predominated that we lack an awareness of some of its main cost and operating features. For this reason it is helpful to see the contrast between the old and the new systems through the eyes of the British parliamentary committee. Their report shows clearly their awareness that "assembling" a firearm was a technical innovation of major proportions. Henry Ford, who was later to bring the system to a more advanced stage of sophistication, also understood the point well. In his article, "Mass Production," which appeared in the twenty-second edition of the *Encyclopaedia Britannica*, he laconically observed: "In mass production there are no fitters."

Interchangeable components, the elimination of dependence upon handicraft skills, and the abolition of extensive fitting operations were, in turn, all aspects of a system whose central characteristic was the design and utilization of highly specialized machinery. The ability to invent, design, modify, and produce specialized machinery linked these characteristics together into a larger system of low-cost mass manufacture of standardized products. As the degree of precision in tool operation increased, and cheaper and more effective measurement devices became available, the interchangeability actually achieved on a complex machine increased markedly and the amount of hand labor accordingly declined. At the same time the technique of interchangeable parts penetrated into a wider range of metal-using products— clocks and watches, sewing machines, agricultural implements, locomotives, locks, hardware, ammunition, typewriters, bicycles, and, early in the twentieth century, automobiles. Some of the products of this new technology were household words for generations: Colt revolvers, Jerome clocks, Waltham watches, Yale locks, McCormick reapers, Singer sewing machines, and Remington rifles and typewriters. At length the production of the specialized machinery itself became a specialized activity undertaken by a well-defined group of firms in the capital-goods sector.

Rise of the machine-tool industry. This last development, the emergence of a new industry designing and producing highly specialized machinery, is so fundamental to the development of a technology of "machinofacture" (as Marx called it) that it demands more detailed examination. Industrialization at many points requires the same specialized skills and knowledge developed and employed in machinery design and production. Much learning, of wide application, took place in the few firms in that industry. The rate of industrialization was strongly affected by the speed with which technical knowledge was diffused from these points of origin to other sectors of the economy where it had further practical application. The role of the machine-tool industry, then, was a dual one: to develop new skills and techniques in response to the demands of specific customers, and to serve as the main transmission center for the transfer of new skills and techniques to the entire machine-using sector of the economy.

Around 1820 it would have been impossible to identify a distinct collection of firms whose primary activity was the production of machinery. Some machinery was made by firms in the metal or wood-products industries, whose skills and facilities could be applied to the manufacture of machinery. Machines were also produced by their ultimate users on an *ad hoc* basis. Machinery-producing firms can first be observed, in embryo, as adjuncts to textile firms in New England, such as the Amoskeag Manufacturing Company in Manchester, New Hampshire, and the Lowell Mills in Lowell, Massachusetts. The more successful of these shops undertook not only the manufacture of textile machinery for sale to other firms, but the production of a range of other kinds of machinery as well. These included steam engines, turbines, mill machinery, and machine tools. At this early stage, then, skills which had been acquired in the production of one kind of machine were transferred to other sectors by the simple expedient of an expansion and diversification of output on the part of a successful producer of one type of machinery. For example, the railroads were introduced during the 1830s, the Lowell Machine Shop, which had previously produced textile machinery, undertook to produce locomotives. In this new activity it was highly successful, and by the mid-1840s it became independent of its textile origins. By a parallel development, early locomotives were produced in New Hampshire by the Amoskeag Manufacturing Company and in New Jersey by some of the cotton textile firms in Paterson. The Baldwin Locomotive Works in Philadelphia, the most successful of all American locomotive builders, grew out of a firm whose highly diverse output had earlier included textile-printing machinery. This increasing specialization in machine production, in response to a growing market for machinery, was duplicated elsewhere. The production of the heavier, general-purpose machine tools—lathes, planers, boring machines—was initially undertaken by the early textile-machine shops to supply both their own firms' requirements and those of the new railroad industry. The lighter, more specialized high-speed machine tools—turret lathes, milling machines, precision grinders—grew out of the production requirements of the makers of firearms. In this period the firearms industry was instrumental in the development of a whole array of tools and accessories upon which the production of precision metal parts depended: jigs, fixtures, taps and gauges, die-forging equipment, the highly versatile turret lathe, and the milling machine. In addition, the complex problems of shaping the stock of a musket had led to the invention of lathe techniques which could be—and subsequently were—applied to producing all sorts of irregular shapes out of wood.

The machine-tool industry originated, then, out of a series of responses to the machinery requirements of a succession of particular industries. While still attached to their industries of origin, these establishments undertook to produce machinery for other industries, because the technical skills which they had acquired had direct applications to production problems in other industries. That this should have been so is hardly surprising: It is the essence of industrialization that it involves the introduction of a relatively small number of broadly similar productive processes to a large number of industries. This characteristic follows from the fact that industrialization in the nineteenth century involved the growing adoption of a metal-shaping technology which relied increasingly upon decentralized sources of power.[20] Eventually, with the combined growth in demand for an increasing array of specialized machines, machine-tool production emerged as a separate industry consisting of a large number of firms, most of which confined their operations to a narrow range of products—frequently to a single type of machine tool and with only minor modifications with respect to size, auxiliary attachments, or components.

The machine-tool industry, then, came to constitute a pool or reservoir of the skills and technical knowledge essential to the generation of technical change throughout the machine-using sectors of the economy. Precisely because it came to deal with processes and problems which were common to an increasing number of industries, it played the role of a transmission center in the diffusion of the new technology. That pool of skill and technical knowledge was added to as a result of problems which arose in particular industries. Once the problem was solved, the solution became available, with perhaps minor modifications and redesigning, for employment in the growing number of technologically related industries. Alternatively stated, the existence of a well-developed machine-tool industry induced a higher rate of technological change by lowering the cost of innovation throughout the metal-using sectors of the economy.

In this fashion a growing family of metal-shaping tools was built during the nineteenth century. The strategic role which the requirements of firearms production had once played in inducing new inventions was now played by a number of industries : the sewing-machine industry after 1850, the bicycle industry after 1890, and the automobile industry after 1900. Each of these industries was responsible for techniques which were widely used throughout the metal-using sector, and each borrowed much of the technology of the earlier ones. Thus, sewing-machine producers drew heavily upon the methods of firearms makers, as did the bicycle manufacturers upon those of the sewing-machine manufacturers, and, finally, as did the automobile industry upon the bicycle industry.

In all these cases machines were designed and adapted to perform highly specialized functions. Even though a basic tool was capable of performing a wide range of tasks, it was designed and adapted for the high-speed and increasingly automatic performance of narrowly defined operations. A further aspect of this technology was, necessarily, a proliferation in the number of specialized machines. This meant a sequential productive process involving large numbers of special-purpose machines, each of which advanced the product one small step further toward its final shape. Where the demand

---

[20] The use of machinery in the cutting of metal into precise shapes involves, to begin with, a relatively small number of operations (and therefore machine types) : turning, boring, drilling, milling, planing, grinding, polishing, and so on. Moreover, all machines performing such operations confront a similar collection of technical problems, dealing with such matters as power transmission (gearing, belting, shafting), control devices, feed mechanisms, friction reduction, and a broad array of problems connected with the properties of metals (such as ability to withstand stresses and heat resistance). It is because these processes and problems became common to the production of a wide range of disparate commodities that industries which were apparently unrelated from the point of view of the nature and uses of the final product—for example, firearms, sewing machines, and bicycles—became very closely related on a technological basis.

for the final product was sufficiently large, and where the standardization of the product was sufficient to permit use of inflexible, special-purpose machinery, very low per unit costs were attainable. These two preconditions help explain why this technology originated in the production of military firearms and was carried on in clocks, watches, sewing machines, bicycles, and the automobile.

The assembly line.   Growing sophistication in the use of machine technology culminated, in the early twentieth century, in the assembly-line system, a system whose contribution to the growth in productivity derived from organizational as well as technical innovations. Its emergence is inextricably linked with the early work of Henry Ford in the automobile industry. The roots of this system, however, lie in rather strange and unexpected places: grain mills and slaughterhouses.

Oliver Evans, one of America's authentic mechanical geniuses, had in the late eighteenth century perfected a highly labor-saving, continuous-flow production process employing many of the techniques for moving material— endless belt conveyors, screw conveyors, and bucket conveyors—which were to be used in twentieth-century factories. Evans' "factory" was a grain mill in which grain flowed through each of the several milling processes "without human intervention":

> In 1783 the model of the automatic mill was complete and in the two following years, 1784–5, the mill itself was built in Redclay Creek valley. This mill could load from either boats or wagons: a scale determined the weight and a screw conveyor (or "endless Archimedean screw" as Evans calls it) carried the grain inside to the point where it was raised to the top storey by a bucket conveyor (or "elevator for raising vertically"). It handled three hundred bushels an hour. From this elevator, the grain fell on the mildly inclined "descender—a broad endless strap of very thin pliant leather, canvas or flannel, revolving over two pulleys." This belt was set in motion by the weight of the grain and, as Evans adds, "it moves on the principle of an overshot waterwheel." A prominent mechanical engineer remarks a century later: "It is the prototype of belt conveyor of the present day, usually used for horizontal movement." After intervening operations, the grain was carried down to the millstones and from the millstones back to the top storey. Thus it made its way . . . through all the floors, from bottom to top and top to bottom, much as the automobile bodies in Henry Ford's plant in 1914.[21]

Appropriately enough for a country which was still primarily agricultural, the next major step forward in mechanical materials handling also dealt with food processing. In the slaughterhouses of Cincinnati the "disassembly" of pigs was carried out by a technique involving workmen at fixed stations while a system of overhead rails suspended from the ceiling moved the carcass, hanging from a hook, at a carefully predetermined rate from one phase to the next. Each man performed a single operation: One split the animal, the next removed its entrails, another removed specific organs— heart, liver, and so on—and the last man washed down the carcass with a hose. Although it was impossible to eliminate the reliance upon the human eye

[21] Siegfried Giedion, *Mechanization Takes Command: A Contribution to Anonymous History* (New York: Oxford University Press, 1948), p. 82. Illustrations of Evans' mill appear on pages 81 and 83.

and human skill in the slaughterhouse, the skillful handling of materials, the rationalized positioning of the workers, the elimination of time loss between operations, the minimization of energy expended by the workers in handling heavy carcasses, and the minute subdivision of the task brought about very substantial increases in the productivity of labor. This system was certainly in existence in Cincinnati packing-houses in 1860 and may even have been there, in somewhat more primitive form, as much as 25 years earlier.

The automobile assembly lines which were introduced in Detroit in the second decade of the twentieth century thus embodied several historical trends and applied them to a highly complicated product containing thousands of separate parts, many of which moved and interacted at high speeds. Henry Ford tentatively experimented with a conveyor-belt system for the assembly of magnetos in 1913. Similar methods were quickly applied to chassis assembly. Much experimentation was carried out in determining optimum assembly-line speeds, the best positioning of workmen, the most convenient height for the performance of each task, and the most efficient methods of material routing, machine layout, and so on. By 1916 the Ford Motor Company alone was selling well over half a million Model T's at a retail price of less than $400. Seven years later the total number of passenger cars produced in the United States was 3.6 million (see Table 7.2). Such output volumes would have been unattainable without the rationalization of the work process,

TABLE 7.2
Factory sales of passenger cars

Year	Number	Year	Number
1900	4,192	1920	1,905,560
1901	7,000	1921	1,468,067
1902	9,000	1922	2,274,185
1903	11,235	1923	3,624,717
1904	22,130	1924	3,185,881
1905	24,250	1925	3,735,171
1906	33,200	1926	3,692,317
1907	43,000	1927	2,936,533
1908	63,500	1928	3,775,417
1909	123,990	1929	4,455,178
1910	181,000	1930	2,787,456
1911	199,319		
1912	356,000	1935	3,273,874
1913	461,500	1940	3,717,385
1914	548,139	1945	69,532
1915	895,930	1950	6,665,863
1916	1,525,578	1955	7,920,186
1917	1,745,792	1960	6,675,000
1918	943,436	1965	9,306,000
1919	1,651,625		

SOURCES: U.S. Bureau of the Census, *Historical Statistics of the United States* (Washington: U.S. Government Printing Office, 1960, 1965); and *Statistical Abstract of the United States*, 1966 (Washington: U.S. Government Printing Office, 1966).

particularly the technique of progressive assembly of parts, involving the systematic use of mechanical conveyors in the movement of materials. These techniques were applied in turn to a widening range of products: numerous products connected with the electrical industry—motors, washing machines, refrigerators, telephones, radios—and a wide assortment of consumer durables, many producers' durables such as farm machinery and equipment, and processed foods.

The productive process itself has been made increasingly automatic, a development for which the term "automation" was coined after World War II. Individual machines have been made fully automatic by the use of numerical control systems which guide the machine tool through its sequence of operations by coded instructions punched on paper tape. Electronic control devices employing feedback mechanisms have eliminated the necessity for human supervision of or intervention in a wide range of productive processes. "Detroit-type" automation has exploited automatic work transfer and positioning devices to link together the operation of successive machines.

Twentieth-Century Technology

If the widening scope of mechanization and the diffusion of a machine technology provided a unifying theme for our approach to technological change in the nineteenth century, no such common denominator is available for the twentieth. Indeed, the sheer diversity in the sources of technological change is one of the most distinctive features of this century. It does appear possible, however, to discern a trend underlying this diversity, a trend which can be most conveniently thought of as tracing its origins to the 1860s. A guide through the maze lies in the fact that an increasing proportion of technological changes have depended upon prior advances in systematized knowledge, a knowledge which has brought with it a much more deeply rooted understanding of the forces of nature and the physical universe. In this respect, the contrast between the nineteenth and twentieth centuries should not be overstated. There was considerable reliance upon science in the inventive process in some areas in the nineteenth century, and a huge amount of inventive activity in the twentieth century has remained totally innocent of any such basis. The trend toward a science-based technology, however, is notable and pervasive. From 1916 to 1945, the number of patents granted annually grew much more rapidly in classes dependent upon the application of knowledge from scientific disciplines such as chemistry and physics, than in classes dependent upon empirical or practical knowledge and mechanical ingenuity.[22] The number of scientists and technologists has also been growing more rapidly than the labor force as a whole since 1870. These indexes of the shift only confirm what is a matter of common observation.

The machine-based technology which emerged in the nineteenth century owed relatively little to scientific knowledge. As A. P. Usher has pointed out: "At the lower levels, mechanical invention involves little more than some

[22] Schmookler, *op. cit.*, pp. 39–41.

improvements in the skills required for the making of simple tools, and as long as invention is essentially empirical, even the development of relatively complex mechanisms does not seem to involve abstract thought or organized scientific knowledge."[23] Usher's observation is particularly applicable to the various standardized products we have already mentioned. In addition to mechanization, however, a succession of new sources of new technology developed in the twentieth century. Chemical, electrical, electronic, biological, and nuclear engineering have developed, depending upon the mastery of complex bodies of knowledge far beyond the crude empiricism of earlier generations.

Ferrous metallurgy.   In order to understand what is so novel and significant about the twentieth-century approach to technological change, a brief glance at its development in a specific field is useful.

In ferrous metallurgy, an activity fundamental to tool making and construction, progress was based before the present century on trial-and-error procedures. America made no advances over British industrial leadership in the first half of the nineteenth century in this area. The New World continued to rely upon the transfer of basic innovations originating in the Old. Important technological breakthroughs were possible, employing no more than a crude empiricism, as long as inducements existed for large numbers of individuals to experiment with untried techniques and to employ novel material inputs. The smelting of iron with a mineral fuel instead of charcoal, for example, was developed in the eighteenth century after many unsuccessful or half-successful efforts by English ironmasters—the Sturtevants, Rovensons, and Dudleys—throughout the seventeenth century. Abraham Darby succeeded—probably in 1709—in substituting coke for charcoal in his blast furnace at Coalbrookdale in Shropshire. His success was largely due to the fact that the coal in his locality was of a chemical composition peculiarly appropriate for smelting purposes. Even though the chemical transformations in iron refining were not understood, strong economic incentives were eventually successful in uncovering new techniques as well as the raw materials which were appropriate to these techniques. Similarly fortuitous circumstances accounted for the initial success of Bessemer's steel-making experiments, reported to the British Association for the Advancement of Science in August 1856. British ironmakers who had quickly purchased lease rights to the Bessemer process found, to their dismay, that they could not employ it successfully. It happened that Bessemer had conducted all his experiments using Swedish charcoal iron, the purest form of pig iron available to him. Bessemer's technique worked only when certain chemical conditions were precisely fulfilled; it failed to produce a satisfactory steel with ores which contained even very slight traces of phosphorus. This fact was not immediately understood, and the determination to establish the causes of failure led to a prolonged, systematic study of the chemical processes involved in iron and steel production. The next major innovation in steel making, the "basic" process

[23] A. P. Usher, *A History of Mechanical Inventions* (Cambridge, Mass.: Harvard University Press, 1959), p. 56.

developed by the chemists Thomas and Gilchrist in 1878, was a direct outcome of these studies. Through their examination of the chemical processes involved in steel production, they were able to develop a technique for refining iron which, among other things, made it possible to utilize major sources of iron ore whose phosphorus content had prevented their use in the Bessemer process.

In a very real sense, modern metallurgical science may be said to have begun in this immediate post-Bessemer period. It rested upon an inquiry into the basic structure and composition of metals which had been initiated by difficulties experienced in the production of iron and steel. The ability to conduct this inquiry was immensely advanced by technological innovation in other spheres. Most important was Henry Clifton Sorby's development, in 1863, of a technique for examining metals under a microscope by the use of reflected light. This technique immediately opened the door to an understanding of the microstructure of steel.

> From steel, the technique spread to show the behavior of microcrystals of the nonferrous metals during casting, working, and annealing. By 1900 it had been proved that most of the age-old facts of metal behavior (which had first been simply attributed to the nature of the metals and had later been partially explained in terms of composition) could best be related to the shape, size, relative distribution, and interrelationships of distinguishable microconstituents.[24]

Another fundamental improvement in experimental technique which was first announced in 1912 was the discovery of x-ray diffraction and its application to the study of solids. For "it at once gave a measurable physical meaning to structure on an atomic scale, and made this as real as the larger-scale structures that had been revealed by Sorby's microscopic methods half a century earlier. It was a physicist's method par excellence, and a fundamental one, which served to relate much of the unconnected data of the chemist and the metallurgist."[25]

Other materials.   The improvements in experimental techniques originating in metallurgy contributed to and joined with the wider stream of understanding of all materials. (Indeed, in recent years this merger is receiving explicit terminological recognition in the substitution of the term "materials science" for "metallurgy.") This broader, fundamental advance in our understanding of the physical world derives from our insight into the atomic and molecular basis for the behavior of *all* matter—an understanding which dates from Mendelejeff's formulation of his periodic table of the elements in 1869. Mendelejeff's periodic law and classification not only provided the basis for explaining the properties of the known elements, but it also correctly predicted the properties of elements which were unknown at the time ; for example, gallium, germanium, and scandium. The knowledge revolution in materials science of the past century is based upon a continuous deepening in our understanding of the general rules determining how atoms and molecules

---

[24] C. S. Smith, "Materials and the Development of Civilization and Science," *Science*, vol. 137 (May 14, 1965) p. 915.
[25] C. S. Smith, "Materials," *Scientific American* (September 1967), p. 75.

combine together into progressively larger and more complex groups. Once these rules are mastered it becomes possible to manipulate materials, to alter their characteristics, to maximize desirable properties, and even to create entirely new and synthetic materials with desired combinations of properties. Our recently acquired knowledge of molecular architecture makes it possible to create synthetic materials with combinations of properties which have no counterparts in the natural world. The burgeoning new industries exploiting these manmade organic polymers—the vast range of plastics, synthetic fibers, packaging materials, synthetic rubber, light-weight thermal insulation, water-repellent coating, and high-strength adhesives—are the direct, legitimate offspring of this knowledge of high-polymer chemistry.

The basis for technological progress in these newer industries is thus totally unlike that in the old metallurgical industries, in which trial and error and intelligent empiricism led to considerable advances over the centuries. No conceivable amount of experimentation, such as once brought slow progress, could ever have generated modern synthetic polymers. The production of these polymers required an adequate theory of molecular structures, and a full appreciation of the staggering complexity of these structures in turn required a highly sophisticated collection of instruments—x-ray diffraction equipment, the ultracentrifuge, the electron microscope, and the viscometer, among others. Similarly, the remarkable advances in the electronics industry after World War II—the breakthrough in semiconductor technology at Bell Laboratories in 1947–1948 with the development of the transistor, the replacement of the vacuum tube by the transistor, the application of semiconductor devices to electronic data processing and to an expanding field of military and commercial uses—were dependent not only upon complex techniques of instrumentation but also upon the development of quantum mechanics in the mid-1920s. For quantum mechanics provided the essential theory which made it possible to understand the determinants of electrical conductivity in terms of the atomic structure of crystalline solids.

Furthermore, the growing usefulness of knowledge of chemical processes in the transformation of materials has greatly expanded the inudstrial area to which such knowledge is now relevant. All industrial activity which changes the nature of its material inputs is, in effect, dealing with a chemical process. In this sense,

> chemical industries include practically all metallurgical refining; all refinement of fuels such as petroleum, natural gases, and coal; the processes of refining materials leading to the production of cement, rubber (whether "natural" rubber or other basic raw-materials), glass, etc.; and all industries, in short, engaged either in breaking down the molecular or atomic structure of materials into their physical components (analysis), or in reassembling them to make new compounds or materials (synthesis). The emphasis is on the *nature of the process*, and not upon the type or state of raw or finished materials. It makes no difference whether the activating agents be heat, electricity, catalysts, or bacteria; so long as a change is effected in molecular or atomic structure—so long as the material undergoes inner transformation—the process is a chemical process.[26]

[26] Robert A. Brady, *Organization, Automation and Society* (Berkeley: University of California Press, 1961), p. 203. The emphasis is Brady's.

Agriculture.   The effect of the knowledge revolution upon agriculture has been, in many ways, strikingly similar to its effect upon materials. Since biological processes are intimately involved, technological adaptation and improvements in agriculture have always reflected a quite explicit Darwinian mechanism of random variation and natural selection. Human intervention in this area until quite recently had very little to do with new knowledge of the biological processes involved. It took the form primarily of a rather blind experimentation with seed varieties in new ecological environments, small variations in the techniques of planting and cultivation, and breeding methods that were haphazard or guided by mistaken principles. The success of a particular crop often depends upon a delicate combination of environmental qualities—topography, rainfall, chemical composition of the soil, temperature variations, amount of sunlight, and so on. Many cereal strains, for example, are so highly photosensitive that they will fail when transferred relatively short distances from one latitude to another. But as long as large numbers of individual agriculturalists were continuously engaged in productive activities involving minor variations in practice, and as long as a reasonably effective communications network existed among them, market forces could be relied upon to select and to diffuse the best practices.

This process of modification and adaptation has been particularly evident in the settlement of virgin regions like the American West, where populations are pushing out into areas involving new combinations of soil, terrain, and climate. The American prairies constituted an environment quite alien to the cultural heritage of Western European settlers. Many serious blunders were committed, partly because of the unfamiliarity of the settlers with such environmental peculiarities as substantial variations in annual rainfall. Out of a prolonged period of experimentation, however, certain plants and animals were found to possess biological capabilities well suited for survival in different parts of this environment. The British Hereford proved to be the best suited of the various breeds of beef cattle over the widest area of the plains ; whereas Indian Brahman cattle were found to be better adapted to the special climate of the hot, dry southern plains. Experimentation with the available range of wheat varieties eventually established the clear adaptive superiority of the hard spring and winter wheats of Eastern Europe. Similarly, the experimental process led to the selection and introduction of African and Asiatic sorghums and Mediterranean alfalfa.

It is essential to note, however, that no alterations were consciously made in the biological characteristics of the plants and animals involved in these transfers. Indeed, the biological mechanisms were not understood, and in the late nineteenth century existing knowledge certainly did not provide a sufficient basis for a more active human intervention in the adaptive process such as is involved in hybridization and genetic mutation.[27] Modern genetics may be said to have begun in the mid-1860s, with the work of Mendel, who

---

[27] Some selective breeding of animals had long been practiced, and it, too, yielded results even though it was based upon a crude empiricism. The mule, after all, is a very old hybrid.

established mathematical laws of inheritance in accounting for the characteristics of garden peas. Mendel's work was ignored for the remainder of the
nineteenth century, but became the starting point for the study of heredity in
the twentieth.

A large part of the social, political, and economic history of the United
States could be written around the bare statistical information that the proportion of the American labor force in agriculture was 63 percent in 1840 and
8 percent in 1960. But whereas in the nineteenth century the main sources of
productivity growth which made this transformation possible were mechanization, transportation improvements, and regional crop specialization, in the last
few decades such growth has been based increasingly upon the advancement
of knowledge dealing with the fundamental biological processes of life and
growth—especially genetics and biochemistry. This recently accumulated
intellectual capital enables the human agent to assert an initiative in growth
processes which was never before possible. Instead of experimenting with
existing seed strains to determine which one is best adapted to the ecological
conditions of a given locality, it is now possible, once local requirements have
been ascertained, to *create* new seed strains possessing the desired characteristics.

The commercial introduction of hybrid corn in the United States beginning
in the early 1930s provided dramatic evidence of the potential benefits of
this new biological sophistication. Hybrid corn, it should be understood, is
not a single strain uniformly superior in different localities. It is, rather, the
outcome of a complex process of continued self-pollination together with a
selection procedure which may be employed to breed a superior type of corn
for a specific locality. Although the increase in output resulting from the use
of hybrid corn varies considerably, the most generally cited figure is an increase
of 20 percent in corn yields. In an important article, Griliches estimated the
social rate of return over the period 1910–1955 to the public and private
resources committed to agricultural research which resulted in the development of hybrid corn. He estimated these returns to be of the order of 700 percent. Since Griliches was deliberately overconservative in his calculations,
this estimated rate of return may be regarded as a lower bound.[28]

Griliches has shown, moreover, that both the spatial and chronological
diffusion of hybrid corn can be largely accounted for in terms of economic
variables. The earlier and the more rapid adoption of hybrid seeds in the corn
belt, and the later and slower diffusion elsewhere, can be explained in terms of
the profit expectations of farmers and seed suppliers. The clear superiority of
the hybrids over the open-pollinated varieties of corn resulted in a sweeping
displacement of open-pollinated corn in the corn belt in a very short period
of time, with lagged as well as slower rates of adoption in the South and other
more marginal areas. In Iowa, where hybrid corn was particularly well suited
and the shift highly profitable, it took only four years for farmers to shift from
10 to 90 percent of their corn acreage to hybrid corn (Figure 7.4). On the

[28] Zvi Griliches, "Research Costs and Social Returns: Hybrid Corn and Related Innovations," *Journal of Political Economy*, vol. 66 (October 1958), pp. 419–431.

FIGURE 7.4
Percent of total corn acreage planted with hybrid seed

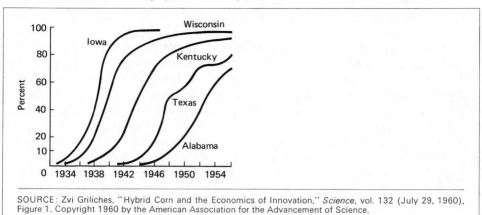

SOURCE: Zvi Griliches, "Hybrid Corn and the Economics of Innovation," *Science*, vol. 132 (July 29, 1960), Figure 1. Copyright 1960 by the American Association for the Advancement of Science.

western fringes of the corn belt—specifically, in the western portions of the Dakotas, Nebraska, and Kansas—where the land was not well adapted to growing corn, the acceptance of the hybrids was much slower.

In some very significant ways the earlier and continuing movement toward mechanization in agriculture and the more recent genetic–biological sources of productivity growth are now merging. Plant breeding raises productivity in many ways: by increasing the size and improving the quality of the plant, by developing plants that are disease-resistant, or require a shorter growing season, and so on. In addition, however, a major thrust of current plant breeding is the development of new plant varieties which lend themselves more successfully to the requirements of mechanization, particularly at the labor-intensive harvesting stage. The highly adaptable modern combine, uniting as it does the reaping and threshing operations in a single machine, now makes possible the totally mechanical harvesting of grain. Furthermore, the plants themselves are now being "redesigned," as were guns and cutlery in the nineteenth century, so that they can be produced more effectively by machinery. Similar changes are occurring in other crops: (a) In cotton, breeding has been directed toward simplifying the mechanical picking of the crop; (b) entirely new strains of rice have been developed which, with the great increase in fertilizer inputs, will resist lodging; and (c) tough-skinned tomatoes which will withstand mechanical handling (and which are also uniform in size and ripen at the same time) are being successfully bred.

The long-term rise in agricultural productivity was dramatically accelerated in the years after World War II.[29] A strong inducement to mechanization was imparted by the growing demand for labor in the nonfarm sectors during the war, which raised wages and led to a large-scale movement of labor out of

---

[29] Quantitative data supporting the assertions in the next two paragraphs, and a further discussion of technological change in agriculture, may be found in Chapter 11.

agriculture. Whereas in the 1920s much of the mechanization had constituted a substitution of machines for animal power as the internal combustion engine became a major supplier of traction power, after 1940 the main impact of mechanization was to bring about a sharp reduction in labor requirements per unit of output. This was made possible by increases in the versatility of machinery, by changes in size and design, by the use of a growing family of attachments, and by reductions in the price of machine power—that is, higher-compression engines. The result was a striking reduction in labor requirements in the post-World War II years.

World War II serves also to mark a transition to substantially higher yields of output per acre, a rise which greatly exceeds anything in our earlier experience. These increases are the outcome of several factors, including the varietal improvements made possible by the growth of biological knowledge, greater use of irrigation facilities, and the shifting patterns of regional specialization as production was concentrated in areas best suited to particular crops.[30] The most important single factor, however, has been a growing utilization of chemical inputs in agriculture: herbicides and insecticides and, far more important, commercial fertilizers, especially synthetic nitrogenous fertilizers. The quantity of fertilizer inputs into American agriculture increased more than four times between 1940 and the mid-1960s. This increase, in turn, was induced by a drastic decline in fertilizer prices relative to product prices and the prices of other inputs.[31] Underlying the relative decline in the price of fertilizer were technological improvements in chemical engineering and in power production, since power is a major component in the cost of synthetic fertilizer. Here, too, as in so many other areas, the shift in the material basis of productive activity was from reliance upon organic materials to a reliance upon inorganic sources of supply.

The materials revolution.   The broad parallels between the impact of the knowledge revolution on materials and on agriculture are wide ranging in their significance. In both areas highly developed scientific disciplines now make it possible to go far beyond the much more passive adaptations to natural surroundings to which man was previously restricted. In both agriculture and the world of industrial material inputs it is now possible to initiate new things—hybrids and seed varietals in agriculture and new alloys and synthetic polymers in materials. We are no longer confined to establishing, through rather haphazard empirical techniques, which corn will grow best in a particular environment or which iron ore will work most successfully with a given coal supply. Now it is possible, in a serious sense, to improve upon nature. We can exploit our knowledge of genetics and biochemistry in agriculture and of molecular architecture in materials to create new seeds and new synthetic materials with optimum characteristics for satisfying human requirements.

---

[30] In some cases this change was related to the specific requirements of mechanization. For example, mechanical cotton pickers work much more effectively on a flat terrain than on a hilly one, and the introduction of the mechanical cotton picker, which began in the 1920s, therefore played an important role in the shift of cotton cultivation out of the Old South and into Texas and California.

[31] The motivation to raise output per acre has also, of course, been strengthened by government programs involving acreage restrictions.

A major thrust of twentieth-century technology, based upon the knowledge revolution, has been to reduce dependence upon specific natural-resource inputs. In some respects this is not a new phenomenon. After all, industrial technology since the seventeenth and eighteenth centuries has been preoccupied with liberating productive enterprise from severe constraints imposed by dependence upon organic sources: food products, wood for fuel and construction, animal energy, and plant and animal fibers and materials—wool, leather, cotton, silk—for clothing and textile products generally. The classic Industrial Revolution in Britain substituted cheap coal for wood as a source of fuel and power and cheap and abundant iron for vanishing timber resources. The great achievements of the Industrial Revolution—precise and reliable machinery, railroads, large-span bridges, great iron ships, and innumerable feats of engineering virtuosity—would have been impossible in the absence of cheap iron.

The more recent materials revolution may be regarded as carrying this liberation process to an entirely new level. Not only are materials being produced and alloyed in ways which make them much more "finely tuned" to specific human purposes (e.g., the precisely articulated needs of the space program[32]), but entirely new products are being synthesized which bear only the remotest relation to materials occurring in nature.[33]

Although it is somewhat less obvious, the current biological revolution in agriculture is part of the same process of reducing human dependence upon the raw facts of nature, more particularly upon its organic products. Although food products continue to be grown on land, the productive contribution of land relative to other inputs has been declining. One way of looking at the impact of technological change in agriculture over the past century is to say that a growing portion of farm output is produced by nonfarm inputs and a smaller proportion is attributable to the input of land itself. This is measurable by looking at the ratio of purchased inputs to total agricultural output, a ratio which has been rising for several decades. In contrast to the long-term trend toward the mechanization of American agriculture, the major effect of which was and continues to be labor saving, the effect of the growth in the economically relevant stock of biological knowledge in recent decades has been to impart a pronounced land-saving bias to technological change.

The American farmer is now much less self-reliant than he was 100 years ago, when he in fact produced his own power sources (draft animals) as well as their fuel (oats, hay, etc.), in addition to providing many of his own consumer goods and services. Furthermore, whereas his son could adequately equip himself for the life of a farmer through the on-the-job training he received at his father's side, the sophisticated skills and decisions required of modern farmers make a university education highly desirable. In these respects, the American farmer has shared in the growing reliance upon specialist suppliers

---

[32] Thus, the nose cones of reentry vehicles are plastic materials which (*a*) are light, (*b*) are resistant to mechanical shock, (*c*) possess a high degree of thermal stability, (*d*) are thermally nonconductive, and (*e*) are easy to fabricate.

[33] Although some synthetic materials have counterparts in nature after which they are modeled—rubber, leather, fibers, fur—synthetic resins have no such counterparts and cannot be identified with particular materials.

of materials, goods, and services which has become so characteristic of the rest of the economy, including the household sector. He is now dependent in his operations upon purchases from a long chain of materials suppliers: dealers in commercial fertilizer, feed for livestock, seeds, and insecticides, as well as machinery and fuel. Moreover, he utilizes knowledge inputs which are made available to him through a complex network including the United States Department of Agriculture; land-grant colleges; agricultural experiment stations; government meteorologists; seed, equipment, and commercial-fertilizer producers; and county agents. Although the family farm still shows a sturdy persistence as a producing unit, it is now hopelessly inadequate for the acquisition and diffusion of knowledge.

This growing skill in offsetting the scarcity of particular natural resources by exploiting alternative, more abundant sources, by innovations which reduce resource requirements per unit of output, and by the development of synthetic materials has falsified the dismal predictions of classical economics.[34] Ricardo and Malthus saw the prospects for an industrial society such as England's as dominated by the inability to offset the resource constraints imposed by the limited supply of land.[35] Their intense interest in foreign trade of course followed from this basic vision. But we now see that technological change has provided another highly effective set of possibilities for reducing the dependence of a growing industrial society upon its natural-resource inputs. Resources in their unprocessed state have, in fact, been playing a role of demonstrably diminishing importance. If we express the value of resource output as a percentage of GNP, this figure has been declining since 1870, the earliest date for which figures are available. The resource/GNP ratio was 36 percent in 1870, 27 percent in 1900, 17 percent in 1930, and 12 percent in 1954 (see Table 7.3).[36]

Interindustry competition. Modern technology may now be said to have displaced the primacy of natural resources in determining a country's growth prospects. Obviously this does not mean that natural resources are unimportant. But it does mean that the human agent is vastly more powerful and *resourceful* than, say, 100 years ago, and this technological mastery has immensely expanded the options available to him. Resource endowment continues to play a major role in determining the relative cost of alternative actions. Maine will doubtless continue to resist the temptation to grow bananas in hothouses; the recent growth of the synthetic fiber industry in the South was heavily

---

[34] Mention should also be made here of the increasing skill in exploiting low-concentrate, "inferior" raw materials. Low-grade mineral deposits such as shale oil and taconite iron ore are available domestically in enormous quantities and will become increasingly practical as the supplies of more abundant, high-quality deposits are exhausted and as technological mastery of their exploitation grows. Since the utilization of many of these low-quality sources, like that of bauxite, is highly sensitive to fuel and power costs, innovations which reduce these costs will also give a strong impetus to their exploitation.

[35] Similarly, the distinguished English economist, W. S. Jevons, in his book *The Coal Question,* published in 1865, warned of the impending decline of British industry due to the inevitably rising costs of coal extraction.

[36] The ratio, of course, is a reflection of a variety of factors. As consumers' incomes rise, they shift their expenditures to goods and services where raw-material costs are less important than in food products. Furthermore, even the final prices of food products now incorporate a much larger proportion of processing, fabrication, packaging, transportation, and distribution costs than was the case in the nineteenth century. Therefore, even in the case of food purchases, a smaller fraction of each dollar of expenditure represents the cost of purchasing raw materials.

TABLE 7.3
Output of resources as a percent of GNP (1954 prices)

Year	All Resources	Agriculture	Timber Products	Minerals
1870	36	27	4.00	1.5
1880	32	25	3.70	2.0
1890	29	21	3.90	2.8
1900	27	19	3.90	3.4
1910	22	15	2.80	4.2
1920	21	14	2.00	4.9
1930	17	11	1.20	4.3
1940	16	10	1.00	4.1
1950	13	8	.77	3.6
1954	12	8	.69	3.3

SOURCE: Joseph Fisher and Edward Boorstein, *The Adequacy of Resources for Economic Growth in the United States*, Study Paper no. 13, prepared in connection with the Study of Employment, Growth, and Price Levels, 86th Congress (December 16, 1959), p. 43.

influenced by its dependence for its basic raw materials upon the petrochemical plants of the Southwest; and the location of steel mills continues to be influenced by the desire to minimize the cost of transporting their bulky input requirements.[37]

The point here is one of great general importance. By increasing the number of good substitutes for any input, the growth in knowledge is adding a new and effective form to the competitive process, a form which is not adequately perceived by the conventional examination of market structures and industry concentration ratios. A direct consequence of the knowledge revolution, a revolution whose immediate consequence is to widen the range of substitute inputs and outputs, is to make the economy more effectively competitive. It is, for example, impossible to appreciate the nature of competitive forces with respect to steel by focusing solely upon the steel industry, where there appears to be abundant evidence of concentration and market power. The competition which increasingly matters for the steel producers is not that of other firms in the steel industry but the behavior of a whole range of firms producing materials which are in most respects quite unlike steel but which are highly effective substitutes for steel *in particular uses.*[38] Aluminum has successfully displaced steel in many of its traditional markets, especially where lightness and resistance to corrosion are highly desired, as have magnesium and titanium on a smaller scale. (All three metals, of course, have been important in the development of modern jet aircraft.) Structural concrete has become a formidable competitor to steel for many construction purposes, especially as its performance characteristics have improved. There is now abundant visual evidence of this substitution in American cities. As the major

[37] The fact that mineral deposits are generally less widely diffused than agricultural and forestry resources is, by itself, a powerful factor in according locational advantages to specific areas. Improvements in transportation technology, on the other hand, tend to reduce the size of these advantages.

[38] The steel industry has also been deeply affected by some "internal" developments such as the increasing prominence of steel alloys and the reuse of scrap steel.

plastics groups continue to decline in price they too have come to constitute a growing competitor to steel, as well as to many other materials. Polyethylene pipe, for example, has largely displaced stainless steel pipe in certain corrosive applications. Increasingly tough and durable plastics are being developed, and are being used even in parts such as gears and bearings.

This new form of the competitive mechanism exerts itself in so many directions that an orderly approach on the basis of conventional definitions of industrial boundaries is an essentially meaningless exercise. Aluminum has replaced steel in many uses, but it has also, due to its comparative cheapness and lightness, been accepted as a substitute for copper in the long-distance transmission of electricity. Aluminum, together with plastics, has displaced wood in many of its former uses, such as construction and packaging.[39] Plastics, in turn, have substituted in different contexts for natural fibers, wood, rubber, leather, glass, and many metals.

The growing importance of manmade materials and the relative (and in some cases absolute) decline of the older, more traditional materials is evident in Table 7.4, which shows production figures for a variety of materials over a recent decade. The phenomenal rise of synthetic materials from a longer time perspective may be indicated by the fact that, between 1931 and 1966, output of plastics grew at an annual rate of almost 17 percent. In the latter year, more than 13.5 billion pounds of plastics were produced with a sales value in excess of $2.7 billion.

The rise of synthetic materials in the form of manmade fibers for use in textiles has now reached the point where these new materials are surpassing the traditional natural fibers, especially cotton. In recent years synthetic

TABLE 7.4
Output of selected materials, 1956–1966

	1956	1966	Percent Change
Plastics[a]	3,977	13,585	+240.0
Rubber, synthetic[a]	2,420	4,414	+ 82.5
Aluminum[b]	1,697	2,968	+ 77.0
Alloy steels[b]	10,338	15,369	+ 49.0
Copper[b]	1,443	1,711	+ 18.6
Steel[b]	115,216	134,101	+ 16.4
Zinc[b]	984	1,025	+ 4.2
Rubber, natural[a]	1,260	1,241	− 1.6
Lumber[c]	38,629	36,128	− 6.3

[a] Millions of pounds.
[b] Thousands of short tons.
[c] Millions of board feet.

SOURCE: U.S. Department of Commerce, *Business Statistics* (Washington: U.S. Government Printing Office, 1967).

[39] Technical change has also brought about methods which economize upon wood requirements without substituting competitive materials, or which substitute cheaper woods—for example, plywood and wood veneers—for more expensive ones.

fibers have been introduced in clothing, carpeting, drapery and upholstery fabrics, and home furnishings (sheets, pillowcases, bedspreads, tablecloths). Their great popularity, especially in clothing, is attributable to special character-istics, many of which are achieved by blending (including blending with natural fibers), such as greater strength, ease of laundering, lightness, crease retention, and fast drying. In the United States in 1968, the quantity, by weight, of synthetic fibers actually surpassed that of natural fibers for the first time. The new materials have had a great effect in revitalizing the textile industry in recent years.

This new form of the competitive process may also energize other old, established industries. This is a form of competition about which conventional economic theory has had relatively little to say. There are numerous historical instances in which an outside threat to a well-established industry has had a potent effect and has galvanized its members into action far surpassing that aroused by competition among its members. The sailboat, for example, was subjected to important improvements in design and construction after the advent of the steamship. More recently, the major steel producers, who for a long time did not appear very actively involved with intraindustry competition, seem to have responded with both energy and imagination to interindustry competition. The encroachment of aluminum upon the traditional domain of steel seems to have been responsible for the establishment of new research laboratories and an awakening of interest in product engineering. These efforts have met with at least partial success.

Interindustry competition has also been particularly important among different forms of fuel—wood, coal, oil, natural gas—and among different forms of transportation. It is conceivable that such competition may even revive portions of the railroad industry which have long been regarded as moribund. In any case it is certainly true that possible monopolistic restrictions in the railroads did not have the deleterious consequences they might have had because of competition from a succession of new forms of transport—trucks, planes, automobiles, and pipelines.

The Case of Energy

A modern industrial economy utilizes enormous amounts of mineral-derived energy in the manufacture and transportation of goods and in the running of its domestic households. The index of energy consumption from mineral, hydropower, and fuel-wood sources in the American economy quadrupled between 1850 and 1900 and more than quadrupled again between 1900 and 1955. In 1850 mineral fuels supplied less than 10 percent and wood more than 90 percent of all fuel-based energy (see Table 7.5). The other energy sources were water power, wind power, and, of course, animal and man power. The abundance of wood and water power (and the trans-Appalachian location of the major coal deposits) kept the United States dependent on those resources long after Great Britain had switched to coal. In 1850, most of the power employed in manufacturing was supplied by water; even as late as 1869, water power accounted for 48 percent of primary power capacity in manufacturing. In the second half of the nineteenth century, however, changes in relative costs as well as technological developments favoring the use of mineral resources in the manufacture of iron and steel and the production of steam power brought about a rapid shift to coal. In the last decades of the nineteenth century, steam power relying upon coal grew to the peak of its influence, and in 1899 steam power accounted for over 80 percent of primary power capacity in manufacturing. Among the material sources of energy, coal had largely displaced wood by the early years of the twentieth century. From a position of overwhelming dominance in 1859, wood declined to less than 10 percent of total power sources by 1915 (Table 7.5). Subsequent decades are largely the story of the declining importance of coal—a decline in which dieselization in transportation and the loss of household markets played major roles—and the rise of liquid and gaseous fuels[40] (Table 7.5).

Superimposed upon the expansion and changing composition of the primary sources of power is electrification, a process whose many ramifications for twentieth-century technology defy any brief summary. Purely within the context of a discussion of the uses of energy, however, the electric motor represents an extraordinarily versatile technological innovation which made it possible to "package" and deliver power in ways which have had very far-reaching consequences for the growth in manufacturing productivity.

Electrification began in the last decade of the nineteenth century but commenced its rapid growth only after the steam turbine had been brought to a level of efficiency which created thermal power stations and the highly centralized generation of electric power. This development was mainly responsible for the decline in the coal-using steam engine which had come to dominate the provision of power to industry by the beginning of the twentieth century. The minimum size of the steam engine had always exceeded the needs of small plants and thus limited the more thorough diffusion of power: Large engines were highly inefficient when they had to supply small quantities of power. Moreover, the steam engine required clumsy techniques of belting and shafting for the transmission of power within the plant. These transmission systems not only were highly wasteful in their energy use, but severely constrained the organization and flow of work, which had to be grouped, according to its power requirements, near the power source.

The advent of "fractionalized" power which was made possible by electricity and the electric motor meant that power could be made available in very small, less costly units and in a form which did not require the generation of excess capacity in order to provide small or intermittent doses of power. In addition to its direct energy-saving and capital-saving effects (not the least of which was in floor space), the new flexibility made possible a wholesale reorganization of work arrangements and, in this respect, made a major contribution to mass-production techniques.

---

[40] Natural gas, the use of which has grown so spectacularly in recent decades and is now the primary source of household fuel, was largely wasted until the development of transportation techniques which made it possible to transport gas long distances from oil fields. The technological breakthroughs which made this possible were high-pressure pipes, improved welding methods which made leakproof pipelines feasible, and the introduction of heavy power equipment to reduce the cost of laying pipe.

Shortly after steam power began to yield to electricity, installation of electric motors called attention to the obvious restraints placed upon efficiency by the steam engine. Its systems, practices, and factory organization became almost visibly redundant. Thus, as "unit drive" electric power grew in plant after plant, thoroughgoing reorganization of factory layout and design took place. Machines and tools could now be put anywhere efficiency dictated, not where belts and shafts could most easily reach them. [41]

If it is true that American industry rests firmly—or, according to some harbingers of mineral supply exhaustion, precariously—upon the conversion of mineral fuels into energy, [42] it is equally true that technological innovation is also improving the efficiency with which these mineral sources are utilized. During the twentieth century there has been a continuous series of technical improvements in the efficiency of centralized thermal power plants, the cumulative effects of which have been enormous improvements in fuel

TABLE 7.5
Specific energy sources as percentages of aggregate energy consumption, five-year intervals, 1850–1955 (Btu's)

Year	Bituminous Coal (1)	Anthracite (2)	Total Coal (3)	Oil (4)	Natural Gas (5)	Natural Gas Liquids (6)
1850	4.7	4.6	9.3	—	—	—
1855	7.3	7.7	15.0	—	—	—
1860	7.7	8.7	16.4	.1	n.a.[a]	—
1865	9.6	8.9	18.5	.3	n.a.	—
1870	13.8	12.7	26.5	.3	n.a.	—
1875	19.9	13.4	33.3	.3	n.a.	—
1880	26.7	14.3	41.1	1.9	n.a.	—
1885	33.4	16.9	50.3	.7	1.5	—
1890	41.4	16.5	57.9	2.2	3.7	—
1895	45.8	18.8	64.6	2.2	1.9	—
1900	56.6	14.7	71.4	2.4	2.6	—
1905	61.2	14.5	75.7	4.6	2.8	—
1910	64.3	12.4	76.8	6.1	3.3	—
1915	62.7	12.2	74.8	7.9	3.8	—
1920	62.3	10.2	72.5	12.3	3.8	.2
1925	58.4	7.3	65.6	18.5	5.3	.6
1930	50.3	7.3	57.5	23.8	8.1	1.0
1935	45.6	6.3	52.0	26.9	9.4	.9
1940	44.7	4.9	49.7	29.6	10.6	1.1
1945	44.8	4.0	48.8	29.4	11.8	1.5
1950	33.9	2.9	36.8	36.2	17.0	2.2
1955	27.2	1.5	28.7	40.0	22.1	2.9

[a] n.a.: not available.

SOURCE: Sam H. Schurr and Bruce C. Netschert, *Energy in the American Economy, 1850–1955* (Baltimore: The Johns Hopkins Press for Resources for the Future, Inc., 1960), p. 36. Reprinted by permission of the publisher.

[41] Richard B. Du Boff, "The Introduction of Electric Power in American Manufacturing," *Economic History Review,* vol. 20 (December 1967), p. 513.
[42] The relative insignificance of hydropower sources is clearly attested to in Table 7.5. Hydropower has never been responsible for as much as 5 percent of aggregate energy consumption.

efficiency. Much of this improvement has involved the exploitation of seemingly inexhaustible economies of large-scale production but, in addition, a stream of minor improvements in plant design, a shift to higher pressures and temperatures, and numerous other small improvements have sharply raised the output of energy derived from a physical unit of input. The magnitude of this improvement is evident in the fact that, whereas it required nearly seven pounds of coal to generate a kilowatt-hour of electricity in 1900, the same amount of electricity could be generated by less than nine tenths of a pound of coal in the 1960s. Even this figure, however, understates the full improvement in the utilization of energy sources.

During the 50-year period 1907–1957 reduction of the total energy required or lost in coal mining, in moving the coal from mine to point of utilization, in converting to electric energy, in delivering the electric energy to consumers, and in converting electric energy to end uses have increased by well over 10 times the energy needs supplied by a ton of coal as a natural resource.[43]

Total Liquids and Gaseous Fuels (7)	Total Mineral Fuels (8)	Hydro-power (9)	Mineral Fuels and Hydro-power (10)	Fuel Wood (11)	Year
—	9.3	—	—	90.7	1850
—	15.0	—	—	85.0	1855
n.a.	16.5	—	—	83.5	1860
n.a.	18.8	—	—	81.2	1865
n.a.	26.8	—	—	73.2	1870
n.a.	33.6	—	—	66.4	1875
1.9	43.0	—	—	57.0	1880
2.2	52.5	—	—	47.5	1885
5.9	63.8	.3	64.1	35.9	1890
4.1	68.7	1.2	69.9	30.1	1895
5.0	76.4	2.6	79.0	21.0	1900
7.4	83.1	2.9	86.1	13.9	1905
9.3	86.1	3.3	89.3	10.7	1910
11.8	86.6	3.9	90.5	9.5	1915
16.3	88.8	3.6	92.5	7.5	1920
24.4	90.0	3.1	93.2	6.8	1925
33.0	90.6	3.3	93.9	6.1	1930
37.1	89.1	4.1	93.2	6 8	1935
41.3	91.0	3.6	94.6	5.4	1940
42.8	91.6	4.5	96.1	3.9	1945
55.4	92.1	4.6	96.7	3.3	1950
65.0	93.7	3.7	97.4	2.6	1955

[43] U.S. Bureau of the Census, *Historical Statistics of the United States: Colonial Times to 1957* (Washington: U.S. Government Printing Office, 1960), p. 501.

These magnitudes in fuel economy are worth dwelling on, not only because of their obvious quantitative significance, but because of the light they shed upon the nature of technological change itself. In thinking about technological change, most attention is accorded the dramatic innovations which constitute sharp departures from earlier techniques. Much less attention is accorded the small, frequently anonymous improvements in design, the substitution of slightly improved materials or the achievement of better tolerances, the minor adjustments and modifications in practice which are as frequent as they are unspectacular. The cumulative impact of these small improvements, however, can be enormous, and any perspective on technological change which fails to recognize this is necessarily distorted and incomplete. The huge cumulative effect of a large number of small changes is also evident in the iron and steel industry. Here gradual increases in size of blast furnaces and modifications in their design, the introduction of more effective auxiliary equipment for handling materials and other purposes, and continual improvement in the control of combustion and temperature have brought major long-term improvements in the productivity of the resources employed in this industry.

CONCLUDING OBSERVATIONS

It is obvious from the foregoing account that technological change in American economic growth has been extremely uneven. Technological change has never visited all sectors of the economy in a uniform, lock-step fashion. Each sector has experienced great variations over time in the rate of inventive activity, in the speed of diffusion of new techniques, and in the specific forms which these new techniques have taken. Indeed, a large part of this chapter has been directly concerned with understanding these developments in terms of the economic forces which generated them and determined their shapes, as well as in terms of their economic consequences. It seems appropriate, in closing, to emphasize the formative role played by technological forces themselves in determining the pace and direction of technological advance.

One useful way of looking at economic growth is as a progressive relaxation of two sets of supply constraints. One set, as we have seen, is imposed by limitations in the stock of knowledge and is relaxed as this knowledge frontier is shifted outward. Thus, hybrid corn required a sophisticated knowledge of genetic processes, and synthetic materials required an advanced understanding of molecular theory. *Within* these limits, however, there is the second set of constraints imposed by the extent to which techniques that are possible with a given state of knowledge are actually realized. Thus, as we have seen, much of the innovation in nineteenth-century mechanization involved an increasing mastery of metal-working techniques, but these techniques were available with no significant growth in the stock of knowledge. Most of what was accomplished in nineteenth-century mechanization involved increasing skills in the precision working of metals and the development of techniques which required imagination and mechanical ingenuity, but no fundamental breakthroughs in basic knowledge.

The direction in which this expansion of knowledge is likely to go in the future is difficult to predict for many reasons. In some measure it obviously depends upon allocation decisions as to the kinds of research activities which deserve to be supported. But, in addition, it depends upon the fact that the realm of the unknown is not uniformly resistant to human probings. Some aspects of the natural world are simply more complex than others and therefore inherently more difficult to unravel. The chemical structure of Vitamin B_{12} is much more complex than those of Vitamin B_1 or Vitamin C, and therefore took longer to synthesize and place in commercial production. Amorphous materials, as a group, are much more complicated in their atomic structure than crystalline solids, and therefore understanding them involves a greater research effort. It appears, more generally, that we may be moving up a scale of increasing complexity in the knowledge base underlying our economic activity—from the mechanical to the electrical to electronic, chemical, biological, and so on. Our increasing reliance upon systematized science is a natural concomitant of this movement.

It is not possible to draw a sharp distinction between the two sets of supply constraints. In a certain sense, after all, it is possible to attribute *all* constraints on what is attainable at any moment in time to limitations of knowledge. But what is more important for our present purposes is not so much strict clarity between the two categories of constraints as the recognition that there are wide variations in the complexity of the problems with which we are confronted and that their degree of difficulty plays an important role in determining both the timing and the direction of inventive activity. Instances abound of cases in which innovations were conceptualized but not realized because they were beyond the technical capacity of the day. Da Vinci's notebooks are full of sketches of novel machinery which could not be produced with the primitive metal-working techniques of his time. Breech-loading cannon had been made as early as the sixteenth century but could not be used until precision in metal working made it possible to produce an airtight breech and properly fitting case (or, in the case of firearms, cartridge). Christopher Polhem, a Swede, devised many techniques for the application of machinery to the quantity production of metal and metal products, but could not successfully implement his conceptions with the power sources and clumsy wooden machinery of the first half of the eighteenth century. The Frenchman LeBlanc, who, Thomas Jefferson reported, was making muskets on an interchangeable-parts basis in the 1780s, seems to have experienced a similar fate, although facts concerning his life and activities are limited.

In the development of machinery to perform specific functions, the differences in the degree of difficulty at the technological level are an important factor influencing the timing of inventions. In the textile industry the mechanization of cotton preceded that of wool partly because differences in the nature of the raw materials made cotton much more amenable to mechanized processes. Although the innumerable attempts to mechanize the picking of cotton go back to the 1820s (as the patent records will testify), a successful cotton picker was developed by International Harvester only in the 1920s, and it was not introduced until the 1940s. A mechanical cotton picker had to imitate (or substitute for) the complex actions of human fingers. A mechanical grain reaper, on the other hand, which imitated the much simpler sweep of the human arm, was successfully developed in the 1830s. Similar considerations explain why a corn picker took so much longer to develop than a cultivator.[44]

Finally, we may close with brief mention of the computer, not only because it has already been responsible for so many changes in the organization and conduct of economic activity, but also because its history nicely illustrates both of the supply constraints which have been mentioned as influencing the timing and direction of inventive activity. Charles Babbage had already conceived of the main features of the modern computer over 100 years ago, and had incorporated these features in his "analytical engine," a project for which he received a large subsidy from the British government. Babbage's failure to complete this ingenious scheme was due to the inability of the technology of his day to deliver the components and methods which were indispensable to the machine's success. Now that the electronic computer is a reality, a century later, its speed and capacity have made possible the advance of scientific knowledge in many directions which would not have been possible without its assistance. Thus, not only does science contribute to the advance of technology, but improvements in technology have become, in turn, critical to the further advance of science.

SUGGESTED READING

Denison, Edward F. *The Sources of Economic Growth in the United States and the Alternatives Before Us*. New York: Committee for Economic Development, 1962.

Fishlow, Albert. *American Railroads and the Transformation of the Ante-Bellum Economy*. Cambridge, Mass.: Harvard University Press, 1965.

Fogel, Robert W. *Railroads and American Economic Growth*. Baltimore: Johns Hopkins, 1964.

Habakkuk, H. J. *American and British Technology in the 19th Century*. Cambridge, England: Cambridge University Press, 1962.

Hunter, Louis. *Steamboats on the Western Rivers*. Cambridge, Mass.: Harvard University Press, 1949.

Kendrick, John W. *Productivity Trends in the United States*. Princeton: Princeton University Press, 1961.

Mansfield, Edwin. *The Economics of Technological Change*. New York: Norton, 1968.

National Bureau of Economic Research. *The Rate and Direction of Inventive Activity*. Princeton: Princeton University Press, 1962.

Perloff, Harvey, *et al. Regions, Resources and Economic Growth*. Baltimore: Johns Hopkins, 1960.

[44] Obviously this discussion is intended to suggest not that technical complexity is the entire story, but merely that it is important. Wheat, for example, had a peculiarly urgent seasonal peak labor requirement, which was not true of cotton or corn, and in this sense the demand for the reaper may be said to have been more urgent. See also the discussion in Chapter 11.

Rosenberg, Nathan (ed.). *The American System of Manufactures.* Edinburgh: Edinburgh University Press, 1969.

Rosenberg, Nathan (ed.). *The Economics of Technological Change.* Harmondsworth, Middlesex, England: Penguin Books, 1971.

Schmookler, Jacob. *Invention and Economic Growth.* Cambridge, Mass.: Harvard University Press, 1966.

Schurr, Sam H., and Bruce C. Netschert. *Energy in the American Economy, 1850–1955.* Baltimore: Johns Hopkins, 1960.

Strassmann, W. Paul. *Risk and Technological Innovation: American Manufacturing Methods During the 19th Century.* Ithaca, N.Y.: Cornell University Press, 1959.

Temin, Peter. *Iron and Steel in 19th Century America.* Cambridge, Mass.: M.I.T. Press, 1964.

8
CAPITAL
AND GROWTH

The economic development of the United States has been, at least in part, underwritten by increases in capital stock. In the course of that development, changes in resources, technology, tastes, and the spatial distribution of economic activity have required important changes in the nature of that stock. These changes are the focus of this chapter.

DEFINITIONS

People frequently have trouble distinguishing among capital, investment, and finance, and it appears useful to make these distinctions early. By *capital* we mean the stock of real (i.e., not financial) resources produced in previous periods and currently available to aid in the production of goods and services. Narrowly defined, this stock includes buildings and other structures, machinery and other durable producers' equipment, and inventories of partially finished products awaiting finishing and of finished goods awaiting sale. More broadly defined, capital includes also goods in the hands of consumers (houses and their furnishings, transport and kitchen equipment, etc.) and the intangible capital stored up in human beings represented by expenditures on their professional education and improved health. *Investment* (sometimes termed *capital formation*), on the other hand, includes those goods and services that are presently being produced to be added to the capital stock for use at some later time. It follows that if one were to add up the investment of past periods and then subtract the items that have been removed from the capital stock because of age or obsolescence, one would have the present net capital stock.

While the terms *capital* and *investment* refer to actual physical assets, *finance* refers to certain claims against these assets in the form of stocks, bonds, bills, notes, or money. In the balance sheet of a nonfinancial corporation the real capital items (e.g., buildings, equipment, inventories) are listed on the left side among the things that the firm owns; but the corporation's financial items are listed on the right side, and they reflect some of the methods that the firm has used to command the real resources that appear on the asset side.[1] Of course, a firm may also acquire (finance) real assets by expending its own saved profits. These appear as "undistributed surplus" on the right side of the account. Indeed, without borrowing or stock issues, an enterprise could acquire capital assets only through its own saving. By issuing these pieces of "symbolic capital" however, it is possible to bring together the savings which other persons or firms wish to place at the firm's disposal.

Finally, by the word *savings*, we mean that fraction of real income that is not consumed in the present period, but is available for use in later periods. Actual savings are the share of current income not spent on consumption goods or paid to the government in taxes. *Saving* represents purchasing power withdrawn from the markets of the economy. Investment represents the spending by private firms or persons on final output other than consumption goods (i.e., capital goods). Clearly, as a matter of arithmetic, savings "realized" in this sense in any one year must equal the private spending on nonconsumer (investment) goods. But this definitional identity does not mean that the savings people plan to accumulate at the beginning of the year and the investment firms plan to make are equal. Further discussion of these phenomena must be left to a book on the theory of income determination. Here we will assume that income recipients do determine the level of savings, that capital users determine the ultimate form that the capital financed by those savings will take, and that the two interact to determine the distribution of savings among competing uses.[2] The question of forced saving (withdrawals from consumption over which the savers have no control) is reserved for Chapter 17, and the relation between the productivity of capital and the level of savings, although acknowledged, is not explored here.

SAVINGS AND THE GROWTH PROCESS

As an analytical device, economists link inputs to outputs through a theoretical construct that they have dubbed a *production function*. For most of the particular functions that economists have found useful for explaining firm behavior, an increase in capital (at least over some range) will increase total output and average output per unit of the other factors. Moreover, given constant or increasing returns to scale, additional capital, when coupled with proportional additions to the inputs of other factors, causes output to rise at least proportionately. It is possible to talk not only of a production function for a particular firm, but also of an aggregate function for the entire economy.[3] If the aggregate function displays some of the characteristics of the firm

[1] This explanation may be slightly misleading. Any financial items that the firm owns (cash, accounts receivable, shares in other companies) appear on the left side.

[2] Thus, for simplicity, it is assumed that aggregate savings are interest-inelastic, but that individual savers will move their savings to the activity offering the highest return.

[3] It is certainly possible to talk about an aggregate production function. Many economists have, although the concept remains quite hazy.

functions, over some ranges of output increased capital per worker will yield increased output per worker, and given a gradually increasing labor force (the product of positive population growth), some increases in the capital stock are necessary, if there is no technical change and output per worker is not to decline. It is for these reasons that economists have tended to emphasize the process of capital accumulation in economic development.

The aggregate production function, like that for a firm, relates inputs to outputs at some given level of technology. If technology is improving over time, then the same inputs can yield greater output. While technical change can, in fact, be embodied in any factor of production (labor, for example, can become more productive if the workers are better trained; land can become more productive if a new cereal strain is developed), it frequently has been assumed that a substantial part of the changes in technology are embodied in capital equipment. If change is embodied in capital, then another benefit is felt from higher rates of capital accumulation. Since older capital does not embody the latest advances, the new technology is transmitted through the economy only by investment in new capital. Thus the more rapid the rate of accumulation (assuming entrepreneurs will introduce the new techniques), the more rapid is the diffusion of the new technology and the more rapid the increase in output.

If, over time, capital becomes more efficient, the output of a piece of new capital will be higher than the output of the same amount of capital withdrawn from the stock. As a result, over time, the stock of capital will become more productive, and it will be possible to achieve increases in worker output even if the dollar value of the stock does not change. It is therefore possible to have increases in per worker output with zero net savings if the rate of technical progress is sufficient.[4]

Recently, estimates of the contribution to economic growth of each of the variables in the aggregate production function have been made. Although the methodology appears at most very flimsy, the exercises probably do provide a fair estimate of the actual orders of magnitude. In the most well-known of these exercises, Edward Denison has concluded that increases in the capital stock accounted for about 35 percent of per capita growth in the U.S. economy between 1909 and 1929, and about 15 percent of the total in the more recent past. If these estimates were to be pushed back into the nineteenth century, when capital was almost certainly scarcer in relation to population and natural resources, it is probable that the contribution of the growth of the capital stock would have been even larger.

---

[4] A careful examination of the trends in capital accumulation in the United States shows that capital consumption (the difference between gross and net investment) has been increasing greatly in the recent past. It appears useful to digress for a moment and explain the economic implication of capital consumption. Capital consumption does not represent nonrepairable wear and tear on the capital stock alone, but to a larger extent is a dollar offset made to the price of a piece of capital to reflect the changing value of that item as tastes and technology change. That is, given new tastes or technologies, it is possible for the same amount of dollars to buy a piece of capital that is "better," and the depreciation charge is intended to reflect just how much better. Thus, for example, the charge on a machine reflects the difference in productivity between the old machine and a new one that could now be purchased, and the reduction in the value of a house reflects the difference between the location of that house and a new one in a neighborhood that is currently thought more desirable.

Thus, capital accumulation has apparently had a substantial impact on American economic growth, and most economists feel that that process has also played an important role in the development of the rest of the "developed" countries. There is, however, still some substantial debate about the amount of accumulation that is required to underwrite sustained growth. There is a thread of argument that runs through the works of some authors—Arthur Lewis and W. W. Rostow, for example—that says that to industrialize success-fully, an underdeveloped country must increase its rate of capital accumulation (and since investment comes from savings, its savings rate) from the 2 or 3 percent net that characterizes most of the underdeveloped world to about 12 percent net (20 percent gross).[5] This argument is founded on a simple theoretical proposition and bolstered by some very casual empiricism. It is argued that if the capital/output ratio is about four to one (a figure that appears to be something of an average of the actual values in most under-developed countries), and if population grows at 3 percent per annum, then a 12 percent rate of savings is necessary for the country to hold its own. More-over, these authors look quickly at the history of countries like the United States and the United Kingdom and find evidence of a 12 percent rate, and conclude that such a rate is a necessary precondition for growth. Given the assumptions, the results follow logically, but there may be serious questions about the usefulness of the assumptions and about the relevance of the model to its conclusions. Moreover, upon close examination, the empirical evidence appears less strong than the authors have assumed. While the United States has always had a relatively high rate of savings, the magical 12 percent probably was not achieved until the middle of the nineteenth century. At the same time, recent research has indicated that savings rates in Great Britain did not reach 10 percent until the 1850s, and touched 12 percent only in the period 1856–1879. Moreover, during the entire nineteenth century, a substantial portion of British savings flowed overseas. Thus, while most economists still argue that some positive level of savings is a requirement for successful industrialization, there is much less agreement over the minimum size of that figure. However, even a downward revision of the required savings rate does not, of course, deny that, if full employment can be maintained, higher rates of savings can lead to higher rates of growth.

THE SAVINGS—INVESTMENT PROCESS —AN OVERVIEW

Given that some level of savings is necessary, what are its sources? With a few exceptions, no country can depend entirely on the accumulations of

[5] Ever since Marx published *Das Kapital*, Marxian economists have argued that original capital accumulation is a necessary prerequisite for economic growth, although there has been some discussion over the source of that original accumulation. Among non-Marxian economists the idea of the need for an increase in the rate of savings before successful industrialization can take place has also been widespread. Although the argument differs from one to another, W. W. Rostow, W. Arthur Lewis, and Alexander Gerschenkron all assign a central role to such an increase in their theories of economic development. W. W. Rostow, *The Stages of Economic Growth, A Non-Communist Manifesto* (New York: Cambridge University Press, 1960); W. Arthur Lewis, *The Theory of Economic Growth* (Homewood, Ill.: Irwin, 1955); and Alexander Gerschenkron, *Economic Backwardness in Historical Perspective, A Book of Essays* (Cambridge, Mass.: Harvard University Press, Belknap Press, 1962).

other countries; however, foreign savings can play a significant role. The post-World War II experience of the United States (and to a lesser extent the countries of Europe) has shown that, with the possible exception of a resource-rich country like Kuwait, one cannot expect miracles from infusions of foreign capital. However, the history of the United States attests to the fact that foreign capital can underwrite a wave of investment (the transportation network in the 1830s, for example) for a few years, at least, before it can be supported by domestic accumulations. In this way the process of development can be speeded up. At the same time, since savings in a developed country are apt to be more mobile than in an underdeveloped one, it is likely that foreign savings can be channeled into new industries and regions more easily than can domestic savings. Again, the U.S. experience attests to the greater mobility of savings originating in more developed areas. It is, for example, very likely that the British were willing to make finance available to transport projects in the American Midwest several decades before investors in the eastern portion of the United States.

Although the United States did receive substantial benefits from foreign capital, most of the accumulations came from domestic sources, and the U.S. experience is probably not very different from that of most other nations. Domestic saving can be either voluntary or involuntary. Sometimes as a precaution, sometimes in anticipation of the future, sometimes because it is profitable, people decide to save a greater portion of their income. At the same time, it is possible for people to consume a smaller portion of income without making any conscious decision to do so. A government policy of high taxes may reduce disposable income and free resources for investment. In fact, the Russian government, both under the later czars and under communism has depended on this type of involuntary saving to underwrite their programs of capital accumulation. The same end can be achieved through an increase in the money supply (either by government or by the commercial banks) that reduces the real value of money incomes and transfers resources from income recipients to the government or to bank borrowers. The United States has supplemented its voluntary domestic accumulation with both types of involuntary saving.

Accumulation, although necessary, is by itself not enough. If capital is to be employed efficiently, there must be a mechanism capable of transferring the savings from the surplus-savings units to the deficit-savings (borrowing) units. In a Robinson Crusoe economy, this second problem is nonexistent. There, the saver and the user of those savings are the same person. A similar situation is frequently found in today's underdeveloped countries. In these primarily agricultural economies, most savings are generated in agriculture and employed on the same farms that produced them. As an economy develops and becomes more specialized, however, the probabilities of a one-to-one correspondence between saver and investor become increasingly small. In fact, since the term *development* almost always denotes a change in the structure of production (a shift in the composition or the spatial distribution of economic activity), problems of mobilization are almost inherent in economic development.

In underdeveloped economies characterized by lack of education and experience, savers are often unwilling to place their accumulations in activities far outside their normal experience. In part, therefore, the process of mobilization is the process of saver education. Education, however, is not the entire story (perhaps not even the greatest part of that story). In an economy without efficient financial markets, there are substantial costs that must be paid if a potential saver wants to seek out and invest in activities far removed from his usual experience. The process of mobilization, then, is in part the process of developing a set of financial markets and intermediaries capable of reducing the costs of search and easing the flow of funds. It also includes, of course, the more traditional processes of matching the time and risk preference of savers and investors. It is in these processes that finance and financial instruments play an important role in economic growth.

CAPITAL FORMATION IN THE UNITED STATES

Levels and Rates

Some question exists about the rate at which capital formation occurred before the Civil War, but the United States clearly has been marked by a rapidly growing capital stock since that time. Between 1869 and the mid-1950s, the level of gross capital formation (gross investment) has increased about nine times (from an annual level of $3.5 billion to almost $30 billion). Over the same period, the net level (excluding military capital) has risen from about $2 billion to $10 billion. The difference, of course, reflects the very rapid increase in capital consumption allowances. In the early stages of growth there was a need for heavy investment in buildings and in social-overhead capital. However, once the stock of these items had been built, the additional demands were much smaller. As a result, there was a shift from more slowly depreciating construction to more rapidly depreciating producers' durables.

Despite this rapid depreciation, the rate of net capital formation remained high (see Table 8.1), and given this rate the stock of capital grew swiftly. In the years since 1869, the gross stock (excluding military equipment) grew about twenty-four times and the net stock grew about fifteen (from $27 to $419 billion). While the first of these measures overstates the actual productive value of the stock, the latter underestimates it. The gross stock less capital retired from the productive process, an alternative measure that may provide a more realistic estimate, grew about seventeenfold (from $36 to $649 billion).

It would be of considerable analytical interest to distinguish between increases in the capital stock that reflect nothing but increases in the size of the economy and increases that reflect actual changes in factor proportions. That task is almost impossible, but it may be feasible to gain some understanding of the relevant magnitudes by examining changes in capital per

TABLE 8.1
Level and rate of growth in capital stock, gross and net,
1929 prices, in population, and in labor force, 1869–1955

		Total Capital Stock (billions of dollars)				
Years[a]		Gross (1)	Net of Capital Retirements (2)	Net of Capital Consumption (3)	Population (millions) (4)	Gross (5)
Volumes						
Total Stock						
1.	1869	45.0	36.0	27.0	40.0	1.12
2.	1879	71.0	56.0	42.0	49.7	1.42
3.	1889	116.0	89.0	68.0	62.5	1.86
4.	1899	190.0	143.0	108.0	75.1	2.53
5.	1909	296.0	224.0	165.0	90.9	3.25
6.	1919	430.0	323.0	227 0	105.9	4.06
7.	1929	607.0	440.0	306.0	122.3	4.96
8.	1939	727.0	480.0	319.0	131.8	5.52
9.	1946	895.0	547.0	374.0	142.0	6.30
10.	1955	1191.0	649.0	442.0	165.9	7.18
Total Stock[b]						
7a.	1929	597.0	437.0	304.0	122.3	4.88
9a.	1946	820.0	501.0	328.0	142.0	5.77
10a.	1955	1085.0	626.0	419.0	165.9	6.54
Percentage Rate of Growth per Decade, Total Period						
1869 to 1955						
11.	Total stock	46.4	40.0	38.4	18.0	24.10
11a.	Total stock[b]	44.8	39.4	37.6	18.0	22.70
1869 to 1929						
12.	Total stock	54.3	51.8	49.9	20.5	28.10
12a.	Total stock[b]	53.9	51.6	49.7	20.5	27.70
Percentage Rate of Growth per Decade, Subperiods						
Total Stock						
13.	1869 to 1889	60.8	57.6	58.9	25.1	28.60
14.	1889 to 1909	59.4	58.4	55.7	20.6	32.20
15.	1909 to 1929	43.3	40.1	36.2	16.0	23.50
16.	1929 to 1955	29.6	16.1	15.1	12.4	15.30
Total Stock[b]						
13.	1869 to 1889	60.8	57.6	58.9	25.1	28.60
14.	1889 to 1909	59.4	58.4	55.7	20.6	32.20
15a.	1909 to 1929	42.1	39.7	35.7	16.0	22.50
16a.	1929 to 1955	25.9	14.8	13.2	12.4	11.90

[a] Mid-year date for absolute volumes.
[b] Excluding military.

SOURCE: Simon Kuznets, *Capital in the American Economy: Its Formation and Financing* (New York: National Bureau of Economic Research, 1961), pp. 64–66. Reprinted by permission of the publisher.

Capital Stock per Capita (thousands of dollars)			Capital Stock per Member of Labor Force (thousands of dollars)		
Net of Capital Retirements (6)	Net of Capital Consumption (7)	Labor Force (millions) (8)	Gross (9)	Net of Capital Retirements (10)	Net of Capital Consumption (11)
.90	.68	12.8	3.52	2.82	2.11
1.12	.85	17.0	4.16	3.27	2.49
1.43	1.09	22.3	5.22	4.01	3.06
1.90	1.44	28.5	6.66	5.01	3.79
2.47	1.82	37.4	7.90	5.99	4.41
3.04	2.15	41.6	10.32	7.75	5.46
3.60	2.50	48.4	12.54	9.09	6.33
3.64	2.42	52.8	13.77	9.08	6.04
3.85	2.63	58.0	15.44	9.43	6.45
3.91	2.66	65.6	18.15	9.89	6.74
3.58	2.49	48.4	12.33	9.04	6.28
3.53	2.31	58.0	14.13	8.63	5.65
3.78	2.53	65.6	16.54	9.54	6.39
18.60	17.30	21.0	21.00	17.00	14.40
18.10	16.60	21.0	19.70	15.20	13.70
26.00	24.40	24.9	23.60	21.50	20.10
25.90	24.30	24.9	23.20	21.40	19.90
26.10	27.00	32.1	21.70	19.30	20.30
31.30	29.20	29.6	23.00	22.20	20.10
20.70	17.40	13.8	26.00	23.20	19.80
3.30	2.40	12.4	15.30	3.30	2.40
26.10	27.00	32.1	21.70	19.30	20.30
31.60	29.20	29.6	23.00	22.20	20.10
20.40	17.00	13.8	24.90	22.80	19.30
2.10	.70	12.4	12.00	2.10	.70

person or per worker. No matter which of these measures is chosen, it is obvious that at least over the last three quarters of the past century, there was a substantial increase not only in the total stock but also in the proportion of capital to other factors. In constant dollars, capital per person increased about three and a half times, while capital per worker rose about three times (from $2100 to $6400).[6] It is hardly surprising that the productivity of the American worker advanced spectacularly during the period.

While all of these magnitudes have risen over the past century, they have increased more slowly in the recent past. This apparent retardation has been a subject of some concern to Kuznets and other economists interested in America's long-term growth. Certainly the depression of the 1930s, marked as it was by high unemployment, low income, and negative corporate profits, saw sharp declines in the level of capital formation however measured and injects a strong downward bias in any average that includes those years. Even if that decade is ignored, however, and the postwar decades compared with the earlier period, there is still substantial evidence of a downward drift in the rates of increase of additions to the capital stock (see Table 8.2). Both gross and net capital formation (excluding military) were increasing at more than 50 percent per decade in the 1870s and 1880s, but by the post-World War II decades, the rate of increase of the gross stock was down to about half that level and the increase in the net stock had diminished to little more than a quarter that level. Since the capital stock is merely the sum of additions to that stock, it should not be too surprising that its rate of growth displays a similar retardation. The decline is not alone a function of fall in the rate of growth of population, since retardation in the rate of increase is also clearly marked in the per capita and per worker figures (Table 8.1). In fact, while those figures were rising by nearly 20 percent per decade in the nineteenth century, they have shown practically no increase at all in the more recent past. Nor does retardation appear to have been a short-run phenomenon associated with the postwar decades. While the rates for all series show little change between 1869 and 1909, growth was uniformly slower in the first two decades of the twentieth century and has been slower yet since World War II.

To a large extent, however, this retardation may be a statistical illusion resulting from the narrow definition of capital. The definition (structures, producers' durables, and net changes in inventories) ignores those resources that are diverted to investment in human capital, and those that go into household durables. A part of the retardation can almost certainly be explained in terms of a substitution of these forms of investment for those traditionally included. Certainly casual observation suggests that the economy has greatly increased the resources devoted to both formal education and on-the-job training. Recent work by Juster and Lipsey tends to confirm these impressions. They have found that expenditures on housing and consumer durables have risen as a proportion of consumer expenditures, and by moving these items

---

[6] Constant-dollar conversions involve the revaluations of new capital at old prices or old capital at new prices. Either method involves serious problems, but in this instance the results of both are similar and highly suggestive.

TABLE 8.2
Level and rate of growth in capital formation,
gross and net, 1929 prices, 1869–1955 (billions of dollars, averages per year)

Periods	Gross Capital Formation (1)	Capital Consumption (2)	Net Capital Formation (3)	Ratio of Column (2) to Column (1) (4)	Capital Retirements (5)	Ratio of Column (5) to Column (1) (6)
Volumes						
Total						
1. 1869–1888	3.48	1.46	2.02	.42	.87	.25
2. 1889–1908	8.68	4.03	4.65	.46	2.18	.25
3. 1909–1928	15.50	8.39	7.12	.54	4.72	.30
4. 1929–1955	22.70	17.30	5.44	.76	14.50	.64
5. 1946–1955	33.00	25.10	7.88	.76	21.40	.65
Total, Excluding Military						
3a. 1909–1928	15.00	8.00	7.00	.53	4.33	.29
4a. 1929–1955	19.10	14.40	4.69	.75	11.60	.61
5a. 1946–1955	29.70	19.30	10.50	.65	15.60	.52
Percentage Rate of Growth per Decade, Total Period						
Total						
6. Line 1 to line 4	34.40	47.60	16.90		55.80	
7. Line 1 to line 5	36.70	48.40	20.80		56.10	
Total, Excluding Military						
6a. Line 1 to line 4a	30.80	43.50	14.20		50.50	
7a. Line 1 to line 5a	34.70	43.10	25.70		49.40	
Percentage Rate of Growth per Decade, Subperiods						
Total						
8. Line 1 to line 2	58.00	66.10	51.80		58.70	
9. Line 2 to line 3	33.70	44.30	23.80		47.10	
10. Line 3 to line 4	17.70	36.10	−10.80		61.10	
11. Line 3 to line 5	26.60	40.90	3.20		60.40	
Total, Excluding Military						
8. Line 1 to line 2	58.00	66.10	51.80		58.70	
9a. Line 2 to line 3a	31.50	40.90	22.70		40.90	
10a. Line 3a to line 4a	10.90	28.60	−15.70		52.20	
11a. Line 3a to line 5a	23.80	31.60	13.30		49.10	

SOURCE: Kuznets, op. cit., p. 56.

from consumption to the capital account they show that the ratio of gross capital formation (GCF) to GNP has actually risen slightly over the period 1929–1962.[7] Second, they also found that broadening the definition of capital to include certain intangibles (education and medical care) produces a marked upward increase in the ratio, since expenditures on these items have doubled since 1929.[8]

[7] F. T. Juster and R. Lipsey, "A Note on Consumer Asset Formation in the United States," *Economic Journal,* vol. 77 (December 1967). Over the period the proportion of consumption expenditures spent on housing rose from 2.5 to 3.8 percent; that spent on major durables, from 7.0 to 9.4 percent; and that on minor durables, from 4.1 to 9.8 percent.

[8] F. T. Juster, *Household Capital Formation and Financing, 1867–1962* (New York: National Bureau of Economic Research, 1966).

Still it is likely that the economy has experienced some retardation in the growth of the net capital stock, although the actual decline is almost certainly less than the figures indicate. While demand factors appear to be of paramount importance in determining the composition of the stock, and although saving may be somewhat responsive to changes in relative prices, it appears that there are certain factors operating to put an upper limit on the rate of capital accumulation. Moreover, an examination of these factors suggests that, in the long run, they tend to induce a fall in that limit. An analysis of the factors that underly the supply of savings is reserved for the next section; however, one additional point should be made. Marxian economists have talked about the inevitability of declining profits in a capitalist society. Such a decline could certainly lead (by reducing the demand for capital) to a decline in the rate of capital accumulation. The evidence, however, suggests that in the late nineteenth and twentieth centuries in the United States at least, there has been no such secular decline in the profit rate, nor, for that matter, any substantial change in the number of potentially profitable ventures.

Some Comparisons

Given the trends in the capital series for the United States over the past century, it is interesting to compare those trends with (a) the United States in the earlier period and (b) other developed countries over the same period. The data are not all one might ask for, but the comparisons are interesting nonetheless.

In the case of the United States, a study of the growth of reproducible wealth per capita (a magnitude not much different from per capita gross capital formation) suggests that the rate of accumulation in the first half of the century was not far different from that which obtained later.[9] The study is based only on 1805, 1850, and 1880 benchmarks, and the conclusions, even if they are correct, suggest nothing about movements within the three long subperiods. For the longer periods, however, the findings indicate that the stock of tangible wealth grew by 2.2 percent per year over the first half of the nineteenth century as compared with 2.5 percent in the last half and 1.9 percent in the first half of the present century.

Robert Gallman's more detailed study of the period 1835–1858 appears to substantiate the conclusion that the rate of capital accumulation was fairly high in the antebellum decades.[10] In addition, he finds that the level was increasing at a fairly high rate. His evidence suggests a growth of about 50 percent per decade in the stock of capital (not far different from the rates found by Simon Kuznets in the late period), with the 1850s in particular displaying a very rapid increase in level.

While most authors appear to agree about the direction of change in the levels of capital accumulation, there is some disagreement about the levels

[9] Raymond W. Goldsmith, "The Growth of Reproducible Wealth in the United States of America from 1805 to 1950," in International Association for Research in Income and Wealth, *Income and Wealth of the United States: Trends and Structure* (Income and Wealth, Series 2) (Cambridge, England: Bowes & Bowes, 1952).

[10] Robert E. Gallman, "Gross National Product in the United States, 1824–1909," in *Output, Employment, and Productivity in the United States After 1800*, Dorothy S. Brady (ed.), Studies in Income and Wealth, vol. 30 (New York: National Bureau of Economic Research, 1966).

themselves. Gallman's recent work, however, suggests that the ratio of gross capital formation to national product, while rising between 1835 and 1860, stood substantially below the levels reached in the latter part of the century. His figures indicate that the ratio was only about 15 percent in the 1830s compared with almost 30 percent in the postbellum years. The series unfortunately are not complete enough to separate the long-term element of the increases from those induced by the Civil War itself. It is clear, however, that the level rose and that the new levels prevailed at least until the end of the century.

Not only has Simon Kuznets been responsible for most of the quantitative work on the American past, but his work on other countries also makes it possible to put the U.S. experience in its international setting.[11] As usual, however, additional data appear to invoke as many new questions as they answer. Table 8.3 displays the trends in savings–income proportions and rate of economic growth for twelve countries. The most striking feature of the table, and the feature that *a priori* theorizing is least able to explain, is the poor correlation between savings/income ratios and growth rates. Of the twelve countries for which we have data, four have experienced high ratios of capital formation to income as far back as we have records, but the remainder appear to have achieved these levels only much more recently. Given the model of aggregate production that we discussed earlier, one would expect that the countries that first achieved the high ratios should have experienced the most rapid rates of growth. However, the data do not support this conclusion. Four of the five "early achievers" have experienced continued growth of income, but their savings ratio has begun to decline in the more recent past. Perhaps capital formation itself is not the crucial variable, but merely a response to savings decisions on the one hand and a particular set of demand conditions in each country's capital markets on the other.

Some additional light on this important question may be shed by a more detailed examination of the trends in the capital/output ratio in the United States and a comparison of those trends with the experience of other developed nations. The movement in the United States has not been monotonic. The latter decades of the nineteenth century were marked by a rise in the ratio, but in the present century there has been a steady fall. *A priori* one might expect the capital/output ratio to decline over time, since any positive rate of technical change causes capital to become secularly more productive. In fact, the relationship is not so simple. In the United States, for example, not only did the capital-intensiveness of particular industries change, but the industrial structure itself also changed, affecting the ratio. In the case of the railroads, for example, a large part of early investment took the form of right-of-way and structures. This fixed capital was not highly productive, but once these investments had been made, further additions had lower capital/output ratios. Similarly, in the case of agriculture, initial development involved heavy

---

[11] Most of the material in this section is taken from Simon Kuznets, "Quantitative Aspects of the Economic Growth of Nations, VI: Long-Term Trends in Capital Formation Proportions," *Economic Development and Cultural Change*, vol. 9, no. 4 (July 1961).

TABLE 8.3
Trends in capital-formation proportions: ratios of domestic capital formation proportions
to rates of growth of output per worker, successive long periods,
selected countries (based on current price proportions)

Country, Output Concept, and Period for Rate of Growth of Labor Force	Duration (years) (1)	Labor Force (2)	Output per Worker (3)	Ratio to Column (3) of	
				GDCF/ GDP (4)	NDCF/ NDP (5)
United Kingdom, NNP					
1. 1821 and 1831 to 1851 and 1861	30.0	.93	1.14		6.5
2. 1851 and 1861 to 1871 and 1881	20.0	.71	1.54	5.6	4.5
3. 1871 and 1881 to 1891 and 1901	20.0	.81	2.19	3.9	3.1
4. 1891 and 1901 to 1911 and 1921	20.0	.73	.40	23.5	19.2
5. 1921 to 1938	15.0	.72	1.30	6.8	2.5
6. 1950 to 1958	8.0	.90	1.59 G	9.7	5.0
Germany, NNP					
7. 1851–1855 to 1871–1875 (1913 boundaries)	20.0	.73	1.99	6.7	4.3
8. 1871 to 1886–1895 (1913 boundaries)	19.5	1.41	1.02	17.3	11.2
9. 1886–1895 to 1907 (1913 boundaries)	16.5	1.69	1.17	19.4	12.8
10. 1925 to 1939 (1925 boundaries)	14.0	.56	1.09	12.3	5.3
11. 1950 to 1958 (West Germany)	8.0	2.10	4.91	4.9	3.4
Italy, GDP; NDP					
12. 1861 to 1881	20.0	.19	.73 G; .68 N	13.4	6.8
13. 1881 to 1901	20.0	.20	.77 G; .72 N	13.9	6.9
14. 1901 to 1911 and 1921	15.0	.33	1.82 G; 1.72 N	8.0	4.6
15. 1921 to 1936	15.0	.45	1.96 G; 1.78 N	9.2	5.4
16. 1950 to 1958	8.0	1.00	5.52 G; 5.27 N	3.8	2.5
Denmark, GDP; NDP					
17. 1870 to 1889	19.0	.68	2.02 G; 2.06 N	4.9	2.4
18. 1889 to 1909	20.0	1.12	2.35 G; 2.35 N	5.8	3.7
19. 1894 to 1914	20.0	1.19	2.46 G; 2.46 N	5.9	3.8
20. 1921 to 1939	18.0	1.28	1.87 G; 1.85 N	6.7	3.9
21. 1950 to 1958	8.0	.40	2.47 G; 2.38 N	7.4	5.4

Key:
GDCF: Gross Domestic Capital Formation
GNP: Gross National Product
GDP: Gross Domestic Product
NDCF: Net Domestic Capital Formation
NNP: Net National Product
NDP: Net Domestic Product

SOURCE: Simon Kuznets, "Quantitative Aspects of the Economic Growth of Nations, VI: Long-Term Trends in Capital Formation Proportions," *Economic Development and Cultural Change*, vol. 9, no. 4 (July 1961), Part II, pp. 34–35. Reprinted by permission of the author.

TABLE 8.3 (continued)

Country, Output Concept, and Period for Rate of Growth of Labor Force	Duration (years) (1)	Labor Force (2)	Output per worker (3)	Ratio to Column(3) of	
				GDCF/ GDP (4)	NDCF/ NDP (5)
Norway, GDP; NDP					
22. 1865 to 1885	20.0	.85	.83 G ; .78 N	13.6	8.8
23. 1885 to 1905	20.0	.73	1.29 G ; 1.27 N	10.0	6.1
24. 1895 to 1915	20.0	.93	1.46 G ; 1.42 N	9.9	6.7
25. 1900 to 1920	20.0	.93	1.53 G ; 1.48 N	10.8	7.4
26. 1920 to 1940	20.0	1.10	2.09 G ; 2.09 N	8.3	5.4
27. 1950 to 1955	5.0	.51	3.00 G ; 2.87 N	10.0	7.7
Sweden, GDP					
28. 1861 to 1880	19.0	.89	2.08	5.3	3.3
29. 1880 to 1900	20.0	.37	2.31	4.9	3.1
30. 1900 to 1915	15.0	1.22	1.99	6.7	4.2
31. 1910 to 1930	20.0	1.57	.71	19.0	12.1
32. 1930 to 1950	20.0	.57	3.63	5.4	3.5
33. 1950 to 1958	8.0	.40	3.11	6.9	4.5
United States, GNP; NNP					
34. 1874 to 1889	15.0	2.77	2.67 G ; 2.55 N	7.9	5.5
35. 1889 to 1914	25.0	2.42	1.14 G ; 1.09 N	19.4	11.8
36. 1919 to 1939	20.0	1.20	.75 G ; .77 N	23.5	7.8
37. 1946 to 1956	10.0	1.45	2.76 G ; 2.78 N	7.8	3.1
Canada, GNP					
38. 1870 to 1910 and 1920	45.0	2.13	1.50	13.1	7.2
39. 1890 and 1900 to 1910 and 1920	20.0	2.70	1.27	18.0	10.2
40. 1920 to 1939	19.0	1.89	1.24	12.4	3.6
41. 1945 to 1953	8.0	.78	3.09	7.5	4.4
Australia, GDP					
42. 1861 to 1881	20.0	3.24	2.34	6.9	5.3
43. 1881 to 1901	20.0	2.86	−.52	negative	
44. 1891 and 1901 to 1914/15	18.5	1.43	1.33	10.8	7.0
45. 1919/20 to 1938/39	19.0	2.02	.55	30.0	19.6
46. 1947 to 1954	7.0	2.26	1.32	20.1	16.4
Japan, GNP; NNP					
47. 1883–1887 to 1903–1907	20.0	.95	2.82 G ; 2.78 N	3.5	1.9
48. 1893–1897 to 1913–1917	20.0	.55	2.58 G ; 2.54 N	4.2	2.3
49. 1918–1922 to 1938–1942	20.0	.86	4.23 G ; 4.18 N	4.0	2.8
50. 1950 to 1958	8.0	2.40	4.26 G ; 3.53 N	6.6	6.2
Argentina, GDP; NDP					
51. 1895 to 1914	19.0	3.70	.54 G ; .23 N	62.8	negative
52. 1920 to 1940	20.0	2.37	.92 G ; .74 N	29.8	17.6
53. 1935 to 1955	20.0	1.93	1.15 G ; 1.39 N	20.5	6.5
Union of South Africa, GNP; NNP					
54. 1919/20 to 1938/39	19.0	2.10	2.44 G ; 2.47 N	7.5	5.1
55. 1945/46 to 1951/52	6.0	1.50	3.46 G ; 3.36 N	7.7	6.5

investment in land clearing, irrigation, and structures, but additions were less capital-intensive. It is therefore not surprising that the latter nineteenth century should have seen a fall in capital/output ratio. This fall was partially offset by changes within the manufacturing sector. In that sector there was a shift from light to heavy industry in the latter half of the nineteenth century, with a concomitant increase in the ratio. More recently the traditional industries have become less capital-intensive, and in addition, because of changes in tastes, technology, and the resource base, there has been a shift away from heavy toward light manufacturing and the service sectors. These latter activities are, of course, marked by lower capital/output ratios.

For the world as a whole, there appears to have been an upward drift in the ratio similar to that observed in the United States in the nineteenth century. In countries that are initially both underdeveloped and marked by a relative shortage of capital, profit maximization should lead entrepreneurs to substitute against the scarce factor (capital). At the same time, because of the primitive institutional arrangements, productivity would be low but the potential gains from economic reorganization would be very high. If these conditions hold, one would expect an initially low ratio, since capital would be conserved for the most productive uses and initial development would be reflected in rapid output growth as the largest gains from reorganization are realized. At a slightly later period, however, the ratio would rise as further economic reorganization yielded smaller gains in output and as the now less scarce capital was applied to low-productivity industries (e.g., transportation). This latter investment—frequently termed investment in social-overhead capital—must be made if the economy is ever to develop further, but at the time it represents a commitment to industries that are characterized by low direct capital productivity. Indirectly, of course, the long-run productivity of that investment may be very high. Still later the ratio may begin to decline as the investment in social-overhead capital is completed, as the demand for investment shifts from structures and producers' durables to investments in humans, as capital requirements are further reduced by the "second Industrial Revolution," and as the further shifts in the industrial sector are toward the service industries with their very low capital/output ratios. The experience of the United States conforms closely to this theoretical description.

If noncapital factors are as important elsewhere as they were in the United States, the trend in the capital/output ratio would depend to a large extent on the industrial structure of the country under consideration and the shifts in that structure. The evidence suggests that there was no single trend experienced in all countries. While the United Kingdom shared with the United States the "inverted U" shape, other countries have not. Once again it appears that it is not the presence or absence of capital that determines the shape of economic development, although that factor may determine the speed and the limits of such change.

The Structure of the Capital Stock

Additional support for the primacy of demand considerations in the determination of the structure of the capital stock can be found by an analysis of the components of that stock. In fact, it is almost possible to write an economic history of the United States in terms of changes in that magnitude. Looking first at the totals, Table 8.4 displays the changes in the relative proportions of construction, producers' durables, and inventories in both gross and net capital formation. At first glance, it may appear that the most striking feature of the composition of gross capital formation is the decline in inventories, a decline an economic historian might well attribute to improvements in communications and transportation (improvements that should reduce goods in final inventory and transit), as well as the innovation of scientific management and mass-production techniques that ought to reduce goods in process. Unfortunately for this type of implicit theorizing, the decline in the proportion of inventories is missing from the net capital formation figures. The divergence between the two trends is in part explained by the increasing importance of capital consumption allowances. If inventories made the same contribution to output as they did a century ago, they would account for the same proportion of the net figures; but because they do not depreciate, they represent a much smaller part of the gross. However, changes in depreciation do not explain why improved transport, communication, and managerial skill have not caused the proportion of inventories in net capital formation to fall. On this question, the profession has no final answers, but perhaps the gains from these sources have been offset by increases in the demand for highly styled or otherwise specialized commodities and wider ranges of goods (and thus higher inventories) that result from attempts by consumers with much higher incomes to diversify their market baskets.

Assuming that the trends affecting inventories were offsetting, the important shifts in the composition of the capital stock have been between construction and producers' durables. If military capital is excluded, construction declined from about 70 percent of both gross and net figures in 1869 to less than half of both totals in recent decades. Within the construction sector, government construction has risen substantially as government has grown in importance. Nonfarm residences have changed but little as the nation's lagging rate of population growth (a factor that should cause a decline in the rate of housing construction) appears to have been offset by higher incomes. But the "other construction" component (nonagricultural plant, roadways, utilities, and office buildings) has fallen sharply. Since the decline in construction is just another side to the changes in the capital/output ratio, it is not surprising that the same factors caused both. Thus the trends both within industries to become less construction-intensive and in the industrial structure as a whole away from construction-intensive industries have underwritten the shift. Utilities, for example, demand a great deal of capital for construction while they are being built, but once built they last a long time and need relatively little additional investment. At the same time, the next generation of firms (those that buy the output of the utilities), are likely to be characterized by a substantially lower capital/output ratio.

Proportions must add to 100, and in this case the decline in construction has been offset by an increase in producer's durables, an item that more than doubled in both gross and net terms. The explanation of this rise appears to lie

TABLE 8.4
Structure of capital formation, by type of capital good,
1869–1955 (billions of dollars)

		Total Capital Formation			
		Percent Distribution of Column (1)			
Periods	Average Volume per Year (1)	Con- struction (2)	Producers' Durables (3)	Net Changes in Inventories (4)	Net Changes in Claims Against Foreign Countries (5)
Gross Capital Formation, Current Prices					
Total					
1. 1869–1898	2.23	63.9	22.9	14.9	−1.8
2. 1879–1908	3.44	64.4	23.8	9.9	1.9
3. 1889–1918	5.67	57.0	27.5	8.3	7.2
4. 1899–1928	10.81	53.2	29.9	9.1	7.8
5. 1909–1938	12.89	52.9	33.8	6.5	6.9
6. 1919–1948	20.38	45.6	43.9	5.3	5.2
7. 1929–1955	37.01	47.6	47.3	4.0	1.1
8. 1946–1955	61.29	48.3	45.0	4.9	1.8
Total, Excluding Military					
3a. 1889–1918	5.48	57.6	26.3	8.6	7.5
4a. 1899–1928	10.48	53.7	28.9	9.4	8.1
5a. 1909–1938	12.44	53.7	32.5	6.7	7.1
6a. 1919–1948	17.42	50.7	37.0	6.2	6.0
7a. 1929–1955	31.91	53.1	41.0	4.7	1.2
8a. 1946–1955	55.78	51.8	40.7	5.4	2.0
Net Capital Formation, Current Prices					
Total					
17. 1869–1898	1.26	63.9	12.8	26.4	−3.1
18. 1879–1908	1.88	64.7	13.8	18.0	3.5
19. 1889–1918	2.88	53.9	15.6	16.4	14.2
20. 1899–1928	5.16	47.3	17.4	19.0	16.3
21. 1909–1938	4.75	37.9	25.9	17.5	18.6
22. 1919–1948	6.26	25.2	40.7	17.3	16.8
23. 1929–1955	9.38	51.4	28.5	15.9	4.2
24. 1946–1955	15.50	67.1	6.2	19.5	7.2
Total, Excluding Military					
19a. 1889–1918	2.71	54.6	12.9	17.4	15.1
20a. 1899–1928	5.10	46.9	17.4	19.2	16.5
21a. 1909–1938	4.69	38.3	25.1	17.8	18.9
22a. 1919–1948	5.21	27.0	32.0	20.8	20.2
23a. 1929–1955	9.14	52.0	27.4	16.3	4.3
24a. 1946–1955	19.57	55.4	23.4	15.4	5.7

SOURCE: Kuznets, *Capital in the American Economy . . .*, *op. cit.*, pp. 146–149.

	Domestic Capital Formation			Durable Capital Formation		
	Percent Distribution of Column (6)				Percent Distribution of Column (10)	
Average Volume per Year (6)	Con-struction (7)	Producers' Durables (8)	Net Changes in Inven-tories (9)	Average Volume per Year (10)	Con-struction (11)	Producers' Durables (12)
2.27	62.8	22.5	14.7	1.93	73.6	26.4
3.37	65.7	23.4	10.1	3.03	73.0	27.0
5.26	61.4	29.6	9.0	4.79	67.5	32.5
9.96	57.7	32.5	9.8	8.98	64.0	36.0
12.00	56.8	36.3	6.9	11.17	61.0	39.0
19.33	48.1	46.3	5.6	18.24	50.9	49.1
36.62	48.2	47.8	4.1	35.13	50.2	49.8
60.17	49.2	45.8	5.0	57.15	51.8	48.2
5.07	62.3	28.4	9.3	4.60	68.7	31.3
9.63	58.4	31.4	10.2	8.65	65.0	35.0
11.56	57.8	35.0	7.2	10.72	62.3	37.7
16.37	54.0	39.4	6.6	15.29	57.8	42.2
31.52	53.7	41.6	4.7	30.03	56.4	43.6
54.65	52.9	41.6	5.5	51.64	56.0	44.0
1.30	62.0	12.4	25.6	.96	83.3	16.7
1.82	67.1	14.3	18.6	1.48	82.4	17.6
2.47	62.7	18.2	19.1	2.00	77.5	22.5
4.32	56.5	20.8	22.7	3.34	73.1	26.9
3.86	46.6	31.8	21.6	3.03	59.4	40.6
5.21	30.2	48.9	20.8	4.13	38.2	61.8
8.98	53.7	29.7	16.6	7.49	64.6	35.6
14.38	72.3	6.7	21.0	11.36	91.5	8.5
2.30	64.3	15.2	20.5	1.83	80.9	19.1
4.26	56.1	20.8	23.0	3.28	72.9	27.1
3.80	47.2	30.9	21.9	2.97	60.4	39.6
4.16	33.9	40.0	26.1	3.07	45.8	54.2
8.74	54.3	28.7	17.0	7.26	65.4	34.6
18.45	58.8	24.8	16.4	15.43	70.3	29.7

in exactly the same factors that caused the decline in "other construction." As industries develop they tend to require less new construction, but they frequently need more producers' durables. Similarly, industries with low construction components frequently have high producers'-durables requirements. Thus, the railroads, with their roadways built, turned to a larger proportion of investment in rolling stock; and their replacement, the airplane, requires practically no construction but a heavy investment in producers' durables. The firms that developed because they could buy power from the established utilities were often manufacturing plants with less need for construction but greater needs for machinery. In general, therefore, it appears that economic development goes hand in hand with a declining ratio of structures to equipment.

Demand factors alone probably do not account for all of the substitution of producers' durables for construction; certain supply considerations also appear to have been important. Of all the capital-goods industries, construction has experienced the slowest growth of productivity. This fact can be seen very clearly by comparing the relative importance of construction in capital formation in constant dollars with its importance in current dollars. As a comparison of Tables 8.4 and 8.5 suggests, the decline is much less in the latter instance, an indication of the relative increase in price of construction compared to the price of durables and inventories. Given this increase in relative price, profit-maximizing businessmen should choose to substitute less expensive producers' durables for more expensive construction. In transport, for example, there has been a substitution of trucks for railroads; and in manufacturing, a substitution of producers' durables built by mass-production techniques for construction-intensive factories.

Although the evidence is very tenuous, it appears that this substitution is not a product of the recent past, but is rooted in some earlier period. Although the magnitudes are small, even the period 1834–1859 saw a slow decline in the proportion of construction and an offsetting increase in the importance of producers' durables.

Moreover, the shift away from construction does not appear to have been characteristic of the American economy alone. Of the twelve countries for which there are data, only three (the United Kingdom, Canada, and South Africa) fail to show the decline in construction; and the data for the United Kingdom are probably unreliable. The other two countries are both frontier areas engaged in the process of opening new lands, and to this extent they may reflect conditions prevailing in the United States a century ago. If the experience of these two countries can be viewed as support for the general proposition instead of evidence against it, one would expect Australia to show a similar pattern. Although those figures are not available, they should act as a test for the general hypothesis relating economic development to the structure of the capital stock.

Thus far we have limited our discussion to changes in the capital stock narrowly defined, but recent work by F. Thomas Juster has provided some estimates of changes in the stock of intangible capital (capital invested in improving the quality of the labor force and in technical change). We have already seen that including such intangible items (an inclusion that logically ought to be made) reverses the apparent decline in the ratio of gross capital formation to gross national product. Table 8.6, although providing very rough estimates of only a part of total intangible investment, is nontheless quite revealing. It suggests that the real expenditure on education has almost tripled since 1940, while expenditure on research and development has risen more than ten times. One might conclude that, as the economy becomes more and more developed, ideas and men trained to effect those ideas replace machines in the same way that machines replaced tools at an earlier stage of development. It would be interesting to compare intangible investment in the United States with that undertaken in the eleven other countries in the Kuznets survey.

From the viewpoint of understanding economic change in the American past, it is useful to examine not only the form of capital, but also the types of economic activity that have utilized the additions to the capital stock (see Table 8.7). Even if military capital is excluded, the government's share of the total has tripled (from 4 to 13 percent) during the past century, while the share of business has remained fairly constant and the proportion used by households has declined slightly.

In the case of the government, the increase clearly reflects that sector's changing role in the economy; however, the distribution between levels of government is something of a surprise. It is easy to assume that it is the federal government that has become so important in the present century, but this is clearly not the case as far as investment activities are concerned. State and local government accounted for between 80 and 90 percent of all government investment in the nineteenth century, and maintained this proportion well into the twentieth. Only the depression of the 1930s led to a decline in their share to below 80 percent; and even in the postwar decades, they continue to account for about three quarters of the total (see Table 8.8). Clearly, nonmilitary public investment remains largely the domain of the local units of government. The addition of military capital, of course, changes the picture markedly.

The lack of significant change in the share of households in total investment that is so obvious in Table 8.7 is probably more a statistical illusion than a reflection of the actual characteristics of the American economy in the past two decades. On the one hand, it mirrors the heavy weight of the 1930s and early 1940s in the latter time periods and, on the other, the definitional exclusion of consumer durables from and the inclusion of multifamily housing in household capital formation.

There can be little doubt that the depression of the 1930s and the building restrictions of the World War II period brought private home building almost to a halt. Furthermore, the decline in the rate of population growth (the product of falling domestic birth rates and the alien exclusion acts of the 1920s) should, other things being equal, reduce the rate of increase of the demand for housing. The Depression and war were, however, essentially short-run phenomena, even if in this case the "short run" lasted almost 20 years.

TABLE 8.5
Structure of capital formation by type of capital good, 1869–1955 (billions of dollars)

		Total Capital Formation				
			Percent Distribution of Column (1)			
Periods	Average Volume per Year (1)	Con-struction (2	Producers' Durables (3)	Net Changes in Inventories (4)	Net Changes in Claims Against Foreign Countries (5)	

Gross Capital Formation, 1929 Prices
Total

9.	1869–1898	4.68	70.5	20.8	9.9	−1.2
10.	1879–1908	7.29	68.2	22.9	7.1	1.8
11.	1889–1918	10.26	62.6	25.2	6.2	6.0
12.	1899–1928	13.76	57.4	28.6	6.6	7.4
13.	1909–1938	14.42	55.0	33.2	4.8	7.0
14.	1919–1948	18.32	45.9	43.7	5.4	5.0
15.	1929–1955	23.90	43.1	50.3	5.0	1.6
16.	1946–1955	32.98	41.5	49.2	6.8	2.6

Total, Excluding Military

11a.	1889–1918	10.04	63.0	24.5	6.3	6.2
12a.	1899–1928	13.42	57.9	27.8	6.7	7.6
13a.	1909–1938	13.95	55.9	32.0	4.9	7.2
14a.	1919–1948	15.87	50.6	37.4	6.2	5.8
15a.	1929–1955	20.27	48.4	43.8	5.9	1.9
16a.	1946–1955	29.72	45.0	44.6	6.7	2.9

Net Capital Formation, 1929 Prices
Total

25.	1869–1898	2.62	73.4	11.1	17.8	−2.2
26.	1879–1908	3.96	70.6	13.1	13.1	3.3
27.	1889–1918	5.23	62.2	13.9	12.1	11.8
28.	1899–1928	6.58	54.0	16.8	13.8	15.4
29.	1909–1938	5.25	42.4	25.4	13.1	19.1
30.	1919–1948	5.63	24.5	41.6	17.5	16.3
31.	1929–1955	5.70	34.2	38.1	21.0	6.7
32.	1946–1955	7.88	55.3	5.5	28.5	10.8

Total, Excluding Military

27a.	1889–1918	5.04	62.9	12.2	12.6	12.3
28a.	1899–1928	6.50	5.37	16.8	13.9	15.6
29a.	1909–1938	5.17	42.8	24.5	13.3	19.4
30a.	1919–1948	4.69	26.3	33.1	21.0	19.6
31a.	1929–1955	5.19	35.5	34.1	23.1	7.4
32a.	1946–1955	10.45	43.9	26.5	21.5	8.1

SOURCE: Kuznets, *Capital in the American Economy . . . , op. cit.,* pp. 146–149.

| | Domestic Capital Formation | | | | Durable Capital Formation | | |
| | Percent Distribution of Column (6) | | | | | Percent Distribution of Column (10) | |
Average Volume per Year (6)	Con-struction (7)	Producers' Durables (8)	Net Changes in Inven-tories (9)	Average Volume per Year (10)	Con-struction (11)	Producers' Durables (12)
4.74	69.6	20.6	9.8	4.28	77.2	22.8
7.16	69.5	23.3	7.2	6.64	74.9	25.1
9.64	66.6	26.9	6.6	9.00	71.3	28.7
12.75	62.0	30.9	7.1	11.84	66.7	33.3
13.42	59.2	35.7	5.1	12.73	62.3	37.7
17.40	48.4	46.0	5.7	16.42	51.3	48.7
23.52	43.8	51.2	5.1	22.32	46.1	53.9
32.14	42.6	50.5	7.0	29.89	45.8	54.2
9.42	67.2	26.1	6.7	8.79	72.0	28.0
12.41	62.6	30.1	7.3	11.50	67.6	32.4
12.95	60.2	34.5	5.3	12.26	63.6	36.4
14.95	53.7	39.7	6.6	13.97	57.5	42.5
19.88	49.4	44.6	6.0	18.69	52.5	47.5
28.87	46.3	45.9	7.8	26.62	50.2	49.8
2.67	71.8	10.8	17.4	2.21	86.9	13.1
3.83	73.0	13.5	13.5	3.31	84.4	15.6
4.61	70.5	15.7	13.7	3.98	81.7	18.3
5.66	63.8	19.9	16.3	4.66	76.2	23.8
4.25	52.4	31.4	16.2	3.56	62.5	37.5
4.71	29.3	49.8	20.9	3.72	37.1	62.9
5.32	36.7	40.8	22.5	4.12	47.4	52.6
7.03	62.0	6.1	31.9	4.79	91.0	9.0
4.42	71.7	13.9	14.3	3.79	83.7	16.3
5.48	63.6	19.9	16.5	4.58	76.2	23.8
4.17	53.1	30.4	16.5	3.48	63.6	36.4
3.77	32.7	41.2	26.1	2.78	44.3	55.7
4.81	38.3	36.8	24.9	3.61	51.0	49.0
9.60	47.8	28.8	23.4	7.36	62.4	37.6

TABLE 8.6
Estimates of gross investment in tangible and intangible assets, selected categories and years (billions of dollars)

| | Tangible Assets | | | | | | Intangible Assets | | | Grand Total (10) | Ratios to GNP | | |
| | Enterprises | | Households | | Govern- ment Civilian Structures (5) | Total (6) | Educa- tion (7) | Research and Develop- ment (8) | Total (9) | | Total Tangible Assets (11) | Total Intangible Assets (12) | Grand Total (13) |
Years	Struc- tures (1)	Equip- ment (2)	Struc- tures (3)	Equip- ment (4)									
Current Prices													
1900	1.44	1.01	.27	.35	.21	3.28	.40	.04	.44	3.72	17.7	2.4	20.0
1910	1.99	1.66	.78	.92	.55	5.90	.81	.07	.88	6.78	17.6	2.6	20.3
1920	4.05	5.10	1.35	4.44	1.19	16.13	2.51	.18	2.69	18.82	17.7	3.0	20.6
1930	4.49	4.51	1.40	4.57	2.83	17.80	4.97	.34	5.31	23.11	19.5	5.8	25.4
1940	2.47	5.64	2.58	5.18	3.24	19.11	6.33	.57	6.90	26.01	19.0	6.9	25.8
1950	10.15	18.94	12.15	21.87	6.82	69.93	17.00	2.84	19.84	89.77	24.6	7.0	35.1
1960	20.56	27.56	20.61	30.14	15.95	114.82	37.85	13.89	51.74	166.56	22.8	10.3	33.0
1929 Prices													
1900	2.96	2.05	.56	1.01	.44	7.02	.81	.07	.88	7.90	18.8	2.4	21.1
1910	3.69	3.04	1.47	1.58	.93	10.71	1.36	.11	1.47	12.18	19.1	2.6	21.7
1920	3.10	4.18	1.14	3.24	.86	12.52	2.02	.15	2.17	14.69	17.1	3.0	20.0
1930	4.83	4.74	1.43	5.12	2.98	19.10	5.16	.35	5.51	24.61	20.2	5.8	26.0
1940	2.41	5.71	2.53	7.31	3.28	21.24	7.44	.67	8.11	29.35	18.0	6.9	24.8
1950	4.67	11.17	5.64	14.86	3.67	40.01	10.92	1.82	12.74	52.72	21.9	7.0	28.8
1960	6.90	11.90	7.38	19.41	6.49	52.08	19.00	7.09	26.09	78.17	20.6	10.3	30.9

SOURCE: F. T. Juster, Household Capital Formation and Financing, 1867–1962 (New York: National Bureau of Economic Research, 1966), p. 112, Table 8.6. Reprinted by permission of the publisher.

TABLE 8.7
Structure of domestic capital formation, by category of user, 1869–1955

Periods	Gross, Current Prices			Gross, 1929 Prices		
	House-holds[a] (1)	Busi-ness Firms (2)	Govern-ments (3)	House-holds[a] (4)	Busi-ness Firms (5)	Govern-ments (6)
Total						
1. 1869–1898	22.6	73.2	4.3	27.9	67.4	4.7
2. 1879–1908	21.4	73.3	5.3	25.0	69.5	5.5
3. 1889–1918	17.5	72.2	10.3	21.0	69.9	9.1
4. 1899–1928	18.9	68.7	12.4	20.5	68.2	11.3
5. 1909–1938	17.3	65.2	17.5	18.5	64.5	17.0
6. 1919–1948	14.3	57.0	28.8	14.5	57.8	27.7
7. 1929–1955[b]	15.1	57.3	27.6	12.6	58.2	29.2
8. 1946–1955	16.9	61.7	21.4	14.2	64.6	21.2
Total, Excluding Military						
3a. 1889–1918	18.1	74.9	7.0	21.5	71.5	7.1
4a. 1899–1928	19.6	71.1	9.4	21.0	70.1	8.9
5a. 1909–1938	17.9	67.7	14.3	19.2	66.9	13.9
6a. 1919–1948	16.8	67.3	15.9	16.9	67.3	15.9
7a. 1929–1955[b]	17.5	66.6	15.9	14.9	68.8	16.3
8a. 1946–1955	18.6	68.0	13.4	15.8	71.9	12.3

[a] Nonfarm residential construction.
[b] 1949–1955 given the weight of a decade.
SOURCE: Kuznets, *Capital in the American Economy ...*, *op. cit.*, p. 178. Because of rounding, detail will not necessarily add to total. Percentages, except those for 1946–1955, are based on three-decade moving totals of absolute volumes.

Other things have not remained equal in the housing market. In particular, the demand for housing (and those consumer durables that ought to be included in any estimates of household capital formation) appears to be quite interest-elastic. Moreover the past two decades have been marked by rapid increases in disposable income.

The magazines and newspapers of the 1950s and 1960s talked of a "consumer revolution," and in fact the recent work of Juster and Lipsey suggests that there have been important changes in consumer buying habits. Moreover, these changes to a large extent have taken the form of increased expenditures on housing (an item that is included in household capital formation) and consumer durables (an item that should be included). Table 8.9 shows the increase in the demand for one-family housing; Table 8.10 indicates the increase in the demand for consumer durables. It is interesting to note that the latter increase is not a function of the innovation of the automobile alone, but also shows the impact of the widespread consumer acceptance of television, radio, and other electrical appliances as well as increased expenditures on furniture to fill those new "better" homes.

While the aggregate supply of capital appears to have been affected primarily by savings considerations, demand factors have apparently shaped

TABLE 8.8
Distribution of government gross capital formation, current prices, between federal,
and state and local, 1869–1955 (percentage shares in total nonmilitary)

Periods	State and Local, Including Federal Aid (1)	Federal Aid (2)	Direct Federal (3)	Military as Percentage of Nonmilitary (4)	Percentage Share of Federal in Total Including Military (5)
1. 1869–1898[a]	84.5	0	15.5	0	15.5
2. 1879–1908[a]	83.9	0	16.1	0	16.1
3. 1889–1918[a]	87.0	.3	13.1	54.1	43.6
4. 1899–1928[a]	92.6	3.1	7.4	36.5	32.2
5. 1909–1938[a]	87.2	14.0	12.8	27.1	31.4
6. 1919–1948[a]	72.2	15.4	27.8	113.7	66.2
7. 1929–1955[a][b]	72.5	11.4	27.5	101.7	64.1
8. 1946–1955	77.1	7.2	22.9	75.2	56.0
Decades (except line 17)					
9. 1869–1878	82.3	0	17.7	0	17.7
10. 1879–1888	87.0	0	13.0	0	13.0
11. 1889–1898	83.2	0	16.8	0	16.8
12. 1899–1908	83.5	0	16.5	0	16.5
13. 1909–1918	89.5	.3	10.5	93.8	53.8
14. 1919–1928	92.2	4.6	4.8	23.2	22.7
15. 1929–1938	81.1	23.8	18.9	13.9	28.8
16. 1939–1948	53.7	14.7	46.3	234.9	84.0
17. 1949–1955	77.2	6.6	22.8	75.7	56.1
18. 1946–1955	77.1	7.2	22.9	75.2	56.0

[a] Percentages based on three-decade moving totals of absolute volumes.
[b] 1949–1955 given the weight of a decade.

SOURCE: Kuznets, *Capital in the American Economy* . . . , *op. cit.*, p. 187. Flow of nonmilitary producers' durables to governments is excluded.

the stock of capital. The impact of demand is readily seen in an examination in the industrial composition of business capital. Table 8.11 shows a rough industrial breakdown of the stock of private durable capital and the flow of net domestic formation for the period 1880–1948, and Table 8.12 shows a breakdown of durable wealth for the period 1805–1948.

While the flow of capital to agriculture has changed little over the period covered, the proportion of the capital stock invested in that industry has declined substantially, as Table 8.11 shows. It appears, therefore, that the capital flows into agriculture must have been substantially higher in some earlier period, an observation that Table 8.12 confirms and that conforms with our knowledge of changes in the industrial structure of the economy. It also explains in part the early and continuing need for agricultural finance that has played such an important role in our agricultural development (see Chapter 11).

The regulated industries show a substantial decline in terms of both the stock and the present-flow figures. This is, of course, the result that one would postulate if he believed that relative rates of return determine the structure of

TABLE 8.9
Construction of new nonfarm one-family structures, GNP,
and personal consumption expenditures, 1900–1916, 1919–1929, and 1945–1964

Year	Expenditures on New One-Family Non-farm Homes, (millions of dollars) (1)	GNP (2)	Personal Consumption Expenditures, (billions of dollars) (3)	Ratio (percent): Expenditures on New Nonfarm One-Family Homes to	
				GNP (4)	Personal Consumption Expenditures (5)
1900	281	18.57	13.4	1.51	2.10
1910	666	33.41	24.7	1.99	2.70
1920	1,361	91.26	62.2	1.49	2.19
1929	1,976	103.10	77.2	1.92	2.56
1946	4,202	208.50	143.4	2.02	2.93
1950	13,601	284.80	191.0	4.78	7.12
1960	14,111	503.80	325.2	2.80	4.34
1964	15,097	628.70	398.9	2.40	3.78

SOURCE: F. T. Juster and R. Lipsey, "A Note on Consumer Asset Formation in the United States," *Economic Journal*, vol. 77 (December 1967), p. 838. Reprinted with permission of the publisher.

investment. Rapid development of the transport network was a characteristic of the nation in the latter decades of the nineteenth and the early years of the twentieth centuries. Moreover, as mentioned previously, transportation was very capital-intensive in that formation period. It should be expected, therefore, that the industry's share both of the stock, which reflects flows before 1880, and the flow would be quite high. These early demands explain, as we will see, the role of that industry in early capital mobilization. More recently, developments have tended to reduce both the relative importance of the industry and its capital requirements, although it still continues to absorb a significant share of total capital formation.

Mining, too, behaves as a reading of economic history might suggest. That industry's share of capital formation rose rapidly through the first quarter of the twentieth century, but it has declined to almost nothing in the more recent past. The earlier decades were periods of exploitation of new sources of mineral wealth: iron from the Mesabi, copper from the Rockies, and petroleum from the Southwest. To open new fields requires heavy capital investment, but to maintain operations requires much less. Although advances in technology have made it possible to utilize additional ores from established areas, it is initial exploitation that is particularly capital-intensive, and the new resource areas are located overseas.

In the case of manufacturing, it is easy to explain the early rise of its relative position (up to the 1920s). Not only was that sector increasing in size, but also within the sector there was a shift from light to heavy (capital-intensive) industry. The continued rise since that period (an era marked by no relative

TABLE 8.10
Ratios of consumer expenditures on durable goods to total consumer expenditures,
alternative measures and concepts, current dollars (percent)

	Total Durables			Major Durables, Including Auto-mobiles (Gold-smith)	Minor Durables (Gold-smith)	Auto-mobiles (Gold-smith)	Major Durables, Excluding Auto-mobiles (Gold-smith)
	Kuznets	Kuznets–Commerce, 1929 Link	Gold-smith				
	Kuznets	Kuznets–Commerce, 1929 Link[a]					
Period	(1)	(2)	(3)	(4)	(5)	(6)	(7)
1899–1908	8.0	8.4	8.2	3.1	5.1	.3	2.8
1904–1913	8.2	8.6	8.5	3.7	4.8	.9	2.8
1909–1918	8.4	8.8	9.1	4.8	4.3	2.0	2.8
1914–1923	9.5	9.9	10.5	6.2	4.3	3.0	3.2
1919–1928	10.8	11.3	11.8	7.5	4.3	3.8	3.7
1924–1933	10.3	10.8	11.0	7.0	4.1	3.5	3.5
1929–1938	9.1	9.5	9.7	6.0	3.7	3.0	3.0
1934–1943	9.0	9.3	9.5	5.5	4.0	2.6	2.9
1939–1948	9.4	10.0	10.3	5.5	4.8	2.2	3.3
1944–1953	11.5	12.8	13.3	8.2	5.1	4.2	4.0
1949–1958	—	14.3	14.8	9.9	4.9	5.4	4.5
1954–1962	—	14.1	14.2	9.4	4.8	5.2	4.2

Column group header: "As a Ratio to Total Consumption Estimates Based on" — column (1) under "Kuznets"; columns (2)–(7) under "Kuznets–Commerce, 1929 Link[a]".

[a] Kuznets data for 1899–1928 linked to the U.S. Department of Commerce data for the period 1929–1962 by the ratio of the two series for the period 1929–1938. The ratio was 1.0831.

SOURCE: Juster and Lipsey, *op. cit.*, p. 842.

growth of the manufacturing sector and probably a trend toward less capital intensity within the sector) is more difficult to explain. In all probability, however, the increase reflects the rising importance of the service sector with its very low capital requirement; and it is to that sector that one should turn for an explanation.[12]

[12] Despite all that has been written about the potential misallocation effect of corporate savings, the evidence suggests that, over the past three quarters of a century, the allocation of capital between competing uses has been accomplished quite efficiently. For example, there appears to have been a steady shift out of declining and toward expanding industries. It is possible that if corporate savings were transferred to stockholders, the system might have operated more efficiently, but as it is, the transfer has been in the direction that competitive theory would imply, and the costs incurred by lack of dividend distribution do not appear to have been unbearable.

TABLE 8.11

Industrial structure of apportionable net private durable capital formation, 1929 prices, 1880–1948 (billions of dollars)

Periods	Agriculture (1)	Mining (2)	Manufacturing (4)	Regulated Industries (4)	Totals, Columns (1)–(4) (5)
A. Capital Stock and Capital Formation					
1. Stock, June 1, 1880	6.57	.37	1.88	11.80	20
2. Net capital formation, June 1, 1880–June 1, 1900	2.20	1.20	5.76	9.18	18
3. Stock, June 1, 1900	8.77	1.57	7.64[a]	20.98	38
			7.16[b]		38
4. Net capital formation, June 1, 1900–Dec. 31, 1922	6.56	3.70	14.88	14.41	39
5. Stock, Dec. 31, 1922	15.33	5.27	22.04	35.39	78
6. Net capital formation, Dec. 31, 1922–Dec. 31, 1948	3.21	.06	12.74	9.90	25
7. Stock, Dec. 31, 1948	18.54	5.33	34.78	45.29	103
B. Percent Distribution of Capital Stock and Capital Formation					
8. Stock, June 1, 1880	31.90	1.80	9.10	52.20	100
9. Net capital formation, June 1, 1880–June 1, 1900	12.00	6.50	31.40	50.10	100
10. Stock, June 1, 1900	22.50[a]	4.00[a]	19.60[a]	53.90[a]	100
11. Net capital formation, June 1, 1900–Dec. 31, 1922	22.80[b]	4.10[b]	18.60[b]	54.50[b]	100
12. Stock, Dec. 31, 1922	16.60	9.40	3.70	36.40	100
13. Net capital formation, Dec. 31, 1922–Dec. 31, 1948	19.60	6.80	28.20	45.40	100
14. Stock, Dec. 31, 1948	12.40	.20	49.20	38.20	100
	17.80	5.10	35.50	43.60	100

[a] Comparable with entry for 1880.
[b] Comparable with entry for later years.

SOURCE: Kuznets, *Capital in the American Economy* .... *op. cit.*, p. 198.

TABLE 8.12
Composition of reproducible tangible durable wealth of United States, 1805–1948

Year	Total Consumers' Durables Inclusive (1)	Exclusive (2)	Nonfarm Consumers Resi- dences (3)	Con- sumers' Dur- ables (4)	Agriculture Struc- tures (5)	Equip- ment (6)	Inventories Live- stock (7)	Crops (8)
A. Absolute Figures in Current Prices (billion dollars)								
1805	.58	.54	.1	.02	.21	.03	.06	.03
1850	4.15	3.85	.8	.20	.65	.15	.54	.15
1880	24.70	22.40	4.9	1.90	2.00	.40	2.00	—
1890	43.30	38.90	10.8	3.80	2.70	.50	2.60	—
1900A	61.00	55.00	15.0	5.20	3.60	.80	3.30	—
1900B	56.90	50.90	15.9	5.20	3.30	1.20	3.10	1.40
1912	107.20	93.60	25.7	11.70	5.60	2.20	5.60	2.60
1922	242.10	211.10	57.3	27.20	12.40	3.30	5.40	3.10
1929	327.30	285.10	91.2	38.40	12.20	3.90	6.50	3.00
1939	308.60	276.10	87.9	30.00	9.00	3.50	5.10	2.20
1948	709.10	618.20	190.7	83.00	25.60	12.90	14.70	7.50
B. Share in Total Reproducible Wealth in Current Prices								
1805	100.00	93.10	17.3	3.50	36.20	5.20	10.30	5.20
1850	100.00	92.80	19.3	4.80	15.70	3.60	13.00	3.60
1880	100.00	90.30	19.7	7.70	8.10	1.60	8.10	—
1890	100.00	89.60	24.9	8.80	6.20	1.20	6.00	—
1900A	100.00	90.20	24.6	8.50	5.90	1.30	5.40	—
1900B	100.00	89.50	27.9	9.10	5.80	2.10	5.40	2.50
1912	100.00	87.30	24.0	10.90	5.20	2.10	5.20	2.40
1922	100.00	87.30	23.7	11.20	5.10	1.40	2.20	1.30
1929	100.00	87.20	27.9	11.70	3.70	1.20	2.00	.90
1939	100.00	89.40	28.5	9.70	2.90	1.10	1.60	.70
1948	100.00	87.20	26.9	11.70	3.60	1.80	2.10	1.10

SOURCE: Raymond W. Goldsmith, "The Growth of Reproducible Wealth in the United States," in International Association for Research in Income and Wealth, *Income and Wealth of the United States, Trends and Structure* (Income and Wealth, Series 2) (Cambridge, England: Bowes & Bowes, 1952), pp. 306–307.

Consumers' Durables (9)	Nonagricultural Business			Government (including nonprofit institutions but excluding military)			International	
	Structures (10)	Equipment (11)	Inventories (12)	Structures (13)	Equipment (14)	Inventories (15)	Gold and Silver (16)	Other (17)
.02	.08		.07	.02	—	—	.02	—.08
.10	1.14		.45	.12	—	—	.15	—.30
.50	5.8	2.4	4.60	.60	.2	—	.60	—1.10
.70	10.3	4.9	7.00	1.20	.4	—	1.20	—2.80
.80	14.3	7.8	8.50	2.10	.7	—	1.70	—2.80
.80	12.9	5.3	5.40	3.10	.1	—	1.60	—2.30
1.90	23.5	11.3	8.40	7.90	.2	—	2.50	—2.10
3.70	45.9	27.4	24.00	19.60	.2	.1	4.40	8.20
3.80	59.1	33.9	28.40	28.90	.6	.1	4.80	12.40
2.60	54.1	29.9	22.10	39.10	.8	1.0	19.60	1.70
8.00	97.8	75.9	63.00	79.10	4.8	2.1	27.40	16.60
3.40	13.8		12.10	3.40	—	—	3.40	—13.80
2.40	27.5		10.80	2.90	—	—	3.60	—7.20
2.00	23.4	9.7	18.50	2.40	.8	—	2.40	—4.40
1.60	23.8	11.3	16.20	2.80	.9	—	2.80	—6.50
1.30	23.4	12.8	13.90	3.50	1.2	—	2.80	—4.60
1.40	22.6	9.3	9.50	5.40	.2	—	2.80	—4.00
1.80	22.0	10.6	7.90	7.40	.1	—	2.30	—2.00
1.50	19.0	11.3	9.90	8.10	.1	.0	1.80	3.40
1.10	18.1	10.4	8.70	8.80	.2	.0	1.50	3.80
.90	17.5	9.7	7.20	12.70	.3	.3	6.30	.60
1.10	13.8	10.7	8.90	11.10	.7	.3	3.90	2.30

SUGGESTED READING

Gallman, Robert E. "Gross National Product in the United States, 1824–1909." In *Output Employment, and Productivity in the United States After 1800*, edited by Dorothy S. Brady. Studies in Income and Wealth, vol. 30. New York: National Bureau of Economic Research, 1966.

Goldsmith, Raymond W. "The Growth of Reproducible Wealth in the United States." In International Association for Research in Income and Wealth, *Income and Wealth of the United States, Trends and Structure*. Income and Wealth, Series 2. Cambridge, England: Bowes & Bowes, 1952.

Juster, F. T. *Household Capital Formation and Financing, 1867–1962*. New York: National Bureau of Economic Research, 1966.

Kuznets, Simon. *Capital in the American Economy: Its Formation and Financing*. New York: National Bureau of Economic Research. 1961.

Kuznets, Simon. "Quantitative Aspects of the Economic Growth of Nations, VI: Long-Term Trends in Capital Formation Proportion." *Economic Development and Cultural Change*, vol. 9, no. 4 (July 1961), Part II.

9
SAVINGS SOURCES AND UTILIZATION

In Chapter 8 the role of capital in the growth process was examined, and the trends in capital formation in U.S. history were sketched out. Capital formation, however, involves the diversion of part of the stream of national income away from consumption and a commitment of those resources to buildings, machinery, and inventories. That diversion—termed "savings"—rests on the conscious decision of someone that more should be saved and less consumed, and it is to an understanding of the savings decision that this chapter is addressed.

SAVINGS

It is capital combined with land and labor that increases output, but it is the decision of income-receiving units to refrain from consumption that releases the resources for capital formation. The data on saving in the United States are even more sparse than those on capital formation; but, since realized investment must be equal realized savings, something can be inferred from the capital-formation figures about the savings income ratio actually obtained. Gallman's estimates suggest that the savings/income ratio in the pre-Civil War decades averaged only about three fifths of the level since attained; however, these figures are still substantially above levels achieved in most developing nations today. Moreover, between the Civil War and the 1930s, the gross savings ratio remained fairly constant at about 25 percent, although the shift in the composition of capital toward more rapidly depreciating producers' durables caused a gradual decline in the net ratio.[1] There can be little doubt that the United States has been a high saving nation throughout most of its history (see Table 9.1).

Much of the analysis of savings has been drawn from Raymond W. Goldsmith's *A Study of Saving in the United States* (Princeton: Princeton University Press, 1955 and 1956). No attempt is made to cite this work each time it is used, but the reader should be aware of the source.

[1] We have, of course, seen that the inclusion of intangible capital results in a gradual increase in the gross ratio since the turn of the century.

TABLE 9.1
Saving/income ratios of major saver groups:
standard social accounting concept; economic periods, 1897 to 1949 (percent)

		Personal Saving				Government Saving		
Period	National Saving (1)	Non-agricultural Individuals (2)	Agriculture (3)	Unincorporated Business (4)	Corporate Saving (5)	State (6)	Local (7)	Federal (8)
1897–1908	13.7	14.2[a]	1.1	6.0[a]	33.4	7.7	12.1	6.1
1909–1914	12.8	13.3	2.2	6.3	24.2	10.3	15.3	11.5
1915–1921	10.7	16.7	−6.8	16.5	40.4	18.8	−1.8	−79.7
1922–1929	16.2	14.7	1.8	3.5	26.3	25.8	13.8	25.2
1930–1933	−6.8	4.8	.4	−73.6	−175.3	17.8	−5.7	−49.2
1934–1938	1.9	5.2	7.5	10.9	−27.0	17.6	8.2	−51.9
1939–1945	1.6	21.3	30.7	24.8	29.5	23.9	5.5	−125.8
1946–1949	15.0	14.5	1.9	41.4	10.5	2.9		5.7
1897–1949	8.6	14.7[b]	9.5	7.4[b]	22.4	18.0	5.8	−54.6
Normal period	12.6	12.9	4.6	6.3	26.1	15.6	7.4	−2.8

[a] 1899–1908.
[b] 1899–1949.

SOURCE: From Volume 1, Introduction; Tables of Annual Estimates of Saving 1897 to 1949 in Raymond W. Goldsmith, *A Study of Saving in the United States* (Princeton: Princeton University Press, 1955), p. 241. Reprinted by permission of Princeton University Press.

Since the 1930s, this conclusion has been less clear. The Depression, marked as it was by rapidly falling incomes and negative corporate profits, resulted in a dramatic decline in the savings ratio. While there has been some recovery in the more recent past, it still appears that the gross savings ratio, as traditionally defined, has remained somewhat depressed. This decline is very pronounced if military capital is excluded, but it is apparent in any case. If, however, the definition of savings is broadened to include expenditures on improvement in human capital (such as education) and consumer durables, the decline disappears. Over the long run, the early nineteenth century probably saw some increases in the ratio; the period from 1870 to 1930 was marked by a high and stable propensity to save—a stability that has probably continued into the present.

While the savings ratio has been stable in the long run, it has displayed marked variability in the short run. Half the years since 1890 were marked by variations of at least 50 percent from the trend value. Moreover, there is and has been a high positive correlation between the savings ratio and the level of income—a correlation that appears both in cross-section (i.e., at a moment in time) and in short-term (i.e., cyclic) time series.

If, however, one wants to explain the characteristics of the level of savings, it is necessary to go behind the figures to the savers themselves. Savings are, after all, a commodity that economic units purchase just like any consumption alternative, and it is in the motives of the "buyers of savings" that the explanation of the trends must be found. As Table 9.1 suggests, most saving (about seven tenths of the total) is done by individuals. Corporations account for about one fifth (although a somewhat larger proportion of gross savings), and government (although its share has been subject to wide variation) accounts for the remainder.[2]

Government Saving

Although higher levels of savings may well be desirable, it appears unlikely that, in the United States at least, either the corporate or the government sector could increase its rate of savings substantially. In the case of government, while there are some investment activities (highways, for example) that the voters appear quite willing to support, there appears to be considerable political resistance to any great expansion of government activity—a resistance that is underscored by the number of school bond failures in the past few elections. At the same time, wars tend to produce heavy dissaving, and the politics of the mid-twentieth century seem more war- than peace-oriented. In other countries, the channels for government saving are well worn; and in those places, the government contribution has been larger in the past, and can well be an important source of additional savings in the future. This has certainly been the case in Russia and, on this side of the Iron Curtain, in France. Some underdeveloped countries, too, have come to lean much more heavily on government savings than does the United States, although for many who depend on the government for capital formation, the government itself dissaves. The American economy may have depended somewhat on government savings in the nineteenth century, but our evidence is far from clear. For example, the estimates indicate that about two thirds of antebellum transport investment was government financed; however, the government could have borrowed from other sectors. Even if the government was the source of these savings, most of them must still come from individuals.

Corporate Saving

Corporations, while almost certainly generating a greater proportion of savings today than they did in the nineteenth century, do not appear to be able to continue to expand their contributions indefinitely. Corporate income is, after all, only a fraction of total income, and, of total corporate income, firms can save no more than the sum of profits plus depreciation. If, for example, all corporations saved a full one half of their profits, the corporate sector would contribute little more than 3 percent of the nation's net savings/income ratio.

In fact, however, corporations usually cannot even save that much. If stockholders thought corporate savings were as productive as dividends, then a corporation could save all its profits. If, however, investors on balance prefer corporations that distribute dividends to those that retain profits, then the market price of the securities of those that retain earnings will decline. Such a fall could drive the value of a corporation's stock below the present

---

[2] The government saves any time that its income exceeds its expenditures.

value of its future income stream, and if that occurred, it probably would induce a "raider" to buy in and dispose of the company's assets.[3] The results would probably be less rather than more savings. Montgomery Ward is an excellent example of a corporation that attempted to pursue a high savings policy but was forced to abandon it in the face of a raid. For some firms where control is firmly held by an inside group (Ford Motor Company is probably the best example), there are no limits on potential saving except the firm's profits; but for most corporations, there is an upper limit set by the preference of the investing public.

While corporations with high profits tend to save more than those with low profits, corporate savings averaged about 30 percent of total profits from 1897 to 1930 and have remained at about the same level since World War II. During the 1930s, corporations with low and sometimes negative profits frequently attempted to maintain their traditional dividend policies, and, as a result, corporate savings were negative.

Personal Saving

Because of these limitations on corporations and government, it is the household sector that generates the bulk of savings. Moreover, the data indicate that it is in the experience of that sector that the explanation for the recent secular decline in the savings ratio must be found. Over the entire period 1890 to 1950, households have on the average saved about one dollar in every ten of income, but the ratio has been declining.[4] Much of the saving is done by the very rich who simply can't spend all their income, but since there is little reason to believe that their habits have changed, it is unlikely that changes in their behavior can account for the drift. Raymond Goldsmith, in his monumental *Study of Savings*, finds that three major reasons underlie the typical household's decision to save: (a) the desire to acquire durable tangible assets, (b) the need to provide for future expenses (e.g., retirement, estate, education, and emergencies), and (c) a wish to mass sufficient funds to enter into business or to expand their present business. While all three remain compelling motives, there are economic forces at work to reduce the impact of some, and although others may be increasing in intensity, that increase appears insufficient to maintain aggregate household savings. Thus, greater life expectancy should increase the need for retirement funds, but greater income stability tends to reduce the need for emergency funds. The shift of the population from farm to city tends to reduce savings both because the demonstration effect (i.e., "keeping up with the Joneses") is greater in the city than on the farm and because farmers are more likely to own their own business than are city workers. Similarly, throughout the economy there has been a movement from employer to employee status, and employees are less likely to save for

---

[3] The present value of a future income stream can often be determined by solving the present value formula:

$$PV = \frac{R_1}{r} + \frac{R_2}{(1+r)^2} + \cdots + \frac{R_n}{(1+r)^n}$$

where the R's refer to future income, and the r's to the rate of discount.

[4] Some, of course, have saved more and some have even dissaved.

business purposes than are employers. Moreover, although it is widely argued that present social services are insufficient, the past half-century has seen a rapid growth in public education and the widespread innovation of "socialized" emergency insurance schemes, and both of these developments have reduced the need for individual saving. Finally, the American economy has been characterized by a high degree of social mobility, but new groups have tended to "buy" their way into higher social strata by consumption expenditures. In many ways the problem is similar to the one that the United Kingdom faced in the nineteenth century, although in the United States it is not restricted to upper-income groups. It yields an interesting paradox: Social mobility aids the process of economic growth, but by reducing savings, it may indirectly make growth more difficult to achieve.

At the same time, the reader should bear in mind that the taxonomy that places almost all educational and health expenditures in the consumption category induces an artificial decline in the savings/income ratio when (as has happened in the recent past) those items increase as a percentage of the total budget. Just as the rate of capital formation could be increased by a change in definition, so could our measures of national and personal savings. Moreover, as we have seen, from almost any logical point of view, some proportion of the resources devoted to those two classes of "consumption" should be included in savings and investment.

Foreign Investment

Thus far the discussion has been limited to domestic saving, but it is perfectly possible for development to be based on foreign accumulations. Recently John Knapp has argued that overseas investment has played at most a miniscule role in the development of any country, and that, among today's great industrial powers only the United States availed itself of large amounts of foreign capital.[5] Moreover, Knapp suggests that even in the case of the United States, the transfers were not necessary to augment domestic accumulations, but were merely ways of overcoming the poor state of the American capital market. Recent research, however, has suggested that while foreign capital has never been a large proportion of total capital formation in the United States, it did make a substantial contribution to growth during certain short periods. That is, the availability of foreign capital made it possible to underwrite periods of very rapid expansion in the capital stock which would have been impossible on the basis of domestic accumulations alone.

Table 9.2 indicates that the aggregate foreign indebtedness of the citizens, companies, and governments of the United States increased throughout most of the nineteenth century. Although there were short periods of capital outflow, the nation was a heavy capital importer in most decades before 1890. Moreover, the heavy borrowing relative to domestic capital formation in the 1830s and 1850s was directly connected with major expansions of the

---

[5] John Knapp, "Capital Exports and Growth," *Economic Journal*, vol. 67 (September 1957).

TABLE 9.2
Aggregate indebtedness, United States to the rest of the world,
1820–1900 (millions of dollars)

Year	Aggregate	Net Flows
1820	86.7	
		−6.4
1825	80.3	
		−5.4
1830	74.9	
		+83.2
1835	158.1	
		+98.3
1840	266.4	
		−53.4
1845	213.0	
		+9.1
1850	222.1	
		+134.2
1855	356.3	
		+12.9
1860	379.2	
		+295.2
1865	674.4	
		+581.3
1870	1255.7	
		+695.7
1875	1951.4	
		−348.2
1880	1603.2	
		+258.0
1885	1861.2	
		+1045.3
1890	2906.5	
		+391.7
1895	3298.2	
		−807.3
1900	2490.9	

SOURCES: Douglass C. North, "The United States Balance of Payments, 1790–1860," and M. Simon, "The United States Balance of Payments, 1860–1900." Both works appear in Trends in the American Economy in the Nineteenth Century, William N. Parker (ed.), Studies in Income and Wealth, vol. 24 (New York: National Bureau of Economic Research, 1960), p. 581 and pp. 700–705. Reprinted by permission of the publisher.

interregional transportation net, an expansion that will be explored in detail in Chapter 13. The canals of the 1830s and the railroads of the 1850s greatly speeded the expansion of the nation's economy, and it appears doubtful they could have been built as soon as they were without the importation of foreign capital.

Although the United States drew savings from almost every country in Europe, the bulk appears to have come from the United Kingdom. England was truly the world's banker in the nineteenth century, and the United States was almost certainly its best customer. From 1870 to 1913, the high-water mark of British overseas investment, the United States absorbed between 20 and 25 percent of Britain's foreign-bound savings (see Table 9.3). The

TABLE 9.3
British investments in foreign countries between 1871 and 1941 (millions of pounds)

Beginning of Year	United States	Canada	Australasia	India (including Ceylon)	Argentina	Brazil	South America (total)	Russia	Spain	Peru	South Africa
1871	200	—	73	153	5	11.0	—	50	15	17.50	—
1875	—	—	—	—	—	—	—	—	—	16.25	—
1876	—	—	—	—	35	43.0	(50)	—	—	—	—
1880	—	—	133	—	—	—	—	—	—	—	—
1881	(100)	—	—	180	—	—	—	—	—	—	—
1884	—	112	200	260	—	—	—	—	—	—	—
1886	—	—	—	—	46	46.6	—	—	—	5.60	—
1888	525	—	285	—	—	—	115.5	—	—	—	34
1899	—	—	—	—	—	—	—	—	—	—	—
1900	—	—	289	—	200	—	—	—	—	—	—
1902	—	205	—	—	—	—	—	—	—	—	—
1911	688	373	380	351	270	94.0	587.0	38	19	32.00	351
1914	755	515	—	379	319	148.0	722.0	—	—	—	—

SOURCE: A. K. Cairncross, *Home and Foreign Investment* (New York: Cambridge University Press, 1953), p. 185.

tastes of the British investor did change, however. In the 1830s he preferred state government bonds (frequently issued in support of some transport activity); the 1850s saw him shift to private rails; and in the latter third of the century, he chose a diversified selection of local and municipal governments, railroads, public utilities, and a very few manufacturing firms.

By the end of the century, however, the position of the U.S. economy in relation to the rest of the world had changed drastically. The nation had become the world's largest industrial power, achieved a high rate of domestic saving, and developed a fairly adequate domestic capital market. As the returns to capital declined at home, foreign investment began to look attractive to American savers. By the 1920s, almost one tenth of American savings were going abroad, and the vast bulk was drawn from private sources. The stock-market crash and the subsequent depression, however, resulted in the temporary withdrawal of the private American saver from the foreign markets. The postwar period was marked by the emergence of the American government as a supplier of savings to the rest of the world, but the 1950s and 1960s saw private investment once again rising until at present flows are largely private (see Table 9.4).

Causes of the Increase in Saving

For the period before 1890, our knowledge of the factors underlying the saving trends is poorer than our understanding of the causes of the trends in capital formation. Kuznets has suggested that there may have been a peak in

TABLE 9.4
External capital flows, United States, 1900–1966 (millions of dollars)

	U.S. Net[a]				Foreign Net[b]		
		Private					
Year	Government	Direct	Other Long-Term	Short-Term	Long-Term	Short-Term	Net Capital Imports[c]
1901–1910	−40[d]	−812	−212	—	927	—	−137
1911–1920	−10,187	−696	−3,458	—	−1,486	822	−15,005
1921–1930	447	−3,018	−4,619	−1,244	1,759	1,397	−5,278
1931–1940	−40	−109	+1,415	+1,962	1,226	1,998	6,452
1941–1950	−13,796	−2,846	−1,150	−1,027	93	4,827	−13,899
1951–1960	−5,999	−20,027	−6,932	−3,467	10,421	13,134	−12,870
1961–1966	−7,105	−22,747	−8,371	−5,687	8,582	10,617	−24,711

[a] Changes in assets or in investments of the United States abroad.
[b] Changes in liabilities of the United States to citizens of foreign countries, or changes in assets held in the United States by residents of foreign countries.
[c] Algebraic sum of preceding columns.
[d] Minus sign signifies capital exports.

SOURCES: U.S. Bureau of the Census, *Historical Statistics of the United States*, Series U-185–190 (Washington: U.S. Government Printing Office, 1960), p. 560; and U.S. Bureau of the Census, *Statistical Abstract of the United States, 1968*, Series 1202 (Washington: U.S. Government Printing Office, 1968), 791.

the savings ratio in the two decades following the Civil War. His conclusion is based largely on intuition—an intuition that leads him to believe that income probably became more unequally distributed because of the great windfall profits of the war and because of postwar movements toward monopolization and capitalization. Given the cross-section correlation between income and savings, redistribution would probably lead toward greater savings. Whether Kuznet's reasons are correct or not remains to be seen, but the evidence does suggest that there was a substantial increase in the savings/income ratio about the middle of the nineteenth century.

In theory, at least, a change in the aggregate ratio could come from (a) a change in the utility of savings; (b) a change in the mix (or proportion) of savings groups, or a change in the distribution of income between groups; and (c) an exogenous change that altered the costs or revenues from savings. One cannot draw any final conclusion about the utility of savings; but, while the data are not very good, it is possible to suggest something about the effects of changes in the second and third categories over the course of the last half of the nineteenth century.

Changes in mix.   Since the latter part of the nineteenth century was marked by the rapid growth (both absolutely and proportionately) of the corporate sector, and since (in the recent past, at least) corporations have tended to save more than unincorporated businesses, corporate growth might account for the increase in the savings ratio. In the case of manufacturing enterprises, however, the evidence (although admittedly very skimpy) suggests that their savings rates in the nineteenth century were much below those of their current counterparts and not significantly above the levels presently attained by unincorporated businesses. The corporate transport sector also grew rapidly, but that sector does appear to have been a heavy saver. Over the middle decades of the century, savings averaged about 50 percent of profits; however, while transport may have accounted for a part of the increase in the gross savings rate, because its capital was subject to very small capital consumption charges its contributions to changes in the net ratio must have been greater.

Changes in the government sector also do not appear to have made any significant contributions to the increase in the savings rate. The federal government was small, and within that sector savings were less than 10 percent of income. Moreover, the periods of rapid government growth (the Civil War, for example) were periods of heavy dissaving. Nor do state governments appear to have increased their savings significantly over the period. Finally, local government, while apparently contributing more to savings than either of the other levels, displayed little trend in its savings rate over the relevant decades.

Thus, insofar as the rate increase reflects a shift either in mix or utility, that change must lie rooted largely in the environment or behavior of the consumer sector. It is doubtful that the relative importance of that sector changed markedly; however, it is possible that shifts within it could account for the increase. In the early years of the twentieth century (years for which we do have data), both the farm and the unincorporated nonfarm sectors tended to save less than the rest of the "personal" savings sector. This tendency has been reversed since World War I, but it was characteristic of the earlier period. Thus, the nineteenth-century shift in the relative weights of farm and nonfarm and of employer and employee status might have contributed to the observed increase in the savings/income ratio, but it probably was not an important factor. Probably more important was the change in the age structure of the population. Since the very young save little, the increase in the nation's median age, resting as it did on an increasing proportion of males in the age group 40 to 60, should have underwritten an increase in the savings rate. Finally, any increase in income inequality (and there is no evidence of any increases in equality), also would have reinforced the tendency toward higher rates of saving.

Financial intermediaries.   These shifts in "mix," while tending to support an increase in the rate, can hardly account for the substantial increases that did occur. Most likely, the largest part of the increase came from the development of a set of financial intermediaries that greatly altered the costs of and the revenues from savings. Improvements in the process of financial intermediation increase the savers' options, and the impact of these trends are evidenced by the increasing diversity of savings (see Table 9.5).

Before the period shown in Table 9.5, the number of intermediaries was smaller and their impact was almost certainly much less. Between 1830 and 1880, the number, size, and variety of the nation's financial intermediaries increased substantially and they spread into the newly settled regions in the West. Free banking legislation was passed in most northern and western states, and these laws made state charters easier to obtain for anyone who wanted to open a commercial bank. In the same vein the passage of the National Banking Act in 1863 opened an alternative route to charter even in states with very restrictive banking laws. In 1830 savings banks had been the only important nonbank intermediary, but by 1880 the life insurance industry commanded assets almost half as great as those controlled by the savings banks. Moreover, unlike the savings banks, whose activities had been confined to the Northeast, the life insurance companies were operating in all sections of the country.

The nation's population increased about three times over the five decades, while the assets of the commercial banks increased over seven times, and those of the mutual savings banks in excess of one hundred times.[6] The mutual life insurance companies—no more than an idea in the 1830s—had grown into a major force in the capital markets with the introduction of tontine and industrial insurance. Intermediation in the South grew slowly— the war had badly torn the sector's institutional fabric—but by 1880 even the West had a substantial number and variety of local intermediaries. Gradually too, as the markets became less local, a national capital market began to emerge. In the short-term capital markets the penetration of commercial-

---

[6] The price level increased only slightly (5 to 10 percent) over the period in question.

paper firms (firms who bought commercial paper from banks in high-interest regions and sold them to banks in low-interest areas) into the Midwest and Far West provided the basis for a single market. In the long-term market progress was slower, but increasing management sophistication coupled with a gradual relaxation of legal restrictions governing the investment policy of savings banks and insurance companies was also aiding the development of a single capital market.

Economic theory would suggest that the emergence of a financial inter-mediary should reduce the market rate of interest, and this reduction should be coupled with an increase in the net returns to savers and a decline in the net cost to the borrowers of financial capital. The intermediary should reduce the search cost of the saver (he no longer has to find someone who wants to use his savings—a search which is almost certainly subject to increasing returns), and, since this cost must be subtracted from the saver's total return, his net should rise.[7] Moreover, by using the services of the intermediary the saver is buying a claim on a portfolio of financial investments rather than putting all his savings into only a few alternatives. In a sense, he is buying insurance, and that purchase should reduce the variance of his return. We know that most small savers today place a very high value on safety and it appears likely that this was an even more marked characteristic of the unsophisticated small saver in the nineteenth century. At any given average return, therefore, the saver should have been happier with a reduction in the variance. Finally, by supplying a known investment alternative for the less well known IOU of the primary borrower, the discounts that the saver applied to the possible returns because of the uncertainty attached to them must have been reduced. Since most people prefer certainty to uncertainty, this too should have increased the satisfaction the saver derived from any given level of actual returns. Taken together, the direct effects of increased intermediation—on costs, variance, and uncertainty—should have acted to induce the saver to save more at any given level of income.

Intermediation, however, also results in increased spatial and industrial financial mobility, and this increase has secondary effects whose impact on the savings/income ratio is less obvious. Mobility makes it easier to transfer finance to sectors offering the highest returns, and therefore, from the point of view of the entire economy, it produces the most productive capital stock. However, by moving savings from one sector to another, increased mobility raises interest rates in some areas and lowers them in others. The total impact of the increase on the level of savings will depend on the relative elasticities of the demand and supply for capital in the surplus- and deficit-capital areas. If the demand for capital in the deficit sector is more elastic and the supply of capital is less elastic than the demand and supply in the surplus sector, the volume of savings should rise with an increase in mobility. The opposite elasticities, however, would produce the opposite results.

There is no way to deduce from theory the relative elasticities of demand

---

[7] The same cost-reduction argument could be made from the point of view of the borrower.

TABLE 9.5

Personal saving by major components: social accounting concept, current values; quadrennial period averages, 1898 to 1949 (millions of dollars)

	1898 to 1901	1902 to 1905	1906 to 1909	1910 to 1913
1. Residential real estate	63	394	642	709
2. One- to four-family	55	358	595	646
3. Multifamily	8	36	47	63
4. Other nonfarm real estate	157	152	175	146
5. Farm real estate	93	117	132	172
6. Real estate	313	663	949	1,027
7. Producer durables	27	98	123	124
8. Consumer durables	191	292	375	439
9. Inventories	— 50	123	— 27	8
10. Livestock	76	38	6	74
11. Tangible assets other than real estate	243	550	477	645
12. Total tangible assets	556	1,213	1,426	1,672
13. Currency	66	66	— 9	28
14. Commercial bank deposits	458	484	192	629
15. Demand deposits ⎱ of nonagricultural	108	114	— 16	164
16. Time deposits ⎰ individuals	112	184	235	274
17. Deposits of agricultural and unincorporated business	237	185	— 27	190
18. Savings bank deposits	140	145	117	174
19. Savings and loan associations	— 7	13	43	76
20. Other deposits	6	6	7	10
21. Life insurance reserves (gross)	126	192	248	283
22. Private pension reserves	0	0	0	0
23. Government insurance reserves	1	1	1	1
24. U.S. savings bonds	—	—	—	—
25. Other U.S. government securities	36	— 18	— 24	8
26. State and local government securities	33	20	103	100
27. Other bonds	259	378	409	312
28. Preferred stock	144	46	68	98
29. Common stock	221	428	657	532
30. Mortgage holdings	55	65	62	337
31. Other claims	1	2	2	4
32. Intangible assets	1,538	1,828	1,876	2,591
33. Residential mortgage debt	43	127	171	267
34. One- to four-family	32	100	135	209
35. Multifamily	10	26	36	58
36. Nonresidential mortgage debt	34	57	69	95
37. Farm mortgage debt	81	94	109	375
38. Consumer debt	39	53	68	97
39. Policy loans	13	26	56	54
40. Borrowing on securities	110	80	34	37
41. Borrowing on bonds	—	—	—	—
42. Borrowing on stocks	110	80	34	37
43. Other short-term liabilities	225	258	169	224
44. Tax accruals	19	16	16	54
45. Liabilities	565	711	718	1,202
46. Total net saving	1,529	2,331	2,584	3,061

SOURCE: Goldsmith, *A Study of Saving . . . , op. cit.*, pp. 300–301.

1914 to 1917	1918 to 1921	1922 to 1925	1930 to 1938	1934 to 1937	1938 to 1941	1942 to 1945	1946 to 1949	1898 to 1949
567	534	3,273	− 909	− 716	1,039	−1,056	3,570	838
501	487	2,951	− 842	− 627	1,051	− 993	3,533	774
66	47	322	− 67	− 89	− 12	− 63	36	64
114	143	525	− 40	− 320	− 164	− 406	334	120
264	349	70	− 226	− 134	− 1	− 91	1,040	144
945	1,026	3,868	−1,174	−1,171	874	−1,553	4.944	1,102
116	117	93	− 426	126	412	276	2,434	291
472	93	1,883	−1,190	908	1,702	−1,307	8,199	1,081
126	494	64	− 626	58	196	434	58	60
193	− 104	− 122	47	− 128	167	36	− 207	7
907	601	1,918	−2,196	963	2,477	− 562	10,484	1,438
1,852	1,627	5,786	−3,370	− 208	3,350	−2,115	15,428	2,541
274	98	20	313	224	866	4,081	− 351	434
1,928	786	1,845	−2,094	1,934	1,830	10,020	1,847	1,523
612	− 54	422	− 7	696	1,035	3,050	510	463
776	555	1,216	−1,362	739	120	3,121	1,188	587
540	285	208	− 725	500	675	3,850	150	473
201	352	453	521	282	207	1,730	1,196	462
101	210	500	− 202	− 202	214	712	1,382	268
22	30	33	− 2	58	100	148	289	57
344	550	924	986	1,406	1,728	2,745	3,662	1,125
0	2	22	50	60	59	431	988	131
5	37	118	4	600	1,405	4,081	3,386	757
125	125	− 200	0	207	1,167	9,445	1,584	957
693	2,510	− 994	572	11	− 264	4,275	−1,272	343
239	476	447	396	− 282	− 111	− 179	571	168
929	1,149	1,550	181	− 718	− 518	− 828	− 313	334
210	315	464	72	− 56	− 27	− 86	149	164
660	1,118	1,017	563	398	506	692	1,590	820
600	1,040	− 10	− 133	− 52	− 174	48	1,270	346
6	11	20	30	30	35	43	56	21
6,336	8,808	6,210	1,258	3,901	7,023	37,359	16,032	7,908
388	652	1,653	− 601	− 77	624	− 122	4,499	768
304	496	1,171	− 613	− 60	621	− 46	4,285	643
84	156	482	12	− 137	4	− 77	214	125
132	200	550	15	− 56	− 74	− 96	502	149
458	1,042	− 238	− 453	− 114	− 133	− 422	183	75
122	169	360	− 800	790	551	− 770	2,701	305
39	64	99	342	− 82	− 114	− 239	69	43
232	102	715	−1,283	− 236	− 154	894	− 764	14
—	—	—	—	—	—	474	− 369	8
232	102	715	−1,283	− 236	− 154	421	− 396	6
678	545	− 101	390	− 274	769	− 230	1,091	30
424	84	77	26	245	618	− 48	207	152
2,472	2,858	3,115	−2,363	195	2,087	−1,034	8,487	1,805
5,716	7,576	8,885	251	3,498	8,270	36,278	22,973	8,644

and supply in the deficit and surplus areas. In general, however, in the context of American development there is a strong likelihood that intermediation increased the volume of savings. The capital-deficit areas were in the newly developing regions and industries, and one would expect that these sectors would be characterized by a wide selection of potentially profitable investment alternatives—in short, by a fairly elastic demand schedule for capital. At the same time in these newly developing sectors much of the saving was being done by persons who owned their farm, shop, or factory and were saving to improve and expand that enterprise. Given the usual responses of ownership, one would assume that the individual savings supply schedules of these owners were relatively interest-inelastic (the amount of leisure that a frontier farmer chose to devote to land clearing was probably not very responsive to changes in the rate of interest). In the surplus-capital sectors (largely already developed regions and industries) the range of profitable opportunities was probably narrower (many had already been exploited—that, after all, is the definition of development), and savings were less likely to be attached to a particular enterprise. If these assumptions are correct, we can infer that the growth of intermediation probably did increase the savings/income ratio, and in fact may have been one of the most important determinants of the 1830–1880 shift.

Let us turn, then, to a more careful examination of the growth of financial intermediation.

CAPITAL MOBILIZATION

The Problem in a Comparative Setting

If savings are to be economically employed, it is necessary that they be transferred from the saving unit to some economic unit that wishes to use them. Output will be maximized if they are transferred to the use in which they are most productive, but the transfer process itself is largely ignored in most economic theory. Within the framework of traditional theory (given the assumption of profit maximization, once allowances are made for the cost of transporting capital and the discounts that must be applied to uncertain returns), it follows that capital will automatically seek its highest return. Unfortunately, the theory, since it fails to allow for changes in transport costs and uncertainty discounts, is of limited usefulness in examining the problems of capital mobilization in a changing economy.

At an early stage of an economy's development, there is often no single capital market. Instead, there are a number of local markets (perhaps loosely tied together), each encompassing some particular geographical area, or some industry, or some group of savers, and separated by high transport costs or large uncertainty discounts. In the absence of central reserves or some institution capable of effecting intrasectoral clearings, all transactions must be accompanied by the means of payment and the costs involved in moving that volume of funds are relatively high. In addition, in the absence of adequate information about rates of return in other sectors, the uncertainty attached to any intrasectoral investment is very high, and the discounts that must be applied to the potential returns to produce "certainty equivalents" are, therefore, concomitantly large. In the process of development, institutions capable of reducing those costs and discounts are innovated to make it possible for capital to flow smoothly between markets.

To analyze these changes, a lagged supply model appears appropriate. The demand for capital tends to be highest in industries and regions experiencing the most rapid growth. In the United States these have tended to be new industries and regions. Savings, on the other hand, tend to be concentrated in already established industries and regions. These, after all, are the sectors in which population is concentrated and that in the past have generated the income from which savings have accrued. The result is a relative capital scarcity in the new sectors and a relative surplus in the established ones. These differences are reflected in relative prices, and capital commands a higher price in the new regions than in the old. Because capital markets are not designed to effect a transfer to new sectors, there is no formal mechanism capable of effecting intermarket arbitrage. Large potential profits exist for any person or institution capable of transferring funds in the absence of formal markets, and the short run is usually characterized by monopoly profits for those with this ability. Moreover, because of the market imperfections, the capital movements induced by these informal arrangements are frequently insufficient to arbitrage out of the market. The long run, on the other hand, is marked by the evolution of a set of formalized institutions that both reduce the monopoly profits and are capable of effective arbitrage. Profit potential induces institutional innovations, and after some lag, capital moves from the low-productivity to the high-productivity market.

This process of lagged adjustment is very much like the process of innovation in the more traditional analysis of technical change, a subject that has been covered in detail in Chapter 7. Like technical change (in the narrow sense), if alternative institutional technologies are known, the process of innovation is apt to be rapid. If, however, innovation must wait on invention, the delay is longer, and there is no certainty that the emergence of potential profits will result in institutional reorganization.

The problem of effective capital mobilization has certainly not been restricted to the United States. In Great Britain, for example, the savings rates apparently have always been fairly high, but there were substantial barriers to the transfer of these savings to would-be investors. Most of the original accumulations were in agriculture and trade, but during the late eighteenth and the nineteenth centuries there was an increasing demand for capital in manufacturing. The bulk of these accumulations were located in London and the Southwest, while the demand for capital was in the Midlands and the North. Even in a country with the world's most sophisticated capital market institutions, the differential demands were not met by the existing arrangement, and not until the middle of the nineteenth century did invention and innovation in capital market institutions produce an efficient domestic market.

Other European countries had more serious problems of accumulation, but even there the mobilization problem was apparent. In Russia, the savings/income ratios were very low, but what savings did exist tended to flow into traditional activities. In the late nineteenth century, the czarist government designed a tax policy to increase savings rates, and it directed these funds into new industries and regions. In France, while savings rates were higher than in Russia, the absence of effective market forms channeled those savings into agriculture.[8] As in Russia, the government stepped in to provide an institutional organization for mobilizing funds; however, rather than taxation, the government established a bond market to serve as the mechanism for transferring French savings. Governments have both political and economic goals, and in this case a significant proportion of French savings were channeled into the Russian military establishment—an activity marked by low economic returns but high political benefits. Again, in Germany, the processes of accumulation and mobilization were accelerated through the evolution of a set of large private commercial banks that made long-term credit available to manufacturers. These banks, by inflating the money supply, were able to generate forced savings and, by their selective loan policy, were able to direct these savings toward German industry.[9] In each instance, differential demands induced institutional innovation; however, the form of that innovation varied widely from country to country.

In the case of the United States, savings rates were a high proportion of income (about 12 percent net or 20 percent gross) as far back as the last third of the nineteenth century; and even before that, they appear to have been above those usually found in underdeveloped nations today. While accumulation was no problem, however, a variety of economic, political, and social factors made mobilization much more difficult than it had been, for example, in the United Kingdom. Original settlement was in the eastern United States; however, the focus of investment shifted steadily toward the South and West. Original capital accumulations came from agriculture, fishing, and foreign trade; but over time, the demand for capital shifted first into transportation and light industry, then into heavy industry, and finally into the service sector and knowledge-related light industries.

If the United States is compared to the United Kingdom, for example, it is clear that the strains placed on the existing capital market institutions were much greater on this side of the Atlantic. Not only was Britain an older economy with better-developed institutions, but it also had less spatial and industrial relocations with which to contend. It was almost certainly easier to find ways to move capital from London to an already established city (Manchester, for example) than it was to move the same volume of capital

---

[8] In our brief summary of the French experience we have ignored the traditional story of the French peasant's proclivity for hoarding. Insofar as they did keep their savings in gold hoards (and it is far from clear that they did), the impact of this behavior depends upon the source of the gold. If it is domestic, then hoarding makes it possible for other units (the banks or the government) to increase the money supply and mobilize capital resources without recourse to inflation. If the source is foreign, the effect is similar to that of using domestic income to purchase consumption items of foreign origin.

[9] The role of commercial banks in the generation and mobilization of involuntary savings is discussed in detail in Chapter 10. Forced saving is, of course, only another name for involuntary saving, discussed in Chapter 8.

from New York to Denver. At the same time, the industrial structure of the British economy changed much less over the course of the nineteenth and twentieth centuries than did its American counterpart.

Capital Mobilization in the United States: Interregional and Interindustrial

The existing data suggest that the American market only gradually began to move funds from region to region and industry to industry during the course of the nineteenth century. There appear to have been wide interest differentials between regions (even after risk was accounted for) as well as little correlation between short-term interest movements in the various areas. Over time, however, interest rates tended to move more closely together, and short-term fluctuations in one area began to be transmitted quickly to other areas.

The period from 1825 to 1840 was marked by a continuing demand for finance to underwrite the construction of a transportation network capable of supporting interregional specialization and trade between the West and the Northeast. Some finance did move in response to this demand, which was reflected in large premiums on capital in the West; but while a portion came from eastern savers, a substantial part was foreign. This pattern is consistent with the revisionist argument that the demand for foreign capital reflected less a national shortage of capital than the immature state of the domestic capital markets. Firms unable to tap foreign sources were often forced to depend on local accumulations. The dependence on local capital was characteristic of most western economic activity, including agriculture, milling, meat packing, and the production of agricultural machinery. But although some eastern short-term capital moved into these enterprises as early as the 1840s, long-term capital was mostly local until almost the end of the century.

In the South, the evidence for the antebellum years is even sketchier, but the problem was no less real. In the 1820s and 1830s, the area now called the Deep South drew its capital from the already established regions, but the transfers occurred outside the formal capital markets. In fact, most frequently it took the form of a physical transfer of capital as a farmer in the older regions moved with his slaves and implements to the new areas. At the same time, the cotton factors—firms specializing in marketing southern cotton —provided the basis for a movement of short-term capital from the Northeast to the South. Although these arrangements may have been sufficient for antebellum agriculture, they proved inadequate in the postwar decades. Long-term capital had never been divorced from its owners, and after the 1850s, while capital still was needed, agricultural entrepreneurs were not. The factoring system collapsed with the war and was not reestablished. Thus there was no mechanism for the transfer of even short-term finance except the mercantile credit offered the country store. As a result, the South—a region of relatively low capital prices in 1860—became a region of relatively high prices by the end of the nineteenth century. In fact, it was the last area to be integrated into the national capital market.

The transfer of capital between industries was very personal in nature before the innovation of formal capital market mechanisms. An examination of milling, meat packing, oil refining, agricultural machinery, and steel (all among the growth industries of the late nineteenth century) indicates that in almost every instance the initial investment was drawn from the local area or from similar activities and that in the early years expansion was based almost entirely on retained earnings. Moreover, in those cases in which some capital was drawn from a different area or industry, the transfer was almost always effected through a personal connection rather than through any formal market. In one instance, the connection was a brother in a New York financial house; in another, close friendships with local bankers; and in another, close personal ties in the Philadelphia business community. Firms that could not draw on personal sources did not get "foreign" capital. Despite the potential profitability of investment and despite the continued search for these foreign funds, capital was not being efficiently mobilized across regional or industrial borders through at least the first four fifths of the nineteenth century.

The "disinclination of capital to migrate" is reflected in the trends in regional interest rates, as well as in the histories of the newly developing industries. Figure 9.1 displays the trends in short-term interest rates over the period 1870–1914. It shows wide dispersion of rates at the beginning of the period and a gradual disappearance of the differential. The later 1870s saw near-equality achieved between New York and the cities of New England and the Middle Atlantic states. The early 1890s were marked by the merger of these eastern markets with those in the cities of the Midwest, and in the next decade the Pacific Coast cities were brought into the national market. Over the same period, while complete equality was not achieved, the differentials between the "national" city market and the markets in the cities of the plains and mountains were substantially reduced. Only in the South is there little evidence of the penetration of the national market. While cities were joined before the rural areas, the same trends also appeared, after a time lag, in the countryside. Here too, the South fails to conform to the national pattern.

While there are fewer data for the long-term market, those that exist suggest that (a) interregional differentials existed there as well; (b) there was some tendency for the differentials to decline over time; but (c) by the beginning of World War I, the movement toward a national market had not proceeded as far as it had in the short-term market. The 1890 census contained a survey of mortgage loans for the period 1880–1890, and this enumeration showed interregional interest differentials similar to those in the short-term interest series. (Rates in that decade averaged, for example, less than 6 percent in New England and almost 11 percent on the Pacific Coast.) There was some decline in the interregional variance over the decade. The next survey, and one that unfortunately is not strictly comparable, was made by the Department of Agriculture in 1914; and it indicates little reduction of the differentials between 1890 and that date. By 1930, however, the differences between markets had largely disappeared.

Data on mortgage rates drawn from the records of life insurance companies

FIGURE 9.1
Three-year moving average net returns of city banks

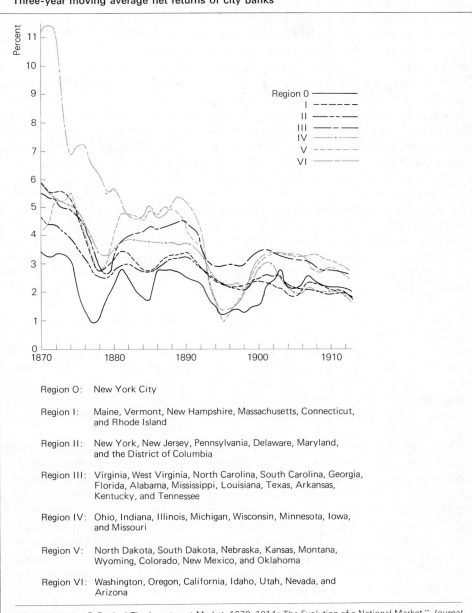

Region O: New York City

Region I: Maine, Vermont, New Hampshire, Massachusetts, Connecticut, and Rhode Island

Region II: New York, New Jersey, Pennsylvania, Delaware, Maryland, and the District of Columbia

Region III: Virginia, West Virginia, North Carolina, South Carolina, Georgia, Florida, Alabama, Mississippi, Louisiana, Texas, Arkansas, Kentucky, and Tennessee

Region IV: Ohio, Indiana, Illinois, Michigan, Wisconsin, Minnesota, Iowa, and Missouri

Region V: North Dakota, South Dakota, Nebraska, Kansas, Montana, Wyoming, Colorado, New Mexico, and Oklahoma

Region VI: Washington, Oregon, California, Idaho, Utah, Nevada, and Arizona

SOURCE: Lance E. Davis, "The Investment Market, 1870–1914: The Evolution of a National Market," *Journal of Economic History*, vol. 25 (September 1965).

suggest the same differentials, but in this instance there is little evidence of a more regular reduction. The data were collected by the location of the insurance company, rather than by the location of the mortgaged property. The variations suggest that in the early years companies tended to lend at home and that there were wide variations among rates, but that the differentials declined as they began to move their capital toward the areas of highest return.

In general, the evidence appears to indicate marked early difference, some movement toward a national long-term market through the 1880s, and some retardation in the rate of equalization between 1890 and World War I. The insurance companies became increasingly aware of and able to exploit the differences in rates, but they were too small to effectively arbitrage the market by themselves. The years after 1914 were marked by the emergence of additional private market institutions and by the entry of the government into the mobilization process (first in agricultural credit and then in the housing market). By the 1930s there appears to have been an effective national market for both long- and short-term finance. Because adjustment had to await the invention of new institutions, the lag was long. It is interesting to note that differential rates of economic growth still cause disequilibria between East and West, and that some parts of the nation (cities in the North, for example) are more closely tied together than others (some cities and southern rural areas, for example).

There were also substantial barriers to the movement of capital between industries in the early years of the nineteenth century, and these barriers too were only gradually overcome by the emergence of institutions capable of effecting intermarket arbitrage. While a brief glance at the early transfers from fishing and foreign trade to transport and light manufacture would suggest that capital was highly mobile, deeper study indicates that such transfer occurred only when there was a shift of the owners of that capital as well.

The cotton textile industry, for example, was one of the first recipients of external capital: That industry was organized along corporate lines, with its shares quoted on the Boston Stock Exchange as early as 1820. However, examination reveals that its shares were almost never traded. The roster of the industry's management reads like a guide to the overseas traders of a decade earlier, and once the initial capitalization had been obtained through the sale of securities to these "insiders," growth was almost entirely financed through retained earnings and by loans from financial institutions controlled by the same group. Despite the obvious locational advantages, there was no movement of capital into the southern textile industry until almost the end of the nineteenth century. While some capital transfer did take place in the 1820s and 1830s, little mobility was achieved for another half-century.[10]

The same pattern emerges in the history of the manufacture of woolen goods. Initial capitalization came from trade and agriculture, but in almost

[10] Lance E. Davis, "The Investment Market" and "Stock Ownership in the Early New England Textile Industry," *Business History Review,* vol. 27 (Summer 1958); and Lance E. Davis, "Sources of Industrial Finance: The American Textile Industry, a Case Study," *Explorations in Entrepreneurial History,* vol. 9 (April 1957).

every case the transfer involved both the capital and its owners. In the case of wool, it was not the South but the West that presented obvious locational advantages. The heavily capital-intensive worsted firms, however, remained firmly rooted in the East long after all economic factors except the availability of capital dictated a move elsewhere.

Nor do the examples have to be drawn from the early period of U.S. history. The steel industry, although removed in time, conforms to the outline of the textile example very well. Given the demand of the railroads and the Civil War, it might be reasonable to expect that the discovery of the Bessemer process would have precipitated a rush into steel making. (In England, this is exactly what had occurred.) However, entry was slow, and growth was severely retarded by the inability to mobilize the requisite finance. The original mills were finished only because of informal ties either with the already-established iron industry or with the railroads that wanted the product. Even Andrew Carnegie, the first large-scale steel producer, financed his operations not through the formal financial markets but through his network of friends and acquaintances. It was not until after J. P. Morgan launched U.S. Steel in the first decade of the present century that nonpersonalized finance began to flow regularly.

Similar examples can be found in almost every industry. Regular institutional provision of long-term agricultural credit awaited the mortgage banks of the 1880s and, after the failure of those institutions, the entry of the government into the credit market in the 1920s and 1930s. The cases of meat packing and milling have already been cited, and even in the railroad industry, much of the western network was initially financed through personal connections or through the accumulations realized in eastern roads.

As the capital markets have improved in the twentieth century industries have fared much better. Automobiles represent something of a transitional case. Henry Ford was so disgusted with his inability to acquire financial capital outside the industry that he cut himself off completely from the capital markets, and General Motors was initially financed by highly personal capital. However, in the latter instance, it was personal capital on a much broader base than anyone had previously imagined, and once the initial capitalization had been achieved, the firm was able to turn to the formal markets for additional finance. Moreover, the companies that came later (although less successful than Ford and General Motors) were able to draw on formal capital markets for needed loan and equity finance. More recently, the aircraft industry shows something of the change that has occurred. Initially established in the 1930s and 1940s, frequently drawing even initial capital from the formal markets, it has turned to the government and to firms in other industries for supplemental finance during the war and in the postwar period. This latter development—interindustry transfers engendered by the desire of established firms to diversify—opens yet another route for capital to travel.

Although mobilization may still be far from perfect, it is clearly much more efficient now than it was 100 years ago. In fact, the evidence clearly suggests that a national capital market (both long- and short-term) had developed by the 1920s. This conclusion is borne out by the increase in the dependence on external finance among households (a rise from 26 to 35 percent of total household finance), governments (from 8 to 49 percent), and (to a lesser extent) businesses in the present century. Although the business increase has been small, there has been a shift from less mobile equity to more mobile debt. Moreover, the data came only from the present century, and if they could be pushed back 100 years, they would almost certainly show a continued increase in external finance throughout the nation's history.

Investor Education and Effective Mobilization

The mechanism for effecting these changes in finance has been the innovation of new and the adaptation of old financial institutions. These institutions have responded to changes in the demand for finance and in the tastes of savers. Firms and households desire financial arrangements that old institutions cannot provide; saving takes new forms and appears in the capital market in new ways; and as people collect in cities, they find less use for personal investment and easier access to formal markets. Successful capital mobilization involves, therefore, on the one hand the process of saver and investor education and, on the other, the invention, innovation, and diffusion of capital market institutions capable of bringing together the savings of the surplus-savings sectors with the demands for capital of the deficit sectors. It is these changes that are reflected in the declining interregional and inter-industry interest differentials and in the increased flow of funds between sectors.

The corporation. While changes in the savers' utility functions and in the choice of institutional forms were of prime importance in increasing capital mobility, changes in legal arrangements also acted to make certain forms of savings appear more attractive. The widespread innovation of the corporate form of business organization made it possible for an investor to divorce the business in which he wanted to invest from the life of its owner and to divorce his investment in it from his total accumulation. At the beginning of the nineteenth century, the only corporations (that is, business institutions with legal lives of their own) were organized by special legislative charter and their numbers and activities were, as a result, severely limited. During the second decade, however, states began to pass general incorporation laws that made it easier to organize corporations and gave the legislatures less control over their activities. By 1875 most states had some form of general incorporation law and some of them were very loose indeed.

In the same period, the courts began to interpret the rights of corporations and contract much more strictly, and these developments, too, made paper investments appear more attractive. In *Fletcher* v. *Peck* (1810), for example, the Supreme Court made the first of a series of decisions on the right of contract that, taken together, have produced the foundation for American business relationships. Again, in *Dartmouth College* v. *Woodward* (1819), and in *Bank of Augusta* v. *Earle* (1839), important precedents were set that limited the power of government to interfere with the operations of a corporation.

Easy incorporation, the right of corporations to operate anywhere in the United States free of "illegal" government interference, and contracts protected by the law all made the process of capital mobilization easier. Since their life was unlimited, but the liability of any stockholder was not, corporations could attract funds more easily than more primitive business forms. At the same time, investments in corporations appeared much safer, since the saver had recourse to the courts to protect him from fraud and capricious management.

Saver education.   While the law made paper investments seem more attractive, the saver was also becoming more sophisticated. In an underdeveloped country in which uncertainties about almost everything run high, savers tend to be concerned primarily with safety. Often it appears that safety means an ability to "touch" an investment. In a one-man economy, saving and investment are carried on by the same economic unit, and to remain close to one's investments presents no insuperable problem. In a more complex society, however, unless the savers themselves are mobile, their accumulations are quite immobile. If capital is to become mobile, it must be depersonalized, and savers must be willing to touch the symbolic representation of their wealth (that is, pieces of printed paper or notations in passbooks), not the factories, forms, and machines themselves.

Investor education comes in many ways, but in part it comes from on-the-job training. The first canals and railroads depended in larger part on investors who could, in fact, touch them. The Erie Canal, for example, obtained much of its initial finance from people who lived along the right-of-way and who saw the direct benefits accruing from the system. Once these investors had made the decision to hold a paper security, they must have found it easier to make similar decisions even when they could no longer touch the real investment. In the same way, the profits that northern savers earned from their investment in government bonds during the Civil War almost certainly helped them buy private bonds in the postwar decades. In fact, Jay Cooke, who had so successfully sold governments during the war, shifted to private issues at the war's end and maintained many of his earlier customers.

Although they have oftimes been cast as "robber barons"—perhaps not always without cause—the educational impact of financiers like Cooke and J. P. Morgan should not be underestimated. Their names (for a time, at least) were synonymous with success, and by placing their personal sanction on an issue, they made the stocks and bonds of such organizations as the Northern Pacific Railroad and the United States Steel Company appear much safer. The effects of the process of saver education were already visible by the end of the century. At that time, a financier reported with some surprise that the Midwest—an area populated by hicks and Hoosiers—was already becoming a substantial market for the sale of paper securities.

The reluctance of savers to hold indirect financial obligations was further overcome by making paper investments appear more attractive. Financial intermediaries did much along this line. Thus, mutual savings banks, guaranteed as they were by the "establishment," made savings held in this form appear particularly safe. Life insurance companies, mixing savings and insurance as only they can do, sold savings plans to consumers who thought they were buying only insurance. More recently, pension plans have become a route to retirement, and the Social Security Act has equated savings and taxes. These and other innovations in "savings forms" have certainly made it easier to divorce the saver from his accumulation.

Financial intermediaries. The invention and innovation of new varieties of financial institutions also speeded the process of mobilization. Intermediaries can make distant investments appear more local (it is possible to touch a bank building) and, therefore, safer, but that is not their only contribution to the mobilization process. In the first place, if individual accumulations are small and there is some minimum investment size, the ability to pool savings in an intermediary and invest this pool in a variety of paper securities can help individuals insure against the failure of any one investment. Thus, by reducing the variance of the returns, intermediaries can reduce the cost of mobilizing funds. From the point of view of the saver, they can greatly reduce the costs of searching for potential opportunities. Consider, for example, the costs incurred by an eastern capitalist interested in the 1870s in investing in western farm mortgages. Either he or his agent had to travel to the West, search out alternative mortgage situations, and assess the potential profitability of each. Unless the capitalist was interested in investing a great deal of money, it is highly unlikely that it would pay him to incur the necessary costs. An intermediary, on the other hand, can spread the cost of such a search over a large number of investment dollars and (since it is continually in the market) can routinize the search procedure. At the same time, the costs to potential savings-using firms can be reduced by the negotiation of a single contract rather than a number of small contracts, one with each potential investor.

Although the data are far from perfect, it is quite apparent that financial intermediaries increased greatly in importance in the century before World War I. Since there were almost no intermediaries at the beginning of the period and a great number at the end, there was certainly an increase. Moreover, for those types for which we have data (mutual savings banks and life insurance companies), it is readily apparent that they grew not only in absolute terms, but also relative to almost any imaginable index of the economy's growth.

Goldsmith's figures indicate that by 1900, nonbank intermediaries accounted for about 60 percent of household mortgages, 25 percent of farm mortgages, 25 percent of the total holdings of domestic corporate bonds, and about 50 percent of the total issues of local governments. (A century before, there had been no nonbank intermediaries.) Nor has the trend toward increased intermediation slackened in the present century. By 1950 these institutions had increased their holdings of corporate bonds to almost 90 percent of the total, they accounted for 20 percent of outstanding corporate equity issues, and they had doubled their holdings of federal government securities. Only in the case of local government issues had their importance declined.

It is impossible to trace the history of every one of the myriad intermediaries, but a look at a few selected examples can help to bring the role of these institutions in the mobilization process into better focus. The first such institution to have an important impact on the economy was the mutual savings bank. Designed to provide a safe place for small savers to hold their accumulations, these banks tended (partially because of legal restrictions and partially because of the provincialism of their management) to have a relatively limited regional and industrial horizon. Despite this limitation, they did act to mobilize substantial blocks of capital for the New England textile industry. The Erie Canal and the railroads of the Northeast also drew funds from the mutual savings banks—funds that probably would otherwise have been invested in housing if they had been saved at all. As late as the Civil War, these banks remained the most important financial intermediaries in the economy, but their popularity never spread outside the Northeast, and their contribution to interregional mobilization was quite small.

Although life insurance was sold in the United States as early as the eighteenth century, life insurance companies experienced no significant growth until the development of adequate mortality tables in the 1840s, and rapid growth awaited the innovation of tontine and industrial-insurance contracts after 1870. Almost any insurance plan involves the creation of some potentially investable reserves, a straight life contract creating somewhat more than a term policy and a savings scheme even more. As insurance grew more and more popular, life insurance companies rapidly became the most important type of intermediary, a position they retain today. Like the mutual savings banks, life insurance companies were at first limited in the scope of their investments by law and custom; but unlike them, they were never restricted to a single geographical region and they tended to overcome these handicaps. In the last quarter of the nineteenth century, most state regulations were altered to permit the firms to invest in any part of the country and, as they developed, their management was quick to see the profit potential from investment in high-interest regions. Although they were not large enough in the 1880s and 1890s to arbitrage out the long-term market themselves, they did contribute to a steady and growing flow of finance across regional and industrial boundaries. Although the legislative reaction to the Armstrong Committee investigation of 1905 produced a movement toward greater regulation, that regulation never seriously hampered their investment policy. Moreover, this trend has been reversed in the twentieth century. Some restrictions have been lifted, and life insurance has continued to mobilize capital throughout the economy.

Innovations in the capital markets continue today. In the more recent past there appears to have been a shift in savers' tastes toward a concern for old age (a result, most likely, of higher incomes and longer life expectancies), and the economy has seen the rapid growth of both private and government pension funds. Potential profits in this area have, after a lag, caused new types of institutions to be innovated and markets to be arbitraged. The result has been a smoother passage of savings from the saver (the person saving for his old age) to the user of those savings (the business firms that need finance now).

Commercial-paper firms. Institutional innovation occurred not only among financial intermediaries, but in other parts of the capital markets as well. In the short-term capital market, for example, the development of a market for commercial paper provided an organizational structure capable of transferring short-term funds across regional boundaries. Because of the legal restrictions on commercial banking—rules that regulated both the investment and the operational aspects of banks—the United States never evolved a system of branch banks serving all parts of the country, a feature of both the Canadian and the English economies. Moreover, so provincial was the attitude of even the federal regulatory authorities, that solicitation of interbank deposits was frowned on officially. To overcome these legal barriers and make it possible to move short-term funds from the low-interest East to higher-interest regions, a different institutional form was required.

Firms specializing in buying commercial paper from banks in high-interest areas and selling it to banks in surplus-savings regions began to appear in the East in the 1840s. It was, however, 1880 before the West North Central region was drawn into the market and the first decade of the present century before the cities of the Southwest and Pacific Coast were included. Penetration into the rural portions of any region lagged behind the inclusion of the cities, but by 1913 there were commercial-paper firms operating in almost every major city outside the South. The absence of the market in the South is, of course, consistent with the failure of interest rates in that region to correspond with those prevailing elsewhere in the country.

The history of the commercial-paper market, however, suggests how little is actually known about the process of institutional innovation. While it is possible to talk in very general terms about the process, it is very difficult to specify it more closely. Why, for example, did it take 60-odd years for the market to spread across the country, and why did it not penetrate the South for another three decades? Until these and similar questions can be answered, it will be very difficult to attain any real understanding of the mechanics of economic development.

The stock market. The market for long-term capital also underwent important institutional changes not associated with the process of intermediation. Here, however, it was the development of a direct market for financial instruments that was important. It is possible to raise some finance by the issue of paper securities even in the absence of a defined securities market; however, if the system is to be more than a cover for personal financial transactions, some formal market is necessary. Such a market reduces the search cost for both saver and investor, and, while perhaps not increasing the safety of paper investments, at least increases their liquidity. The holder of paper finance may be unable to sell his investment for as much as he would like, but he is at least able to sell it. Thus, for example, on Black Thursday, during the height of the 1929 stock-market crash, 15 million shares of stock were sold (and purchased).

The nineteenth century and the first decade of the twentieth saw the gradual development of a single securities market encompassing the entire nation and almost the entire range of economic activities. While there were markets for paper securities as early as the late eighteenth century, these markets were local and were limited to a very narrow range of securities. As late as 1830, for example, there were a fairly large number of local exchanges; and at least two of them, Philadelphia and Boston, were as important as that in New York. Moreover, the markets handled little besides government and transport issues, and industrials were almost totally absent from the list of securities traded. Even in Boston (the center of the market for industrials), it appears that manufacturing stocks, though listed, were seldom exchanged.

The decades between 1840 and 1880 were marked by the centralization of the securities market in New York City. The demise of the Second Bank of the United States removed much of the financial support from the Philadelphia market. At the same time, the increasing importance of New York as a center for interregional and international trade provided the base for an active short-term money market, and such a market is a prerequisite for a major securities exchange. Although regional exchanges continued to exist, they concentrated more and more in local issues and, as far as national issues were concerned, became merely satellites for the central exchange in New York.

It was well after the Civil War, however, before the exchange began to broaden its activities beyond government, transport, and public-utility issues. In 1885 it organized a department of unlisted securities, and it was through this channel that the issues of the first manufacturing firms located far from New York reached the "big board." Discrimination still existed, however, and it was harder to borrow on industrials than on other types of equities. The success of J. P. Morgan in underwriting industrial ventures made such securities appear more desirable, and gradually more and more issues were traded. By World War I, manufacturing securities were no longer discriminated against by banks making brokers' loans, and the majority of brokerage houses had broadened their activities to include manufacturing stocks and bonds.

In many ways the 1920s were the heyday of the stock exchange. Capital from all over the country was mobilized for an ever-expanding number of domestic and foreign activities. The debacle of 1929 scared away many potential investors, but the effect was short lived. By the 1940s the market had largely resumed its earlier role. The regulatory authority of the Securities and Exchange Commission (SEC) did much to reassure potential investors. However, certain factors were at work to reduce the market's relative importance. As long as the financial intermediaries were relatively small, they dealt through the formal markets themselves. As they have grown larger, however, they have found it increasingly profitable to bypass formal markets and deal directly with potential capital users. In recent years, these direct placements have become even more important—a trend which suggests again that the institutional adjustment to changing demands for and supplies of capital continues today.

Capital Mobilization—Its Economic Impact

The costs of the capital immobilities of the nineteenth century included a slower aggregate growth rate and a bias in both the industrial composition and the spatial distribution of economic activity. In addition, there appear to have been other less obvious results. Some economic dogma suggests that industrial concentration and economic growth are not likely to be found together. It is usually observed that cartels or other semimonopolistic agglomerations are defensive reactions to declining markets, and that rapid growth is anathema to monopoly. In the case of the United Kingdom, the evidence conforms closely to the theoretical conclusions. The late nineteenth century was marked by rapid technical change and growth in steel, brewing, and chemicals; but in each case the growth was shared by a substantial number of firms. What concentration did occur was localized in those industries that were stagnant or declining.

In the United States, on the other hand, concentration frequently went hand in hand with rapid growth. In the postbellum decades, steel, meat packing, and petroleum all underwent substantial technical advance and the output of all three industries grew very rapidly. In each case, however, an industry that had begun the period with a highly competitive industrial structure ended it with much of its output very heavily concentrated in a few firms.

The explanation of this trend toward concentration lies both in the nature of the technical changes in the industries' production processes and in the barriers to capital mobilization. In each instance, the new technology yielded substantial cost savings, but the new process appears to have been subject to substantial returns to scale. Thus, large firms could produce more cheaply than small, and as a result, a substantial premium was placed on the ability to acquire the finance needed to underwrite the innovation of the new technique. Given well-developed capital markets (as existed, for example, in the United Kingdom), innovations should have produced some reduction in the number of firms, but this reduction ought not to have gone so far as to concentrate production in the hands of a very few. The U.S. capital markets were, however, far from perfect, and few firms had access to the requisite finance. As a result, the degree of concentration appears to have been much higher than technology alone would have dictated. Andrew Carnegie was the nation's largest steel producer not because he knew how to produce steel better than his competitors, but because he could informally organize the necessary finance. John D. Rockefeller was able to create the Standard Oil monopoly not because of his skill as an oil refiner, but because he could draw on the Cleveland banking community for loans when others could not. The same story is repeated again and again in the industrial history of the United States in the late nineteenth century.

While imperfect credit markets tended to produce concentration and monopoly profits, improvements in the markets tended to reduce both the profitability and the extent of financially induced concentration. J. P. Morgan made a fortune personally mobilizing sufficient finance to underwrite ventures like United States Steel, but once he had done so it was easy for others to imitate his method. The channels he developed became formalized in the capital markets, and thereafter the profits accruing to the financial capitalists were much less and the pressures from financial sources for industrial concentration were much reduced.

Well-oiled capital markets are, however, not entirely costless. The innovations that helped bring about the smooth flow of resources from saver to investor also brought about fluctuations in prices, economic instability and many other short-term costs associated with "speculative" activity. These costs are examined in more detail in Chapter 10.

SUGGESTED READING

Davis, Lance E. "Capital Immobilities and Finance Capitalism: A Study of Economic Evolution in the United States, 1820–1920." *Explorations in Entrepreneurial History,* Series 2, vol. 1, no. 1 (Fall 1963).

Davis, Lance E. "The Investment Market, 1870–1914: The Evolution of a National Market." *Journal of Economic History,* vol. 25 (September 1965).

Davis, Lance E., and Robert E. Gallman. "The Share of Saving and Investment in Gross National Product During the Nineteenth Century, United States of America." In *Papers of the Fourth Congress of the International History Association.* Bloomington: University of Indiana Press, forthcoming.

Goldsmith, Raymond W. *A Study of Saving in the United States,* vol. 1. Princeton: Princeton University Press, 1955.

Greef, Albert. *The Commercial Paper House in the United States.* Cambridge, Mass.: Harvard University Press, 1938.

Myers, Margaret. *The New York Money Market:* Vol. 1, *Origins and Development.* New York: Columbia University Press, 1931.

North, Douglass C. "Capital Accumulation in Life Insurance Between the Civil War and the Investigation of 1905." In *Men in Business,* edited by W. Miller. New York: Harper & Row, 1952.

Sobel, Robert. *The Big Board, A History of the New York Stock Market.* New York: Free Press, 1965.

Williamson, Harold F., and Orange A. Smalley. *Northwestern Mutual Life.* Evanston, Ill.: Northwestern University Press, 1957.

10
BANKS AND THEIR ECONOMIC EFFECTS

In Chapters 8 and 9, capital formation was related to the process of economic growth, the role of savings in capital formation was explored, and the twin problems of capital accumulation and mobilization were examined. Rapid economic growth is aided by high rates of savings. If savings are to be utilized effectively, however, they must be channeled into economically productive activities. In the context of American development, the evolution of a set of financial intermediaries contributed both to a rapid rate of capital accumulation and to effective capital mobilization. The role played by the commercial banks in capital accumulation and mobilization in the United States was critical, and their history is therefore the subject of this chapter.

The commercial banks are treated separately from other financial intermediaries because their power to create money gives their lending activities a far greater impact than that of the typical intermediary. Before turning to the history of commercial banking in the American economy, let us examine the nature of the difference between commercial banks and other financial intermediaries.

THE ROLES OF COMMERCIAL BANKS

Involuntary savings can come from (a) forced levies (i.e., taxes) that reduce consumption and the directing of those released resources to investment purposes, or (b) increases in the money supply that provide investing units with more and consuming units with less of the money claims on goods and services. The size of the money supply can be increased either by the government's decision to print more money or by the commercial bankers' decision to make more loans. Without totally ignoring the government's role in the process of money creation, let us concentrate on the behavior of the commercial-banking sector. Since bankers constitute a nonpublic body which is in the position to affect powerfully the allocation of resources, the rate of economic growth, the distribution of income, and the degree of economic instability, it appears particularly useful to examine their role in the savings–investment process.

Since money provides a command over goods and services, there is, at any moment of time, a demand by economic units for loanable funds to effect desired transactions. The demand is the sum of consumers' demand for cash to finance consumption expenditure, businesses' demand for funds to carry out investment decisions, governments' demand for money to implement their budgetary decisions, and foreigners' demand for domestic claims to allow them to purchase American goods and services. The total demand for money is a function of the level of income and the rate of interest. The greater the level of income, *ceteris paribus*, the greater is the need for funds to underwrite each sector's transactions demands. Lower rates of interest imply that consumers must forego smaller returns if they choose to consume and/or that their costs are lower if they choose to borrow. For businesses, lower interest rates mean lower costs of borrowing, and that fact makes more projects profitable. Thus, the total demand for funds is greater at lower rates of interest.

The supply of funds, in turn, is the sum of changes in the holdings of cash outside banks, changes in the volume of bank-created demand deposits or bank notes, the stream of funds currently being released to business in the form of additions to depreciation or depletion reserves, and the funds set aside as savings or those currently dishoarded by income recipients. The supply of legal tender is, of course, largely a function of government policy. The quantity of bank money, although constrained at the upper limit by the threat of drain or by legal requirements, is largely the product of decisions by the banking sector. *Disentanglings*, while not particularly subject to short-run variation, are related to the size of the capital stock.[1] And, finally, the level of current savings is the result of consumption–savings decisions by the consumer sector. The level of savings tends to respond to changes in both income and interest rates, and insofar as the capital stock is related to some past level of income and this year's income is related to last year's income, the disentanglings probably are loosely related to income. On the other hand, there is no reason to believe that the supply of legal tender or bank money is particularly responsive to changes in either the rate of interest or the level of income.

Given a normally large demand for costless money and a limited supply of that commodity, loanable funds usually command a positive price (that price is, of course, the rate of interest). Moreover, like any other commodity, changes in the demand for or supply of loanable funds are transmitted to the decision-making unit in the economy through changes in that price.

Since the demand for funds is a function of income, increases in the size of the economy (increases in population, the capital stock, or land area) cause the demand curve to shift to the right. If this shift is not matched by a supply response, the increase in demand will cause interest rates to rise, and that

---

[1] Disentanglings are the funds released by depreciation and depletion policies that are available for investment.

increase will reduce the number of investment projects undertaken (and therefore the rate of capital accumulation) and ultimately the rate of growth. A strong argument can be made for a secular increase in the money supply sufficient to offset the tendency for interest rates to rise.

If, in addition, people are willing to pay for the use of funds, this demand creates still another pressure on commercial banks for increasing the money supply. An increase in the supply of money will, at full employment, cause prices to rise. If the newly created balances are held by people who want to devote them to investment expenditures and if at least some of the holders of the original balances demanded them for consumption purposes, the price increase will, by transferring purchasing power from original to new balance holders, provide the mechanism for transferring resources from consumption to investment. Similarly, if the new balances are held by government, the price rise provides the mechanism for transferring resources from the private to the public sector. Money creation, through printing paper or by selling bonds to banks in exchange for deposits, has in fact been the technique most often employed by the federal government when it has needed to mobilize resources for war.

The government could, of course, create money and use the new funds to support private investment, but such a policy, while common abroad, has not been characteristic of American development. This fact, however, does not deny that involuntary savings have been an important source of private investment, for the government is not alone in its ability to create money. As long as the commercial banks need only fractional reserves, they can create money as efficiently as the government.[2] Today bank money takes the form of book-keeping entries (demand deposits). In the nineteenth century, when checking accounts were rare, bank notes were more common. The only physical difference between bank notes and government money was the pictures on the notes and the paper they were printed on.[3] In economic terms, of course, the difference lay in the backing and in the risk attached to either form. In the case of demand deposits, although there are physical differences between them and government money, they are analytically identical.

Thus, the commercial banks are in a position to force involuntary saving on the economy just as effectively as the government. There is, however, one important difference. The government can always select a method that is not inflationary, but the commercial banks can only induce saving by credit creation—a technique that is by its very nature inflationary.[4] Thus bank-induced involuntary saving (even if it leads to increases in the rate of growth) can be criticized on two grounds. First, it is destabilizing and may involve any of a whole series of costs that go hand in hand with instability (increased uncertainty, semiexplosive price movements, or fluctuations in real output, to cite only three). Second, while price increases are the instrument for effecting

---

[2] Under normal conditions neither the need to meet day-to-day demand nor the law requires that banks maintain more than a small fraction of their deposits as reserves.

[3] Since the federal government did not have the legal right to print (as opposed to coin) money until the 1860s, the only paper currency circulating was that printed by the commercial banks.

[4] The government could always offset any inflationary pressure by an appropriate tax policy.

transfer from consumers to investors, those same price increases almost always induce some income redistributions and that redistribution may have undesirable social, political, or economic effects.[5] To anticipate a conclusion, criticisms leveled at the commercial banks have led to legislative attempts to mitigate their impact, and these attempts have, in turn, limited the banks' ability to increase the level of savings.

Commercial banks are unique because of their ability to create money; however, in their role as lender they act to allocate finance like any other financial intermediary. Whether they are creating money to make loans or merely lending out funds left as time deposits, they act to allocate funds between competing uses. Like any other intermediary, their ability to mobilize capital and channel it toward the most profitable use is circumscribed by both law and custom. In this area, too, complaints voiced against the banks' destabilizing and redistributing powers have produced legislation that has adversely affected their ability to mobilize capital. The process of capital mobilization in the United States has been aided by the emergence of a large commercial-banking sector, but its effect has been less than it might have been because of the legal restrictions not aimed at, but nevertheless hitting, its mobilization powers.

At this point, two notes of warning should be introduced. First, in periods of full employment, commercial banks can induce an increase in the level of involuntary savings only to the extent that they can cause prices to rise. Since the effects of their actions may be masked by other events, it is not possible to deduce any estimate of the magnitude of the involuntary savings from a simple examination of the changes in the price level that followed an increase in the volume of bank money.[6]

Second, while one may argue that the costs have been excessive, it is clear that the commercial banks could have increased the rate of capital accumulation. There is, however, no rule that limits a bank's customers to those business firms that want to use the funds for investment. In fact, presently about one seventh of all commercial-bank loans are made to consumers who wish to purchase consumer durables. Insofar as bank loans are of this latter variety, the creation of bank money—while still producing price increases—does not lead to involuntary (or any other kind of) saving.[7] Instead, it merely effects a redistribution from one consumer to another (or perhaps even from a business firm to a consumer). The justification for these loans can hardly rest on their contributions to growth.

With these caveats in mind, let us turn to an analysis of the impact of commercial banks on American development and certain other facets of

[5] It is, of course, possible that banks loan not to persons desiring to finance investment projects, but to persons who want to finance consumption. In this case there are no forced savings, and if some original holders were potential investors, forced savings may be negative.

[6] For example, productivity increases (*ceteris paribus*) would cause prices to fall and induce an income redistribution in line with that decline. If the banks had created additional deposits (or bank notes), the two tendencies might offset each other and there would be no change in the price level. In fact, however, the situation is quite different from what it would have been had the banks not created the additional money. There has certainly been a relative inflation and an implicit income redistribution. It may be that such an implicit redistribution produces fewer " obvious " effects, but there is no doubt that it has occurred.

[7] Unless, of course, you include consumer durables in capital.

American financial history (for example, the Gold Rush and the battle over "free silver") that can easily be discussed within the structure of our analysis of banks and the money supply.

A MODEL OF FINANCIAL DEVELOPMENT

Since the process of involuntary saving, bank-induced inflations, and the impact of regulation on growth and stability are extremely complex topics, it appears useful to introduce a very simple economic model. Reference to that model, it is hoped, will make it possible to sort out the effects of changes in a number of economic magnitudes while, at the same time, not overly confusing the reader.

Let

$T =$ the theoretical maximum amount of bank money that the commercial-banking system can support.

$B =$ the actual amount of bank money that the banks have chosen to supply. Before the 1870s, these were largely bank notes; later, mostly demand deposits.

$M =$ the total money supply (bank money plus cash and specie outside of banks).

$c =$ the amount of government money and specie outside the commercial-banking system. Initially, it appears useful to assume that c is a constant, but later we can make it an exogenous variable (that is, one determined outside of the system).

$R =$ the cash and specie reserves held by the banking system.

$RR =$ the percentage reserves that the bank must hold to support its bank money. In the period before legal reserve requirements, this amount was the percentage of liabilities that bankers thought they must hold in cash or specie to protect themselves against internal drain from other banks and from their own depositors' desires to substitute cash for bank money. Later it was either those reserves or the legal reserve requirement, whichever was greater.

$k =$ the reciprocal of the velocity.[8] For purposes of exposition, it is assumed that there are no idle balances, and that velocity is the same for consumers (who make initial bank deposits) and business-men (who receive all the bank loans). Like c, as a first approximation, k is assumed to be a constant, but later that assumption will be slightly relaxed to make the velocity depend both on the extent to which nonbank intermediaries have penetrated the economy and on certain other exogenous changes in the economic environment.

$P =$ the price level. Since in our simple model there is only one kind of output, both consumer- and investment-goods prices are identical.

$Q_c =$ the quantity of output that is consumed.

---

[8] The student should remember that velocity is the measure of the number of times a dollar is spent in a year.

Q_i = the quantity of output that is invested.

q = the maximum quantity of output that the economy can achieve if all resources are fully employed. At any moment in time, q is fixed, although its value can increase over time.

B_c = the bank money held by consumers.

B_l = bank money produced by bank-money creation (that is, business loans).

Y = the value of output in the economy.

The model itself combines these magnitudes into eight equations with T, M, P, Q_c, Q_i, Y, and B_l as endogenous variables.

$$T = R \frac{1}{RR} \tag{1}$$

$$T = B \tag{2}$$

$$\text{or } T > B \tag{2a}$$

$$M = B + c \tag{3}$$

$$M = kY \tag{4}$$

$$Q_i + Q_c \leqslant q \tag{5}$$

$$Y = P(Q_c + Q_i) \tag{6}$$

$$B = B_l + B_c \tag{7}$$

$$Y = \frac{B_l + (B_c + c)}{k} \tag{8}$$

Equation (1) is, of course, nothing but a mechanical relation (an institutional production function, if you like) relating the maximum amount of bank money that can be created given the level of reserves and the percentage reserve requirements. It does, however, indicate that anything that changes R and/or RR can affect B. Equation (2) is, however, behavioral and says something about the way bankers will react to the existence of excess reserves. It is a very strong assumption, since it assumes that bankers will always continue to make loans until excess reserves are zero.[9] If Equation (2) does hold, then anything that changes the level of reserves or the reserve requirement will have an effect on the money supply. If, however, (2a) rather than (2) best describes the economy, then there will be no necessary connection between the exogenous variables in (1) and the money supply. Although the historical example may be oversimplified, it appears that throughout most of the nineteenth and early twentieth centuries, Equation (2) represents a reasonable model of banker behavior; but during periods of panic or depression, their behavior was most frequently represented by (2a). In the latter case, no amount of action on the monetary policy variables (R and RR) had much

---

[9] It could be weakened somewhat and written as $B = B(T)$, where the function is known to be positive and the results would not be altered by much.

effect on M. Equation (3) defines the money supply as bank money plus cash outside of banks. Equation (4) is behavioral and implies not only that payments equal receipts but also that the velocity of money is a constant. While the assumption of a constant velocity is a very strong one, for heuristic purposes it appears useful. Equation (5) ties output to some full-employment level, but if full employment is not achieved, implies that the relation between the money supply and the price level is not automatic, but that changes in the money supply might affect the quantity of output as well as (or instead of) its price. Equation (6) implies that income is the sum of the value of consumer and investment goods and shows that if the economy is at full employment, increases in Y (such as might be caused by an increase in the supply of money) can come about only through increases in the price level. Equation (7) is also definitional and says merely that the total supply of bank money is the sum of that held by consumers and that created in the process of making loans.[10] Finally, Equation (8) is not independent but shows that the claims on income Y are divided between producers and consumers in proportion to their holdings of money. Thus, the creation of bank money can effect a redistribution of income from consumers to producers. With this model in mind, let us trace through a few simple operations.

In a world without commercial banks, all claims on income are held by the consumer sector, which holds all the money. If we introduce banks into this idyll, and if some reserves appear in the banks (by the deposit of some of c in the bank, perhaps), then, if the bankers make loans to reduce their excess reserves, the results are higher prices and a redistribution of income from the consumers to the business community. The new loans create additional money, which in turn increases the value of output. But if the economy is at full employment, physical output is fixed and only its money value (prices) can increase. At the new prices consumers have the same number of dollars, but they are worth less. As a result, they receive a reduced share of income. Businessmen, on the other hand, now have money equal to the value of their borrowing (where they had none before), and they can lay claim to some share of output. The banks have generated involuntary savings (the consumers did not want to save, but found their purchasing power reduced through inflation). The mechanism of that reduction was the increase in the price level. Thus, forced saving and price instability go hand in hand.[11]

[10] In this model, banks make only business loans. If they also make other types of loans, then B_c should be the same for loans to businessmen, consumers, government, or foreigners.

[11] There is sometimes a feeling that once touched off the inflationary process has no end, but in this context it does. The initial increase in the money supply would cause interest rates to fall, and this should cause an increase in the demand for investment. However, as prices rise there is a fall in the real value of money, and the nominal money supply is no longer adequate to support the new higher level of transactions. As a result, businessmen substitute against bonds and for cash, this substitution increases the rate of interest and reduces the excess demand in the real sector (the substitution will continue as long as there is any excess demand) and will ultimately result in a return of the rate of interest to its initial level and therefore no changes in the real sectors. However, prices will have increased proportionately with the increase in the money supply.

As long as Equation (2) holds, anything that affects R or RR will also affect the money supply, the price level, and the volume of involuntary savings. Today we are used to thinking of the important changes in the two monetary variables as stemming from the actions of the Federal Reserve System. In an earlier period, the changes were likely to come from increased banking competition (that by increasing the threat of internal drain would cause banks to hold a greater proportion of reserves) or from a sudden infusion of new reserves: the product of a gold discovery or a sudden alteration in the balance of payments.

THE RISE OF THE COMMERCIAL-BANKING SYSTEM

Although there had been private banks previously, the first commercial bank organized as a corporation in the United States was chartered to help finance the Revolutionary War. At the end of the war, the bank took a Pennsylvania charter and continued to operate as a commercial bank. Its monopoly position did not, however, last long. While the number of banks was still small in 1800, there was at least one bank in every major port city and several in some. Since then, growth has been very rapid, and banks have extended their activities both in their depth of coverage in the East Coast cities and in the breadth of coverage across the country. The statistics are notoriously bad, but they probably do serve as some indicator of growth. They show an increase in the number of banks from 88 in 1810 to 30,000 just 120 years later. Banks increased not only in absolute terms but also in proportion to population. Thus, from 1860 to 1914, the number of banks rose over five times as fast as population; and since that time, while the number of banks has actually fallen, their assets have risen almost nine times as rapidly as population growth.

An increase in the number of banks, if it involves an increase in the volume of reserves, will (assuming, of course, that the banks lend on the basis of their excess reserves) increase the supply of money and, if the loans are used to finance investment, the volume of involuntary savings. The mechanism for that rise is, of course, an increase in the price level. Moreover, given the very high ratio of bank notes to reserves that most of the early banks strove to obtain, the leverage that the entry of even a few banks had on prices was very impressive.[12] In the years before 1828 there were no such things as legal reserves, and many bankers had little commitment to even the concept of reserves. The literature of the early period is full of references to banks like the famous one in Cape Frear, North Carolina, that managed to support several hundred thousand dollars of bank notes on only a few dollars of reserves.

Loan Ratios

Two forces could have operated to limit loan ratios of the commercial banks. In the first place, there was always a considerable threat that the depositors would want their money. The banks were, however, fairly successful in countering this threat. Throughout the nineteenth and early twentieth centuries, any general attempt, either in a local area or in the country as a whole, to convert bank money into specie led to local, statewide, or economy-wide bank suspensions. During a period of suspension, the banks refused to redeem their notes and deposits. If one bank refused to make such a conversion, it could be forced to close; but if all of them suspended payments, there was

---

[12] The reader should remember that bank money can take the form of either checking accounts (demand deposits) or bank notes. In this early period, while demand deposits were not uncommon in the largest cities, bank notes were the usual way of effecting loan transactions. Each bank issued its own notes, and by 1860 it is estimated that there were over 6000 different kinds of bank notes circulating in the United States. Since the value of any individual note depended on what one thought he could get for it and that value depended (among other things) on the certainty of ultimate redemption, it is not surprising that there was a great lack of uniformity in the value of bank notes. Commerce was therefore difficult.

little that could be done. The state of Pennsylvania, for example, had a law that required any suspending bank to surrender its charter. Despite numerous suspensions, there is no evidence that any significant number of banks ever lost their charters. While such suspensions must have made the public more wary of the workings of the commercial-banking system, the fact that the banking community usually accepted them meant that banks did not need protection from the internal drain to competitors in times of crisis. In fact, it was usual for the banks in any community to agree to suspend payment when faced by a potential run. If cooperation was successful, the required reserves were reduced and the potential volume of bank money increased concomitantly.

It is important to note the need for cooperative action. Any single bank suspending payment could be forced into bankruptcy almost regardless of its size. In 1841, the Bank of the United States of Pennsylvania (formerly the Second Bank of the United States) desperately wanted a general suspension to ease pressure on it. The New York banks refused; even the threat of a mass presentation of notes did not persuade them to alter their views. As a result, the nation's largest financial institution was forced into bankruptcy.

The second limitation on loan ratios was imposed, except during periods of suspension, by the threat of internal drain. That is, while depositors were unlikely to want their deposits on any particular day, any bank whose notes turned up in a competitive institution knew that it was certainly going to be faced with a demand for payment. On the average, of course, the more competitors, the more likely that one bank's notes would appear as deposits in another bank. As a result, banks in large cities usually had to hold a fairly high proportion of reserves unless they could collude with their competitors (and recent work in experimental economics has suggested that when the number of competitors gets larger than about three, such collusion is very difficult). On the other hand, banks located at a distance from their competition were not so severely constrained. The name "wildcat banking" was applied to banking in areas in which there were "more wildcats than people." Such banks were faced by a minimum threat of internal drain and were able to sustain very high bank note/reserve ratios. It should be no surprise that Cape Frear was not near any commercial center populated by a set of competing banks. Moreover, internal drain could be even further reduced if, given the poor state of transport, ways could be found of issuing notes in areas other than that in which the bank was located. It was possible, therefore, for two banks in different regions to reduce their reserve ratios by exchanging notes and giving these "foreign" notes to their borrowers.

Despite this potential handicap, the willingness of the American business community to accept suspensions, coupled with the insulation provided by the size of the American continent, did permit these early banks to generate a substantial volume of involuntary savings. The costs of these savings, as Equations (4) and (5) suggest, were either a steady inflation or a rate of price decline lower than the rate of productivity growth would have dictated. In either case, the consumers lost claims on assets to the business community.

Types of Loans

In this early period, commercial banks were almost the only type of financial intermediary. It is not, therefore, surprising that they attempted to accommodate all types of loan demand. While they originally had been established to provide the short-term credit that was necessary to underwrite the trading activities of city merchants, that focus had been dictated by the structure of the economy (mercantile activity was almost the only type of economic activity other than agriculture) and not by any overriding economic law. As the economy developed, other types of business began to feel the need for finance, and the commercial banks tried to accommodate them.

Thus, by 1830 commercial banks in the East Coast cities were supplying both short- and long-term credit to industry. In the South banks were involved in providing long-term mortgage financing to the cotton plantations, and in the West both industry and agriculture benefited from bank loans. The records of early meat-packing firms in Cincinnati show a heavy dependence on local bankers, and there is some evidence of short-term loans to Ohio cattle ranchers about the same time. In New England, the records of the large textile mills show that commercial banks were providing the bulk of short-term external finance and that they also made some contribution to the long-term finance solicited by those firms. Moreover, it is a well-known "fact of banking life" that a short-term loan can become a source of long-term finance if it is continually renewed. Such renewals apparently were common practice. Although there is a shortage of data, indirect evidence makes this conclusion appear very reasonable. The Savings Bank of Baltimore (not a commercial bank, but a bank whose loan activities, contemporary commentary suggests, were similar to those of the commercial banks) made a 90-day loan in 1845 which was still out and drawing interest in 1919, some 74 years later. Moreover, drafters of the Forestall legislation regulating Louisiana banks, which served as a model for other regulatory laws, went to considerable length to attempt to prevent this practice. Not only did they make such renewals illegal, but they also required that any bank receiving a request for renewal post the name of the requester on the door for all to see.

The 1840s, however, saw a substantial change in the type and maturity of commercial-bank loans. Throughout the previous decade, the growing demands for long-term finance by the transport, industrial, and southern agricultural sectors had induced more and more banks to make long-term loans. In fact, some bank charters were issued specifically to provide long-term capital to one or more of these types of enterprises. The Morris Canal and Banking Company, for example, was essentially a commercial bank whose assets consisted of long-term loans to the canal company. The panic of 1837 and the depression of 1839–1842 placed considerable pressure on the banking system, and the least liquid banks (those with the lowest reserve ratios) were placed under the heaviest pressure. The model suggests that the system cannot stand any sudden attempt by depositors to substitute specie for bank money, and banks with no reserves and few liquid assets are less able to stand the attempt than those with higher reserves and more liquid assets. Given an adequate temporal balance in a bank's portfolio and operating markets for bank assets, there is no reason to suppose that a bank with some long-term loans is substantially less liquid than one with nothing but short-term notes in its portfolio. But during the 1840s there were few markets for bank assets and the bankers had only the haziest ideas of adequate balance. For better or worse, the experience of the 1840s convinced both bankers and the legislatures that regulated their activities that long-term loans were "bad." In the 1840s they may have been so, but the policies that grew out of that period severely restrained the activities of the banks long after the conditions of the 1840s had disappeared.

The 1840s were thus marked by a change in bank portfolios that saw banks' lending activities more and more restricted to short-term commercial credit. This change was underwritten both by the passage of restrictive bank regulations by state legislatures (the Forestall Act in Louisiana, for example) and by the establishment of "sound banking" canons that tended to govern the behavior of commercial bankers for over a century. As a result, commercial banks were almost entirely excluded from the long end of the capital market, and their capital-accumulation and mobilization activities were largely restricted to the short end. Only in the past 30 years, for example, have commercial banks become an important force in the home mortgage market, and only in the last 15 years have they gradually begun to extend long-term credit to business.

Chartering and Regulation

Another characteristic of American banking, and one that not only set it apart from banking in other countries but also had a significant impact on the timing and direction of U.S. economic development, was the primacy of state laws in granting "life" to corporate banks. The first banks were chartered by special acts of the state legislatures, but even after charters became easier to obtain, it was the state governments that granted them. Until 1863, with only two exceptions, all bank charters were issued by state governments. Moreover, unlike those of other corporations, commercial-bank charters limited banks to the state of charter for their deposit, if not their loan, business. Most laws were not even that liberal, and many banks were not permitted statewide operation. Even today, while California and North Carolina permit unrestricted branch banking throughout the state, most states restrict the geographical area of operation. In Indiana, for example, branching is, at most, permitted only within counties; branching across townships (a subcounty unit) is permitted only if the bank wanting to establish a branch can show "need"—which the bank commissioners have defined as the absence of any other bank. Some states prohibit any branch banking. In Illinois, for example, a bank cannot have a branch that is not physically connected to the main office, and it took a State Supreme Court ruling to permit one bank to maintain a drive-in branch connected to the main office at the end of the block by a tunnel.

In 1863 the National Banking Act authorized federal charters for banks satisfying certain conditions. The act itself says nothing about branches, and it should have been possible under its terms to establish national branch banking similar to the systems currently operating in Canada and the United Kingdom. With national branching, one of the worst defects of the American banking system could have been overcome, since the system would have allowed the commercial banks themselves to effect capital mobilization at the national level.

With few exceptions, however, successive Comptrollers of the Currency (the official charged with supervision of the national banks under the National Banking Act) not only have shown a willingness to go along with state laws but also have gone out of their way to support them. With few exceptions (and no Comptroller has been willing to rewrite the rules), the Comptroller has never hesitated to affirm the dictum that to permit national banks broader geographical coverage than those of the state banks in the area that they serve would be to provide "unfair competition." Moreover, while interbank lending could have effected capital mobilization across regional boundaries, it would have undercut the monopoly position of banks in high-interest regions. Throughout most of the last quarter of the nineteenth century, the Comptroller took a strong stand against such loans; and in annual report after annual report, he warned of the hazards of such relationships and slapped the wrists of the bankers engaged in these "dangerous" transactions. In the recent past, James J. Saxson's suggestion that national banks be permitted to branch across state lines engendered such a political storm that the proposal was quickly dropped. Thus, in 1971 the area in which a bank (be it state or national) can operate was still limited by the whims of the state legislature, and in some cases (e.g., Illinois) the area is very small indeed.

What are the economic costs of these limitations? The record suggests that for the first four fifths of the nineteenth century they were probably quite high. More recently, however, certain innovations in other institutions have reduced them substantially. Banks could, of course, always make loans anywhere they wanted. They were prohibited only from opening branch offices and conducting deposit business. Aside from foregone interest, the major costs of any loan include the costs of search for potential borrowers, the costs of credit investigation, and the administrative costs of closing and collection. All three of these latter costs can be reduced if they are carried on as part of a complete banking operation. If, however, they must be supported at a distance from the bank itself, they may become prohibitively expensive. The costs interfere little with the ability of the commercial-banking system to generate involuntary savings, but they do tend to prevent the banks from effectively mobilizing this capital across regional boundaries.

Capital Mobilization

While it has been only in the recent past that the commercial banks have made a substantial contribution to interindustry mobilization, institutional changes in the last third of the nineteenth century made it possible for them to effect interregional transfers with a fair degree of efficiency by World War I. The principal new institution was the commercial-paper market. That market permitted banks in capital-deficit areas to sell their commercial paper (the IOUs they received in their short-term loan transactions) for cash (and therefore, by replenishing their reserves, enabled them to make additional loans) and for banks in capital-surplus areas to buy the paper from the high-interest areas (and, as a result, to earn more than they could had they been limited to making local loans). The market itself was first organized in the 1840s (and there is some evidence of informal transactions ten years earlier), but it was restricted to the eastern United States. In the 1870s the old Northwest Territory was brought into the market and, while it never had an important impact in the South, from that date the market moved westward at a fairly steady pace. By the first decade of the twentieth century, it effectively spanned the continent.

The importance of the market in the process of mobilization is reflected in the history of East–West interest differentials. Wide differences were characteristic of the economy before the market had penetrated (in the 1870s, 3 percent after-loss rates in the East compared with rates of 13 percent in California). After market organization, however, rates between eastern and western cities equalized within a year or two, and rates in rural areas tended to fall into line within five years as the commercial-paper firms established in western cities gradually extended their coverage. By 1910, with the exception of the South, the new institution had circumvented the banking laws, and the commercial banks in conjunction with the market were able to contribute to the process of interregional capital mobilization. The process had, however, not been instantaneous (it took, after all, almost a century) and the economic costs were 100 years of inefficient mobilization.

In the last 50 years another development has made the commercial-paper market almost obsolete. While national branch banking could effect interregional transfers directly, the same result could be accomplished if borrowing firms (or some substantial proportion of them) had offices in all regions. The past half-century has seen the rise of the national firm, and these firms, able to borrow in one region and use the funds in another, have made spatial mobilization possible without the intercession of a special market. In 1880 only Standard Oil was able to borrow in New York to finance its Cleveland refineries; but by the 1960s any of several thousand firms were able to underwrite operations in any part of the country with finance borrowed in some other region.

Ease of Entry

Since the number of banks can affect the money supply and through it the volume of involuntary savings and the price level, the ease with which new banks can (or cannot) enter the industry is important. Historically, more banks have meant more reserves and therefore a larger money supply [Equation (1)].[13] As mentioned, until the late 1830s, banks could be given corporate

---

[13] It is, of course, possible that one bank may have the same dollar level of reserves as the total of a large number of competing banks, but given the rules against branch banking, in the United States more banks have meant more geographical coverage and, as a result, more reserves (reserves that arise either from cash deposits or from equity sales).

life only through a special act of a state legislature. As one might surmise, during this period the growth of the commercial-banking sector was slowed by this requirement, which made charters both slow and expensive to procure. The difficulties are nicely summarized in Aaron Burr's attempts to obtain a charter. He was able to get the required law through the New York legislature only after he disguised it as a bill to charter a corporation to supply water to the city. And again, a caricature is seen in the Mormons' attempts to gain a charter for a bank in Ohio: since they were turned down, they opened an "antibank" instead.[14] This state of events meant monopoly profits for those banks that could obtain charters, and it certainly limited the role that the commercial banks could play in the accumulation of capital.

In a growing economy, there was continual pressure for an easing of chartering laws. This pressure came both from potential bankers thirsting after a share of the profits and from businessmen who wanted more and cheaper loans. The period from the late 1830s to the 1870s was marked by a gradual easing of the restrictions on entry. In particular, this easing was associated with the general diffusion of the institution of free banking and the passage of the National Banking Act.

Free banking acts, first passed in 1838 in New York and Michigan, took the power of bank incorporation away from the legislature and made it possible (in theory at least) for any group of individuals to obtain a bank charter merely by filing a notice of intent with the Secretary of State. Once innovated, the laws were diffused through the East and West in the decades before the Civil War and in the South in the postbellum decades. The result was a dramatic increase in the number of banks and also apparently, since banks were chartered where there had been no banks before, in the size of the commercial-banking sector. Since total reserves were greater and many of the new banks were located in areas characterized by substantial demands for banking services, entry yielded more bank money and a higher rate of involuntary saving.

Changes in federal law, too, altered the conditions of entry and, therefore, the number of banks. The National Banking Act, by opening an alternative route to charter, should have eased entry somewhat—particularly in those states that still did not permit free banking. The amendment of 1865, however, had the opposite intent and effect. The revision placed a 10 percent tax on state bank notes (the most common form of bank money), and this tax forced state banks to take a federal charter or to exit from the industry. In states with loose banking regulations, either course of action reduced the volume of bank money. If a state bank (either existing or potential) chose to take a national bank charter, it was forced to conform to higher capital requirements, and this stipulation must certainly have reduced the number of banks. At the same time, in many instances the reserve requirements established for national banks were higher than those that had prevailed for state banks. As Equation (1) suggests, this increase almost certainly reduced the amount of bank money that any dollar of reserves could support. The closing of a bank transforms

[14] The "antibank" issued antibank notes and acted in all other ways just like a bank—in fact, the courts held that, despite its title, it was a bank.

"high-powered" reserve money[15] into cash outside of banks (if this money is not redeposited in another bank) and, if the banks are even partially loaned up, probably reduces the total amount (bank and cash) of money in circulation.

It is hard to determine whether the authors of the National Banking Act thought that the law would restrict or support bank growth; however, in the decade after 1865, it almost certainly was restrictive. By the mid-1870s, however, the substitution of demand deposits (an untaxed form of bank money) for bank notes led to a resurgence of state banking. Once state banks could exist along with national banks, a large part of the restrictions imposed by the act on bank growth was removed. Still, since the national banks continued to support the bulk of bank activity, the threat of internal drain imposed by these banks with their higher reserve requirements must have forced the state banks to conform to the expansion limits that they set.

Since the 1870s, state laws have gradually changed to slow the entry of new banks into the system. While free banking is now almost universal (in the sense that state legislatures do not grant charters), bank charters are not as easily obtained as charters for other corporations. It is common for a potential banker to have to prove financial stability and to justify his proposal by demonstrating that the community "needs" another bank. Need is most often undefined, but existing banks (who, after all, do not want more competitors) are given a chance to show that such need does not exist. The net result is frequently to make entry more difficult and to slow the growth of the number of banks and, perhaps, the total volume of bank money.

Since 1933, the Federal Deposit Insurance Corporation has also served as an additional screen for not only national but also state bank charters.[16] The FDIC was established not to police state banks, but to provide deposit insurance. As it has actually functioned, however, since it is extremely difficult for an uninsured bank to operate, FDIC approval is an almost necessary step in the formation of a new bank. FDIC stability rules have almost certainly limited the number of new state banks in the past 30 years, and again this limitation has affected the processes of capital accumulation and mobilization.

In summary, then, the past century and a half has seen a great deal of growth (both absolute and relative) in the size of the commercial-banking sector. This growth has certainly resulted in the banks' underwriting a substantial volume of involuntary savings, although the magnitude of that stream is still in doubt. On the other hand, certain forces have also been at work that have tended to limit the role that the banks have been able to play in the processes of capital accumulation and mobilization. These have taken the form of restrictions (both legal and managerial) in the types of assets that banks can hold, in the area over which banks are permitted to operate, and in the ease of entry to the industry. A number of institutions have also emerged whose function is to limit the amount of bank money that any single bank can support, and it is to the growth of these regulatory institutions that we now turn.

---

[15] In Milton Friedman's terms, reserves are "high-powered money."
[16] The FDIC was established as part of the emergency banking legislation in the early days of the New Deal.

THE GROWTH OF BANK REGULATION

As we have seen, the process of involuntary saving involves income redistribution through changes in the price level. While these changes benefit borrowers, they certainly do not benefit the consumers—at least immediately. Moreover, when banks reduce their lending, the result is a decline in prices. If all that decline involves is a redistribution away from borrowers and toward consumers, it may give that group a chance to recapture their savings. It is, however, possible that these reductions may go further and cause a decline in output and employment in addition to the price falls [$Q_i + Q_c$ in Equation (5) is upper but not lower bounded]. Finally, any multiple expansion based on fractional reserves—be it in bank notes, demand deposits, or some other form of money—cannot survive a general attempt to substitute specie for bank money. This fact makes the system very vulnerable to short-term financial crises. Thus the whole process of involuntary saving resting on the ability of the commercial banks to create money is inherently destabilizing.

Since there are always some sectors in the economy that must bear the costs of this instability, and since these are not always the same groups that reaped the benefits of the involuntary saving, it is not surprising that there have been attempts to regulate the banks to minimize instability. The liquidity problem (the inability of a bank to meet the demand of its depositors for cash) affects borrowers, banks, and consumers, and any easing of liquidity crises tends to help everybody. The instability of prices, output, and employment that comes from the redistribution of income may aid banks and borrowers, but it injures consumers. However, any attempt to regulate banks to minimize these destabilizing effects makes it less possible for banks to affect involuntary saving. A banking system based on 100 percent reserves is perfectly stable, every loan is fully backed, no bank money is created, and there can be no effect on the price level; but it provides no capital accumulation, since it acts only to mobilize the savings of its depositors. American financial history in one dimension can be viewed as a tug-of-war between those who want more rapid accumulation and those who desire economic stability. Postponing for the moment the discussion of those institutions that have emerged to provide greater liquidity, let us examine this legal tug-of-war.

Reserve Requirements

In the absence of any legal reserve requirement, the ratio of reserves to deposits [RR in Equation (1)] is determined by the banker's estimate of the cash drain that his loan activities will generate. The more a bank can insulate itself from these drains, the greater the amount of bank money that can be supported on any given level of reserves. In the early nineteenth century there were no legal reserves. As a result, banks in areas in which competition was present (cities) found their loan activities severely restricted compared to banks in rural areas. In this environment, regulation frequently took the form of new institutional arrangements that increased the threat of drain on these "insulated" banks.

The first successful attempt to regulate some insulated banks dates back to 1819–1821, and the organization of the Suffolk system by the banks of Boston. That cooperative institution was the city banks' response to the "unfair" competition of the country banks. Country banks were able to provide more loans at lower rates of interest than the city banks with their higher reserve requirements. The system itself was relatively simple. Banks in the city would pool their holdings of the notes of country banks that were pursuing a "too liberal" lending policy and suddenly present these pooled notes for payment. Since the country bank had too little specie to make such a payment, it was forced to come to terms with the city banks or face bankruptcy. This type of blackmail was very effective. Not only did the Suffolk banks manage to increase the reserve ratios of their country competitors, but they were also able to force the country banks to hold their reserves as deposits in the city banks. One result was a very stable monetary system in New England—so stable, in fact, that only in that region did all local bank notes pass at par. Another result was greater profits for the Boston banks. But there were also costs. Among them were lower profits for country banks and, more important, significantly fewer total loans and therefore less involuntary saving.

What the Suffolk system managed in New England the Second Bank of the United States could have managed for the economy as a whole. That bank was the nation's largest financial institution and was in a position to bring any other bank to its knees. Moreover, since its charter permitted it to branch in any state, it was in a position to administer policy cheaply. This power was, of course, not spelled out in the bank's charter, and during its first years of operation no one could conclude that it had pursued such a policy. In fact, it tended to be among the most liberal of the lending institutions. Under its third President, Nicholas Biddle, however, the bank began to act as a regulatory agency attempting to minimize bank-induced inflations. Bankers in the 1830s argued that this action may have been the result of the bank's desire to eliminate competition, but in part it is clear that Biddle thought that the bank should act to stabilize the economy.

While many historians still maintain that the Jackson–Biddle fight over recharter was a result of Jackson's hard-money attitude, recent study has indicated that the opposite was the case. Jackson listened to the group of largely eastern bankers and businessmen who wanted to be free to pursue an easy-lending, high-accumulation policy even if the costs involved substantial short-run instability. The recharter fight was directed at removing an institution that could maintain stability, and it represents one of the few victories for the forces supporting higher rates of involuntary savings and growth in all of U.S. history.

Even before the demise of the Second Bank, those groups interested in regulating the activities of the commercial banks had begun to talk of legal reserve requirements. By requiring that banks hold a certain portion of their bank money in the form of specie reserves, it was generally assumed that the loan activities of the banks could be limited (which was true) and that the resulting system would be less subject to short-term instability (which was not necessarily true). Reserve requirements, then as now, were minimum require- ments, and there was no mechanism offered to change the legal ratios with ease. Thus, there was nothing in the system that could ease the decline in output and employment that could follow from a rapid contraction of loans by the commercial banks. The panic of 1834, for example, may have been touched off by the loan contraction that was Biddle's last shot in the bank war.

The first mention of legal reserves appears in 1828 in the Safety Fund Act in New York, but those requirements were seldom enforced. The trend, how- ever, had been set. The New York and Michigan Free Banking Acts both contained provisions for legal reserves, and the Forestall Act in Louisiana had even more stringent requirements. The effectiveness of the legal reserve requirements were largely a function of the state regulatory bodies, and as they diffused across the country, state-to-state differences developed. In Louisiana, for example, the requirements were enforced very strictly, and the results were stable banks (the Louisiana banks did not suspend during the panic of 1857) but a lower rate of capital accumulation. On the other hand, the Michigan bank examiners frequently reported that the same coins appeared in the reserves of one bank after another's as the examiners moved across the state. In this case, it does not appear that the legal change had much impact on the rate of capital accumulation, but faster accumulation was pur- chased at the price of less stability. Nor were all these stories products of the early nineteenth century. As late as 1916, an Illinois banker was jailed for having loaned his reserves to a new bank down the street so that they could satisfy the examiners. Now, of course, legal reserves are part of every state's banking laws, and there is much less room to maneuver around enforcement.

Nationwide uniform regulation, however, was a product of the Federal Reserve System. The panic of 1907 and the specie suspension that accom- panied it gave the "regulators" the impetus they needed to effect a far-reaching set of rules governing commercial-bank activity. Like most political decisions, however, this one took time, and it was 1914 before the regulations were written into the law. By that time the Democratic party had captured both houses of Congress and the executive mansion, and the final legislation reflected the great fear of Wall Street that still dominated the thinking of that party. In place of a single central bank regulating the activities of all commercial banks, there were 12 district banks, each one charged with regulation in some part of the country. The only central institution was the Federal Reserve Board, and its powers were solely advisory. Although the act established reserve requirements for member banks, it gave the 12 Federal Reserve banks no power to alter them. The only control that the district banks had over the level of bank money was their power to set the rediscount rate (the rate at which member banks could borrow additional reserves from the Federal Reserve banks). In Great Britain, where banks have a long history of con- tinuous borrowing from the central bank, such a control has been an effective weapon of monetary policy. In the United States, however, banks had no such history, there was strong moral pressure within the banking community against it, and even the Federal Reserve banks tended to view such loans as privileges rather than rights. Not too surprisingly, therefore, the rediscount rate has been largely ineffective as an agent of monetary policy. While putting some upper limit on bank creation through the reserve requirement, the Federal Reserve Act furthered hardly at all the search for stability. In fact, from the point of view of those who wanted more involuntary savings, the act probably represented a minor victory. The average reserve requirement under the new law was less than it had been under the old National Banking Act.

Despite this inauspicious beginning, during the 1920s the Federal Reserve banks innovated a new regulatory mechanism that permitted them some discretionary powers over the level of commercial-bank activity. The original act had, as an afterthought, permitted each of the 12 district banks to buy and sell government bonds so that they could adjust their portfolios in the face of changing economic conditions. No one thought that there should be any economic impact from these transactions, and as long as the banks acted independently, there was none. In the early 1920s, however, Benjamin Strong, President of the New York Bank, realized that purchases of government bonds increased member-bank reserves and sales reduced them. If the 12 banks could coordinate their transactions, they would have an important effect on the maximum amount of bank money that the commercial-banking system could support [Equation (1)]. Moreover, if, as Equation (2) implies, the banks' loans responded to changes in their reserve position, the money supply, and through it the price level, could be affected. Some question has recently been raised as to the Federal Reserve Bank's understanding of these open-market operations in the 1920s, but there can be no doubt that the system's account (the information network that underlies the purchases and sales) and the Open Market Committee (the institutional arrangement that provided the necessary interbank coordination) were both introduced in this period. Moreover, the operations were used to stabilize the economy during the incipient depressions of 1924 and 1927. It is, however, also true that because of (a) a lack of understanding; (b) a set of inconsistent goals (the New York Federal Reserve Bank, for example, was the recognized leader in the system, and it is not clear that that bank was committed to a policy designed to stop runaway stock prices); (c) the inability of any monetary control to affect the money supply if, as is frequently the case during serious depressions, bankers choose not to lend more; or (d) some combination of the first three factors, open-market operations combined with the power to set the rediscount rate were insufficient to head off or alleviate the depression that followed on the heels of the 1929 crash.[17]

The result of this demonstration of weakness was a complete rewriting of the Federal Reserve Act in 1935. The Bank Act of that year established a single

---

[17] Friedman and Schwartz argue that at least a part of the blame lies with the Federal Reserve Board for taking inappropriate action; Wicker, on the other hand, suggests that the Federal Reserve Board had no understanding of what appropriate action was and that their fault was not one of commission but one of ignorance. See Milton Friedman and Anna Schwartz, *A Monetary History of the United States, 1867–1960* (Princeton: Princeton University Press, 1963); and Elmus Wicker, *Federal Reserve Monetary Policy, 1917–1933* (New York: Random House, 1966).

central bank by making the 12 district banks satellites of the Federal Reserve Board and giving the board the power to affect both the level and the efficiency of bank reserves. Thus, while individual district banks continued to set the rediscount rate, the board was given the power to approve whatever rates they set. In addition, the Open Market Committee was given legal status, but while the committee continued to have 12 members, 7 were now appointed by the board and only 5 were appointed by the district banks. Finally, the board was given the power to set and to change the reserve requirement within very broad limits. Those who supported bank regulation and stability as opposed to easy loans and involuntary savings had definitely triumphed.

The history of the Federal Reserve System since 1935, however, does not indicate that we have managed to solve all our monetary problems, even if our concern is only for stability. In the first place, all the controls remain permissive; and if the bankers do not choose to lend their excess reserves during a depression (and any banker who behaved differently would probably soon be bankrupt), there is no way that changes in the volume or efficiency of reserves can have any effect on the supply of money [Equation (2a) holds, instead of Equation (2)]. This fact became obvious soon after the rewriting of the law. The early attempts of the Federal Reserve Board to substantially increase the supply of money in the depth of the 1930s depression failed completely.[18]

In the second place, all the legislation in the world cannot offset stupidity. Thus, the logic behind the Federal Reserve Board's concern about inflation in 1936 (when the economy still had 9 million workers unemployed), and their actions to increase reserve requirements and to sell bonds on the open market defy logical analysis. In a similar vein, the chairman's concern with depression in 1968 was also something that no amount of economic theory or new laws will ever clarify. Such understanding will have to await a contribution by the psychologists to a theory of institutional behavior.

Increasing Liquidity

The growth-versus-stability conflict has been resolved in favor of stability, but the nineteenth and early twentieth centuries also saw the evolution of a series of institutions that managed to make the system more liquid and less subject to sudden financial crises. In this case everyone gained. The attempts to ease the periodic financial crises that were a characteristic of the economy from as early as 1819 to as late as 1929 have taken two forms. They have been aimed, on the one hand, at preventing the mass substitution of specie for bank money that underlies every panic; and, on the other, at maintaining as much liquidity as possible during periods of general bank suspension. A solution to the first problem would permit banks to hold fewer reserves and therefore to increase the level of their loans, while at the same time reducing

---

[18] The amount of bank deposits increased in the period 1935 to 1939, but by less than the increase in reserves; thus, reserves increased about 60 percent, while deposits rose by only about 33 percent. Moreover, despite increases in the reserve requirement, excess reserves increased about 10 percent over the period.

the probability of violent movements in the level of reserves. A solution to the second would make it possible for banks to continue to support some loans even during a liquidity crisis and a shortage of reserves. The first would tend to reduce the chance of crisis; the latter would mitigate such a crisis if it were to occur.

The set of controls aimed at preventing the substitution of specie for bank money includes the attempts to provide insurance for holders of banking liabilities (notes or deposits). The most famous of the early attempts was the New York Safety Fund system enacted in 1828. Although it did contain some provisions for bank regulation, the law was directed at providing insurance for depositors and note holders. Each bank was required to pay a fraction of its capitalization into the fund, and the fund (or if that was exhausted, the general credit of the state) was to be used to pay the obligations of any defaulting bank.

There were obvious technical difficulties with the law as it was written. The basis for the insurance was clearly wrong, for example. It penalized those banks with the highest capital/bank-note ratios and benefited those with lower ratios. City bankers whose competitive position required that they keep large reserves were very unhappy. Still, if technical details could have been ironed out, the act, by insuring depositors and note holders, should have prevented panic substitutions of specie for bank money. Unfortunately, the claims on the fund during the panic of 1837 and the subsequent depression exhausted it, and the system was thrown onto the general credit of the state. Although the legislature appropriated sufficient funds to make up the deficiency, the cost was more than they had bargained for and the law was not renewed.

Similar schemes were tried in a number of western states in the early years of the twentieth century, but once again the state provided an insufficient basis for insurance.[19] Scheme after scheme died as the agricultural depression of the 1920s led to the bankruptcy of banks with more liabilities than the pools could meet. It was not until 1935 that the federal government stepped in, and the FDIC provided insurance for banks throughout the country. That scheme has successfully convinced depositors not to substitute against bank money, and since its inception, there have been practically no runs on insured banks.

The second line of development was aimed not at preventing runs, but at minimizing their costs once they had begun. In many panics, banks faced with legal reserve requirements found themselves forced to call in loans (and, therefore intensify the collapse) not because they wanted to, but because they found that they could not convert claims on other banks into reserves. In this instance, the organization was not carried out through the government but by a voluntary cooperative association of the banks themselves. Acting through the banks' clearing-house associations, it began to issue clearing-house certificates during periods of bank suspension. The certificates were merely

---

[19] Eight states passed deposit insurance laws between 1908 and 1917.

formal recognition of interbank liabilities that had not been cleared because of the suspension, but the banks treated them like reserves. Although the banks were in technical violation of the law, both the bankers and most state governments were satisfied. The certificates first appeared after the Civil War, and they helped ease every financial panic after 1873. They were widely accepted (in fact, they were sometimes used as hand-to-hand currency), they alleviated at least some of the pressure of the periodic suspensions, and they were made legal reserves for national banks by the Aldrich–Vreeland Act of 1909. However, once the Federal Reserve System could act as lender of last resort, its loans could solve the liquidity problem and the certificates no longer played any role in the economy.

EXOGENOUS INFLUENCES

Thus far we have explicitly assumed that both the sum of bank reserves plus cash and specie outside of the banks $(R + c)$ and the velocity of money $(1/k)$ were constant. However, a great deal of American financial history has been written about changes in parameters, and it appears worthwhile to talk about the effect of some exogenous events on them. In particular, let us focus on three developments in the American economy: the California Gold Rush, the battles over bimetallism and free silver, and the growth of nonbank intermediaries.

The discovery of gold at Sutter's Mill in 1848 touched off a rush of people to California and a rush of gold from California to the eastern states. While some of the new gold flowed overseas to help pay for additional imports, part of it became net additions to the supply of money. Since nothing affected the public's desire to hold specie, it appears that a substantial portion of the increase flowed into the reserves of the commercial banks. Had the specie been left in circulation, the money supply (and therefore income and prices) would have increased, but only in proportion to the increase in the public's holdings of gold. In the case of the deposits in the commercial banks, however, the results were additional reserves with the potential of supporting a multiple increase in the supply of money. Although we know little directly about the banking system's response to these added reserves, they appear to have loaned out a substantial portion of their excess reserves. The period of the late 1840s and 1850s was marked by a steady increase in the price level. The increase, in turn, appears to have gone hand in hand with an increase in the level of involuntary savings—savings that permitted the growth of manufacturing and the expansion of railroad mileage that are so evident in the history of that decade.

From the middle 1880s until the end of the century, the question of free silver was an important issue in almost every election at the local, state, or national level. While the views of the citizens of the silver states represented obvious enlightened self-interest, the most pressing economic reasons for the inflationist agricultural sectors to support free silver had been largely removed almost before the movement had begun. As we have seen, the 1865 amendment to the National Banking Act placed a tax of state bank notes sufficient to force the banks either to accept national bank charters or to exit from the industry. The effect of either action was a reduction in the money supply. In the first years the issue of greenbacks and federal expenditures may have offset some of the most deflationary effects, but within a very short time, prices began to fall and fall rapidly. The Warren–Pearson index of all commodity prices that had reached 193 in 1864 stood at 85 twenty years later. For sectors that were net debtors, there can be little question that political action aimed at reversing the trend should have appeared quite profitable.

As even a casual reader of U.S. history knows, the economy was legally on a bimetallic standard for most of the early nineteenth century; but since gold had been overvalued since the 1830s, there had been almost no monetary silver. In the 1870s, however, new discoveries increased the supply of silver. At the same time the demand for silver was falling as other countries abandoned the silver or bimetallic standard for gold. The result was a fall in silver prices, and, had the old coinage law still been on the books, there certainly would have been a rapid increase in silver coinage and *pari passu* an increase in the money supply. In the interim, however, silver had been demonetized (the "crime of 1873"); thus, there was no increase. Inflationists who wanted more and easier credit began to argue that the free coinage of silver would offset the increases in reserve requirements, make loans easier, and raise prices. The model shows that even if silver had remained as hand-to-hand currency, there would have been an increase in M; and if some of it flowed into the banks and the bankers loaned out even some fraction of their excess reserves, M would have increased by some multiple of the additions to the monetary stock.

The economics of the free-silver argument make good sense; however, by the time "free silver" had become a popular political slogan, the initial conditions had changed and the need was much less urgent. With the widespread innovation of check money, there was a resurgence of state banks— banks that were less subject to the stringent reserve requirements—as well as an increase in the total number of banks, and the money supply increased without the addition of silver to the monetary stock. Thus, between 1870 and 1900 the per capita money supply rose from $323 to $838.[20] While free silver could have produced an even greater increase, the most restrictive limitations of the National Bank and Specie Resumption Acts had been removed by the widespread innovation of check money ten years before William Jennings Bryan was attempting to prevent mankind from being "crucified upon a cross of gold."[21]

Finally, as Chapter 9 outlined, the nineteenth century was marked by the rapid growth of nonbank intermediaries. Although these institutions cannot

[20] These figures are not quite correct, since they include cash outside of banks plus *all* commercial-bank deposits (demand and time). They are, however, the best estimates. Friedman and Schwartz, *op. cit.*, app. A-1.
[21] Checks had, of course, existed since the eighteenth century, and they were common among eastern city businessmen in the early nineteenth century. Widespread use, however, awaited the postbellum decades.

create money, they do increase the velocity of money. Rewriting Equation (4) we can get

$$\frac{1}{k} = \frac{Y}{M}$$

and it becomes obvious that the growth of intermediation, by reducing k, causes Y to increase unless there is some offsetting decline in M. Thus, even nonbank intermediaries can have an effect on output and prices, and their growth may have been in part responsible for the secular price increases that set in after the mid-1890s. Recently some economists have begun to argue that the nonbank intermediaries, like the bank intermediaries, should be regulated in the interest of stability. Our model, however, should make it clear that such regulation is unnecessary even if the goal is stability. An increase in velocity produced by an increase in intermediation can be offset by proper monetary policy aimed at reducing M.

Despite the growth of financial intermediation, over most of the nineteenth century there appears to have been a downward drift in velocity averaging (at least since 1869) about 1 percent a year. While this trend has been reversed in the past two decades, it was characteristic of the American economy over most of its history. Its explanation probably lies both in the relatively high income elasticity of the demand for cash balances (cash balances are a luxury, and as income rises people tend to substitute away from other commodities and toward them) and in the secular downward drift in interest rates that has reduced the opportunity cost of holding such balances. From the point of view of economic stability, the decline in velocity has reduced somewhat the instability engendered by changes in the money supply. As Equation (4) implies (it can be rewritten in terms of changes as $\Delta M/k = \Delta Y$), the smaller the velocity (the larger k), the smaller will be the change in Y associated with any given change in M.

TRENDS AND FLUCTUATIONS IN PRICES

Finally, no financial history of the economy would be complete without some comments on the movements of prices over the past century and two thirds.

As Table 10.1 suggests, while there have been both violent short-term fluctuations and apparent long waves in prices over the course of American history, that history has been characterized by a high degree of secular stability. It would be pleasant to attribute this stability to the effectiveness of monetary policy, but not only has conscious monetary policy been a reasonably recent development, it also has not been particularly effective even since its inception. Sheer accident, in fact, provides a much more reasonable interpretation of the secular pattern. It appears that a long-term downward trend in prices has been offset every half-century or so by a short period of rapid inflation. Moreover, with one exception, each of those inflations has been the result of increases in the money supply effected by the government in its

TABLE 10.1
Wholesale price indexes, all commodities, 1779–1969

Year	Index	Year	Index	Year	Index	Year	Index
1779	226.0	1826	99.0	1873	133.0	1921	142.5
		1827	98.0	1874	126.0	1922	141.2
1780	225.0	1828	97.0	1875	118.0	1923	146.9
1781	216.0	1829	96.0	1876	110.0	1924	143.2
1782	—			1877	106.0	1925	151.1
1783	—	1830	91.0	1878	91.0	1926	146.0
1784	—	1831	94.0	1879	90.0	1927	139.3
1785	92.0	1832	95.0			1928	141.2
1786	90.0	1833	95.0	1880	100.0	1929	139.1
1787	90.0	1834	90.0	1881	103.0		
1788	—	1835	100.0	1882	108.0	1930	126.1
1789	86.0	1836	114.0	1883	101.0	1931	106.6
		1837	115.0	1884	93.0	1932	94.6
1790	90.0	1838	110.0	1885	85.0	1933	96.2
1791	85.0	1839	112.0	1886	82.0	1934	109.4
1792	—			1887	85.0	1935	116.8
1793	102.0	1840	95.0	1888	86.0	1936	118.0
1794	108.0	1841	92.0	1889	81.0	1937	126.0
1795	131.0	1842	82.0			1938	114.8
1796	146.0	1843	75.0	1890	82.0	1939	112.6
1797	131.0	1844	77.0	1891	81.5		
1798	122.0	1845	83.0	1892	76.2	1940	112.7
1799	126.0	1846	88.0	1893	78.0	1941	125.2
		1847	90.0	1894	69.6	1942	141.5
1800	129.0	1848	82.0	1895	71.2	1943	148.0
1801	142.0	1849	82.0	1896	67.9	1944	149.1
1802	117.0			1897	68.0	1945	151.7
1803	118.0	1850	84.0	1898	70.8	1946	173.2
1804	126.0	1851	83.0	1899	76.2	1947	212.7
1805	141.0	1852	88.0			1948	230.1
1806	134.0	1853	97.0	1900	81.9	1949	218.8
1807	130.0	1854	108.0	1901	80.7		
1808	115.0	1855	110.0	1902	86.0	1950	227.4
1809	130.0	1856	105.0	1903	87.0	1951	253.4
		1857	111.0	1904	87.2	1952	246.3
1810	131.0	1858	93.0	1905	87.7	1953	242.9
1811	126.0	1859	95.0	1906	90.2	1954	243.4
1812	131.0			1907	95.2	1955	244.2
1813	162.0			1908	91.8	1956	252.0
1814	182.0	1860	93.0	1909	98.9	1957	259.4
1815	170.0	1861	89.0			1958	263.0
1816	151.0	1862	104.0	1910	102.8	1959	263.6
1817	151.0	1863	133.0	1911	94.8		
1818	147.0	1864	193.0	1912	100.9	1960	263.8
1819	125.0	1865	185.0	1913	101.9	1961	262.8
		1866	174.0	1914	99.4	1962	263.6
1820	106.0	1867	162.0	1915	99.4	1963	262.8
1821	102.0	1868	158.0	1916	124.8	1964	263.3
1822	106.0	1869	151.0	1917	171.6	1965	268.6
1823	103.0			1918	191.7	1966	277.5
1824	98.0	1870	135.0	1919	202.4	1967	278.0
1825	103.0	1871	130.0			1968	284.8
		1872	136.0	1920	225.4	1969	296.1

SOURCES: U.S. Bureau of the Census, *Historical Statistics of the United States* (Washington: U.S. Government Printing Office, 1960, 1965), Tables E-1 and E-13; and U.S. Bureau of the Census, *Statistical Abstract of the United States, 1970* (Washington: U.S. Government Printing Office, 1970), p. 339, Table 517.

attempt to finance a war. It was apparently the War of 1812, the Civil War, and World Wars I and II that created the inflationary movements and established the new base from which the deflationary bias of productivity gradually went to work. The same pattern began after World War II, but the continued Cold War coupled with a greater government concern about full employment has led to almost stable prices for the two postwar decades—a stability that was broken only by the inflation associated with the Vietnam conflagration.

The sole exception to this pattern was the relatively slow rise in prices that marked the period from 1896 to the beginning of World War I. Even here, however, the explanation probably lies not in any structural change in the American financial sector, but rather in the changing balance-of-payments position of the United States coupled with the gold discoveries in Alaska and South Africa, which greatly increased monetary reserves.

Since the entire period was characterized by a rapid expansion in both the number of banks and the money supply (both absolutely and relative to population), the fact that prices still tended downward between wartime highs suggests the strength of the productivity gains that apparently underwrote that decline. The downward price drift also suggests the importance of the "relative" inflation alluded to earlier. If one were restricted to the view that the impact of the banks and other credit-creating agencies was limited to actual price increases, it would be difficult to argue that such institutions had engendered any involuntary savings. Given, however, what we know about increases in the money supply, we can be certain that in the absence of these financial developments the deflation would have been much more rapid. Thus, the impact of banks on the level of savings is, in fact, masked by the productivity movements.

SUGGESTED READING

Bloomfield, Arthur. *Monetary Policy Under the International Gold Standard, 1880–1914.* New York: Federal Reserve Bank of New York, 1959.

Chandler, Lester V. *Benjamin Strong: Central Banker.* Washington: Brookings Institution, 1958.

Friedman, Milton, and Anna Schwartz. *A Monetary History of the United States, 1867–1960.* Princeton: Princeton University Press, 1963.

Goldenweiser, Emanuel. *American Monetary Policy.* New York: McGraw-Hill, 1951.

Hammond, Bray. *Banks and Politics in America from the Revolution to the Civil War.* Princeton: Princeton University Press, 1957.

Smith, W. B. *Economic Aspects of the Second Bank of the United States.* Cambridge, Mass.: Harvard University Press, 1951.

Trescott, Paul. *Financing American Enterprises.* New York: Harper & Row, 1963.

Wicker, Elmus. *Federal Reserve Monetary Policy, 1917–1933.* New York: Random House, 1966.

part IV
INDUSTRIES AND ACTIVITIES IN THE PRODUCTION PROCESS

11
AGRICULTURE

Much of American agrarian history is not ready for textbook treatment—and much can never be unraveled from the extant materials. The difficulty lies partly in the immense regional differences, the complex technology, the vast numbers of enterprises. Accompanying size, variety, and unregulated organization is a lack of data. The only comprehensive source of nineteenth-century microeconomic data, the manuscript returns of the federal censuses, exists only for 1840 through 1880; the scope and reliability of the information conveyed is not all that a modern sample survey would desire; and the scientific utilization of it in economic history is in its infancy.[1] The only other sources of information are farm documents (diaries and account books), which even for the southern plantations are not very abundant or revealing; the farm newspapers, which flourished in the middle and late nineteenth century; the reports of state and county agricultural societies; and the publications of the departments of agriculture of the various states and of the U.S. government. Thus materials do exist for the individual enterprises, for local groups of producers who faced similar problems, and for the study of agriculture as a branch of engineering and as a national industry. This chapter draws on all these sources and on the studies based on them. The model implicit in the discussion in the following three sections of this chapter is that of a competitive industry of small-scale producers making decisions with respect to location, product, factor use, and techniques within the larger natural, social, and technological environment of nineteenth- and twentieth-century America. The fourth and sixth sections examine why such an organization arose and persisted in this environment and at what points it broke down. The fifth section shows the income and welfare results of this activity for the farmers themselves. The larger question of the effects of the production responses in agriculture on

---

[1] Use has been made of these records by the agricultural historians, James Malin and Allan Bogue and Margaret Bogue, and by Frank Owsley and his students. Recently a sample of cotton farmers drawn from the 1860 census returns has served as the basis of a group of studies [*Agricultural History*, vol. 44 (January 1970)].

the growth of the economy as a whole is best examined in conjunction with the other studies in this volume, and so is not explicitly treated here.

We may focus first on the elements in the massive opportunity for expansion and productivity increase which American agriculture has enjoyed over the past two centuries. Three main lines of opportunity can be identified:

1. The availability of new lands in the West, with new conditions of soil, terrain, and climate
2. The growth of markets for farm products, both abroad and at home, on farms and in cities; and, in conjunction with this market growth, the transport improvements and geographically more perfect factor markets which encouraged regional specialization
3. The improvements in technical knowledge of farming, fertilizers, and mechanical equipment

Each of these elements has a history of its own. The western lands attracted continuous *westward movement* from the first settlements until the exhaustion of the usable public domain in the 1910s. *Market growth* began in the colonies with the demand for tobacco and rice from the South; codfish and timber from New England; and dried beef, barreled pork, and flour shipped from the middle colonies to the sugar islands of the West Indies. The urban and industrial growth on both sides of the Atlantic, and the drastic transport changes of the nineteenth century, commercialized agriculture rapidly and thoroughly—not only in America but in the world at large. *Technical change* has been a human activity since the prehistoric origins of agriculture, but the union with basic science developed only after 1850 and began to reap a rich reward after 1940. All three elements are interwoven in U.S. agricultural history. The adaptation of seeds, breeds, and practices, for example, was a technical change accompanying and accelerating the westward movement, and the growth of trade diffused the knowledge and materials on which technical improvement in agriculture depended.

Looked at each in isolation and decade by decade, the westward movement, market growth, and technical change all appear to have been subject to sudden spurts. Figure 11.1 shows roughly the historical course of these lines of opportunity. The traditional colonial markets were cut off by the Embargo Act of 1808. The cotton gin (1793) thrust new supplies into world markets after 1820. The Erie Canal, breaking a transport bottleneck in 1825, put western lands in direct reach of eastern markets. The mechanical reaper, invented in 1834, was diffused rapidly in the 1860s. The foreign market for wheat, pork, and beef expanded in the decades from 1870 to 1900. The frontier as defined in the federal census closed in 1890. These spectacular events might be supposed to have had a revolutionary impact on agricultural history. They are so numerous, however, and the processes of change are so interwoven in the lives and production decisions of farmers, that their combined result, from the perspective of two centuries, is one of continuity, of gradual, steady expansion and improvement. Until 1940, no combination of

FIGURE 11.1
Historical succession of expansion opportunities, 1630–1970

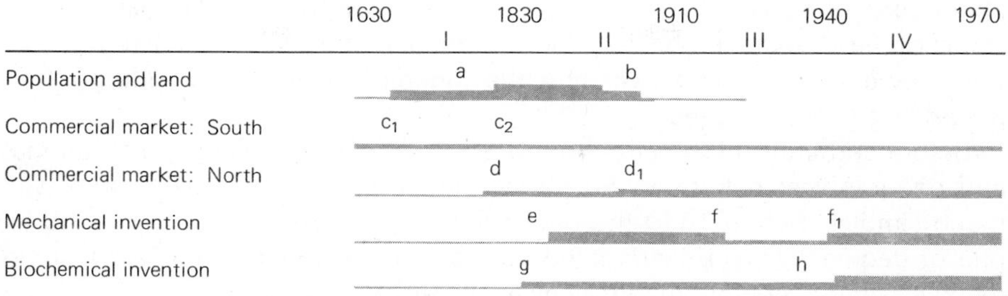

	1630	1830	1910	1940	1970
	I	II	III	IV	
Population and land	a	b			
Commercial market: South	c_1	c_2			
Commercial market: North	d	d_1			
Mechanical invention	e	f	f_1		
Biochemical invention	g	h			

			Periods		Active Elements
a	Western lands opened up		I	1630–1830	Population and land
					Colonial markets
b	End of "frontier"				Tobacco and food
c_1	Tobacco		II	1830–1850	Expansion of land supply
					Cotton market in North and abroad
c_2	Cotton				General market growth in North
					Transport change
d	Transport improvements, urban growth				Random improvement
d_1	Refrigerated transport		IIa	1850–1910	Expansion into new land
					Market growth in North and abroad
e	Reaper, thresher, and cultivator				Transport change
					Mechanization
f	Tractor				Random improvement
f_1	Cotton and corn harvesters, small combine		III	1910–1940	Tractorization
					Random improvement
g	Random improvement		IV	1940 . . .	Market growth
					Further mechanization
h	Organized research payoff				Biochemical invention and diffusion

SOURCE: U.S. Bureau of the Census, *Historical Statistics of the United States*, Series K–156 (Washington: U.S. Government Printing Office, 1960, 1965), p. 43.

the elements of change occurred so intense, cumulative, and restricted in time as to produce a drastic break with the past in less than a generation.

Figure 11.1 is an effort to show schematically the major breaks in the overlapping processes which have permitted the expansion of output and productivity. For westward expansion the 1890s were terminal, with an afterglow of expansion in acreage within the settled frontier in response to wartime demands in the 1910s. Particularly following the transport improvements after 1830, and the growth of urban markets in the Northeast, overseas, and in the midwest itself, westward movement occurred in a sharply intensified commercial environment. Between 1830 and 1850, too, mechanical invention in grain harvesting and improved horse-drawn implements for the row crops, corn and cotton, made themselves strongly felt. By the 1890s the possibilities of horse-drawn technology were nearly played out. These overlapping trends in the three major elements of opportunity in 1830–1890 account for its particularly intense character. In these central decades, inventions occurred along with extensive expansion and market growth. Economies of scale and regional specialization were mingled with higher yields on new lands and higher labor productivity through the substitution of horsepower for human power and the ingenious devices for putting that power to a variety of uses.

Before and after these central decades, in which the essential institutional and geographical pattern of American agriculture was set, the picture was much simpler. Before 1830 the difference was not so much one of kind as one of degree. Western lands filled up, commercial markets appeared, some technical improvements made themselves felt. But without the railroad, the steamship, the reaper, and the massive urban demands for grain and meat, the processes of change moved slowly; and marked and sustained rises in productivity almost certainly did not occur.

The period from 1910 to 1940 marks another lull in the processes of change, disturbed by only one major development—the replacement of animal power by the tractor. The tractor speeded up field operations, saved labor, and permitted machinery to do some jobs which previously could not be done at all. At the same time, by substituting gasoline for hay and oats, it released within four decades 90 million acres of crop land (one quarter of the acreage under cultivation) to other uses. Thus, although the expansion of acreage ended in the 1910s, this one invention expanded by roughly one third the acreage available for dairy pasture and food crops. No better example of the complex interrelations among developments in our three lines of opportunity could be imagined.

These main developments then may be conceived of schematically as producing the periodization shown in Figure 11.1, as follows:

1. 1630–1830: Simple expansion, combined with production responses to market opportunities—for the South, in tobacco, rice, and indigo to Europe; for the Middle states, in food to the West Indies; for New England, in fish and timber to the mother country
2. 1830–1910: Complex patterns of opportunity, including: (a) continued expansion and settlement, under improving technology of settlement; (b) enormous growth in the size and complexity of markets, with continued shifts among optimal locations and crop patterns set by changes in market location, transport, and the pull of both the West and the cities on farm labor; and (c) horse-powered mechanical technology affecting operations in field and barn to various degrees
3. 1910–1940: Little expansion in total land supplies, unstable but not strongly expanding markets, minor technical improvement, replacement of animal by mechanical power
4. 1940–present: Expansion and increased complexity of markets, striking improvements in mechanical and nonmechanical technology

Taken together, these trends represent the movements in the opportunity that faced American farmers, that bounded their activity and invoked their response. That farmers responded with considerable vigor and perspicacity is shown by the record of production and productivity growth, which several observers have recently tried to measure.[2]

Developments since 1940 are of a wholly different order from all that has gone before. Figure 11.2 shows the nature of this break in land and labor productivity up to 1960, and data since that date show that the technical revolution in American agriculture has not yet come to an end. Its sharpness and suddenness, and its widespread ramifications in all branches of production, appear to be the result of two features of the modern environment: (a) the massive application of scientific methods to the life processes with which agriculture is concerned, and (b) the reduction in the risks of innovation and the corresponding increase in the speed with which improvements can be diffused. It may be noted, too, that as communication improves and as the number of decision-making units in agriculture falls, the task of diffusion is simplified. Thus a beneficent cumulative process has been set to work in modern agriculture, the end of which has not yet been reached in America, much less in the world at large.

The developments since 1940 are the payoff on a continental scale of the whole U.S. agricultural history: the expansion of a commercially minded farm population over the soil, the development of the institutions and attitudes from which scientific agriculture could grow, and the raising of productivity and national wealth to levels at which capital formation—in the soil, in equipment, in ideas, and in the training of human beings—could proceed.

The connection between agriculture and the rest of the economy is usually judged by agriculture's performance in three respects: (a) the provision of food and fiber to final consumers, (b) the release of manpower to nonfarm employment, and (c) the demand generated on farms for the products of urban and village industry and service industries. Some of these effects are discussed in Chapters 2 and 6 and later in this chapter. Figure 11.3 shows the growth in farm output since the first census of agriculture. Taken in conjunction with Figure 11.2, it shows that increases in output of from 4 to 15 times between 1840 and 1960 have been accompanied by only a sixfold growth in land under cultivation and a growth of 1.7 times in labor employed in agriculture.[3] The difficulties of measuring changes in the quantity of capital over a long period are notorious. Under no condition, however, can it have increased more than fivefold (in constant prices).[4] The great fact in American

---

[2] This measurement has been carried out either by simple calculations of output per unit of the various inputs, by index numbers, or by fitting equations expressing a functional relationship between output and inputs to the data over a period of time. See Glen T. Barton and Ralph A. Loomis, *Productivity of Agriculture: United States, 1870–1958*, U.S. Department of Agriculture Technical Bulletin no. 1238 (Washington: U.S. Government Printing Office, 1961); John W. Kendrick, *Productivity Trends in the United States* (New York: National Bureau of Economic Research, 1961); Lester B. Lave, "Empirical Estimates of Technological Change in United States Agriculture, 1850–1958," *Journal of Farm Economics*, vol. 44 (1962), pp. 941–952; Charles O. Meiburg and Karl Brandt, "Agricultural Productivity in the United States: 1870–1960," *Food Research Institute Studies*, vol. 3, no. 2 (May 1962), pp. 63–85.

[3] The greatest increase in land under cultivation occurred between 1840 and 1930, but this increase was only slightly more than sixfold. However, the greatest increase in the labor force, which occurred between 1840 and 1910, was substantially larger than that which occurred between 1840 and 1960: namely, 3.3 as compared to 1.7.

[4] Using the available data for 1870 and 1950, the increase in capital is approximately 2.7 times. Allowing for large relative increases in capital in the 1840s, 1850s, and 1860s, an estimate of a maximum fivefold increase in capital would still seem reasonable.

FIGURE 11.2
Output per acre and per man-hour in the major crops, 1840–1960

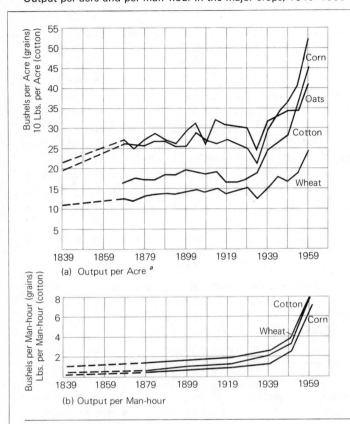

(a) Output per Acre [a]

(b) Output per Man-hour

[a] Estimated trend, 1839–1869, and at five-year intervals thereafter.

SOURCES: Figure 11.2(a)

Corn, oats, and wheat
 1839: William N. Parker and Judith L. V. Klein, " Productivity Growth in Grain Production in the United States, 1840–60 and 1900–10," in *Output, Employment, and Productivity in the United States After 1800*, Dorothy S. Brady (ed.), Studies in Income and Wealth, vol. 30 (New York: National Bureau of Economic Research, 1966), p. 532, Table 1.

Corn
 1869–1959: U.S. Department of Agriculture, *Agricultural Statistics, 1967* (Washington: U.S. Government Printing Office, 1967), pp. 33–35, Table 38. Estimates are five-year averages, centered on the given year, except for 1959, which is a three-year average.

Cotton
 1869–1959: Ibid., pp. 73–74, Table 85. Estimates are five-year averages.

Oats
 1869–1959: Ibid., pp. 44–45, Table 50. Estimates are five-year averages.

Wheat
 1869–1959: Ibid., pp. 1–2, Table 1. Estimates are five-year averages.

SOURCES: Figure 11.2(b)

 1840–1940: U.S. Bureau of the Census, *Historical Statistics of the United States, Colonial Times to 1957*, Series K-87, K-92, and K-97 (Washington: U.S. Government Printing Office, 1960), p. 281.
 1950–1960: U.S. Bureau of the Census, *Historical Statistics of the United States, Colonial Times to 1957, Continuation to 1962 and Revisions*, Series K-87, K-92, and K-97 (Washington: U.S. Government Printing Office, 1960, 1965), p. 42.

FIGURE 11.3
Production in the major crops, 1839–1959/60

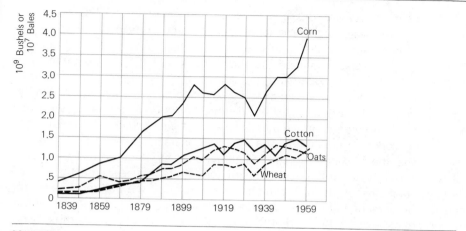

SOURCES

Corn

1839–1859: U.S. Bureau of the Census, *Census of Agriculture: 1959, General Report,* vol. 2, *Statistics by Subjects* (Washington: U.S. Government Printing Office, 1962), Table 2.
1869–1959: U.S. Department of Agriculture, *Agricultural Statistics, 1967, op. cit.,* pp. 33–35, Table 38. Estimates are five-year averages centered on the given year, with the exception of the figure for 1959, which is a three-year average.

Oats

1839–1859: U.S. Bureau of the Census, *Census of Agriculture: 1959...,op. cit.,* p. 681, Table 2.
1869–1959: U.S. Department of Agriculture, *Agricultural Statistics, 1967, op. cit.,* pp. 44–45, Table 50.

Wheat

1839–1859: U.S. Bureau of the Census, *Census of Agriculture: 1959 ..., op. cit.,* p. 681, Table 2.
1869–1959: U.S. Department of Agriculture, *Agricultural Statistics, 1967, op. cit.,* pp. 1–2, Table 1. Estimates are five-year averages.

Cotton

1839–1859: U.S. Bureau of the Census, *Census of Agriculture: 1959 ..., op. cit.,* p. 688, Table 2.
1869–1959: U.S. Department of Agriculture, *Agricultural Statistics, 1956, op.cit.,* pp. 73–74, Table 85. Estimates are five-year averages.

agriculture has been the saving of land, labor, and directly employed capital alike due to productivity increases arising from the sources considered in this chapter. The sensitivity of American agriculture to demand changes and the elasticity of its long-run response are shown also by the changes in the product mix with changing conditions of demand and cost. Closer measurement of the efficiency of the sector through relative price and profitability measures for different products lies beyond the scope of this chapter. A full study of the output and input record, however, would make apparent two major shifts: (a) the shifts in output mix toward products of high income elasticity of demand (beef, dairy products, fruits, and vegetables) as consumers' incomes have risen; and (b) shifts in animal diets from more to less land-using feeds (from range to concentrated feeds) as the country has become more densely settled.

EXPANSION AND REGIONAL SPECIALIZATION

Extensive Expansion

In the great central decades of American agrarian history, 1830–1910, the movement westward onto new lands was continuous. An entire school of American historians, developing the insights first advanced by Frederick Jackson Turner,[5] has examined the social aspects of the movement in some detail—its origins, its rate and incidents, and its effects on American institutions and the American character. Western settlement may also be looked at as an economic process, in which risks were borne in return for knowledge—knowledge of climate, soils, and terrain—which might ultimately be put to work in agriculture.[6] The principal obstacle to settlement was not the Indians, the Mexicans, or the federal land policy. It was ignorance : complete uncertainty about the conditions of agriculture in a new area, the risks of Indian attack, insect plagues, climatic variations, and the nature of soils and terrain. Settlement involved an immense learning process by which these uncertainties were converted into defined, experienced, measurable, and even insurable risks. Planned expeditions and surveys—discussed in Chapter 4—could yield much knowledge, but the process also required the painful experience and accumulated wisdom of a generation of settlers. A productive buffer zone of frontiersmen, trappers, speculators, adventurers, and first settlers lay between the wilderness and settled agricultural production.

Risks, when known, were not necessarily an obstacle to rapid or skillful settlement. With high risks also went high rewards. What was important was that the level of risk should be suited to the gambling instinct of the settlers. The risks had to be brought below the level of Russian roulette ; a modicum of safety from attack by Indians and voracious neighbors was required. In each new area, in the "back country" of the colonies, the "Old Northwest," the territories of the Louisiana Purchase, the Southwest, and California, the institutions of a capitalistic agriculture—a free market in land, and safety to persons and property—were provided. Then an eager population was found to bear the risks of a new area, to try out its soils and climate, and to seek out the commercial markets which its resources could supply. At least before 1830, the danger—from the viewpoint of efficient expansion of the nation's agriculture—was not that migration would be too slow, allowing returns in the East to sink to excessively low levels before migration set in ; it was rather that

[5] Turner's famous essay "The Significance of the Frontier in American History" was presented at the 1893 meeting of the American Historical Association in Chicago. For recent studies of the Turner thesis see Lee Benson, *Turner and Beard: American Historical Writing Reconsidered* (New York : Free Press, 1965) ; and Richard Hofstadter, *The Progressive Historians: Turner, Beard, Parrington* (New York : Knopf, 1968).

[6] Martin L. Primack has computed the new land cleared by type of cover and region for each decade from 1850–1859 to 1900–1909. His totals for the United States are as follows (millions of acres) :

	1830–1839	1860–1869	1870–1879	1880–1889	1890–1899	1900–1909	Total
Forest	39.7	19.5	49.3	28.6	31.0	22.4	190.5
Nonforested	9.1	19.4	48.7	55.7	41.1	51.6	225.6

["Farm Capital Formation as a Use of Farm Labor in the United States, 1850–1910," *Journal of Economic History*, vol. 12 (December 1962).] Primack shows that average labor requirements for clearing land were 32 and 1½ man-days for forested and nonforested land, respectively. The simple movement west in this respect had strong labor-saving effects.

uncertainties would be underrated, risks too eagerly borne, and the East too rapidly emptied out.

Given the qualities of western lands, the effect of migration on the average level of productivity in agriculture depended on how rapidly and in what sequence the lands were taken up. Since average yields per acre in the two major grains—corn and wheat—were not much, if any, higher in the Midwest than in New York and Pennsylvania, the observed direct effect of westward movement, taken alone, on measured productivity growth was probably not very great. But it is hard to imagine how population growth or technological change in the East would have been affected by the absence of western lands. Perhaps a seaboard economy could have followed an English model and developed trade and manufacture while drawing ultimately on agricultural supplies from abroad. In fact, however, the main function of the West was to absorb a portion of the growing eastern farm population. The relative stability of yields in the major crops from earliest record through the late 1930s attests to the success of the West in forestalling diminishing returns until such time as agricultural science could come to the rescue. Figure 11.2 shows the steadiness of yields and labor productivity in the face of the rises in output before 1920.

Market Growth and Specialization

Reduction of the uncertainties and risks of settlement helped bring in new, and sometimes better, land during each decade in the nineteenth century (see Chapter 4). At the same time, after 1830, the growth of concentrated markets and the fall in transport costs had certain productivity-raising effects.

The shifting geographical pattern of crops and the development of specialized regions came about through the interplay of three separate influences: (a) the changing differential in the costs and conditions of transport to concentrated markets for various products, (b) the differing natural suitability of land for various crops, and (c) the changing degree of evenness in the distribution of productive factors—labor and capital—over the land area.

The exact effects of each of these influences have never been sorted out, and the economic history of regional specialization needs closer scrutiny. The three do indeed seem partly to run counter to one another. Transport cost is minimized when perishables are produced nearest the market; bulky, low-value commodities next; and compact, high-value commodities farthest away. From colonial times on, we can identify village gardens and urban hen coops and milksheds, areas of hay production for urban livestock, wheat zones, and farther away the compact, high-value commodities—whisky and preserved pork[7]—beyond which lay the cattle range. On this pattern were

---

[7] Before the railroad, livestock furnished their own transportation, moving in droves on the hoof, eating as they went. They might be raised to adulthood at scattered locations and moved to the market to be fattened. Before much refrigeration or refrigerated transport, slaughtering was a widely diffused activity. Long-distance shipments of fresh meat, which began in 1867, combined with economies of scale in slaughtering to push livestock production away from markets, finally locating it at the great stockyards in Cincinnati, Chicago, Omaha, and Kansas City. Since 1940 a reverse movement pushing slaughtering closer to the range or farm, and the spread of both markets and feed supplies has closed these stockyards and brought livestock production still closer to the sources of feed.

overlaid the effects of the higher labor/land ratios which existed nearer markets strengthening the advantage of dairying—which needed labor—over other animals products, of the perishable truck crops over the staples, while pushing the grazing of sheep and meat animals toward the perimeter of the market area. Some of the westward shifts in regional cropping patterns and variations in techniques were due presumably to the changing distribution of the labor force over the land and the growing perfection of the capital market. However, after 1830, as transport costs fell and labor and capital markets grew more perfect, the natural advantages of regions came through. The areas naturally suited to pasture could be devoted to that use; feed and grain could occupy their large belts; and the areas of special advantage for cotton, tobacco, and vegetables found their advantages reinforced.

It should be noted that the adjustment of cropping patterns to differentials in transport costs between various crops does not increase physical productivity in agriculture itself. Specialized locations to minimize transport-cost inputs would occur even if the land were equally well suited to the production of all crops. Given that all land is not of equal quality, transport-cost minimization and production-cost minimization may run counter to one another. In terms of the physical efficiency of production operations, growth of markets may cause a less productive locational pattern to be utilized. It was then, only the *fall* in transportation costs described in Chapter 13 which freed production from the transport constraint and permitted the regions' natural advantages to have their productivity-raising effects. The more even distribution of the labor force and the integration of a national capital market (described in Chapters 6 and 8) must similarly have had the effect of bringing into play the natural production advantages of the great agricultural regions.

These shifting patterns, theory tells us, must have been present, but the data are not available to measure the effect of these shifts in all their complexity. One small effort to get at this question for the grains is contained in some recent research into hypothetical history. Here the question was asked: How would manhour productivity have altered by 1910 if nothing had changed *except* the redistribution of the crop among regions, at the regional yields and labor inputs of the 1850s? The answer (9 percent for wheat, 23 percent for oats, 30 percent for corn) involves so many hypothetical conditions as hardly to qualify as a statistic at all.[8] Taken together, the gains from westward movement and specialization were probably just sufficient to counteract the pressures of population and markets on the land. They counteracted—with a little net gain—the costs of the spreading out of farming over the land with the resultant long hauls of products to serve concentrated markets.

By the end of our central period in the 1890s, these changes had worked themselves out over the land. Figures 11.4–11.7 show the regional shares of output of the various crops by census districts. In the grains, the distributions

    [8] William N. Parker and Judith L. V. Klein, "Productivity Growth in Grain Production in the United States 1840–60 and 1900–10," in *Output, Employment, and Productivity in the United States After 1800,* Dorothy S. Brady (ed.), Studies in Income and Wealth, vol. 30 (New York: National Bureau of Economic Research, 1966), Table 2.

FIGURE 11.4
Shares of census regions in crop production, corn

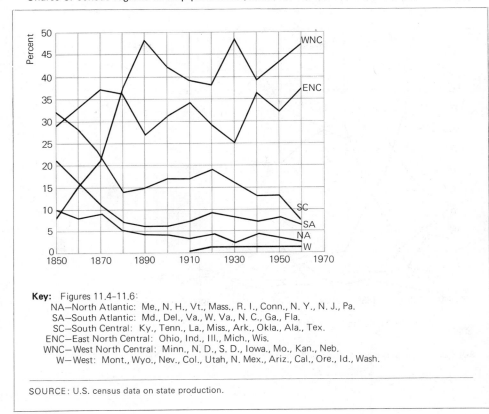

Key: Figures 11.4–11.6:
  NA—North Atlantic: Me., N. H., Vt., Mass., R. I., Conn., N. Y., N. J., Pa.
  SA—South Atlantic: Md., Del., Va., W. Va., N. C., Ga., Fla.
  SC—South Central: Ky., Tenn., La., Miss., Ark., Okla., Ala., Tex.
  ENC—East North Central: Ohio, Ind., Ill., Mich., Wis.
  WNC—West North Central: Minn., N. D., S. D., Iowa., Mo., Kan., Neb.
  W—West: Mont., Wyo., Nev., Col., Utah, N. Mex., Ariz., Cal., Ore., Id., Wash.

SOURCE: U.S. census data on state production.

reached by 1890 have remained approximately stable up to the present. The same is true of the distribution of the dairy herd and of pork production since 1890. In beef production, the loss of open range and the growth of feed grains have permitted somewhat more complex production patterns to emerge. Cotton, too—always a laggard—has continued its shift west, as shown in Figure 11.7, though the western region including Texas has accounted for about 45 percent of the output since 1920. With these two exceptions, one may speak of the character of the main types of farming regions in the United States as established for the various crops between 1890 and 1920. Whether the technological changes, transport changes, and population redistribution of the middle and late twentieth century will break up this pattern in agriculture, as they have done in other areas—for example in heavy industry —remains to be seen.

MECHANICAL INVENTION: SOURCES AND IMPACT

The spread of crops and livestock across the American continent required the reproduction and adaptation of seeds and breeds in new physical environments. The "folk" process of improvement by which this occurred is described

FIGURE 11.5
Shares of census regions in crop production, oats

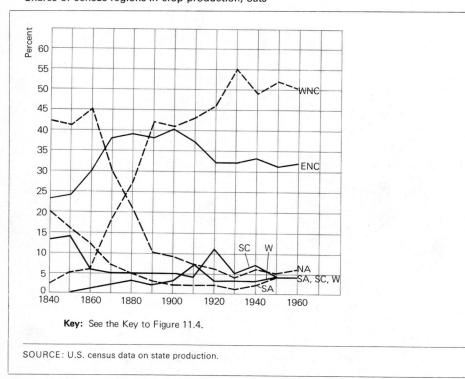

Key: See the Key to Figure 11.4.

SOURCE: U.S. census data on state production.

in the next section. Mechanical invention—the adaptation of implements to new soils and crops—at first involved a not dissimilar process of trial and error in the nineteenth century. The spirit of improvement abroad in the farm population, intensified by market growth, cheap land, and rapid transport, was communicated and enforced by the competitive structure of agriculture. The payoff was greater and came sooner to mechanical improvements in farm operations than to the biochemical processes in farming for a number of reasons rooted in the economic, intellectual, and institutional history of modern times.

The "economic" explanation of the course of American agricultural invention hangs on its adjustment to American factor proportions. An abundance of land and a scarce but strenuous population pressed for the means to save labor, and turned to improving implements and to devising the means by which nonhuman power might be utilized. This explanation—essentially a sociopsychological as well as an economic one—accounts for the widespread

FIGURE 11.6
Shares of census regions in crop production, wheat

Key: See the Key to Figure 11.4.

SOURCE: U.S. census data on state production.

generalized interest in labor-saving improvements. It explains in particular the pressure to save labor at peak periods, as in small-grain harvesting, in which the weather produces a time constraint on the operation. But it does not explain the incidence of mechanical invention from one crop or operation to another, the lags in development of inventions, the specific form of the inventions, or the differences in the speed of their adoption. Moreover, the non-mechanical improvements—increases in yields of seeds and stock—are often both labor- *and* land-saving, and have since 1940 proved as cost-reducing as new machinery.

To understand why tinkering with implements and equipment was a favorite occupation of farmers, and why it paid off so early and so handsomely, we must hypothesize a *supply function* for inventions in which their costs and likelihood of success can be identified.[9] Neither economists nor

[9] This and other points in this section appear also in Chapter 7 on technology, and were developed by the authors in conversation while these chapters were being written.

FIGURE 11.7
Shares of census regions in crop production, cotton

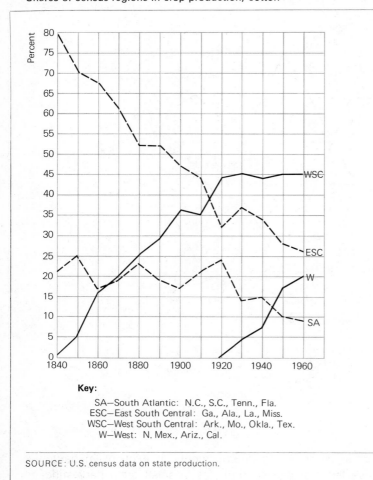

Key:

    SA—South Atlantic: N.C., S.C., Tenn., Fla.
    ESC—East South Central: Ga., Ala., La., Miss.
    WSC—West South Central: Ark., Mo., Okla., Tex.
      W—West: N. Mex., Ariz., Cal.

SOURCE: U.S. census data on state production.

historians of science have done this, but it is clear that, over the range of
economic activities, the mechanical processes yielded more readily to human
contrivance than the more deeply hidden secrets of biochemistry. One can
suggest many reasons; the most direct one is simply that mechanical principles
and relationships are visible to the naked eye, while the observation of
chemical and biological processes requires an advanced scientific technique
and instrumentation. Partly because of this, industrial change in the eighteenth
and nineteenth centuries was largely mechanical in nature. The inventions in
farming were an extension of mechanical engineering that had already found
expression in the making of textiles, shoes, and machinery. Indeed it was the
link with industry which made the mechanical inventions in agriculture so

abundant. Seeds and breeding were matters peculiar to the farm. Earth-moving operations such as plowing, harrowing, and farm building were activities shared with civil engineering and construction; but harvesting, threshing, cotton ginning, and similar semimanufacturing operations performed on the crop could share in the general advance of manufacturing technology.

Inventions in these operations had two further advantages over inventions in seeds, fertilizers, and farm practices. Since they applied to the crop in the later stages of production, they were less dependent on specific situations of soil and climate for success. Seeds are often of no special value beyond a few hundred miles of their locality of origin; breeds adapted to New York may do poorly in Tennessee. But threshing and ginning are nearly the same everywhere. This greater generality of mechanical inventions was accompanied by a second advantage, which they shared with inventions in manufacturing and not with those of agriculture as such. This was their embodiment in specific, marketable forms—and hence their patentability. Improved farm techniques—for example, feeding practices—could not be monopolized or concealed. Nor could new strains of plants or breeds of stock, although the original breeder might retain a temporary advantage. Even in machinery, wherever the work was not beyond the skill of a local blacksmith or craftsman, patents were almost impossible to enforce, as even Eli Whitney discovered. At a certain stage of complexity, however, the production of farm implements required machinery, skills, and business organization; and here as elsewhere in manufacturing, economies of scale in production and market power in merchandizing drove out village workshops and gave an advantage to the larger producer and to the holder of a patent.

By the 1860s the farm machinery industry, concentrated in Illinois with the McCormick Works as its center, had become a large manufacturing industry like any other. The whole apparatus of industrial capitalism—rationalizing production, advertising, merchandizing, giving credit through local dealers, and eventually monopolizing the market somewhat—was brought to bear on this branch of farm technology. The scale of the family farm, discussed below, was probably too small for some machinery; in the case of threshing, this difficulty was overcome by mobile threshing units selling their services from farm to farm or by cooperative arrangements. In other cases, the overcapacity probably did little harm, since the scale of machinery production which it encouraged permitted scale economies and falling prices. Machinery was produced for northern farms in abundance, and the institutions of industrial capitalism—patents, stock companies, factories, and sales organizations—were well adapted to its dissemination. When one compares the histories of the machinery companies with the unhappy and abortive adventures of many seed companies and the amateur efforts to commercialize on feed formulas and breeding stock, one sees clearly how difficult it was to master the science required to standardize commercial production, to reduce risk, and to mono-polize and market identifiable products. The institutional equipment needed to produce the modern agricultural revolution is described in the following section. Neither its organization and scale nor the knowledge needed to make it productive was available in the nineteenth century.

The successes and failures of nineteenth-century mechanization emphasize the ambiguities of causation which permeate U.S. economic history. In
three areas, the successes and failures are especially revealing. First, the
degree of adjustment of the machinery to the flat lands of the Midwest is
often cited as a notable success. Here certainly was the ideal terrain for
machinery, and, as productivity calculations show, the interaction between
the falls in labor costs in Midwest grain and the increasing concentration of
the crop in that area was very strong.[10] The small grains moved into the
Midwest so completely by 1910 because machinery had been invented which
was ideally suited to the terrain. The adaptation of this machinery to the
smaller fields and less even terrain in the East was relatively slow, and the
small combine was not perfected technically until the 1940s. But is it then
correct to say that the inventions were in any sense "caused" by the ideal
conditions for their use? It seems more satisfactory to say that a process
resembling natural selection was at work among the stream of inventions
thrown up in mid-century. The characteristics of that stream were partly
conditioned by the kinds of tasks that the inventions tried to tackle, but the
degree of technical success depended on the mechanical ideas and equipment available and on their suitability to the tasks at hand. Some inventions
were easier to hit upon than others, and of the stream of such technically
practicable inventions, those which were suited to a wide economic opportunity flourished. In retrospect the opportunity appears to have caused the
invention, whereas in fact the occasion only selected one invention over many
others which were technically or economically impracticable.

This characteristic of the process of mechanical invention in agriculture is
seen all the more clearly when we look next at the inventions which were not
successful and the operations and crops which remained unmechanized.
Why, we may ask, were cotton picking, corn picking and husking, and milking
not mechanized when the reaper was invented for wheat? With respect to
both cotton and corn, ambiguity again clouds our view. It is possible to
argue that in these crops the picking time was not narrowly limited by
weather, as it was with wheat. This natural fact, it may be argued, worked
through the demand for inventions to reduce the attention paid to the mechanization of these operations. This argument is reinforced for cotton by the
presence of an abundant labor force in the South—that is, the presence of
different factor proportions there than in the Midwest. But these arguments,
while intuitively appealing to an economist and based on true—or partly true—
premises, miss several important features of the question. Milking occurred in a
labor-scarce region and had an even stronger time constraint than wheat
harvesting. While it could use child or female labor, it often did not do so, and

[10] Parker and Klein's study on labor productivity, cited above, affords some rough calculations. Taking the
regional distribution of the crop and the level of yields per acre at their 1850 values, the fall in labor costs per
acre due to the mechanization which had occurred by 1910 would have produced labor productivity indexes in
1910 on an 1850 base as follows: wheat, 246; oats, 186; corn, 227. Combining these effects of mechanization
with the redistribution of the crops in 1910—that is, the strong shift to the Midwest where the falls in labor cost per
acre due to mechanization were strongest—raises these indexes to 377, 372, and 330, respectively. Since yields
per acre are fairly stable, the interregional shift and mechanization taken together account for nearly the whole
productivity increase. (Parker and Klein, *op. cit.*, p. 533, Table 2.)

labor of all forms had many other tasks. In any case, the substitution of capital for labor here would seem as profitable as in many other operations—for example, spinning—in which mechanical substitutes were found. Furthermore, there is evidence of some interest in mechanizing all these operations—particularly corn harvesting—in the nineteenth century in the form of many patented but unsuccessful devices. Surely the most plausible single answer is that these operations were all inherently difficult to mechanize without radical alteration and improvement of basic elements in the prevailing technology. In the case of the corn harvester, the problem of harvesting the ear separately from the stalk, while preserving the stalk for forage, was hard to solve. In cotton picking, the need to make several passes over the field as the bolls ripened prevented a crude solution.[11] The possibility of mechanical milking was hardly dreamed of, except by cranks, before the gasoline engine and electric power. It is no accident that in all three cases, the mechanical problem was to imitate complex motions of the human hand rather than the simple sweeping actions of the arm required in reaping and threshing.

The need for mobile inanimate power and the failure of nineteenth-century technology to furnish it provides a third example of the interaction of a demand working against an unresponsive supply. The steam engine found widespread application only in its stationary form in operations on the harvested crop—for example, in ginning and threshing. In the field, efforts were made to apply it to pulling a plow on a cable across a field. But in any form, steam was cumbersome, hard to regulate and embody in mobile equipment. Here again questions of scale and cost overlap the purely technical considerations.[12] With cheap gasoline and repair service, George Washington might have used a jeep to get around Mount Vernon, and Daniel Webster might have plowed his land, even given the enormous plow he invented, with a small tractor. But even when the gasoline tractor was introduced, it was large and cumbersome, adapted to heavy tasks on large acreages. To be sure, the scale on which farms cooperated to employ such equipment might have been enlarged, but patterns of farm size and farmer behavior were too rigid for that to be done easily. Until the 1940s at least, it proved easier to adapt the gasoline-powered technology to the organizational and technical structure of agriculture. After the gasoline engine was developed, it could be adjusted to economic conditions. But its development depended on the particular constellation of technical and economic conditions in the early twentieth century. As long as the steam engine was the only mechanical substitute for

[11] Heywood Fleisig, in an unpublished study of costs and yields in the 1850s, concluded that a simple stripper, while losing much of the cotton and lowering the quality of what was picked, would still have been profitable under many conditions of labor costs and cotton prices. Even such a simple device was not invented until the 1910s, when some farmers in Texas, desperate for labor, dragged a picket fence through the field. Neither economic nor intellectual obstacles, but rather social obstacles and communication failure appear to have been involved. It is interesting that, as cotton cultivation was beginning, intercourse between North and South was close enough to expose Eli Whitney to the ginning problems of the widow of Nathaniel Greene. But that whole episode has an eighteenth-century flavor of easy mobility between educated classes in the North and South—a spirit quite foreign to the grim, evangelical, and self-righteous sectional fervor that grew up later. See Constance McL. Green, *Eli Whitney and the Birth of American Technology* (Boston: Little, Brown, 1956), pp. 40–62.

[12] Clarke C. Spence, *God Speed the Plough: The Coming of Steam Cultivation to Great Britain* (Urbana: University of Illinois Press, 1960).

the horse, cheapness and adaptation to the tasks and organizations of field operations could not be achieved.

The result was the development of horse-drawn equipment to a degree approaching the bizarre.[13] The characteristics of animal power in turn gave certain characteristics to farm organization. The scale of the power unit was small, though not infinitesimal, unless horses could be rented out or shared. Moreover, in addition to their capital cost, horses had the unfortunate habit of consuming fuel (feed) even when idle; and they required personal care and upkeep. The physical difficulties of massing a sizable amount of power by combining a number of horses in a team were immense, even though in California and in the northern Plains, teams of 20 and 30 were put in the field to pull combines in the 1890s. The need was felt to schedule operations throughout the year, to relate the scale of the labor force to the power unit, and to avoid tasks and terrains where two or at most four horses could not do the job. Thus the family-size team was a central feature in the family-size farm. The initial problem for the manufacturers of the tractor was to adapt it and its equipment to this scale. Just as the automobile took over many of the features of carriage design—including the position of the engine—so, too, farm equipment was based at first on the simulation of human motions and on the power scale of an animal. By the 1940s, however, the adaptation of the tractor, the development of complex machinery, the adaptations in crops and farm practices all made possible a more efficient use of mechanical power in the field. This complex "package" of technology began then to affect the scale of the acreage and capital controllable by a single farm entrepreneur. The organizational structure of farming was sufficiently flexible to accommodate the new technology, including large amounts of expensive equipment, with ample access to credit and a redefinition of the meaning of the term "family farm." The resulting increases in the number of power units on farms for field operations and in the various types of machinery are shown in Figures 11.8 and 11.9. But such series tell only part of the story. As the farm equipment industry has grown, the variety of machines has increased and prices have fallen. More important, equipment has gained an adjustability to task, crop, and farm organization that makes it a powerful part of the total package of modern technology.

The slow adjustment of machinery to the whole range of field operations, and of power sources to the types of machinery, was matched in the twentieth century by a lag in the distribution of electricity in rural areas and of electric devices for farm use. The organizational problems on which electricity generation and distribution depended fall outside the limits of this chapter, but they bear a strong similarity to those considered in the next section on biochemical technology. The high fixed overhead costs of distribution made the economy of electricity doubtful, except on a very large scale and often with

---

[13] One of the most bizarre examples was the Mott combine, in which "propulsion was divorced from operation by putting the engine as well as the cutting and threshing mechanism on a truck drawn by twelve horses." [Leo Rogin, *The Introduction to Farm Machinery in Its Relation to the Productivity of Labor in the Agriculture of the United States During the Nineteenth Century* (Berkeley: University of California Press, 1931), p. 123.]

FIGURE 11.8
Power on farms and number of farms, 1910–1965

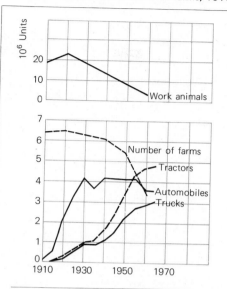

SOURCES

Tractors
1910–1925: U.S. Bureau of the Census, *Historical Statistics of the United States, Colonial Times to 1957,* Series K-150 (Washington: U.S. Government Printing Office, 1960), p. 285.
1930–1965: U.S. Department of Agriculture, *Agricultural Statistics, 1967, op. cit.,* p. 522, Table 644.

Automobiles
1910–1925: U.S. Bureau of the Census, *Historical Statistics of the United States, Colonial Times to 1957,* Series K-152 (Washington: U.S. Government Printing Office, 1960), p. 285.
1930–1965: U.S. Department of Agriculture, *Agricultural Statistics, 1967, op. cit.,* p. 522, Table 644.

Trucks
1910–1925: U.S. Bureau of the Census, *Historical Statistics of the United States, Colonial Times to 1957,* Series K-151 (Washington: U.S. Government Printing Office, 1960), p. 285.
1930–1965: U.S. Department of Agriculture, *Agricultural Statistics, 1967, op. cit.,* p. 522, Table 644.

Work animals
1850–1910: J. Frederick Dewhurst and Associates, *America's Needs and Resources, A New Survey* (New York: Twentieth Century Fund, 1955), app. 25–3, p. 1108, Table A, Col. 1.
1920–1950: U.S. Bureau of the Census, *Historical Statistics of the United States, Colonial Times to 1957,* Series K-213 (Washington: U.S. Government Printing Office, 1960), p. 290.
1960: U.S. Bureau of the Census, *Historical Statistics of the United States, Continuation to 1962 and Revisions,* Series K-213 (Washington: U.S. Government Printing Office, 1965), p. 45.

governmental participation and support. This was especially true because, in operations other than milking and pumping, electricity's contribution to farm life lay more on the consumption than on the production side of farm accounts. Electrification of the farm home required incomes of a certain level and a willingness to spend income on modern living as well as on productivity-raising equipment. The connection with the outside world made possible by the radio was electricity's greatest contribution to farm life during the 1920s and 1930s. Together with the automobile (which also required high public capital costs in the development of rural roads), radio and television made possible the transformation of rural culture from the nineteenth-century mold centered on family, church, and village to one much more assimilable to the

FIGURE 11.9
Farm equipment and number of farms, 1910–1965

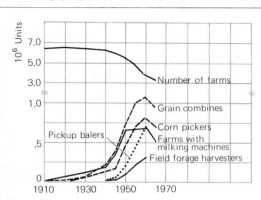

SOURCES

Grain combines
   U.S. Department of Agriculture, *Agricultural Statistics, 1967, op. cit.,* p. 522, Table 645.
Corn pickers
   Ibid.
Pickup balers
   1910–1955: U.S. Bureau of the Census, *Historical Statistics of the United States, Colonial Times to 1957,*
   Series K-156 (Washington: U.S. Government Printing Office, 1960), p. 220.
   1960: U.S. Bureau of the Census, *Historical Statistics of the United States, Continuation to 1962 and Revisions*
   Series K-156 (Washington: U.S. Government Printing Office, 1965), p. 43.
Farms with milking machines
   U.S. Department of Agriculture, *Agricultural Statistics, 1967, op. cit.,* p. 522, Table 645.
Field forage harvesters
   1910–1955: U.S. Bureau of the Census, *Historical Statistics of the United States, Colonial Times to 1957,*
   Series K-157 (Washington: U.S. Government Printing Office, 1960), p. 284.
   1960: U.S. Bureau of the Census, *Historical Statistics of the United States, Continuation to 1962 and Revisions,*
   Series K-157 (Washington: U.S. Government Printing Office, 1965), p. 43.

culture of urban industry. Such an assimilation in turn continued the incentive to farm families to maintain and increase their income levels and, in order to do so, to resort not only to government support but also to the adoption of complex technology and heavy investment.

Mechanical technology, then, has been active in American agriculture since the eighteenth century. That it shared both the ideas and the business organization of the developing machinery industry was a major source of its strength and its advance beyond the technology of materials and life processes more peculiar to the agricultural sector. Some inventors were luckier than others in finding needs which mechanical equipment could serve and to which the state of the art of machinery construction and power generation was appropriate. Thus lags appeared among the crops, especially in their harvesting (where the peculiarities of plant and terrain were most strongly felt). A noticeable delay occurred in the modernization of the power source for similar technical reasons. The inventions that were successful proved to have strong labor-saving effects, felt more sharply in some crops and regions than in others. This circumstance fitted well with the American factor endowment and was no doubt partly abetted by it. Unlike Europe, the United States had the good luck to have a factor endowment which mechanical technology could readily match. It was said, in this country's happier days, that God took care of fools, drunkards, and the United States of America; and we may be in the presence of one instance of this providence. Twentieth-century mechanical technology was less kind to American agriculture—except in providing the tractor—until after 1940, when it formed part of a revolution that had its basis in the laboratories and greenhouses rather than the workshop.

THE DEVELOPMENT OF A SCIENTIFIC AGRICULTURE[14]

The " Folk " Process of Invention

The westward movement of men and farming areas required and encouraged incessant innovation not only in equipment but also in farm practices and in seed and animal strains. The state of scientific knowledge about biochemistry and genetics in the nineteenth century was one of profound ignorance on many points. Successful innovation was largely a process of trial and error. In livestock breeding, for example, there could be no definite rules. The relation of the physical points of an animal to its efficiency as a piece of capital equipment was not known, and—even if the linked physical and economic characteristics had been known—there was little understanding of how such characteristics were transmitted. In the history of wheat, corn, and cotton improvement, a farmer observing a specially fine plant might save the seed and inbreed one or two generations to obtain a new variety. Such techniques had proved moderately effective, but without knowledge of the underlying science, many mistakes were made and many false claims created. Every farmer did things a little differently from his neighbor and was sure his own way was best.

This variation in practices—a reflection of the independence of farmers' jugdments—was the seedbed of novelty. The important problem for agriculture at large was not to produce new forms; both nature and human nature were doing that in abundance. Rather it was to provide a means of testing the ideas and new materials to ensure their widespread adoption if they were valid. Here a very great difference existed among the innovations in their degree of suitability to a national or even a regional market. Some practices, seeds, and equipment were suitable only in the localities of their origin; others had widespread use wherever a crop or an operation appeared. But no innovation could be adopted until the estimate of the risk attaching to its use in a given neighborhood was reduced. Risk reduction was essential to the diffusion of a technique across a variety of farms and farmers. Something could be done by the system of communication, by official reports, advertisements, salesmen's pitches, and exhibits at county fairs. But the most powerful persuader was an actual practical exhibition nearby under conditions that a

[14] This section has been adapted from an unpublished paper delivered at the Second International Conference on Economic History at Munich (August 1965). Recognition is due Professor Allan G. Bogue of the University of Wisconsin for helpful criticism.

farmer recognized to be similar to his own. And if the farmers were usually "from Missouri," the crust of skepticism was sometimes surprisingly thin—too thin often for their own good. The susceptibility of the nineteenth-century farming public to fads and manias was the reverse side of the eagerness to innovate.

Since local demonstration was important, it was important also that risk takers be widely scattered and that communication of their activities be easy. Here the structure of rural society must have played an important part, far beyond what we are able to trace. The wealthier farmers—though hardly rich landowners by European standards—were the most prominent innovators, partly because any given innovation involved them in less proportionate risk. But such innovations may have been tried by farmers whose fortunes suffered when they failed. A high degree of venturesomeness was often looked on—in America as elsewhere—as a form of insanity. But grouped around the county seats in the rural areas were men whose opinions counted and whose examples might be followed. And the motives for talking about one's practices, as the literature reveals them, are interesting to consider. The simple love of talk and boasting by hard-working, half-educated men was an important source of conversations about farming. Occasionally one wonders whether a definitive answer to a moot question would have been welcomed, since it would have destroyed the source of the controversy and so of the entertainment. To introduce a practice and to benefit financially from it was only half the game; the rest was to show one's neighbors that one was right. The purely competitive organization of the industry put no premium on keeping an invention secret unless it could be patented and sold to other producers. To talk about a successful innovation added pleasure and prestige to the profit.

The farmers in a county acquired various reputations—some as rash and hair-brained; some as backward, lazy, and ignorant; and some as sound, progressive, and prudent. Tolerance of innovation admitted a great deal of experiment, and skepticism exercised an effective control over excess. Around the level set by the interest in innovation and by the pressures for money income, competition separated good from bad. Natural selection was at work among farmers as among plants. Suitable adaptations and practices were rewarded; too many errors would make a farmer sink in the "agricultural ladder" and drive him eventually out of farming. The level of debts set the upper limit of tolerance to money losses, but even where these were met, disappointment and discouragement in an atmosphere so full of promise and hope could winnow out the farmers with bad judgment or luck as effectively as bankruptcy. Between ownership and abandonment of the land lay gradations of tenancy in which a farmer could function with some loss of control over entrepreneurial decisions.

The process of trial and error has gone on in agriculture since Neolithic times; it represents the standard behavior of farmers—or anyone else—in a new situation. In nineteenth-century America, it occurred in a hothouse atmosphere provided by the sheer numbers of farm families scattered over the land, the tension of a growing market opportunity, and the glimmerings of an

agricultural science. Empirical "rules of thumb" were found by hard experience, and, not surprisingly, extravagant claims were made. In this way
many right and wrong notions about seed selection, about the soils best
suited to corn, about standards of livestock judging were evolved. Behind the
efforts to improve seeds and breeds, to find the right crops and feeding formulas, lay the implicit assumption that some general rules or solutions could be
obtained. The premature effort was made to form a scientific agriculture before
the empirical basis was wide enough, the range of variation in conditions fully
enough explored, statistical methods and tests developed, or a theoretical
basis available for understanding or predicting results or for controlling
experimentation.

The Institutions of Scientific Agriculture

To achieve the foundations for an innovating agricultural science in the United
States required innovation of another kind: the development of social institutions to sponsor research and disseminate the results. The difficulties of
employing the patent system and the apparatus of industrial capitalism in this
area have been referred to above. Much progress in fundamental science was
needed before research could be considered a directly profitable use of the
investment funds of a large private corporation and before patentable and
standardized products—such as fertilizers, hybrid seeds, and insecticides—
could become suitable subjects for commercial marketing. When that began
to occur after 1920, development could proceed with ever increasing speed.
Until then, a patron was needed to sponsor risky and massive experiments in
abstract science, remote from immediate problems.

In Europe, intellectual capital formation at a deep and abstract level had
been sponsored since the sixteenth century by the state and nobility as a
kind of secular successor to the priestly functions of the Church in the Middle
Ages. When science became a faith of princes, support for its practitioners
seemed a natural act of piety. In Europe, too, where concentrated land holding
obtained, it was easy and plausible for wealthy farmers to devote part of their
energies and investments to efforts at agricultural improvement. In England,
where the landowners had early become capitalists in some sense themselves,
large-scale efforts to improve agricultural practices could go forward as
vigorously as similar efforts in industry—though with somewhat smaller payoff. In nineteenth-century Europe, these two strains of innovation—field
experiments to achieve improvement and laboratory work to discover the
principles of agricultural science—were lodged in the universities working
with government research institutes or stations. Where the role of a priestly
intelligentsia was taken over by universities and that of a noble patron of
improvement by a government institute, a formidable organization for advances
in science and technology was achieved. The efforts of Lawes and Gilbert in
England and Liebig in Germany to develop a soil science based on chemical
analysis were a fruit of this cooperation. Even by 1900, this effort in Europe
was restricted, however, by the lack of understanding of much of the basic
chemistry of the biological processes of growth and reproduction.

In the United States, the structure of society made the development of scientific institutions of the European sort extraordinarily hard to achieve. The difficulty of commercializing the product was only part of the problem. The wide distribution of agricultural wealth and the lack of a landed gentry limited the private resources likely to be channeled in these directions. And the democratic character of the government meant that its expenditures had to produce rather immediate and tangible help for a substantial portion of the electorate if they were to be justified. To overcome these obstacles, however, American society had certain favorable features. First and most important was the commercial nature of agriculture itself, almost from the very outset. The need for constant innovation on the frontier prevented encrusted and anti- quated techniques from surviving. The habit of joining together in frontier projects persisted in the formation of agricultural societies, and the respect for education—so enormous in post-Reformation European culture—made a university a plausible object of public expenditure. By the mid-nineteenth century, it became apparent that could adequate institutions be devised, the scale and variety of domestically supported American agricultural science might exceed anything Europe could create. Tax-supported institutions could draw on a layer of wealth untouched by princes and noble patrons, and the superior scale of the American national enterprise, compared with any in Western Europe, was an immense advantage. A national government had the added advantage of including regions of widely differing characteristics among which communication could yield the data for an empirically based science. A central organization on top of many local ones promoted this communication without prematurely destroying the originality and variety of research at local levels.

The instrumental institutions which finally developed—the land-grant colleges and the experiment stations—proved very effective in the task of developing agricultural science and disseminating its results. They combined in one system a division of labor between theoretical and applied work, and they gained the advantage of good communication and some central direction without losing local initiative and a closeness to local problems. The grants under the Morrill Act (1863) stimulated in every state the founding of the stipulated colleges for the agricultural and mechanical arts. These colleges introduced a variety of theoretical and applied courses, but they related the work directly to studies in chemistry and biology going on in the scientific curriculum at these and related institutions. The experiment stations, at least one in each state, based on the German model, were introduced under the Hatch Act of 1887 and strengthened by the Adams Act of 1906. Their original purpose was to work directly on the needs and possibilities of the agriculture of their respective states. Defined narrowly, this was taken by some administrators to mean the testing of seeds and fertilizers on the market and the dissemination of existing best-practice techniques. But the demands, ambitions, and curiosity of the farm population and its leaders were too great to permit so narrow a definition of research. Instead, problems of all sorts were tackled indiscriminately. Since the intellectual, as distinct from the administra- tive, history of the experiment stations has not yet been written, it is not possible to trace the development of research ideas within them. The improvement in the selection procedures and the focusing of research on a few major lines, with adequate use of fundamental science and statistical methods, were essential steps. Such a history would show a succession of human effort, evolving from the random empiricism of an energetic folk culture, through quackeries and false leads, to a body of interconnected experiments, closely linked in purpose and controlled by intelligent awareness of a developing scientific theory. It took a high degree of statesmanship in the Office of Experiment Stations in the Department of Agriculture to guide this work without stifling its variety and originality. With a semi-centralized organization reaching into states and—through the Agricultural Extension Service—into counties, an extraordinary network of communication was produced. Every bulletin of every station was distributed to the libraries of all the others, and abstracted and elaborately indexed in Washington. Through the Extension Service, results and other relevant developments were made known in a practical way to the farm population. It was a system which overcame completely the lack of commercial incentive. While existing in reasonably happy symbiosis with the system of private producers, it acted also as a test and a check on the farm inputs sold on commercial markets. It is a tribute to the farmers' faith in science that the experiment stations were allowed to function for 60 years without producing an agricultural revolution. Their record was good, but not brilliant, and was more notable in the plant and animal sciences than in soil science. As knowledge developed about soil and plant chemistry, the large chemical companies themselves took over much of the research and development in chemicals.

After 1940, then, three major strands of invention came together and intensified one another: (a) the machinery inventions, produced to fit crop, terrain, and farm size; (b) the biological inventions, notably hybrid seed and improved feed and fertilization techniques for animals; and (c) the chemical and medical inventions—feeding nutrients from soil to plant, and controlling disease and natural enemies. The ingenuity in adapting inventions of each type to those in the other areas has been extraordinary. Intensive fertilizer applications have necessitated changes in plant breeds to absorb them and bear a heavier yield. Plants are also bred to meet the characteristics of machinery. The ability of insects and plant diseases to breed around man's efforts to exterminate them has required continuous innovation in insecticides and fungicides. So widespread has been the application of this technology that fears are now expressed that the natural balance of the environment has been upset. The end of these cumulative developments is not in sight, though the whole history of technology leads us to expect that the end, at least in the lines now most fruitful, will be reached before long.

ORGANIZATION OF AGRICULTURAL PRODUCTION

The Family Scale of Production

Behind the American record of output and productivity growth have lain many production and investment decisions made by millions of separate economic units. Farmers who made these decisions were small businessmen holding from thirty to a few hundred acres; their chief source of labor (outside of slaves and sharecroppers in the South) was themselves and their own families. How did such a production structure come into being, uniformly across the country, through all the variations in climates, crops, and terrain? Why did it multiply like a simple many-celled organism across the continent? How did it maintain its essential character for 300 years, through changes in technology, government, and the price level, during a time when family firms and even small corporations in industry and transport were swallowed up in mergers, chains, and monopolies? These questions form one of the most interesting puzzles to the student of American agrarian history, and the effort to explain them casts interesting sidelights on economic processes in American society.

It should be realized first that—at least before World War II—not all American economic life had succumbed to "bigness." In the distribution and construction trades, the very small unit (the "ma and pa store") was as prevalent as the family farm in agriculture—and for some of the same reasons: positive economies yielded by a widespread locational pattern and few economies accruing to production on a large scale. The family unit has been a common production organization in much of the world's agriculture, though ownership by village or tribal groupings or in large estates has also been prevalent. In the United States the farmers were not huddled in a village, but lived apart from each other—like lords in the midst of their holdings. The basic ownership and production, or management, unit was the same (with some exceptions, noted below); and with so peasant-like an individualistic and organization, commercial considerations and risky innovation, rather than family security and self-sufficiency, were dominant. The phenomenon is worth closer examination, although we can see only partially the relationship between this structure and the spirit and behavior of those who grew up in it and made it work.

Consider, first, what has set the *scale of production unit* in American agriculture: the acreage and equipment under single direction. A basic factor is the time taken by workers to travel between home and fields. Beyond a point, it is obviously more economical for workers to remain where they are at work, rather than return to their home or village. By itself this would argue for a wholly nomadic labor force; only economies of scale in consumption and the simple needs of social life group workers in farmstead residences or in villages. Indeed, it is evidence of the priority given by farmers to efficiency over comfort and social needs that American farms were isolated, with the farmer living along a road, if possible near the center of his fields, rather than in the villages characteristic of Europe and Asia and derived there from the defense requirements and social needs of a communal agriculture. Much of the lonesomeness and barrenness of American rural life sprang from this isolation, as did much of the demand for good roads and rapid transport.

Given a farm population scattered over the soil, why should the grouping and the size of the labor force under single control be just the family, with auxiliary harvest labor and sometimes, especially on dairy farms, a "hired man"? The most direct answer is simply this: If the family was indeed the minimal unit of *social* life, there were few technical or economic reasons for making the minimal *production* unit in agriculture any larger in terms of labor requirement. In manufacturing such larger units grew up under the factory system as market growth encouraged a division of labor, and the assembly of workers in factories around a collection of power-driven equipment yielded fantastic productivity gains. In agriculture no such gains were available to large groupings of workers cooperating in a set of tasks. The succession of tasks over the year defined a seasonal division of labor, one in which only a labor force migrating with the seasons could begin to perform repeatedly a specialized operation for more than a few weeks of the year. And, as we have seen, the lag in the invention of power equipment meant that until 1920 a horse and a modest collection of horse-drawn machinery formed the center of a farmer's capital in the field crops. Herds of sheep and beef cattle on the range called for some hired labor, but the labor requirement relative to the number of animals herded was very low. The farm livestock operations producing milk and pork could be run on a very small scale with family labor.

Technically, then, it was not cheaper to group laborers in larger-than-family units on the land, and there were strong reasons of a different sort that allowed the family to work more cheaply than hired labor. The members of a family were not free; they were bound to the entrepreneur by ties of custom, law, fear, and affection. And the entrepreneur, the farmer—head of family, was himself a slave either to an ideal of personal and family success, or to fear and ignorance of alternative opportunities. We shall refer to the implications of these circumstances for farm income in the next section; here it is sufficient to note that family farms could out-compete any appreciably larger-scale organization of a labor force, and did so rather decisively when put to the test. Only in fruit and vegetable harvesting, in which larger quantities of seasonal labor were required and mechanization was slow, is a persistent exception to be noted.[15] A similar exception might have occurred in cotton and tobacco after the end of slavery if the system of family tenancies on shares, discussed briefly in the next section, had not largely taken its place.

Apart from his privileged access to cheap labor, the family farmer had also the advantage of an intimate knowledge of the physical conditions of his land and the difficulties of cultivating it. Obviously this knowledge, gained from experience and family training, was the more precious as scientific knowledge was the more untrustworthy. It was a less prominent feature of the environment in America than in the countries of settled peasant agriculture, where frontier conditions were long past and changes of crops to suit commercial markets were less frequent and less radical. Still, in the absence of technical knowledge of wide applicability—of reliable "book farming"—the

---

[15] In the "bonanza farms" of the Red River Valley of the North in the 1880s, large labor forces were assembled to complement large-scale land holdings and equipment. They died out in the early 1890s, victims of depressed wheat prices and of a shift to dairying in part of their area. After 1892 they were nibbled away as the family farmers—Swedes and Yankees—moved in. [John L. Coulter, *Industrial History of the Red River Valley of the North* (Bismarck, N.D.: North Dakota State Historical Society, 1910).]

acquisition of the particular knowledge required to farm a modest area was the task of a generation living on the soil, surviving through risk and frequent failure, and transmitting this knowledge to its successor. Farms were amateur research laboratories and technical schools as well as production organizations, and these functions have been shed only slowly as scientific agriculture has grown reliable and dominant.[16]

The Family Scale of Ownership

Granted that its production advantage over the farm with hired labor was secure, why did the family farm also constitute such a prevalent *ownership* unit in America? Table 11.1 shows the level of tenancy in 1880 and 1930—dates when it was in fact rather high—and in 1950. What advantage did the family-owned farm have over that operated by the family of a tenant? The answer to this question takes us into the subject of capital sources and investment opportunities in the United States.

First, the exceptions which "prove" the rule, in the sense of both testing and establishing it, should be noted. The most striking exceptions to the description of American agriculture outlined above lay in the organization of black labor in the South, as discussed in the next section. If slaves are considered as capital rather than labor—then in the antebellum South, too, we may say that family ownership and family labor prevailed. The tenancy system which succeeded slavery made explicit the use of black labor in family units, but it,

TABLE 11.1
Level of farm tenancy, by region, 1880, 1930, 1950

Census Region	Percent of Farms Operated by Tenants		
	1880	1930	1950
New England	8.5	6.3	3.7
Middle Atlantic	19.2	16.2	7.9
East North Central	20.5	27.3	19.8
West North Central	20.5	39.9	28.2
South Atlantic	36.1	48.1	32.1
East South Central	36.8	55.9	36.6
West South Central	35.2	62.3	33.7
Mountain	7.4	24.4	16.0
Pacific	16.8	18.9[a]	11.6[a]
U.S. total	25.6	42.4[a]	26.9[a]

[a] Includes Alaska and Hawaii.

SOURCE: U.S. Bureau of the Census, *Census of Agriculture: 1959*, vol. 2 (Washington: U.S. Government Printing Office, 1960), Table 25.

[16] A further advantage of a family as a source of farm labor derives from the combination of types of tasks on a farm and the possibility of fitting tasks to a family labor force. The coincidence of residence and work place has meant that much part-time labor has been available, and many tasks, especially in livestock care, could be done by part-time and substandard labor. Farm operations, though set in a broad schedule by nature, are much more flexible in hour-to-hour or day-to-day scheduling than are manufacturing operations employing continuous processes and power-driven equipment.

too, obviously differed from the free farm organization of the Midwest. Outside the South the major incidence of tenancy was in the upper Plains—in Iowa, Nebraska, and the Dakotas, where a steady current of tenancy was accelerated by falling prices in the early 1890s and 1930s. In this area generally adverse conditions pushed farmers down the "ladder" that led to full ownership. Elsewhere, a normal level of tenancy was incidental to the system of inheritance and served as an alternative to status as a mortgage. Frequently an aging farmer might turn over his farm to a son, accepting rental payments for life or until the prospective heir proved his credit with a bank or local moneylender. The mortgage debt, which also constitutes a limitation on full operator ownership, was large in American agriculture. However, Figure 11.10 shows that 75 to 80 percent of long-term farm finance before 1900 and as much as 40 percent in the 1940s was furnished directly by local sources: other family members or small-town magnates.

FIGURE 11.10
Farm mortgage debt, by type of holder, 1910–1962

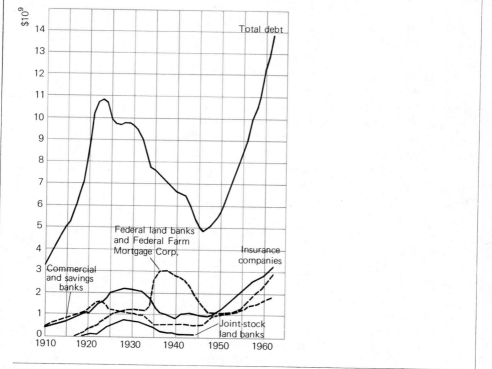

SOURCES

1910–1955: U.S. Bureau of the Census, *Historical Statistics of the United States, Colonial Times to 1957*, Series K-162–K-167 (Washington: U.S. Government Printing Office, 1960), p. 286.

1956–1962: U.S. Bureau of the Census, *Historical Statistics of the United States, Continuation to 1962 and Revisions*, Series K-162–K-167 (Washington: U.S. Government Printing Office, 1965), p. 43.

The reason for the diffuse ownership pattern, then, is a simple economic one. It derives from the proportions of land, enterprise, and credit on the American scene in the nineteenth century and from the availability of investment opportunities outside farming. The land system was slanted sufficiently toward owner–operators to place land in their hands early in the settlement process. Preemption and squatters' rights, enforced by the law or local pressure, kept outsiders away from land auctions and helped settle the land in local ownership. Such early owners were not all simple sons of the soil, by any means. Their ambition was often to farm only a portion and to share in the rise in land values by selling the rest. Such ambitions, and the holdings derived from them, were often dissipated by the claims of children; and the selling-off, when it occurred, simply established another small local owner. Once small pockets of rural wealth had become established with title to the land, they formed a source of credit to others; and once the land was vested in the operator, it shared with family labor the farmer's tendency to overprice it on the external market and underprice it for home use. The market in land was freer in law than the market for family labor, but it was perhaps no more perfect. Both labor and land became instruments for the father–farmer's entrepreneurial ambitions.

Land policy set the ownership pattern in the farmers' favor only because other capitalists with more abundant resources were not interested in buying up farming land. That regular commercial tenants were hard to find reflects the fact that land, capital, and ambition were available on a small scale. Even large-scale speculators, who might hold land temporarily in idleness or as a cattle range, sold out as the density of settlement increased, and avoided the risks of large-scale supervision of tenants. Agriculture was left largely to itself as an object of investment until very recent years also because alternative objects of investment in industry, trade, and transport were abundant. The capital created in cities tended to stay there, or to move to other cities and to growing industrial areas. Where it entered the countryside, its purpose was to provide manufactured goods or distribution services to farmers, or to handle the movement of crops, not to hold land or to finance the living of farmers while they worked it.

Here as elsewhere (see Chapter 8), we observe that capital moved until recent decades in deep channels set by the assessment of risks, which depended in turn on the sphere of personal experience of the capitalist or his agent. Farm capital tended to stay on farms, and it was available in thousands of small lots to finance land holding by the farmers themselves; the separateness ordained to agriculture by its geographical spread and the peculiar characteristics of its techniques was fortified by the separateness in its access to credit. The family-operated farm was strengthened and reinforced in its organization by a high degree of independence born of family ownership; the separateness of the agricultural sector as a whole was increased by the dependence of farmers on other farmers or on ex-farmers for the means of long-term finance.

Slavery and Sharecropping as Exceptions to Family Scale

To those familiar with the realities of agriculture in the South, such comfortable talk of family farming has a hollow ring. Before 1860 were not the major southern commercial crops—tobacco, rice, cotton—grown almost wholly by slave labor in holdings running from ten to a hundred slaves? And were not the plantations transformed by emancipation into sharecropping tenancies, with little increase either in wealth or in independence for the black farm laborers? Even where blacks were kept together as families under slavery or became tenants of their former masters, their economic position can surely not be identified with that of the northern farm family.

A close examination of southern conditions shows that the system of plantation labor did not rest on technical or natural economic causes, but rather on the social power of southern owners to exploit black labor. It should be noted first that outside of the main commercial crops, most southern farmers were family farmers, though of a poorer sort. Cotton was the main cash crop of the South from at least 1820 on; it was grown on over half of the farms in the states from Tennessee and North Carolina south in 1860, and slaves accounted for perhaps 80 percent of the labor used in growing it. But at least half of the southern farms had no slaves; these were family farmers selling food crops to some of the plantations or living in near self-sufficiency with little cash income. The concentration of cotton growing in the hands of the slave owners in the antebellum period and the general weakness of the southern market resulting from it meant that these farms did not share in the progressive developments of northern agriculture. But family farms they were, and their main difference from their northern counterparts lay in their lack of commercial opportunities and in the competition which the plantations gave them for the better land of the region.

The southern plantations themselves were not "large," as the world's agriculture has reckoned large holdings. Except for some of the sugar and cotton plantations in the lower Mississippi Valley, the southern plantation was smaller than those devoted to sugar or tropical crops in the Caribbean Islands or in Brazil. Even before 1865 some plantations in the Southeast organized labor under a family system, with the slaves settled in huts and tilling specified areas or fulfilling assigned "tasks." Perhaps, along with some slave breeding, the organization of American slave holdings helped the slave population to grow about as fast as the white population up to 1860, whereas elsewhere in the Western hemisphere the slave populations could be maintained only by continual imports.

The important fact is that the viability of the plantations does not appear to have rested on economies of scale. Slavery became fixed in the South rather than the North at an early period because of the availability of European commercial markets for the southern crops in the seventeenth and eighteenth centuries. Once the system was established, the slaves became a form of capital in which continued investment was profitable. The advantage which the free family farm had over hired labor—that is, its willingness to work at lower wages—did not apply in the competition with slavery. It is plausible, then, to explain the dominance of the plantation under slavery in the South, not on the basis of economies of scale in the use of labor, but on the ability to exploit a form of labor, and on the impulse in such a system to reinvest earnings along accepted lines. Plantations were indeed family farms, with an investment in slave labor for commercial crops—an investment which the later timing of market development for northern products denied to the northern farmers.

This line of reasoning is supported by reference to the operation of the system after emancipation. A period of chaos from 1864 to the mid-1870s, with efforts to utilize hired black labor, resulted in the settlement of the former slaves as tenant families on the estates, in a pattern which resembled the "hutting" of slaves in the Roman Empire in the fifth and sixth centuries. The scale of the average southern farm as a production unit, as defined by the census, fell from 121 improved acres in 1850 to 56 acres in 1880, and tenancy on shares became the principal means of maintaining a labor force. The independence of the black operators was undermined by the "crop-lien system," by which the landowner or a storekeeper furnished supplies and working credit against a lien on the crop. It requires little imagination to understand why the black tenants could not readily rise to the status of independent operators according to the northern pattern, although in fact a small number were able to do so.[17] As a system of management, sharecropping was probably more injurious to the long-run economic development of southern resources than slavery had been. But the explanation for the tragedy of southern agriculture— so long an exception to the generally happy picture painted here—does not lie in any peculiarities of southern crops or resources which made them especially suited to slave or tenant labor, nor in any unusual wickedness residing in the southern white population. Its explanation is not technological or economic, but purely historical and psychological : the result of an evil system which, attaching itself profitably at a certain period in a society's development, shaped that society around it and took a toll on master and slave alike.

Vertical Disintegration of Farms and Farming

Although American farms have been commercially oriented to a degree unusual in the world's agriculture, the family farm has been until recently relatively self-sufficient as a production and living unit. Many of the deficiencies of an individual farm were made up for by other farms, so that as a sector, agriculture's self-sufficiency surpassed that of its constituent units. The destruction of this self-sufficiency and the splitting off of functions from the agricultural to the industrial and commercial sectors, and from the individual farm to market sources, has affected all areas of farmers' productive and social lives.

We have already observed some aspects of this splitting off of functions from the farm to other production units. The movement after 1920 toward nonfarm sources of finance shown in Figure 11.10 was only one of the symptoms of farmers' growing dependence on the urban-based economy in the United States, and of the integration of the rural and urban economies into one. The functions of research and training of the labor force were

---

[17] In 1900 in the South, 25 percent of black farm operators were full or part owners, and the remaining 75 percent were tenants; whereas 63 percent of white farm operators were full or part owners, and only 36 percent were tenants.

slowly lost by farms in the twentieth century as the scientific institutions previously described became operative. As research findings became better based, many young farmers profited from book training acquired through the extension agent or at college. Equally important in destroying the farm's function of educating by precept and experience was the reduction of the risk of innovation as knowledge improved. Techniques became communicable and farmers could change farms more easily, relying on a body of knowledge which was the common property of all.

Long before they lost these basic functions, farms were shedding many industrial operations and tasks. Domestic industrial operations were affected first and most strongly. Weaving, spinning, finally (despite the sewing machine) dressmaking, carpentry and all forms of woodworking, soap making, and even many operations of food preservation—all these home tasks were shifted from farm to local craftsmen and then largely to enterprises covering regional or national markets by 1900 (see Chapter 12). Some were replaced quite early, as the frontier advanced; others disappeared across the rural economy within a decade or two as a result of some striking technical change. American industrial history follows a sequence of inventions and cost-reducing improvements from the supply side and from the side of demand, its course was fixed by the order in which farmers replaced home manufacture by purchased industrial products.

In farming itself, semimanufacturing operations on the marketed product —milling, ginning, and the slaughter and butchering of meat animals—split off first. Beginning with cattle, local slaughterers had replaced farm slaughter in much of the Midwest in the 1860s. Then with refrigerated rail transport began the growth of central meat-packing installations, for pork as well as beef, in Cincinnati, Kansas City, Omaha, and Chicago. Considering the variety of equipment available by 1900, and the flexibility possible in the use of work stock, it is surprising that many more farming operations were not separated from the individual farm. Early stories of prairie plowing indicate that sod-busting, which required a large team and a special plow, was often performed by hired labor. Mobile threshing machines, or combines, working from farm to farm, were also much used. Villages and migrants in many areas supplied harvest labor, and on dairy farms, first cheese making and then butter production were turned over to creameries. But even in 1910 the main bulk of the labor in all crops over the year came from the farm family, which grew a share of its food supply ranging between 25 and 80 percent, and produced the feed for most of its meat animals and work stock. The tractor made great inroads into this pattern by making farms and farming as a whole dependent on the industrial sector for fuel. Electrification, the automobile, and the assimilation of farm demand into the pattern of American consumption, homogenized by mass distribution and advertising, continued the development. Finally, the growth of the consumption of fertilizers and other nonfarm inputs and the growth of purchased equipment requiring repairs and maintenance expense brought farm operations under the immediate pressure of current conditions in input markets.

Since 1940, farms have been rapidly transformed from units which comprehended the whole natural cycle of birth, life, death, decay, and regeneration to much simpler production organizations—small factories pouring industrial inputs into the land over the year and extracting a raw product for immediate sale. With this vertical disintegration of the operations once included in farming has come a higher gross cash income to be spent on nonfarm products, for the home, field, and barn. And with that, in turn, has gone an ever-closer dependence on the markets for farm products by which the very means of life and continued operation can be sustained. Gone is the last buffer between the farm family and the vagaries of markets. What this has meant for farm incomes and finally for the forms of organization in the agricultural industry is described in the two succeeding sections.

THE MOVEMENT OF FARM INCOME

As a sector in the national economy, the 2 to 6 million family farms that have operated in the United States since the mid-nineteenth century have been lodged and have earned their living in the "economic space" between input prices and the prices of their output. Figure 11.11 shows something of the movements of these prices as they affected the determination of "parity" prices and incomes—a subject we shall have more to say about in the next section. Farmers could increase net income by selecting just the right combination of output, suited to markets and to the inputs they had on hand or could buy. They could try to increase incomes by economizing on inputs and by adopting the productivity-raising innovations described in the preceding sections. But the relative price movements of outputs and inputs still circumscribed their income-earning opportunities. Even great skill in production

FIGURE 11.11
Prices received and prices paid by farmers, 1910–1967 (1957–1959 = 100)

SOURCES

1910–1953: U.S. Department of Agriculture, *Agricultural Statistics, 1967, op. cit.*, p. 508, Table 628.
1954–1967: U.S. Department of Agriculture, *Agricultural Statistics, 1968* (Washington: U.S. Government Printing Office, 1968), p. 429, Table 621.

and great luck with new practices and the weather might be wholly negated by a short downward turn of markets. The productivity improvements themselves, inasmuch as they meant expansions of output, meant lower farm prices and, in view of the price inelasticity of demand for farm products, would have meant lower total gross farm incomes if demand had not grown simultaneously. The competitive nature of the industry insured that improvement was rather readily passed on to consumers in the form of lower prices.

In considering the movement of farm income, it is most important to distinguish among a number of phenomena and the different problems arising from each:

1. The long-run position of farm income relative to the incomes of nonfarm families
2. Long-run fluctuations in this relative income position
3. Short-run instability in earnings
4. Unevenness in the distribution of income among the farm population as a whole

Erratic or lagging adjustments of production to changes in markets, techniques, and factor supplies were the root of all these phenomena; but some have required for their remedy small changes, while others required large changes in agricultural organization.

The Labor Market and Farm Income Levels

To the extent that they have been integrated enterprises producing much of their own materials, capital, food, and consumer goods, farms have been of course somewhat sheltered from the movements of market prices. Since land has been a factor specific to farming, its price was a result of expected returns in farming, rather than an independent determinant of costs. Ultimately, especially before the dependence on mechanical power, most farm costs were reducible to the cost of farm labor, the cost of finance for land holding, and the cost of purchase of some equipment. These, together with taxes which themselves varied with land values, set the necessary costs farmers had to meet. But what *was* the necessary cost of farm labor?

In the slave economy of the South, the cost of slaves was ultimately reducible to the cost of raising them. On free farms, the cost of labor was the earnings needed to keep a family or some of its members from moving out of farming. This opportunity cost for farm labor depended loosely on the attractions of nonfarm work—that is, on the state of income and employment in the industrial and commercial economy of the country, particularly in those lines in which farmers and their sons might work.

The importance of the general labor market for incomes in farming was heightened by several historical factors. First, the rate of natural increase of the population was higher on farms than elsewhere; even under very favorable conditions of demand for farm products and under supply conditions that did not economize on labor, some migration off farms would have been necessary. But, in fact, the demand for farm products, even with large accessions of export demand, did not grow as fast as total demand in the American economy, and technical change in agriculture was, as described above, heavily labor-saving. The demand factors important to the course of farm family incomes, then, were partly the demand for farm output, but equally the off-farm demand for farm-grown labor. But where could such labor fit into the American labor force? The problem is most interesting in the North because of the simultaneous inflow of large numbers of Europeans, drawn or displaced mostly from European agriculture, to jobs in the growing urban centers and industrial districts from the mid-1840s on. The phenomena of migration and labor-force formation are discussed in Chapter 6. It is enough to observe here that migration off farms proceeded rapidly in the North; in the South between 1860 and 1920 labor piled up in rural areas, and only after the shutting off of European immigration did the movement of blacks and poor whites begin to provide substantial relief.

The ability of farms to insulate themselves to a degree from factor markets was thus a source of both strength and weakness to farm families. To some degree, farms were sheltered from the bankruptcy that threatened with fluctuations of markets and weather. More than purely commercial operations, they could absorb the shocks of instability by compressing their own incomes and standards of living. Only where fixed interest charges, debt repayments, and taxes were high was a depression of income fatal. Thus in parts of the Midwest in the 1870s and early 1890s and again the early 1930s, price deflation continued long enough to affect the whole structure of farm ownership. Relatively low farm wage rates were favorable, too, to farmers in their roles as entrepreneurs and hirers of labor. On the other hand, farmers and their families were also furnishers of labor. The farmers' dependence largely on one input—the labor of the family—meant that labor remained in farming until freed by the promise of considerably better economic and social conditions elsewhere. The isolation and distinctness of American farm life was a hindrance to ready migration off farms, but also a barrier to a return flow as relative income conditions altered.

The result of these conditions in American agriculture was that—despite its commercial character and its productivity growth—measured farm family income remained low relative to nonfarm income, at least after 1869. But though widening and narrowing from time to time, the gap between agriculture and industry did not show a strong tendency to increase as income levels in industry advanced. Figure 11.12 shows something of the relationship in recent decades. Too much should not be made of these figures, but in the United States, as in nearly every country where such measures have been compiled, this gap appears and persists. That it is not wholly a phenomenon of measurement is shown by the fact that some gap was necessary to produce the continual movement of labor off farms. The continued need for such movement is evidenced by the persistence of the gap up to the latest statistics. On the other hand, it is clear that with the changes in communication between farms and cities and the increasing dependence of farms on industrial inputs, this gap must largely disappear. As it has diminished in importance

FIGURE 11.12
Per capita personal disposable income, farm and nonfarm, 1934–1967

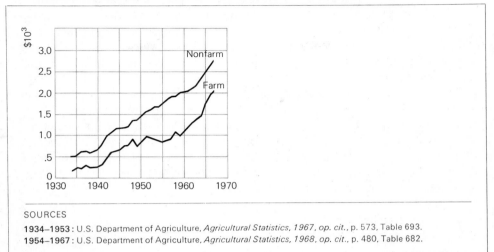

SOURCES
1934–1953: U.S. Department of Agriculture, *Agricultural Statistics, 1967, op. cit.*, p. 573, Table 693.
1954–1967: U.S. Department of Agriculture, *Agricultural Statistics, 1968, op. cit.*, p. 480, Table 682.

within the American economy, one source of general productivity increase for the whole economy through the more efficient allocation of labor has been eliminated.

Demand Instability

Farm income in the United States kept up, though at a distance, with the growing incomes of the population as a whole. Its ability to do this was—as indicated above—largely the result of the readiness of labor to move off farms. It was also partly a result of agriculture's ability to change its output structure to keep up with the shifting composition of urban demand and to meet demands appearing overseas. As income grew in the United States, and as the occupations of the population changed, demand for some goods grew and that for others declined. The chief gainers in this shift were beef, dairy products, fruits, and vegetables. The chief losers were pork and wheat—whose demand, however, was sustained on the export market. The ability of agriculture to shift the directions of its growth to meet these changes was high; farm incomes benefited from the possibility of selling higher-value products.

These favorable aspects of agriculture's income record were responses to gradual and continuous change. Within these trends, however, the response to more sudden changes in the economic environment was less favorable. Export markets, for example, unlike domestic demand, were susceptible to sudden changes as a result of crop fluctuations in importing and other supplying countries. The demand in Europe for American wheat depended on the weather in Canada, Russia, and Argentina as well as in Europe itself. Export markets could experience sudden cutoffs due to tariff acts or quality or sanitary restrictions enforced to benefit the home producers. This source of instability affected different products differently. It was not serious in cotton, in which foreign competition was relatively slight and demand growth was steady. Beef and pork, however, experienced great vicissitudes and the instability of the world wheat market was notorious. Added to this instability was the movement of domestic demand with business and employment conditions in the industrial economy.

The demand fluctuations by themselves did not have serious long-run effects on farm income except when they were very large and continued over several years. Such was the case with the boom in 1915–1918, whose collapse left wheat, cotton, and beef production drastically overexpanded throughout the 1920s. Similarly, the collapse of foreign and domestic demand in all directions in the early 1930s, coming on top of incomplete recovery in the 1920s, produced acute and prolonged loss of income.

Supply Instability

Great events like these would have upset even the smoothest-running supply adjustment mechanism. But the supply response of American agriculture was not very smooth or exact when changes in opportunity, either on the demand side or on the cost side, occurred. On the side of costs and supplies, the opening up of new territory in the nineteenth century or the rapid diffusion of a new invention or technique often brought a rush of investment and expansion with prices pushed for several years below their long-run equilibrium level. These expansions had the effect of crowding out producers on marginal lands and those who were slow to adjust. But if the expansion overshot the mark, a general compression of incomes resulted. Nor were such upsets limited to the great events of frontier expansion and technical change. A small fluctuation in supplies caused by the weather, insects, or disease could set similar shorter-run fluctuations in motion.[18] Such disturbances produced an initial rise in prices and an overexpansion of output in the following year. In the case of animal products, the output response was delayed for several years—long enough to bring new arrivals to maturity. It is easy to see that if such price fluctuations were not accompanied by a growth of demand, the expansion they evoked would be excessive, leading to excessively low prices and incomes in a later period. Thus the famous cycles in agricultural prices, output, gross income, and net income were generated and propagated. Figure 11.13 shows the instability in the markets for cattle, corn, and hogs. The cycle in pork production is discernible from the earliest annual statistics and, working in relation to corn prices, became a normal expectation in the industry. Beef cycles were longer and more violent, particularly before 1890, when great expansions of herds on the open range were possible. The overstocking of the range and the terrible collapse, which brought about the starvation of millions of cattle in the hard winter of 1886–1887, is the most spectacular event of this history.

[18] For a standard exposition see W. J. Baumol, *Economic Dynamics: An Introduction*, 2nd ed. (New York: Macmillan, 1960), chap. 7.

FIGURE 11.13
Production of beef, pork, and corn, 1870–1957

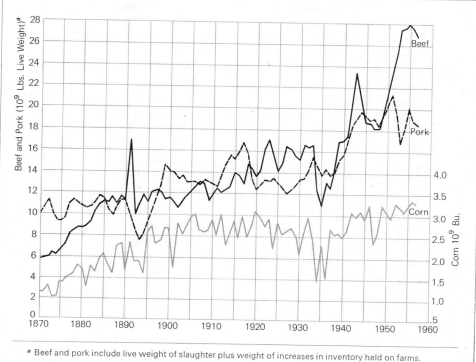

^a Beef and pork include live weight of slaughter plus weight of increases in inventory held on farms.

SOURCE: Neal Potter and Francis T. Christy, Jr., *Trends in Natural Resource Commodities* (Baltimore: Johns Hopkins, 1962), p. 176, Table AO-28, Col. 1.

Income Effects of Instability

The instability of farm prices and output produced unstable gross incomes. Since short crops were accompanied by high prices and large crops by low prices, the gross receipts of farmers fluctuated less than prices of output. Several factors, however, made for sharp fluctuations in net farm incomes and for greater inflexibility in contracting than in expanding production. First, the price elasticity of demand was over a sizable range less than unity. Hence crop expansions were overbalanced by price falls, and actual contractions in gross receipts could occur. The paradox of a large output bringing less than a small one was bitter to farmers. Furthermore, the price behavior of inputs and consumption goods purchased from the industrial sector, and the movement of fixed charges—rents, interest, taxes—did not correspond to changes in farm prices. Hence net money incomes were compressed when farm prices fell. The terms of trade of farm products against industrial products worsened and real incomes declined.

As we shall see in the next section, the instability of farm incomes from year to year and decade to decade was the major source of a discontent which took many forms and outlets. Some of the instability was attributable to inflexible fixed charges and input prices, as farmers claimed. Some was attributable to inevitable natural factors—weather and the length of the production period of many crops. Some was attributable to the slowness of farmers to contract output and the inability, especially on specialized wheat and cotton farms, to shift readily among crops. But for the most part, whatever the cause, the solution was time. In time the two favorable trends—the gradual growth of demand and the movement of farm workers to industrial jobs—relieved the pressure on farm incomes. The growth of productivity in agriculture and the growth of demand and productivity in the economy at large made themselves felt in farm incomes through the confusions and disappointments of short-run disturbances.

The economic mechanism by which these changes occurred was becoming apparent between 1900 and 1914, when the agricultural instability of the late nineteenth century, with the discontent and crank remedies it had evoked, was receding into history. The depression of demand in the 1920s and 1930s, however, undermined faith in market mechanisms. The high demand of the 1940s and 1950s and the successful adjustment to technological change improved the outlook. But by that time the changes in the role of govenment in agricultural markets and supply conditions had sharply modified the organization of the agricultural industry.

Income Distribution

The demands for government action, induced by acute and prolonged instability, were sharpened in the 1930s and 1940s by one other feature of the growth in farm incomes; this was its uneven incidence. The data are not available to measure changes in the spread of incomes within farming; one oft-quoted recent statement is that the gap between the richest and the poorest groups of farmers in the United States is as wide as that between the average incomes of the richest and the poorest countries of the world. Whatever the extent and trend of income disparity, the mechanism by which it has been created and maintained, as investigated by Schultz, Nicholls, and others, has become apparent.[19] Two features have been important: first, a natural selection process that takes place in any agricultural society; and, second, the differential impact of market growth and technical change deriving from the uneven geographical incidence of market opportunities and communication improvements.

Prior to the strong market growth and technical change of the late nineteenth century, differences in wealth among farmers made themselves manifest as a result of different skills, abilities, and luck. Farmers coming early to an area secured the best locations and often the best land, and, striking early the best combinations of crops in good years, they began to amass some wealth. The distribution of the gains from the rise in land prices during settlement was a

---

[19] See Theodore W. Schultz, "Reflections on Poverty Within Agriculture," *Journal of Political Economy*, vol. 58, no. 1 (1950), pp. 1–15; William H. Nicholls, "Industrial–Urban Development and Agricultural Adjustments, Tennessee Valley and Piedmont, 1939–1954," *Journal of Political Economy*, vol. 68, no. 2 (1960), pp. 135–149; and Anthony M. Tang, *Economic Development in the Southern Piedmont: Its Impact on Agriculture* (Chapel Hill: University of North Carolina Press, 1958).

most important source of wealth inequality. In the Southeast in particular, inequality in original land grants set the process of widening inequality in motion. Changes in this distribution were then affected by the counteracting influences of two elements: the higher savings and easier access to capital for further investment open to holders of wealth, and the breakup of individual holdings through inheritance. Taken by themselves, these two forces have probably produced a fairly stable wealth distribution in many peasant societies in modern times where adequate internal checks to population growth were present. In the United States, however, the distribution was strongly affected by the breakup of slavery, which turned one third of the southern population into poor farmers, tenants, or landless laborers, and later by the dynamic intrusion of localized market growth and technical change in the country as a whole. The rather sharp adjustments of regions to new markets, products, and processes were not without cost. In each adjustment, some farmers were left behind; in regions less well favored by transport—in the hill country of New England, the Appalachians, and the Ozarks; in the cutover country of northern Minnesota; in areas of the Southeast with damaged soils; and in the southern Plains—the vicious circles characteristic of agriculture in underdeveloped countries appeared. People, removed from progressive farming by isolation, poverty, and ignorance, developed a fairly self-sufficient rural culture at a low level of subsistence which tended to perpetuate the poverty and ignorance on which it was built. High birth rates in such areas allowed for an out-migration which often left the weaker bodies and poorer spirits behind.

As we shall see, the problem of poverty in agriculture has not been much affected by government programs designed to raise the income level of agriculture as a sector. These may even, to some degree, have exaggerated the differences. The solution, of course, is the one suggested for raising farm income as a whole—increased shifts of poor farmers out of farming, with or without migration out of poor farming areas. In the case of southern blacks, it is possible to understand (though hard to sympathize with) the barriers that kept them largely confined to poor farms and rural areas. The massive migrations since the 1920s—particularly after the displacement of their labor on cotton farms—has exported much of the problem to urban areas. The solution for poor whites is the same, and the consolidation of farms and the penetration of transport, communication, and technical improvements into remote rural areas has done much. Nevertheless, it seems likely that as long as a meager independent living can be eked out on scrub farms, there will be people to occupy them. Poverty in agriculture, as measured by tangible income measures, can probably never be completely overcome; but population control, continued out-migration, and rehabilitation of depressed rural areas can keep the problem from growing worse.

NONCOMPETITIVE ELEMENTS
IN AGRICULTURAL ORGANIZATION

The impression of low and fluctuating farm income, inflexible industrial prices, and wide margins between the farm and retail prices of farm products has produced "agrarian discontent" in various forms and focused on various objects during the last 100 years. Farmers' faith in untrammeled individualism was modified by demands that "something be done" by government or by voluntary association to stabilize farm incomes and to improve and maintain the relative standing of family farmers in the economy. The most deeply distressed groups within the farm economy—tenants, migratory laborers, sharecroppers —were considerably less vocal than average farmers with disappointed expectations. This was true partly as the result of the farmers' submerged position in the national society, and partly because the evident remedy for their poverty was not agricultural reform, but migration out of agriculture. In the 1870s and 1890s, and in a lesser way even in the 1920s and 1930s, farm discontent also had a noneconomic component. It reflected the anxiety of a group which had dominated the national society, its politics, and its values since the first settlements, and had reached the high point in its culture in the mid-nineteenth century. It was clear after 1870 that industry was the business of America and that cities were its most characteristic social expression. But agrarian discontent had for a long time a tinge of nostalgia, a reactionary urge to preserve the Jeffersonian ideal forever. Given the active and enterprising spirit of many of its producers, the competitive and small-scale organization of America agriculture had traditionally been a great source of strength. But even the most individualistic farmers found it increasingly necessary to act in voluntary association with one another or through the organs of established government. Such activities fell into two groups : (*a*) those in which the disadvantages of the small-scale farm were overcome by splitting the activity off and organizing it cooperatively on a larger scale ; and (*b*) those in which the taxing and police powers of government were utilized to accomplish ends which farmers sought.

Group Organization Without Government

The ability of farmers to combine for obvious local purposes has been evident throughout American history. On the frontier and behind it, the barn-raisings and the husking bees provided examples of the readiness of groups to form and cooperate. American rural society, it has often been pointed out, combined individualism with a readiness to cooperate when some positive production advantage could be obtained. Nor was it always an innocent advantage that was pursued. The "claim clubs" of Iowa farmers to bid on lands at auctions and keep away outsiders were said to have defended early settlers and squatters against the intrusions of speculators.[20] They were also a means to the perpetuation of small local monopolies. Though economically isolated and living in a scattered pattern over the land, rural neighborhoods were not without group feeling and had the means of expressing it and enforcing it when the occasion arose. The church and the school were important centers for expressing and reinforcing commonly held values, but social life also rotated around the business and legal affairs in the small town. Crops, prices, railroad rates, and trading margins, as well as farm practices, were subjects of conversation at

---

[20] Allan G. Bogue, "The Iowa Claim Clubs : Symbols and Substance," *Mississippi Valley Historical Review*, vol. 44 (September 1958), pp. 231–253.

meetings of every rural social organization; and such organizations formed the basis for economic activities or for political action for economic purposes.

The reorganizations of agriculture in response to market pressures and opportunities have been the subject of earlier sections of this chapter. So long as these involved no innovations in ownership forms, they were readily assimilable under a system of market capitalism. Changes in specialization, in mortgaging or tenancy, in the complex of functions included under one owner have occurred and left the family farm and the competitive organization of farming unchanged. Even the growth in the size of capital and land holding in the farm unit has not made a drastic change. A striking innovation since 1940 has been the growth of contracts tying farms to food processors and distributors. Here the effort on the part of the buyer has been to avoid the price risks inherent in weather and other natural problems while insuring the producer against market fluctuations by guaranteeing him a fixed price for his output. In some cases, where needs or supplies are furnished by the purchaser, the effect of such contracts has been to change the farmer's status from that of an independent producer to one of a semidependence. These contracts have become most frequent in the perishable crops—fruits, vegetables, milk, and poultry—and control in some crops as much as 90 percent of the production. The development of large corporate farms, proceeding with some delays in the Midwest in the 1960s, represents a similar modification in farming's organizational structure.[21]

Before these recent changes, the major modification of the competitive organization in farming occurred with the cooperative movement that grew rapidly between 1880 and 1910, and continued to grow in the bad times of the 1920s and 1930s. The cooperative movement itself was an important feature of the organizational change which occurred in western countries in the middle and late nineteenth century. In Europe, in workers' districts, housing cooperatives and buyers' cooperatives appeared in conjunction with the growing trade-union movement. Formation of such units at the consumer level furnished a continuing concrete activity around which group action for wages and working conditions could be organized. Mutual insurance schemes were examples of such work. In farming, particularly in Germany and the Scandinavian countries in which peasant farming was combined with long traditions of village solidarity, the cooperative farm appeared in credit institutions and the sale of dairy products. How the seminal idea of this organizational form was imported from these European sources is not exactly known. Certainly the movement appeared first and strongest in the dairy regions of Wisconsin and Minnesota among farmers with German and Scandinavian antecedents. It grew and spread in the Midwest and into the South in cooperatives for the purchases of fertilizer and supplies. In the Far West, complicated cooperative arrangements and pools for the grading and marketing of fruits and vegetables were a prominent development after 1920.

---

[21] It is interesting that these organizational changes—cooperatives and contract sales—have appeared most frequently in perishable crops, where the seller is at a special disadvantage in disposing readily of the product. Where storage is relatively cheap, the producer has greater control over the marketing.

The purpose of all these arrangements was, of course, to secure for the farmers participating in them some of the control over prices and conditions of purchase or sale which size and a semimonopoly position could give. Viewed by many as defensive arrangements against the power of local merchants and money-lenders, shippers, railroads, and "big business," they had surprising success in many instances, though not always on the scale or with the spirit to fulfill the utopian ideals of some of their founders.

Government as an Agent of Group Action

Cooperatives worked for farmers through the market economy; their efforts resembled those of an individual farmer to raise himself by his bootstraps. Over small areas, cooperatives improved the conditions and timing of sales and bought a few specific supplies at wholesale prices. But farmers' complaints were steadily directed at problems that they felt demanded more fundamental solutions. In particular, government, with its power over the behavior of both the nonfarm sector and unwilling and uncooperative farmers, was called into play. Agrarian individualism, which had flourished in a period of free land and expanding markets, came to be modified in a direction leading to a major alteration in the market organization of the economy. Farmers, through political parties and their own semipolitical organizations, came to demand controls over the economy as a whole and ultimately over the behavior of farmers in particular.

The extreme doctrine of laissez faire had never, it should be noted, been a part of the thinking of American farm leaders and politicians. The indispensability of community organization was learned on the frontier, when projects of drainage, road building, and defense were obviously beyond the scope of the individual, and where even voluntary association was not enough to carry out the common purpose. The origins of government itself are seen in the early history of pioneer communities, and democratic local government with its parties, elections, taxes, and social expenditures—particularly on schools and roads—early became a part of rural life.

At a local and state level, in the South and west of the Alleghenies, the farm interest was dominant and expressed itself in the West before 1860 in a demand for internal improvements. The powers of taxation and withdrawal of land for public use were invoked on behalf of chartered companies to secure transportation improvements, particularly in the canal movement. Since canals generally did not run over several states, they did not require federal sponsorship. But even before the Civil War, the great national issues—money and the banking system, the tariff, the public land policy, slavery, and national transportation network—intimately affected the prosperity of farmers and planters and became objects of rural political organization.

Farmers' activities and attitudes in federal politics, however, cannot be understood without an appreciation of the social structure of the rural community and particularly of the regional differences in that structure between the South and the Midwest. In the South before 1860, the planter class, though composing only 3 to 4 percent of the population, was dominant. It held in slavery about 35 percent of the southern population, and—even more significantly—the racism inherent in the fact that the slavery was black slavery permeated the values and activated the fears of the rest of the white population. The preservation of slavery and of the cotton agriculture which utilized the slaves, overrode all questions of small farmers' welfare. The Democratic party, as the vehicle of this interest and policy. increased its dominance after the Civil War and the unpleasant experience of Republican Reconstruction. The primacy of the issue of local social structure in the South meant that the Democratic party's main concern there was to keep the federal government and federal programs at a distance. Subsidiary to this, the party acted as an agrarian party, advocating low tariffs, expansion of foreign markets, and banking and monetary policies which might help the agricultural sector. Even when industrial growth and a measure of urbanization came to the South after 1880, the party and the politics of the area remained dedicated first of all to the maintenance of the white-dominated society, without Yankee interference, and secondarily to low tariffs and a weak federal power.

In the North, the interest corresponding to that of the planters in the South was that of small-town businessmen whose values and attitudes were the model for the farmers' enterprise. Before the Civil War, free farmers, afraid of the extension of slavery and excited by business hopes and interests, joined this class and gave birth to the Republican party which, being the "party of business," came under domination of its conservative eastern wing. High tariffs, producing strong domestic markets, were sold to American farmers and much of the laboring population as essential to economic welfare and expansion. So in both regions the national political parties became instruments for preserving the hegemony and interests of a class other than that of the mass of the rural population. Of the two parties, the Democratic party was in a better position to represent the interests of those whose lives and fortunes were completely dedicated to farming so long as the race issue did not interfere. On tariffs and on the issue of the monetary standard, the programs of the Democrats were designed to appeal to the farmer. But in the North they failed often to make that appeal because of the close local connection between the more enterprising farmers and local business interests. And when the Democratic party came to represent also the interests of the mass of immigrant workers in the large eastern and Great Lakes cities, its usefulness as a purely agrarian party was further damaged.

Farmers, then, could use the national political system on occasion and could influence the platforms of the major parties. Where their interests were coincident with general national expansion, as for example in the development of the transportation network and the agricultural research and extension system, there was no problem. On tariffs the Democrats could represent the interests of farmers and laborers as consumers, although it was not a stand that both groups appreciated as their own. On the monetary issue and the control of corporations, the urban interests of the Democrats and the relative indifference of the southern politicians muddied the party's policy. In these peculiar national political circumstances, the alliance of small farmers in the

North and the South would seem to have been a natural one; and in the Populist movement between 1870 and 1900, the effort was made to establish the most plainly class-based party in American history. Its program included a graduated income tax, regulation of trusts and railroads, and bimetallism—and much of it was shared by the major parties or eventually taken over by them. But its thoroughgoing agrarian philosophy prevented it from capturing a presidential election.

But if farmers had somewhat limited success in shaping national economic policy to their interests, they were no less successful than other interest groups in getting the national government to do things for them. The United States Department of Agriculture, beginning as part of the Patent Office in the 1840s, established itself as a separate agency under a commissioner in 1863 and as a department with cabinet rank in 1876. Under a series of able secretaries, particularly James Wilson (1900–1912), its size and service functions to farmers increased. Then in the 1920s came a series of efforts to revive foreign markets for farmers, culminating in the establishment of the Federal Farm Board in 1929. These attempts tried to organize agricultural markets somewhat as it was imagined that industrial markets were organized and controlled. But they foundered, like most other sales cartels in history, from the inability to control farmers' production. The natural step under the New Deal was acreage and production control.

The Agricultural Adjustment Acts of 1933 and 1938, which began today's farm programs, were founded on two principles: (a) the idea of "parity," and (b) the right of the government acting on behalf of some farmers to force acreage control on all, so that parity might be achieved. *Parity* meant a relation first of farm prices, then after 1936 of farm incomes, to industrial prices and incomes which would approximate those prevailing in 1910–1914. The instrument by which farm prices were to be controlled was the marketing quota on the acreage allotment. In marketing quota programs, when 67 percent of the producers in a crop agreed, the total ouput marketed was to be controlled at a level estimated to yield parity prices or incomes, and each farmers' allotment was to be curtailed by a proportion to keep the total at the desired level. Acreage allotment programs have had a similar purpose, with payments being made to farmers to withhold acreage from planting in the controlled group. Such programs produced, of course, an incentive to increase the yield on the allotted acres. Loans or payments have been made to farmers to make up the difference between the market and the parity price or to compensate for acreage taken out of production, and the government has stored portions of the crops until their sale would not depress prices. The agricultural programs thus have been essentially a powerful cartel enforced and subsidized by the federal government.

However, it is wrong to think of government intervention as coming only in the form of this interference with the market economy. Since the early 1930s the federal government has adopted a whole series of measures to improve rural life directly and to strengthen the private institutional structure in agriculture. In crop insurance and in farm credit—from mortgage loans to short-run production credit—federal finances have supported semicommercial operations. The 1930s were alive with schemes to improve the condition of tenants and sharecroppers, although much actual change had to wait for economic forces and mechanization to drive many to the cities during World War II and the following decades. Rural electrification, sponsored by the Rural Electrification Administration in the 1930s, encouraged cooperatives to overcome the problems of scale in bringing lines to the countryside. The Tennessee Valley Authority vastly altered life in the upper South Central region, and federal dams, programs of flood control, woodland conservation, and federal highways have penetrated all sections of the country. Ironically—from an old agrarian point of view—such programs, while improving conditions of life and production in farming, have undermined the isolation of, and thus the features peculiar to, rural society. They have encouraged both the out-migration of farmers and the diffusion of industry in rural areas and so have gone far toward destroying the case for special agricultural programs.

Government activity in agriculture has been continuous, varied, and extensive. It has derived its effectiveness both from the superior size and scale of governmental agencies and from the taxing and police power of the state. The framework of local and state government early permitted the construction of the public-overhead capital demanded in rural areas. State governments, dominated by farmers, not only sponsored large public works in the nineteenth century, but also tried to control commercial and financial practices in their areas—though not necessarily always for the average farmer's good. More clearly at the federal than at the state level, government failed to give farmers full control over policies. Nevertheless, in the nineteenth century, the land policy, the public improvement policy, and the aids to agricultural research—all were guided by the demands of the farming community. When the price level fell after 1873 and as demand fell off after 1920, the efforts farmers made to change the drift of the economy through lower tariffs and easier money were unsuccessful. In particular, the effort to form an agrarian party, uniting the poorer class of farmers in the South and Midwest, came too late to overcome the divisions which race in the South and business interests in the North created among the rural classes. Farm organizations, operating like labor unions outside the national parties, were constrained to act as a special interest, lobbying within the national parties for favorable legislation.

Partly through their efforts, and through the response of the New Deal to agricultural distress, a framework of federal institutions grew up to strengthen and supplement the private economy as it functioned within and in relation to agriculture. The numerous services of the United States Department of Agriculture were expanded by a system of farm credit institutions, by crop insurance, by a federal highway program, and by the sponsorship of rural electrification.

Most interesting for an economist and most important for the economic health of agriculture have been the efforts to regulate the marketing of farm products and ultimately to control acreage and production at the source. The United States has not been alone in establishing such marketing and production controls. Other surplus producers, notably France, have been pushed into similar efforts to satisfy the agricultural interest and to maintain farm purchasing power through cartel-like controls sponsored by the government. Here, as in the markets for transportation services, many industrial products, and labor, the shift from unorganized freedom to conscious manipulation and control has accompanied the growth of productivity and the rapid changes in technology in the twentieth century.

It is an anomaly to many that the United States should be engaged in controlling farm output while starvation and malnutrition exist in the world, and indeed among some groups in the United States itself. The anomaly was most painfully evident in the early 1930s when the first control programs were accused of killing pigs and plowing under corn already in the field while unemployment and distress in the national economy were widespread and growing. Farm surpluses may indeed be an important instrument in a national and international war on poverty. However, on an international scale they are not great in relation to the world's needs, and they cannot be distributed with many strings attached. Although the new technology has made American agriculture immensely more productive, it has also raised prospects of similar improvements in productivity in native agricultures throughout the world. Perhaps American agriculture's best contribution to the world is not food but knowledge of how to grow it. That knowledge can best be developed and distributed on the basis of a sound and unsubsidized commercial agricultural economy at home.

SUGGESTED READING

Benedict, Murray Reed. *Farm Policies of the United States, 1790–1950: A Study of Their Origins and Development.* New York: Twentieth Century Fund, 1953.

Bidwell, Percy Wells, and John I. Falconer. *History of Agriculture in the Northern United States, 1620–1860.* Washington: Carnegie Institution, 1925. Reprint. Gloucester. Mass.: Peter Smith, 1941.

Bogue, Allan G. *From Prairie to Corn Belt; Farming on the Illinois and Iowa Prairies in the Nineteenth Century.* Chicago: University of Chicago Press, 1963.

Danhof, Clarence H. "Agriculture." In *The Growth of the American Economy,* edited by Harold F. Williamson. Englewood Cliffs, N.J.: Prentice-Hall, 1951, chap. 8.

Danhof, Clarence H. *Change to Agriculture: The Northern United States, 1820–1870.* Cambridge. Mass.: Harvard University Press, 1969.

Gates, Paul Wallace. *The Farmers' Age: Agriculture, 1815–1860.* New York: Holt, Rinehart & Winston, 1960.

Gray, Lewis Cecil. *History of Agriculture in the Southern United States to 1860.* Two vols. Washington: Carnegie Institution, 1933. Reprint. Gloucester. Mass.: Peter Smith, 1958.

Griliches, Zvi. "Hybrid Corn: An Exploration in the Economies of Technological Change." *Econometrica,* vol. 25, no. 4 (October 1957).

Hathaway, Dale E. *Government and Agriculture: Economic Policy in a Democratic Society.* New York: Macmillan, 1963.

Knoblauch, H. C., E. M. Law, and W. P. Meyer. *State Agricultural Experiment Stations; A History of Research Policy and Procedure.* U.S. Department of Agriculture Miscellaneous Publication no. 904. Washington: U.S. Government Printing Office, 1962.

Rasmussen, Wayne David. *Readings in the History of American Agriculture*. Urbana: University of Illinois Press, 1960.

Ross, Earle Dudley. "The Expansion of Agriculture" and "Agriculture in an Industrial Economy." In *The Growth of the American Economy*, edited by Harold F. Williamson. Englewood Cliffs, N.J.: Prentice–Hall, 1951, chaps. 20 and 36.

Schmidt, Louis Bernard, and Earle Dudley Ross. *Readings in the Economic History of American Agriculture*. New York: Macmillan, 1925. Reprint. New York: Johnson Reprint, 1966.

Shannon, Fred A. *The Farmer's Last Frontier: Agriculture, 1860–1897*. New York: Holt, Rinehart & Winston, 1945. Reprint. New York: Harper & Row, 1968.

U.S. Department of Agriculture. *Century of Service: The First 100 Years of the United States Department of Agriculture*. Washington: U.S. Government Printing Office, 1963.

U.S. Department of Agriculture. *Yearbook of the United States Department of Agriculture, 1899*. Washington: U.S. Government Printing Office, 1900.

True, Alfred Charles. *A History of Agricultural Experimentation and Research in the United States, 1607–1925, Including a History of the United States Department of Agriculture*. U.S. Department of Agriculture Miscellaneous Publication no. 251. Washington: U.S. Government Printing Office, 1937. Reprint. New York: Johnson Reprint, 1970.

Webb, Walter Prescott. *The Great Plains*. Boston: Ginn, 1931. Reprint. New York: Grosset & Dunlap, n.d.

12
MANUFACTURING

The manufacturing sector of the economy grew rapidly in the century and a half following 1800. The volume of manufacturing production rose about 6 percent a year throughout the nineteenth century, and at varying, but also generally high, rates through the world wars and the Great Depression. As a result of this rapid growth, manufacturing came to play an ever more important part in the national product. From a very minor position in 1800, it rose to constitute about one fourth of the national product in 1900 and about one third in 1950. It is no wonder that industrialization is often taken to be synonymous with economic growth.

In this chapter we shall discuss both what happened within the manufacturing sector and how these developments were related to the rest of the economy. We shall use a somewhat artificial dichotomy that allows for wide variation in the level of abstraction. To describe changes within the manufacturing sector, we shall follow the progress of two leading industries from the start of the nineteenth century up to the present. To show the relationship of manufacturing to other parts of the economy, we shall stop every half-century and survey what has happened to industry in general.

Any two industries would do for the detailed case histories. They are not intended to be encyclopedic chronicles of particular industries, but rather examples of the kind of experience found in many. Nevertheless, there is a value in studying industries long recognized as central to industrialization, and continuity is gained by studying the same ones throughout the entire period.

The first industry to be studied here is cotton textiles, which makes yarn and cloth out of raw cotton. Traditionally this has been the first industry to change over to a factory organization in the course of industrialization. In Britain, Japan, and many other countries, it was the cotton textile industry whose progress foreshadowed the more general growth of manufacturing. The reasons for this initiatory role are not all clear, but the progress of this industry does show the emerging dominance of factory production in manufacturing. As our time period progresses, we can examine the fate of a "mature" and then an "old" industry in a dynamic economy.

The other industry we shall follow in depth is iron and steel. This is the industry that made iron and then, after the Civil War, steel from iron ore and other raw materials. It generally supplies iron and steel to other industries which make it into finished products, although there are prominent exceptions to this rule. The growing complexity of iron and steel production illustrates the increasingly "indirect" pattern of manufacturing—that is, the increasing number of steps used to make a finished product for consumption. In addition, since the manufacture of steel is characterized by large-scale plants, and since large-scale plants tend to lead to monopolistic and oligopolistic behavior in the industry affected, the steel industry provides a contrast to the competitive cotton textile industry in its organization. We can therefore give some index of the range of industrial organization by examining two such extreme examples.

THE ANTEBELLUM PERIOD

The Cotton Industry

"About 1760 a wave of gadgets swept over England."[1] This quotation from a schoolboy's essay opens T. S. Ashton's famous chapter on the transformation of British industry in the final third of the eighteenth century. The transformation was most marked in the production of cotton textiles, as a series of newly invented machines revolutionized production. The spinning jenny allowed one woman to spin several threads at once. The water frame permitted water —and later steam—power to be used for spinning. The mule, which combined features of both these innovations, produced by the new methods a thread comparable in quality to those produced on a spinning wheel.

The result was an expanding supply of cotton thread which cheapened the weavers' inputs. The golden age of hand-loom weavers, however, was shortlived. The pressure on weaving to keep up with spinning encouraged people to search for ways to mechanize this part of the industry too, and the result was the power loom. The wages of hand-loom weavers were driven down again, and this group became a classic example of those left behind in the process of industrialization.

The British attempted to maintain a monopoly of the new methods of making cotton textiles, but it is easier to embargo goods than ideas, and production by the new means soon spread across the Atlantic. In 1790 a young man named Samuel Slater, who had been attracted to America by advertisements for men knowing how to build British cotton-spinning machinery, built the first mill in America to use Arkwright's water frame successfully. It is conventional to date the American cotton industry from this date, although there were already

[1] T. S. Ashton, *The Industrial Revolution* (London: Oxford University Press, 1948), p. 58.

several mills employing spinning jennies in America at this time. Slater's activities symbolized Britain's failure to monopolize its knowledge, and they are remembered for this reason.

Slater and his partner, Moses Brown, prospered. Their mill at Pawtucket, Rhode Island, was joined by others, and the production of cotton yarn expanded. New England with its many streams furnished an ideal setting for these small, water-powered spinning mills, and the cotton textile industry was concentrated in that region for the first two thirds of the nineteenth century. The mills produced only yarn, which was woven into cloth on hand looms in separate establishments.

Additional prosperity came to the fledgling cotton industry during the Embargo and the War of 1812, which virtually eliminated imports from 1808 to 1815. Unfortunately this protection soon came to an end, and the cotton industry found itself in a crisis. The price of cotton textiles—together with the prices of almost all other goods—fell drastically after 1815 as a result of competition from inexpensive British imports into the newly reopened American market.

The cotton textile manufacturers felt themselves to be under pressure, and they took steps to improve their profits. Their most potent response was the introduction of power looms, which lowered the costs of producing cloth and enabled some producers to survive the depression. The loom was introduced independently in Massachusetts and in Rhode Island by men who had been to England and acquired some knowledge of the power looms introduced there in the late eighteenth century. The change in Massachusetts has received more attention than the one in Rhode Island because it was accompanied by an organizational change that was of equal importance to the industry.

In 1813 Francis C. Lowell established the Boston Manufacturing Company, which began production at Waltham, outside Boston. Lowell was one of the men who had learned about the British looms, had he and Paul Moody utilized this knowledge to introduce the power loom at Waltham. But the use of the power loom was not the only thing that distinguished the Boston Manufacturing Company from its predecessors. It was an integrated firm, performing both the spinning and the weaving operations that had been separated previously. It used girls instead of children as operators, a change dictated by the inability of children to work the new looms. And it had a large capitalization. The second change was the most visible, as the firm recruited girls by advertisements and by providing living accommodations in boarding houses that—except for the long working hours—bore some similarity to college dormitories today. But the third, plentiful capital, was the most important.

Capital was needed to provide time—to build the machines and to begin production—before the sale of cloth could begin to produce profits. The early history of American manufacturing is replete with the stories of firms that failed from insufficient capitalization. For example, Alexander Hamilton was instrumental in the formation of the Society for Useful Manufactures, a firm that was organized to spin cotton in New Jersey in the early 1790s. The firm was not a success in the production of cotton for many reasons, but one of the main ones was the lack of capital supplied by its founders. People organizing firms realized that they would have to build or purchase machinery and buildings, but they failed to realize that they needed capital to employ labor and to operate the machines until they could begin to make a profit. Without this "working capital," firms were susceptible to accidents and succumbed to small difficulties. It was one of Lowell's more important contributions that he understood this problem and saw the means to avoid it.

With the introduction of the power loom and the organizational principles of the Boston Manufacturing Company, the cotton industry had acquired the tools for its rapid expansion. The quantity of cotton goods produced in mills increased by leaps and bounds after 1815. Measuring this output from the temporary peak in 1815 to another prosperous year, 1833, we discover that it had been growing at an average annual rate of about 16 percent. This is an extraordinarily rapid rate of increase; contemporary interest and pride in the cotton industry is not hard to understand. As the quantity of goods produced rose, the price fell, implying that the ability to make cotton textiles more cheaply after 1815 led to the increase in output. But was the rise in output due entirely to a change in the supply of cotton textiles? Output is determined by supply and demand. What was happening to demand?

This problem has been posed by Robert B. Zevin, and we shall follow his formulation here.[2] The most plausible single explanation for the rapid growth of the cotton textile industry between 1815 and 1833 is that the improvements in manufacturing methods lowered the price of cotton goods, and that people consequently bought more. It is undeniably true that this happened. On the other hand, the assertion that this was the *only* thing that happened implies that if the price had not changed, the quantity of cotton textile production would not have grown. However, there were at least five changes during this period that could have caused the quantity of cotton textiles produced to rise even if its price had not fallen. To assess the importance of the fall in price, we must ask how important these other changes were. In more technical terms, we are asking how important shifts in the demand curve—that is, increases in the quantity people would buy at a given price—were, relative to shifts in the supply curve—that is, increases in the quantity bought as a result of the increased productivity of cotton mills.

A glance at Figures 12.1 and 12.2 will clarify this question. The heavy lines in each graph represent possible supply and demand curves for cotton textiles. The hypothetical supply curves, *S*, slope upward, expressing the normal assumption that an increase in the price will induce producers to make more textiles. The hypothetical demand curves, *D*, slope downward, since we normally assume that an increase in the price will decrease the amount of textiles consumers wish to buy.

Two points are identified on both graphs; *they are the same points.* Let us assume that these points represent the data we are seeking to explain. The

[2] Robert Brooke Zevin, "The Growth of Cotton Textile Production After 1815," in *The Reinterpretation of American History*, Robert W. Fogel and Stanley L. Engerman (eds.), (New York: Harper & Row, 1971), pp. 122–147.

FIGURE 12.1

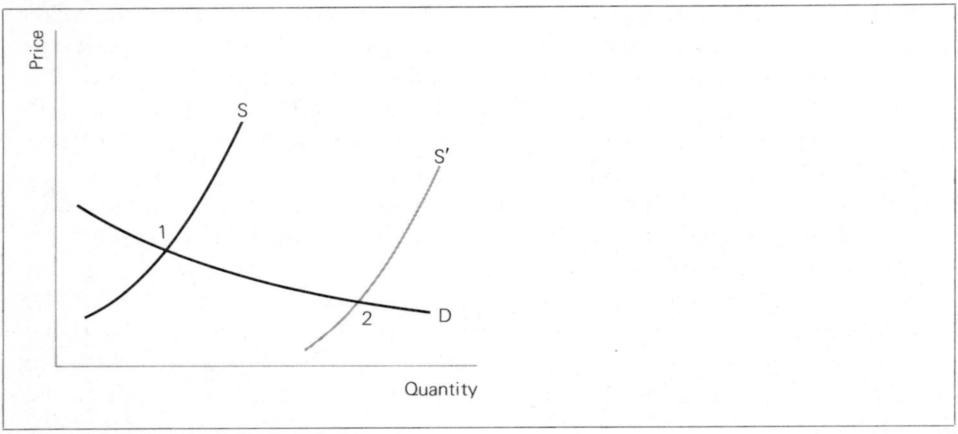

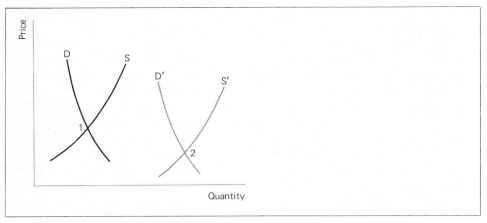

FIGURE 12.2

curves, then, represent alternative explanations of the given data. In the case at hand, the output of cotton textiles rose over time while the price fell. Point 1, representing a later time period than point 1, therefore lies to the right and below point 1. What are the possible explanations for the move from point 1 to point 2?

We assume that the market is in equilibrium at both points—that is, that the goods flowing into the market are sold at that price without raising or depleting inventories. We may then rephrase our question to ask: What are the possible configurations of supply and demand curves that will pass through point 1 at one time and point 2 at a later time? We begin with the supply curve.

Supply curves slope upward. It is therefore not possible for both points to lie on one supply curve, and our data on prices and quantities confirm the hypothesis that the supply curve for cotton textiles did indeed expand. But the magnitude of the shift—that is, the rise in the quantity that would be supplied *at a given price*—is not known. While any upward-sloping supply curve would have had to move to the right between the two periods, a supply curve that was close to horizontal would have had to move farther to the right to go through both points than would a more vertical one. To use the economist's language, a more horizontal curve is a more elastic curve, and a more elastic supply curve would have had to shift farther to pass through point 2 than a less elastic curve. Without knowing the elasticity, we cannot say how large the shift actually was.

We turn now to the demand curve, for which a similar indeterminacy exists. In fact, we cannot even tell from the two points alone that the demand curve shifted at all. Because the demand curve slopes downward, it is possible that a single curve passed through both points. In this case, the increase in quantity would be explained entirely by the shift in supply, as the traditional story of the cotton industry implies. This possibility is illustrated in Figure 12.1.

But there is another possibility. Since point 2 lies far to the right of point 1 without being too far below it, a demand curve has to be almost horizontal to pass through both points. As with supply curves, we term a horizontal curve an *elastic* curve. If point 2 represented conditions in this industry in 1833 while point 1 showed conditions in 1815, illustrating the fact that the quantity of cotton textiles sold rose much faster before 1833 than the price fell, then the demand for cotton textiles would have had to be very elastic to pass through both of them.

What does it mean for a demand curve to be very elastic? As Figure 12.1 shows, it means that a small change in price will produce a large change in the quantity demanded. In other words, a demand curve is elastic when people are very sensitive to changes in price—when a small change in price causes them to revise sharply their purchasing plans. It is possible that the demand for cotton textiles was of this sort, but it is also possible that people did not purchase many more cotton goods when the price fell.

This latter possibility is shown in Figure 12.2. The demand curve *D*, in this figure is less elastic (steeper) than the demand curve of Figure 12.1. Because it is so steep, it cannot pass through both of the observed points. Therefore, *if* the demand curve was not very elastic, then the demand curve must have shifted to the right between time 1 (1815) and time 2 (1833). In this case, the observed expansion of output would have been the result of an expansion of both the supply and the demand curves, in contrast to the traditional uni-causal explanation.

How are we to decide whether Figure 12.1 or Figure 12.2 is more accurate? How are we to discover the true elasticity of demand? These are the questions Zevin has attempted to answer, and we may begin our attempt by listing the five changes causing the demand curve to move to the right after 1815.

1.   Population was growing at this time, as it was throughout the early nineteenth century, at a rate of about 3 percent a year. If everything else stayed the same, each individual would have wanted to buy the same amount of

cotton goods at the beginning and end of our period. But since there were more people at the end than at the beginning, the total amount of cotton that everyone together would buy at the same prices (and incomes) would have risen approximately 3 percent a year, and we may therefore say that the demand curve shifted outward at a rate of about 3 percent a year. Of the 16 percent growth rate of production, 3 percent was accounted for by this growth in demand. The falling price of cotton textiles therefore accounted for no more than a 13 percent rate of growth, the rate of increase of per capita consumption.

2.   The United States had a tariff on cotton textiles throughout most of the antebellum era. The protective tariff was another response to the British textile imports that flooded into the United States after 1815. Nevertheless, the tariff was not a factor in the growth we seek to explain. Our base period, 1815, was taken to be the time when American cotton textile production was at a peak because the War of 1812 offered the same kind of protection to the American producers that the tariff did later.

The tariff instituted in 1816 had a minimum—that is, a fixed monetary amount was paid on every yard of cloth imported, no matter how cheap the cloth was. As the prices of cotton textiles fell, the effective rate of tax rose; by 1820 the tariff rate was high enough to reserve most of the American market for American producers. Had we calculated our growth rate from the depths of the depression, we would have found a higher growth rate, part of which would have been attributable to "import substitution." As we started from a period when there were very few imports, however, we have already taken a large degree of protection for granted in our estimate of the rate of growth.

3.   This was a period of great improvements in the transportation network of the United States. The most important single new link in this network was the Erie Canal, which greatly cheapened the cost of transporting goods from New England to the area west of the Allegheny Mountains. In addition, the introduction of the steamboat on the Mississippi River reduced the cost of an alternate route to the West—by the sea to New Orleans and then up the Mississippi —and provided another inexpensive way to ship goods from New England to the interior of the country. Most machine-made cotton textiles were produced in New England, and the lower cost of transportation broadened the market for them. Even if there had been no change in manufacturing methods and the price of cotton textiles at the mills had not fallen, the lower cost of transporting textiles to the consumers would have made retail prices throughout the country lower. The consumers would have bought more at the new prices, and the production would have grown.

4.   If people receive more income, they normally buy more goods and services. If the incomes of Americans had been increasing, per capita consumption would have risen. Unfortunately, we do not know whether incomes were rising (see Chapter 2). It seems clear that they were rising between 1820 and the Civil War, but it is also possible that they fell between 1815 and 1820. You will recall that 1815 was the height of wartime production, and that the succeeding few years were years of great depression. If the fall after 1815 was large, then the rise in income after that date would have only regained ground

lost in the earlier years. It would not then have led to an increase in the consumption of cotton. It seems more likely, however, that per capita incomes were not below the level of 1815 for very long and that the growth of income did in fact lead to a growth in demand.

5.   Finally, in our list of factors increasing demand, comes what economists call "changes in tastes." It is possible that people decided they *liked* cotton textiles. They were lighter than wool, they could be washed, they could be printed with bright colors. If people were willing to buy more cotton because they liked it—not because its price was lower—a change in tastes occurred. However, it is very hard to know whether people buy a new product because their tastes have changed, or whether they buy it because it is cheaper than the old product they had been buying before.

Having listed these various factors, can we say how much of the increase in the per capita consumption of machine-made cotton textiles was due to them—that is, to an expansion of demand—and how much was due to an increase in the supply? To do this, we must broaden the scope of our inquiry to include the entire antebellum period. We can learn more from the contrast between conditions before and after 1833 then we can from a look at the earlier period alone. In the period from 1833 to 1860, the growth of cotton textile production was far slower than it was in the years before 1833; the average rate was about 5 percent, down from 16 percent before 1833. This meant a growth in per capita consumption of about 2 percent, as the rate of population growth did not change. The price of cotton textiles fell at a rate of about 1 percent a year.

The growth of production did not fall abruptly from 16 percent per annum to 5 percent per annum in 1833, of course. There was a gradual slowing down of growth in the antebellum period, and an annual calculation of growth rates would show a rather smooth descent. For the sake of simplicity, we have broken the period in two. The first subperiod contains the years of most rapid growth, and its growth rate consequently is significantly higher than the growth rate of the second subperiod. The large discrepancy between 16 and 5 percent does not indicate an abrupt shift in 1833; instead, it indicates that the rate of growth was falling quite rapidly throughout the antebellum years. (The succeeding comments about the contrast between conditions before and after 1833 need to be interpreted in the same light.)

Was the demand for cotton textiles still increasing after 1833? The effects of the initial introduction of cheap transportation to the West may have been wearing off, and the novelty of machine-made cotton textiles may have been fading. Nevertheless, transportation continued to become less expensive, albeit at a much slower rate, and the income of people buying cotton was undeniably rising. It is unlikely that demand was growing more slowly than about 1 percent a year, leaving only about 1 percent to be attributed to the fall in the price. In other words, the falling price tells us that supply was increasing faster than demand, but a good part of the increase in the quantity sold was due to the growth of both supply and demand. Figure 12.2 is a more accurate representation of the growth of the industry *after* 1833 than Figure 12.1.

Now let us return to the period before 1833. In these years, the quantity had been rising more rapidly than in the years between 1833 and 1860, and the price had been falling more rapidly. In fact, all prices were falling in the years after the War of 1812. If all prices were to fall equally, there would be no reason to expect people to buy more of one good than another. Consequently, it is the extent to which the price of cotton textiles fell *relative* to other prices that is important. (The overall price level did not change between 1833 and 1860.) The fall in this relative price was about 3 percent a year.

The two periods may be compared by looking at Figure 12.3. The three points identified on the graph show the prices and quantities in 1815, 1833, and 1860, respectively. Point 2 is considerably closer to point 3 than to point 1 in a horizontal direction because the quantity of cotton textiles produced rose much more rapidly before 1833 than it did later. It is slightly farther from point 1 than from point 3 in a vertical direction, a result of the slightly more rapid price fall in the earlier period.

Supply and demand curves have been drawn through points 2 and 3, similar to the ones in Figure 12.2. No single supply curve could pass through point 2 and point 3; thus, the supply curve must have shifted between 1833 and 1860. A single demand curve *could* have intersected both points, but we have asserted that the demand curve was probably shifting to the right in these years. Consequently, D_2 has been drawn as too inelastic to pass through point 3, and a new demand curve, D_3, has been drawn for 1860.

Turning to the earlier period, we see that no single supply curve could pass through point 1 and point 2. As we have said before, the supply curve shifted outward after 1815, and it can be seen from the graph that it was shifting far more rapidly before 1833 than later. The innovations of the late eighteenth century in England allowed a large shift in the supply curve, and most of the shift took place in one great leap of productivity in the years just following 1815. A single demand curve could have passed through points 1 and 2, as in

FIGURE 12.3

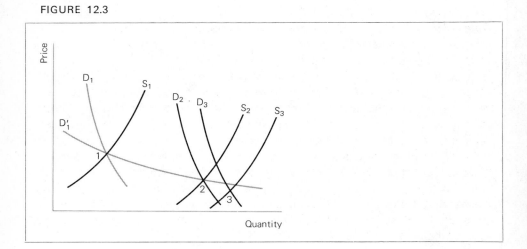

Figure 12.1 and the traditional description of the industry; such a curve, D_1', is drawn as a light line in Figure 12.3. It is far more elastic (horizontal) than D_2 and D_3, however, and it is hard to imagine why the elasticity of demand—that is, the shape of the demand curve—would have changed dramatically in or around the 1830s. (It passes above point 3—it is even more elastic than a demand curve that passed through both points 2 and 3 would be!) On the other hand, if the elasticity did not change between the two subperiods, then the demand curve in 1815 looked like the other light curve in Figure 12.3, D_1, and there was a pronounced decrease in the rate of expansion of demand (the rate at which the demand curves shifted to the right). We have given some reasons why the demand curve might have been expanding particularly rapidly in the years just after 1815, but the implied slowdown in the rate of expansion in the late antebellum years still seems quite extreme.

It is likely that the true demand curve lies somewhere between D_1 and D_1', and that both the elasticity and the rate of growth of demand fell in the antebellum period. There was some fall in elasticity as machine-made cotton cloth became more of a necessity and less of a luxury, and the rate of expansion slowed as the savings from the Erie Canal were incorporated into the economy.

Return now to the power loom. This innovation increased the consumption of cotton goods by lowering their price. But our discussion of the demand curve has shown that the per capita production of cotton would have risen rapidly even if the price had not fallen. The use of this machine was aided by the growth of population, the decline in transportation costs, the rising income of the country, and changing tastes. The combination of these factors and the power loom produced growth that was not merely rapid, but truly spectacular.

The Iron Industry

The iron industry, like the cotton industry, was revolutionized by innovations in eighteenth-century Britain. A complex of changes affecting every part of iron production—from the production of pig iron from ore to the production of wrought iron from pig—reduced costs and increased the output of iron in Britain. These changes were instrumental in making Britain the "workshop of the world," but they were slow to spread to other countries.

The production of pig iron in America, for example, rose at the comparatively modest average rate of 6 percent per year throughout the antebellum period. The rate of growth was slightly higher in the 1840s and somewhat lower during the great agricultural booms of the 1830s and 1850s, but the overall rate was not nearly as large as that of the American cotton industry in its early years. Even more surprising, this growth was accomplished without a significant fall in the (relative) price. The production of pig iron per capita grew about 3 percent a year, and most of even this moderate increase must be credited to the simultaneous expansion of supply and demand, not to the results of a lower price. Can we explain why the expansion of supply and demand moved at this relatively slow rate?

Turning first to the supply side, we need a little technical background. Iron ore is a mixture of iron and oxygen, as is rust. In order to transform the iron into usable form, it is necessary to remove the oxygen. This is done by heating the ore in a container called a blast furnace, where the ore and a fuel are mixed together and burned. Fuels are composed of carbon, and the net effect of the operation is to replace the oxygen in the ore by carbon from the fuel. The resultant mixture of iron and carbon is called pig iron. It melts easily and can be cast into many shapes; on the other hand, it is brittle and cannot be forged. Wrought iron, which can be forged or wrought, is made by removing the carbon from pig iron, this process being cheaper than making it directly from iron ore. Steel was made from wrought iron before the Civil War, but it was very expensive and little used.

The traditional blast-furnace fuel was charcoal. This fuel has several disadvantages, one of which is that it can be used only in a small blast furnace. As a result, increases in the quantity of pig iron made with charcoal were provided by increasing the number of blast furnaces, rather than by increasing their size. The knowledge to operate a blast furnace was easy to acquire; iron ore was available in the necessary small quantities in many places, and wood for charcoal was not scarce. Thus there were no obstacles to the construction of new blast furnaces, and the production of pig iron with charcoal could be extended easily without a large increase in the price. This appears to be what happened in the antebellum United States. There was a great increase in the number of charcoal blast furnaces, which accounted for most of the increase in production. There was a movement along a very elastic supply curve, as opposed to a shift in the curve itself. This situation is shown in Figure 12.4, where only a slight fall in a very elastic supply curve is shown. (Had the supply curve not changed *at all*, point 2 would have been virtually unchanged also.)

This is very strange. The British cotton industry was transformed by innovations, and Americans soon copied, adapted, and superseded them. The British iron industry was similarly transformed, but the American iron industry

FIGURE 12.4

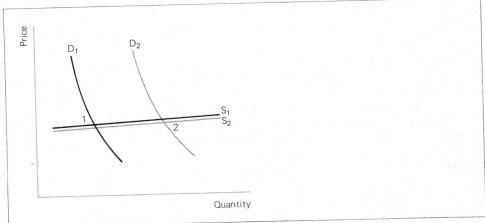

continued to use the traditional technology. Why the contrast? The answer appears to be in the nature of American raw materials.

The innovation that transformed the making of pig iron in Britain was the substitution of coal and, more importantly, coke for charcoal in the blast furnace. To do this, coal that could be coked was needed. This was *bituminous* coal—that is, coal containing gas or bitumen. There was bituminous coal in America, too, but the American coal had two important disadvantages. First, it contained sulfur. This impurity weakened the resultant pig iron, which reduced its value and hence the inducements to use coke. Second, it was located west of the Allegheny Mountains. This meant that it was far from the Atlantic Coast where consumption was initially largest, and that it was in a less well-known part of the country. Both of these disadvantages were temporary. As the country expanded, the demand for iron "moved" west, the area west of the Allegheny Mountains was settled and explored, and coking coal free from sulfur was discovered. But for most of the antebellum period, the production of pig iron with coke was very small.

On the eastern slope of the Alleghenies, there was a different kind of coal, *anthracite*. This coal did not contain either gas or sulfur. The absence of gas was a disadvantage, as it meant that the methods of using coal discovered in the eighteenth century could not be employed. The absence of sulfur, on the other hand, was an advantage, for it meant that if pig iron could be produced with anthracite, it would be of good quality. The techniques necessary to use anthracite were discovered around 1840, and were introduced simultaneously in Britain and the United States. The use of anthracite lowered the price of pig iron slightly, but not nearly as much as the use of coke would have done, because anthracite was more expensive than coke and harder to use. To the extent that there was a fall in the price after 1840, however, the expansion of pig iron production was partly a result of a shift in the supply curve. Americans, being unable to adopt the English fuel immediately, temporized with less adequate fuel. The effect of this substitute on price was small, but it contributed to the expansion of production without a rise in price.

Turning to the demand for iron, we may ask what caused the increase in demand noticed earlier. People did not use pig iron the way they used cloth. It was necessary to make the pig iron into something a bit more accessible before it could be sold to its eventual user. There were two ways in which this could be done, and we shall consider them in turn.

When the carbon was removed from pig iron, the resultant product was wrought iron that could be rolled or hammered into different shapes. Carbon would "evaporate" from iron spontaneously, but heat was needed to speed the process. This heat was traditionally supplied by a forge which had the disadvantage of heating only a small area at a time. In the eighteenth century, a way of containing heat over a wider area was introduced, enabling each worker to work with more iron. The need for work was by no means eliminated, and "puddling," as the new process was called, was not a trivial job. Nevertheless, the new process was more efficient than the old, and its adoption increased the production of wrought iron at any given price.

Puddling, together with the use of rollers in place of hammers to shape the wrought iron, was adopted in the United States in the early nineteenth century. The price of wrought iron consequently fell, even though the price of pig iron did not. The extent of this price fall is not known with any exactitude, but it appears to have been about 2 percent a year. The production of wrought iron in the United States rose about 4 percent a year in the years before 1850, but this change cannot be compared to the growth rate directly, since imports of wrought iron also rose. The consumption of wrought iron—as opposed to its production—rose about as fast as the production of pig iron, about 6 percent a year. Per capita consumption consequently rose about 3 percent a year. As the price was falling about 2 percent a year, this could have been simply a movement along a stable demand curve.

Sometime around the middle of the nineteenth century, the consumption (and the production) of wrought iron rose to about 8 percent a year. There does not seem to have been any change in the supply of wrought iron at this time ; instead, the expansion was the result of a growth in demand. The reasons are not hard to find. The railroad had been introduced to the United States in the years before 1850, and the construction of railroads had grown rapidly. By the middle of the century, the demands of railroad construction were large enough to have an impact on the total demand for wrought iron. Trains run on rails, and it was discovered that wrought iron combined the properties of malleability, resilience, and strength that are needed for rails better than other materials existing at the time. When railroads became a prominent part of the American scene, they caused the demand for wrought iron to shift outward.

Not all pig iron was used to make wrought iron. Some was used as pig iron to make castings. Puddling could use a wider range of materials than the earlier methods of making wrought iron, and a result of the introduction of puddling was the substitution of scrap for pig iron in the manufacture of wrought iron. While this process was going on—in the years before about 1850—the production of wrought iron was not rising rapidly, and the demand for pig iron to make wrought iron consequently did not rise much at all. That the production of pig iron rose more rapidly than would have been required for the production of wrought iron alone is evidence that the demand for iron castings was rising. In fact, the production of iron castings rose at a rate of over 10 percent a year in the two decades preceding 1850. After 1850, this rate slowed to about 5 percent, or about 2 percent per capita.

In eighteenth-century Britain, the introduction of coke had stimulated the use of castings in two ways. It had reduced the price, and it had altered the characteristics of pig iron. Pig iron made with coke was less suitable for wrought iron than pig iron made with charcoal, but it made better castings. In America, coke was not used widely in this period, and pig iron made with anthracite shared the characteristics of pig iron made with coke to only a limited degree. The use of coke in Britain encouraged the use of castings by increasing their supply. The parallel, later movement toward castings in the United States was primarily the result of a shift in demand.

It would appear that the use of castings in Britain was an easily apparent benefit of the new technology. The Americans were determined to reap the same benefits, even before they could locate American resources that would let them use the British technology. They increased their use of castings as the British had done, although they did not have the price incentives the British had to do so. In other words, the Americans were willing to pay more than the British in order to imitate them. It is possible that they paid enough more to cancel out the advantages to be gained from the new materials—cast iron is superior to wood for many uses only if it does not cost too much more—but we do not know enough to make a judgment. When this imitative process takes place today, we call it a "demonstration effect." It is a shift of the demand curve deriving from a change in tastes. (See item 5 on page 425.)

We can identify three main uses for cast iron. First, there were stoves. Fires were used for heat and cooking, and it was found that the efficiency and convenience of a fire could be enhanced by enclosing it in cast iron—that is, by using a stove. The stove could be located within a room, so that it radiated heat in all directions, while a fire was surrounded on three sides by brick and radiated from only one. In addition, the stove was easier to cook on, as it had a surface on which to place pots. A particularly fine stove was introduced by Benjamin Franklin near the middle of the eighteenth century, and the use of stoves spread rapidly. In the nineteenth century, many foundries separated themselves from blast furnaces and specialized in the production of stoves. Although this does not seem to have reduced their price, it may have served to make more stoves available without an increase in price; in other words, it may have made the supply of stoves more elastic.

Second, cast iron was substituted for wood in machinery and other implements. The substitution that used the largest amount of iron was probably the conversion of municipal water systems from wooden pipes—hollow logs—to cast-iron pipes. Many eastern cities became conscious of the lack of water in the city and constructed water systems in the early nineteenth century. Increasingly, they used cast iron for their pipes. More diverse, but still important, was the growing use of cast iron for plows, steam engines, reapers, and other machines. The use of iron in plows enabled farmers to plow more deeply and to replace plows less often. The use of iron in steam engines permitted the use of high-pressure steam and a consequent growth of efficiency. The durability, rigidity, and adaptability of cast iron to diverse uses increased the efficiency of machines, and the demand for cast iron rose.

Third, cast iron was used for ornamentation. House fronts were made of cast iron; pillars were made of cast iron; any kind of curlicue or flourish that would demonstrate the versatility of the metal and the architect was used. Cast iron, it turned out, was a strong and durable material for construction, but its utilitarian appeal was almost overshadowed by its visual attractions. Cast-iron ornamentation was the most visible symbol of the new age.

Why then did the production of castings stop growing at its rapid rate? People did not stop cooking, or using machines, or building buildings. Yet the growth of demand slowed markedly after the middle of the nineteenth century.

The movement was not as sharp as the data presented above may have suggested. The comparison of average rates from two periods emphasizes the differences between them without illuminating the transition from one to the other. Even if the slowdown in the growth of demand was not sudden, however, it was nevertheless large and calls for explanation.

The supply curve of pig iron made with coke had not yet shifted to increase the attractiveness of cast iron relative to other materials. Wrought iron was becoming less expensive, however, and the use of rollers to shape wrought iron was providing a way to shape it more easily. The advantages of wrought iron increasingly overshadowed the initial appeal of cast iron, and the composition of demand shifted. People did not decrease their demand for iron after the middle of the nineteenth century; they just used iron in a different form. This change was most apparent in railroads, but many products other than rails also came to be made of wrought iron after the middle of the century. The same transition was taking place in Britain, although it did not follow with such precipitous haste the adoption of cast iron: The use of cast iron in Britain expanded in the eighteenth century, and the use of wrought iron waited until the nineteenth. In the United States, progress in blast furnaces came later and demand was more volatile. The use of cast iron spread wildly for a brief time, only to be replaced by wrought iron and, later, steel.

Industry in General Up To 1860

Cotton textiles and iron were the leading symbols of the new age, but many other industries were also expanding and progressing in the early nineteenth century. Manufacturing had been a comparatively minor activity in the eighteenth century, when most people were farmers. There were, of course, iron furnaces and forges, flour mills, rope walks (to make ropes for ships), and other large-scale establishments. But most manufactured articles were produced either at home by families of farmers or by specialized individual craftsmen. Most families made cloth, soap, candles, or leather themselves; more specialized craftsmen made shoes, saddles, hats, iron implements, and men's clothing. In the years before 1860, these articles were made increasingly in factories.

The ten largest industries as given in the census of 1860 are shown in Table 12.1. They are ranked by their "value added"—that is, by the amount by which the value of their output exceeded the value of their raw-material inputs. Cotton goods head the list as a result of the phenomenal growth of this industry. Woolen goods, from which most ordinary clothing was made before the rise of cotton, was also one of the largest industries in 1860, but by no means the largest. The technical innovations that revolutionized the cotton industry were applicable also to the woolen industry, but there was just enough difference between the animal and the vegetable fibers to make the transfer difficult. Technical progress in the woolen industry lagged behind progress in the cotton industry by about 30 years, and the cotton industry reaped most of the rewards from the innovations as a result.

TABLE 12.1
The ten largest industries in 1860, by value added

	Value Added (millions of dollars) (1)	Employment (thousands of workers) (2)	Value Added per Worker (thousands of dollars) (3)
Cotton goods	55	115	.48
Lumber	54	76	.71
Boots and shoes	49	123	.40
Flour and meal	40	28	1.43
Men's clothing	37	115	.32
Iron	36	50	.72
Machinery	33	41	.81
Woolen goods	25	61	.41
Carriages and wagons	24	37	.65
Leather	23	23	1.00
All manufacturing	815	1474	.55

SOURCE: U.S. Bureau of the Census, *Census of the United States: 1860*, vol. 3 (Washington: U.S. Government Printing Office, 1861), pp. 733–742.

The iron industry appears in the list also, its modest place reflecting its modest growth rate. The value added per worker in the iron industry, shown in Column (3) of Table 12.1, was higher than in the textile industries, although it was not as high as in flour and meal production. This quantity is called *labor productivity* by economists, and differences in labor productivity among industries raise questions to be answered. Rather than ask specifically about the difference between iron and textiles, let us examine the general question of why labor productivity varies.

Value added is a measure of the extent to which the value of an industry's products has been increased by the process of manufacture. Products are increased in value by the use of workers (labor) and of machines (capital), and labor productivity measures the ratio of this increment only to the number of workers used. Accordingly, there are two reasons why labor productivity could be high. If most of the work were being done by capital—that is, if there were many machines or large machines for each worker—then the number of workers required to produce a given value added would be small. Alternatively, if the workers and the machines used were very productive, labor productivity could be high even though there were not so many machines in use. To be more formal, we may say that labor productivity can be high either because the capital/labor ratio (the amount of machines used per worker) is high or because total productivity is high.

If we know the amount of machinery used per worker, we can decide which of these reasons is applicable in any specific case. Unfortunately, however, the quantity of capital is an elusive concept and measurements are hard to make. The problem is that while there is a natural unit of labor—the worker—there is no natural unit of capital. A machine by any other name may still be a machine, but two machines need not be alike. If one lathe can produce twice as many chair legs as another, should we call it one lathe or two? And if it can in addition produce fancier legs than the other, does that make it three? We normally settle questions like this by looking at the market: Do such lathes sell for twice and three times the price of the original one? But this solution has its own problems. Prices change over time, and we need some way to deflate for changes in prices. This is done by dividing the price in any year by the price of a standard unit in the base year—which is only possible if we have decided what a standard unit is.

It seems advisable to sidestep this hornets' nest and to see if the discrimination can be made on other bases in individual cases. As our theory about changes in the capital/labor ratio is better developed than our theory about changes in overall productivity, we ask first if differences in the capital/labor ratio can explain differences in labor productivity.

Of the industries shown, the one producing flour and meal had by far the highest labor productivity. This is not surprising: flour and grist mills were large combinations of machinery operated by very few men. About one third of the steam engines in the antebellum economy were used in these mills, and these engines were not the only machines used. Oliver Evans, a Philadelphia millwright in the late eighteenth century, invented a series of machines that automatically moved the grain and meal around the mill. These machines were used widely, improving labor productivity in flour mills and involving Evans in endless patent litigation. Evans' machinery may have been better than the machinery used elsewhere. Nevertheless, without other information, it seems wiser to attribute the high labor productivity achieved with his machinery to its large size rather than to its quality—which is hard to compare with machinery in other industries.

It is often said that Evans' purpose in introducing these machines was to save labor, since the machines did in fact decrease the labor needed to produce a given output by half. Nevertheless, the fact that the invention saved labor is not by itself evidence that its primary purpose was to do so. The new machines saved costs in many ways, and there is no evidence that Evans thought the reduction in labor requirements was the most important of these. Evans calculated the savings to be made by using his machines in an advertisement dating from 1810. Only about 10 percent of the savings were calculated to come from the reduction in labor costs, while fully three quarters were said to come from the increased quality of the flour produced. We do not know whether this advertisement was accurate, nor do we know the extent to which it reflected Evans' motives for making the inventions, but the nature of the benefits in his calculation would seem to offer prima facie evidence that his motives were more general than just saving labor (see Chapter 7).

At the opposite end of the spectrum lay the production of men's clothing, with the lowest labor productivity recorded in Table 12.1. The sewing machine was only just beginning to be used in 1860, and most clothing was made by hand. This was slow work, involving almost no machinery, and labor productivity was low as a result. Boots and shoes were produced by similar methods and had a similar labor productivity. The sewing machine would revolutionize production here too.

This discussion raises a general question about the progress of American manufacturing. Knowing the availability of land in the United States, English visitors to the United States at mid-century expected to find only rudimentary manufacturing. When they discovered a sophisticated and advanced manufacturing sector with high labor productivity, they asked what had caused it. And, paradoxically, they said it came about *because* of the availability of land.

The argument went like this: Workers in agriculture could earn a high wage because the land was plentiful and productive. Just as the use of more or better machines in manufacturing raises labor productivity there, the use of more or better land in agriculture raises labor productivity in farming. Since workers in agriculture were very productive, their wages were high. In order for manufacturers to attract workers from farms, therefore, they had to offer high wages also. In order to offer high wages, manufacturers had to have workers with high labor productivity; and in order to improve the labor productivity of workers in manufacturing, they used more or better machinery than English manufacturers. As a result, the British visitors said, American manufacturing was more productive than English.

Just as it is hard to compare the quality of Evans' milling machinery with that of Lowell's power loom, it is hard to compare the quality of American machinery as a whole with that of British machinery. The English visitors were very impressed by the American methods, but they did not stop to ask if the American machines were better, larger, or merely different. We must ask two questions as a result: First, did the availability of land create an inducement for manufacturers to use better machines? And second, did it lead to an inducement to use more machines?

The argument about the *quality* of machines is based on comparative advantage. It says that the United States had a comparative advantage in agriculture, and that something "extra" was needed in manufacturing to attract labor away from agriculture. As just stated, the argument maintains that this extra something was better machinery. But there was an alternative to the use of better machinery: the tariff. If manufacturers could get Congress to impose tariffs on imported manufactured goods, they would raise the price of manufactures in the United States and thus increase labor productivity in manufacturing by raising the price of the goods produced—as opposed to increasing the quantity. As explained in Chapter 17, the manufacturers were very successful in their incessant endeavors to levy and raise tariffs. Thus this argument loses its force once the tariff is taken into account.

The argument about the *quantity* of machinery is a little different. It asserts that the plentiful supply of land took labor from the manufacturing sector, either directly or by attracting immigrants to the countryside rather than the city. This process left a relatively large supply of capital in manufacturing with a small labor force; high labor productivity was the result.

This argument has all the appeal of a traditional economic position. It requires, however, some strong assumptions about the way the economy operates to be applicable. In particular, it assumes that the extension of agriculture in the United States would deny labor to manufacturing, but not capital. For if capital were needed on the farms also, we would not know if more labor or more capital were taken from manufacturing. As capital clearly was needed in farming (land had to be cleared, buildings built, and machinery used —see Chapter 11), this argument is too simple to use as an explanation of American industrial efficiency.

An alternative argument, alas, is hard to find. The general issue is discussed in Chapter 7. Here we will note only that the impressions of the British observers were not spread over the broad spectrum of American industry. The visitors talked primarily about two areas, which deserve special comment.

The first area was the production of "locks, clocks, and small arms"—that is, light manufacturing. These industries used what came to be called the American system of manufacturing. They made their locks or clocks or guns out of many smaller *interchangeable parts.* The parts could be produced separately and then assembled much more quickly and cheaply than complete individual items could be made. To be assembled easily, the parts had to be truly interchangeable, a situation which required that they all be the same size. It was not possible to guarantee a constant size before the nineteenth century, and the use of interchangeable parts was in part the exploitation by one segment of the manufacturing sector of progress made in another. Metal-working machinery or machine tools and measuring devices were improved greatly in the first half of the nineteenth century, and they enabled the American system of manufacturing to grow and eventually to be exported to Britain.

The name of Eli Whitney is associated with this advance, and the story is told of his contract with the army to build muskets for the War of 1812. A more commercial story might serve even better: About 1840, an American clock maker discovered how to make a one-day brass clock using interchangeable parts for less than 50 cents—far less than individually made clocks were worth. He sent a shipment to England for sale, valuing them, naturally, at 50 cents each. The British customs authorities, knowing the price of British clocks, assumed that these clocks were undervalued, confiscated them, and paid the importer the invoice price. The clock maker was delighted to find an immediate buyer for his clocks with no selling expense on his part, and he promptly sent a new and larger shipment of clocks to England. The British government seized them also, paying only the invoice price. But when a third and even larger shipment arrived, the British government abandoned the clock business and let it in.

The other area noticed prominently by the British visitors to America was woodworking. Americans used a great deal of wood, and they were very skillful in its use. In England, there were fewer trees, and iron was much cheaper (for reasons we have seen). The English consequently used iron where the Americans used wood, and they were better at metal working than the Americans at mid-century. This is hardly surprising. Industry, at least in its early stages, is tied to the raw materials available to it. Americans used wood in manufacturing, and they also used many other materials from the land. Over half of the ten largest industries in 1860 used materials directly from agriculture, forestry, or mining. Cotton, wool, corn and wheat for milling, and leather all came from agriculture. Wood for lumber came from the forests, and iron ore was mined. As the country grew, more and more manufacturing industries used as inputs the products of other industries. But that is a story largely of the century after 1860.

1860–1910

The Cotton Industry

The cotton textile industry was one of those hardest hit by the Civil War. Cotton was grown in the South and made into cloth in the North; the war could not have done otherwise than disrupt this process. When, in addition, southern ports were blockaded in an effort to starve the South of foreign exchange, the hardships of both the American and British cotton industries were ensured. It is common in Britain to talk of a "cotton famine" during these years, and that is exactly what it was. In the North, at the peak of prices in 1865, the price of cotton in terms of wheat was ten times its price in the South. The relative price of cotton cloth was consequently high, and people bought wool during the war.

After the cessation of hostilities, the cotton industry quickly regained its antebellum size and approximated its earlier growth rate. Measuring its growth from the years just before the Civil War to the years just before World War I, we find that the output of the cotton industry grew about 4 percent a year. This is a little slower than the industry was growing in the last antebellum years, but the population of the country was also growing a little slower—2 instead of 3 percent a year. The growth of per capita production was thus about the same in the two periods, about 2 percent.

During this period the price of cotton relative to other goods changed very little. It fell slightly, but the rate of fall was less than $\frac{1}{2}$ of 1 percent a year. As a result, unless the demand curve was more elastic than most people think, one element in the expansion was an increase in the size of demand of approximately 2 percent a year. This was about the rate at which per capita income was rising, and it is reasonable to suppose that the demand for cotton goods rose with income in these years.

What about the supply of cotton goods? If the supply was inelastic, then the supply curve must have shifted outward with the demand curve for the price to have stayed relatively constant. On the other hand, if the supply curve was infinitely elastic—that is, perfectly horizontal—then it would have had to shift only slightly to cause the observed change in relative price. What would have made the supply inelastic? There was no shortage—except during the war years—of the raw material. The efficiency of cotton cultivation fell after the Civil War, but the quantity of cotton grown continued to increase without a rise in the price. There was no shortage of labor; the ever-increasing tide of immigrants furnished an adequate supply for the industry. Capital too was freely available to what had become a well-established industry. Finally, the knowledge and the ability to make cotton machinery and to run cotton mills had become widespread. Thus there were no barriers to the expansion of the cotton textile industry at a fixed price after 1860; the expansion of the industry—like the expansion of the antebellum production of pig iron—was more a movement along the supply curve than a shift in the curve itself. The progress of the postbellum cotton industry, like the antebellum iron industry, is summarized by the curves of Figure 12.4.

It must be remembered that we are talking of *relative* prices. When we say that the price of cotton textiles did not fall, we are saying that they did not fall faster than the average price of other goods, since almost all prices were falling in the late nineteenth century. When we say that the supply curve was not falling, therefore, we mean that the supply curve of cotton textiles was not falling faster than the average of the supply curves of other industries. There is no intent to deny or ignore the changes that took place in the production of cotton cloth; we want only to say that these changes did not create incentives at constant prices for people to drop other activities and turn to the production of cotton goods.

A few changes in cotton production may be mentioned to redress the balance. There was in this industry—as in many others at this time—a proliferation of machines to do simple jobs and of automatic devices to make the machines less dependent on human control. Raw cotton was moved around the mill by fans mounted in wind tunnels; knots were tied in broken yarn by little devices worn on the hands of the girls tending the machines; empty bobbins on looms were automatically replaced by full ones without stopping the loom. In addition, the mule spindle—which had been introduced into America by Samuel Slater in 1790—was being replaced by the ring spindle. The latter had been invented in 1831, but it was not until many years thereafter that it was improved to the point where it could compete with the mule spindle throughout the industry. Adapted to coarse rather than fine yarns, to hard rather than soft finishes, to ordinary rather than quality goods, the ring spindle only gradually became of value to the industry as a whole. As its range was extended, the inherent simplicity and efficiency of the ring spindle allowed it to replace the mule in the American cotton industry. The British industry, which made higher-quality products, continued to use the mule spindle.

Another important change was taking place behind the apparently static supply curve. The cotton industry had been located almost exclusively in New England before the Civil War; by 1910, there were two thirds as many spindles in the South as there were in the North. This shift in location is often spoken of as a "migration" of the industry, as its "center of gravity" moved South. These metaphors are illuminating, but they should not obscure the fact that the industry was growing in both the North and the South and that the migration in this period consisted solely of a more rapid growth in the South than in the North.

The effect of the southward migration was to open up a new source of labor for the industry. It therefore contributed to the maintenance of the elasticity of supply that was mentioned above. But while the effects of the move to the South are well known, the *causes* of this shift are still in doubt. Let us turn our attention to this question.

We are not trying now to explain the growth rate of the cotton textile industry as a whole, but rather why conditions in the South were more favorable to its growth in the late nineteenth century than conditions in the North. The reason most often given is directly related to the effect just mentioned. It is said that the industry moved South to use cheap southern labor.

During the Civil War, a large amount of southern capital was destroyed. Buildings were burned, railroads torn up, machinery smashed. As a result, capital earned high rates of return in the postbellum South, and labor received a low wage. This condition created an incentive to use more labor for a given unit of capital in the South than in the North, and to import capital from the North to the South. There is strong evidence that capital did in fact flow southward, comprising an actual migration as opposed to the metaphorical migration of the cotton industry. Capital was loaned and invested by northerners in a wide variety of southern activities. Not only cotton mills benefitted; there were loans to planters, to merchants, and to ironmasters. And herein lies the problem. For the low southern wage rate was an inducement for capital to move South; it was not an inducement for it to move into the production of cotton textiles rather than other activities. Furthermore, it was not an incentive for southerners to invest in cotton mills as opposed to other activities. And although the importance of northern capital in the rise of the "New South" is not to be denied, the southern cotton industry was also sustained by southern capital.

The low-wage argument, then, is correct but irrelevant. It can be used to explain differences between North and South and the flow of capital from North to South. But it cannot be used to explain the shift of activity within the South. For southerners to have decided to invest in cotton mills when they had previously been investing in cotton plantations or tenant farms and for northerners to do likewise, there must have been a shift in the relative prices within the South. The profitability of cotton mills must have risen relative to the profitability of cotton cultivation. The scarcity of Southern capital provided an incentive to invest in all southern activities, and if all other things had been equal, the southern economy should have expanded with the aid of northern capital without changing its composition. That cotton textile production expanded faster than other activities still needs to be explained.

One possibility is that the cotton industry used more labor relative to capital than other industries and that it consequently benefited more from the fall in the wage rate. The data in Tables 12.1 and 12.2, however, show that the cotton industry was not the most labor-intensive industry even among the top ten. In addition, the cultivation of cotton was very labor-intensive, and there was no reason why capital had to be invested in manufacturing rather than agriculture. It does not seem likely that the cotton industry gained more from the change in the relative price of labor and capital than other activities, or at least that it gained sufficiently to explain its growth.

Another often-mentioned possibility is that the southern cotton industry gained from its proximity to the areas in which cotton was grown. This argument has two parts. First, it is asserted that the southern cotton mills saved on transportation costs by being near their source of supply. Second, it is asserted that the southern mills were more able to take advantage of special situations by being on the spot. Neither of these is convincing. The southern cotton mills were located primarily in the states along the Atlantic Coast, in the Carolinas, and in Georgia. Cotton cultivation, on the other hand, had moved west and was concentrated in the states of the Mississippi Valley. The southern cotton mills consequently often received their cotton by ocean shipment in the same way the New England mills did. The costs of water transportation are not very sensitive to the distance of transport, and the savings were not great. In addition, the cotton textiles produced in southern mills often were sold in northern markets, and the gains achieved in getting the raw materials to the mills were lost in getting the textiles from the mill to the market.

Similarly, the benefits with reference to special situations are largely illusory. Communication was very rapid by this time, agents of northern mills were not scarce, and the ability to capitalize on inside knowledge depended as much on the availability of investible capital—which northern mills had in greater abundance than southern—as on the knowledge itself. While there were undoubtedly some savings deriving from proximity to cotton farms, they do not seem to have been large enough to have caused the expansion of cotton mills in the South. (If they were, of course, we would have to explain why cotton mills did not thrive before the Civil War.)

The factors leading to the expansion of cotton textile production in the South in the late nineteenth century were probably more closely connected to the institutional changes brought about by the Civil War than the arguments just presented suggest. The westward movement of cotton cultivation had started well before the Civil War. The western states had more fertile land, and as the settlement of these states progressed, planters in the eastern states found their returns from growing cotton diminishing. As Conrad and Meyer have shown, however, they were able to keep up their total income by supplying slaves to the rapidly expanding western areas. There was a well-developed market in slaves that allowed them to be taken where they would be most productive and also provided an income for slave owners in older areas of the South that obviated the necessity of finding a more productive use for slaves than growing cotton.

The freeing of the slaves put an end to this arrangement. True, the freedmen could move to the productive areas of the "Black Belt," but the former slave owners of the coastal states could no longer benefit from their movement. In other words, the profits of growing cotton in the coastal states were reduced relative to the profits of other occupations by the withdrawal of an important profit-generating activity. In the western states, where the cotton cultivation itself provided the profits, there was no such change. Cotton mills were therefore established in the coastal states, but not in the Gulf states. The shift from agriculture to manufacturing, whose start was hailed as the birth of a "New South," was the result of the fall in the comparative profitability of agricultural activities attendant on the freeing of the slaves.

But, still, why cotton mills? The argument just stated tells why people investing in the Carolinas would turn their attention to manufacturing, but it does not say why they built cotton mills rather than other industrial plants. This problem is not unique to the South. The English Industrial Revolution began with the cotton industry; the American did too. In fact, the start of industrialization in many countries has been signaled by the adoption of modern techniques in the cotton textile industry. There are several reasons for this. The technology of the industry is not too difficult; the machines do not require highly skilled labor. The materials and the products are relatively easy to transport, and the demand for them is widespread. Thus, we cannot be too surprised that the American South started its industrialization with cotton textiles, particularly when cotton had long been central to the southern economy.

Iron and Steel

While the cotton industry was undergoing its stately advance, the methods of making iron and steel were being revolutionized. The iron industry was being transformed into a radically different steel industry by the impact of a new technology.

In the discussion of the antebellum period we noted that pig iron contained a large amount of carbon, that wrought iron contained little carbon, and that wrought iron was made from pig iron. Steel contains an intermediate amount of carbon. It represents an intermediate stage between pig and wrought iron, and—like many compromises—it has qualities superior to either extreme. It can be shaped more easily than iron with the same strength; it is stronger than iron that is equally malleable. On the other hand, the process by which steel was made before the Civil War was very expensive, and little steel was produced. Steel was made from wrought iron, and since it was very difficult to melt wrought iron, the carbon had to be insinuated into the solid material by a long and expensive heating process. As long as this method was used to make steel, it would remain a luxury good.

Just before the Civil War, an Englishman named Henry Bessemer introduced a new method of making steel. The problem with earlier methods was that they operated with a solid material; Bessemer set out to keep the iron liquid. It was not difficult to melt pig iron; wrought iron was made from molten pig. But the melting point of iron rises as the quantity of carbon in it falls, and the iron solidified as it was transformed into wrought iron. (In the terminology of the day, it "came to nature.") To keep the iron molten, it was necessary to add more heat than had previously been possible. Bessemer did this by using the heat generated by the transformation of the iron itself. He blew air through liquid pig iron, providing the means of continuing the elimination of carbon at a rapid rate. The speed of this process generated enough heat to keep the iron molten. Carbon and silicon were removed by this process; under the original arrangement, phosphorus was not. (It took until 1879 to discover a way to remove phosphorus. Until that time, only nonphosphoric iron ore could be used to make Bessemer steel.)

The Bessemer process, therefore, was a way to remove carbon from pig iron while keeping it liquid. The efficient use of the heat generated in the removal of carbon, which had started with the introduction of puddling, was thus completed. But the Bessemer process was still only a better way of making wrought iron; it did not yet make steel. Or at least, it did not yet make what we now call steel. In the nineteenth century, the terminology was not as rigid as it has now become, and the product of the Bessemer process was often called "mild steel." Wrought iron was solid by the time it was finished, and any impurities in the iron were mixed in with it. There was no way to remove these impurities, and one characteristic of wrought iron was its inhomogeneity. Certain kinds of steel were produced by melting the inhomogeneous product obtained by impregnating solid wrought iron with carbon to produce homogeneity. This steel, of course, was even more expensive than the inhomogeneous steel produced directly from wrought iron. Before the Bessemer process was introduced, however, it was the only malleable product that had a uniform composition. Now, however, since the iron never solidified during the Bessemer process, the impurities in it—which were lighter than the iron and floated on top of it—could be poured off at the end, leaving a homogeneous product. It was natural—and it sold more metal—to call this product "steel."

Nevertheless, the qualities of Bessemer steel could be improved by increasing the amount of carbon it contained, and efforts were bent to this end. Bessemer's plan was to arrest the process part way, before all the carbon had been removed by burning. Unfortunately, the great speed of the process precluded this. The entire transformation took approximately 15 minutes, and a small delay along the way radically altered the carbon content. The resulting product was too uneven, and Bessemer's idea was abandoned. A superior suggestion was to remove all the carbon—that is, to let the combustion of impurities run its course—and then to add some carbon in place of that just removed. This was the same process used in the traditional method of making steel, with the crucial distinction that it could now be done while the iron was liquid, not solid. Instead of solid wrought iron being heated over a period of days to impregnate it with carbon, a bag of carbon was simply thrown into the molten product of the Bessemer process. The bag burned, and the carbon was spread throughout the iron by convection. In this manner, Bessemer steel was made.

The Bessemer process was a spectacular innovation, and the dramatic flaming of the changing iron soon became the symbol of a new age. The dour economic historian, however, notes that an alternative way of accomplishing the same end was introduced only a decade later. The problem with the puddling process and with the traditional methods of making steel was that sufficient heat could not be generated to keep the iron molten. If more heat could be added to the familiar puddling furnace, the benefits of the Bessemer process could be achieved in a quieter fashion. This is precisely what William Siemens, another Englishman, did during the 1860s. He used a furnace that operated more efficiently than its predecessors by tapping the previously wasted heat in the various waste gases. The Siemens–Martin or open-hearth process was less spectacular than the Bessemer process because it stayed closer to the existing technology. In addition, it was initially less efficient than the Bessemer process, and it was not adopted on a large scale.

As the nineteenth century approached its end, however, consumers of steel noticed that the Bessemer steel was not as reliable as they had at first thought. It performed well in laboratory tests, but it was subject to mysterious breakages in actual use. Open-hearth steel did not suffer from this defect, and it replaced Bessemer steel in an increasing number of uses. A vocal, but not overly coherent, controversy erupted between the supporters of the two kinds of steel, but it is only too clear that the source of the difficulty was not within reach of nineteenth-century technology. The scientists and engineers had isolated several variables they thought important in determining the characteristics of steel. As luck would have it, however, the critical variable was not among them. It will be recalled that the Bessemer process consisted of blowing air through molten iron. Air consists largely of oxygen and nitrogen. The oxygen combined with the carbon and other impurities ; that is what we mean by saying the impurities burned. The nitrogen, it was thought, passed through the iron without effect. We now know that some of the nitrogen dissolved in the iron and that this dissolved nitrogen produced what is known as "aging." There was no difference between the qualities of Bessemer and open-hearth steel at the time they were made, but the presence of nitrogen in Bessemer steel caused it to become progressively more brittle in use. This did not happen with open-hearth steel—as air had not been blown through it—and its lack of brittleness was the result.

The transition from iron to steel followed rapidly on the introduction of these new methods of making steel. The new steel competed more with wrought iron than with the old types of steel, and prices soon reflected this development. Taking railroad rails as an example, the price of Bessemer steel rails was approximately double that of iron rails when they were first sold commercially in 1867. Five years later, the price of steel rails was only 30 percent higher than the price of iron rails, and shortly after 1880, the price differential disappeared entirely. As steel rails lasted far longer than iron rails, no one bought iron rails thereafter except for special purposes. The change was slower in other uses, but the direction was uniform.

Then, at the turn of the century, consumers became aware of the quality difference between the two types of steel, and the demand for open-hearth steel rose. The supply of this type of steel expanded because it could use a wider range of raw materials than the Bessemer process, and production of open-hearth steel began to rise rapidly. The comparatively omnivorous open-hearth process used scrap as part of its raw materials, and it could also use many more of the vast Lake Superior iron ore deposits than the Bessemer process. Thus both supply and demand forces aided the shift from Bessemer to open-hearth steel.

What difference did all this make to the industry as a whole? How were the technical changes just described reflected in the growth of the industry? The paradoxical answer is, comparatively little.

The production of pig iron traditionally has been the measure of the growth of the iron and steel industry; we used it as such in the antebellum period. For the entire period from 1860 to 1910, the production of pig iron rose at an average annual rate of 7 percent. Population grew at a rate of about 2 percent per year, making the growth of per capita production about 5 percent. During these same years, the price of pig iron fell relative to the prices of other goods about 1 percent a year. This means that supply was expanding more rapidly than demand, and the expansion of production resulted at least in part from a movement along the demand curve. The expansion of the demand curve itself consequently was less than 5 percent per year. As it is unlikely that the demand for iron was extraordinarily elastic, the demand curve was probably shifting outward by about 2 or 3 percent a year (see Figure 12.2). The expansion of demand in the antebellum period was about 3 percent a year; the difference was not spectacular. Our task is now to discover why.

It is useful to separate the period into two parts at 1880. Before that time the price of steel was falling relative to the price of wrought iron; afterward, the relative price was more or less constant. From 1860 to 1880, the production of pig iron rose at an annual rate of about 6 percent, or at a per capita annual rate of about 3 percent. The relative price of pig iron *rose* during these two decades, and the expansion of demand consequently was larger than 3 percent. This situation is illustrated in Figure 12.5, where point 2 is higher than point 1. As a result, the horizontal distance between D_1 and D_2 at any price is larger than the horizontal distance between point 1 and point 2. This is the first example we have seen of the demand curve shifting sufficiently faster

FIGURE 12.5

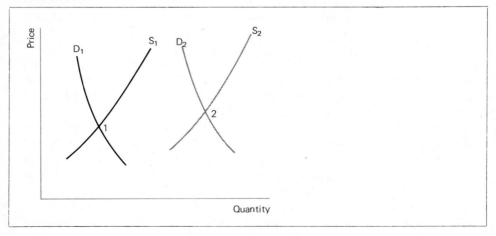

than the supply curve to cause a movement upward along the supply curve, although this must have been happening often in industries we have not examined.

Pig iron could be used either for castings or for conversion into wrought iron and steel. The price of wrought iron neither rose nor fell relative to the prices of other goods, and the expansion of its production by 7 percent a year must be attributed to an equally rapid rise in demand. (See Figure 12.4.) It was during these years that steel began to be substituted for wrought iron in many uses, but expanding steel production did not have a large effect on the demand for wrought iron because the production of steel was still relatively small. The steel industry's phenomenally rapid growth rate therefore affected that of the iron industry only slightly.

As the production of wrought iron and steel grew faster than the production of pig iron, the other use of pig iron—castings—must have grown more slowly. In fact the growth of castings was even slower than would be thought from this fact alone. Puddling was an omnivorous process, and considerable amounts of iron scrap were added to pig iron to make its input. The Bessemer process had more rigid chemical requirements, and the amount of scrap that it could use was limited. The amount of pig iron used to make wrought iron and steel thus rose more rapidly than the output of these products as the industry shifted from wrought iron to steel.

There was a temporary spurt in the demand for iron from 1860 to 1880. While the Civil War prostrated the cotton industry, the iron industry was booming. Guns—large and small—were made from iron, and guns were needed for war. Iron was also needed to build military railroads during the war and to help reconstruct destroyed southern railroads afterward. The use of iron for ships may even have been a factor in raising the demand. And the growth of the economy after the war was rapid enough to generate new demands for iron unrelated to the military.

After 1880 the price of pig iron began to decline, falling at an annual rate of about 2 percent a year until World War I. The production of pig iron rose only slightly faster than it had during the years before 1880; the rate was about 7 percent. While the demand for pig iron was still rising, it rose less rapidly after 1880 than before.

The prices of wrought iron and steel also fell about 2 percent a year. The continuing substitution of steel for wrought iron was the result of a slow process whereby consumers learned to take advantage of the superior qualities steel offered at no extra cost. The production of steel rose at an annual rate of about 10 percent after 1880, while the production of wrought iron was actually lower just before World War I than it had been in 1880. As a result, the combined sum of wrought iron and steel products rose at an annual rate of about 6 percent. (Castings grew at this same rate; the difference between this figure and the growth rate of pig iron is accounted for by the higher demands of steel production than of puddling for pig iron.)

The growth of demand was therefore in the neighborhood of 4 percent, not very different from the growth of cotton production or national income. This is not surprising. Iron and steel were used throughout the economy by 1880, and the expansion of demand thereafter came from the growth of industry as a whole. What is surprising is that the technical changes described above did not produce a greater change in the supply curve, leading to a lower price and a greater growth in production. Before 1880 the new technology had almost no effect on the size of total production; after 1880 it probably did not contribute more than 2 or 3 percent a year to the growth rate.

On the other hand, the new technology had effects apart from its impact on the total size of production. For example, it affected the kinds of products that were made from iron and steel. While steel was superior to wrought iron for most uses, it was not uniformly better; and the substitution of steel for iron encouraged the substitution of some products for others.

Approximately one third of all wrought iron and steel production in the third quarter of the nineteenth century was made into rails. This product was for many years that mainstay of the industry, and its production was enormously encouraged by the introduction of Bessemer steel. Practically all Bessemer steel was used for rails before 1880, and the increased supply of steel encouraged the production of rails. Starting about 1880, however, the demand for rails began to rise less rapidly than the demand for other iron and steel products, and the change in demand offset the change in supply. Before the Civil War, the increasing supply of wrought iron had been coupled with an increasing demand for wrought iron rails which led to a rapid growth in their production. After the war, the changing supply curves of the industry still encouraged the production of rails, but the pattern of demand had shifted. The pace of railroad construction slowed relative to other activities in the late years of the nineteenth century, and—despite the favorable supply influence— the production of rails became less important to the iron and steel industry.

As the demand for steel rails declined in importance—although not in absolute size—its place was taken by the demand for plates, sheets, and structural shapes. The demand for such steel products was either rising rapidly or very elastic, we cannot tell which. In any case, although their production was not encouraged initially by the shift from iron to steel, their demand for steel rose dramatically after 1880. They were used to build heavy machinery, to make transportation facilities of all sorts, and to construct the steel skeletons of the new skyscrapers. As the economy expanded, demand for these products expanded even faster.

From these few examples, it can be seen that the impact of new technology was diverse and interconnected with other changes. Still other developments brought about by the new technology will be discussed below.

Industry in General Up To 1910

The Civil War was the first modern war in its extensive use of the railroad, but it was the last ancient war in its effect on industry. During the war, there were strains on industry, but they had little influence on the long-run trend of manufacturing. The cotton textile industry suffered from an inability to get southern cotton, but the interregional network of trade was speedily re-established after the war. Iron was in demand for cannon and ironclad ships, but the important technological changes taking place in that industry were largely independent of the war. And so it went in other industries.

But although the Civil War had little direct impact on the growth of industry, it was followed by the greatest industrial growth the country has seen. Industry as a whole grew rapidly, firms expanded, and the size of individual plants shot up. Americans became conscious of living in an *industrial* economy, a consciousness that was not altogether welcome. It interacted with the "closing of the frontier"—announced by the Census Bureau in 1890—to produce a variety of policies designed to preserve the rural nature of America. Although we still fight some of these battles today—conservation and immigration, to name two—the character of the United States is no longer agricultural.

The causes of this great flowering of industry are not clear. Charles and Mary Beard saw them in the wartime "destruction of the planting aristocracy," and the "triumph of a new combination of power: northern capitalists and free farmers."[3] The results were many: high tariffs, the national banking system, land grants to railroads (see Chapter 17). Nevertheless, the connection between these policies and the growth of industry is still obscure. They undoubtedly pushed in the right direction, but the magnitude of their influence has been called into question.

The progress of industry in the postbellum years can be seen from Table 12.2, which does for 1910 what Table 12.1 did for 1860. Each of the industries

TABLE 12.2
The ten largest industries in 1910, by value added

	Value Added (millions of dollars) (1)	Employment (thousands of workers) (2)	Value Added per Worker (thousands of dollars) (3)
Machinery	690	530	1.29
Lumber	650	700	.93
Printing and publishing	540	260	2.08
Iron and steel	330	240	1.37
Malt liquors	280	55	5.01
Men's clothing	270	240	1.18
Cotton goods	260	380	.68
Tobacco manufactures	240	170	1.44
Railroad cars	210	280	.73
Boots and shoes	180	200	.91
All manufacturing	8529	6615	1.29

SOURCE: U.S. Bureau of the Census, *Census of the United States: 1910*, vol. 8 (Washington: U.S. Government Printing Office, 1913), p. 40.

[3] *The Rise of American Civilization*, vol. 2 (New York: Macmillan, 1927), p. 99.

shown had grown rapidly in the intervening half-century, as had manufacturing as a whole. More importantly, labor productivity (the value added per worker) rose also. For manufacturing as a whole, it rose from $550 per worker in 1860 to $1290 per worker in 1910.

Labor productivity could have risen either because the price of the goods produced rose or because the quantity produced rose. Prices doubled in the five years following 1860—the period of the Civil War—but they fell steadily thereafter almost until the end of the nineteenth century. As a result, prices in 1910 were only slightly above prices in 1860. Most of the change in value added between 1860 and 1910 therefore was due to an increase in the quantity of goods produced.

The ability of labor to produce goods can be increased either by supplying more capital or by increasing overall productivity, as we saw earlier. Despite the difficulty of measurement, most observers believe that the quantity of capital used per worker rose in the latter part of the nineteenth century. But most observers also agree that this rise was not enough to explain the rise in labor productivity shown in Tables 12.1 and 12.2. We conclude that the manufacturing sector was not only becoming larger; it was also becoming more efficient.

The general question of technology is treated in Chapter 7; we turn here to the diversity of experience within manufacturing. At one extreme we find the cotton industry, with labor productivity of just over half the average for all manufacturing. The increase in labor productivity from 1860 to 1910 was smaller in the cotton industry than in any other industry appearing in both Tables 12.1 and 12.2. As we saw above, the cotton industry had been transformed in the antebellum period, and its production methods remained relatively unchanged in the following half-century. By way of contrast, the men's clothing industry, which had the lowest labor productivity shown in Table 12.1, had the fastest rise in labor productivity between 1860 and 1910 of the industries shown. Mechanization (the sewing machine) standardization, and "sweat-shop" production combined to increase the value of clothing produced per worker.

At the opposite extreme from the cotton industry stand the producers of malt liquors. Breweries, like the flour mills of the antebellum period, utilized a lot of capital and comparatively few workers. Like the flour mills also, breweries used the products of efficient American agriculture, and the great size of this industry shows once again the close connection between agriculture and industry. It also shows the connection between science and industry and immigration and industry. The barrier to beer production before the late nineteenth century had been the difficulty of storing it. Beer is produced by fermentation, but the fermentation has to be arrested at the appropriate point if the beer is to be stored. Until the late nineteenth century, there was no way to do this without spoiling the beer. The work of Louis Pasteur is often thought of today in connection with milk, but it was equally important for the production of beer. Pasteurization stopped fermentation without destroying the beer because it was heated enough to kill the bacteria, but not enough to erase their effects. And if the use of pasteurization illustrates the impact of science, the impact of immigration is shown by the title selected for the brewers' trade journal established in 1868, *Der Amerikanische Bierbrauer.*

Returning to Table 12.2, we find illustrated there a phenomenon widely duplicated in the history of other countries: the growing importance of producers'-goods industries. (A producers' good is a product used by another producer, as opposed to a consumer. Machinery is an example.) In a primitive society people tend to make consumer goods directly, out of materials and with tools that they can grow or make themselves. As the economy develops, people begin to use purchased materials and more specialized tools made by tool builders. As this process continues, the tools and possibly the raw materials are made in part from purchased materials and with purchased tools also. The industries that sell to other industries grow faster than the industries that sell to consumers.

The production of cloth is an excellent illustration. In the eighteenth century and before, most people made their own cloth by weaving thread they had spun themselves from the wool of their own sheep. When they started to buy cotton cloth, they were buying from an industry that made cloth with machinery too large and expensive to be made by each individual who used it. There was a specialized set of shops that made textile machinery. This machinery originally was made of wood, which was easily available, but wood was gradually replaced by iron. More iron had to be produced. Then, as the machines became more complicated, machines were needed to make the machines to make cloth. These metal-working machines are called "machine tools," and the demand for them rose, too. Then the cotton industry began to switch from water power to steam power. Steam engines and coal were needed. Cotton cloth was transported over increasingly long distances, and railroad cars were needed. Finally—in the twentieth century—the raw materials for many textiles came to be produced in industry rather than agriculture. This last step belongs to the next section, but enough happened before 1910 in this and in other industries to change the shape of American industry. In 1860, three out of the top four industries made consumer goods; in 1910, three out of the top four made producers' goods.

The lone consumer-goods industry among the top four deserves some comment because it illustrates the combined impact of increasing technical sophistication and a growing market that is found so often in the history of American manufacturing. The rapid growth of printing and publishing was due to changes on both the supply and the demand sides. On the supply side, paper made from pulp replaced paper made from rags in the late nineteenth century. The great timber resources of North America thus aided the growth of two of the largest industries in 1910, lumber and printing, although wood for pulp and wood for lumber are very different. The change for rags to pulp cheapened paper considerably, but not without a loss of quality. The change was permitted by the scientific discovery of a process using sulfur which produced a new kind of paper. Anyone who has delved into nineteenth-century sources is familiar with the difference between the paper used in the early nineteenth-century books and newspapers and that used in later sources. The earlier paper is heavy and rather rough; more important, it is still flexible. The latter paper is smoother, lighter, often shiny, and it has a disturbing propensity to crack when bent. This brittleness is causing libraries a great deal of concern, but it did allow paper to be made much more cheaply at the time. Labor productivity was also high in printing and publishing. There was considerable investment in this industry, and printing presses were built which were able to run with little attendance before World War I.

On the demand side, printing and publishing gained from the growth of education and of cities. Increased educational achievements opened up the world of books—albeit dime novels—to many people. Urban residents needed some way of finding out what was happening in a city too large to be served by word-of-mouth communication. The "penny press" satisfied this market, informing the always-interested readers about the more sensational aspects of urban life. The combination of higher demand and cheaper supplies meant rapid growth.

The progress of this industry thus combines three factors that are seen over and over again in varying proportion in the history of different industries. The supply of industrial products was increased by the exploitation of both an increasingly sophisticated technology and America's fabulously rich resources. And these two supply influences were accompanied by rising demand stemming from rising income. It would have been possible to grow on the basis of modern technology or plentiful resources alone, but the combination of these two with a strong demand made the United States one of the leading industrial nations by 1910. The history of any industry in America can be written in terms of these three influences, and variations in their relative importance go far toward explaining the differences in the histories of different industries.

The growth of a new technology was the most important element in the expansion of a group of industries not shown in Table 12.2 because they were not large enough, but whose nineteenth-century origins are remembered because of their later importance. Primary among these was the group using electricity as its source of power. The telegraph had begun to use electricity commercially before the Civil War, and the telephone also used it in the late nineteenth century. But it was its utilization for light that began to shape the technology of electricity we know today. For while the telegraph and telephone used minute quantities of electricity, lighting used much more. In addition, if electric lighting was to be installed along city streets or in people's houses, there had to be a way of generating large amounts of electricity and transporting it from the generator to a series of light bulbs.

Thomas Edison introduced a central generator and a lighting system in New York in the 1880s. He used a direct current—that is, current in which the electrons always flow in one direction. George Westinghouse challenged this decision in the following decade. He championed alternating current, in which the electrons move back and forth in a series of rapid cycles, and which turns out for technical reasons to be easier to transmit than direct current. With the victory of alternating over direct current, the way was open for electricity to be used in large quantities for power as well as light. The first electric generator at Niagara Falls was built in 1895. The electric street railway began to change the shape of American cities at the end of the nineteenth century by permitting the growth of suburbs. And the electric motor, which could be made in practically any size and used practically anywhere, began to introduce a new flexibility into the American factory. No longer did factories have to be organized around a power source; they could be organized for efficient work, and the power could be supplied where it was needed.

Another new industry in the late nineteenth century was the automobile industry. Most of the technical problems of the horseless carriage were solved by the end of the nineteenth century, although the automobile was not yet cheap enough to be used widely. The chemical industry also got its start before World War I, although its greatest expansion came later (helped by the capture of German patents in the war). The chemical industry is really two industries, making organic and inorganic chemicals, respectively. Organic chemicals are based on hydrogen and carbon and are obtainable from coal and petroleum. They are made from the waste products that used to be thrown out in the manufacture of coke from coal, and the growth of this part of the chemical industry is the story of progressive utilization of previously unusable wastes. The inorganic chemicals are acids, bases, and other products used in manufacturing. They were made by various processes, many of which were dramatically improved in the late nineteenth century.

All this discussion of the size of industries tends to ignore an important aspect of industrial growth: the growth in the size of the individual business firm. Before the Civil War, firms were small enough so that ambitious entrepreneurs could run more than one. In the late nineteenth century, the leading businessmen were associated with one firm only. The firm had outgrown the managers. Andrew Carnegie, that archetypal American success, began his career as the son of an immigrant hand-loom weaver. At the end of the Civil War, when Carnegie resigned from the Pennsylvania Railroad to make his fortune, he was already active in making iron, bridges, and sleeping cars, owned part of a fast-freight company, and was speculating in oil. In the depression of the 1870s, when Carnegie decided to go into steel, he sold all his other holdings and concentrated his energies on the growth of the company that bore his name. Many other examples could be found of men who in the 1850s and 1860s engaged in multiple activities and whose entire energy in the 1880s and 1890s was devoted to the promotion of a single firm, although not many people could be cited who made the transition as successfully as Andrew Carnegie.

Firms grew because the unit of production grew, and they also grew because various units of production were combined increasingly into one firm. Although horizontal and vertical integration often went together, vertical integration—the combination of plants performing different stages in the production of a single good—increased most in the late nineteenth century. Horizontal integration—

the combination of plants making the same product into a single firm—increased in the early twentieth. American Tobacco, Armour, Swift, and United Fruit were all combinations of firms processing agricultural products. Singer Manufacturing and International Harvester made machinery. U.S. Steel and Standard Oil, the two largest firms in 1910 measured by the size of their assets, utilized the output of mines and wells to make a familiar range of products.

The reasons for the growth of these industrial giants are obscure. It has been traditional to ascribe it to the actions of John D. Rockefeller, Andrew Carnegie, J. P. Morgan, and other "robber barons." But without denying the drive and ability of these extraordinary men, it may be objected that there have been ambitious, energetic, and intelligent leaders at other times too. Why was it that these men chose to direct their energies into business and that they were so successful in building their businesses in the years before World War I?

One popular explanation gives rise of the the large urban market as the crucial factor (see Chapter 15). The growth of this market enabled firms to utilize centralized distribution facilities and to advertise extensively. This, so the argument goes, gave an advantage to the large firm, which was able to buy out and absorb its competitors. This argument is not convincing for two reasons. First, the extent to which profits could be improved by these methods is not known, nor is the range of industries which could exploit them. And second, it is not clear that the use of centralized facilities and advertising owes its growth to the growth of cities, as opposed to other changes in late nineteenth-century life and technology.

Another explanation cites the role of the capital market (see Chapter 9). This argument states that the growth of industry in America had put great strains on the capital market so that not everyone could get financing with equal ease. People with the ability to raise capital were in a position to absorb their suppliers or their competitors and expand. Many of the new companies were holding companies, running the purchased firms as independent units rather than as parts of an integrated enterprise. This situation suggests that there were few incentives to cut costs by reorganizing production. The captains of industry were able to extend their empires and sometimes to reduce the competition they faced, but they probably were exploiting imperfections in the capital market rather than the market for goods as they did so.

The result of this expansion, needless to say, was a tremendous increase in the range of goods available to the consumer. As an 1895 advertisement for Macy's department store in New York said:

Follow the crowd and it will always take you to

R. H. MACY & CO.

What better evidence do you wish that ours is

The All Around Store

of New York City? Ride our bicycles,

read our books, cook in our saucepans,

dine off our china, wear our silks,

get under our blankets, smoke our cigars,

drink our wines

—Shop at Macy's—
and life will
Cost You Less and Yield You More
Than You Dreamed Possible.[4]

THE TWENTIETH CENTURY

The Cotton Industry

The production of cotton textiles rose between 1910 and 1960 at an annual rate of slightly less than 2 percent a year, or slightly slower than the population. The cotton industry, as a result, is absent from the table of the ten largest industries in 1960. The price of cotton textiles neither rose nor fell relative to other prices, and we must infer that both the supply and demand for cotton textiles rose more slowly than the population (or that supply was very elastic and remained unchanged while demand grew slowly).

On the demand side, this slow growth was the product of two factors. The cost of substitutes for cotton fell drastically, and people switched to them from cotton. For most uses, artificial fibers—rayon, nylon, and so on—were substituted; but paper and plastics were also suited for some uses. This factor alone cannot explain the slow growth, for the consumption of all fibers rose at an annual rate of less than 2 percent a year. Although cotton was losing out to other fabrics, the market for all fabrics was not growing as fast as the population. (Most textiles were still cotton even in 1960, which is why the growth rate for all textiles was so close to the growth rate for cotton textiles alone. See Chapter 7, Table 7.9.)

Economists look first to the price for an explanation of changes in the quantity demanded. The relative price did not change in this instance, however, and we must look to the next most likely variable: income. The income of consumers was rising in the twentieth century, and it is possible that the increase in income led to a decrease in the consumption of fabrics. In other words, as people became richer, they could afford to use substitutes for fabrics. Instead of warm clothing, they heated their houses. Instead of curtains, they used Venetian blinds.

If the rise in income was the cause of the decline in per capita consumption of textiles, we would say that textiles were "inferior goods" at the level of income achieved by Americans in the twentieth century. It is hard to find examples of inferior goods, and it would be nice to know of others. The most common example is potatoes: The Irish ate potatoes when they could not afford meat. American examples are corn meal and pork. But we cannot be sure that textiles really are an inferior good. Had nothing else changed between 1910 and 1960, we might be willing to attribute all changes in the quantity demanded to changes in prices and income. But since we know that very little else remained constant, we must be wary of doing so. In particular, those items that economists lump under the term "tastes" changed markedly

[4] Ralph M. Hower, *History of Macy's of New York* (Cambridge, Mass.: Harvard University Press, 1943), p. 273.

over this half-century. To take the most obvious example, women stopped wearing voluminous floor-length dresses, appearing instead in dresses that stayed closer to their form and stopped well above the floor. Part of this change was due to the rise in income already mentioned; many-layered clothes were not needed for warmth. But only a foolish man attributes the changes in women's fashions to "real" variables such as income. The changing position of women in society, the changing concept of house furnishings, the changing architectural styles, all were important in determining the demand for textiles. It is probably true that the per capita demand for textiles would not have risen rapidly in the absence of changes in tastes, but we cannot say with any assurance that it would have fallen.

On the supply side, there was an absence of marked technological change in the production of cotton textiles that investigators have noted with great frequency. Without denying the accuracy of this observation, let us take a different tack and note the parallels with the history of the iron and steel industry in the half-century before 1910. The lack of technological change, it will be shown, is as much a result of our industry classification as of conditions in the economy itself.

The iron and steel industry, it will be recalled, produced iron almost exclusively in 1860. Steel was an expensive luxury good, used only in small quantities where the finer qualities of steel were worth enough to justify the substantial premium charged for them. The Bessemer process changed all this by making a new material by a new process. This new material was called "steel," and it was thought that it would replace the earlier form of steel. As the production of Bessemer steel was made more efficient, however, its price approached that of wrought iron, and Bessemer steel emerged as the successor to wrought iron, not to steel. The new product, in other words, did not remain a luxury good; it became the common material of the new technology. The production of wrought iron stagnated, and there was little technological change to improve its competitive position vis à vis steel.

An analogous development took place in the manufacture of textiles, and we need a little technical background to understand it. Natural fibers acquire their properties from the presence of cellulose, an organic molecule composed of long chains of a rather simple unit. These chains have a fair amount of rigidity, and they will combine with each other to form long strands that can be combined in turn to form fibers. Cellulose is the common building block of all living plants; it provides the stiffness in cell walls that enables plants to maintain their shape. In fibers, the chains of the cellulose molecule are aligned in a single direction, giving continuity to the material at the cost of lateral strength.

There are four major natural fibers: cotton, wool, linen, and silk. Of these, silk is the most expensive and the most luxurious. If one were to make an artificial fiber, it would be natural to attribute to it all the qualities of silk. This was done in the 1890s, when a new fiber was introduced. Cellulose, it turns out, is more or less the same, no matter what plant it comes from. If man could discover a way of disassociating the cellulose molecules from their existing combinations and recombining them in a linear fashion, he would have discovered a new way to make fibers. In the late nineteenth century, a new fiber was made from wood—that is, from the cellulose extracted from wood—in this fashion. It was hoped that this new fiber would compete with silk, and it was called "artificial silk."

Note the parallel with the iron industry. In each case a new product was made by circumventing an existing productive process. In the iron industry, this process was puddling; in the textile industry, the production of fibers by growing cotton, sheep, flax, or silkworms. In each case the new material was designed to compete with the most expensive previous product and given a name to match.

In each case also, the old and new processes used the same raw material. Bessemer steel was made from pig iron, the raw material from which wrought iron was made. And artificial silk was made from cellulose, the basic component of all natural fibers. But while pig iron was produced within the iron industry, cellulose was not produced by man at all. The Bessemer process used a material already processed by the iron industry to produce a product competing with iron. It was clearly a part of the same industry, and it has been treated as such by the census and in the discussion here. The production of artificial silk, however, started with a raw material not utilized directly by the textile industry. The textile industry had always purchased its fibers, and the introduction of a new fiber was therefore outside the scope of the industry classification.

It turned out that the new fibers could be made into fabrics by the same machinery used for cotton, but the practice of labeling textile factories by the nature of their raw materials was too ingrained to be broken. Consequently, the production of artificial silk was not considered part of the cotton textile industry. It was a separate industry, and the manufacture of the fibers themselves were designated as part of the chemical industry. (The production of natural fibers, of course, was not part of industry at all.) There was thus a great deal of technological change going on in the production of textiles, but not in the production of cotton textiles. It would be equally true to say that there was change in the manufacture of iron products in the late nineteenth century, but not in the production of wrought iron. The difference was that, while we are aware of a "cotton industry," we are not aware of a "wrought-iron industry."

The parallels with the iron industry continue. Artificial silk was not produced in any substantial quantity before World War I, but its production rose more rapidly than the production of cotton thereafter. Its price also fell relative to the price of cotton. It was three times as expensive as cotton between the world wars, but it was about the same price after World War II. Like Bessemer steel, the new product was initially designed and labeled to compete with the highest-quality product of the industry, but it too approached the price and competed with the largest-volume product. Unlike Bessemer steel, however, artificial silk was renamed to take account of this development. In the 1920s the term "rayon" was adopted for all types of artificial silk. By this time there were several different fibers made by man from cellulose, and rayon was adopted as the generic name for all of them. This change in terminology preceded the decline in rayon's price, and rayon competed primarily with silk for several years after the change. As one commentator said in 1938: "From fiber to fabric wool remains wool; cotton, cotton; silk is—apt to be —rayon."

The introduction of rayon greatly broadened the raw-material base of the textile industry. The industry had been dependent on the natural production of fibers, particularly the production of cotton, before the introduction of rayon. Thereafter, cellulose from any source could be used. The common sources were wood pulp and cotton linters, the cotton fibers left on the seeds after the long fibers used to make cotton textiles had been removed by ginning. In each case, a waste material was utilized as a new raw material.

But the production of textiles was still limited to the use of natural cellulose in the 1930s. This was not an important constraint because of the prevalence of natural cellulose, but once the idea of replacing part of the natural process by manufacturing methods had been realized, the idea of replacing the rest was a natural successor. Late in the 1930s, the first truly synthetic fabric—nylon—was produced. This fabric was composed of artificial polymers—chain-like recursive molecules made in a laboratory or factory, not derived from a naturally fibrous material. Much as Bessemer steel was replaced by open-hearth steel, rayon was replaced after World War II by completely synthetic fibers. At the start of World War II, 90 percent of women's stockings were made of silk, the balance being composed of rayon. After the war, nylon had replaced both silk and rayon. In 1946, about two thirds of the stockings were made of nylon; by 1960, almost all.

The production of stockings was unusual, however; artificial fabrics had not replaced natural ones in all uses by 1960. At the start of the half-century under review, 90 percent of all fibers consumed in the United States were cotton, the remainder being mostly wool. (Silk accounted for only 1 percent.) By 1960 the proportion accounted for by cotton had fallen to 65 percent, the proportion accounted for by wool had fallen to 6 percent, and man-made fibers had taken over the remainder. While cotton textiles have been losing out to the newer competitors, they have by no means been pushed out of the market.

So the story of the cotton industry is really a rather familiar one. It is a story of technological change, of the replacement of old methods of manufacture by new, of the increasing exploitation of scientific knowledge. For the reasons that we have seen, the changes did not take place within a single industry; they took the form of the replacement of one industry by another. But whichever form it takes, the process pervades the economy. The demand for textiles was growing slowly, and the textile industry as a whole consequently grew slowly, but this should not mask the existence of dynamic elements within it.

The Steel Industry

By 1910, the principal product of the "iron and steel industry" was steel. Iron had become in large part an intermediate good in the production of steel, and we will not do too much violence to our story if we talk only of steel.

The production of steel ingots rose at an annual rate of about $2\frac{1}{2}$ percent between 1910 and 1960. This was faster than the growth of cotton output, but still not as fast as the growth of national product. The relative price of steel also rose in this period—a sharp contrast with its behavior in the nineteenth century. It rose slowly, about 1 percent a year, but the rise still indicates that the growth of demand was outrunning the growth of supply. (See Figure 12.5).

Demand, we may infer, was probably rising at about the same rate as national product as a whole. Steel was widely used by 1910, and the growth in its demand came from the general expansion of the economy. On the other hand, supply was rising considerably more slowly than the economy as a whole. The slowness of this growth might have been due to a growing scarcity of the raw materials needed to make steel. In fact, the industry was concerned late in this period with the exhaustion of the high-grade ores found around Lake Superior that had been its chief source of supply in the late nineteenth century. But there was no general scarcity of raw materials. The exhaustion of the high-grade ores meant that ways had to be found to use lower-grade ores, but these ways were found. Lower-grade ore could be "enriched" before it was used in a blast furnace, and it could be "pelletized" to make it more uniform. These extra operations had a cost, but the cost turned out to be surprisingly small.

If raw materials were not scarce, the slow growth of supply must have come from a slow rise in the efficiency with which these resources were used. Productivity was rising throughout the economy, and its growth may have been slower than average in the steel industry. Why this should have been so is a mystery, but one possible explanation concerns the role of U.S. Steel. This giant corporation, so the argument runs, exploited a monopoly position to ignore new technological developments. The oxygen process, for example, is an important recent technological discovery. In the Bessemer process, it will be recalled, air was blown through molten pig iron. The oxygen in the air turned the iron to steel, but the nitrogen in the air rendered the steel inferior. It was natural, once oxygen could be isolated cheaply, to try blowing oxygen alone through the iron. Not only did this speed the steel-making process, it avoided the problems of Bessemer steel. It was introduced in Europe several years before it found wide use in the United States or in U.S. Steel, and many people have said that U.S. Steel was laggard in adopting it. This argument has its problems and its opponents, and the theory of technological change is still too rudimentary to allow us to test it. Nevertheless, the existence of U.S. Steel was certainly important for the industry, and we should discuss its role more fully.

The technical changes that transformed the iron and steel industry in the late nineteenth century have already been described. One aspect of these changes that has not been mentioned, however, is the increase in the scale of individual production units. The Bessemer process used complex machinery and handled large amounts of steel at a time. It was necessary to build a large mill to make the production of steel economical, and in 1880 the average Bessemer steel mill was ten times as large as the average iron-rolling mill. The switch from iron to steel therefore was accompanied by a drastic fall in the number of plants in the industry.

Steel mills also were integrated backwards—that is, they combined the production of pig iron and steel in one plant. This development enabled the pig iron to be taken from the blast furnace to the Bessemer converter in its molten state, avoiding the expense of solidifying and remelting it. Whether from contact with the steel makers or from independent causes, economies of scale began to increase in blast-furnace operation about the same time that steel was introduced. Blast furnaces grew in size, they acquired a retinue of mechanical aides, and they produced ever more iron under the influence of "hard driving." This last item was one of the innovations characteristic of American industry; it consisted essentially of working a given unit of capital equipment harder than it had been worked before. A blast furnace worked by having air pumped into a mixture of coal and ore to induce combustion. "Hard driving" was the act of pumping more air under higher pressure into the blast furnace. British iron-masters, who did not take to hard driving, objected that the linings of the furnace wore out more quickly, that unit costs were not reduced, and that hard driving was showmanship—the Americans were always talking about blast-furnace production records—rather than good business. Nevertheless, the Americans continued the practice, and the scale of blast furnaces grew. Somewhere around the turn of the century, the limit had been reached even for the Americans, and the size of blast furnaces stabilized. But the new, large size was another factor diminishing the number of plants in the steel industry.

The number of firms could be no larger than the number of plants in the industry, and the steel industry of the 1870s was composed of about ten firms. In the depression of that decade, the steel producers watched the price of their product decline. (It should be recalled that, in addition to the price decline attendant on the depression, the price of steel was falling rapidly in response to what we call technological change, which the producers referred to—without much justification—as "excess capacity.") They became concerned that the price would continue to drop and take their profits with it, and they met together to form the Bessemer Association, the first of many attempts to restrict the output and raise the price of steel.

The efforts at combination continued throughout the last quarter of the nineteenth century with limited success. Only in the 1890s did the pools appear to raise the price of steel rails above a level that could be produced by competitive forces. By this time, however, the number of steel-producing firms had fallen below the number of steel mills, and the stability of the pool was uncertain. In Pittsburgh, Andrew Carnegie had bought out all the mills started in competition with his, and he owned three of the most efficient steel mills in the country at the turn of the century. In Chicago, the Illinois Steel Company had been formed by a merger of three members of the old Bessemer Association; the new firm had four Bessemer steel mills at its disposal. Late in the 1890s, J. P. Morgan was instrumental in transforming the Illinois Steel Company into the even larger Federal Steel Company; Morgan and Carnegie then faced each other—so the traditional story goes—in a titanic struggle for control of the steel industry.

The titanic struggle never took place, and we cannot test the veracity of the traditional account. Instead, the giant steel firms were merged in 1901 into a truly giant firm: the largest firm the country had seen, the first billion-dollar corporation—U.S. Steel. The profits earned in the merger itself were very large, and they might have provided sufficient incentive for Morgan to undertake it even without the threat of a "war" with Carnegie.

U.S. Steel produced somewhere between one half and three quarters of the steel industry's output at its formation, the proportion depending on the product chosen as an index. Its share of the market declined slowly over time, but this one firm still produced one third of the industry's output in 1960. There are two questions that emerge naturally from this observation: How did United States Steel come so close to maintaining its large relative size? And what was the effect of this firm's enormous size?

The first question may be rephrased to read: Why didn't other steel firms grow faster or more new firms come into being? We normally expect that un-less there is some sort of barrier to entry into an industry or to growth within it, one firm will not be able to maintain a large share of a particular market for over half a century. One possible barrier would be the economies of scale mentioned in connection with the formation of U.S. Steel. These economies, however, seem to have been gained at a comparatively small size. Using the sizes of plants in the largest firms as an index, the optimal-size plant toward the end of our period produced only 1–2.5 percent of the national market, or 2.5–6.25 percent of the largest recognized submarket. Assuming that these proportions can be projected back into the past, we may conclude that the steel industry would never have consisted of more than 50 or 100 firms, but that the economies of scale in the industry would not by themselves cause the number to be significantly less than this. In particular, U.S. Steel did not lower its operating costs below those of its rivals by attaining its enormous size.

The main barrier to entry in the steel industry in the twentieth century was the difficulty of obtaining iron ore. The industry drew its ore from the rich de-posits around Lake Superior, and these deposits were closely held. The for-mation of U.S. Steel, in fact, can be seen as a device to bring together the ex-tensive ore holdings of Carnegie and Morgan (and Rockefeller) to achieve control over the industry. While U.S. Steel never acquired anything like all of the Lake Superior iron ore, the ownership was never subsequently dispersed. In the middle of the twentieth century, over nine tenths of the Lake Superior iron ore was produced by no more than four steel firms and four ore companies affiliated with steel firms. (The remaining percentage was supplied by four more steel firms and twelve more ore firms, bringing total membership in the ore business up to only twenty-four firms.) Iron ore is needed to make steel, and the existing steel makers were in a position to dictate to a newcomer the terms under which he could obtain that ore throughout the twentieth century.

Concentrated ownership of ore thus preserved concentrated production. But what difference did this make? Was it any easier to maintain pools in the twentieth century than the nineteenth? Was the price of steel higher than it might otherwise have been?

U.S. Steel was a holding company for many years, and the firms making up the big corporation continued to function as independent operating departments. They participated in pools much as they had done before joining U S. Steel, but the pools seemed to be more lasting. No one who has looked at a price series for steel rails can fail to be impressed by the persistence of a stated price of $28 per ton from 1902 to 1913 and similar plateaus at later dates. The mechanisms for achieving this stability were various, and we will examine them in a minute, but we should ask whether the prices were *higher*—as opposed to more stable—than they would have been in a free market.

One index that can be used is the ratio of the price of steel to the price of pig iron. Pig iron is the principal raw material used to make steel, and an upward movement of the ratio of the two prices would show either higher costs in making steel or higher profits. Costs did not change much in the first decade of the twentieth century, and large movements of the ratio could be attributed to profits. On observation, however, it turns out that this ratio was lower than it had been during the pool of the 1890s. This seems to indicate that U.S. Steel was not earning a monopoly profit on its steel production. However, it must be remembered that U.S. Steel was an integrated firm. It produced more pig iron than it used, and the price of pig iron consequently was a price it charged, not a price it paid. In other words, the price of pig iron was purely an accounting device for U.S. Steel, although it was a cost to independent steel makers. By setting the price of pig iron high, U.S. Steel showed its profits in the making of pig iron rather than the making of steel, and it kept the profits of independent steel makers down at the same time. Similarly, by setting a high price on ore, the firm pushed its profits back further into the production of ore, and reduced the profits on independent blast furnaces. Without further analysis, therefore, we cannot say that U.S. Steel was not making monopoly profits in its early years. We can only say that if it was, it was making them at the stage in which it had a monopoly (that is, in the production of ore) in order not to encourage its competition.

The techniques by which prices were set varied over time. The use of formal pools was abandoned early in the century as it came under pressure from the courts. Pools were replaced first by the so-called Gary dinners. These were dinners given by Judge Gary, the President of U.S. Steel, at which prices were discussed and informal agreements were made. The system worked well until the Justice Department brought suit against U.S. Steel in 1911 for violation of the Sherman Act and attempted to dissolve the giant firm.

U.S. Steel survived the government's suit—which was concluded only after World War I—and new forms of price control were introduced. Prominent among these devices was the use of "Pittsburgh plus." This was a form of basing-point pricing, in which all steel was sold f.o.b. Pittsburgh. Under this system, a purchaser of steel paid the cost of manufacture plus the cost of transportation from Pittsburgh, whether or not the steel was made in Pittsburgh and shipped to him from there. This system had two effects. Steel was cheaper in Pittsburgh than anywhere else, and users of steel in Pittsburgh consequently were favored over users in other cities. The system encouraged the continued growth of Pittsburgh and—its opponents complained—militated against the growth of the industry in other parts of the country. A producer with a particularly favorable location could not lower his price to expand his business. On the other hand, since steel producers outside of Pittsburgh earned larger profits on the "phantom" freight for which they were paid, the total effect of this formula is hard to know.

Pittsburgh plus introduced too many strains into the marketing of steel, and it was replaced in 1924 by multiple-point pricing, under which steel was sold as if it had been produced in any of a small number of locations. Price maintenance broke down in the Depression and was not reestablished until after the post-World War II scarcity of steel had abated. When "normal" conditions returned to the steel industry, U.S. Steel renewed its price leadership. Basing-point pricing was pronounced illegal in 1948, and U.S. Steel's leadership has been on an informal basis since then.

But to return to our original inquiry: What was the effect of all this on the supply of steel? Many people have asserted that after World War II the steel industry raised prices faster than a competitive industry would have done. If so, the rise in the price of steel that we observed from 1910 to 1960 was due partly to the exploitation of monopoly power within the industry, and the slow growth of supply was in part a monopolistic restriction of supply. The existence of U.S. Steel could have retarded the growth of supply in the steel industry in two ways. The firm could have been laggard in the adoption of new technology, and it could have kept prices "artificially" high while adopting new technology. The difference between these possibilities from the point of view of a steel user is minimal; he pays high prices in either case. From the point of view of society as a whole, the first implies that more resources are being used to make steel than need to be, while the second implies that profits in the steel industry are higher than they might be. Extant evidence favors the first possibility over the second, as U.S. Steel's stated profits have not been very high. But whether either of these hypotheses describes the true situation is still moot, and we shall have to let the dust of history settle a little before we can answer such highly controversial questions.

Industry in General Up To 1960

The 50 years after 1910 were quite unlike the century that preceded them. The nineteenth century had been a period of comparative peace in America. With the notable exception of the Civil War, industry was free to supply the needs of consumers without being asked also to cope with the needs of war. Someone has called the years from 1915 to 1945 "the second Thirty Years' War." Twice in that time, American industry has been asked to turn from peacetime production to war material. Competition was abandoned in favor of government controls during the periods of actual conflict, and the government has never withdrawn from industry to return to the degree of separation that existed in the nineteenth century.

During the "truce" that separated the two wars, there was also the greatest depression the country has ever known, whether measured in terms of the magnitude or of the duration of the decline of output. The government tried to alter or to supersede the market during this period to alleviate the depression. These aspects of governmental action have proven even more durable than the wartime controls, and industry emerged from "the second Thirty Years' War" far more tightly enmeshed with the government than when it had gone in.

The ten largest industries in 1960 are shown in Table 12.3, although the manufacturing sector had become so complex by 1960 that it is much more difficult to classify production into industries than it was in the nineteenth century. For example, "machinery" was the largest industry in 1910. It still was in 1960, and it had grown so large that data were collected separately on two separate parts of its production. Consequently, the two largest industries in Table 12.3 are both *machinery*.

The most startling change between Tables 12.2 and 12.3 is the increase in labor productivity; value added per worker rose from $1290 to $13,400 between 1910 and 1960. As a result of the wars, prices were 2.5 times as high in 1960 as in 1910; thus, part of the difference is the increase in the price—not the quantity—of output. Nevertheless, the quantity produced per worker had increased by a factor of four in the half-century before 1960. Labor productivity —considering changes in quantities only—had doubled in the half-century before 1910; it doubled *and redoubled* in the half-century after that date. The quantity of capital used in industry did not increase nearly fast enough to explain this acceleration; the pace of technical change rose dramatically in the twentieth century. This phenomenon has been called by some people the "Second Industrial Revolution" (see Chapter 7).

TABLE 12.3
The ten largest industries in 1960, by value added

	Value Added (billions of dollars) (1)	Employment (thousands of workers) (2)	Value Added per Worker (thousands of dollars) (3)
Nonelectrical machinery	14.38	1,012	14.2
Electrical machinery	13.07	950	13.8
Motor vehicles	10.12	571	17.8
Steel	7.69	504	15.2
Aircraft	6.45	410	15.7
Basic chemicals	5.10	161	31.7
Beverages	3.20	116	27.8
Dairy products	3.17	134	23.6
Structural metal products	2.93	239	12.3
Newspapers	2.92	160	18.3
All manufacturing	163.57	12,185	13.4

SOURCE: U.S. Bureau of the Census, *Survey of Manufacturers, 1959 and 1960* (Washington: U.S. Government Printing Office, 1962), pp. 28–47.

The three industries whose nineteenth-century origins have already been chronicled—electricity, automobiles, and chemicals—were among the largest industries in 1960. By the mid-twentieth century, electrical machinery performed a great range of functions. The number of electrical household appliances alone is vast. To this must be added the many industrial uses of electricity. Electricity can be used to produce heat, light, or motion. It is easily transmitted. It can be used in large quantities or small, by large machines or small, in almost any locale. To a nineteenth-century observer, the omnipresent electrical machine would be one of the most startling facets of a mid-twentieth century home or factory.

It must be remembered, however, that electricity is not a prime mover—that is, a *source* of power. Electricity by and large is a way of transmitting power, not a way of creating it; and most electricity is generated by water or steam power, the traditional sources for the nineteenth century. New sources of energy—like nuclear power—are awesome in their potentiality, but they are as yet largely potential. The use of electricity consequently provides yet another example of the increase in the indirect nature of production. Rather than generate power at the factory, whether by water wheel or steam engine, most firms prefer to have the power generated separately. Power is generated in one place by one group of people and used elsewhere by other people. The result of this increased specialization—even though the source of the power is unchanged—is a reduction in cost.

One suspects that most of the motors that are not electric are used for automobiles and trucks. The problem of storing and carrying power has led to the use of gasoline, which is easy to carry, rather than electricity, which is not, in car motors. The result, as everyone knows, has been a great increase in urban pollution.

This brings up a general point. The pollution created by car exhausts is an example of what economists call "external diseconomies"—that is, side effects of an activity that are not sold and that do not have a price. No one buys polluted air; no one chooses whether he will at any moment breathe from a pure or a contaminated atmosphere. Similarly, the congestion caused by traffic is an external diseconomy. If everyone drives to work, traffic moves slowly, and everyone is delayed. Yet no one is charged for the time he forces other people to spend on the road because he is there too. As a result, the air is more polluted and the roads are more crowded than they would be if each driver were billed for the costs he imposes on others. The competitive system will not tend toward an optimum allocation of resources under these circumstances because the market cannot value all the effects of the activities involved.

Many people say that automobile and gasoline taxes are too high. The prevalence of external diseconomies in this sector provides reason to think that they are too low. Since we cannot charge everyone directly for spreading fumes or choking the roads, we can impose a cost on those who own cars or on those who use gasoline in them that will approximate the cost to society of their doing so. Of course, if these taxes go into a fund that can only be used to build more roads, the extra roads will encourage more people to use cars—offsetting the effects of the taxes and quite possibly leading to an increase rather than a decrease in automobile traffic. To discourage driving, taxes on driving and related activities should be high, and these taxes should be used for purposes that will not encourage people to drive.

Unlike the use of electricity or automobiles, the use of chemicals is hard to describe. Two thirds of the value of the chemical industry's output is organic chemicals—materials made from coal, oil, or even wood (for cellulose). Dyes and cleaning fluids, explosives and plastics, rayon, vinyl, and photographic film all are made from these seemingly simple raw materials. The remaining chemicals are still more varied. Nitrates which were originally made from guano now are obtained from the air. Potash and sulfur for sulfuric acid are mined. Soda ash is extracted from common salt. These substances are used in the production of soap, paper, fertilizer, glass, rayon, and many, many other products. As might be inferred from its name, the chemical industry is based in large part on the exploitation of modern science, and its workings are hard to see without examining the technical details of production.

We noted earlier that the growth of American industry was dependent both on the use of a sophisticated technology and on the prevalence of abundant raw materials. The chemical industry represents a divergent trend because progress in this industry has created many substitutes for traditional materials. Nylon can be used in place of cotton; plastics, in place of steel. Increasingly efficient use is being made of natural resources such as coal and wood, decreasing the amount that is needed for a given level of production. As the range of materials that can be used for industry is broadened, dependence on the possession of specific raw materials is lessened.

Returning now to a topic that has been discussed for the nineteenth century, it should be noted that six out of the top ten industries are producers'-goods industries. The increasing complexity of manufacturing means that more and more industries are created to sell products to other industries. The four consumer-goods industries are similar to the consumer-goods industries found in previous tables. Two are food-processing industries, one is a part of printing and publishing, and the remaining one produces transportation equipment (automobiles).

Table 12.3 contains two industries producing transportation equipment, automobiles and airplanes. The aircraft industry is a twentieth-century industry, and it is also the product of a close—some would say incestuous—relationship between business and government. Airplanes were something of a curiosity before World War I, and the military demand for aircraft found the industry unprepared. A crash program was instituted to construct planes, but it bogged down after a few initial technical breakthroughs. Airplanes had been built from a variety of relatively scarce materials before the war. The wartime demand could not be filled without either expanding the supply of these materials or finding substitutes. Both were done, but it took time, and almost no planes were produced before the armistice.

After the war, the Post Office undertook to supply airmail service using military planes. During the 1920s, however, the Post Office substituted contracts with private companies for its own operations. These contracts initially were subject to competitive bidding and frequent renewal, but the airlines were not eager to take them on this basis. The contracts therefore were increased in duration, and they came to carry with them exclusive operating rights over selected routes. Thus they became desirable indeed, and the Postmaster used the awarding of contracts as a tool to promote consolidation and reform of the airlines.

With government subsidies through the Post Office, the airlines expanded rapidly. The demand for planes expanded too, and the aircraft industry grew. With the introduction of the DC-3, which was a rough analogue to the Model T automobile, the aircraft industry may be said to have come of age. The military demand expanded again in World War II and—unlike its earlier pattern—continued thereafter. Much of the cost of introducing new planes subsequently has been underwritten by the government, either directly or because the civilian planes are simply variants of military planes. Many planes are purchased by the government, and the government essentially guarantees the continued operation and expansion of the airlines—the primary alternative purchasers of airplanes.

The aircraft industry, as a result of this government support, has come to be a leading part of something called the "military–industrial complex." This loose term describes the military establishment and a group of industries closely connected with it: aircraft, electronics, munitions, and so on. The term, however, is not merely descriptive; it is also pejorative. It is used by opponents of American military activities to suggest that these activities are undertaken to increase profits among the firms concerned.

No one would deny that it is possible to make profits by supplying the military needs of the government. The question is rather one of causation. Does the government engage in wars to keep its supplying firms in business, or do these firms exist because the government wages war? The answer to this question probably does not emerge from facts alone. Each person answers it according to his view of causation and his theory of economic change. Most people today would probably say that the problem cannot be answered by making a simple choice. The government is affected by the nature of its suppliers, but these suppliers exist because of the requirements of national policy and the technology of modern warfare.

Although the government encouraged the growth of large and powerful corporations by its military procurement policies, it also discouraged the growth of large firms by its antitrust policy. Starting with the Sherman Act of 1890, the government has sought by several means and under the influence of several different definitions to maintain "competition." When the Sherman Act was passed most people thought that there was no conflict between the goals of free competition and economic efficiency. They thought that the small-scale business unit, working independently of other similar units, was the most efficient form of economic organization. Unhappily, the growing importance of economies of scale and patentable discoveries has rendered that belief obsolete in the twentieth century. Faced with a choice, the courts generally have decided in favor of efficiency; if a firm was acting in accordance with traditional business behavior, then—even if it was large relative to other firms in the industry—it was competitive. Only gradually did the balance of opinion shift and the definition of competition become more strict. The trend now appears to be toward a definition of competition based on market structure rather than efficiency, but the trend is neither rapid nor clear cut.

Not surprisingly, the results of such a weak and ambiguous antitrust policy have not been marked. The industries producing for a national market at the middle of the twentieth century can be divided into three groups roughly equal in size. In the first group, the eight largest firms produce over half the industry's total output, and the twenty largest firms produce over three quarters of it. In such industries, there is a strong presumption that the dominant mode of behavior is oligopolistic, not competitive. In the second group, the eight largest firms produce over one third of the output, but the twenty largest do *not* produce three quarters. Some of these industries show competitive behavior, while others do not. The large group of small firms acts as a potential restraint on the few large ones, and there is no general presumption about the kind of behavior that will be found. In the third and final group, there are no large firms and the behavior of the industry is competitive. Consequently, somewhere between one third and two thirds of the industries with a national market do not operate in a competitive fashion.

American industry in the twentieth century, then, differs quite sharply from its nineteenth-century predecessor. It has a faster rate of technical change. It uses the results of science more extensively and more consciously. It is less dependent on the natural resources of the United States because scientific advances continue to discover substitutes for traditional materials and fuels. It is more connected with the government, particularly with the national defense. It uses larger-scale plants. And it appears to be less competitive although our data on competition in the nineteenth century are too poor to warrant a definitive judgment. This change has contributed to the unprecedented wealth of America, but it has also led people to ask if some of the benefits of America's large and efficient industry might not be sacrificed to alleviate some of its less fortunate consequences. Destruction of oligopolies and elimination of pollution involve costs, but people wonder increasingly if the costs of ignoring these problems are not greater than the costs of solving them. Very little has been done in these areas; only time will tell how much will be.

SUGGESTED READING

Adams, Walter (ed.). *The Structure of American Industry: Some Case Studies.* 4th ed. New York: Macmillan, 1971.

Chandler, Alfred D., Jr. *Strategy and Structure: Chapters in the History of Industrial Enterprise.* Cambridge, Mass.: M.I.T. Press, 1962.

Clark, Victor S. *History of Manufactures in the United States.* Three vols. New York: McGraw-Hill for the Carnegie Institution of Washington, 1929.

Cole, Arthur H. *The American Wool Manufacture.* Two vols. Cambridge, Mass.: Harvard University Press, 1926.

Kirkland, Edward C. *Industry Comes of Age: Business, Labor, and Public Policy, 1860–1897.* Vol. 6 in The Economic History of the United States, edited by Henry David *et al.,* New York: Holt, Rinehart & Winston, 1961.

McGouldrick, Paul F. *New England Textiles in the Nineteenth Century: Profits and Investment.* Cambridge, Mass.: Harvard University Press, 1968.

Taylor, George Rogers. *The Transportation Revolution, 1815–1860.* Vol. 4. in The Economic History of the United States, edited by Henry David *et al.,* New York: Holt, Rinehart & Winston, 1962.

Temin, Peter. *Iron and Steel in Nineteenth-Century America: An Economic Inquiry.* Cambridge, Mass.: M.I.T. Press, 1964.

Tryon, Rolla M. *Household Manufactures in the United States, 1640–1860.* Chicago: University of Chicago Press, 1917.

Ware, Caroline F. *The Early New England Cotton Manufacture.* Boston: Houghton Mifflin, 1931.

13
INTERNAL
TRANSPORTATION

The United States was the first country of continental proportions to develop in the nineteenth century. This result was largely the consequence of the development of internal transportation in the nineteenth and twentieth centuries. Through a combination of an unprecedentedly large investment in the transport sector and the initiation of and receptivity to newer and more efficient transport modes, the original coastal settlement reached out to an ever-wider hinterland. The rich interior, with its better soils, was integrated into a regionally specialized whole. Without the allocation of resources to transportation on a large scale and the succession of nineteenth-century transport innovations, particularly the canal and railroad, the contours of the American economy would have been far different.

In this chapter we examine how the interplay of American market conditions and social intervention functioned to evoke transport investment in great abundance; how these facilities lowered the costs of movement and widened the market; and how the benefits were distributed to the rest of the economy. We begin by discussing some of the effects of transport investment. The second section treats the motives, magnitudes, and financing of the succession of transport innovations undertaken in the nineteenth and early twentieth centuries. It also deals with their success in lowering rates and attracting traffic. The third section examines the variety of economic effects attributable to the nineteenth-century transportation revolution. The fourth section covers the mature industrial economy of the twentieth century and its different transport requirements. The final section briefly reviews the entire experience to see what conclusions may be drawn from it.

THE EFFECTS OF TRANSPORT INVESTMENT
As background for the discussion which follows, it will be helpful to consider the effects of transport investment, many of which can be illustrated with the

FIGURE 13.1

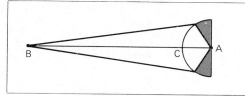

aid of a simple diagram.[1] Consider an area of uniform agricultural fertility, as shown in Figure 13.1, producing a single product for which there is a perfectly elastic demand. Prior to construction of a railroad from the coastal city A to B, the extent of economic settlement is limited to the semicircle around A. At the border of the semicircle the cost of transport plus the cost of production exactly equals the price in A. Hence the land earns zero rent and is at the margin of cultivation. At all points within the area of cultivation, and proportional to the proximity to market, positive locational rents are earned.

The construction of the railroad, by reducing transport costs, immediately widens the area of profitable cultivation, as shown. Now along the margins of the triangle, and at B itself, the sum of the lower transport costs and constant production costs equals the former revenue. Moreover, within the previous boundary, at all points outside the shaded segment, it is now cheaper to use a combination of railroad and overland transport. Rents will rise in this new zone, reflecting the new lower supply costs and the profits potentially earned on land brought closer to the market. Those located at C are especially favored. Previously on the margin of cultivation, and therefore with the largest ton-mile shipments, such settlers receive the greatest benefits from the railroad. These manifest themselves in increased rents, which are nothing more than the annual value of the direct benefits of the transport investment.

Obviously the creation of new economical production sites within the compass of the market will encourage settlement in the area and lead to new output. Aggregate real income will rise by the entire extent of the new cultivation. But since much of the increase is due to the influx of more labor and capital, per capita income increases more modestly. Its growth is determined by the savings in transport costs on goods shipped to market. These lower charges have their analogue in reduced factor inputs, thereby releasing some inputs previously engaged in transportation to other productive activities. Figure 13.2 illustrates the direct benefits that can be ascribed to the road as area ABCD. The area represents the difference between what persons would have been willing to pay in transportation charges and what they actually paid. Since their willingness to pay is based on the exact equality of the sum of transport charges and costs of production with revenues, this difference is exactly the same as the locational rent discussed above. Note that we do not

[1] For a fuller treatment see A. A. Walters, *The Economics of Road User Charges,* World Bank Staff Occasional Paper no. 5 (Baltimore: Johns Hopkins, 1968), chap. 5.

FIGURE 13.2

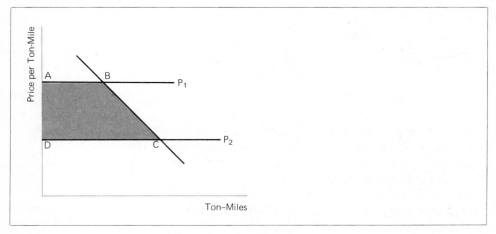

Ton–Miles

evaluate the differential cost of the total traffic *DC* after the road has opened, because that figure overstates its benefits; it is necessary also to take into account how the transport demand, and thus the resources potentially freed, depend on the rate charged.

This straightforward case can be extended to more complicated, and more realistic, alternatives without much alteration. For example, if settlement had already occurred between *A* and *B* and a limited production for subsistence were already present, a much larger per capita income increase would have to be ascribed to the road. This is because the same aggregate real income increase could occur with a much smaller addition of new factors. Similarly if, given a larger market area, it is now feasible for *A* to specialize in manufactures at a lower production cost than the costs of previous imports or home manufacture, there is a further gain to the community. It is also easy to accommodate the case of differential fertility or of less than perfectly elastic demand.

Perhaps the most important modification is to introduce explicitly the capital costs of constructing the road. The price line P_2 in Figure 13.2 will in general include only the variable costs of operation, for once the railroad is constructed that is the relevant measure of the resource input. The decision to construct the road or not must depend upon the size and time profile of the benefits relative to the capital costs. Or if we wish to interpret the price as including some normal return on the capital, we must compare the *sum* of net revenues (receipts minus operating costs) and benefits (measured on a price rather than cost basis). If the road is costly, then although it will have a favorable effect on real income, it may not be economical. It may be better to invest in improved techniques of cultivation, for example, and to lower the costs of production, rather than to reduce the costs of transportation.

In making such calculations, we emphasize the necessity of taking into account the totality of benefits, not merely the private profits, for an essential attribute of transport investment, particularly when embodied in a more advanced technology (as when the canal superseded the turnpike or the railroad the canal), is that its social returns tend to be large. This is typically the case because transport serves as intermediate input into a variety of final outputs, and because of its spatial fixity. These characteristics lend to transportation routes a quality of essentiality. When the railroad is initially opened from *A* to *B*, it does not matter that there may already be a whole series of prior investments linking other cities. They are of no value to the immediate area because their capacity cannot be utilized there. When investment proceeds to the point at which duplication of facilities occurs, the indirect benefits drop off quickly. The same is true when the technical characteristics of successive innovations leave little basis for choosing between them.

The indivisibility of transportation facilities in their early phase thus makes for quantum jumps in traffic carried, and large benefits. It also simultaneously poses a problem to private investors. They cannot recapture through their charges all of the benefits conferred by the road. Any single tariff will lead to smaller private revenues than benefits, since the latter represent the maximum that could be obtained through a set of perfectly discriminated prices (charging each potential user a different price based on his personal advantage, and thereby absorbing all of the locational rent). This problem does not arise with the usual investment because it typically involves small enough changes in output to allow the private revenues obtained to approximate the social benefits. Indivisibility also operates on the cost side to increase the capital that must be mobilized to construct the road. As larger sums are required, the risk increases and finance becomes less readily available.

To the effects creating a divergence between social and private rates of return we may add still others. The durability of the typical transport investment makes it necessary to take into account a flow of revenues far into the future. The reduction in transport costs will set in motion ancillary investment— agricultural settlement in the example in Figure 13.1—and these will affect the profitability of the original transport facility. If the private investor is myopic, he will understate the true, dynamic outcome and will focus upon the more limited current traffic. These *forward linkages*, as they have been termed, reflect themselves at least in traffic increases and thereby in revenues. (Of course, for reasons of indivisibility it may be impossible to capture all the benefits by charges.) The *backward linkages*, or effects upon suppliers to the transport sector, do not impinge upon the investor in the same way. The ultimate technological or scale impact of, say, the number of rails ordered upon the iron industry will only partially register itself through the indirect route of iron price reductions. Very rarely will such considerations enter into the individual investment decision. To the extent that the original transport investment sets in motion a unique sequence of further investment and technological change, the uncoordinated action of the market does not reward that initial investment sufficiently. Consequently, some socially desirable investments may not be undertaken.

Even if the private sector responds appropriately in constructing the right facilities, there may still be a problem of price determination. Transport investments, particularly in their early phases, confer natural monopolies upon their owners and operators. Users typically have no option among alternative routings. While optimal social policy requires that price be equal to marginal costs, the profit-maximizing monopolist will equate marginal revenue to marginal cost and produce less. Hence there will be insufficient utilization of the carrying capacity of the road if market power is not restrained. The problem is further complicated by the existence of economies of scale that make any pricing rule based upon marginal cost privately nonviable: Only a subsidy to compensate for intramarginal losses can make it feasible.

It is no surprise, in light of the defects of the market signals, that the history of internal improvements has been intimately tied up with government policy. Whether because of the desire to stimulate transport investment for its wide-ranging indirect effects, or because of the necessity for regulation, the public interest has asserted its presence even when the pure price system has ruled supreme in the rest of the economy. Yet compared to other national transport development, the role of the private sector in the United States was surprisingly vigorous, as we shall see.

THE NATURE OF NINETEENTH-CENTURY TRANSPORT EXPANSION

The Turnpike Era, 1800–1820

The earliest expression of the postcolonial demand for internal improvement was in the construction of better overland facilities. In the process the precedent was created of a strong reliance upon private enterprise and initiative. This emphasis was to characterize much of the subsequent investment in transportation. It was not that the public or common road was unknown: In 1800, before there was any sizable turnpike mileage, post roads already aggregated more than 20,000 miles. Rather, reliance upon independent local construction and repair, financed largely by labor services, seemed unable to evoke a system of anything approaching adequate quality. And small wonder. Since passage on the roads was not limited to local residents, some part of the benefits devolved on others without compensating payment. Moreover, in the context of a seasonal agriculture, the additional costs in time and effort of inadequate transportation to market did not conflict with productive labor. It was preferable to give up leisure after the harvest than be subject to the cash levies required for a more efficient road network.

Improvement in the road system therefore took the form of turnpike construction rather than investment in public thoroughfares. Beginning with the prosperity engendered by the surge of commercial activity in the 1790s and ending with the rise of canals and railways, somewhat more than 11,000 miles of turnpikes were constructed in the northern states before 1830. The majority were completed by 1820, and in New England even earlier. All indications point to modest southern turnpike construction, despite Virginia's claim to the first road in 1785; nor was much done in the West until the era of plank roads. Thus the New England figures require an adjustment of only 10–20 percent to reflect the national picture.

Table 13.1 provides rough estimates of the magnitude, location, and timing of the investment. Since it is derived from the systematization of literary accounts of individual New England turnpikes, various state reports, fragmentary additional references, and distribution of cumulative totals by reports of incorporation, the tabulation is less exact than we should like. Nonetheless, the general contours are probably valid enough.

The data reflect the early and rather complete system of roads radiating from commercial and political centers such as Boston, Concord, New Haven, Hartford, Albany, New York, Philadelphia, and Baltimore. Subsequent construction in the Middle states extended already completed trunklines westward and interlaced their larger territories. The more expensive and serious character of the Philadelphia and Baltimore links to the Ohio Valley, well surfaced according to the McAdam design, show up in the much higher costs per mile registered in Pennsylvania and Maryland. The total investment required to finance the construction of turnpikes, conservatively estimated at about $30 million, represented some 60 percent of the expenditure for all canals in this period.

TABLE 13.1
Cumulative turnpike construction in the New England
and Middle Atlantic states (costs in thousands of dollars)

	1810		1820		1830	
	Mileage	Cost	Mileage	Cost	Mileage	Cost
Maine	35	35	35	35	35	35
New Hampshire	455	455	527	527	527	527
Vermount	341	341	410	410	455	455
Massachusetts	767	1,851	843	1,966	964	2,086
Rhode Island	78	78	133	133	172	172
Connecticut	1,148	1,148	1,302	1,302	1,459	1,459
New York	1,100	2,000	4,000	8,000	4,500	9,000
New Jersey	200	600	500	1,000	550	1,100
Pennsylvania	500	1,500	1,800	6,400	2,500	8,800
Maryland	60	300	250	1,200	300	1,500
National road	—	—	130	1,561	200[a]	2,689
Total	4,684	8,308	9,930	22,534	11,662	27,823

[a] In process of construction; approximately 200 miles completed.

SOURCES

New England: Frederick J. Wood, *The Turnpikes of New England and Evolution of the Same Through England, Virginia and Maryland* (Boston: Marshall Jones Co., 1919); Albert Gallatin, "Report on Roads and Canals," Document no. 250, 10th Congress, 1st Session. Vol. 1 in *American State Papers: Miscellaneous,* (1810).
Middle Atlantic: Joseph A. Durrenberger, *Turnpikes: A Study of the Toll Road Movement in the Middle Atlantic States and Maryland* (Valdosta, Ga.: Southern Stationary and Printing Co., 1931); J. L. Ringwalt, *Development of Transportation Systems in the United States* (Philadelphia: J. L. Ringwalt, 1888); George H. Evans, Jr., *Business Incorporations in the United States, 1800–1943* (New York: National Bureau of Economic Research, 1948).
National road: Thomas B. Searight, *The Old Pike* (Uniontown, Pa.: Thomas B. Searight, 1894).

This substantial sum, unlike the outlays for canals, was secured predominantly from private coffers. Apart from federal finance for the National Road, substantial state assistance was limited to Virginia, Ohio, and Pennsylvania during the period in question. (Kentucky, Indiana, and Illinois became involved in the 1830s.) Only the Keystone State, attentive to regional interests, completed an extensive system, and there the proportionate contribution of the state came close to 30 percent. Taken as a whole, about $25 million was raised privately, an amount that was twice the private commitment to canals.

Such a feat was made possible by the decentralized character of the turnpike corporations. The average turnpike size in Massachusetts was less than 20 miles, and it was smaller still in Connecticut. The route between Philadelphia and Pittsburgh was operated by eight turnpike and three bridge companies. Few exceeded $100,000 in capitalization, and all relied quite heavily upon local contributions which were widely distributed in the communities. State charters frequently placed a maximum upon the number of votes a shareholder might cast and required immediate cash deposits upon subscription. The motivation for the investment seemingly was not the direct financial return but the indirect advantages accruing to those with access to better roads. Whatever the expectations, however, little direct profit was actually realized.

Even the Philadelphia and Lancaster Road, well constructed in a region already experiencing vigorous trade, and originally oversubscribed, could not remunerate its proprietors satisfactorily. Gallatin reports a net income of $12,000 upon a total cost of $465,000 for a return of less than 3 percent; and profits did not exceed 4 percent even in later years, after the successful extension to Pittsburgh. The detailed accounts of the Massachusetts turnpikes likewise chronicle financial disappointment. The Salem Turnpike was well situated and excellently constructed; yet its average returns on cost were below 5 percent. The high cost of construction, $15,000 per mile, cannot be blamed. Less expensive turnpikes in western Massachusetts fared little better, and more frequently worse. For New England as a whole, only 5 or 6 out of 230 turnpikes have been identified as profitable.[2] In light of this, the Gallatin Report's attribution of an 11 percent return to the Connecticut roads in the first decade seems exaggerated.

What explains this lack of profitability, surprising because of both the continuing flow of private investment and the widespread eagerness for transport improvement? Among the reasons given are high overhead expenses, avoidance of tolls through the device of shunpikes, and construction in sparsely settled regions incapable of generating sufficient traffic. The most important factors, however, were the limitations of the available technology and the marginal advantage over common roads the turnpike represented.

The only innovative feature of the turnpike was its better surface which reduced friction. This gain in carrying capacity was calculated at 125 percent over that possible on ordinary roads in an 1831 Pennsylvania Canal Commis-

[2] George R. Taylor, *The Transportation Revolution* (New York: Holt, Rinehart & Winston, 1951), p. 27

sioners' report. Translated into transport costs, it converts to a 50 percent reduction. Whether such ideal technical characteristics reflected themselves exactly in market prices is difficult to ascertain. The apparent decline in wagon rates during the turnpike era is in the right direction. Nevertheless tariffs remained high. The rates most frequently quoted were between 12 and 17 cents per ton-mile, and sometimes higher. At such prices, long-distance hauling of all but the highest-valued commodities continued to be excluded. Over the range of price reduction, the demand for long hauls was not very elastic. For shorter hauls, the disadvantages of a lighter load and lengthier elapsed time on common roads seemed to be less than the toll charges. These were determined by the type of vehicle rather than the load carried. For maximum load, the typical toll was 2 cents per ton-mile, but upon smaller shipments it became proportionately higher. This increased cost could become a significant deterrent where population density was limited and shipments small. The reports of the Pennsylvania and New York Turnpikes confirm that "long distance traffic was the chief source of revenue on all turnpikes except a few situated near the larger centers of population."[3]

Two final points should be kept in mind. First, the turnpike corporation was limited to toll receipts without any possible additional profit on the transportation services themselves. A similar handicap was to harass canals, but their much lower charges frequently evoked a traffic large enough to compensate for it. Under such circumstances, the companies were able to appropriate to themselves only a part of the total transport savings. The increased profits accrued to stage operators and teamsters upon their investments in equipment. Second, as we have seen in the discussion of Figure 13.1, no charge could have recaptured the total benefits, because of externalities.

Ultimately, the unsatisfactory private financial outcome determined the turnpike's fate. Even before the competition of canals and railways had made itself felt, many turnpikes had fallen into disrepair, unable to repay even variable costs. The technology could not justify the cost. Peak mileage was reached about 1830, although the investment rate had been greatest some 15 years previously. The turnpike was to be partially responsible for far greater transport consequences, however. Completion of the Pittsburgh Pike and National Road, however inadequate, had given Philadelphia and Baltimore advantages in the western trade vis-à-vis New York. Out of that confrontation emerged the Erie Canal and, in reflex, the Baltimore and Ohio Railroad. We now turn to these other innovations.

The Age of Canal Expansion, 1815–1843

Water as an internal transport medium retained the disadvantage of slowness, but compensated with sharply reduced friction. Large loads could be carried cheaply with a minimal expenditure of energy. This principle had been applied since ancient times. Yet natural waterways were not always adequate or

[3] Joseph A. Durrenberger, *Turnpikes: A Study of the Toll Road Movement in the Middle Atlantic States and Maryland* (Valdosta, Ga.: Southern Stationery and Printing Co., 1931), p. 118.

ideally located. The Duke of Bridgewater's success with his canal, begun in 1759 in England, set off a wave of imitation that involved an expenditure of some £13 million in Great Britain in the last 40 years of the eighteenth century.[4] The response in the United States was longer in coming, but ultimately more ambitious.

The delay in American response until the 1790s is easily explained by the Revolutionary War and the unsettled decade immediately following. Thereafter economic factors played a more decisive role in inhibiting canal construction. The large average size of most planned ventures, and the substantial costs per mile, made total capital requirements a significant deterrent. Moreover, there were no immediately paying propositions, such as the coal-carrying canals of England represented; the poor financial results of the pioneering Middlesex and Santee Companies reinforced such skepticism. It took the Erie Canal to undermine it.

That epic undertaking, 364 miles in length, linking the Hudson to Lake Erie, was begun in 1817 and completed in 1825.[5] Its roots extend much earlier. The initial step was taken in 1792 when the Western Inland Lock Navigation Company was authorized to connect the Hudson River to Lake Ontario and Seneca Lake. Harassed by shortages of funds, compensated only partially by state assistance, the canal could not be completed to either of its termini. Nor was river improvement, which constituted the bulk of what was in fact done, efficient enough to compete successfully with neighboring turnpikes. The expenditure of $400,000 yielded little or no return. Yet that failure ultimately had the following consequences: (*a*) It established a precedent for the necessity of state intervention rather than reliance on private initiative; (*b*) it was the basis for later consideration of an all-canal alternative, constructed in a more technically satisfactory fashion; and (*c*) it also meant a more sympathetic hearing for an alternative route to the Lakes, via Lake Erie.

For many years, no such beneficial effects were apparent. Not until the Gallatin Report of 1808 included a proposal for the federal government to construct a canal from the Mohawk River to Lake Ontario did a significant revival of the earlier scheme take place. In 1810 one of the directors of the Western Company suggested that the legislature appoint a commission to examine the possibilities of further westward expansion by that enterprise. A resolution emerged empowering a commission to explore the entire route and to propose a program to the next session. Finally, in 1811, an expanded board was voted with additional financial support. By this time it was clear that private enterprise was not sufficient to the task. Federal funds were sought to fulfill the original Gallatin scheme. But that report, solicited in the commercial euphoria of 1807 and concluded after the Embargo Act, was not about to receive implementation in the less satisfactory economic and political climate of 1810 and thereafter. The state itself, if anyone, would have to shoulder the burden, now estimated at $6 million. The legislature cautiously

[4] T. S. Ashton, *An Economic History of England: The Eighteenth Century* (London: Methuen, 1955), p. 75.
[5] We have drawn extensively, in this and succeeding paragraphs, upon Julius Rubin, "An Innovating Public Improvement: The Erie Canal," in *Canals and American Economic Development*, Carter Goodrich (ed.) (New York: Columbia University Press, 1961).

followed its commission, authorizing in 1812 the borrowing of $5 million for the project, but retaining for itself the final decision to proceed.

The presages of early success proved false. The War of 1812 intervened to eliminate the possibility of a European loan and to diminish the enthusiasm of the legislature. Only an extensive campaign led by DeWitt Clinton, abetted by the postwar recovery and the rapidly increasing population of western New York, revived and consummated the proposal in April 1817. In addition to the Erie route, a canal was authorized linking the Hudson River to Lake Champlain, a plan which had been the unrealized intent of the earlier private Northern Company.

The Erie and its imitators.   Few public investments were so well rewarded or so immediate in their impact. Prior to completion to its full length, the Erie Canal had collected almost $1 million in revenues. The annual *net* gain on the Erie and Champlain Canals over their first decade of operations, 1826–1835, amounted to almost 8 percent of the cost. Emulation did not await the ultimate confirmation of the success of the venture. Old projects were revived; new ones cogitated; and above all, large quantities of capital began to be expended.

Not the least of the reactions occurred in New York State itself. A general canal law was passed in 1825 providing for extensions through much of the state, many of which did not justify the expenditure. The Erie, too, was an object of interest as the legislature voted for enlargement of the main canal, commencing a stream of expenditures that continued until the Civil War. By 1860 the original $9 million cost for the Erie and Champlain Canals had increased to almost $55 million.

The second largest contributor to the canal boom was the state of Pennsylvania. For Philadelphia, the challenge of New York City's route to the West could only evoke immediate response. Already in ascent after the War of 1812, New York now threatened a death blow from which Philadelphia commercial interests would never recover. The inadequacy of the Pittsburgh Pike as a competitor to the Erie Canal was never in doubt. Neither was the willingness of the state to stand behind its premier city. The tradition of state financial support had already been established in the turnpike era, and was not the subject of extensive debate.

The choice of technology, rather, was the crucial question. Nature had not treated Pennsylvania as kindly as New York. Only 655 feet of lockage was required to surmount the Appalchian barrier by the Erie route. A Pennsylvania canal implied 3358 feet of lockage and a 4-mile tunnel. Under such adverse circumstances, the railroad alternative, although still visionary, was not excluded. The successful application of locomotive power on the Stockton and Darlington Lines in England in September 1825 intensified an already keen interest in the new form of transport. In March, an emissary of the Pennsylvania Society for the Promotion of Internal Improvement, William Strickland, had been dispatched to England to prepare a firsthand report on the subject. His favorable disposition to railways set off a brief but bitter debate between railroad and canal supporters that culminated in victory for the latter. Construction of the canal began on July 4, 1826.

Reality compelled substantial modification of the original scheme. A portage railroad substituted for the projected tunnel in the mountains, but not until 1831 did its construction begin. At its easternmost end, the narrow Union Canal was forsaken as the principal link from Philadelphia to the Susquehanna, and another railroad was authorized, the Philadelphia and Columbia. Its 81 miles were begun in 1828 and completed in 1834. The entire mainline became operative in the same year. The final result, a hybrid of canal and railroad, replete with inclined planes, has been much maligned. Its cost of $12 million for the 395 miles was never adequately compensated by traffic over it. Whereas the annual profits on the Erie were 8 percent of cost in its first decade, those on the Mainline were not a fourth as large.[6] Nor did finances improve considerably thereafter. More relevant from the standpoint of its motivation, through tonnage on the route both early and late compared even less favorably to the Erie results. This performance is still poorer considering that the Ohio Valley was at that time a more important source of surplus than the Great Lakes region served by the Erie Canal. The Mainline could not divert agricultural exports from their southward course over the Mississippi nor generate enough return transport in manufactures to make its existence worthwhile. Such a result is readily explained: Handicapped by multiple transhipments, a system in which the state provided only motive power and not freight cars on the Philadelphia and Columbia Lines, and less favorable grades of shipments, the Mainline always exceeded the Erie Canal in transport costs by a goodly margin.

Nonetheless, it is both unfair and inaccurate to criticize the decision to proceed with the venture too harshly.[7] In 1826, a delay of four or five years to verify the possibilities of railroads was not a feasible solution to Philadelphia's rapidly deteriorating commercial position. Apart from the completion of the Erie Canal, there was underway construction of a system of Ohio canals designed to link the Ohio Valley to it. Immediate response or acceptance of secondary status were the options. With full hindsight, the latter is recognized as the inevitable outcome. Choice of a railroad technology would not have been a successful strategy. Costs at that early date were prohibitive. None of the great trunk lines succeeded in their objectives. When they finally did, it was with a technology that was only beginning at that late date to compete successfully with the alternatives afforded by the Erie Canal and the Mississippi River. The decision for the canal, moreover, was more ample in scope than construction of the Mainline alone. It encompassed a state *system* of canals, whose feeders cost an additional $6.5 million, as a price for state support of the commercial aspirations of Philadelphia. A through railroad, because it did not lend itself to similar extensions, had no guarantee of equivalent funding. The Pennsylvania Railroad was built in the 1850s under private auspices with only limited government support, primarily from Philadelphia

[6] A. L. Bishop, "The State Works of Pennsylvania," *Transactions of the Connecticut Academy of Arts and Sciences*, vol. 13 (November 1907), pp. 238–239, 278–280.
[7] For a view less sympathetic to the Pennsylvania decision, see Julius Rubin, "Canal or Railroad?" *Transactions of the American Philosophical Society*, vol 1, Part 7 (1961).

and Pittsburgh. Parts of the statewide system did function reasonably well in serving local interests, moreover. The Delaware Division turned a net profit of $2.5 million from 1830 until its sale in 1858 for $1.8 million; its rate of return was about 5 percent over this interval; the Eastern Division of the Mainline did about as well.[8]

Overall, however, the public works were clearly a financial failure, even a disaster.[9] The total investment in construction was over $33 million. The sale value was only $11 million, augmented by cumulated net revenues of an additional $8 million. More impressive still was the constant drain on the public treasury—$43.5 million in interest was disbursed from initiation to sale. Much of the state loss originated in ventures which were begun but not completed ($10 million plus interest thereon), and in failure to undertake until a very late date technical improvements that could have rendered the results more palatable. The experience is not an impressive argument for public investment.

Another response to the Erie, equally unsatisfactory, was the Chesapeake and Ohio Canal.[10] This was the successor of the Potomac Company, formed in the 1780s under the presidency of George Washington, which had successfully bypassed the rapids north of Georgetown, but had done little more. The idea of an extension to Cumberland and thence to the Ohio River was revived in the 1820s by the power of example. What made the Chesapeake and Ohio unique was the extent of national sponsorship. Congress subscribed $1 million in May, 1828 toward a projected expenditure of $4.5 million for a canal to be completed to Cumberland; Maryland contributed an additional $500,000, as did Alexandria and Georgetown, the termini; Washington allocated $1 million in addition. All told, only $606,400 was forthcoming from private sources.

This auspicious financial reserve was counteracted by mounting costs as construction began. Federal support was not an unmixed blessing, since it imposed standards far above those of the original plans or of other works under way. It required five years to reach Harper's Ferry, 65 miles distant, and the original capital was already exhausted. Andrew Jackson was not as favorably disposed to national assistance as his predecessor, and refused further involvement. Maryland alone was forced to rescue the project by a direct subscription totaling $5 million in 1839, as well as an additional loan of $2 million. Work continued until 135 miles were completed in 1840; the additional 50 miles to Cumberland were bridged a decade later and only after further debt had been contracted.

By that time, the canal faced the competition of the Baltimore and Ohio Railroad for transport of general merchandise. It was a losing struggle. The shipment of coal generated the largest part of its revenue, that commodity amounting to some two thirds of tonnage in the 1850s. Some such specialized canals in the anthracite region of Pennsylvania did well; the Chesapeake and

[8] Bishop, *op. cit.*, pp. 278, 281.
[9] *Ibid.*, pp. 228–229.
[10] See Walter S. Sanderlin, *The Great National Project: A History of the Chesapeake and Ohio Canal* (Baltimore: Johns Hopkins, 1946).

Ohio did not. Net receipts were actually negative during the 1850s, and while the canal continued to be used into the twentieth century, its financial status never significantly altered for the better.

The Erie excited not only emulative response from the commercial empire of the Middle Atlantic states seeking to extend their hinterlands westward, but also from the interior. The first and largest system was that of Ohio.[11] Begun in 1825, its objective was to connect Lake Erie to the Ohio River in both the eastern and western portions of the state. The eastern link was completed in 1833; the western was delayed by the economic decline of the late 1830s and not consummated until 1845. The cost for the 731-mile system, plus 91 miles of slack-water navigation, was almost $16 million. As in New York and Pennsylvania, no small part of this total was due to the uneconomical feeders constructed to the mainlines. Revenues from the canals never succeeded in returning costs before their eventual demise due to the railroad. Although the eastern segment was by far the more remunerative, its annual net revenues did not exceed 4 percent of cost, and only did that for 15 years. This was insufficient to pay the current interest on the debt, let alone amortize the investment. The canal did continue in operation into the twentieth century on a lease arrangement initiated in 1861. But in the absence of continuing improvements, its competitive position steadily worsened.

Despite this unfortunate denouement, the early success of the Ohio canals found ready imitators. There was no room in the calculations for eventual displacement by the railroad, and thus for sharply truncated earnings. Present benefits counted more than future payments on state debt. It was in such a spirit that Indiana and Illinois undertook their contributions to the wave of canal construction.[12] For Indiana, the vehicle was the Wabash and Erie Canal, supported in part by a federal land grant in 1827. Construction proceeded slowly, but in the gradually accelerating inflation of values and expectations of the 1830s—which had seen New York, Pennsylvania, and Ohio greatly expand their commitments—Indiana did not balk at initiating branch extension simultaneously. When depression descended in 1839, much was in process, but precious little was completed. Not until 1843 did the Wabash and Erie reach Lake Erie at Toledo, and not until ten more years had passed was it terminated at Evansville on the Ohio River. Its 450 miles made it the longest single canal in the United States, constructed at a cost of over $6.5 million. Completion to the full extent antedated abandonment of the southern section by less than a decade, and total net operating revenues of $1.3 million made the canal's financial performance among the least satisfactory of all antebellum ventures.

Illinois, too, received a grant of federal lands in 1827 to finance the Illinois and Michigan Canal, the missing link between Chicago and the Mississippi River. Construction began in 1836, along with an elaborate railroad network

[11] For a factual treatment of the Ohio Canal, see C. P. McClelland and C. C. Huntington, *History of the Ohio Canals* (Columbus: Ohio State Archaeological and Historical Society, 1905). For a more analytic and recent study emphasizing public policy, see Harry Scheiber, *Ohio Canal Era* (Athens: Ohio University Press, 1969).
[12] The two standard histories are those by Elbert J. Benton, *The Wabash Trade Route in the Development of the Old Northwest* (Baltimore: Johns Hopkins, 1903); and James W. Putnam, *The Illinois and Michigan Canal* (Chicago: University of Chicago Press, 1918).

intended to dissect the state, and encountered the same depression-caused limitation of capital common to other projects. The canal was completed under new management and on more modest scale in 1848. The construction cost was $6.5 million, augmented by continuing interest charges during the period of dormancy. The characteristically checkered early history augured the characteristic result: financial disaster. After 1879, expenditures for repairs and maintenance exceeded tolls. Only rental revenues from land holdings prevented the situation from deteriorating more. Peak traffic on the canal was realized in 1882, and the more adequate Chicago Sanitary and Ship Canal largely replaced it in the twentieth century.

Thus far we have described great interregional works undertaken with extensive state aid. These made up the majority, both in mileage and investment, of the canals constructed before the railroad. A second group of canals, smaller in extent, largely attached to coal interests like the original English model, and privately funded, also inherited the enthusiasm engendered by the Erie. They were to be found almost exclusively in the anthracite region of eastern Pennsylvania, from which they descended to serve the markets of New York and Philadelphia. In many instances canals were owned by the coal-mining enterprises themselves. In this category, the Delaware and Hudson, Lehigh, Schuylkill, Navigation, and Morris were the most prominent. All were undertaken in the 1820s, completed shortly thereafter, and, with the exception of the last, became almost immediate financial successes. The Lehigh and the Schuylkill Navigation both underwent difficult periods in the 1840s, but recovered again in the 1850s to continue effectively for some time. The Schuylkill bowed to railroad competition sooner, helped along by a disastrous 1869 flood, while the Lehigh continued to operate, albeit in diminishing proportions and under railroad direction. The Delaware and Hudson remained one of the most attractive investments both before and after the Civil War. Its peak traffic was reached in 1872, and thereafter the coal tonnage diminished as railroad transportation, likewise owned by the company, replaced it. The Morris became a dividend payer in the 1850s and 1860s, but its useful life was likewise brought to an end by railroad purchase.

The three investment cycles. Table 13.2 summarizes the investment undertaken in the canal expansion just described. The first period, through 1834, includes the construction of the Erie Canal, the Pennsylvania Mainline, the commencement of the Chesapeake and Ohio, the completion of the Ohio and Erie, and the private eastern canals. In all, more than 2000 miles were constructed at this time, with the large state-financed systems making the most important contribution. Two thirds of the capital emanated from public sources.

The character of the second cycle, covering the latter 1830s, is different. Apart from the ventures in Indiana and Illinois, its major components were the continuation of works already under way—the Chesapeake and Ohio and the west branch of the Ohio system, for example—and the construction of feeders to supplement the already-opened trunk lines. Governmental participation actually rose slightly in this period due to the earlier completion

TABLE 13.2
Canal investment (millions of dollars)

Period	Total	Public
1815–1834	58.6	41.2
1834–1844	72.2	57.3
1844–1860	57.4	38.0

SOURCE: Adapted from Harvey Segal, "Cycles of Canal Construction," in *Canals and American Economic Development*, Carter Goodrich (ed.) (New York: Columbia University Press, 1961), p. 215.

of the private anthracite canals. This is not the only difference between the two periods. Whereas foreign investment accounted for one fourth of the finance in the earlier cycle, 60 percent originated in Europe during the second. Much of this amount entered after 1836, when a number of states passed legislation enlarging upon their original aspirations. This dependence on foreign funds created a vulnerability to financial conditions that was to prove disastrous. As the flow halted, investment declined from a peak outlay of $14.2 million in 1840 to $1 million in 1843.[13] Little mileage was brought to completion because the larger ventures did not construct consecutively.

The final investment cycle, the recovery from this trough, was surprisingly large due to the completion of many projects cut short previously. Continuation of work on the Erie enlargement and completion of two extensions to the New York canals account for almost half the total amount. The rest was expended on the completion of canals in Indiana and Illinois and the termination of the Chesapeake and Ohio. Less than 900 new miles were added after 1844, a measure of both the intensive character of the expenditure and the absence of new ventures as the railroad emerged as an alternative.

Canal transport services. The almost $200 million in canal investment created a substantial potential supply of transport services. Table 13.3 presents estimates of the actual ton-mileage carried by canals at two points during the antebellum period and at a third later date approximating their peak utilization. Note the independence of the construction cycle and the growth of ton-mileage. Although new mileage built after 1844 was limited, traffic increased quite rapidly until 1859, and beyond. Only with the later abandonments and decreased demand provoked by more intense railroad competition did the absolute ton-mileage diminish. In not a few instances railroad ownership was responsible for a premature demise: "In nearly every case where a canal had passed under the influence of a railroad the volume of canal traffic has decreased. In some cases it is apparent that railroads deliberately endeavored to kill off traffic by water route."[14] Railroads by 1909 owned 90 percent of the 632 active miles of private canals; in all, in 1909, there were

---

[13] Harvey Segal, "Cycles of Canal Construction," in *Canals and American Economic Development*, Carter Goodrich (ed.) (New York: Columbia University Press, 1961), pp. 188, 192.
[14] *Report of the Commissioner of Corporations on Transportation by Water in the United States*, vol. 4 (Washington: U.S. Government Printing Office, 1909–1913), p. 64.

TABLE 13.3
Canal transportation services (millions of ton-miles)

	Annual Average 1837–1846	1859	1880
New York system	227.5	544.3	1223.6
Chesapeake and Ohio	9.6	58.8	104.8
Mainline	49.0	65.8	51.7
Pennsylvania Lateral Canals	23.0	172.8	—
Delaware	17.4	88.1	119.6
Lehigh Navigation	13.8	104.6	43.1
Schuylkill	23.4	169.9	50.4
Morris	4.6	51.0	42.2
Delaware and Raritan	11.2	75.0	67.4
Union	7.2	18.2	2.1
Chesapeake and Delaware	2.9	6.9	13.4
Susquehanna	11.1	29.1	10.9
Ohio system	79.5	70.4	83.7
Wabash and Erie	13.2	13.0	—
Illinios and Michigan	—	25.7	52.6

SOURCES

1837–1846: Harvey Segal, "Canals and Economic Development," in *Canals and American Economic Development*, Carter Goodrich (ed.) (New York: Columbia University Press, 1961), p. 242; New York system calculated by multiplying average tonnage by 1856–1859 average haul, 145 miles; Morris Canal calculated by using 1845 tonnage only; Chesapeake and Ohio calculated by applying 1851 tolls per ton-mile to 1837–1846 tolls; Susquehanna calculated by averaging receipts from 1840 to 1946 and applying a 7 mill ton-mile rate; Ohio system based upon receipts and a 6 mill ton-mile rate; Wabash and Erie, 1846 receipts and an 8 mill charge; Pennsylvania Lateral Canals, receipts and an 8 mill toll.

1859: Albert Fishlow, *American Railroads and the Transformation of the Ante-Bellum Economy* (Cambridge, Mass.: Harvard University Press, 1965), p. 21.

1880: U.S. Bureau of the Census, *Census of Population: 1880*, vol. 4, *Transportation* (Washington: U.S. Government Printing Office, 1883); *Annual Report of the Auditor of the Canal Department for the Year 1881*, New York State Assembly Document no. 38, vol. 3 (1882), p. 41.

almost 2000 miles still in operation, but at utilization rates well below their 1870–1880 peaks.

The singular and extraordinary success enjoyed by the Erie Canal, the principal component of the New York state system, also stands out in Table 13.3. It alone among the canals operating in 1880 substantially exceeded its pre-Civil War performance, despite the parallel line of the New York Central and the competition of the Erie Railroad. The performance was not effortless, however. Progressively lower tolls made revenues fall off quite rapidly after 1870, until the legislature abolished tolls altogether in 1882. Such sacrifice only delayed the inevitable. Continuing advances in railroad technology and rate discrimination made possible charges as low as those on the waterway. The course of the decline may be seen in the means of arrival of western grains at tidewater shown in Table 13.4.[15]

This is the most favorable comparison possible, focusing upon the trade in which the canal system remained most competitive. Of total ton-miles transported in New York State, the canal share shrank from 86 percent in

[15] U.S., Congress, Senate, *Preliminary Report of the Inland Waterways Commission*, Senate Document no. 325, 60th Congress, 1st Session (1908), p. 235.

TABLE 13.4
Shipment of western grains (thousands of bushels)

Year	Canal	Total	Percent Canal
1868	44,012	45,788	96.1
1880	69,346	143,856	48.2
1890	30,185	94,970	31.8
1898	19,407	161,115	12.0

1853 to 5 percent in 1898.[16] Nonetheless, that early period of superiority was sufficient to establish the Erie's financial profitability. During the period of toll collection before 1822, the surplus earned after operating expenses was $92.2 million. This figure implies a rate of return on cost in excess of 10 percent, without assigning a value to the canal's facilities at that date. This unique record of private profitability, however, was not sufficient to offset the $4.2 million loss of the branch canals on an investment of equal magnitude. Thus, even the New York State system as a whole did not satisfy an accounting criterion of success: earnings sufficient to amortize the canal debt and to pay the accumulated interest.

The Erie Canal both ushered in the age of canal construction and also terminated the era of canal utilization. In the intervening half-century an irrevocable change in transport rates had occurred. Ton-mile charges, even on the best turnpikes, remained over 10 cents, and closer to 20, prior to the canal. The canal introduced rates on the order of 2.3 cents per mile, including tolls. By the 1850s the average costs for bulk commodities verged upon 1 cent per ton-mile, and even less in the case of the anthracite canals.[17]

Increased cargo capacity was the prime factor in increased canal efficiency; between 1835 and 1859, tonnage per vessel more than quadrupled from 38 to 143.[18] Thereafter technical gains were more modest. The principal contributor to reduced transport costs came to be reductions in tolls as canals struggled unsuccessfully to maintain their share of the transport market. Charges on Erie Canal tonnage in the early 1880s were less than .5 cent, but the gain was modest relative to the 7 mills already attained in the late 1850s. Attempts to introduce steam power on canals to lower costs of carriage further were unsuccessful.

Unlike the turnpike, the canal left an indelible mark on nineteenth-century transportation rates. The water technology was incomparably superior to the horse-and-wagon alternative even given well-surfaced roads. Its principal deficiency was geographic inflexibility: Not all areas were equally well suited to canal construction. One important nineteenth-century innovation utilizing steam power, the steamboat, compensated by making transportation

[16] *Ibid.,* pp. 228–229.
[17] Taylor, *op. cit.,* pp. 133–138.
[18] U.S. Auditor for the Treasury Department, *Report for 1881* (Washington: U.S. Government Printing Office, *1881*), p. 38.

on the naturally abundant navigable rivers and streams much more efficient. To that subject we now turn.

The Exploitation of the River and Lake System, 1815–1900

Canal construction, for all its advantages, was of limited extension. The system of naturally navigable waters—rivers, lakes, and the coastal perimeter—possessed by the United States was many times larger. Rivers alone totaled more than six times the 4000 accumulated miles of canals that the canal era had seen through to completion. Nor did exploitation of the water routes await the nineteenth century. From the beginning all manner of vessels were employed for commerce—sailing ships, flatboats, barges, keelboats. Economic activity was concentrated along bodies of water wherever possible to maximize access.

Antebellum diffusion.   Development of the steamboat in the early nineteenth century extended the importance of water commerce, particularly upon the western rivers.[19] Not until considerably later would steam navigation become the preferred form for all water transport, both internal and international. The interest in the West, however, was immediate. Little time elapsed between Fulton's successful demonstration on the Hudson in 1807 and the first trip of the *New Orleans* from Pittsburgh to its namesake (1811). The feasibility of downstream navigation thus proved, four more years elapsed until the *Enterprise* negotiated the more difficult return trip against the current. It was the unique capacity of the steamboat to master the upstream voyage that led to its rapid acceptance. In fact, however, downriver commerce always dominated, and by the time the West had developed to the point that return imports might have been significant, there were direct links to the East.

The early growth of steamboat tonnage on western rivers is documented in Table 13.5. Until 1840, western steamboats represented half the national

TABLE 13.5
National and western steamboat tonnage, 1820–1860

Year	United States	Western
1820	—	13,890
1830	62,409	29,481
1840	182,925	83,592
1845	261,034	98,246
1850	371,819	141,834
1855	559,508	173,068
1860	640,906	162,735

SOURCE: Adapted from Louis C. Hunter, *Steamboats on the Western Rivers* (Cambridge, Mass.: Harvard University Press, 1949), p. 33. The national tonnage has been adjusted by the difference between Hunter's series of tonnage on western rivers and the official one.

[19] This section has depended heavily upon Louis C. Hunter, *Steamboats on the Western Rivers* (Cambridge, Mass.: Harvard University Press, 1949).

tonnage; after that date, the geographic domain of steam expanded. The steamboat's position on western rivers, moreover, was dominant. Keelboats and barges outfitted for upstream travel were the first to be dislodged by the competition of the steamboat, although the keelboat lingered longer, particularly on the upper Ohio. Flatboats, on the other hand, showed a much greater vigor. They were used only for downstream transportation, and given the opportunity to sell the lumber from which they were made in New Orleans, the crew could return inexpensively and reasonably rapidly by steamboat. Thus the two transport forms were partially complementary. Not until 1846–1847 did flatboat arrivals at New Orleans reach their peak, a level five times their pre-steamboat rate. Yet relatively, they had long before begun to recede in importance. As early as 1830, the volume of freight carried by steamboats probably exceeded that by all other craft. Not until after the Civil War would the flatboat emerge reincarnated as a complement to steam power in the towing system.

The western steamboat not only made upstream commerce feasible, but also, as it evolved technologically, meant substantially lower rates and greater speed as well. The earliest trips from New Orleans to Louisville by steamboat required 30 to 35 days; by 1833 the duration had been reduced to 7 days and 6 hours, gradually declining thereafter to regular runs of $5\frac{1}{2}$ to 6 days in the 1850s. This meant an average speed of 10 miles an hour; traveling south, the speed was closer to 15. Smaller boats, 200 to 300 tons, went perhaps half as fast. By contrast, keelboats and barges had required 3 to 4 months for the same upriver voyage.

Rates followed a corresponding tendency. The steamboat rate in 1816 was originally 4 to 5 cents per pound for delivery from New Orleans to Louisville. Gerstner in the late 1830s reported an average rate for freight of all kinds of .625 cents. Adjusting for the difference in price levels, the reduction is still more than fourfold. By the 1840s and 1850s, in part due to the imbalance caused by significantly larger downstream shipments, the upriver rate converged with the lower downriver charge. This meant a further reduction to perhaps half the previous amount by 1860. Per ton-mile, railroad distance, rates in the 1840s and thereafter for a variety of shorter routes averaged about 4 cents; for the longer hauls they were much less than 1 cent. On the eve of the Civil War, in short, the steamboat had cheapened upriver transportation by a factor of ten, and downstream trips by a ratio of between three and four.[20]

One important element in this downward trend was the widespread competition in the industry. This was particularly noticeable in the 1820s as tonnage rapidly mounted. The very nature of the innovation ideally fitted the competitive model. Unlike turnpikes and canals, which constituted a capital-intensive and geographically fixed medium over which private conveyances might travel for a toll, the innovation of the steamboat required little direct investment and yielded early returns. Steamboats cost between

[20] *Ibid.*, pp. 374–377, 658–659; Thomas S. Berry, *Western Prices Before 1861* (Cambridge, Mass.: Harvard University Press, 1943), pp. 42–70, 557–561.

$75 and $100 a ton.[21] A medium-sized boat by the standards of the 1850s could be constructed for a total investment of $30,000. Returns were immediate, although they varied considerably due to the hazards of navigation. Insurance was only partial in its coverage. To those with enough good fortune and good management to keep their ships afloat longer than the four-year average, the gains were especially generous. It is difficult to generalize about the average rate of return because of the dispersed and individual character of the enterprises, and also because complaints about lack of profit were rife, biasing the limited reports available. The competitive character of the industry, along with a possible tendency among owner–captains to overestimate their own capacity for good fortune should have made for a relatively modest return. Because of the small units of investment, that private return probably approximated the social gains more satisfactorily than those of other indivisible, capital-intensive innovations. The market could and did work without public intervention.

The usual form of ownership was the partnership: About half of the pre-1860 tonnage was owned by groups of two to four, with another 20–25 percent being held by individuals.[22] Divided ownership with representation in different river cities was common. This arrangement assured direct access to the supply of capital in those larger commercial centers which had a direct interest in improved transportation. It thereby eased the possibility of entry. Such widespread ownership also assured that boats would compete directly for the same traffic.

Competition and the rapid rate of depreciation assured the rapid diffusion of technological advance. Such technical progress was the ultimate determinant of the trend in charges. Improvement expressed itself in two complementary forms—evolution of the structure of the boat and refinement of the power source. Length and breadth increased as depth was reduced to enhance maneuverability under the low-water conditions of western rivers. The high-pressure engine was favored for its lesser bulk, and its continued expansion in power led to a ratio of horsepower to tonnage that went from 1:3 to the opposite 3:1. Both developments together made for larger boats and a more than proportional increase in capacity. Cargo capacity which had stood in a 1:1 ratio to measured tonnage (actually a cubic foot measurement) had by the 1850s exceeded it by 50 to 75 percent. The additional speed, moreover, meant the possibility of more intensive utilization of the boat and decreased capital costs per individual trip.

Despite the low rates that were thereby made possible, particularly in the Ohio–Mississippi system, the steamboat fell victim to railroad competition, as had the canal, and for the same reasons of directness, convenience, and speed. Insurance costs, too, represented a financial burden that could add as much as a third to steamboat charges that were superficially lower. Relevant as well was the uncertainty of the river depth; in the crucial decade

[21] Hunter, *op. cit.*, pp. 110–111.
[22] *Ibid.* p. 311.

of the 1850s, during the height of the railroad struggle, the Ohio remained consistently low until quite late in the year. As soon as the Pennsylvania and Baltimore and Ohio Railroads directly linked the eastern ports to the Ohio Valley, steamboat arrivals went into decline at Pittsburgh and Cincinnati; in the former, the 3000 entries in 1848 dwindled to less than 600 in 1858. Total tonnage on western rivers was smaller in 1860 than in 1855. On the southern reaches of the Mississippi, due to a slower pace of railroad construction in the South and to the greater ease of river shipment, the steamboat maintained its dominion and thereby offset the rapidly declining arrivals at New Orleans from the West. Increasingly, cotton replaced western foodstuffs in the commerce of the Crescent City.

Post-Civil War decline. After the Civil War, the pattern of decline continued and extended to the South. Steam tonnage on western rivers recorded an unbroken decline, as shown in Table 13.6. The statistics of the major river ports are equally dolorous. St. Louis in 1891–1895 received and shipped by water only 62 percent of the 1871–1875 level; in the first decade of the twentieth century there was a further reduction. By 1890 St. Louis trade by rail amounted to eight times its river commerce.[23] As in the 1850s, the lower river traffic was more resistant to diversion, but no longer fully so. Arrivals in New Orleans were 29 percent fewer in 1880 than in 1860. However, almost two thirds of the cotton continued to come by river. By 1890, the proportion was 20 percent, and the steamboat had become a minor factor even in New Orleans commerce.[24] This occurred despite efforts to stem the tide. Barge towing substituted for individual steamboats, each with its own cargo. Although this practice had been tried in the coal trade from Pittsburgh in 1860, it was applied much more widely thereafter. The same principle was adapted to the grain and lumber trade from the northern Mississippi southward. The innovation reduced capital costs by a factor of as much as four.[25] In 1889 more than two thirds of all shipments were handled

TABLE 13.6
National and western steamboat tonnage, 1868–1889 (yearly average)

Period	United States	Western Rivers
1868–1869	1,012,056	332,279
1870–1874	931,402	265,269
1875–1879	983,665	231,584
1880–1884	1,169,999	246,184
1884–1889	1,392,347	217,014

SOURCE: Adapted from Hunter, *op. cit.*, p. 565. These measurements are in the new-measure tonnage for western rivers established in 1865; for comparison with the tonnage on western rivers given in Table 13.5, it is necessary to reduce them by about 45 percent.

[23] Frank H. Dixon, *Traffic History of the Mississippi River System* (Washington: U.S. Government Printing Office, 1909), p. 53.
[24] *Ibid.*, p. 59.
[25] Hunter, *op. cit.*, pp. 567–575.

in this way, although general merchandise and upriver freight continued to be transported in the more conventional fashion. Accordingly, a large part of the post-Civil War steam tonnage on the western rivers consisted of tow-boats. In 1880 the ratio was 1:4; in 1890, 1:3.[26] Still, such methods did not alter the increasing superiority of the railroad, because their success depended on very large scale. The entire Mississippi system transported less than 4 billion ton-miles in 1890, or no more than the Pennsylvania Railroad alone.

The western steamboat represented the most dramatic, but not exclusive, application of steam power. Eventually steam power on the lakes and in the coastal trade—not to mention in international commerce—came to supersede its importance in the West. By the post-Civil War period the western steam tonnage represented only 15 percent of the national total. On the other hand, sailing vessels persisted much longer in these other trades. Steam did not power a majority of shipping in the lake trade until 1884; in the coastal trade, until the later 1890s; and in international trade, until the twentieth century. The gradual rise of the participation of the steamboat in its diverse uses is indicated in Table 13.7.

Sailing vessels dominated until much later in nonriver use for a variety of reasons. Long-distance routes afforded a problem of fuel storage, adding to the space already taken up by bulky machinery; on the river this was no problem, since wood and later cheap coal were readily available at any number of places. Moreover, the costs of construction of sailing vessels were quite low due to the abundance of wood, and this fact gave an edge to sailing vessels in initial capital requirements. Technical advances such as the iron hull for greater buoyancy, the screw propeller which provided more efficient drive than the paddle wheel, and progress in the construction of the engine and boilers themselves later combined to make the steamship more economical. Almost from the earliest, propellers were applied to lake steamboats: half the 1860 fleet was so equipped. Nevertheless, the United States, which boasted an initial lead in the application of steam propulsion on the western rivers, lagged badly in its generalization to the ocean-going merchant marine. The success of the clipper ship, the satisfactory performance of wooden sailing vessels in general, and the lesser role of foreign trade made for this curious lapse of innovative energies.

Investment in domestic shipping.   The expenditure generated by steamboat construction may be crudely calculated by applying a price of $100 a ton to construction prior to 1860; for the year 1880 and thereafter, we have direct census data. Until the Civil War, the gross cumulative outlay may thus be estimated at $150 million, an amount quite closely comparable to the total cost of canals over the same period. Much of this sum, however, went toward replacement rather than adding to the effective capital stock. As a consequence, the value of the accumulated 1860 capital was much smaller than that of canals and was worth probably no more than $33 million.

---

[26] *Ibid.*, p. 638.

TABLE 13.7
Tonnage, by trade and by type, 1851, 1870, and 1890 (thousands of tons)

	1851	1870	1890
Foreign[a]			
Total	1726	1517	947
Steam	62	193	197
Coastal			
Total	1548	1647	2120
Steam	150	478	804
Barges and canal boats	—	397	285
Northern lakes			
Total	216	685	1063
Steam	77	143	653
Barges and canal boats	—	277	81
Western rivers			
Total	136	398	294
Steam	136	262	205
Barges and canal boats	—	133	89

[a] Includes whale fisheries.

SOURCES

1851: U.S. Senate, Executive Document no. 42, 32nd Congress, 1st Session, 1853.
Foreign
    Total and Steam: from Commerce and Navigation Reports.
Coastal
    Total equal to total tonnage employed in internal trade (from Commerce and Navigation Reports) minus lake and river totals.
    Steam: total equal to Senate Executive Document no. 42 total for coastal minus registered steam tonnage as given in Commerce and Navigation Reports.
Northern lakes
    Total and Steam tonnage: taken from Israel Andrews, *Report on Trade and Commerce*, Senate Executive Document no. 112, 32nd Congress, 1st Session, 1853.
Western rivers: Steam tonnage assumed to be total.
1870 and 1890: Commerce and Navigation Reports.

Inclusion of all vessels engaged in domestic commerce, including sailing ships and canal boats, increases construction outlays by $190 million and the 1860 capital stock by some $65 million.[27] The net 1860 value of $100 million for *all* vessels does not match the canal interest. Post-Civil War comparisons, on both a gross and net basis, concede to steamboats and other craft even less relative importance. In 1880 some 6000 miles of railway were completed at a cost in excess of $210 million; steamboat construction consumed about $10 million in resources. Census valuation in the same year was

[27] The 1860 value of steamboats is calculated as .6 times the investment in the tonnage existing in that year. This recognizes that part of the capital stock had already undergone depreciation. The implicit rate employed is about 10 percent. Such an estimate corresponds closely to the observed .7 ratio between investment and value reported in the 1880 census.

For other vessels engaged in domestic commerce an average cost per gross ton of $50 was employed [cf. John G. B. Hutchins, *The American Maritime Industries and Public Policy, 1789–1914* (Cambridge, Mass.: Harvard University Press, 1941), pp. 280–281]. The number of vessels destined for the domestic trade was estimated at one third the total number constructed from 1800–1815, and one half thereafter. A ratio of .7 was applied to the cumulated investment in nonsteam tonnage engaged in domestic commerce to obtain the 1860 value.

For construction series of both sailboats and steamboats and tonnage engaged in domestic commerce, see U.S. Bureau of the Census, *Historical Statistics of the United States, Colonial Times to 1957*, Series Q-180, 181, and 166 (Washington: U.S. Government Printing Office, 1960).

$80.2 million for steamboats; $5.2 billion for railways.[28] If we were to consider all ships, including vessels engaged in foreign trade, the annual flow and stock valuation would have to be adjusted by a factor of less than two.

Yet if the cost was small, this fact makes the services of internal water commerce that much more impressive.. Only canal ton-mileage statistics are available before 1889. At that late date, a total of 35.9 billion ton-miles was transported by water—excluding canals—or nearly half the comparable railroad total.[29] Specialization on long hauls of coal and iron ore, where water enjoyed a competitive advantage, accounts for this good showing. Earlier estimates are quite precarious because of data limitations. Extrapolation back on the tonnage engaged in coastwise and internal trade would suggest an 1860 total of 20 million ton-miles. The information in the 1853 Andrews Report justifies assuming such a high level of activity. Thus, extraordinarily enough, even though railroad diversion had steadily eaten into the canal and Mississippi River system traffic during the 1850s, the *total* volume of waterborne domestic commerce continued to exceed railroad ton-mileage by a factor perhaps as high as eight or ten. The important, and largely ignored, role of the coastwise fleet is central to this result. Not until the unparalleled railway extension of the 1870s and 1880s would the natural and inexpensive routes of ocean and internal waterways yield their position.

The Ascendancy of the Railroad, 1830–1860[30]

The canal and steamboat marked important steps in the solution of the American transport problem. Between them, they afforded access to market for large parts of the interior. Yet neither was to prevail as the nineteenth century unfolded. The torch, instead, passed to the railroad, the first rapid and efficient overland transport innovation. The basic principles underlying the railway were simple enough: a smooth surface, consisting of rails, to reduce as far as possible the friction of wheels passing over it, and efficient application of steam, by means of the locomotive, to expand carrying capacity. The first serious experiments in England in the 1820s rapidly proved the merits of the technology, and the United States thereafter became its leading practitioner.

Early ventures. The proximate impetus, as in the rise of canal construction, was the Erie Canal. Baltimore, dissatisfied with the projected Chesapeake and Ohio Canal because its terminus would favor Alexandria, determined instead to construct a railroad of over 200 miles. The decision, even from this vantage point, was one of heroic folly. How else can one label an enterprise of that magnitude undertaken before steam locomotion had fully proven itself and when the few existing railroads in the world were modest ventures to exploit the coal trade? Impelled by the same urgency as Philadelphia,

[28] U.S. Bureau of the Census, *Census of Population: 1880*, vol. 4, *Transportation* (Washington: U.S. Government Printing Office, 1883), pp. 5, 702.
[29] Harold Barger, *The Transportation Industries, 1889–1946* (New York: National Bureau of Economic Research, 1951), p. 254.
[30] For a more complete treatment of this period, see Albert Fishlow, *American Railroads and the Transformation of the Ante-Bellum Economy* (Cambridge, Mass.: Harvard University Press, 1965).

Baltimore in the end wound up little better. The railroad was completed to Wheeling, its Ohio River terminus, only in 1853, well after the issue of western trade had been decided. The projected cost of $5 million became a realized investment in excess of $20 million.

Once under way, the Baltimore and Ohio served as a powerful incentive to imitators, and for very good reason: Few locations were so well favored that water transport could fully satisfy their needs, or better, their aspirations. The railroad also held out the prospect of more rapid and convenient passage, a not irrelevant consideration in the already densely populated coastal region. When its technical properties were proven, future financial problems could no longer diminish enthusiasm. Charleston business leaders, dissatisfied with their attempted canal solution to the problem of Savannah's competition, read and responded to reports issuing from Baltimore. In 1833 they completed what was then the longest railway in the world, 136 miles to Hamburg in the interior. Pennsylvania adopted the technology for parts of its route to Pittsburgh where canals were not feasible. Boston interests watched developments in Baltimore carefully before initiating their modest challenge to New York. More in the original English tradition, feeder roads, often relying upon horsepower and limited in mileage, were built to canals in the coal regions. Commercial men in various population centers along the fall line saw an opportunity to capitalize upon the demands of a traveling public, from which emerged such projects as the Boston and Providence, the Camden and Amboy in New Jersey, and the Richmond and Petersburg, among others.

Railroad mileage increased rapidly in the 1830s, fed on the one hand by buoyant economic conditions and a relative abundance of capital, and on the other by glowing expectations. The expansion was a learning process. English methods were rapidly discarded. Iron rails were replaced by wood with iron bars; tunnels were avoided; great tolerance was exhibited for curvatures and gradients found in the terrain. In general, costs of construction were compressed as far as possible. More than substitution economies emerged, as American ingenuity was applied to the adaptation of both locomotive and rail design. American locomotives designed with a flexible truck to adapt to curves rapidly replaced imports. Experimentation with rails to support maximum weight with minimum iron input led to a prototype of the soon to be universal "T"-rail.

By the end of 1839, more than 3000 miles of railway were in operation. A potential system of sorts was emerging. One axis lay East–West, the intent of the original Baltimore and Ohio. The Western Railroad in Massachusetts, the ill-fated Erie Railroad of New York, the individual ventures later to be consolidated in the New York Central, and the two Pennsylvania lines auxiliary to the canal completed this interregional category. A second axis was North–South, comprehending the roads paralling the coast and oriented to the passenger traffic. In terms of completed mileage, these constituted the largest part of the emerging rail network. A third group of enterprises was in the western interior and was constructed under state auspices to feed into the great natural water courses serving the region. A final miscellaneous category includes the many coal roads in Pennsylvania and what Chevalier termed "the railroads which, starting from the great cities as centers, radiate from them in all directions."[31]

The depression lasting from the end of 1839 until 1843 played havoc with two important elements of this design. The east–west roads were forced to halt far short of their goal, with the exception of the Western, which struggled through with state aid, and the earlier completed and predominantly canal Pennsylvania Mainline. The interior western roads were affected more adversely. States, unable to borrow abroad after 1839, could not maintain construction out of their limited revenues. Abandonment of roads was not infrequent, resulting in additions to public debt without corresponding assets. The same dependence upon public assistance marked many southern ventures and with similar consequences. In general, the less ambitious the undertaking, and the greater its private finance, the better it emerged after 1839.

This setback did not diminish enthusiasm for the innovation or alter conviction in its substantial benefits. It merely emphasized the problem of finance. For this reason, the locus of construction was in New England and the East in the 1840s, while the South and West gradually recovered. Capital was more readily available in the settled regions and was independent of the foreign investment that had permitted public ventures to multiply in the interior. Appeals for funds were couched in terms of indirect gains as well as pecuniary rewards. Investment was concentrated in local railroads in the form of equity, partially in the hope of securing advantages to one community or another. This aim was most obvious in the 600 miles of railroad making up an alternative Boston route to the Great Lakes, which promised a more successful New England showing in the western trade.

At the end of the decade, despite the sluggish start, total railroad mileage had doubled to more than 7500. Massachusetts, Connecticut, and New Hampshire possessed roughly half the mileage they would have a century later. In the 1840s, the East–West lines also began to emerge from their dormancy. The Baltimore and Ohio pushed on; the Pennsylvania Railroad was initiated to give that state an all-rail connection to the West; the group of independent New York railroads in the Mohawk Valley was completed from Buffalo to Albany—although these were useful primarily for passenger traffic; and the Erie Railroad reorganized in 1845 and completed over 200 miles toward the lake thereafter.

Extension to the West and South.   The full-blown emergence of the railroad awaited the 1850s. In ten years the network more than quadrupled to 30,000 miles, making it possible to speak meaningfully of rail shipment and travel throughout the nation. It was possible to travel from New York to Dubuque, Iowa entirely by train. Hogs could be shipped from the Illinois prairie to slaughterhouses in Boston; manufactures could be delivered from Philadelphia to Holly Springs, Mississippi. Serious problems of articulation

[31] Michel Chevalier, *Society, Manners, and Politics in the United States* (Garden City, N.Y.: Doubleday, 1961), p. 260.

remained, however. There were few bridges over major rivers; a variety of gauges impeded continuous shipment; schedules were chaotic in the absence of time zones. Still, the tendency toward integration was clear.

The West and East had been joined overland, not once, but at least four times. The principal trunk lines—the New York Central, the Erie, the Pennsylvania, and the Baltimore and Ohio—each extended from tidewater to western termini by 1853. Festivities were widespread celebrating the joining of the areas, not to mention the realization of profits on a through traffic for the first time.

The western interior was the principal arena of new construction. Feeders not only linked the waterways of the regions but, more important, directly connected with the trunk lines as they were completed. Chicago emerged as a rail center second to none, the node for ten different railroad lines which, with branches and extensions, totaled more than 4000 miles. Ohio possessed on the eve of the Civil War almost 3000 miles of railroad, closely followed by Illinois with more than 2700, and Indiana with over 2000. The Mississippi had been bridged, and the railhead verged on the Missouri; Wisconsin and Iowa, admitted as states a few years earlier, together could claim 1500 miles of track. In all, 10,000 miles were constructed in the West during the 1850s, more than the national total at the beginning of the decade.

This accomplishment was not the product of a unique American willingness to build ahead of demand, as Schumpeter and others have argued. It was rooted in the more prosaic, but frequently more effective, profit motive. The large majority of these western railroads in fact earned net revenues from the beginning; they were built through areas of previous and abundant settlement and successfully attracted private funds. These points merit brief elaboration because they run counter to earlier views.

The relationship with settlement shows up strikingly in the regular progression of construction over time from more to less densely settled areas. Ohio, the most settled area, by 1852 already possessed one third of the mileage it was to acquire by the end of the decade; at the opposite extreme, Wisconsin and Iowa at that time had practically none. The same searching out of favorable opportunities exhibits itself at the regional level. Of the total number of miles of railroad built in Illinois by the end of 1853, over 60 percent can be found in the eleven leading wheat counties and the eight largest corn counties, both as measured by the census of 1850. The disproportion of railroad density—these counties represented only 25 percent of the land area—is clearly due to the existing level of settlement and economic activity. Wisconsin illustrates the point even more dramatically. There 10 percent of area accounted for over half the mileage at the end of 1860 and three fourths at the end of 1856.

These early railroads, directed to immediate sources of demand, were rewarded by high profits. For the West as a whole, net earnings in 1855–1856 reached 7.2 percent of the cost of construction, exceeding the corresponding returns in New England and the Middle Atlantic states. Receipts per mile were smaller, but so were costs. The western railroads adapted their construction practices to the initially lower absolute demands in the region.

Such aggregate results do not accurately convey the varied fortunes of individual roads. Many railroads in older parts of the region, in Ohio and Indiana, did poorly over time because of excess competition. Railroad rivalry, induced by high fixed costs, produced an excess of feeder roads; commercial rivalry, responding to the high costs of inadequate transport facilities, abetted such a tendency by guaranteeing local subsidies. The consequence of overbuilding was lower profits in 1855–1856 in the established railroad states than in the newer ones.

The receptivity to western railroad securities in eastern money markets affords another clue to the worthiness of the early projects. Bonds were negotiated with relative ease until the tightness commencing in late 1854, as the market shared the view that "western roads are to be our best paying lines, and the great success that has followed the opening of the few roads in that section has done much to confirm this opinion."[32]

Access to capital markets was crucial due to the predominantly private character of the investment.[33] The unhappy experiment of the 1830s left a legacy in the West of constitutional prohibitions against state aid to internal improvements. Federal aid was sought and ultimately obtained in the form of land grants, but it came too late to influence the course of events prior to the Civil War. Local funds were sought, and successfully, but not in amounts sufficient to alter the dominant role of private profit motivation. Indiana communities contributed no more than 4 percent of total construction costs. In Illinois the ratio was not much greater. Significantly, Chicago gave nothing; it was the lesser towns that paid their tribute, hoping for a place in the sun that they only infrequently gained. Even in states farther west such as Wisconsin and Iowa, where the undertakings might seem more risky, local support probably did not much exceed 10 percent of the investment. In fact, as much was expended by Ohio communities as by those in Indiana, Illinois, and Wisconsin together. Their contributions were defensive, designed to assure that they would not be bypassed by the new era. The benefits realized were always less than anticipated because all areas acted similarly; but the potential costs of a refusal to contribute made the behavior explicable, if not globally efficient. To be sure, local assistance could on occasion be catalytic and even crucial to obtaining other subscriptions. But it is well to contrast the passive character of this municipal assistance—sought *after* the railroad was decided upon by the initiative of others—and the state aid of the 1830s, which was clearly directive and in advance of demand.

Not only in the West, but also in the South, the sharp decline in activity in the 1840s was compensated by a robust rebound in the 1850s. The reaction was longer in coming and less a private response to potential profits than was true in the West. The natural river access enjoyed by the South had facilitated a cotton-based commercial agriculture well before western expansion, and

---

[32] *American Railroad Journal*, vol. 25 (February 21, 1852), p. 121.
[33] Carter Goodrich, *Government Promotion of American Canals and Railroads, 1880–1890* (New York: Columbia University Press, 1960), presents the fullest accounting of governmental assistance and stresses its importance more than is done here.

rivers remained as a powerful competitor to railroad interests. The traumatic experience of the late 1830s was possibly even more influential in reducing enthusiasm for railroad investment. By the late 1850s, however, the debacle of earlier public assistance had diminished as a deterrent, and aid was once more forthcoming. The success of the railroads apparent elsewhere was an important incentive. States financed the competition of their ports for the commerce of the interior: The same motivation had spurred the beginning of the railroad era 30 years previously. New Orleans, Mobile, Memphis, Savannah, Charleston, Norfolk, and Wilmington, North Carolina, were the major participants. Louisville also was actively involved in seeking to divert the trade of the Ohio Valley southward. While aid was liberally given at both state and local levels, private investment was also encouraged by the favorable operating experiences of the southern roads completed earlier: Dividends commonly were being paid in 1855 in the seaboard states. Once under way, the commercial contest led to rapidly accelerating construction, with much mileage being brought to fruition only on the eve of the war. While western investment perceptibly peaked in 1854, investment in the South and Southwest halted only slightly in response to economic conditions and continued upward until 1859.

The magnitude of the investment. Table 13.8 recapitulates the cycles of antebellum investment. The concentration of expenditure in the East in the 1840s and the subsequent boom in the West and South are patent. So too is the extraordinary magnitude of investment. Already by the early 1850s, more resources had been devoted to the railroad than to canal, steamboat, and turnpike construction together before the war. And as we shall later see, this margin accelerated for the remainder of the century.

To the more than $1 billion capital stock at the end of 1860, public treasures had contributed about 25 percent. The role of public subsidy was largest in the South, where it amounted to more than 50 percent over the period, and convincingly contradicted the image of uninvolved laissez faire. The greatest influence of public aid came during the first upward surge, when it exceeded one third of the total investment. It was at its smallest in the 1840s, when

TABLE 13.8
Antebellum railway investment (millions of dollars)

Period	New England	Middle Atlantic[a]	West[b]	South	Total
1828–1843	29.7	64.9	9.7	33.0	137.1[c]
1844–1850	79.5	52.8	20.2	19.7	172.3[c]
1851–1860	40.5	126.4	370.3	199.4	737.3[d]

[a] Includes Maryland and Delaware.
[b] Includes Missouri.
[c] May not add due to rounding.
[d] Includes $.7 million investment in California.

SOURCE: Adapted from Fishlow, *op. cit.*, p. 53.

privately financed construction in New England dominated. In absolute terms, aid reached its largest level in the 1850s as publicly financed southern involvement rapidly increased. Exact proportions are difficult to calculate due to uncertain factual bases and conceptual problems. State guarantees of bonds, for example, are included in some calculations, although they represent no transfer of resources. Nor for that matter do state loans that are repaid, except to the extent of an interest rate differential favoring the sale of state securities over private instruments. For the purpose of determining the share of immediate financial contribution, however, loans are a present transfer even if they are subsequently amortized. It is this broader concept that is applied here.

Public assistance to railroads differed from aid to canals in its form and its relative importance. Canal construction was underwritten to the extent of nearly three fourths its total antebellum cost. Almost universally, the political unit from which assistance flowed was the state; and equally commonly, the form it took was direct ownership and operation. Railroads received a relatively smaller financial incentive and were operated as private corporations even when they received a capital subsidy. This difference derives in part from the technological characteristics of the innovations—state control was much easier when tolls alone were involved—and in part from their historical sequence. Railroads came later, when private sources of capital were more abundant. Moreover, the ability of railroads to draw upon private savings was enhanced because they were constructed in response to present demands.

Railroad traffic and productivity. Table 13.9 measures the results in transportation services of the $1 billion prewar investment. Of interest is the substantial initial dependence of railroads upon personal travel for their revenues. Not until 1849 do freight receipts exceed the income from passengers. Although canal freight service at that time continued to exceed railroad ton-mileage, the newer innovation had already monopolized the movement of persons. By the end of the following decade, the railroad succeeded in edging out the canals in freight, although total water commerce in all its forms bulked much larger, as we have seen. Rapid railroad growth presaged ultimate victory in that contest as well, and not too far in the future.

TABLE 13.9
Railroad output (millions of miles and dollars)

Year	Passenger Receipts (1)	Passenger Miles (2)	Freight Receipts (3)	Ton-Miles (4)
1839	4.5	90.1	2.5	32.8
1849	13.6	468.1	14.1	347.0
1859	45.8	1879.6	66.5	2577.7

SOURCE: Data from Fishlow, *op. cit.,* app. A.

Acceptance of the new technology cut short the profits on canals and led to the abandonment of many ; it also generated quite respectable net revenues for the railroad owners. Table 13.10 presents net earnings corrected for depreciation as a proportion of the capital stock for various benchmark years. These data, indicating rising profitability through the mid-1850s, help explain the continuing interest in railroad investment. Such ratios are not the equivalent of rates of return, which take into account the future stream of earnings over the lifetime of the enterprise. The latter are more impressive, since much of the capital was newly placed in 1855–1856 and 1859, and thus was not yet fully utilized and held prospects of a rapidly growing revenue flow. For example, a conservative annual net receipts growth of only 2 percent for 30 years from 1859 implies an average *private* return of some 6 percent. This is not a bonanza gain by any means, but it stands out in a sector in which private investors had previously been singularly unfortunate. That such a return was capable of evoking the private investment it did testifies to the appeal of indirect benefit in attracting local finance, and to the optimistic expectations which magnified the real possibilities.

Railroads earned profits because they overtook the canals in the volume of traffic carried. They successfully competed because they reduced the initial rate differential in favor of canals to such a degree that it was relevant only in the immediate vicinity of waterways. During the 1830s railroad rates per ton-mile were about $7\frac{1}{2}$ cents ; passenger fares were only 5 cents per mile. By 1859 the absolute level had been drastically reduced. Passenger rates stood at 2.44 cents, and ton-mile charges at 2.58 cents. Even at the earlier tariffs, and with the relative—although by no means absolute—comfort of railroad travel, the railroad easily gained a virtual monopoly in the movement of persons. For freight, canal charges continued to be significantly lower, but as the total differential narrowed on competing routes from 3 cents in 1849 to much less than 2 cents in 1859, the qualitative advantages of the railroad made the difference. Greater speed, all-season utilization, less transshipment, and concentrated responsibility succeeded in capturing the trade not only in highly

TABLE 13.10
Adjusted net earnings relative to net capital stock (percentages)[a]

Year	Including Expenditures on Failed Enterprises (1)	Excluding Expenditures on Failed Enterprises (2)
1839	3.0	3.7
1849	4.5	4.8
1855–1856	5.9	6.0
1859	4.7	4.7

[a] Adjusted net earning are net receipts minus depreciation not charged to current account : the latter is calculated as the difference between total capital consumption and replacement of equipment, ties, and rails. Expenditures in failed enterprises are deducted in making the calculations in Column (2).

SOURCE : Data from Fishlow, *op. cit.*, apps. A and B.

valued merchandise, but also in the less bulky agricultural commodities : Flour and livestock, in particular, began increasingly to utilize the railroad, leaving the transport of grains and coal as the greatest source of the canals' demand.

Such a reduction in railroad rates was made possible by increased factor productivity, as Table 13.11 indicates. Between 1839 and 1859, productivity slightly more than doubled; that is, input requirements were halved. An appropriately weighted rate index correspondingly declined by 42 percent. The contributing factors to the productivity growth undoubtedly include some technological advance even in that experimental period. The average tractive force of locomotives considerably more than doubled between 1839 and 1859 ; eight-wheel freight cars began to be introduced and were by far the most common type in 1859, except in the carriage of coal where they were introduced more slowly; rails had been improved from simple bars of iron on wooden stringers to edge rails of 50 to 60 pounds per yard. Yet during these first decades, what is most impressive is the effect of increasing utilization of the stock of capital. The capital/output ratio declined quite markedly after 1839 as traffic increased and the indivisible capital stock could be more fully employed. Such increased utilization, taking 1859 as a base, explains more than half of the rise in productivity observed before 1860. The constancy of the productivity index between 1849 and 1859 results from the absence of further reductions in the capital/output ratio. The rapid extension of the railway system during the 1850s caused capital accumulation to match the growth of output. In this sense of incompletely utilized potential capital services, it is quite legitimate to speak of construction being ahead of demand before 1860. In so doing, however, one must note that the imbalance between capital and output was considerably greater in 1839 than in 1859, that the 1859 capital/output ratio was actually somewhat smaller than in 1849, and that in 1859 output was artificially low due to cyclical influences. Taken together, these facts still do not add up to *increasing* excess capacity in the 1850s.

The ascendancy of the railroad before the Civil War marked a virtual end to the diffusion of the other transport innovations of the period. Not until the

TABLE 13.11
Productivity change in the railroad sector, 1839–1859 (1910 = 100)

Year	Output	Labor	Capital	Fuel	Total Input	Total Factor Productivity
1839	.08	.3	.8	.07	.5	16.0
1849	.46	1.1	2.2	.20	1.4	32.8
1859	2.21	5.0	10.1	1.50	6.6	33.5

SOURCE: Adapted from Albert Fishlow, "Productivity and Technological Change in the Railroad Sector, 1840–1910," in *Output, Employment, and Productivity in the United States After 1800*, in Dorothy S.Brady (ed.), Studies in Income and Wealth, vol. 30 (New York: National Bureau of Economic Research, 1966), p. 626. Output is changed from this original version, being now based on 1910 weights and thereby altering the total factor productivity index.

twentieth century, and the era of the automobile, would a new challenge arise. Further advance in the nineteenth century depended upon continued railroad extension and increasingly efficient transport capacity. Let us now examine the post-Civil War experience.

The Reign of the Railroad, 1860–1910

Impressive as were the first three decades of American railroads—the 30,000 mile network existing in 1860 represented half the world total—more epic still were the decades to follow. Whether the measure be quantitative, such as construction activity or output, or qualitative, such as the speculative performances of the great railroad entrepreneurs, the post-Civil War decades make the earlier epoch pale by comparison. By 1890 an *additional* 140,000 miles of railway were in place, and railroad mileage was destined to reach over 250,000 by 1916. The 2.6 billion ton-miles of 1859 escalated to 80 billion by 1890, and trebled again by 1910. And what casual student is unaware of the exploits of Vanderbilt, Cooke, Gould, Morgan, and others who stood out among the rising robber barons?

Late nineteenth-century expansion: the postwar surge. Like the earlier growth, the expansion after 1860 was not a smooth one, temporally or geographically. Table 13.12 portrays the three great waves of later nineteenth-century expansion in the periods 1868–1873, 1879–1883, and 1886–1892. Mileage continued to be constructed after these dates, but in lesser annual increments. The first acceleration occurred in the wake of the virtual cessation of investment during the Civil War. Railroads emerged from that conflict in excellent financial condition, since rapid output increases were absorbed without the necessity of substantial additional investment. For 1867, when Poor's tabulations effectively begin, a ratio of net earnings to capital account of 9 percent is shown.[34] Supply ultimately responded to this rising demand in the first three regions enumerated in Table 13.12. These areas were precisely those which previous construction had exploited and which afterward were even more intensively served. In 1873 the number of miles of railroad per square mile in these regions was .092; in the rest of the country it was .015.[35] In economically more meaningful terms, the Northeast per dollar of income had 60 percent as much mileage as the rest of the country. Such potential demand provided an important and continuing impulse to the ongoing investment in this region.

A second factor was the land grants conceded by Congress, both prior to 1860 and in support of transcontinental extension thereafter. Of the trackage brought to completion in 1868–1873, some 10,000 to 12,000 miles arose from this source. They were located largely in the Pacific region, and in the states of the Western North and South. The single most dramatic event in the course of this federally supported construction was the junction of the Central

---

[34] U.S. Bureau of the Census, *Historical Statistics, op. cit.,* p. 428, based on *Poor's Manual of the Railroads of the United States* (New York: H. V. and H. W. Poor, 1884).
[35] Calculated from *Poor's Manual . . . , op. cit.* (1873).

TABLE 13.12
Railroad mileage constructed, by groups[a]

Area[b]	1868–1873	1879–1883	1886–1892
New England	1,376	358	605
Middle states	3,833	2,873	2,557
Central North	3,847	7,539	6,839
Western North	3,749	9,036	9,396
South Atlantic	1,937	2,881	6,639
Gulf	2,041	2,323	4,409
Western South	5,709	10,343	11,754
Pacific	2,097	4,200	4,619
Total	29,589	39,553	46,818

[a] Differences of total mileage in operation between the specified years.
[b] Key

New England: Me., N.H., Vt., Mass., Conn., R.I.
Middle States: N.Y., N.J., Pa., Md., D.C.
Central North: Ohio, Mich., Ind., Ill., Wis.
Western North: Iowa, Minn., Neb., N.D., S.D., Wyo., Mont.
South Atlantic: Va., W.Va., N.C., S.C., Ga., Fla.
Gulf: Ala., Miss., Tenn., Ky., La.
Western South: Mo., Ark., Tex., Kan., Col., N.Mex., Okla.
Pacific: Wash., Ore., Cal., Nev., Id., Ariz., Utah

SOURCE: Data from *Poor's Manual of the Railroads of the United States* (New York: H. V. and H. W. Poor, 1869–1893).

Pacific and Union Pacific at Ogden in 1869; only later would the allure of that accomplishment be tarnished by reflection upon the large profits accuring to private enterprises undertaking such large and risky ventures.

Noteworthy as the completion of the first transcontinental line was, the total mileage completed in the least settled areas by it and similar projects was limited. Kansas, Nebraska, Minnesota, and Texas ended up with more than twice the mileage of Colorado, Utah, Nevada, Wyoming, and the Dakotas. Even in an era of federally subsidized construction ahead of demand, designed to bind the Pacific states to the East, the attraction of a ready market was not altogether forgotten or uninfluential. Indeed, the Union Pacific yielded a price-adjusted ratio of net returns to construction cost of 6.7 percent by 1871, only two years after completion; for the first decade of operation, the ratio was 11.6.[36] This favorable operating performance resulted from an adjustment process similar to that of the 1850s. The railroads constructed to less populated regions charged proportionately higher rates for their services to compensate for the smaller demand.

What was relevant for the financial solvency of the new enterprises was current net earnings relative to capitalization, not the ratio of real profits to investment. Many fewer projects, whether in the East or the West, passed this test. In fact, average net earnings for all railroads during the 1870s did not exceed 5 percent on capital.[37] Of total railroad mileage, 18 percent was in the hands

[36] Robert W. Fogel, *The Union Pacific Railroad: A Case Study in Premature Enterprise* (Baltimore: Johns Hopkins, 1960), pp. 95, 102.
[37] U.S. Bureau of the Census, *Historical Statistics . . .*, op. cit., p. 428.

of receivers at the beginning of 1877, and probably a still larger proportion of railroad bonds had been in default.[38] The reason for such a poor showing was threefold : (a) the desire for immediate profits during construction and discount below par on securities sold, which led to excessive capitalization ; (b) a declining price level that increased real interest payments on the substantial funded debt previously issued ; and (c) a cylical decline in the 1870s that owed its origins largely to the deceleration in railroad investment. Construction ahead of demand was secondary in the poor financial showing during the decade.

Excessive capitalization was a consequence of paying contractors with securities rather than cash. Stocks and bonds were accepted only at a substantial discount, at prices which were frequently even lower than what was justified by risk. Construction companies charging high prices were frequently formed by the railroad promoters in order to gain an immediate return. With knowledge of this situation, potential bondholders could be cajoled into holding debt only under the most favorable terms. Sales at prices below par were the common mechanism of adjustment, rather than high interest rates. Issuers gained the advantage of postponing some part of the interest burden by this mechanism. Part of the discount on bonds has a place in construction costs, since it reflects the higher interest costs that must be paid during the period of construction. Typically, however, the entire discount was included, thereby greatly exaggerating the cost. Likewise, all shares issued were counted at par. This watered stock, without corresponding assets, became the basis for dividend payments and aroused a continuing controversy over what railroads claimed was an inadequate return and what users claimed were excessive profits. It was estimated in 1884 in *Poor's Manual* that the true investment in railroads did not exceed the sum total of the floating or funded debt, implying an excess capitalization of 50 percent.[39]

As net earnings in current dollars began to increase less rapidly because of the general price decline, annual interest payments, which remained fixed, became an increasing real burden. Market interest rates at the time of construction did not reflect an expected decline in prices. Later roads built at lower nominal cost could compete favorably, since their interest rates were not dissimilar and applied to a smaller debt. The reorganization of railroads during the 1870s, which affected especially those newly built, resulted less from sheer overbuilding in ignorance of returns than from an insupportable burden of debt. In most cases, the capital structure was altered to permit the roads to pay lower effective real rates of interest.

The final factor in the disappointing financial performance of the railways in the 1870s was the cyclical crisis that broke, ironically enough, with the failure of the Northern Pacific and Jay Cooke and Company in 1873. Railroad output, which had increased by 115 percent between 1868 and 1873, expanded in the next five years by little more than a third. Net earnings were less

---

[38] Henry H. Swain, "Economic Aspects of Railroad Receiverships," *American Economic Association Economic Studies*, vol. 3, no. 2 (1898), p 70.
[39] *Poor's Manual . . . , op. cit.* (1884), p. iii.

sensitive owing to the curtailed operating costs which were unsuccessfully resisted in the famed railroad strike of 1877. These lower costs explain the capacity of the older and better established lines to maintain their dividends through the crisis.

The boom of the 1880s and its aftermath. Less rapidly but as inexorably as the storm had broken in 1873, it gradually cleared, and railroad construction resumed at a brisk rate in 1878. The course of this investment was largely the less developed regions, the states in the Western South and Western North accounting for some 50 percent of the total, as Table 13.12 illustrates. These efforts represented, most often, a continuation of projects already begun in 1873. Two of the original transcontinental lines, the Southern Pacific and the Northern Pacific, were completed, while the conclusion of the Atchison, Topeka, and Santa Fe permitted an alternative route from St. Louis to the Pacific Coast. The large amount of additional mileage in the southwestern states was a measure of the rising importance of Kansas City and the cattle trade. It also reflected construction of links to the Gulf ports, particularly Galveston, in the hope of funneling grain exports in that direction. In the North Central area, the various lines tributary to Chicago began a series of extensions to the then rapidly settling Dakotas and Nebraska, not to mention further construction in Iowa.

The extent of the construction so far surpassed previous efforts—an annual average of 8000 miles was constructed during the five years 1879–1883— that subsequent characterizations have stressed the speculative and exuberant features of the expansion. *Poor's Manual* retrospectively referred to the surge of investment as a delusion, not once but in almost every phase.

> From 1877 to near the close of 1883 a most singular delusion rested upon the public ... and this delusion was taken advantage of on a vast scale by able and unscrupulous adventurers. Whatever was manufactured and put afloat was seized with avidity by an eager and uninformed public. The delusion was increased and prolonged by payments on a very large scale of interest and dividends from capital. In this delusion, the most loud-mouthed and unscrupulous promoters usually had the greatest success.[40]

Such a judgment, harsh as it was, correctly emphasized the role of abundant capital supply in permitting the boom to go forward. Railroad common-stock prices doubled between 1877 and 1881, and in such a setting it was quite easy for construction companies to sell their shares profitably. Bond yields declined during the expansion, not to reverse themselves until 1883 and then only insignificantly. Price deflation influenced this downward trend but so too did the rapid decline of the federal debt, which liberated capital.

The question is whether these favorable evaluations had any basis in fact. Superficially, it might seem that all was overbuilding. In 1878 the average net earnings relative to the costs of construction in the newer western states were less than elsewhere. The instances of parallel construction—such as the Nickel Plate and West Shore ventures, which were designed primarily for sale at

[40] *Ibid.* p. iii

favorable prices to potential competitors—seem only to reinforce the speculative image. However, all was not quite so socially irrational. Most construction was undertaken by extant systems, either to complete previously demarcated through routes, or to extend into the newer areas whose potential contribution to traffic seemed favorable. This meant that returns could be paid out from older portions of line even while construction was under way. Completion and extension frequently resulted in more than proportional additions to earning capacity. This was natural when the areas between termini were meager sources of traffic. The Atchison approximately doubled its net earnings *per mile* after doubling its extent; the same advantage, albeit less pronounced, was enjoyed by the Southern Pacific and the Northern Pacific. The three most expansion-minded systems were perhaps the Chicago and Northwestern; the Chicago, Milwaukee, and St. Paul; and the Burlington. All experienced an initial increase in net revenue per mile, followed by a falling off; gross output per mile unambiguously increased. Net earnings performed less well due to deteriorating rate conditions which developed from the increasing competition for traffic.

Total demand, however, expanded quite rapidly in the newer states since settlement and commercialization occurred more synchronously than in the pre-Civil War period. An important fillip was added by the great increase in European demand for cereals and meat beginning in 1879. Wheat exports in 1877 of 40 million bushels worth $47 million expanded in 1881 to 151 million bushels worth $168 million, later subsiding. States with significant railroad construction such as Iowa, Nebraska, Minnesota, the Dakotas, and Kansas contributed almost half of the 200,000-bushel increment in the output of wheat between 1874 and 1884.[41] This was the era of bonanza farms. Even where settlement and agricultural growth were not large in scale, there were other sources of demand, such as the silver-mining boom in Colorado. The Denver and Rio Grande did extraordinarily well—to the point of paying dividends—until an ambitious extension to Salt Lake City proved more costly than profitable. It and the Texas and St. Louis were the only significant western lines to pass into receivership after the check to construction in 1884.

Thus, despite the unprecedented magnitude of investment and the great increase in mileage, the boom was more than a delusion. Individual projects could anticipate favorable demand conditions, although admittedly, when the expansion plans of all were taken together, there were instances of excess construction. The rapid resumption of investment in 1886 and its continuation until 1893 in the very same areas previously exploited suggest that such instances were not numerous, and that previous investors were not completely deluded. This last surge was much like its predecessor in motivation: Its aims were completion of an additional transcontinental line to the Northwest, as well as amplification of facilities serving that area; construction of tactical extensions by the large systems to compete for long-haul traffic in newer

---

[41] Calculated from U. S. Department of Agriculture, *Report of the Commissioner of Agriculture for 1874* p. 30, and *Report of the Commission of Agriculture for 1885,* (Washington: U.S. Government Printing Office, 1875, 1886) p. 361. All production in 1874 shown for territories was credited to the Dakotas.

areas; and investment in trackage to provide direct and separate entrances for the major systems into the principal railroad centers, East and West. An additional stimulus was provided by a resurgence of construction in the southern and Gulf states. A combination of renewed economic activity and the passage of time since the debacle of public assistance during Reconstruction contributed to the resumption; the mechanism—expansion by established or newly formed extended systems—was the same as previously.

With the depression of 1893, extensive railway construction came largely to an end. Although an additional 80,000 miles was constructed in the next 25 years, the laying of secondary and yard track and the acquisition of equipment made the larger contribution to investment. Table 13.13 restates gross investment in 1909 dollars from the inception of the railroad era until that year and clearly demonstrates the rapid use of purchases of rolling stock after 1890. Construction of track other than mainlines accounted for approximately $900 million in 1900–1909 and $500 million in the preceding decade. Thus the sum of equipment purchases and intensive track construction equaled extension outlays in 1890–1899 and went on to exceed it by 50 percent in the next decade.

The extent of the investment and its sources. The rapid growth of railroad investment in the 1870s and 1880s stands out in Table 13.13. Within 20 years real expenditures quadrupled, for an annual average rate of over 7 percent for two decades. This expansion retained for railroads its 1860 position as the leading nonagricultural activity in the country, even given the rising manufacturing sector. Railroad capital of $10 billion represented perhaps a sixth of the nation's reproducible wealth in the early 1900s; individual railroad enterprises were numbered among the corporate giants of the time.

In current prices between 1860 and 1910, the gross investment flow into the railway sector was between $9.1 and $15.9 billion, the correct total depending upon the degree of overcapitalization of share capital. The private sector was the principal source of finance. Apart from the land grants authorized in 1862–1871 and a federal loan (later repaid with interest) of nearly

TABLE 13.13
Gross investment in construction and equipment (millions of 1909 dollars)

Period	Track	Equipment	Total
1828–1838	85.3	4.0	89.3
1839–1848	158.5	13.7	172.2
1849–1858	854.3	72.6	926.9
1859–1869	793.1	126.8	919.9
1870–1879	1677.7	332.7	2010.4
1880–1889	3413.4	681.1	4094.6
1890–1899	1755.8	742.8	2498.6
1900–1909	3023.4	1922.4	4945.8

SOURCE: Adapted from Fishlow, "Productivity . . .," *op. cit.,* p. 611.

$65 million to the Central Pacific–Union Pacific project, state and local governments added only $275 million, about the same as their antebellum contribution.[42] Valuation of the land grants is difficult: As a lower bound the price per acre can be set equal to the value at the time of the grant, or less than $1; an approximate upper limit is the average value of sales, or $3.38 an acre. (This accounting is exclusive of the additional 22 million acres granted by states to railroads in the 1850s). Although it includes appreciation due to completion of the railroad and does not discount for the interval until sale, the higher price probably reflects better the real transfer of resources—that is, the present value of federal lands contributed. There was also a quid pro quo involved: reduced rates on transportation of federal property and troops.

For present purposes we can accept an estimate of $400 million for the 131 million acres bestowed by the federal government and the 27 million acres in the state of Texas. Overall, public aid was thus absolutely greater after the Civil War, but it still provided less than 10 percent of needed resources. In the first postwar surge, 1868–1873, especially in the land-grant incentive to undertake large-scale projects, government aid was much more crucial. Indeed, within this single interval, the gross financial assistance was comparable to the relative subsidy granted in the 1830s. Both were experimental periods: the first in the introduction of the innovation, the second for transcontinental systems. After the crisis of 1873, there was a parallel wave of revulsion, constitutional prohibition of aid, and dependence upon private finance.

Land grants were the principal component of assistance after 1860. There was abundant unsettled land in the West, and the grants seemed a costless way to subsidize construction. Since the government retained alternate sections along the right-of-way which could be sold at a higher price, its receipts would not decline and yet construction could be accelerated. In fact, since government sales were not made at higher prices, a financial opportunity cost was involved.[43] More fundamentally, however, the efficacy of the subsidy was diluted by the underlying contradiction of the grants, which impinged differentially upon the railway's construction, land, and transportation interests. The former required that the lands be converted immediately to a liquid asset. Immediate sale did not satisfy this objective, since current prices were low. Rather, the grants secured bond issues, frequently sold at discount in any event, and could thus have been substituted by government guarantees. By withholding lands as they thus frequently did, and by further procrastinating in preempting lands in the wider indemnity zone to compensate for acreage along the right-of-way that had already been settled, the railroads succeeded in causing their value to appreciate. This procedure conflicted with the early development of traffic that the railroad might serve, as well as with the social advantage of earlier settlement. Land grants were therefore not an unambiguously optimal solution.

---

[42] Goodrich, *Government Promotion . . . , op. cit.*, chaps. 5–7.
[43] Paul. W. Gates, "The Railroad Land Grant Legend," *Journal of Economic History*, vol. 19 (Spring 1954), pp. 143–146.

More important than public subsidy after the Civil War was foreign investment. Estimates suggest that as much as $2.5 billion of American securities found their way into European portfolios between the end of the war and the beginning of the twentieth century. Indeed, until the reversal that began in 1893, the net inflow totaled more than $3 billion.[44] The foreign contribution was two thirds in bonds and only one third in shares, a fact which made its role the more significant, since the former were sold at a lesser discount. Between 1865 and 1893, almost half the funded debt issued by railroads was absorbed abroad, and one fourth of the stock, or more than a third of total capital.[45] Foreign investment and public subsidy responded inversely. European participation was perhaps greatest in the last surge of investment in the 1880s and least between 1878 and 1884. The fate of the foreign investors was not always happy. Their extensive finance of the Erie Railroad was always a source of grief, its failure being a regular feature of the American business cycle. On average, financial outcomes were undoubtedly better, however. Bonds of the leading railroads were favored objects of investment, sold at a premium in London in the late 1880s, and yielded a return of between 4 and $5\frac{1}{2}$ percent. Indeed, it was argued that they were undervalued, inasmuch as South American and Balkan railways, albeit government guaranteed, were quoted similarly.[46] English investors were accustomed to much lower returns than American, and the higher yield of the American railroad securities in London adequately compensated for the greater risk, while still securing to railroad promoters an abundant and cheap source of capital.

Despite the size of the foreign interest, the major burden of the investment fell upon Americans. How could such substantial finance have occurred with average returns on capital rarely in excess of 5 percent, frequent receiverships emanating from defaults of interest, and large quantities of stock not paying dividends? The answer lies partially in the already-cited exaggeration of capitalization and in the attraction of capital gains. The first factor meant that returns to investors were always greater than those to the enterprise; the second provided expectations for still-larger individual profits. Securities acquired at discount were increased in value by the completion and operation of the project, if only because its survival was then assured. This capital gain, a compensation for the risk involved, was sufficient to evoke the crucial inflow of domestic capital necessary to undertake construction. Unfortunately, the magnitude and variation over time of such returns is not easily assessed. Security prices rose and fell. Yet there seems to have been ample scope for capital gains. In the decade 1889–1899, an index of share prices fluctuated around a mean value of approximately 67 percent of par; in 1900, the index stood at 80; and in 1901, after a series of good years, it was above par.[47] If,

[44] Matthew Simon, "The United States Balance of Payments, 1861–1900," in *Trends in the American Economy in the Nineteenth Century*, William N. Parker (ed.), Studies in Income and Wealth, vol. 24 (New York: National Bureau of Economic Research, 1960), pp. 698–707.

[45] William Z. Ripley, *Railroads: Finance and Organization* (London: Longmans, Green, 1915), pp. 4–8; Cleona Lewis, *America's Stake in International Investments* (Washington: Brookings Institution, 1938), chap. 8.

[46] S. F. Van Oss, *American Railroads as Investments* (New York: G. P. Putnam, 1893), pp. 178–179.

[47] U.S. Industrial Commission, *Reports*, vol. 19 (Washington: U.S. Government Printing Office, 1902), pp. 270–271.

as has been asserted, real investment was only half the nominal capitalization, the capital gains element must have varied between 34 and 100 percent. This was in addition to a higher current yield, based upon an original purchase price rather than reckoned against par capitalization.

In addition to such influences upon the investor's expected return, another mechanism was operating at the end of the century to assure abundant capital supply. This was the reinvestment of internally generated funds as part of the expansive strategy of existent or nascent consolidated systems. The return on such funds from the viewpoint of the enterprise was quite high, even though it was socially low and, even in realized terms, quite modest. Not to engage in feeder construction and other competitive investment might mean losses on previously sunk capital, even though the actual recorded gains from such investment were small.

In sum, construction was not undertaken for altruistic reasons, nor did investment go without reward. The success of individual financiers like Drew, Gould, Cooke, Vanderbilt, and others exaggerate the average returns, but serve as a vivid reminder that profits were sought and earned.

Transport services and technological change.[48] Yet, impressive as its record of physical expansion and mobilization of financial resources was, the output and productivity performance of the railroad sector were no less spectacular. Ton-mileage grew almost a 100-fold between 1859 and 1910; passenger miles, more than 16 times. As shown in Table 13.14, weighted output increased 7 percent per year from 1870 to 1910, a figure well in excess of such aggregates as national income or total commodity production, and more than that of any other single major sector. The most important factor in the increase was the sheer physical extension of mileage. Intensified demand, more tonnage originating per mile, accounts for only half as much of the change.

TABLE 13.14
Productivity in the railroad sector, 1870–1910 (1910 = 100)

Year	Output	Labor	Capital	Fuel	Total Input	Total Factor Productivity
1870	6.57	13.5	16.6	5.4	13.9	47.3
1880	13.87	24.5	31.5	11.7	25.9	53.6
1890	32.82	44.1	61.9	28.7	49.3	66.6
1900	54.84	59.9	72.3	45.9	63.2	86.7
1910	100.00	100.0	100.0	100.0	100.0	100.0

SOURCE: Adapted from Fishlow, "Productivity ...," *op. cit.,* p. 626

[48] For a more thorough treatment of this question, see Albert Fishlow, "Productivity and Technological Change in the Railroad Sector, 1840–1910," in *Output, Employment, and Productivity in the United States After 1800,* Dorothy S. Brady (ed.), Studies in Income and Wealth, vol. 30 (New York: National Bureau of Economic Research, 1966).

Productivity in the railroad sector likewise exceeded that in the economy as a whole by a goodly margin. The average annual rate of advance from 1870 to 1910 was 2 percent; for the national economy it was approximately 1.5 percent. This aggregate measure encapsules the consequences of extensive organizational and technical changes introduced by railroads in the post-Civil War period. Bridges successfully vaulted natural gaps and the manmade obstacles of gauge differences and confused time changes were overcome in the 1880s. The appearance of fast-freight lines after the war eliminated the inconvenience of breaking bulk at each junction of independent roads, not an inconsiderable bother prior to widespread consolidation. Participating railroads contributed cars in proportion to their share of the traffic, in a precursor of later rental arrangements. Some 40 separate lines were formed and rapidly won the bulk of the through business. Less dramatic was the steady advance in the weight and quality of rails. The Pennsylvania Railroad was the first to introduce steel rails during the Civil War, motivated by the frequency of rail replacement under conditions of dense traffic. By 1880, almost 30 percent of national trackage was laid with steel rails; by 1890, 80 percent was so equipped. Rail weights increased from approximately 50 pounds per yard to a standard 70 pounds at the beginning of the century. On this heavier track, more numerous and more powerful locomotives pulled larger and more efficient freight cars. Tractive force increased by more than 100 percent between 1870 and 1910. Freight-car capacity more than trebled, but without proportional increases in dead weight, altering the ratio of capacity to weight from 1:1 to 2:1. Finally, block signaling devices, automatic couplers, and air brakes made important contributions to the expeditious movement of larger trains.

However, the most important, albeit prosaic, cost-saving change occurred in train size and composition. More powerful locomotives and more efficient freight cars together created a reduction in 1910 operating costs of $749 million, 40 percent over what the 1870 technology could have produced. Because of their increased longevity, steel rails represented a direct saving of another $200 million; and because of their greater strength—which permitted locomotive size to increase—another $279 million was saved. Automatic couplers and air brakes were of significantly less importance. The increased speed and safety they facilitated were translated into much smaller economies of $50 million. Therein lies an explanation for the long delay in their adoption by railroads. Although couplers and brakes both were experimented with as early as the 1870s, national legislation was necessary to secure their installation. Congress acted in 1893 and was forced to extend the period of adoption to 1900 because of the railroads' recalcitrance. The rapid diffusion of steel rails and the continuing and unheralded progress of locomotives and rolling stock, on the other hand, required no legislative enforcement: The market sufficed.

Economies of scale also continued to operate in the post-Civil War period as they had earlier. The capital/output ratio declined by 60 percent between 1870 and 1910. If capital services were proportional to output, economies of scale explain about half the observed productivity advance between these dates. The four innovations examined above—train size and composition, steel rails, automatic couplers, and air brakes—account for the largest part of the remaining half, and in that order.

This productivity gain was translated into lower railroad tariffs. Passenger rates of 2.8 cents in 1870 fell almost one third to a 1910 value of 1.9 cents; average ton-mile costs decreased more sharply, from 2.2 cents to only .75 cents. While some part of the decline in the average is due to a rising share of low-rate commodities, especially coal, the reduction on various identical commodities was only slightly less impressive. Both reductions exceeded the 25 percent fall in the general price level over the same period. Yet during these years railroads and their pricing policies became the object of considerable complaint, publicity, agitation, and ultimately regulation.

The objections centered on the level of rates and discrimination in their application. Such discrimination could be personal, as in the case of rebates to large shippers, or locational, as in the controversy over the relative charges for long or short hauls. The first of these criticisms found national expression in 1874 in a senatorial report, *Transportation Routes to the Seaboard,* and would be repeated locally many times over. The region west of the Missouri River, in particular, complained of rates much higher than those in the trunk-line territory between Chicago and the seaboard. Discrimination did not lack for attention. Farmers especially complained of the advantages bestowed upon larger shippers, which gave to elevator operators a favored position in monopolizing the trade. Yet it was in the oil trade, and the rise of the Standard Oil monopoly, that perhaps the most audacious personal discrimination was found. Finally, the vexing and complicated problem of asymmetry between distance and transport charges could not fail to attract notice. Local rates, which were generally noncompetitive, were set considerably higher than through rates. It was not uncommon for localities lying close to a shipping point to be charged more for transportation than a competitive terminal at the far end of the same line.

In reply to such charges, railroads pointed to their low rates of return and to what their managers considered fair charges. James J. Hill of the Great Northern offered to accept state regulation if it would "guarantee the roads six percent on their actual cost and a fund for maintenance, renewal, and other necessary expenditures." President Dillon of the Union Pacific phrased the issue in a less conciliatory and also less relevant manner: "What would it cost for a man to carry a ton of wheat one mile? What would it cost for a horse to do the same? The railway does it at a cost of less than a cent."[49]

Central to the controversy was the inapplicability of the competitive model to the railroad industry. Competition in other sectors might be relied upon to drive prices down to cost; where there were excessive profits, new firms would enter, and where profits were insufficient, some would exit. But railroads did not lend themselves to such a self-regulating mechanism. Entry was costly

---

[49] Quoted in John D. Hicks, *The Populist Revolt* (Lincoln: University of Nebraska Press, 1961), p. 62.

and irreversible, and frequently predicated upon a profitability later eroded by overconstruction. Individual localities could not have uniform access to the supply of rail services because some were better situated than others. Nor was water competition evenly distributed. A railroad faced differential elasticities of demand at different points along its line. Thus profit maximization required locational discrimination. Economies of scale due to large fixed costs also conflicted with purely competitive behavior, although fostering rivalry. They encouraged personal discrimination and favorable differentials on marginal traffic. They also contributed to excessive construction of feeders, and ultimately to consolidation.

The post-Civil War period saw a playing out of the tendencies inherent in the structure of the industry. Rate wars were frequent, as were cartel arrangements to avoid them. Wars were usually initiated by the railroad most needing increased revenue, and without fear of the ultimate penalty of being forced from the market: Large capital-intensive enterprises are permanent. To farmers, the instability and uncertainty resulting from such wars more than offset the benefits of the often absurdly low rate levels. Discrimination was inevitable. Areas with alternative forms of transportation received better service and lower rates. So did high-income regions generating substantial traffic. Individuals guaranteeing large shipments were always assured favorable treatment. Not surprisingly, because their own situations were not identical, many railroads were eager, by whatever means, to stabilize the potentially disruptive operation of this model. The pools that arose to divide traffic were one manifestation of this desire; the formation of large consolidated systems of railroads was another.

The grievances against the railroad gave little brief to such technically conditioned responses. On more than one occasion, the demands ignored even more obvious facts. North Dakota farmers farther from the market could not expect to receive the same price for wheat as those in Illinois. Prairie farmers benefiting from long hauls *gained* as much as those disadvantaged by short hauls lost to others. Overproduction of agricultural crops and falling prices on world markets could not be compensated proportionally by lower transport costs, which were determined by altogether different considerations. Construction to serve areas generating little traffic could justify itself only by high rates. Seasonal traffic logically also had to bear the expense of additional investment in rolling stock not efficiently utilized. These higher charges did not imply high profits: High-rate railroads west of the Missouri were not singularly profitable. Indeed, the many comparisons of average receipts per ton-mile ignored all differences in the composition of freight and length of average haul; two railroads with identical rate structures could have far different averages if lower-cost transport dominated on one.

This is not to deny that some railroads did ungraciously accumulate profits at the expense of others. It is simply to point out that on average the industry did not grow fat. The degree of competition assured that. Even if overcapitalization had been as large as 100 percent, the average direct return to direct cost would not have exceeded 10 percent in the 1870s, 1880s, and 1890s. And of course, some part of the overcapitalization was a real cost of securing the needed capital. Enterprises in other sectors could not have earned significantly less. The results shown earlier in Table 13.14 are again relevant. Real railroad rates, which could have been expected to decline commensurately with the .5 percent differential between national and sectoral productivity growth, fell even more rapidly. This situation implies that the rate of increase of factor returns in the railroad sector was less than in the rest of the economy, or more simply, that consumers of rail services benefited at the expense of owners of railroad inputs. The fact that railroads were unionized and facing a competitive labor market suggests that the incidence of the differential was borne by investors. The return on *real* investment, without regard to nominal capitalization, probably declined relative to profits in other sectors between 1870 and 1910.

As a further example of the inexorable realities involved, the various efforts at regulation, made in response to the complaints of shippers, did not much alter matters over the period. Despite the decision by the Supreme Court in 1877 in *Munn* v. *Illinois*, which upheld the rights of states to institute regulatory legislation, the Granger Laws setting rail rates were invariably softened, if not repealed. National regulation followed soon thereafter, hastened by another judicial decision in the Wabash case that states could not regulate rates on interstate commerce. The passage of the Interstate Commerce Act of 1887, with the commission it created, was not the punitive action it has sometimes been made out to be. Railroads were by no means completely opposed to regulation as a means of achieving greater stability in the industry—the Iowa pool had finally dissolved in 1885 and other traffic associations were little more effective. Despite the language in the act outlawing pools, its consequences were in fact contrary. Regulation worked initially to the advantage of the trunk lines by increasing through rates to the detriment of long-distance shippers.[50] However, the less discriminatory rate structure and the relative decline of short-haul rates imposed by regulation did work to benefit many localities.

Court decisions in the early 1890s, culminating in the Maximum Rate case in 1897—which eliminated the authority of the ICC to establish rates—set off new wars. The Alabama Midland case in the same year also questioned the commission's authority to reduce short-haul rates; the Court insisted upon consideration of competitive conditions as well as the principle of non-discrimination. This judicial emasculation of the original act was remedied by the Hepburn Act of 1906 and later by the Mann–Elkans Act. Neither altered the fact that decisions of the regulatory agency tended to be strongly influenced by the industry itself, however.

Nor did either reverse the consolidation that had by that time concentrated about two thirds of the extant mileage and 85 percent of earnings in the hands of seven groups. The Vanderbilt roads monopolized movement between New

[50] For a statistical test of the effect of regulation upon through rates, see Paul W. MacAvoy, *The Economic Effects of Regulation* (Cambridge, Mass.: M.I.T. Press, 1965); for a more general, revisionist view of the origins of regulation, see Gabriel Kolko, *Railroads and Regulation, 1877–1916* (Princeton: Princeton University Press, 1965).

York and Chicago; the Pennsylvania interest dominated the lines running westward from Pennsylvania and Maryland; Morgan controlled the Southeast; Gould interests and the Rock Island group were paramount in the Mississippi Valley; Hill railroads functioned in the Northwest; and Harriman's lines were made up largely of the southern and central transcontinental routes. Moreover, these seven were in reality only four, since Morgan was associated with the Pennsylvania, Vanderbilt, and Hill groups, and assured a commonality of interest. Constructed out of the wreckage of the depression of 1893, and given impetus by favorable financial conditions after 1898 which yielded large capital gains to their investment-banker organizers, these consolidated units marked an end to the earlier rivalry. In part they represented a natural evolution of the underlying economic realities of the industry, although the concentration went well beyond such a rationalization. Consolidation did not resolve the problems of the industry, however. The return on capital, which had reached almost 6 percent in 1907, receded to as little as 4 percent in 1914 and 1915, partially as a result of the reluctance of the ICC to grant petitioned rate increases—in spite of a rising price level. For the remainder of the twentieth century, the situation of the railroads was to get little better and frequently worse.

THE EFFECTS OF NINETEENTH-CENTURY TRANSPORT INNOVATION

Transport innovation profoundly altered existing production relationships in nineteenth-century America in three ways. First, it reduced direct resource requirements for producing a given amount of transport services. The lower cost of total input per unit of output led to a correspondingly lower real price for transport services.

Second, this lower price influenced the decisions of consumers of transport services. It made their current level of activity more profitable by virtue of the lower cost of inputs. The reaction to this change varied by sector, depending upon the importance of shipment expense in total costs and the response of consumers of the final product to lower price. The chief beneficiary was agriculture. Not only did transport charges loom large in the total costs of bulk commodities, but the export market was one of elastic demand. In addition, the lower costs of transportation made the abundant land accessible. This development illustrates the unique locational consequences of transport innovation. Other innovations typically lower costs at given sites, and do not carry with them the impetus to geographic extension and specialization. But accelerated settlement and increased marketable surplus were directly associated with the succession of internal improvements.

A third sequence of reactions followed from the demands generated by the transport sector. As canals or steamboats or railroads were introduced, they required engineering talents, marine engines, iron rails, and so on in their construction phase and, as their output expanded, inputs of labor and material inputs. This development occasioned a reallocation of resources. Investment in transportation represented a large share of capital formation throughout the nineteenth century. Moreover, when it declined relatively, the rapid growth of transport services substituted current for capital requirements. Together, they made the sector a potent force.

Note that these backward linkages, because of their technological origins, were more specific than either direct resource savings or forward effects. Canals or railroads could lead to identical price reductions and direct benefits without being substitutable in their impact on other sectors.

This gamut of effects did not go unnoticed. Contemporaries evaluated transport projects with unbridled optimism. Later commentators have not stinted in their praise of what transportation innovation meant for nineteenth-century American economic development. While railroads have received the lion's share of the commendation, canals and steamboats, too, have had their partisans. Let us assess such contentions.

We shall do so from the perspective of the individual innovations, rather than in terms of the entire range of transportation advance. The cumulative contribution made by the transition from the common road through to the railroad is so large and so obvious as to defy accurate calculation. Without the canal, steamboat, or railroad, the contours of development in the United States would have been so different and less satisfactory that we need go no farther. David Wells already resolved the issue in 1889:

> The railway freight service of the United States for 1887 was . . . equivalent to carrying a thousand tons one mile for every person, or every ton a thousand miles. The average cost of this service was about $10 per annum for every person. But if it had been entirely performed by horsepower, even under the most favorable of old-time conditions, its costs . . . would represent an expenditure greater than the entire value of the then annual product.[51]

The interesting question, rather, is the relative contribution of the various technological innovations, and their social rate of return, given the actual historical sequence. In this context, the question of indispensability is of little interest. Without the railroad, say, but with canals, automobiles, and airplanes, the transportation situation would not have totally impeded progress. Indeed, in a complex economy, the range of potential substitution is so great that no single innovation can be regarded as completely necessary. This is not the same as saying that individual advances were unimportant or insignificant. The assessment of importance depends upon the specific benefits of the change and the costs of its introduction. In measuring its effects, we shall consider the situation with and without the innovation, all else remaining the same. We shall *not* inquire into the possible alternatives that could have reduced, or altered, the perceived historical consequences. Nor shall we venture so far beyond the margin of observable adjustments that our analysis becomes vitiated in the process.[52]

[51] David Wells, *Recent Economic Changes* (New York: D. Appleton, 1890), pp. 41–42.

[52] A considerable controversy has sprung up concerning the ability to reach casual conclusions in general, and the importance of transport innovation specifically. For a recent statement explicitly differentiating historical necessity and sufficiency see Albert Fishlow and Robert W. Fogel, "Quantitative Economic History: An Interim Evaluation," *Journal of Economic History*, vol. 31 (March 1971).

Let us now turn to the consequences of the diverse transport innovations in terms of their direct benefits, their backward linkages, and the expansion they created in the using sectors.

Direct Benefits

To estimate resource savings, the following types of information are necessary: (a) the cost of carriage by the new mode, (b) the alternative cost by the existing facilities, and (c) the elasticity of demand. Then it is possible to estimate the consumers' surplus associated with price reduction, or the maximum value that could have been exacted by a discriminating monopolist leaving no gain for users.

This principle is illustrated in Figure 13.3, which is an expanded version of Figure 13.2. Our initial situation in period O is defined by the demand curve D_o and the price P_A. The quantity of transport services P_AF is utilized. By period 1, a more efficient means of transport has been introduced, and the charge is now a lower P_B. The demand curve is now D_1, shifted outward due to changing total income, and more elastic because of the use of a more transport-intensive technology in response to lower rates. Our objective is to measure the direct benefits. In the first instance, we must replace D_1 by the less elastic demand curve D_1' appropriate to the older technology at the same level of income. (We assume that the change is sufficiently small not to have affected the total income substantially.) The correct area is P_AFCEP_B, since the older technology was subject to increasing costs and there is a gain in not extending it further.

In fact, we can easily calculate the sum P_AABP_B, in which we ignore rising costs and apply the price differential $(P_A - P_B)$ to the quantity of transport output observed in period 1. This figure will always overstate benefits if $P_A = P_A'$ because the elasticity adjustment reducing quantity from B to E is

FIGURE 13.3

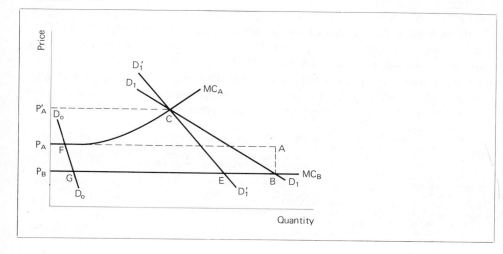

ignored. But if costs are rising, a corresponding undervaluation is introduced whose effect may more than balance this positive bias. In particular, if the new technology is efficient at handling large volumes and the old is not, capacity constraints may make the relevant price P'_A much higher than P_A. Some allowance for rising costs and adjustment for demand elasticities can be introduced in practice to indicate the range within which the benefits can be expected to fall.

Criticism of the method has often ignored its approximative objective. The relevant question is not whether there was any violation of the assumption that price corresponded to marginal cost due to monopoly elements, or whether costs may have been increasing; it is rather the numerical implication of such violations. Evidence already presented concerning rates of return suggests that the monopoly problem was not a serious one. Rising costs have not been adequately shown to be serious enough to vitiate most applications; indeed, one purported demonstration of increased Erie Canal charges during the Civil War actually proves the opposite. The inherent merits of this quantification of benefits stand, and justify its continued use.[53]

Turnpikes.   Estimation of the social benefits generated by the introduction of turnpikes is hampered by the absence of traffic statistics. For two of the largest ones, the Pennsylvania Turnpike and the National Road, unverified reports cite annual shipments of 30,000 and 10,000 tons respectively around 1820.[54] In addition, a fair amount of livestock was driven to market over them. These magnitudes, and a cost differential in favor of turnpikes of 50 percent, imply an annual benefit of about $1 million. These roads cost some $4.5 million, yielding a social profit ratio of 22 percent. However, such a static view exaggerates the roads' true profitability. This reported volume of shipments was not an average annual flow over the life of the investment, but rather a maximum level which occurred after the rapid growth of settlement in the Ohio Valley subsequent to the War of 1812. Nor would it be continued indefinitely after the definitive success of the Erie Canal. Correction to incorporate a rising trend, with a time horizon of 1830, yields an internal rate of return of about 15 percent.

Moreover, this rate cannot be extrapolated to the remainder of turnpike investment. The National Road and the Pennsylvania were among the most densely traveled roads in the country. The private companies along the Pennsylvania route managed to obtain a net return on capital. Even in densely populated Massachusetts, the average financial experience was less favorable. Since total investment in turnpikes exceeded $27 million, of which less

---

[53] For a different view, see Peter McClelland, "Railroads, American Growth, and the New American History: A Critique," *Journal of Economic History*, vol. 28 (March 1968), pp. 102–123. Suffice it to say in rebuttal that most of McClelland's objections, while theoretically sound, are recognized in the works in question. See Fishlow, *American Railroads . . . , op. cit.*, and Robert W. Fogel, *Railroads and American Economic Growth: Essays in Econometric History* (Baltimore: Johns Hopkins, 1964). McClelland's one factual consideration, that Erie Canal rates in the early 1860s increased sharply under increased demand, thereby negating the availability of a low-cost water alternative to through rail shipment, is hardly so damning as he makes out. His own data show that a doubling of canal traffic between 1859 and 1863 left real canal freight rates virtually unchanged! Over the interim, they had temporarily risen owing to adjustment problems, to be sure, but that is totally irrelevant to the long-run question under consideration

[54] J. L. Ringwalt, *Development of Transportation Systems in the United States* (Philadelphia: J. L. Ringwalt, 1888).

than a fifth occurred in these particularly successful projects, the overall results were by necessity much less encouraging. It is doubtful whether any but a handful of projects had a clearly favorable impact. Neither in the absolute magnitude of their benefits nor in their relative return did turnpikes distinguish themselves. This verdict is consistent with the general disinterest Americans subsequently manifested toward nonrail overland transportation until the late nineteenth century.

Canals.   Canals were another matter. Their introduction brought a palpable and dramatic reduction in rates. Equally clear are the rapid tonnage increases and the profitable returns on the Erie. That many of the enterprises constructed in emulation of the New York canal later came to grief due to railroad competition does not necessarily negate their important interim contribution. One student of the subject has approximated their direct benefits prior to the railroad age and concludes that these social gains alone justified the total investment, including the investment in failures: "Canals seem clearly to have conferred upon the antebellum economy direct benefits that exceeded their cost by a substantial margin."[55]

This judgment is based upon the average 1837–1846 traffic on ten heavily utilized canals, and upon a cost differential of 23 cents per ton-mile between canals and overland transport. The calculation denies the feasibility of alternative shipment by water for any part of the total. This assumption appears reasonable in view of the localization of much of the canal business in areas not developed earlier because of lack of access to markets. Less plausible is the assumption of constancy of benefits over the 50-year life span of the investment. For decision makers, *ex ante*, such a horizon and stream of benefits may have been appropriate; for subsequent measurement of the realized average rate of return, it is not. For in fact, within two decades, despite a threefold expansion in canal output, the relevant differential was no longer between canals and roads, but between canals and railroads. This change greatly altered the magnitude of the resources liberated by the relative efficiency of canals. Nor is it entirely appropriate to neglect those canals whose results, even prior to the production of the railroad, were less favorable.

Careful recalculation of the returns upon canal investment is beyond our present scope, but an approximation is possible. Setting the initial returns and cumulative investment both in 1830 to obviate adjustment for present values, substituting a more reasonable rate differential of 17 cents per ton-mile until 1846 and 2 cents thereafter, and using the observed output trend, the average internal rate of return for all canals well exceeds 50 percent. The reason for this impressive figure is simple. At such a large rate differential, the initial capital cost is immediately repaid. This result is admittedly upward biased due to the overstatement of benefits calculated on the basis of observed quantities. If the large terminal bias which is found to obtain on the Ohio canals by comparison of increased rents and direct benefit calculations is applied, the results

[55] Harvey Segal, "Canals and Economic Development," in *Canals and American Development*, Carter Goodrich (ed.) (New York: Columbia University Press, 1961), p. 247.

change somewhat.[56] Such an adjustment reduces the rate of return to the neighborhood of 15 percent. The conclusion remains the same, however. Even this lower figure is impressive considering the short period in which the canal dominated the transport scene. In the years 1837–1846 in particular, the annual benefits may have represented as much as 2 percent of national product.

This favorable evaluation reflects the singular success of the Erie Canal, itself responsible for almost a third of ton-mileage, but representing only 10 percent of investment. One study suggests that as much as 85 percent of government construction may not have yielded a socially profitable rate, largely because of lack of foresight concerning the imminence of the railroad alternative.[57] Projects like the Wabash and Erie barely opened in time to close much of their route, and the high-cost feeders in New York consistently produced deficits. Yet the record of deficits is itself not sufficient to establish lack of social profitability. Development-minded state agencies fixed tolls at modest levels, well below what the traffic might have borne. In any event, there was no way of fully recouping the transport benefits short of a discriminating tariff. Private coal canals did better, either paying dividends or merging transport gains with the profits of extraction.

As a technology, therefore, the canal represented a highly desirable investment solely from the standpoint of its reduced transport charges. More careful planning might have avoided much needless expenditure, to everyone's benefit. Yet even the failures should not be judged too harshly; beyond the direct benefits, there were other consequences which may have tipped the balance favorably in some cases.

Steamboats.   The positive case for steamboats is, if anything, more certain. This is true despite the steamboat's smaller relative advantage compared to canals. Flatboats, keelboats, and barges, while more expensive, were more satisfactory alternatives than the horse and wagon which competed with the canal. The steamboat's special advantage in upstream travel, moreover, was diluted by the considerably smaller traffic in that direction. What made the innovation socially profitable was the limited investment involved. The existence of private returns assures us of its social success. For direct social benefits are the *sum* of net revenues and noncaptured gains. Where the former already justify the investment, there can be no instance of social unprofitability, unless negative externalities are involved.

It is instructive, nonetheless, to attempt to gauge the approximate size of the rents earned by shippers. Ton-mileage has been estimated from arrivals at New Orleans, with a generous conversion to allow for the extensive tributary commerce that never reached that terminus. Given a rate advantage over nonsteam craft of 2 cents per ton-mile downstream and 8 cents upstream, the total annual gains come to $1 million in the 1820s, rising to $6.3

---

[56] See also Roger Ransom, "Canals and Development: A Discussion of the Issues," *American Economic Review*, vol. 54 (May 1964), p. 373, in which the terminal bias is shown to be a factor of six. Such a large magnitude seems unlikely, however, since it implies an extraordinarily high elasticity of transport demand.
    [57] *Ibid.*

million in the 1840s. This takes no account of the passenger receipts and the gains in time afforded to travelers. But the results are already clear. These flows exceed the corresponding net investment in steamboats by a factor of between .5 and 1.5, being greater in the earlier period. As rail diversion began in the 1850s, less favorable results may have been realized.

The evident implication, regardless of later traffic erosion, is of enormous social returns to the steamboat in western waters. Yet the absolute levels also are informative, for, compared to canals the steamboat was much less important. In other words, it was extraordinarily advantageous to adopt steam power, but the investment was not a large enough commitment of resources to influence profoundly the economy as a whole. The slower diffusion of steam power to lake and coastal shipping suggests that its advantage there was less marked. This only reinforces the conclusion of a limited impact.

Railroads. The canal achieved its social profitability from the large initial difference between overland and water rates. The steamboat exhibited extraordinary rates of return on a limited capital input. By contrast, the railroad depended for its importance upon a modest reduction of rates applied to an unparalled extension of output. For this reason its impact awaited a considerable accumulation of mileage. Railroad benefits began to approach canal resource saving in absolute terms only in the later 1840s. Not until the late 1850s, when the railroads' proportion of GNP amounted to some 4 percent, did they surpass the earlier contribution of canals. The time path of benefits, corrected for much of the bias of terminal measurement, is given in Table 13.15. Despite this delayed fruition, a result of the modest pace of railroad construction until the feverish 1850s, the antebellum benefits still represented an average internal rate of return of 15 percent on all investment. That is, even without allowance for the continuing earning capacity of the system after 1860, it already had established its profitability. If our calculations are extended to 1890, the rate increases to 18 percent, as the flow of later investment continued to produce significant benefits.

Railroad technology, despite its expense, was thus a wise investment and

TABLE 13.15
Social return of direct benefits to railroad investment (millions of 1860 dollars)

Annual Averages	Net Capital Formation	Noncaptured Benefits	Net Earnings	Gross Direct Benefits	Gross Direct Benefits Less Net Capital Formation
1828–1835	4.5	.3	.2	.5	−4.0
1836–1840	14.0	3.9	2.0	5.8	−8.2
1841–1845	7.0	14.5	7.1	21.6	14.6
1846–1850	27.9	31.4	15.9	46.2	18.3
1851–1855	72.1	78.7	31.2	109.9	38.8
1856–1860	48.1	155.7	48.5	204.2	156.1

SOURCE: Adapted from Fishlow, *American Railroads* . . . , *op. cit.,* p. 53.

justified its utilization vis-à-vis the alternative already in use. The same excessive enthusiasm that had marked governmental promotion of canals was not lacking to private prosecution of railroads. Excess construction was undertaken in response to competitive pressures. The areas into which duplicate facilities penetrated obviously gained a relative advantage, but at a cost in excess of the additional income generated. To put it another way, had some of this investment been reallocated to areas unserved by railroads, or perhaps not undertaken at all, there would have been better use of resources. Yet, as with canals, the total assessment remains affirmative.

The favorable rate of return is only one aspect of the railroad's contribution; the absolute size of the benefits is another. These were large owing to the sheer magnitude of the railroad interest and its continued dominance throughout the nineteenth century. By 1890, resource saving must have exceeded its 1859 dimensions relative to gross product, since the sector's output and productivity growth was more rapid than that of the economy as a whole. This view differs from other findings which suggest 5 percent as the maximum possible proportion for 1890.[58] This latter conclusion is based upon partial results for interregional and intraregional agricultural shipments. Apart from the problem of extrapolation from a nonrepresentative base, there is a more fundamental methodological problem: that of assessing the alternative costs of shipping 80 million ton-miles long after shipments and rates on water alternatives ceased to have the same significance they possessed before 1860. This difficulty makes the calculation distinctly nonmarginal and uncertain, and almost surely implies an understatement of gains arising from capacity constraints on other overland modes of transport.

Therefore, the 1890 gains probably exceeded 10 percent of national income rather than lying well below 5 percent. Such a performance constituted a significant contribution. In absolute terms, however, there is no useful criterion of what is large and what is small, and individual assessments will differ. The virtue of the rate of return is that it definitively resolves the question in favor of the social profitability of an investment of unprecedented size and duration.

All these transport innovations, then, with the possible exception of the turnpike, earned a social rate of return in excess of current interest rates due to the reductions in cost they introduced. Such direct benefits are but one aspect, albeit the most easily quantifiable, of the consequences of the nineteenth-century transport revolution. A second path of influence was that of backward linkages.

Backward Linkages[59]

The derived demands of transport improvement, and especially those of railroads, have received special attention in recent years due to the role that they play in Walt Rostow's *Stages of Economic Growth*: "Perhaps most important

---

[58] Fogel, *Railroads* . . ., *op. cit.*, p. 223.
[59] See Fishlow, *American Railroads* . . ., *op. cit.*, chap. 3; and Fogel, *Railroads* . . ., *op. cit.*, chaps. 4 and 5, for a more detailed exposition.

for the take-off itself, the development of railways has led on to the development of modern coal, iron and engineering industries. In many countries the growth of modern basic industrial sectors can be traced in the most direct way to the requirements for building and, especially, for maintaining substantial railway systems."[60] Nineteenth-century observers, particularly at the beginning of the railroad age, were less impressed; they were more concerned with the high costs and the limited domestic supplies of needed industrial inputs. Ultimately, as special supply interests developed, attitudes altered and the role of the transport system as a consumer was lauded, though never as enthusiastically as its reduced rates and its role as an inducement to geographic expansion.

One reason for the early reserve was the limited reorientation of demand effected by turnpike and canal construction. Total investment during the turnpike era and in the first wave of canal construction until 1834 neither pressed upon total resources significantly nor was much impeded by capital shortage. Equally relevant, the structure of demand represented no sharp break with past patterns. The principal requirement was skilled labor and locally available building materials; engineering was scarce, but a handful of persons sufficed to direct the major projects, most commonly in sequential order.

The coming of the railroad altered matters in both respects. The magnitudes of investment in the new transport form rapidly made it evident to all that a new element had entered into demand considerations. In their initial decade of development, railroads surpassed canals in the volume of capital expenditure in less than five years. They remained in the lead, despite the large amount of aid for canals granted by the western states in the later 1830s. At that early date, railroads already absorbed almost 10 percent of all resources committed to capital formation. Moreover, railroads represented a break with the past in requiring relatively large quantities of iron and complicated capital equipment like locomotives.

This said, it is necessary to put the technological discontinuity into perspective. The predominant demands in railroad construction remained the ones already familiar from the turnpike and, to a still greater degree, the canal. Expenditures for preparing the right-of-way, which involved the employment of unskilled labor with picks and shovels, always exceeded the more sophisticated industrial demands by a substantial margin, even in the post-Civil War period. In the first decade of construction, expenditures for iron rails and equipment came to perhaps 20 percent of outlays, rising to a third in the next two decades, and thereafter remaining stable until the era of intensive investment that began after 1893. It was as much the magnitude of the railroad impetus as its particular form which led it to consume an increasing share of industrial output.

The divergence of early American technique from the British experience is marked in this respect. Railroad iron demands per mile stood at only one fourth the British level before the Civil War, a reflection of the higher price of iron in

[60] Walt W. Rostow, *The Stages of Economic Growth* (New York: Cambridge University Press, 1960), p. 55.

the United States and the consequent substitution of less durable but cheaper construction practices. Equipment requirements were similarly modified to correspond to the less intense utilization of American railroads. In other features as well, American technology reflected American conditions. Rails were repaired rather than replaced. Locomotives burned wood rather than coal; as late as 1859, outlays for the former were ten times the purchases of mineral fuel.

Later, as the economy and the railways prospered, changes did occur. Use of coal became more common on the well-traveled roads, although wood consumption continued to be reported in the South as late as 1880. Iron rails became heavier, and eventually steel found a natural and economical application in the manufacture of standardized types. Equipment became more sophisticated; railway shops followed suit as maintenance requirements became more industrial in character. Still, by 1880 only about a fifth of all railroad workers were employed in shops, and a fourth of these were carpenters.

Iron and steel.   As technology altered, there was a corresponding magnification of the role of railroad demand in the industries most closely affected. In the first decade of railroad expansion, its demands for iron had virtually no influence upon domestic producers. The tariff of 1830 permitted a drawback reducing the tax on imports of iron to 25 percent ad valorem (rather than the 75 percent represented by the specific duty of $37); two years later, a policy of free imports was instituted which remained in force for 10 years. In the 1840s, because of tariff protection and because English supply was being diverted to rapidly rising English demands, local iron production to satisfy railway demands did begin. Lower tariffs in 1846 and a large reduction in British prices after the collapse of their railway boom combined to direct purchases abroad in the 1850s. Not until the end of the decade did gradually increasing domestic production of rails exceed imports. American production took firm hold only after new construction had passed its peak, and then only because of the specialized character of supply. The willingness of British suppliers to accept payment in securities was a powerful incentive for new roads to import their initial requirements. However, the American practice of rerolling used rail favored production for replacement. By the end of the 1850s, extension of mileage was reduced in importance relative to maintenance demands.

Recent studies have examined the aggregate iron demands of the railroad for rails, equipment, and maintenance. These calculations confirm the small role of railroads until the 1850s. In 1840–1850, total railroad consumption constituted 7 percent of domestic pig iron production; despite extensive rail importation in 1851–1855, the proportion rose to almost a fifth; and by 1856–1860, it was greater still. The comparative incremental results are more informative: Changes in railroad demand absorbed 17 percent of the increased supply of the 1840s and over 100 percent in the 1850s. By 1860, rails constituted in volume more than 40 percent of all rolled iron. Rail mills were the largest mills in the country and functioned as technological leaders; five of the six integrated iron works in the country in 1854 were rail producers.

The antebellum experience was only a precursor to the later effort, however. From 1867 until 1891, rails comprised more than 50 percent of annual Bessemer steel output; until 1880, the average ratio exceeded 80 percent.[61] Mills were specialized to serve the rail demand. Requirements for equipment and its maintenance likewise grew more rapidly than output, broadening the influence of railroads upon the iron industry. An estimate for 1889 would allocate 29 percent of rolled iron and steel production to rails alone.[62] Thereafter, with the reduced rate of railroad investment, the growth in installed iron and steel capacity began to be led by other sources, ultimately by another transportation development, the passenger car. Railroad backward linkages to the iron industry thus became progressively more important during the later nineteenth century until the innovation finally yielded its preeminence to more diversified demands. However, this record cannot be extrapolated backward to the 1840s nor indiscriminately to other branches of industry.

Machinery. The experience of the machinery industry is a case in point. Quite contrary to the gradual initiation of rail production, domestic producers quickly met rolling-stock demands. Of the 450 locomotives in the United States at the end of 1839, only 117 were imported from England, and of these 78 arrived before 1836. This performance has led some to exaggerate the role of the railway in promoting the expansion of the machinery industry. Locomotive demand did not originate machine production. Rather, locomotive supply expanded rapidly because of the prior existence of general firms which converted to the new speciality. The first American locomotive was built by a producer of marine engines. Locomotive shops typically originated either in the production of cotton textile machinery—for example, Rogers, Ketchum and Grosvenor, the Taunton works, Manchester, and Locks and Canal Company—or in general machine work, like Baldwin, Hinkley, Grant, and others. Many firms continued their former line of output until the new demand proved sufficiently large and stable to warrant total conversion. Later entrants, particularly in the West, sometimes proved less cautious. On the basis of the demand engendered by rapid extension of trackage, western producers mushroomed in the early 1850s only to disappear once investment decelerated.

Horsepower comparisons have also been suggested to measure the importance of railroad demands for machinery. Citing estimates that railroads accounted for 435,000 horsepower, or 35 percent of the total, in 1849 and 60 percent a decade later, Rostow concludes that the American engineering industry was a product of the growth of the railroad. More careful calculations lead to horsepower values for railroads that are about half as great. Indeed, they suggest that the steamboat may have been a more important source of demand for engines. Western steamboats developed two and a half times more horsepower than locomotives in 1850, an advantage lost only in the 1850s when the rapid rise of the railroad was coupled with the decline of the

[61] James M. Swank, *History of the Manufacture of Iron in All Ages* (Philadelphia: American Iron and Steel Association, 1892).

[62] Peter Temin, *Iron and Steel in Nineteenth Century America* (Cambridge, Mass.: M.I.T. Press, 1964), p. 276.

steamboat on western rivers. But if the tonnage on the lakes, in the coastal trade, and in foreign commerce are considered as well, the total horsepower developed by steamboats was probably close to three fourths the 1860 railroad total.

Such a static comparison does not allow for the greater annual purchase of marine steam engines relative to stock owing to the fact that they depreciated more rapidly than locomotives. The construction of marine engines between 1851 and 1860 exceeded the extant 1860 total by a wide margin; whereas the cumulative 1860 stock of locomotives exceeded recent purchases. Comparison of engine production in 1859 confirms this impression. One account lists 68 machine shops, employing between 4800 and 4900 men, manufacturing machinery to be used on the western rivers alone; in the same year, locomotive producers employed 4174. From the standpoint of antebellum engine demands, therefore, railroads were secondary to the steamboat.

In a more fundamental sense, railroad-derived demand could not be as crucial in the engineering industry as in iron and steel, due to the inherent diversity of machine output. The machinery industry catered to many users, often in a custom manner. The variety of products increased over time as the techniques embodied in industry progressed in their requirements for exactness. In 1859 locomotive production was valued at $4,866,900; the census accorded to cotton and woolen machinery a barely larger value of $4,902,704. Thus railroads were as important in their demands as the leading manufacturing interest of the country. Total production of the machine sector, however, came to more than $52 million, implying a railroad share of less than 10 percent. In the next census railroad participation rose modestly only to decline thereafter as the variety of producers' goods increased. At the end of the nineteenth century and the beginning of the twentieth, despite significantly larger railroad equipment purchases, the relative magnitude was smaller than in 1869.

Railroads had much greater influence through their development of elaborate repair facilities. They served as a powerful force for geographic dissemination of skills, even as the western steamboat had done for the growing river centers of Pittsburgh, Cincinnati, Louisville, and St. Louis. Railroads, of course, were not confined to watercourses and thus cast their influence more widely. Although the South supported only limited locomotive production, the larger railroads in the region all had extensive shops for the reworking of old metal, renewals of locomotives, and even manufacture of rolling stock. In any discussion of western machine firms, the repair shops of railroads are prominently featured, as well they should be. In Detroit, Cleveland, and other cities, they were among the best-equipped and largest enterprises. The repair function was extended with railroad trackage itself. Chicago became an important center, not to mention lesser cities along the expanding routes which became "railroad towns" whose fate was tied to the giant enterprises. In 1870 railroad repairing and manufacture of locomotives and cars came to 20 percent of the output of the machinery sector, with establishments in 29 states.[63] Research

[63] U.S. Bureau of the Census, *Census of Population: 1870*, vol. 3, *Statistics of Wealth and Industry* (Washington: U.S. Government Printing Office, 1872), p. 455.

facilities were established on the largest roads, standardization of equipment was imposed, and an industrial mentality was emphasized in the apprentice programs.

The railroad's influence on the engineering industry was thus related more to maintenance than to new equipment purchases. It was particularly and specifically important in the geographic dissemination of industrial skills. More machinists in many different states were probably directly employed by railroads than by locomotive works in 1860. Although, as we have seen, railroads and steamboats were an important source of demand for engines, steamboats were more important because of their temporal precedence and their continuing stream of demands.

Coal. A third sector alleged to have been profoundly influenced by rail demand was the coal industry. Neither canals nor turnpikes required fuel, nor did steamboats utilize coal in large amounts. Wood was preferred by the latter because of its relative cheapness—the low cost explains the wasteful inefficiency of western engines. In the East, where wood was no longer abundant, the low-pressure steamboat engines had been almost wholly converted to anthracite by the 1840s. Cheap bituminous found near the Ohio River began to be admixed on western boats during the 1850s, a practice that continued due to the better adaptation of boilers to wood. This factor, plus the decline in steamboating, led to coal consumption by western steam craft of less than a million tons in 1880, not even 2 percent of bituminous production. For all steamboats together, the share of total coal output was not much greater.

Railroad impact before the Civil War was little different, as has already been noted. By the century's end, it was another matter. Beginning in 1880, locomotives consumed close to a fifth of total production, a ratio they maintained until 1910. Yet the larger questions are how railroads influenced the expansion of mining, and why development of a coal industry was crucial to national progress. On both counts, the significance of the backward linkages are diluted. There has been no suggestion that railroad demand altered mining technology or otherwise influenced the structure of the coal industry. Likewise, it is possible to exaggerate the influence of mineral fuel as a source of energy. As late as 1860, coal provided less than 20 percent of total energy consumed in the United States. This fact did not impede the rise of a substantial industrial sector by that date. The coal tonnage carried was probably more significant as a source of revenue to the railroad than the consumption of coal was to mining interests.

A real difference existed between the railroad and its predecessors in the pattern of their specific demands. Larger industrial effects emanated from railroad construction and operation even before 1860. However, such linkages were less significant for both coal and the engineering industry than has been suggested. Not until the 1850s, moreover, were demand effects upon iron production perceptible. After the war, railroad demands exerted a greater influence. What made them more important were technological considerations—the use of coal instead of cordwood, the substitution of iron rails by steel—and, especially, the rapidly growing size of the industry. In 1860, 1 percent of the labor force was employed by railroads; in 1900, the figure was 5 percent. Twice as many were employed by railroads as in iron and steel production before the Civil War; eight times as many in 1900. Gross capital formation by railroads, even at its peak in the 1850s, reached only 15 percent of investment; in the 1880s, it increased to 18. These are shares exceeded only by residential construction and far in excess of the claims on savings by other industries. Such magnitudes not only influenced derived demands but obviously reflected increasing utilization of railroads as well.

Forward Linkages[64]

Reductions in transport rates facilitated significant response by present and potential shippers. The locational advantages bestowed by the various internal transport improvements led to marked regional realignments, sometimes temporary, sometimes permanent in character.

With the best and earliest turnpikes, Philadelphia and Baltimore experienced rapid growth in the first two decades of the nineteenth century. It was not an advantage that withstood the construction of the Erie Canal. Steamboats upon the Ohio and Mississippi Rivers brought better access to market to the southern part of the Northwest and that area flourished after the War of 1812. It, too, fell before the Erie. Locations north of the National Road were no longer disadvantaged and the 1830s saw migration into those areas. Finally, the railroad reinforced the advantages of existing and nascent centers such as Chicago and created others west of the Mississippi in Kansas City, Omaha, and elsewhere as trackage after 1860 penetrated into areas not previously settled.

These dramatic effects do not find equivalents in correspondingly large advantages bestowed upon the aggregate economy. These last depend upon the relative efficiencies of production in one location versus another. These are typically small, since the range of possible alternatives is likely to be large. As always, what counts are the opportunity costs. The improvements in the regional terms of trade due to lower transport costs have already been credited in the direct benefits measured earlier, as have the increases in land value due to greater economic proximity to market. Each measures the distribution of the total gains between sectors and between regions.

Yet there are more than static locational effects involved in transport cost reduction. There is also the flow of immigration to the developing interior. There are the farmers encouraged to save and invest more in response to the new conditions of profitability. There are the technological changes, like the reaper, whose dissemination was facilitated by larger scales of output which permitted their utilization. There are the internal economies made possible by the larger demand following upon lower transport costs, not to mention the impact of the wider market upon the division of labor.

These changes in the rate of supply of factors, and in the efficiency of their combination, are only partially and indirectly reflected in the demand curve

---

[64] See Fishlow, *American Railroads . . .*, *op. cit.*, chaps. 4–7, for an extended treatment of these questions in the antebellum period.

for transportation, and hence are not subsumed in the direct benefits. These latter measure the difference in the efficiency of transportation, not the full difference in resource use set in motion by transport innovation. Thus the consequences of induced immigration show up in the direct benefits only to the extent of the savings realized on the additional goods shipped to market; while its contribution to income, in fact, is the value of the total increment in production. The magnitude of such indirect effects is virtually impossible to calculate in a dynamic process in which transport innovation was but one important element. Nevertheless, they should not be forgotten.

Our effort to examine forward linkages will proceed on a more modest level. In the first instance, we shall consider the effects upon the economy of westward settlement. Secondly, we shall touch on the differential response of manufactures and agriculture to lower transport rates. And finally, we shall explore the way in which the succession of transport innovations altered the traditional patterns of commerce.

Regional redistribution. The question we must ask about the new settlement pattern evoked by better transportation is how much *more* productive was labor upon the newly cultivated areas than it would have been in the older region. Stories abound of a veritable surplus for the taking in the interior, suggesting a large forward effect of transportation. Estimates of regional productivity differentials form a more sober but accurate account. Table 13.16 presents a measure of the efficiency differentials between 1839 and 1910 in wheat, oats, and corn arising solely from regional redistribution of output. The alternative output for 1910 is a reconstruction of production utilizing 1910 technology with the 1839 geographic distribution of acreage. As can be seen, the proportion of the total change explained by differing regional yields is not particularly great. A more sophisticated partition of the regional effect, including its interaction with changes in yields and mechanization, does not alter the general impression. These results allocate to regional effects 17 percent of the increased labor productivity in wheat, 29 percent in oats, and 21 percent in corn. This outcome, although inferior to the influence of mechanization, is not to be underestimated. The gain to the economy in monetary terms for these three crops alone amounted to $521 million, or an addition to the earned

TABLE 13.16
Labor requirements as affected by interregional shifts (man-hours per bushel)

	Wheat	Oats	Corn
Actual 1839	3.17	1.45	3.50
Actual 1910	.76	.40	.96
Alternative 1910 without			
regional redistribution	2.90	1.18	2.70

SOURCE: William N. Parker and Judith L. V. Klein, "Productivity Growth in Grain Production in the U.S., 1840–1860," in *Output, Employment, and Productivity in the United States After 1800*, Dorothy S. Brady (ed.), Studies in Income and Wealth, vol. 30 (New York: National Bureau of Economic Research, 1966).

private profits of railways of more than 60 percent. Nor is this a fully accurate accounting. No allowance has been made for the declining marginal productivity in the East that would have resulted from a geographically limited and intensive agriculture. Other similar calculations relate to the redistributive consequences of westward movement in the 1850s. They are consistent in finding that the regional effect is only a partial explanation of the total productivity change. But again, the monetary amount was not totally negligible: a tenth of the railroad's total direct benefits, a fourth of the resource savings in rail transportation of agricultural products. That this single measurable external economy should be so important would seem to justify more than passing attention to the wider gamut of forward linkages.

The principal beneficiary: the primary sector. The sector in which the total range of forward linkages had greater and more immediate influence was undoubtedly agriculture, as this regional effect suggests. Regional differentialism in costs of production did not exist in manufactures. The relationship between the expansion of manufactures in Massachusetts and the rise of the railway network in that state does not run from the latter to the former. One does not find a great reduction in costs following upon the completion of a region's internal communication system or its better national articulation. Indeed, the period of peak dollar profits for the sizable textile industry preceded railroad investment noticeably and was an important source of capital for it.

Transport costs of raw materials and final products represented a small proportion of the total costs of manufactures. The 1859 estimates of railroad resource saving confirm this observation. Total estimated transport cost savings for nonagricultural commodities excluding coal amounted to 5 percent of value added in manufacturing, and half as much of total value. If all the cost reduction had been passed along in lower prices, the cumulative increment in total industrial demand, presuming an elasticity as great as two, would have been limited to 5 percent of the observed 1859 level. This is too small to have counted much.

This finding holds for the succession of other transport innovations. The steamboat never succeeded in shipping much merchandise upriver from New Orleans because manufactures could bear the high overland rates to the West. To be sure, the Erie Canal created much better access and replaced the turnpike, but the manufacturer was less affected by it than agriculture. New England's industrial revolution of the 1820s preceded the existence of a cheap water route. It did so because industry could survive very well under primitive conditions of transport. Wagon shipment to and from Boston of all the inputs and outputs of Lowell at 1845 prices and levels of production would have occasioned no more than a 4 percent difference in costs. Cotton came by sailing ship, and its leading markets remained along the seaboard for many years.

Manufactures were not immune to the beneficent effects of the transport revolution. But they responded more to an increased internal market created by an agricultural income much more sensitive to transport cost reduction. The introduction of the Erie Canal immediately led in adjacent counties to replacement of home production by factory-produced goods. People turned exclusively to agricultural production for the market, as increases in improved acreage clearly demonstrate. The principal effect of the canal, for many years, was the agricultural surplus it evoked in the western canal counties.

Transport cost reduction invariably brought with it higher relative prices for agricultural products in the regions farther from market. This improvement in the terms of trade did not occur at the expense of consumers but was the consequence of lowering the artificial tariff of distance. The distribution of the total savings in transportation expense depended upon the nature of consumer demand : The more elastic it was, the larger the real income benefit derived by producers. Historically, transport expansion was concentrated in periods of buoyant agricultural demand and directed to areas of immediate supply response. This was true of the expansion of the Erie in New York State, of the railroads in the Midwest in the 1850s, and of the trans-Missouri construction of the 1880s. Foreign export was frequently a key factor in supporting agricultural prices. As a result, farmers retained a goodly share of the transport reductions through favorable terms of trade and higher real income. The decadal pattern of farmland price rises, capitalizing this gain, seems to confirm such an interpretation. The agricultural sector was not exploited as a source of savings for industrial growth or to maintain lower nominal wages in the cities. It was allowed to keep its advantageous terms of trade, which became a strength rather than a liability of subsequent aggregate development.

Another relationship between manufactures and the much more transport-sensitive primary sector was in the rise of the agricultural processing industries. These are frequently given little attention in discussions of the process of industrialization ; they are undramatic and uninteresting. One English visitor at the time of the Civil War refused to consider them as legitimate manufactures. Yet these activities were in fact more capital-intensive than the average. Virtually a fourth of industrial horsepower was developed by the milling in-industry in 1870, much of it by steam engines at interior sites which fed local machine demand.

The United States from 1850 to 1890 showed an increasing share of employment in processing activities. They migrated westward with agriculture itself to be close to the weight-losing material inputs. There evolved a sequential and repetitive natural process of transition from agriculture to processing to a broader industrial base. Milling, meat packing, and tanning contributed to the formation of such urban, and later industrial, nuclei as Cincinnati, Chicago, St. Louis, Minneapolis–St. Paul, Omaha, and Kansas City. They provided a mechanism by which high agricultural profitability could contribute directly to industrialization within the American context.

The flow of commerce and transport innovations.   Our third line of indirect transport effects, the modification of trade relationships due to altered relative costs, is a recapitulation of the competition between steamboat, railroad, and canal for the trade of the West. Exports from that region at the beginning of the nineteenth century could go only by river through New Orleans—a situation which created an important pressure for the Louisiana Purchase. The emergence of the steamboat as a substitute, or more accurately, supplement for flatboats, made that route more attractive. Western foodstuffs arrived at New Orleans in ever-rising amounts, much more than doubling in every decade from the 1810s to the 1850s. Yet even as this advance occurred, an important and irreversible change in the pattern of trade had entered with the canal. Table 13.17 portrays the relative reduction in western exports via New Orleans after 1835 owing to the much-increased tonnage of western exports reaching tidewater via the Erie Canal. The slower growth in southerly shipments through 1849 is not to be attributed to direct competition between river and canal as much as to the accelerated development of the region tributary to the Great Lakes. This new area increased western exports and directed them almost exclusively eastward. The surplus of the Ohio Valley continued to travel southward. Production of wheat in the northern parts of Ohio, Indiana, and Illinois more than doubled between 1839 and 1849 and increased the surplus available for export by an even larger proportion; the area adjacent to the Ohio River experienced a substantial decline in marketable surplus over the same interval, suggesting that New Orleans may have diverted some of the flow from the area tributary to the canal. In 1849, "about a million bushels each from Iowa, from the Illinois River and Rock River in northern Illinois, and from the Middle Wabash River in northern Indiana found its way to the southern gateway."[65] In the same year, however, the newly completed Illinois and Michigan and Wabash and Erie Canals forecast the future pattern by siphoning off corn that had previously moved by river southward.

Between 1849 and 1860, absolute decline in shipments to New Orleans set in, and this time the explanation must be sought in altered market boundaries. The larger wheat surplus of the Ohio Valley was now definitively captured by the railways completed from Baltimore and Philadelphia. The entire decline in flour exports via New Orleans can be explained by increases in the flow to these two cities. The proportion of flour shipped upstream from Cincinnati, or dispatched directly eastward by railway or canal, was 90 percent in 1860;

TABLE 13.17
Proportion of western exports shipped via New Orleans (percent)

	1835	1839	1844	1849	1853	1857	1860
Flour	70	53	30	31	27	34	22
Meat products	—	51	63	50	38	28	24
Corn	98	98	90	39	37	32	19
Whiskey	95	96	95	67	53	48	40
Total foodstuffs[a]	—	49	44	40	31	27	17

[a] Weighted by current prices.

SOURCES

1835: Albert L. Kohlmeier, *The Old Northwest* (Bloomington, Ind.: Principia Press, 1938), p. 20.
1839–1860: Fishlow, *American Railroads . . . , op. cit.*, p. 284.

[65] Albert L. Kohlmeier, *The Old Northwest* (Bloomington, Ind.: Principia Press, 1938), p. 84.

only a decade earlier, the downriver proportion had been 97 percent. A similar, if less drastic decline occurred in provisions, with the larger part following a direct rail course eastward. With the introduction of the railway, moreover, export of livestock became a much more attractive alternative and reduced the supply of processed meat for which the river route might compete.

During the 1850s, another and equally important development was occurring : the decline in re-export from New Orleans to the East and abroad. As the total volume of western receipts fell, New Orleans redistributed larger and larger amounts to other parts of the South and lost its function in interregional commerce. The decade marked the conversion of the river route from the West to the more limited role of supplier of the limited southern consumption of western products. After the Civil War, there was only further deterioration.

Did this diversion of trade have profound economic consequences, as has sometimes been claimed ? Victor Clark, for one, argued that until New Orleans was supplanted, there was a continuing danger of imported manufactures flowing upriver to replace the domestic product. Such a view has little basis. New Orleans, despite the steamboat and its drastically reduced upriver rates, never succeeded in developing an import trade. The principal commodities delivered upriver were salt, coffee, and sugar. But bonds of commerce can have more subtle implications as well, for credit relationships and for diffusion of information about markets and prices. A more direct link was to the mutual advantage of the East and West, as much as it was to the detriment of New Orleans as a commercial center, and possibly to southern development.

THE TWENTIETH CENTURY

The nineteenth century marked the high point of the contribution of transportation to American economic growth. Never again—not even in the heyday of the bus and truck—would investment in transport facilities amount to more than 15 percent of capital formation, as it did in the 1870s. Nor would there be repeated the epic expansion of the United States to its continental limits, made possible by the more than 200,000 miles of railway in operation by the beginning of the twentieth century. Finally, the rate of transport growth, as a whole and not only for railroads, failed to maintain its earlier pace, which was substantially in excess of national product. That, in conjunction with the failure to develop further innovations, meant that the resource savings of transportation became less significant.

Despite the inability to replicate its earlier dominating role, the transport sector was not unimportant after 1900. Patterns of land use changed drastically with the introduction of the automobile and the development of the suburb. The motor vehicle industry, with by far the largest part of its production destined for consumption, advanced from seventeenth rank in value added in 1909 to first in 1925. Derived demands for gasoline and rubber sparked equally vigorous expansion of those activities. Schumpeter, in his classic work *Business Cycles*, found in the automobile the same dynamic force for the earlier twentieth century that the railroad had represented for the mid-nineteenth.

Few in 1900 were so visionary as to foresee the eventual decline of the railroad in favor of motor transport. It was at that time the largest single industrial interest in the country and the principal source of securities traded on the burgeoning New York Stock Exchange. The railroad stood at its moment of triumph. Indeed, its most pressing challenger was not the automobile, but another innovation, the interurban trolley. This substitute promised to compete away much of the short-haul passenger traffic which had been a railroad monopoly since the decline of the stage. Or at least so its promoters thought. Their subsequent disillusionment sheds some light on the operation of market processes.

Interurban Railways

The electric streetcar, the basic technology of the interurban system, owed its development to urban needs at the end of the nineteenth century. The horse-car on public streets presented greater inadequacies with each passing year, the foremost of which was the increasing relative cost of operation. Rapid advances in technology were occurring all around while the basic characteristics of urban transport remained unchanged. Frank Sprague's successful installation of an electric system in Richmond in 1888 marked the beginning of a wave of investment that by 1901 had produced 15,000 miles of electric railway, almost exclusively urban. Whereas in 1890, 70 percent of street railway mileage had still been animal powered, 12 years later, electric cars operated over 97 percent of the trackage.[66]

Extension of the technology to intercity and rural service appeared the next logical step. Its great appeal vis-à-vis railroad passenger service was the much greater frequency of its service, its much larger number of stops, and lower cost. Beginning in the recovery from the collapse of 1893, and especially between 1901 and 1908, more than 11,000 miles of interurban railways were constructed. The apogee was attained in 1916, when the system extended over 15,000 miles. Some $1 billion had been spent. During 1901–1908, the outlays equaled the contemporaneous expenditures on roads and represented as much as 15 percent of the total investment in railroads.

Most of the construction was in the Midwest. Ohio alone possessed a quarter of the national mileage; no town of 10,000 was without service. Indiana, Illinois, Michigan, and Ohio together contained almost half the national total. A dense rural population and the existence of many small urban centers were especially favorable conditions for construction, and they were abundant in the rich heartland of the Midwest as well as in such states as Pennsylvania and New York. Although it was never possible to go directly from New York to Chicago via interurban connections—there being two small breaks in the line in New York State—a true enthusiast could make his way

[66] We have drawn primarily upon George Hilton and John Due, *The Electric Interurban Railways in America* (Stanford: Stanford University Press, 1960), in this and subsequent paragraphs in this section.

continuously for more than a 1000 miles from Elkhart Lake, Wisconsin, to Oneonta, New York.

The decline of the industry was only slightly less rapid than its rise. Between 1921 and 1939, three fourths of the mileage fell into disuse under the pressure of automobile and bus competition. Even at its best, the performance of the interurbans could be described as disappointing. Average return on investment was no better than 3 percent in 1909, and perhaps slightly higher if over-capitalization is taken into account. By that time saner expectations had begun to prevail in the capital market, and the expansion in facilities began to peter out. As returns declined still further, falling below 1 percent in the late 1920s, stagnation gave way to accelerating abandonment.

The interurban episode illustrates both how badly and how well market processes work. Given extensive financial support on the basis of the urban streetcar's success, the interurbans repaid the faith of their backers most un-charitably. Even before the age of the automobile, they were an obvious error, as reflected by the diminished stream of investment after 1908. The market ultimately gave its correct signal, but it was too late for many. The mistake turned into an unmitigated disaster as motor cars and buses flowed off assembly lines.

The Rise of Surfaced Highways

The discussion of surfaced highways properly begins with yet another, but most unlikely, innovation, the rubber-tired bicycle. For it is to the League of American Wheelmen, organized in 1880, that the movement for surfaced roads owes its origins.[67] The good roads movement gathered enough momentum by the 1890s, prior to the automobile age, to secure legislation providing for state aid for road construction in New Jersey, Massachusetts, California, Connecticut, Maryland, Vermont, and New York. The federal government acted as well, establishing in 1893 an Office of Road Inquiry. Its informational function was a significant factor in augmenting the support for good roads, as well as in shaping legislation in the various states. The introduction and rapid dissemination of the automobile substantially intensified the pressures for surfaced highways by creation of a direct client interest. By 1913, all but six states had programs of highway construction, and all but ten, state highway departments. Annual state and local expenditures on construction by that time were running in excess of $200 million and absorbing increasing shares of revenue. Ultimately, in 1916, the largess of the national treasury was tapped; the first of what was to become a series of federal grants for construction was authorized by Congress.

Worthy of note in the good roads movement is the limited role played by agricultural interests until rather late in its history. Farmers, rather than seeking better outlets to market as might have been expected, had to be persuaded of the movement's advantages before joining. Indeed, that persuasion was one of the principal triumphs of the Office of Road Inquiry. Not until 1907 did the

[67] See also Charles L. Dearing, *American Highway Policy* (Washington: Brookings Institution, 1942) app. A.

National Grange declare itself affirmatively. The reluctance of farmers to involve themselves is explained by their fear of being disproportionately saddled with the cost through revenues obtained by property taxes. There were also doubts concerning the real advantages to be obtained. Farmers would be trading increased cash payments for increased leisure, since they themselves did most of the local hauling at very little direct financial expense. Proponents of legislation indicated both the substantial benefits to be derived—an annual saving of $600 million was promised on an investment not to exceed $2.4 billion—and the possibility of diverting urban revenues to rural roads through state and federal aid.

Railroads, however, were quite vocal in favoring better roads. They were viewed as complements rather than substitutes for the existing rail network. Feeder roads could only increase rail traffic, not reduce it. Few envisioned them as capable of long-distance service. By 1910, after the formation of the American Automobile Association, however, the divergent position of the railroad and automotive interests became clear. The latter favored federal construction of 50,000 miles of interstate highways on an integrated basis, leaving to states and their subdivisions the responsibilities for lesser arteries. The railroads, "at the risk of seeming to be actuated by [their] interest," asserted that "if the greatest good is to be done to the greatest numbers, the farmer is more interested in the improvement of the roads of the second class . . . those radiating from a market town or shipping station."[68]

This fundamental issue was not resolved in the 1916 Federal Aid Road Act. It appropriated $75 million in grants on a matching basis to be spent over a five-year period and distributed through state highway departments. The selection of routes to be supported was left, however, to the discretion of the Secretary of Agriculture. By 1921, with over 9 million automobiles and 1 million trucks in use, the direction of the future became clear. The application of federal funds was limited to a designated federal road system, composed of not more than 7 percent of the total nonurban mileage in each state. This not only defined a trunk network, but did away with the 1916 state allocation formula based upon the area's population and the extent of its post roads. Thereafter, at federal, state, and local levels, the rapidly growing automotive interest remained the principal pressure group shaping the extent and type of highway construction.

Magnitude of transport investment. From its modest origins in the propaganda of the League of American Wheelmen, highway construction grew to mammoth proportions. Table 13.18 presents estimates of road expenditures by quinquennia from 1902 to 1961, along with corresponding railroad investment and total investment data. A number of observations may be made. First, there is the rapid growth in highway expenditures themselves. Over the entire interval, these expenditures expanded in constant dollars at an annual rate of 5.5 percent. The advance was not even—the Depression's effects are visible, and the war's even more so—but it was much more stable than other forms of

---

[68] W. W. Finley, President of the Southern Railway, quoted in Dearing, *op. cit.,* pp. 260–261.

TABLE 13.18
Twentieth-century gross investment in highways
and railroads (annual averages in millions)

Year	Highways		Railroads		Total Gross Capital Formation[a]	
	Current Dollars	1929[b] Dollars	Current Dollars	1929[c] Dollars	Current Dollars	1929[d] Dollars
1902–1906	109	190	532	980	5,290	10,800
1907–1911	173	272	574	981	6,350	11,700
1912–1916	260	374	465	754	8,050	13,100
1917–1921	511	424	547	507	16,700	15,200
1922–1926	963	815	854	832	18,000	18,000
1927–1931	1,330	1,375	715	728	16,800	17,400
1932–1936	1,002	1,160	191	228	4,120	4,930
1937–1941	1,279	1,431	314	457	11,720	11,750
1942–1946	541	429	580	471	12,760	9,640
1947–1951	1,902	1,449	1,223	715	45,820	24,040
1952–1956	3,536	2,411	1,160	579	58,720	26,580
1957–1961	5,506	3,603	1,243	527	70,120	27,690

[a] Until 1932, private and public capital formation; thereafter, only private.
[b] For 1915 and thereafter, 1947–1949 base shifted to 1929 = 100; 1902–1914 based upon adjusted total construction deflator.
[c] For 1902–1914, 1914 base shifted to 1929 = 100.
[d] For 1932 and thereafter, base shifted to 1929 = 100 from 1958 dollars; earlier in 1929 dollars.

SOURCES

Highways: Robert E. Lipsey and Doris Preston, Source Book of Statistics Relating to Construction, Series C20, C51, C52 (New York: National Bureau of Economic Research, 1960), pp. 39–40.
Railroads
1902–1914: Larry Neal, "Investment Behavior by American Railroads: 1897–1914," Review of Economics and Statistics, vol. 1, no. 2 (May 1969), pp. 131–132.
1915–1950: Melville Ulmer, Capital in Transportation, Communications and Public Utilities (New York: National Bureau of Economic Research, 1960), pp. 256–257.
1951–1961: Interstate Commerce Commission, Transportation Statistics in the United States and for the deflator Schedule of Annual Indices for Carriers by Railroad, 1914–1964, mimeographed.
Total
1902–1931: U.S. Bureau of the Census, Historical Statistics of the United States, Colonial Times to 1957 (Washington: U.S. Government Printing Office, 1960), pp. 143–144.
1932–1961: U.S. Department of Commerce, National Income and Product Accounts of the United States, 1929–1965, supplement to Survey of Current Business (Washington: U.S. Government Printing Office, 1966).

investment. Massive infusions of relief funds by the federal government to provide employment were responsible for the favorable record in the 1930s. In 1936–1940, more than a third of total construction was financed by this means.

Prewar investment had already converted American roads from haphazard mud trails to reliable, all-season conduits for transportation. It was this change, rather than the geographic extension of the network, that was the principal accomplishment. In 1904, of little more than 2 million miles of non-urban roads, only 7 percent was surfaced, and these usually utilized gravel. There was more railroad mileage than improved highway in the country. Surpassing the railway network in 1914, the progression of surfaced mileage continued until in 1940 such roads extended more than 1,300,000 miles or almost half of all highway mileage. Thus, while total road mileage increased only 50 percent between 1904 and 1940, improved mileage multiplied by a factor of eight! Moreover, high-quality surfaces such as concrete and asphalt had appeared with increasing frequency after federal standards went into effect. Some 150,000 miles of superior roads could be found in 1940.[69]

Even this accounting understates the extent of the change that had occurred. Since traffic is concentrated upon the highly improved portion of the road network, about 50 percent of the motor vehicle mileage had access to modern highways by 1940. At the other extreme, only 10 percent of the vehicle miles were dependent upon unimproved roads, although these were ten times greater in length.[70] By World War II, the more than 30 million registered motor vehicles were increasingly adequately provided for.

Thereafter, as the stock of vehicles trebled, the tendency toward intensive development accelerated. Through the toll road initially, and subsequently under the auspices of the Federal Interstate Highway Act of 1956, a system of nationwide superhighways emerged. These multiple-lane, limited-access roadways were designed for high-speed, nonstop driving. Initially, they more than redressed the technical imbalance caused by the evolution of bigger and more powerful vehicles and longer-distance traffic. But under the pressure of increasing utilization in high-density areas, even such advanced highway design could not eliminate congestion. Nor could improved physical facilities alter the increasingly persuasive arguments against the social costs of vehicle emissions. Yet as attention rightly turns to rapid transit schemes, rehabilitation of railways in densely populated urban corridors, and devices to render the automobile less noxious, the extent and positive aspects of American highway development should not be lost sight of. There are now more than 2 million miles of surfaced highway in the United States, of which a substantial proportion are first class. Mass mobility and an end to rural America have been their irreversible consequences.

The rapid increase in highway construction emerges even more strikingly in contrast with the performance of railroad investment. Maintained at the beginning of the twentieth century by intensive investment in electrification, freight yards, line improvement, and equipment, railroad gross capital formation flagged after 1916. Extension of mileage had reached its natural limit, and the slowing rate of output growth made investment in further improvement less attractive. The Transportation Act of 1920, had it been implemented, might have helped. It was designed to promote increased efficiency through consolidation, while retaining competition. The inconsistent charges and divergent interests of wear and strong lines, long- and short-distance shippers, and poorly and well-served regions, made the task of the ICC an impossible one. Thus unassisted, the railroads entered into precarious maturity during the decade of the 1920s. Rates of return never reached the prescribed 6 percent "fair" return. Passenger output declined by 30 percent between 1920 and 1929

[69] U.S. Bureau of the Census, *Historical Statistics . . . , op. cit.,* p. 458.
[70] Dearing, *op. cit.,* pp. 120–121.

under the pressure of motor-car competition, and freight increases compensated only to the extent of maintaining total output at a constant level.

The 1930s, as the investment data attest, saw an outright decline of railroads. Gross investment became minimal and did not even succeed in offsetting depreciation for many years. The simple replacement of capital required from the 1920s on an annual outlay of $500 million in 1929 prices. While highway extension and surfacing continued apace, the rail network was diminishing in both physical and financial dimensions. The net value of the capital stock was less in 1939 than in 1929, and 14,000 miles of track were abandoned. Railroads were beset simultaneously by an unprecedented reduction in the demand for transport services as a whole resulting from the Depression and increasingly effective competition emanating from the much larger stock of vehicles accumulated during the 1920s. For the first time trucks became a serious factor in intercity traffic. Although federal legislation could assist in the reorganization process that followed upon widespread railroad failure, like the earlier 1920 act, it did not secure consolidation of the industry. Whether even consolidation would have been enough to arrest the railroad decline is open to considerable doubt. The underlying technological efficiency of motor vehicles for short-haul and high-valued merchandise, the unprogressive cast of railway management, and the rail freight rate structure, stand out as persistent problems.

Nor, after the wartime surge in traffic and a brief rise in capital formation, did a more positive tendency assert itself. Despite complete reequipment with diesels, piggy-back transport of truck cargoes, and modern yard handling controls, among other innovations, the postwar investment data as a whole chronicle the continuing decline of the industry. A continuing inability to compete for high-valued, profitable traffic made average profits a dismally low proportion of capital as we shall see. Coupled with a large fixed debt from the past, these profits left precious little room for maneuver. It is not obvious whether merger and consolidation, which are finally being accomplished, will be able to reverse the decline. The best hope for rehabilitation seems to lie in a more integrated, consistent national policy encompassing all transport modes.

The contrast between the declining fortunes of railways and the ascendency of the highway is summarized in the rise of road construction expenditures as a fraction of total investment. By the 1920s, road improvement and extension had come to represent almost a tenth of capital formation. During the 1930s, the proportion rose sharply due to the decline in private investment. (This increase is somewhat overstated by the fact that aggregate gross investment does not include public construction.) Conversely, the emergency circumstances of the war restricted further expansion and reduced the ratio. By the beginning of the 1960s, which saw accelerated construction due to the stimulus of federal grants, highway construction had returned to its 1920s importance. Investment in highways over the postwar period proceeded far more rapidly than total capital formation, and this figure does not include considerable additional expenditure for maintenance and administration. The road system, amounting to more than 3 million miles in 1940, absorbed by that time half as much in the form of recurrent expenditures as was being spent for net extension. Maintenance requirements continued to grow, although their proportion declined to about a third of total capital outlays in the beginning of the 1960s, as investment returned to high levels. By any standard, still another form of transportation had established itself as a voracious consumer of resources.

Yet, construction and maintenance together are far from exhausting the tally. Highway transportation was unlike previous innovations, in which the fixed capital always greatly surpassed the investment in rolling stock. Purchases of automobiles and trucks exceeded in value the expenditures on construction by a factor of at least two in *every* year from 1912 through 1940.[71] The largest part of this expenditure was for consumption purposes. Under this impetus, the automobile industry rose from seventeenth in value added in 1909 to first in 1925. Americans bought more than 4 million cars and 800,000 trucks in 1929, and these levels were not greatly exceeded in the 1950s. Few innovations were so eagerly seized upon. The campaign slogan of Herbert Hoover in 1928 is revealing: "Two cars in every garage, a chicken in every pot." Demand for cars was sustained by increasing incomes, lower relative prices, and—possibly most important—the introduction of credit sales. Installment purchases accounted for more than two thirds of all sales in 1925.[72] The method itself was to be extended to all other consumer durables, and represented an essential element in creating a widespread market for initially costly, but durable items consumed over a number of years.

Aside from its direct production of 12.7 percent of the value of total manufactures in 1929, the automobile industry and vehicle operation contributed substantially to the industrial prosperity of the 1920s. They accounted for 20 percent of steel output and were the largest single source of demand for petroleum, rubber, plate glass, machine tools, nickel, and lead. In some instances, the linkages were nearly one for one: 90 percent of petroleum production was consumed, largely in the form of gasoline; 80 percent of the rubber; 75 percent of the plate glass.[73] During the 1920s, automobiles and the complex activities related to them were the dynamic factor in economic expansion.

Abetting these effects was the stimulus afforded to construction. Although the suburb did not originate with the automobile—it was rather the creation of rail lines entering urban areas—its rapid growth in the 1920s and thereafter was the product of and completely dependent upon a motor-car civilization. This may be seen by the startling disclosure in 1940 that 13 million persons, or virtually a tenth of the population, lived in suburbs without access to any public transportation.[74] Although the residential construction boom gave way to the Depression of the 1930s—having peaked earlier in 1925—the tendency toward suburbanization continued unchecked. Federal Housing Authority finance permitted additional new community development prior to the world

[71] U.S. Bureau of the Census, *Historical Statistics . . ., op. cit.*, p. 462.
[72] George Soule, *Prosperity Decade* (New York. Holt, Rinehart & Winston, 1947), p. 165.
[73] *Ibid.*, pp. 164–165; and John B. Rae, *The American Automobile* (Chicago: University of Chicago Press, 1965), p. 88.
[74] Rae, *op. cit.*, p. 220.

war, and afterward, as residential construction recovered, such housing became the symbol of middle-class affluence.

The automobile industry regained its earlier influence in the years immediately following the end of the war. One of the major reasons the oft-predicted postwar recession did not materialize was the boom in consumer durables. Between 1946 and 1950, such expenditures increased from a tenth of total personal consumption outlays to 15 percent. Purchases of automobiles and parts grew even more rapidly, from little more than 2 percent of consumption to 7 percent. The entire sector, including purchases of gasoline and oil, repairs, and so on, amounted by 1950 to more than 10 percent of consumption, and to almost as much of the economy as a whole.

After this surge, the sector did not retain its dynamic properties. Purchases of cars and parts stabilized to a level between 3 and 4 percent of total product annually throughout the 1950s and 1960s. Individual years showed variation around this level, but without serious cyclical implications. Total expenditures, because they were in part dependent upon the stock of vehicles, which continued to grow, were slightly more buoyant. By the end of the 1960s, they had expanded to 13 percent of consumption and 8 percent of all economic activity.[75] With a total of 90 million cars registered, or almost one for every two persons, the most favorable prognosis seems to be continued proportional advance based upon replacement of existing vehicles and population growth. The growth cycle of the industry has brought it to maturity.

The output record.   The preceding sections have pointed up the dramatic realignment of transport activity in the twentieth century. Table 13.19 chronicles the matter still more directly. From virtually unchallenged supremacy before World War I—coastwise and lake shipments being the exception—the railroad proportion of total freight movement had by the 1960s shrunk to less than 40 percent. More notable still, since 1948, railroad and water shipments have hardly increased while pipelines and intercity trucking have expanded at annual rates in excess of 5 and 8 percent, respectively. Even the total does not behave as it once did. Whereas through the beginning of the twentieth century, freight shipments grew much more rapidly than commodity output, they no longer did so in the 1950s and 1960s. Equality now seems to be the rule.

The passenger segment of the market exhibits even more rapid deterioration of the original modes. Railroads for intercity movement and electric railways for urban transit held undisputed sway in 1900. Soon after the introduction of the automobile in 1919, approximate parity between commercial and private passenger travel was established. Thereafter, the record was one of complete domination by the automobile. The railroad has not been alone in its demise. Intercity bus travel has shown little growth; indeed, it has declined in recent years, and the fate of local transit facilities has been equally pronounced.

These physical statistics clearly understate the emergence of motor trucking as a competitive factor. Since the revenue received per mile is greater by road

---

[75] U.S. Department of Commerce, *National Income and Product Accounts of the United States, 1929–1965,* supplement to *Survey of Current Business* (Washington: U.S. Government Printing Office, 1966).

TABLE 13.19
Transport output

Year	Railroad	Inland Waterway (Great Lakes included)	Pipeline	Intercity Truck[a]	Weighted Index[b] (1939 = 100)
Panel A. Freight Traffic (billions of ton-miles)					
1899	126	n.a.	n.a.	—	22
1909	219	n.a.	n.a.	—	38
1919	367	78[c]	7[c]	1	65
1929	450	98	31	10	87
1937	363	103	45	35	91
1948	641	162	120	116	200
1953	609	202	170	217	268
1963	644	234	253	336	361

Year	Railroad	Intercity Bus	Local Transit[d]	Domestic Airlines	Passenger Total[e]	Automobile Intercity
Panel B. Passenger Traffic (billions of passenger miles)						
1899	15	—	10	—	—	—
1909	29	—	20	—	—	—
1919	47	1	30	—	90	—
1929	31	7	38	—	409	—
1937	25	10	31	—	559	—
1948	41	33	46	6	801	—
1953	32	28	29	15	1088	576
1963	19	22	23	40	1638	766

[a] Includes private as well as common carriers.
[b] Ton-miles weighted by 1939 revenues per ton-mile.
[c] 1920.
[d] Revenue passengers assumed to travel an average of three miles, based upon 1939 revenue per passenger.
[e] Passenger motor vehicle miles multiplied by 25, estimated average number of passengers based upon Barger.

SOURCES: Data from Harold Barger, *Transportation Industries, 1899–1946* (New York: National Bureau of Economic Research, 1951); U.S. Bureau of the Census, *Historical Statistics ..., op. cit.*; and U.S. Bureau of the Census, *Statistical Abstract of the United States, 1967* (Washington: U.S. Government Printing Office, 1967).

than by rail, the shares in receipts give another dimension of the contest. By the mid-1960s, although railroads continued to transport twice as many ton-miles, the revenues of motor carriers and railroads were approximately the same.[76] On the passenger side, the outlays confirm the automobile's advantage. Consumers spent in 1969 more than $73 billion to purchase and nourish their private automobiles. They expended less than $3 billion on purchases of all other forms of land transportation, local and intercity combined. An additional $2 billion went for air travel, a mode of conveyance which has been an increasing factor in passenger transportation.[77] In recent years, airlines have been responsible for more than 5 percent of total intercity movement.

The decline of the railroad at the hands of the motor vehicle repeats many

[76] U.S. Bureau of the Census, *Statistical Abstract of the United States, 1967* (Washington: U.S. Government Printing Office, 1967), p. 552.
[77] *Survey of Current Business,* vol. 50 (July 1970), p. 28.

of the features of its own previous triumph at the expense of the canal. Passenger carriage was the first to be eroded in both instances; the freight diversion was more differentiated, high-valued manufactures moving to the newer mode, bulk commodities being retained by the older. The logical consequence of such market changes was rapidly increased investment in the new mode, as we have seen, and net decline in the old. However, the historical pattern differs in one important respect from the current contest. Whereas the canal was in unequivocal decline within 50 years of the introduction of the railway—only a few specialized waterways continuing in operation—the railroad remains, and is likely to remain, a general-purpose transporter. Over the last decade, the share of rail freight traffic has stabilized, and revenues have fallen at much slower rates.

Central to this result has been the fact that the technology of the truck does not dominate railroads in the same way that railroads surpassed canals. The same advantages of speed and flexibility of the newer mode exist, but their significance is much reduced. There are almost 200,000 miles of rail line covering the most important commercial routes; whereas canals were much more limited in extent when railroads were introduced. Moreover, the all-season capacity of rail versus water transport is not relevant in comparing road and rail alternatives.

The fact that railroads experienced competition from trucks only after reaching their full geographic extension has other implications. On the positive side, it has meant the capacity to utilize the resources generated by depreciation to introduce more modern equipment. Negatively, it has created problems of adjustment from a previous growth pattern to a situation in which output has not increased. Specifically, "featherbedding" requirements come to mind. On balance, the industry has managed surprisingly well over time to reduce its labor inputs and to improve the quality of its capital stock. Productivity in the sector has substantially and continuously increased since 1950. Output per manhour—capital stock has not changed much—has gone up at an annual rate of 6 percent, compared to a total for the private economy of only half as much.[78] Real freight rates have correspondingly declined. This is hardly the profile of a moribund sector which has exhausted its technical capacities.

Why, then, have railroads lost out to the truck? Spokesmen for the industry as early as the 1930s cited unfair competition as the principal cause.[79] Their complaints have been lodged against the implicit subsidy received by motor carriers: The railroad has provided its roadbed at private expense and must pay taxes upon it; the trucker receives the road at public expense and thereby obtains the advantages of reduced capital cost and general taxation financing. There is some merit to these assertions, but their general import is much exaggerated. State construction yields lower capital cost only to the extent that the state can obtain credit on a more favorable basis than private firms. (This is the same advantage the railroads themselves enjoyed during the period

---

[78] U.S. Bureau of the Census, *Statistical Abstract . . . , op. cit.,* p. 237.
[79] See Dearing, *op. cit.,* pp. 191–198, for a statement of the arguments.

of public assistance in the 1830s.) But since highways were constructed largely on a pay-as-you-go basis until the 1950s, the practical significance of the objection diminishes. The same is true of the property tax exemption, which is not a major matter.

Nor can the argument that trucks do not pay their own share of the capital costs be fully substantiated. The successful financial innovation that made highway construction proceed as rapidly as it did was the institution of user levies, principally in the form of gasoline taxes. The predominant share of capital expenditure was underwritten in this manner. Indeed, the early concern was that user revenues, because of their rapid growth, might be diverted to other purposes. Many states enacted constitutional amendments to prohibit such a possibility. Provided that fuel taxes, registrations, and other excises accurately measure capital consumption for different classes of vehicles, commercial truckers are accorded no advantage.

Recent studies based upon incremental costs seem to confirm that these excises do accurately reflect costs, the one exception being large diesel units. In these studies, the cost of facilities adequate for the lightest vehicles was first allocated evenly among all classes. Increments of cost—capital and current—were then charged against the appropriate type of larger truck. This method yielded implicit costs in 1964 of $31 per automobile, $462 per three-axle truck of 45,000 pound gross weight, and $1369 per five-axle diesel-powered unit of 66,000 pound gross weight. Actual taxes paid were $30, $466, and $923.[80] The advantages enjoyed by diesels stem from their relative fuel economy over gasoline engines and the fact that the principal revenues derive from fuel taxes. That there should be such correspondence in the other classes, despite the fact that fuel consumption is not a fully satisfactory proxy for either capital or maintenance costs, is both surprising and encouraging. But it should not deter efforts to find more appropriate taxes that better correspond to the relevant consumption of facilities. Such taxes could be based upon the distribution of weight, speed, and other factors that determine highway costs.

Thus user payments do roughly approximate costs except for long-haul shipments. These studies also reveal the inherent economies of scale that truckers legitimately obtain. Because highways are joint facilities shared by private automobiles and commercial truckers, some part of the overhead is paid by the former. Because the railroad right-of-way is exclusively utilized by the rail companies, full and incremental cost are identical. From the standpoint of efficient social policy, what is relevant is not total, but incremental resource utilization. It is better that trucks utilize a highway principally paid for by pleasure vehicles, if their user taxes cover the additional wear and tear, than that traffic be diverted to railroads requiring larger inputs of resources for shipments. It is exactly such joint use that has made the technology of the motor vehicle efficient and that permits it to compete effectively against the railroad.

Although no large artificial advantage has been created in favor of trucks, this does not mean that the division of traffic reflects the operation of market

[80] Cited in John B. Lansing, *Transportation and Economic Policy* (New York: Free Press, 1966), p. 252.

forces in an ideal manner. There is little doubt that substitution of motor vehicles has gone too far due to ICC regulation and administration of the present railroad rate structure.[81] This set of rates is based not upon relative costs, but upon discrimination according to the elasticity of demand. Low-valued, bulky commodities receive low rates because they cannot bear higher tariffs; manufactures, on the other hand, can afford to pay more—even if the service received is identical. This value-of-service rate-making process was perfectly rational as long as railroads were effectively monopolists in supplying that service; indeed, by increasing private profits, it accelerated the process of construction and the attendant social gains. But it is more difficult to defend now, particularly since motor carriers after 1935 adopted a similar structure—enabling them to meet exactly the price of the competition in the one part of the market in which they were interested.

Price discrimination is effective in maximizing the utilization of resources within the transport sector if the charge is greater than marginal cost and if commodities otherwise would not be shipped. But neither of these conditions is fulfilled in the case of some products for which railroad rates are kept artificially low. Moreover, what may be good for transportation may not be good in general. Departing from the rule that prices should reflect the costs of resource inputs means that distortions will occur in the rest of the economy. Too much of the subsidized, low-rate goods will be produced relative to high-value ones. A discriminatory rate structure is equivalent to an excise tax imposed upon the consumers of manufactures to cover transportation overhead expenses. The difference from an ordinary tax situation is that there is no equity or use principle to justify it. Moreover, given the lack of profitability of many rail carriers, the apparent justification of discrimination for its higher profits seems dubious. In fact, by limiting traffic to low-rate, high-cost commodities, discrimination has probably been partially responsible for the poor financial health of the sector.

A clear consequence of the higher railroad rates imposed upon manufactures has been large-scale erosion of the traffic by trucks through the 1950s. Truck costs and rates would be more efficient only within a range of about 100 miles, were they confronted with true rail costs.[82] This calculation takes into account considerations of time in transit and size of shipment. In fact, however, the *average* haul of common carrier truck cargoes in 1963 was 255 miles, because at equal rates longer-distance motor shipment is preferable to rail.[83] Thus we have an inefficient allocation of resources and responsibilities, and an explanation of the extensive diversion that has occurred.

In recent years, the rate differentials have narrowed, and with this change the position of railroads has ceased to deteriorate as rapidly as it did between 1945 and 1960. This is true even in the face of the continuing greater growth of manufactures, which favor highway delivery. In 1961, railroad carload

[81] John Meyer, M. Peck, W. Stenison, and C. Zwick, *The Economics of Competition in the Transportation Industries* (Cambridge, Mass.: Harvard University Press, 1959), chaps. 7 and 8.
[82] *Ibid.*, p. 190.
[83] *Commodity Transportation Survey*. Vol. 3 in *Census of Transportation: 1963* (Washington: U.S. Government Printing Office, 1966), Part III, p. 13.

revenues from the shipment of manufactures were 1.48 times out-of-pocket costs; for agricultural products they were 1.18; and for mineral products, only 1.06. Here we see clearly the value of the service rate structure. Compared to the 1952 differentials, however, these figures represent a distinct improvement. At the earlier date, the respective ratios are 1.85, 1.37, and 1.25.[84] While all revenues have thus declined relative to costs, those of manufactures have fallen more than those of either agricultural or mineral products.

This change has been associated with more permissive legislation governing ICC administration of the sector. The Transportation Act of 1958 directed that rates *not* be set to protect traffic from other modes, leaving open the possibility of greater competitiveness in future rate decisions. While the clear principle of traffic allocation according to efficiency seems to be accepted by all, the procedure of case-by-case analysis, the imprecision of accounting rather than economic cost concepts, and the necessity of taking into account the "objective of national transportation policy" leave the matter less clearly resolved than it should be. Now that increased attention is being paid to the hidden social costs of vehicular traffic, the need is even more pressing to formulate unequivocal legislation that will provide for a socially efficient satisfaction of transport requirements in the 1970s. It may be that the simple pattern of rise and fall of transport modes that has been characteristic of the past century and a half will be altered in the process.

SUMMARY

The themes of almost two centuries of transport expansion in the United States are few and bold. The basic force stimulating nineteenth-century investment in canals, railroads, and steamboats was that of geographic extension and specialization. In 1800, economic activity in the United States was concentrated east of the Appalachians, and there it was limited to margins of water access. A century later, a national market existed, the frontier had closed, and long-distance transportation of commodities from the site of production to that of consumption was common. This process of extension featured early competition among the diverse transport modes and the ultimate triumph of the railroad—a victory won by a flexibility of location and capacity that permitted it to supply the exponential growth of demand for facilities. The nineteenth century was well served by the choice. Rapid advances in technology permitted railroad productivity to increase at rates greater than those for other sectors, and real transport rates to decline correspondingly. Moreover, the initial provision of efficient access to market brought with it a large and calculable saving of resources. Through the nineteenth century, the social rate of return upon railroad investment from this source alone was of the order of 15 percent.

Yet the railroads themselves earned much less. Indeed, the returns in the 1870s and thereafter had reached such modest levels that every cyclical swing brought with it extensive receiverships and reorganizations. Despite these

[84] Lansing, *op. cit.*, p. 227.

results, it was under predominantly private auspices that the rail network was created. Only in the breaching of the Appalachian barrier, in the infancy of the technology in the 1830s, had public support been prominent—and even then, the canal was the more significant instrument of state transport policy.

Such an apparently mysterious operation of the market is explicable. In the first instance, during the period of rapid extension prior to the Civil War, the private profitability of investment was better than thereafter and served to encourage private investors. Equally relevant, the results after 1865 understate the gain achieved by investors as well as by individual enterprises. The distinction between the two entities is essential. Investors could and did purchase securities at discounts below par: Their expectation and objective were large capital gains after the completion of new projects and actual operation. While such investment was risky, the returns were high to compensate. Such risk showed up in overcapitalization of the enterprises and made the calculated profits relative to investment too small, perhaps by as much as a factor of a half. The effect of this private pursuit of gain was to get the job done, but probably at a higher cost to consumers of rail services, who had to pay the risk premium in their rates. Governmental guarantees might have been more efficient.

In addition to this mechanism for eliciting funds, another continuing characteristic of the American scene made for large-scale private interest in transportation improvement. That was the capacity to internalize the social gains derived from lower transport costs. Internalization occurred in a variety of ways. The most direct example was the instance of private investors in railroads who were simultaneously shippers of commodities and thereby realized additional profits in their diverse enterprises. For them the return on railroad investment was the sum of their shares of the railroad plus their incremental profits in their own undertakings. Another instance of internalization was the optimism so characteristic of most promotions that permitted them to reckon, frequently rashly, the gains from the additional traffic a project would engender. There is no historical counterpart to the simplistic investor of static economic theory who fails to reckon the chain of consequences set in motion by his actions. Both factors operated to assure abundant construction of facilities in the period of expanding demand before the Civil War. Afterward, particularly toward the end of the century, as corporate direction of the investment decision and internal financing became more prominent, the expansion of systems was motivated in parallel manner. For each railroad it was rational to expect increasing returns from extension, since each firm was typically operating with excess capacity and falling costs. When all expanded, the expected gain was diluted and the final results were less profitable than anticipated. While tendencies toward overconstruction thus existed, they were more modest than is often claimed.

This competition among the giant firms had the effect of continuing a process by which private initiative satisfied the need for facilities and occasionally, wastefully, satiated it. Other consequences of competition were rate wars and periodic attempts at pooling and other means of cooperation. None were very successful over long periods. Stability was obtained only after regulation by the ICC, a situation which illustrates how administrative control frequently operated to the benefit of the administered, and not necessarily and unequivocally in the public interest.

Regulation and public involvement are continuing features of twentieth-century development. The leading innovation of the modern period was the motor vehicle, and creation of improved highways was a totally public matter. The resources devoted to this mode of transportation did not approach their earlier relative significance. Yet, taken together with private consumption of automobile services, the total was actually higher. Americans became personally more mobile even as the demand for transport of goods grew at declining rates. Thus the modern transport sector has adopted a smaller role in fostering expansion of the productive system even while it has assumed much greater significance in consumption.

The redistribution of the population to suburban communities close to large market centers not only was dependent upon the motor car, but itself contributed to the diversion of freight traffic. Trucking evolved as a serious competitor to railroads first for shorter hauls and gradually for longer distance hauls. Such substitution was due to the inherent advantages of joint commercial use of highway capacity created primarily for pleasure use. It was combined with an efficient method of finance through fuel taxes. Canals gave way before railroads in part because there was no consumption component that could be taxed; motor trucking flourishes because there is. Such a scheme of taxation, and particularly its local allocation based on fuel consumption, also built in an inherent response mechanism of supply to demand. Diversion has now reached such a point that social efficiency seems to be ill served. The purpose of public regulation is to assure that externalities enter into private calculations. In this instance, however, administrative procedures have developed an independent life divorced from the necessities of an integrated national policy. The establishment in 1967 of a federal Department of Transportation is an encouraging move in the other direction.

The challenge of the past was to maximize investment in transport facilities to serve the continental requirements of the United States. It was met by an unprecedentedly large commitment of resources. Roads and rails span the nation. Private capital markets secured the expansion of railroads in the nineteenth century, and user taxes effected the construction of superhighways in the twentieth.

Public regulation has been less prominent in its allocation achievements. Obviously, in the presence of natural monopoly or even the ruinous competition of giants, the unfettered market will not function perfectly. But it is disturbing to note how administered price policies have served neither to distribute transport demand among alternative suppliers to maximize material gain nor to compensate for the welfare losses of congestion and pollution. Such current problems command our attention and imaginative response as urgently as did the first efforts of our forefathers two centuries ago to escape limitations of natural geography.

SUGGESTED READING

Chandler, A. D., Jr. (ed.). *Giant Enterprise: Ford, General Motors, and the American Automobile Industry.* New York: Harcourt Brace Jovanovich, Inc., 1964.

Dearing, Charles L. *American Highway Policy.* Washington: Brookings Institution, 1941.

Fishlow, Albert. *American Railroads and the Transformation of the Ante-Bellum Economy.* Cambridge, Mass.: Harvard University Press, 1965.

Fishlow, Albert. "Productivity and Technological Change in the Railroad Sector, 1840–1910." In *Output, Employment, and Productivity in the United States After 1800,* edited by Dorothy S. Brady. Studies in Income and Wealth, vol. 30. New York: National Bureau of Economic Research, 1966.

Fogel, Robert W. *Railroads and American Economic Growth.* Baltimore: Johns Hopkins, 1964.

Fogel, Robert W. *The Union Pacific Railroad: A Case in Premature Enterprise.* Baltimore: Johns Hopkins, 1960.

Goodrich, Carter (ed.). *Canals and American Economic Development.* New York: Columbia University Press, 1961.

Goodrich, Carter (ed.). *Government Promotion of American Canals and Railroads, 1800–1890.* New York: Columbia University Press, 1960.

Grodinsky, Julius. *Transcontinental Railway Strategy, 1869–1893.* Philadelphia: University of Pennsylvania Press, 1962.

Kirkland, Edward C. *Industry Comes of Age.* New York: Holt, Rinehart & Winston, 1961.

Lansing, John B. *Transportation and Economic Policy.* New York: Free Press, 1966.

Meyer, John, M. Peck, W. Stenison, and C. Zwick. *The Economics of Competition in the Transportation Industries.* Cambridge, Mass.: Harvard University Press, 1959.

Taylor, George R. *The Transportation Revolution.* New York: Holt, Rinehart & Winston, 1951.

Walters, A. A. *The Economics of Road User Charges,* World Bank Staff Occasional Paper no. 5. Baltimore: Johns Hopkins, 1968.

14
FOREIGN
TRADE

A rapidly growing nation usually enjoys a high rate of growth in both exports and imports and an increasing share of world trade. The volume of American exports grew tenfold between 1790 and 1860, and more than tenfold in the next century; and the U.S. share in world trade approximately tripled during the same period. This chapter asks how the economic development of the United States was affected by the existence and the evolution of world markets, and how it in turn affected American trade with other countries.

Rising exports may be considered a cause of economic growth, a sign of exploitation by foreigners which hinders growth, or simply a result of economic development which would have taken place in the same way even if there had been no trade. Similarly, rising imports can be thought of as a passive accompaniment to development, as a source of vital capital goods which could not have been produced domestically, or as a depressing influence on the growth of domestic industry.

Some of the possible relationships between trade and growth are more subtle or indirect, however. The effects of a change in an industry's output may be diffused throughout many other sectors, through purchases from other industries, the enhancement of the profitability of investments in various types of overhead capital, or the import of foreign factors of production. An example is the influence of railroad investment on other industries, mentioned in Chapter 13.

Even a direct influence may need the cooperation of some less obvious change in domestic or foreign conditions. If foreign demand were highly inelastic, an improvement in American productivity (a rise in the U.S. supply function) might not stimulate the growth of exports, as one might expect, but might result only in a decline of export prices. Despite these complexities, certain relationships between trade and development seem to predominate at particular times or for particular sectors of the economy, and we try in this chapter to identify them.

What benefit does any country, and particularly a new or small country, derive from trade ? There are two almost universal advantages : one, the gains from specialization in the products that a country is most suited to produce ; and the other, the gains from economies of scale.

The gains from specialization arise from the fact that no two countries have the same proportions of land and other natural resources, labor-force skills, accumulated capital, or even technological knowledge and experience. If there were no trade, each country would have to meet its own needs for all products, including those it was ill-suited to make. The crowded industrial country would have to use its precious land to grow food and raw materials, at a great cost in terms of the sacrifice of living space and the diversion of labor and capital to agriculture. The sparsely settled country, rich in land and resources, would have to divert labor and capital to the production of clothing, tools, and other manufactured products, however poor and expensive. The country with no metal ores would have to be content with wooden tools ; the country with a cool climate would have to do without tea, coffee, rice, and many fruits.

With the opening of trade, each country can specialize in what it produces best. The agricultural country can enjoy more manufactured goods by taking capital and labor out of manufacturing and turning them to agriculture, buying its manufactures from the country that is more suited to their production, while the manufacturing country enjoys more food by giving up food production and buying from the agricultural country.

The advantages of specialization via trade are often described in diagrams showing each country's production-possibility and indifference curves before and after trade. The production-possibility curves of Figure 14.1 tell us that the United States is much more suited to the production of wheat than of cloth, relative to the United Kingdom. However, the United States does produce cloth and the United Kingdom wheat if trade is not possible, because

FIGURE 14.1
Before trade

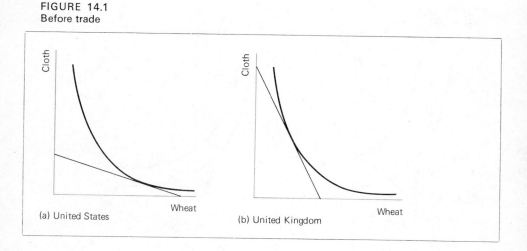

(a) United States

(b) United Kingdom

production is the only way to obtain these products, even though the cloth made in the United States entails a large sacrifice of wheat output and the wheat in the United Kingdom costs a large sacrifice of cloth output. The price of wheat, measured by the slope of the production-possibility curve, is low in the United States and high in the United Kingdom, while cloth prices are high in the United States and low in the United Kingdom.

After trade is opened up (Figure 14.2), the United States specializes in wheat and the United Kingdom in cloth, and the United States exports wheat to the United Kingdom in return for cloth. Both countries move to higher consumption levels (C_B instead of C_A) and the price of wheat rises in the United States and falls in the United Kingdom while cloth prices move in the opposite direction.

The second basis of trade benefits, economies of scale, is of particular importance to a small country. For manufactured products in particular, small-scale production is often inefficient. A small country isolated from the rest of the world, producing everything it needs, will inevitably be making many products in too small a volume for efficiency. If it could import these products, it would be free to concentrate on a smaller number of products which could be produced on an efficient scale. The country could then export these efficiently produced products in exchange for larger amounts of the goods that were formerly produced inefficiently at home.

These gains from trade produce economic growth in the sense of increases in productivity and in the standard of living. However, a larger part of past economic growth, if we measure growth by increases in a country's total real income rather than its income per capita, has come from the rise in inputs : increases in a country's cultivated land area, labor force, and capital stock.

The way in which the opening of trade can promote this type of growth can also be illustrated by Figures 14.1 and 14.2, particularly if we imagine the United States to be a small new country. If that were the case, the price ratio

FIGURE 14.2
After trade

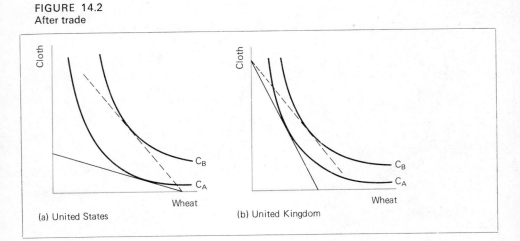

(a) United States

(b) United Kingdom

after trade would be close to that of the United Kingdom before trade, because the U.S. products would be too unimportant to affect prices in world markets. The wheat price would still be high and most of the gains from trade would be reaped by the Americans. In this situation, trade would induce growth in the United States not only by shifting existing U.S. resources from cloth to wheat, but by encouraging a migration of men and capital from other countries to the United States and bringing new land into cultivation to take advantage of the opportunity to produce wheat at low cost and sell it to foreign countries at high world prices.

Descriptions of the influence of trade on the economic growth of new countries can be arrayed between two extremes. One depicts export trade, arising from high or rising levels of foreign demand, as one of the main forces leading to rapid economic growth. The other holds that an undeveloped economy, exposed by trade to competition from more advanced countries, will be unable to develop economically and will be permanently condemned to be a supplier of raw materials and agricultural products to the countries that had a head start in development. A view between these two holds that the main forces leading to the growth of trade are the growth of resources, and therefore of domestic output, and the increase of productivity in the exporting country. The existence of foreign markets, in this intermediate view, may aid development by offering an alternative market to producers when home demand is low or by absorbing the sudden surges of production that occur in new industries, but the role is a secondary one and does not strongly affect the course of economic growth.

None of these theories is usually expressed in terms precise enough to encourage empirical testing. The theories that attribute favorable effects to trade imply long-run increases in supply in the developing country. They differ in that one interpretation emphasizes foreign demand as the force that precipitates the shifts in supply. This force can be either a rise in foreign demand or the existence of a large unfilled foreign demand at costs feasible for the new country. The other implies that the shifts in supply result from techno-logical developments that are independent of changes in demand or are responses to the growth in domestic demand in the developing country itself.

There is no reason to assume that either interpretation is applicable to all periods for the United States as a whole or to all sectors of the economy. We shall try to decide which explanation applies best to each important period and product. One criterion could be the level of, and the course of changes in, the proportion of production exported—that is, the export/output ratio. If foreign demand provided the main stimulus to the growth of the country we would expect that exports would account for a large fraction of production. If foreign demand were the main stimulus for an industry we would expect to find that most of that industry's production, at first, was sold abroad. Only after the industry was mature would it turn from exporting to production for the home market, and the export ratio would then tend to decline.

On the other hand, if an industry's export trade was a consequence, rather than a cause, of improvements in output and efficiency, we would expect to find that industries began producing entirely or mainly for the home market. Only gradually, as they reached a substantial level of sales and gained in productivity from economies of scale achieved in selling to the home market or from innovations or improvements in technique, would exports become important. The export ratio, in this case, would begin at a low level in the industry's early days and then show a rising trend as the industry's size increased.

THE INFLUENCE OF TRADE ON ECONOMIC DEVELOPMENT

Speculations on the Role of U.S. Exports

The potentiality for trade was often, in the New World, the motive for exploration and settlement. Some of the early explorations, such as those of the Portuguese, were aimed at breaking into the profitable trade of the Far East with Europe; others, particularly the Spanish, sought precious metals for export to Europe. The consequence of exploration, as related in Chapter 4, was the opening of new areas to settlement, once their characteristics and possibilities became known. The growth of the new colonies was not the result mainly of increases in the productivity of a fixed set of resources, but rather of increases in the supply of factors of production: newly discovered natural resources, newly cleared fertile land, and a new population of immigrants.

The relationship among costs, prices, and growth described earlier was implied in Adam Smith's discussion of the British government's policies toward colonial products. In explaining the exclusion of some products from the provisions of the Navigation Acts, he suggested that the British government was conscious of the advantages of extensive markets in permitting a greater rise in output than would be economical for an isolated country producing for its own subsistence. In the case of grain, for example, "By allowing them a very extensive market for it, the law encourages them to extend this culture much beyond the consumption of a thinly inhabited country, and thus to provide beforehand an ample subsistence for a continually increasing population. . . ." And in the case of timber, "By allowing the colonies a very extensive market for their lumber, the law endeavors to facilitate improvement by raising the price of a commodity which would otherwise be of little value. . . ." In almost the same words, he said of cattle "By allowing to American cattle . . . a very extensive market, the law endeavors to raise the value of a commodity of which the high price is very essential to improvement. . . ." Just as freedom to export raised prices for a product in the colonies and promoted its cultivation, limitations on exports reduced prices and obstructed economic development: "The prohibition of exporting from the colonies to any other country but Great Britain, masts, yards, and bowsprits, tar, pitch, and turpentine, naturally tended to lower the price of timber in the colonies, and consequently to increase the expense of clearing their lands, the principal obstacle to their improvement."[1]

Smith's argument called for promoting development by raising the prices obtained for export products. The purpose was, presumably, to encourage an increase in the colonies' factor endowment—through the clearing of additional land and, perhaps, through the encouragement to immigration that would come from higher incomes.

The rise in prices that encourages immigration and land clearing can be a result of the increase of foreign demand. The following sequence has been suggested for cotton production in the early nineteenth century: First, a rise in demand (from D_1 to D_2 and D_3) presses against an eventually inelastic supply (S_1), which is limited in the short run by the availability of cleared land (see Figure 14.3). The inelasticity of short-run supply drives up the price and makes the clearing of new land profitable. Once this takes place, supply is increased (to S_2) and the price falls back (see Figure 14.4). Nevertheless, the amount of resources in this industry has been permanently increased.

FIGURE 14.3

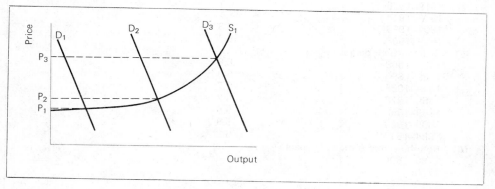

FIGURE 14.4

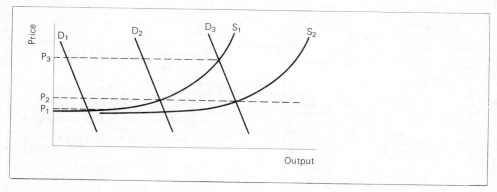

[1] Adam Smith, *The Wealth of Nations* (1776; reprinted, New York: Modern Library, 1937), Book 4, chap. 7.

U.S. Export/Output Ratios

The data for the United States as a whole suggest that export trade was not a major force in stimulating economic growth after the 1830s. From that time through the end of the nineteenth century, the ratio of exports to total output (GNP) never rose above 7 percent in any decade (Table 14.1). After 1900, it occasionally rose to higher levels, particularly during the two world wars, but

TABLE 14.1
U.S. exports as percent of GNP

		Current Dollars
(a)	Commerce GNP data	
	1964–1968	4.0
	1954–1963	4.1
(b)	Kuznets GNP data	
	1954–1963	4.6
	1944–1953	5.6
	1939–1948	6.5
	1929–1938	3.8
	1919–1928	6.1
	1909–1918	8.1
	1904–1913	6.3
	1899–1908	6.7
(c)	Gallman GNP data	
	1899–1908	6.8
	1889–1898	6.9
	1879–1888	6.7
	1869–1878	6.2
	1849–1858	5.6
	1839–1848	5.9
	1834–1843	6.2
(d)	Rough estimates for early years	
	1790–1800	10–15
	1770	15–20
	1710–1720	20–30

SOURCES

Row (a): Exports from various issues of U.S. Department of Commerce, *Overseas Business Reports*; GNP from *Survey of Current Business*, vols. 48 and 49 (July 1968 and July 1969), and from U.S. Department of Commerce, *National Income and Product Accounts of the United States, 1929–1965*, supplement to *Survey of Current Business* (Washington: U.S. Government Printing Office, 1966).

Rows (b) and (c): Simon Kuznets, "Quantitative Aspects of the Economic Growth of Nations: Level and Structure of Foreign Trade. X: Long-Term Trends," *Economic Development and Cultural Change*, vol. 15, no.2, (January 1967), Part II, pp. 113 and 114.

Row (d)
1790–1800: GNP figures are Gallman's 1840 estimate, roughly extrapolated back to 1790 using David's per capita GDP and population figures [Paul A. David, "The Growth of Real Product in the United States Before 1840, New Evidence, Controlled Conjecture," *Journal of Economic History*, vol. 27 (June 1967), Tables 3 and 8 and n. 69] and the Warren and Pearson wholesale price index [U.S. Bureau of the Census, *Historical Statistics of the United States*, Series E-1 (Washington: U.S. Government Printing Office, 1960), p. 115]. An alternative ratio was calculated from income estimates in George Rogers Taylor, "American Economic Growth before 1840: An Exploratory Essay," *Journal of Economic History*, vol. 24 (December 1964). Exports are from U.S. Bureau of the Census, *Historical Statistics of the United States, Colonial Times to 1957*, Series U-11 (Washington: U.S. Government Printing Office, 1960).

The estimates for earlier years are based on the data given in Gordon C. Bjork, "The Weaning of the American Economy: Independence, Market Changes, and Economic Development," *Journal of Economic History*, vol. 24 (December 1964), and "Stagnation and Growth in the American Economy, 1784–1792" (Ph.D. dissertation, University of Washington, 1963), on the colonial population and export tonnage information in U.S. Bureau of the Census, *Historical Statistics of the United States, Colonial Times to 1957*, Series Z-1 and Z-56–Z-75 (Washington: U.S. Government Printing Office, 1960), and on Gallman's calculations in Chapter 2 of this volume.

mainly fluctuated around 6–7 percent until the 1930s and 4–5 percent after World War II.

Part of the decline in export ratios after the 1920s was a consequence of price changes—a larger decline in prices of export goods than in the general price level. In quantity terms, the export ratio has remained virtually stable from the 1820s to the present. By any method of measurement, however, the role of exports appears to have been a fairly minor one, relative to total American output, throughout this century and a half.

For the period before the 1830s and 1840s, we can only speculate about the importance of exports from bits and pieces of statistical data. There is some indication that the export ratios of the 1820s were not very different from the later ones, but that exports were more important in the years before 1820. The ratios were probably between 10 and 15 percent in 1790 and 1800, according to the rough guesses shown in Table 14.1.

The export ratio was probably still higher in 1770 and earlier years. Between the early 1770s and the late 1780s, American exports did not grow substantially in value, while population increased by more than 50 percent and prices rose. The ratio of exports to output must have fallen by a considerable amount during those years—enough to suggest that it was probably at least 20 percent in 1770. The same reasoning applies to the quantity of exports, which hardly held its own, and even declined, while population grew. Therefore, the export quantity ratio must have fallen by at least a third. In other words, it must have been 50 percent higher in the early 1770s than it was in 1790.

Evidence for earlier periods is still more fragmentary, but points in the same direction—that is, that exports were more important relative to total output the further back one looks. Data on the tonnage of export shipments, for example, seem to point to a decline in the physical volume of exports per capita between the early eighteenth century and the 1760s. Tobacco exports to Great Britain, which accounted for about a quarter of the value of the colonies' exports in 1770, had fallen from about 150 pounds per capita in 1700 to less than 40 pounds per capita. In other words, the per capita value of tobacco exports in 1700, in 1770 prices, was almost as great as the value of all the colonies' 1770 exports combined. Thus, even if there had been no growth of per capita income from 1700 to 1770, and if there had been no exports in 1700 except tobacco, the export ratio in 1700, in 1770 prices, would have been as high as it was in 1770. If there were any other exports, or if there was any growth in real income, the earlier export ratio would have been higher. Since there is evidence of a considerable volume of trade other than what went to Great Britain in the early 1700s and of exports of products other than tobacco, such as rice, it seems safe to conclude that export ratios were higher at the beginning of the eighteenth century than in the late 1700s. A somewhat different set of calculations in Chapter 2 of this volume also suggests high export ratios in current dollars in the early part of the eighteenth century.

It seems safe to say, then, that export markets must have played a major role in stimulating American economic growth during the eighteenth century, particularly in the early years. This role was probably considerably larger than it was in the nineteenth-century development that is more frequently cited as an example of the favorable influence of export markets. The earlier experience is often ignored because the quantitative assessment is so uncertain.

The Role of Exports in Individual Industries

Export markets have been far more important to American farmers than to American industry. The ratio of agricultural exports to farm gross product was above 10 percent in all but a few (mainly wartime) years after 1879, and it was over 20 percent in almost half of these years (Table 14.2). These are much higher ratios than those for the economy as a whole given in Table 14.1. The peaks in the importance of exports to American agriculture did not come in

TABLE 14.2
U.S. agricultural exports as percent of agricultural gross product

Years	Percent
1964–1968	27
1954–1963	22
1944–1953	16
1939–1948	12
1929–1938	14
1919–1928	24
1909–1918	20
1904–1913	19
1899–1908	22
1889–1898	24
1879–1888	21
1869–1878	18
1870	12
1860	18
1850	13
1840	13
1830	11
1820	14
1810	11

SOURCES

1960–1968
Agricultural exports
    1967–1968: *Survey of Current Business*, vol. 50 (January 1970).
    1966: *Survey of Current Business*, vol. 49 (January 1969).
    1960–1965: *Business Statistics* (supplement to *Survey of Current Business*), 1967 ed.
Gross farm output
    1968: *Survey of Current Business*, vol. 50(January 1970).
    1964–1967: *Survey of Current Business*, vol. 48 (July 1968).
    1960–1963: *National Income and Product Accounts of the United States, 1929–1965, op. cit.*
1869–1960: Robert E. Lipsey, *Price and Quantity Trends in the Foreign Trade of the United States* (New York: National Bureau of Economic Research, 1963), Table G-14.
1810–1870
    Agricultural gross income: From Marvin W. Towne and Wayne D. Rasmussen, "Farm Gross Product and Gross Investment in the Nineteenth Century," in *Trends in the American Economy in the Nineteenth Century*, William N. Parker (ed.), Studies in Income and Wealth, vol. 24 (New York: National Bureau of Economic Research, 1960).
    Agricultural exports: From U. S. House of Representatives, *Domestic Exports, 1789–1883*, House Miscellaneous Document no. 2236, 48th Congress, 1st Session (1883–1884), compiled by C. H. Evans.

the early stages of American development, however, as is pointed out in Chapter 6. The highest sustained levels in the nineteenth century came in the 1890s, at a time when agriculture's importance in the economy had been declining for three quarters of a century or more (see Chapters 2 and 6). Similar, and even higher, levels were reached just after World War I and again in the 1960s.

Despite the declining importance of agriculture, the second half of the nineteenth century represented a climax in the development of American agriculture and the agricultural export trade. Farm productivity and output per capita grew more rapidly in the second half of the century than in the first, and per capita output reached levels it never attained in later years.

This rapid growth of farm output involved large expansions in the farming area of the United States; the land added to farms in the 50 years after 1850 was almost twice the 1850 acreage. Many of the great increases in farm production were associated with the migration of production to new areas. In the first half of the century, cotton production migrated from Georgia and South Carolina to Mississippi, Louisiana, Texas, and Arkansas. After 1850 the main shift was the migration of grain and meat production from the Atlantic states and the Ohio Valley to the states west of the Mississippi.

These migrations of production involved increases in the U.S. supply of agricultural products. At the same time, the supply of North American agricultural products, as seen from Europe, was increased further by a rapid decline in freight rates both within the United States and on shipments across the Atlantic. The causes and consequences of this fall in transport costs are discussed in Chapter 13.

Rapidly increasing U.S. production and falling prices, combined with the decline of transport costs, enabled American products to drive continental suppliers out of the British market for grains and meat during the years after the Civil War. Eventually the same transport-cost developments, as well as increases in U.S. domestic demand and the development of still newer producing areas such as Canada, Australia, and Argentina brought about a dethronement of the United States as the major supplier of agricultural products to Europe.

The question here, however, is not the influence of these supply changes on trade, but the role of trade in the supply changes. Is this role adequately described by the fact that 20 to 25 percent of farm output was exported? The significance of the foreign market in the nineteenth century was greatest during periods of rapid expansions in agricultural output. While the ratios of agricultural exports to agricultural gross product before the Civil War ranged between 10 and 17 percent, the growth of agricultural exports was more than a fifth of the increase in agricultural output between 1830 and 1860. Similarly, while the post-Civil War ratios of agricultural exports to output ranged between 20 and 25 percent, the increase in agricultural exports was about one third of the increase in output from 1870–1874 to the peak in 1895–1899. Thus, exports absorbed large proportions of increases in agricultural output when agricultural output was growing most rapidly. They sustained agricultural prices, which might otherwise have dropped sharply. In that way, they encouraged the flow of resources (both land and settlers) into new agricultural production. The flow might otherwise have been cut off at an earlier point if large price declines had made new settlement unattractive.

Some of these points can be seen more clearly in the history of individual commodities. Several products fall into the first of the categories mentioned— those initially oriented toward the export market and always mainly dependent on it. Tobacco, for example, was produced largely for export from an early stage in its development, with over two thirds of the crop being exported in 1800 and about three quarters in 1810. Cotton was the epitome of an export crop, 80 percent of the output being exported in the 1830s, when it first reached major importance. Even in the second half of the nineteenth century, when cotton and tobacco had long since declined in significance as parts of American agriculture, the export shares for these two crops remained over 50 percent.

Important as cotton and tobacco were, they accounted for only about a sixth of agricultural output in 1860. They were responsible for less than a fifth of the growth of agricultural exports between 1860 and 1890, although they had provided more than 80 percent of the growth in U.S. agricultural exports between 1800 and 1860. Many of the other agricultural products—even those that were important export items—fell into the second class described above. They began as essentially domestic products but became export goods as American production developed and became cheaper. In other words, they were products for which the export market was not the main impetus in the early stages of development. The course of the trade/output ratios of some of these other products, such as grains, was very different from those of cotton and tobacco. At no time did the grain export ratio reach 50 percent—domestic consumption was always the main destination of grain output. However, the export market did, at times, take a large fraction of increases in the output of grains : In the case of wheat, for example, almost 50 percent of the increase in output from 1869–1873 to 1894–1898 went into exports.

For some products, the export/output ratios are deceptive, because the output is sold to another domestic industry and processed before exporting. Exports of live animals were almost always a small fraction of farm output, but the export of meat products accounted for considerable proportions of the farm sales. In the case of pork products, for example, the rise in exports was at times over 50 percent of the addition to farm income from hogs, although exports never accounted for a high proportion of any year's output. Exports of the animals themselves were negligible.

Thus the situation for grains and meat products differed from that of cotton and tobacco, to judge from the lower export/output ratios and the fluctuations in these ratios. There was, probably, a steady increase in domestic demand with the growth of population and urbanization. Domestic demand was, however, inelastic. That is, a decline in price would not have produced a great increase in domestic food consumption ; and an increase in output, all thrown on the domestic market, would, therefore, have caused severe price declines. Foreign demand, at least in markets in which there were other suppliers to replace, was much more elastic. The United States could increase its sales abroad by replacing other foreign suppliers and did not have to rely on raising the consumption of foods by lowering prices.

Changes in supply were irregular, as in the case of cotton, and also involved large population movements to new farming areas. These population movements were, however, partly autonomous—that is, they were not simply a response to rising prices. If there had been no foreign market, but only the domestic market with its inelastic demand, a period of rising supply from new land settlement would have brought severe price declines.

The role of the foreign market is illustrated in Figures 14.5 and 14.6. In Figure 14.5 there is only a domestic market, with demand inelastic, although gradually increasing. A rise in supply therefore produces a sharp decline in prices. The foreign market, with its much more elastic demand for U.S. products (Figure 14.6), permits surges in U.S. output to be absorbed without such large price declines. In this case, P_2 is only slightly lower than P_1. The rise in supply in Figure 14.6 leads to only a small price decline but to a large shift from domestic sales into exports, with exports taking a larger fraction of the increment to output than of the initial output.

Aside from agriculture, primary industries that were important in exports at the beginning of the nineteenth century, and even more in the eighteenth century, were forestry and fisheries. Both were declining as export industries during the first half of the nineteenth century, and the fisheries had already declined considerably in the final years of the eighteenth. Products of the sea fell from 16 percent of exports in 1770 to 7 percent in 1803–1805 and 2

FIGURE 14.5
Domestic market only

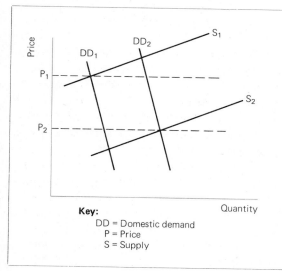

Key:
DD = Domestic demand
P = Price
S = Supply

FIGURE 14.6
Domestic and foreign markets

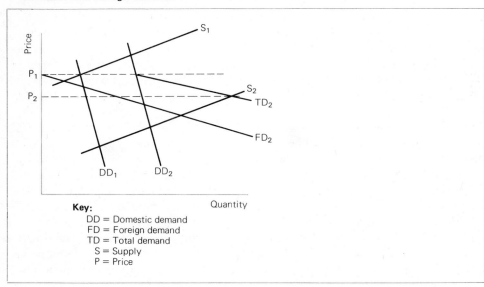

Key:
DD = Domestic demand
FD = Foreign demand
TD = Total demand
S = Supply
P = Price

percent in 1836–1845; and forest products, which accounted for 12 percent of the value of exports in 1770 and 1803–1805, declined to 5 percent in 1836–1845.

The export/output ratio for forestry was probably above 15 percent in the early 1800s. In the case of fishing, exports in the 10 or 15 years before the Civil War appeared to be well over a quarter of the total value of output, and the ratio must have been higher in earlier years. It might well have been a third or more, especially for the whale fisheries, in the 1770s. The importance of export markets thus seems to have been great in a wide range of primary products, including those derived from forestry and fishing as well as farming.

Even in 1869, before the peak in farm exports, the export ratio for agriculture was more than twice as great as the ratio for manufacturing. The few manufactured products that were exported reflected the richness of American resources, rather than American capabilities in processing them. The export ratio was inflated by the figure for food products, mainly grain and meat products, in which a high fraction of the value entering the final cost, over 80 percent, had been added in agriculture rather than in manufacturing.

The petroleum and coal products group, also highly dependent on a resource base, was the only manufacturing industry in which exports played a large role in the early stages of development. Exports accounted for more than half of output in 1869 and 1879, and the share remained above one quarter through 1914. In no other manufacturing industry, even those such as foods which were close to the primary production stage, did the ratios ever go above 15 percent. In 1869, 14 out of 18 manufacturing industries showed export ratios below 4 percent, and 10 out of 18 ratios were below 2 percent.

The proportion of manufactured goods exported increased after the 1880s, and was perhaps three times as high after World War II as in the last half of the nineteenth century. Some manufacturing industries—such as those producing tractors, certain types of machine tools, oil-field machinery and equipment, rubber-working machinery, industrial sewing machines, and certain types of instruments—came to rely heavily on foreign markets, selling a quarter or more of their output abroad during the 1960s. However, the development of these industries clearly did not depend heavily on the foreign market. Rather, these industries were based on the domestic market of the United States and reached such an advanced level in catering to that market that they became strong exporters. The effect of the existence of foreign markets in these cases was to permit the United States to reap additional gains from specialization, but not to stimulate the growth of new industries to any important degree.

In general, there seems to be strong evidence that the dominance of the export trade as a factor in U.S. growth was confined to agriculture and other primary industries. Within agriculture, exports played a major role in two different ways. In some products, particularly in the early decades, the foreign market was the main outlet and the main stimulus to the flow of resources and the growth of production. In others, especially in the second half of the nineteenth century, the foreign market eased the path of rapid growth in output by cushioning the effect of increased supply on price, an effect which we might expect to have been large in view of the presumably low price elasticities of domestic demand for agricultural products.

The role of imports in development is more difficult to quantify. The benefits to the standard of living may be far greater than is indicated by the ratio of imports to consumption. The gain from imports is the difference between their cost in resources used for exporting and the cost that would have been incurred if the same products had been produced at home. For an undeveloped and small country or colony importing mainly manufactured goods and tropical foods, the cost of home production might have been several times the cost of imports.

THE EFFECT OF ECONOMIC GROWTH ON TRADE

While the effect of trade on the rate and direction of economic growth is difficult to measure, the reverse effect, that of economic development on trade, is more obvious. Development, in the sense of the sheer increase in population and output (Chapters 2, 5, and 6), raises a country's ability to produce and export and changes the relative importance of domestic and foreign markets. However, development involves much more than an increase in size; it includes shifts in the composition and prices of productive resources and, consequently, in the kind of productive activity the country finds advantageous. It therefore alters the nature of the country's comparative advantage with respect to other countries and produces changes in the volume of trade, the share of total output devoted to trade, the composition of trade, and the terms at which a country buys and sells in international markets.

The Volume of Trade

It was not only the newness of the American colonies that made trade important for them; it was also the smallness of their population. In 1770, for example, the colonies consisted of about 2 million people. A country with a small population does not contain markets sufficiently large to enable its producers, particularly those producing manufactured products, to reach efficient scales of production by selling a wide range of products domestically. They can specialize in those simple products which do not require large output for efficient production or in those products they can produce so advantageously that they can find outlets for their production in other countries. Thus, the roles of import and export trade are related to the size of a country. A small country cannot sustain the manufacture of the consumption and investment goods it wants, except at an extremely high price. Foreign producers, taking advantage of their own large domestic markets or of markets outside their own countries, can enjoy economies of scale which reduce the cost and price of their products.

If economies of scale are important, we would expect that trade would account for a smaller share of output and consumption in large countries than in small ones because the large ones could achieve efficient production for the home market alone in a greater variety of products. Several studies of the ratio of trade to output in many countries show that this is indeed the case. If the relationship between size and trade had been the same in the nineteenth century as in recent years, the rise in U.S. population from 1790 to 1860 would have been sufficient to reduce the ratio of trade to output by a half in those years. The U.S. market of 1790, in other words, was not large enough to support many types of manufacturing at an efficient scale, and a large part of the consumption of manufactured products was therefore supplied by imports.

The classical belief that the economic development of a country reduces its dependence on foreign trade did not rely only on the effects of population growth. It arose rather from the expectation that industrialization, as it spread throughout the world, would reduce those differences in resource scarcities and skills between advanced and backward nations that were the basis for profitable exchange. Underlying the classical predictions of declining ratios of trade to output was the belief that international trade consisted mainly of the exchange of manufactured goods from the developed countries, which possessed large capital and labor resources but little land, for crude materials and foods from the undeveloped countries, in which labor and capital were scarce and expensive, but land was plentiful and cheap. The industrialization of the backward areas would eventually result in the diversion of their agricultural exports to domestic use and in the replacement of imported by domestically produced manufactured goods.

The basis for these expectations is related to classical theorizing regarding the future terms of trade between agricultural and manufactured products, discussed later in this chapter. It was expected that a rise in agricultural prices in the newer areas, as they matured, would destroy the basis for trade between old and new areas by "narrowing the gap of comparative advantage."

The ratio of exports to GNP in the United States (Table 14.1) was remarkably stable from the 1830s through the beginning of World War I, but fell in the 1920s and still further during the 1930s to little more than half its earlier level. A recovery after World War II left the ratio still below the pre-World War I level.

For U.S. imports there was more of a trend. The ratios of imports to GNP were between 5.7 and 6.7 percent throughout the nineteenth century, but there was a substantial drop in the early years of the twentieth. This was followed by an additional decline in the 1920s and a further one in the 1930s when imports were only half as large, relative to GNP, as they were in the nineteenth century. The recovery after World War II was considerably smaller than that on the export side.

It is clear, then, that over these 125 or so years, both exports and imports declined in value relative to total national output. The proportion of U.S. resources devoted to exporting was smaller in all the years after World War I than before.

If we examine the quantity, rather than the value of trade, and compare it to constant-dollar GNP, a very different picture emerges, however. Export ratios in constant dollars were as high in the 1920s and after World War II as they had been in the years before World War I and back as far as 1820 and 1830. Only in the earliest decades of the country's existence were the ratios higher. Thus the only downward trend in export quantities occurred at the earliest stages of national development, although the 1930s saw a considerable decline which, for a time, suggested a downward trend.

The course of the import ratio in real terms was also far different from that of the monetary values. The quantity of imports declined somewhat relative to GNP between the pre-Civil War period and the early twentieth century, but was comparatively high during the 1920s and 1930s, in contrast to the current values. After falling in the late 1930s and through the early postwar years, the import ratio began to rise steadily, approaching in recent years some of the highest levels of the years before the Civil War.

On the whole, then, the growth in the size of the American economy has not had strong effects on the importance of exports and imports, measured in constant prices, since the early 1800s. What appeared to be downward trends in the 1930s and the early postwar years now seem to have been only temporary shifts. However, the proportion of resources used for exports, described by the current-dollar figures, has declined.

The United States has been one of the world's fastest-growing countries, and the constancy of the trade ratio implies an equally high rate of growth in American trade. This constancy is, in a way, remarkable, because trade involved exporting to, and importing from, countries whose consumption and production were growing much more slowly than that of the United States. American exports were thus supplying a rising fraction of the world's consumption and American imports were absorbing a rising share of the world's production. The share of the United States in world trade approximately doubled during the nineteenth century and again in the first half of the twentieth. Until at least the 1880s, most of the American gains were at the expense of the countries of Eastern and Southern Europe. For the next 70 years, however, the large American gains, as well as those of other countries, were accompanied by a sharp fall in the share of industrial Europe, partly as a consequence of two devastating world wars of which Europe bore the heaviest burden.

To some extent, the difference between the two periods reflects the changing composition of American exports, discussed below. Until the late nineteenth century, the United States was mainly an agricultural exporter. Therefore, U.S. exports competed with those of the less developed countries of Europe, also primary-product producers and exporters, and with the agricultural sectors of the developed countries. As the composition of U.S. exports shifted toward manufactured products, U.S. competition began to be felt by the more developed countries and particularly by the manufacturing sectors of those countries.

The effect of a country's economic growth on its exports is not automatic; a new country must force its way into world markets in competition with older producers. If the newcomer attains any importance in international markets, it affects the prices at which it buys. The main impact presumably falls on the prices of its exports, however, since a country's exports are usually concentrated in fewer products than its imports. We would expect to find, therefore, that the growth in the U.S. share of world trade we have described was related to the terms on which the United States sold its products and bought supplies in the world market.

The Terms of Trade of the United States

A country pays for its imports by exporting its own products. The higher its revenues from exports, the more it can spend on imports. Export revenues depend on both the amount of a country's exports and the price it receives for each unit, while the amount of imports purchased with the export proceeds depends on the amount spent and the price of imports. Given the quantity of exports, the higher the export price, the greater the revenue. Given the amount spent for imports, the lower the import price, the greater the benefit from the expenditures.

Economists have frequently summarized these price relationships in the concept of the terms of trade (sometimes referred to as the "net barter terms of trade"), which is the ratio of the export price index to the import price index. It measures changes in the purchasing power of exports—in the quantity of imports purchased by each unit of exports.

We are accustomed to thinking of a rise in export prices relative to import prices as being beneficial to a country—and it is referred to as an "improvement" in the terms of trade. The country is able to buy more imports for any given amount of exports, and its real income is therefore increased.

If the rise in this price ratio results from a rise in the demand for a country's products, the improvement in the terms of trade is favorable. If, on the other hand, the increase in export prices reflects a rise in costs, resulting from lagging productivity relative to other countries, it may be an unfavorable omen. It may represent a deterioration in the country's ability to compete abroad, and although each unit of exports buys more imports than before, fewer units of exports can be sold.

It has been suggested by a number of writers that countries mainly dependent on primary products, such as farm products—that is, countries in an early stage of economic development—tend to suffer declining terms of trade in the long run. Several reasons have been suggested as to why such a decline is to be expected. One is that price elasticities of demand for agricultural products are low. Increases in world production are not easily absorbed by gains in consumption and therefore result in relatively large price declines. Furthermore, it has been said that income elasticities of demand for food are low, and food prices therefore are not lifted by increases in demand. In addition, it is said that agricultural products are sold in competitive markets and there is little opportunity for producers to exercise monopoly power to raise prices. In contrast, manufactured products are said to be subject to higher demand and income elasticities and to the raising of their prices through monopolistic market practices.

The evidence on this question has been drawn mainly from recent years or, at most, from data for the last century. However, we can examine the terms of trade of the United States over a period of about 200 years, covering the metamorphosis from a primitive economy exporting almost entirely primary products to the world's most highly developed economy, an exporter mainly of the most advanced and sophisticated industrial products.

This long view of the terms of trade of the United States is presented in Table 14.3. On the whole, the picture is one of long-term improvement—perhaps a doubling, or more. The timing of the changes is not what one might expect from a belief that long-term changes in the terms of trade have hurt primary producers. The greatest gains in U.S. terms of trade took place in the earliest years, particularly before 1850, when the United States was almost entirely an exporter of primary—largely agricultural—products. These remained predominant, although not as overwhelmingly, through the end of the nineteenth century, as a gradual rise in the terms of trade continued. In the twentieth century, when the United States has been mainly an exporter of manufactured goods, the terms of trade have improved little, if at all, aside from wide swings resulting from the two world wars and the depression of the 1930s. Within the history of the United States, therefore, we can find no evidence that being in an underdeveloped economic condition leads to an unfavorable evolution of a country's terms of trade. If there is any relationship, it has been in the opposite direction. Part of the explanation for these changes in terms of trade rests with the shifts in the relative importance and relative prices of agricultural and manufactured goods, as is explained in the next section.

TABLE 14.3
Terms of trade of the United States[a] (1913 = 100)

Period	Terms of Trade Index
1964–1968	111
1954–1963	103
1944–1953	113
1939–1948	130
1929–1938	130
1919–1928	111
1909–1918	108
1904–1913	99
1899–1908	97
1889–1898	90
1879–1888	97
1869–1878	87
1859–1868	80
1849–1858	90
1839–1848	77
1834–1843	83
1829–1838	79
1819–1828	65
1809–1818	60
1799–1808	66
1789–1798	58
1784–1792	51
1770–1775	39

[a] Export price index ÷ import price index.

SOURCES

1961–1968: Extrapolated from 1960 by export and import unit value indexes of the U.S. Department of Commerce, as published in various issues of *Overseas Business Reports* and earlier in the *World Trade Information Service*.
1879–1960: Lipsey, *op. cit.*, pp. 442–443, Table H-1.
1860–1878: Extrapolated from 1879 by the indexes in Matthew Simon, "The United States Balance of Payments, 1861–1900," in *Trends in the American Economy in the Nineteenth Century*, William N. Parker (ed.), Studies in Income and Wealth, vol. 24 (New York: National Bureau of Economic Research, 1960), pp. 650 and 652, Tables 6 and 7.
1790–1859: Extrapolated from 1860 by the indexes given in Douglass C. North, *The Economic Growth of the United States, 1790–1860* (Englewood Cliffs, N.J.: Prentice-Hall, 1961), pp. 221, 229, and 273.
1770–1789: Extrapolated from 1790 by index in Gordon C. Bjork, "The Weaning of the American Economy ...", *op. cit.*, p. 554.

The Composition of Trade

The composition of colonial trade was the result of two influences: the trade practices of the colonial powers and the natural endowments of the colonies—their scarcity of men and capital relative to natural resources.

The classical economists envisaged a world trading network based mainly on the exchange of manufactured products from developed countries for the crude materials and foods of the undeveloped countries. The basis for trade was that new or undeveloped regions had an abundance of land to be had for the asking (or without asking). The land had never been cultivated and was far more fertile than that of the parent countries which had long supported crowded populations. The new countries had abundant forests, such as had long since disappeared from Europe, untouched fishing grounds, and un-exploited minerals (see Chapter 4). On the other hand, they were short of labor (see Part II) and capital (see Part III), which their resource-poor mother countries possessed in abundance. It was therefore natural that resource products—such as agricultural, mineral, forest, and sea products—should be relatively cheap in the new countries, while manufactures, particularly those requiring much labor, skill, or capital, were relatively dear. The European countries, on the other hand, with abundant capital and labor relative to their resources, offered cheap manufactured products but expensive foods and raw materials. It was this difference in resource endowments that accounted for the difference in relative prices, or comparative advantage, shown in Figure 14.1, and it was the difference in relative prices of the two types of products that provided the opportunity for trade profitable to both regions.

It was not part of government policy, in the eighteenth century and earlier, to depend for these benefits on free trade in the world market. Governments were not only unsure of the workings of the market, but felt that they could improve on its results.

The policy of European colonial powers toward trade with their colonies was aimed at maximizing the power and income of the parent country rather than the combined income of parent and colony. To that end, the British government, for example, attempted to monopolize both the raw-material exports of her American colonies and the supply of manufactured products to them.[2] The purpose of the monopoly of raw-material exports from the colonies was, Adam Smith suggested, that "our merchants . . . would . . . be enabled to buy them cheaper in the Plantations, and consequently to sell them with a better profit at home." The purpose of the monopoly of supply was similar: to keep up both the share of the market and the prices at which British manufacturers could sell to the colonies.

The measures taken included prohibitions on the export of some com-modities to countries other than Great Britain, high tariffs on manufactured goods imported from the colonies combined with duty-free status for the same commodities in the crude stage, and in some cases complete prohibitions on manufacture or trade.

> While Great Britain encourages in America the manufacture of pig and bar iron, by exempting them from duties . . . she imposes an absolute prohibition upon the erection of steel furnaces and slit-mills in any of her American plantations. She will not suffer her colonists to work in those more refined manufactures even for their own consumption, but insists upon their purchasing of her merchants and manufacturers all goods of this kind. . . . She prohibits the exportation from one province to another . . . of hats, of wools, and woollen products, of the produce of America; a regulation which effec-tually prevents the establishment of any manufacture of such commodities for distant sale, and confines the industry of her colonists in this way to such coarse and house-hold manufactures, as a private family commonly makes for its own use.[3]

[2] "The policy of Great Britain . . . has always been to secure to herself the carriage of the produce of her colonies, to monopolize their raw materials, and to furnish the Colonists with all the manufactures or other imported articles they consume." Smith, *op. cit.*, Book 4, chap. 7.

[3] *Ibid*. See the appraisal of the consequences of British navigation policy in Chapter 17 of this volume.

The pattern of American trade conformed well to this picture of the desirable relationship between a colony and a mother country, in which a colony would export foods, crude materials, and semimanufactures, but not finished manufactures, and would import finished manufactures from the parent country.

In 1770, for example, the colonies exported virtually no finished manufactures, at most less than 1 percent of total exports. The main manufactured items they did export were spermaceti and tallow candles and soap, all closely related to the richness of the colonies' natural resources and dependent mainly on the existence of the fishing industry rather than on any particular advantage in manufacturing.

Even 50 years later, when the United States had been independent for more than 40 years, exports of finished manufactures had risen to only 6 percent of the total. Among imports, on the other hand, finished manufactures were, at this point, more than half the total value (Table 14.4).

On the whole, the colonial and early U.S. trade seemed to fit the pattern implied by mercantilist policy, even after the United States became independent. British regulations apparently had not, up to that point, prevented the colonies from specializing according to their comparative advantage. They had abundant land, the sea, and the forest, while labor and capital were scarce. They therefore specialized in resource-intensive products—products demanding large natural-resource inputs—and the persistence of this pattern

TABLE 14.4
Share of finished manufactures in U.S. exports and imports (percent)

Period	Exports	Imports
1964–1968	60.2	45.1
1954–1963	59.4	30.7
1944–1953	59.9	18.6
1939–1948	62.3	17.7
1929–1938	45.6	22.2
1919–1928	37.7	18.8
1909–1918	33.3	17.7
1904–1913	27.0	21.4
1899–1908	23.3	22.4
1889–1898	16.1	24.8
1879–1888	14.1	28.3
1869–1878	15.9	34.6
1859–1868	15.7	43.5
1850–1858	12.6	47.2
1850	12.6	54.6
1840	9.8	44.9
1830	8.5	57.1
1820–1821	5.8	56.4
1770	.8	n.a.

SOURCES: U.S. Bureau of the Census, *Historical Statistics of the United States*, Series u-61, u-66, u-67, u-72, z-76; U.S. Department of Commerce, *Overseas Business Reports, op. cit.,* various issues. The 1770 data were allocated to commodity classes according to the classification used by the Census Bureau for later years.

for decades after independence suggests that it was not a product of trade restrictions.

Agricultural products were always the main resource-based export of the United States, but products of the forest and the sea were much more significant in 1770 than in later years, accounting for 28 percent of the value of exports. The increase of population and its spread into the Plains states shifted American comparative advantage from sea and forest products—the most resource intensive—to farm products, in which the labor and land content were greater. For the next 90 years, until the Civil War at least, agricultural products increased their share of exports, as first the sea and then the forest declined in importance. The share of agricultural products rose to more than 90 percent of the value of exports in the 40 years before the Civil War. Most of the gain in the agricultural share took place before 1815–1820, although there were slower gains after that.

Following the Civil War, agricultural exports lost some of their importance, but they continued to account for more than three quarters of total exports in most years until the early 1890s. After that, they began a long decline, falling to below 50 percent by the years just preceding World War I and regaining that level only once after the war.

To some extent the decline in agriculture's share of total exports merely reflects the shift in the domestic economy of the United States—the decline in the share of labor force and output accounted for by the agricultural sector (Chapters 2 and 6). However, the share of agricultural products in exports fell much more slowly during the nineteenth century than did the share of agriculture in output and labor force. During the first half of the century, in fact, the agricultural share in exports rose from 85 to over 90 percent. In the second half, despite the continued fall in the domestic importance of agriculture, the share of agricultural products in exports, considerably larger than the share in the domestic economy, remained almost unchanged, until the late 1890s, when it began to decline. Thus, there was a substantial shift toward foreign markets for farm products. The ratio of agricultural exports to farm gross product rose throughout the nineteenth century and reached a peak of 20 to 23 percent in 1880–1900, before a long and permanent decline.

In terms of our earlier description of comparative advantage, the internal development of the United States was reflected in a shift in its production-possibility curve (Figure 14.7) away from resource-based output (agriculture, forest products, and fishery products) toward skill-based and capital-based output (manufacturing), and thus toward a shape more like that of the United Kingdom in Figure 14.1. If there had been no change within Europe, and particularly within the United Kingdom, the result of American development would have been a decline in trade, or at least in the exchange of agricultural products for manufactures, between the United States and Europe. However, the European countries' economies were not stationary, and were, in fact, shifting in the same direction : toward even further specialization in manufacturing (Figure 14.8). Thus, on both sides of the Atlantic, changes in the production-possibility curve favored manufacturing. However,

FIGURE 14.7
U.S. production-possibility curves, colonial period and late nineteenth century

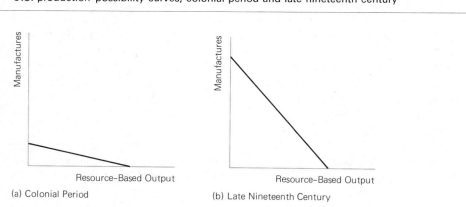

(a) Colonial Period   (b) Late Nineteenth Century

FIGURE 14.8
European production-possibility curves, colonial period and late nineteenth century

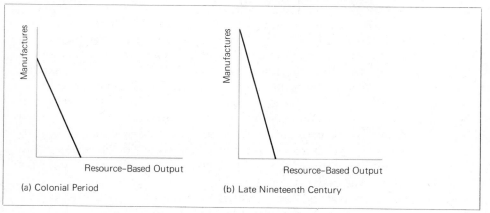

(a) Colonial Period   (b) Late Nineteenth Century

the comparative advantage of the United States vis-à-vis Europe continued to produce an exchange of European manufactured goods for American agricultural products, despite the rise of manufacturing in the United States. The effect of the continuing U.S. comparative advantage in agriculture was reinforced during the nineteenth century by a reduction in British protection of domestic agriculture. This added to the natural advantages of American farming by reducing the cost of American farm products, as compared with British products, to the British consumer.

The other side of this trend was a large growth in the share of finished manufactures in exports, although this had not by the late 1890s encroached substantially on the overwhelming share of agricultural products. After that, however, the growth of manufactured-product exports continued vigorously while that of agricultural products declined to the point that finished manufactures have accounted for close to 60 percent of U.S. exports since World War II (Table 14.4).

The rising share of finished manufactures in U.S. exports tells only a small part of the story of changing U.S. comparative advantage, because manufactured goods are an enormously varied collection of products. At one extreme are simple transformations of agricultural or mineral products, the main value of which consists of the raw material itself, such as the candles and spermaceti wax mentioned earlier, which were closely tied to the fishing industry. At the other end of the scale are complex machinery and scientific equipment in which the cost of the raw material is insignificant. American manufactured-goods exports have steadily shifted toward the latter group. One basic shift was away from products of animal or vegetable origin (such as most textiles) to those of mineral origin. Among the latter, petroleum and coal products, which are closely tied to the production of raw materials, have given way in large part to metal products. Furthermore, the composition of metal products has changed radically. Machinery and transport equipment, a third of all manufactured exports in 1913, accounted for two thirds in recent years. More than half of these products, such as electronic computers, telecommunications equipment, semiconductors, automobiles, and aircraft, were either unknown or of negligible importance in 1913.

What is the nature of the present American comparative advantage in trade implied by this list of exports? One explanation is that the U.S. comparative advantage is no longer in mass-produced, capital-intensive products, but is now in research-intensive products characterized by constant innovations, the production of which requires heavy expenditures on research and development and extensive employment of highly educated members of the labor force. Several studies have shown that the U.S. share of international trade tends to be high in such industries as aircraft, machinery, and drugs, in which scientists and engineers form a large proportion of those employed and research and development expenditures are high relative to sales.

Even within these industries, the comparative advantage of the United States seems to be in the newer products. In office machinery, for example, the United States exports electronic computers and parts, but imports the older product such as nonelectric typewriters and adding machines. Among machine tools, American companies export numerically controlled tools but import older, standard types from Europe. There are many examples in other industries, although there are also some cases in which innovations have appeared in other countries and resulted in American imports of new products.

Changes in the comparative advantage of the United States have been reflected not only in shifts among exports but also in import trade. The changes in the composition of imports were almost directly opposite to those in exports until recent years. The share of manufactures in imports declined from more than half in the early years of the nineteenth century to a little over a quarter in the late 1880s. Then it dropped fairly steadily, in peacetime, to under a fifth just after World War II. Since then, however, there has been a sharp reversal, and the share of manufactures in U.S. imports has more than doubled, reaching a half again in 1968 for the first time since the 1850s (Table 14.4 and underlying data).

Another way in which changes in comparative advantage were reflected in import trade was in the proportion of consumption supplied by imports. Just after the Civil War, foreign countries supplied almost 15 percent of U.S. consumption of manufactured goods (Table 14.5). As the United States advanced in its manufacturing capability, this proportion declined, falling to 6 percent before World War I. Most of the decline in import share came in the 30 years after 1870, during which the import share in consumption of manufactured goods was cut by more than half.

For several major industries, imports still accounted for high proportions of U.S. consumption in 1869—a third for paper products, more than a quarter for chemicals, and more than a fifth for textiles and nonferrous metal products. In the next 40 years, all of these ratios were cut sharply to 6 percent in paper products, 12 percent in chemicals, less than 10 percent in textiles, and 6 percent in nonferrous metals. Other examples are shown in Table 14.5.

TABLE 14.5
Relation of exports and imports to domestic production
and consumption, 1869, 1909, 1947

	Exports as Percent of Production			Imports as Percent of Consumption		
	1869	1909	1947	1869	1909	1947
Manufacturing, Total	3.7	5.2	6.6	14.0	5.9	2.2
Foods	7.8	6.9	5.1	19.8	9.5	3.8
Beverages	.8	.6	1.2	15.2	5.8	1.8
Tobacco products	3.1	1.4	2.7	5.3	3.0	.1
Textile products	.8	1.7	6.3	20.8	8.6	1.7
Leather products	.2	4.7	2.4	4.0	2.1	1.0
Rubber products	1.4	4.5	8.0	10.0	1.0	.1
Paper products	3.6	2.3	2.7	32.8	5.8	8.3
Printing and publishing	.4	.8	1.2	2.8	1.4	.1
Chemicals	9.7	9.0	8.2	26.8	11.8	2.5
Petroleum and coal products	99.3	30.0	8.4	0	.6	1.4
Stone, glass, and clay products	.6	1.3	5.5	11.7	5.5	1.1
Forest products	3.6	4.7	3.6	3.6	3.6	3.5
Iron and steel products	1.7	4.2	6.5	12.0	1.4	.2
Nonferrous metal products	1.7	9.3	4.4	20.1	9.2	5.2
Machinery	3.2	7.7	10.0	.9	.8	.3
Transportation equipment	.8	3.2	15.0	0	.8	.2
Miscellaneous	1.4	3.4	8.5	17.2	5.7	3.1
Agriculture	9.8	10.5	4.8	5.8	8.3	6.0
Fisheries	2.1	2.0	.2	1.1	4.8	15.3
Mining	3.5	4.2	8.6	2.1	7.3	6.0
Total	6.2	6.4	6.9	10.9	6.8	3.2

SOURCE: National Bureau of Economic Research, *Thirty-third Annual Report, 1953* (New York: National Bureau of Economic Research, 1953), p. 78. Data are from a compilation by Phyllis A. Wallace. Reprinted by permission of the publisher.

These declines in import shares suggest that part of the growth of U.S. manufacturing involved import substitution, either in the absolute sense of a replacement of imports by domestic production, with the level of imports declining, or in the relative sense of a decline in the import share without necessarily any fall in the level of imports.

There are at least two apparent cases of import substitution in the absolute sense in broad industry groups. Both appear to have resulted partly from restrictions on imports rather than solely from economic causes. One is a very large fall in the amount of imports of textile products before the Civil War. The domestic industry had grown rapidly under the protection of import restrictions during the Napoleonic Wars and particularly the War of 1812, and of the tariffs on cotton goods that were enacted afterward to protect the newly developed industry. Taussig concluded that it was the earlier period of war restriction, amounting to a complete cessation of trade for part of the time, that provided the main impetus to the domestic industry.[4]

Another case of an absolute decline in imports for a whole industry was that of iron and steel. From 1879 to 1899 the value of imports declined as domestic consumption more than doubled. However, import substitution in the absolute sense could not be considered to have played a major role in the growth of the industry, since the decline in imports was insignificant in relation to the growth of domestic production. In at least two important products, steel rails and tin plate, import substitution was spurred by major tariff changes. Two appraisals of the role of the tariff concluded that, while it hastened the growth of some parts of the industry, particularly tin plate, it was not a major influence in the long run for the industry as a whole.[5]

By World War I, and even more by the end of World War II, the scope of import substitution in manufacturing had been reduced almost to insignificance. The industries in which imports were as much as 3 percent of consumption were almost all resource-related ones—such as foods, forest products, paper products, and nonferrous metals—in which one might expect that comparative advantage was shifting away from the United States. Since the end of World War II, a number of industries have been pleading strongly for protection, not to increase their share of the U.S. market, but to slow the capture of the market by foreign producers.

A look at the type of industry demanding protection reveals the reason for the demand. Two of the industries most stridently demanding protection are the textile industry and the steel industry, both among the great growth industries of the nineteenth century but now in decline. Both have suffered losses of markets to new industries in the less developed countries, just as they inflicted such losses on British industry many years ago.

Relative Prices of Agricultural and Manufactured Products

As economic growth, described by the production-possibility curves of Figure 14.7, alters the composition of a country's production and trade, it also

---

[4] F. W. Taussig, *The Tariff History of the United States*, 8th ed. (New York: Putnams, 1931), chap. 1. See also the discussion of the cotton industry in Chapter 12 of this volume.

[5] *Ibid.*; and Peter Temin, *Iron and Steel in Nineteenth Century America* (Cambridge, Mass.: M.I.T. Press, 1964), pp. 209–214. See also the discussion of the tariff in Chapter 17 of this volume.

changes the relations among the prices of different kinds of products. The classical economists thought that the effect of development was easily predictable. Agricultural prices would tend to rise because any improvements in technique would be more than offset by the loss in productivity due to the increased ratio of population to the fixed supply of land. The prices of manufactures, on the other hand, would tend to fall relatively because increases in the scale of production and in the use of capital would raise productivity in manufacturing.

Exactly the opposite view has been popular in the last 20 years. Agricultural and other primary-goods prices are said to tend to decline, in the long run, relative to manufactured-goods prices, and such a decline is said to have characterized the world trading environment for the last 100 years. The theoretical reasoning behind this belief involves several different ideas, including the belief in low income and price elasticities for food mentioned earlier. Another basic idea underlying the theory is that the developed countries' demand for primary products not only is inelastic but has declined because synthetic replacements have been devised. A third is that monopolistic or oligopolistic pricing practices by firms in developed countries keep manufactured-goods prices high and thereby deprive the less developed countries of the benefits derived from productivity gains in the manufacturing industries of developed nations.

The price trends of U.S. exports seem to confirm the classical analysis rather than the later one. Prices of manufactured exports declined by almost half relative to U.S. agricultural export prices between the 1880s and the period after World War II (Table 14.6). The decline was not a steady one: Most of it took place from 1900 to 1913 and during the two world wars. Since the end of World War II, the direction of change has been reversed, with manufactured-goods prices rising relatively. However, the 90 years as a whole still show a large relative decline in prices of manufactures.

What caused this enormous change in price relationships? The major factor was the shift in the production-possibility curve in the direction expected by the classical economists, shown in Figure 14.7. It was a decline in agricultural productivity relative to manufacturing productivity (output per unit of labor and capital input), as described by Column (2) of Table 14.6. Agricultural productivity rose more slowly than manufacturing productivity during the 60 years or so from the 1880s to the 1940s. Since World War II, however, productivity has grown more rapidly in agriculture than in manufacturing.

These changes in rates of productivity increase have been reflected in relative prices. During the period when manufacturing productivity was rising more rapidly, until World War II, export prices of manufactured goods declined relative to those of agricultural products. Since World War II, as agricultural productivity has raced ahead of manufacturing productivity, export prices of manufactured products have risen in relative terms.

The price and productivity indexes have not moved completely in unison, and the divergences tell a separate story. When the relative price index in

TABLE 14.6
Relation between U.S. manufactured and agricultural product export
prices and productivity (1913 = 100)

Period	Manufactured Export Price Index as Percent of Agricultural Export Price Index (1)	Agricultural Productivity Index as Percent of Manufacturing Productivity Index[a] (2)
1964–1966	89.6	80.9
1954–1963	81.7	78.4
1944–1953	58.4	66.4
1939–1948	64.6	63.8
1929–1938	91.3	73.9
1919–1928	81.5	84.9[b]
1909–1918	93.7	109.1[b]
1904–1913	110.4	118.3[b]
1899–1908	126.8	123.1[b]
1889–1898	138.2	121.1[b]
1879–1888	142.1	136.6[c]

[a] Total factor productivity, including both labor and capital input.
[b] The labor productivity index was used to interpolate the total factor productivity index.
[c] Average of 1879 and 1889.

SOURCES

Prices: Lipsey, *op. cit.*, pp. 451–452. Table H-9, corrected and extrapolated to 1966 by data from the following sources: *Agricultural export prices:* agricultural export values from various issues of *Overseas Business Reports*; agricultural export quantities from Economic Research Service, U.S. Department of Agriculture, *Quantity Indexes of U.S. Agricultural Exports and Imports* (February 1969). *Manufactured export prices:* various issues of U.S. Department of Commerce, *Overseas Business Reports, op. cit.*

Productivity: Lipsey, *op. cit.*, pp. 421–422, Table G-7. These are data from John W. Kendrick, *Productivity Trends in the United States* (New York: National Bureau of Economic Research, 1961), put on a different base. They were corrected and extended to 1966 using data from a forthcoming NBER study by John Kendrick entitled *Postwar Productivity Trends in the United States, 1948–1969.*

Column (1) is lower than the relative productivity index, agricultural prices are higher than one would expect from productivity changes, and agricultural factors of production are being relatively well paid. When this price index is higher, it means that agricultural prices have fallen relatively, to an extent not explained by productivity changes, and that agricultural factors are suffering a period of low returns.

The index in Column (1) was particularly low during 1909–1918 when wartime demands drove agricultural prices up to high levels and produced a particularly prosperous period for American farmers. The index was high in 1889–1898 and 1929–1938, both periods during which agricultural prices were reduced far more sharply than industrial prices and agricultural incomes were therefore depressed.

The U.S. Share of World Trade

The rise in world trade of a new country, a new commodity, or a new supplier of a commodity is often accompanied by a decline in prices relative to established competitors. Price reductions are part of the mechanism by which technological advances or the opening of new lands to cultivation push a new entry into world trade.

Just as American cotton replaced cotton from Brazil and the West Indies in the early part of the nineteenth century, and American wheat drove Russian wheat from the British market at the end of that century, U.S. manufactured products, with relatively declining prices, competed for markets with the older industry of the developed countries, particularly the United Kingdom. The competition took place in the domestic market of the United States, where it took the form of the import substitution described earlier, and in the markets of many other nations.

One indication of the shift in U.S. comparative advantage toward manufactured goods was the growth in the U.S. share of world exports of these products. Between the late 1870s and the turn of the century, the American share almost doubled; and it virtually doubled again by 1929, rising more slowly after that to a peak in the 1950s (see Table 14.7). Even the 4 percent of world exports of manufactures accounted for by the United States in the late 1870s was a large advance over the share of five years earlier, to judge by comparisons with the United Kingdom and France. Relative to those two countries, the U.S. share of manufactured exports more than quadrupled in

TABLE 14.7
The U.S. share in world exports of manufactured goods

Period	Percent
1964–1968	15.9
1959–1963	17.7
1959	21.0
1957	25.3
1955	24.1
1950	26.6
1937	19.2
1929	20.4
1913[a]	13.0
1899[a]	11.7
1896–1900	7.0
1891–1895	4.7
1886–1890	4.1
1881–1885	4.2
1876–1880	4.0
1876–1880	6.9[b]
1871–1875	4.7[b]

[a] Excluding Netherlands.
[b] Percent of United States, United Kingdom, and France.

SOURCES

1959–1968: United Nations, *Monthly Bulletin of Statistics* (March 1965 and March 1970).

1899–1959: Alfred Maizels, *Industrial Growth and World Trade* (New York: Cambridge University Press, 1963), p. 189.

1871–1900: League of Nations, *Industrialization and Foreign Trade* (by Folke Hilgerdt) (Geneva: The League of Nations, 1945), pp. 157–158.

the 40 years before World War I. Even compared with Germany, the most rapidly advancing developed country in Europe, the U.S. share almost doubled between the 1890s and 1913.

The timing as well as the direction of gains in the U.S. share of world trade seem to have been related to price movements. In comparison with Great Britain, for example, there was little change in shares of world trade in manufactured goods between 1879 and the late 1880s, while U.S. and British prices moved together. Between the 1880s and 1913, however, the ratio of American to British export prices fell by almost a third, and the quantity of U.S. exports rose almost four times relative to that of U.K. exports.

The relationship between price changes and trade shares for textiles may have been even closer than that for manufactured products as a group. The major relative gains in U.S. exports took place between 1890 and the early 1900s and between 1907 and 1912, both periods of distinct declines in American prices relative to those of the United Kingdom. Shorter periods of relatively rising U.S. textile prices quickly reversed the main volume trend for short periods.

The peak in the U.S. share of exports of manufactured goods, approximately one quarter, was reached in the 1950s. Since then, the United States has lost ground steadily, at first to the European Economic Community countries and more recently to Japan. The U.S. losses were, in many cases, associated with relative increases in American prices, just as the U.S. gains in the nineteenth century were associated with relatively falling U.S. prices. The effect of price changes can be seen most clearly in the iron and steel industry. The United States lost its foreign market as a consequence of the relative rise in U.S. prices, and foreign steel began to be important once again in some sectors of the U.S. market. Japan, in particular, increased its share of world markets by price reductions, presumably reflecting large productivity gains.

The Trade Balance

A country's balance of trade (merchandise exports minus imports) and its current account as a whole (merchandise and service receipts minus payments) might be expected to pass through several stages as the economy advances. These changes in the current account partly reflect changes in the flow of foreign capital, whose role in financing American development is taken up in Part III. We are concerned here with the reverse relationship: the impact of U.S. development on the trade balance.

At the beginning of development, imports exceed exports. The newly developing country absorbs foreign capital because capital, being scarce, earns a higher return in the new country than in the old. As the new country builds up its capital stock in the course of economic development, the returns to new investment decline, and/or the supply of domestic capital increases to such a point that the country is running a trade surplus and repaying debt; and this stage leads, finally, into one in which the country begins to lend to others.

The main outlines of the trade balance of the United States can be seen in Table 14.8. The United States had negative trade balances (imports

TABLE 14.8
Balance of merchandise trade of the United States, 1790–1968

Period	Annual Average (millions of dollars)
1964–1968	+4039.
1954–1963	+4040.
1944–1953	+5527.
1939–1948	+5394.
1929–1938	+462.
1919–1929	+1380.
1909–1918	+1332.
1904–1913	+476.
1899–1908	+511.
1889–1898	+154.
1879–1888	+97.7
1869–1878	+.5
1859–1868	−63.6
1849–1858	−41.1
1839–1848	+.1
1829–1838	−14.6
1819–1828	−6.7
1809–1818	−20.8
1799–1808	−19.9
1790–1798	−10.2

SOURCES

1790–1860: Douglass C. North, "The United States Balance of Payments, 1790–1860," in *Trends in the American Economy in the Nineteenth Century*, William N. Parker (ed.), Studies in Income and Wealth, vol. 24 (New York: National Bureau of Economic Research, 1960), pp. 600, 605.

1861–1898: Matthew Simon, "The United States Balance of Payments,1861–1900," in *Trends in the American Economy in the Nineteenth Century*, William N. Parker (ed.), Studies in Income and Wealth, vol. 24 (New York: National Bureau of Economic Research, 1960), pp 699–705.

1899–1953: U.S. Bureau of the Census, *Historical Statistics of the United States, op. cit.*, Series U-14.

1954–1968: *Economic Report of the President Transmitted to the Congress, February, 1970* (Washington: U.S. Government Printing Office, 1970), p. 276.

exceeding exports) in almost every year before the 1870s, and then began to run a surplus in merchandise trade that has characterized the U.S. balance of trade ever since the 1880s, with few exceptions. The trade surplus was particularly high during the two world wars, but it remained high after World War II, relative to almost all previous periods, until the last year or two.

The commodity trade balance, although it is known to be more reliable than other measures of international transactions, is only a rough guide to the current account balance, and therefore to the amount of net borrowing or lending. This is because it omits many current expenditures and receipts, such as transport charges and earnings, interest on past lending, and tourist expenses and receipts. The net balance on the whole current account, however, changed in much the same way as the trade balance. It turned positive (current account receipts exceeded payments) in the 1870s. There were several years of negative balances after that until the late 1890s, after which the current account turned positive almost permanently.

The change in the position of the United States from a capital-poor to a capital-rich country can also be seen from the capital flows themselves which, together with specie (gold and silver) movements, are the obverse of the current account balance. The capital flows were a negative factor in the balance of payments—that is, capital was, on net balance, flowing to the United States until the 1890s. After that the United States became a net lender, as it has remained ever since. Although the United States became a source of capital for other countries at the end of the nineteenth century, it remained a net debtor, on account of past borrowing, until World War I, when wartime lending turned it into a net creditor.

American capital exporting has had one characteristic that has set it apart from the nineteenth-century capital importing by the United States and from most other countries' capital exports. Particularly in recent years, U.S. capital has tended to go into direct investment—that is, investment in foreign corporations owned or at least controlled by Americans or American companies, as contrasted with investment in financial assets such as corporate or government bonds or minority stockholdings which do not give control.

The characteristics of American investment suggest something about the nature of U.S. comparative advantage. The United States invests abroad in two main types of industries. One is the type of raw-material production which requires both large amounts of capital and the abundance of resources no longer found in the United States. The other is the type of manufacturing industry in which we said earlier the United States maintains an advantage over foreign firms : industries undergoing rapid technical transformation, industries with large research and development expenditures and high proportions of engineers and scientists in their labor force. The American advantage, then, seems to arise not only from the abundance of U.S capital but also from the extent of research and development, from the possession of certain types of managerial or organizational skills, and from the availability of human capital, as represented by comparatively high skill levels. While capital itself can be exported through lending to foreign countries, this combination of capital and talent is more typically exported by a capital movement within a single enterprise. The American-owned foreign firms resulting from this flow produce far more than the United States exports to foreign countries, and intrafirm shipments account for a substantial share of American exports and imports. One might say that direct investment has become the major element of U.S. international economic relations.

SUMMARY

We have asked two questions regarding the trade of the United States with other countries. One was about the way in which the existence of foreign markets and foreign sources of supply affected the speed and direction of American development. The second was about the way in which U.S. economic development affected American trading and investment relationships with the rest of the world.

The influences of trade on development seem to have been strongest in what are, from a statistical point of view, the almost prehistoric times before

U.S. independence. Large portions of the resource-based industries that attracted immigrants and capital from Europe were almost completely dependent on foreign markets for the sale of their products. Much of the consumption of manufactured goods, such as textiles and metal products, was supplied by Europe at costs far below the real cost of producing those products in the United States at that time. The availability of these imports, and of the ability to pay for them by exports, may have added substantially to the American standard of living and thus to the drawing power of the United States on European resources.

Since independence, the importance of trade has declined relative to total output, and with that decline, the possible influence on aggregate economic growth has waned. However, foreign markets do seem to have played a vital role in the expansion of the farming and settlement area of the United States throughout the nineteenth century. They performed this function by providing a comparatively elastic demand that permitted large expansions of American production without catastrophic price declines. A United States in isolation might have been prevented from rapid settlement of new territories and the corresponding production gains by the depressing effect of these production increases on farmers' incomes.

In the industrial sector it was difficult to see any instances in which export trade was a major factor in the expansion of U.S. production. Instead, imports of manufactured products were gradually replaced by American output. The American producers may, however, have drawn some advantage from the development of markets and channels of distribution which originally served the import trade.

The influence of economic development on trade was manifested in a number of ways. The American economy was, at first, characterized by an abundance of natural resources and a shortage of both labor and capital, and the concentration of American exports on resource-based products reflected this resource abundance. As the forests were cut and the population increased and moved away from the sea, the American comparative advantage shifted, first into agriculture, then into industry, and finally toward skill- and research-oriented industries. In each period, the composition of exports shifted toward the successive specialties while the composition of imports shifted away from them, sometimes toward the products that previously were exported. At first U.S. imports shifted away from manufactures, but they now have moved back to them as less research-oriented industries, such as iron and steel, textiles, and clothing, have become less suited to the American economic environment.

The influence of development also appeared in price trends, with manufactures becoming relatively cheap and agricultural products expensive, mainly as an outcome of productivity changes. These price trends conformed to the expectations of classical economics as to the long-run effects of economic development.

A further reflection of the direction of American development has been the growth of American-owned industries abroad, concentrating on capital-intensive resource industries and on the type of skill-intensive or research-intensive manufacturing industries that have accounted for a large part of exports in recent years.

SUGGESTED READING

Gruber, William, Dileep Mehta, and Raymond Vernon. "The R. & D. Factor in International Trade and International Investment of United States Industries." *Journal of Political Economy*, vol. 75 (February 1967).

Keesing, Donald, B. "The Impact of Research and Development on United States Trade." *Journal of Political Economy*, vol. 75 (February 1967).

Kindelberger, Charles P. *Foreign Trade and the National Economy.* New Haven: Yale University Press, 1962.

Kuznets, Simon. "Quantitative Aspects of the Economic Growth of Nations: Level and Structure of Foreign Trade." IX, Comparisons for Recent Years; X, Long-Term Trends. *Economic Development and Cultural Change*, vol. 13, no. 1, (October 1964), Part II and vol. 15, no. 2 (January 1967), Part II.

League of Nations, *Industrialization and Foreign Trade* (by Folke Hilgerdt). Geneva: The League of Nations 1945.

Lipsey, Robert E. *Price and Quantity Trends in the Foreign Trade of the United States.* New York: National Bureau of Economic Research, 1963.

Maizels, Alfred. *Industrial Growth and World Trade.* New York: Cambridge University Press for the National Institute of Economic and Social Research, 1963.

North, Douglass C. *The Economic Growth of the United States, 1790–1860.* Englewood Cliffs, N.J.: Prentice-Hall, 1961.

Pitkin, Timothy. *A Statistical View of the Commerce of the United States.* 1816. Reprint. New York: Kelley, 1967.

Williamson, Jeffrey G. *American Growth and the Balance of Payments, 1820–1913.* Chapel Hill: University of North Carolina Press, 1964.

15

INDUSTRIAL
LOCATION
AND URBAN
GROWTH

In 1790, the 24 cities of the United States sustained 5 percent of the population. By 1960, the 24 cities had grown to over 5000. These clustered within 162 metropolitanized areas harboring, barely but grimly, nearly 90 percent of the population.[1] In 1960, every metropolitanized area held 50,000 or more people; the largest city in the United States in 1790 was barely more than 30,000. Today several metropolitan areas each contain more people than did the whole of the United States at its first census. This chapter deals with just a few of the causes and consequences of this growth in the number of cities, the growth in the size of particular cities, and the growth in the proportion of the population on which they have clamped their hold, all of which were the not altogether undesirable by-products of the growth of the economy.

City growth is a manifestation of the way firms, households, and governments have chosen to distribute their growing stock of physical capital upon the landscape. Most of this chapter is devoted, therefore, to an abstract representation of how commercial firms which serve agriculture, builders of transport systems, and managers of industrial plants and the capital stock of the remainder of the service sector make their location decisions. This model generates some expectations about what the historical record should be like, and the chapter concludes by comparing these expectations and the pattern of settlement which actually resulted from these independent but interrelated location decisions. The chapter as a whole, then, details the interrelationships between national economic advance and the growth of cities.

The authors would like to thank Sam Nelson, Tom Tietenberg, and Susan Waisbren for their assistance, and Professors Ralph Andreano, Lance Davis, Nathan Rosenberg, and William Parker for their very constructive comments.
[1] Brian J. L. Berry with Peter G. Goheen and Harold Goldstein, *Metropolitan Area Definition: A Re-Evaluation of Concept and Statistical Practice* (rev.), Bureau of the Census Working Paper no. 28 (Washington: U.S. Government Printing Office, 1969), p. 19.

THE SYSTEM OF CITIES IN AMERICAN ECONOMIC GROWTH: A THEORETICAL OVERVIEW

The Network of Commercial Centers Serving Agriculture

At noon on April 22, 1889, to the urging of Cavalry pistol shots, 50,000 people and perhaps half as many horses and a quarter as many wagons stormed into a nearly empty rectangle of 1,900,000 acres of the Oklahoma territory in the last great land rush in the continental United States. Most of the participants planned to stake out a homestead and cultivate the land, but within hours a sizable tent city had been constructed and within months many thousands were working in permanent urban settlements which had already outgrown their initial boundaries. What were the underlying forces which generated a system of towns and villages, an urban labor force, and a network of roads connecting farms to villages, and villages with one another and with the cities in the surrounding states at the very same time that the land was being put to the plow? Let us examine these underlying forces and how they affect the size, spacing, and growth rates of urban centers in a newly settled area, of which Oklahoma was only the last in a long series.

Fundamentally, urban settlements arise out of the interaction of two factors: (a) Laborers specialize in narrow economic functions to get the most from their efforts, while (b) businessmen locate their establishments together to reduce transport costs and thereby maximize their profits. For both these reasons, then, there would be great cities, even if there were no rivers, waterfalls, harbors, mountains, or other natural characteristics such as are often cited to explain why cities are where they are.

Each farmer in the Oklahoma territory could have made periodic trips to Caldwell, Kansas or the other towns in the bordering states to buy his seed, cloth, stogies, and alcohol; but obviously each was better off because some individuals decided not to farm, but rather to specialize in acquiring goods from outside the territory and dispensing them to their neighbors from a general store. Similarly, each farmer in the territory could have tanned his leather, ground his corn, stitched his clothes, and shod his horses. But each of these functions was better left to a specialist, if only one were a reasonable distance away.

For someone to decide to specialize in one of these functions—blacksmithing, for example—it would have to be to his economic advantage to do so. More specifically, for a man to become a full-time blacksmith, he would have to expect to earn as much from one hour at the anvil as he would earn working an hour on the land.[2] Furthermore, a farmer would patronize the blacksmith only if it were cheaper than shoeing his horses or mending his pots and plow irons himself. Both of these conditions could be and were met in Oklahoma and every other area as they were opened by farmers to mass settlement.

---

[2] He would also have to earn as much from a dollar invested in his equipment as he would earn from a dollar spent on land, but to keep things simple, we will concentrate on the return to labor.

Specialization reduces costs in a variety of ways. First, it permits people of different physical attributes, talents, and tastes to concentrate on what suits them best. Secondly, the special and costly tools that are required for certain tasks can be kept in use a greater part of the time. Thirdly, the workmen do not have to waste time moving from one activity to another. Finally, the special knowledge and muscular control acquired from concentrating on a task— learning by doing, as it is sometimes called—reduces the time it takes to complete the business. Hence the specialist—in our example the blacksmith—may, if there is enough demand for his service, be able to offer the farmer a saving over doing the shoeing himself and yet still earn from an hour at the anvil at least what he could have earned from working an hour on the land. The farmer, furthermore, by concentrating on his farming rather than on blacksmithing, for which he has neither special skills nor tools, can also produce more each hour.

Typically, therefore, some farmers began to concentrate, at their farms, on particular nonfarming activities in addition to tending the farm. Some were wheelwrights for their neighbors; others, tool makers; still others, tailors; and so on. Sometimes, of course, the American farmer had previously been a European artisan. All over a newly settled territory appeared a few wheelwrights, a somewhat larger number of tailors, and an even larger number of tool makers, who gradually became primarily artisans and only secondarily farmers. To these were added artisans who came to farm, thought they would ply their trades for a short time to raise the cash they needed, but found themselves by necessity or by greater profit bound to them to the end. In addition, there were instances of craftsmen migrating to the frontier in anticipation of greater profits when and if a tide of farmers engulfed their areas.[3]

However, specialization does not come without cost. If workers specialize, then they must trade with one another for those goods they want but do not themselves produce. If there is trade, goods must be transported from seller to buyer, and transportation raises costs. When the farmer is taking his horse to the blacksmith he is foregoing the opportunity to do something else which would raise his income. The cost-saving advantages of specialization, therefore, must be sufficient to compensate the farmer for his travel as well as provide a saving on the task itself.

The savings from specialization on the one hand and the extra costs of transportation on the other interact to determine the number of specialists of each kind that there will be in an area. The cost reductions derived from specialization vary from activity to activity. While blacksmithing may offer significant cost savings from specialization, sewing, which uses only a meager amount of specialized equipment, probably does not. Similarly, transport costs vary substantially from commodity to commodity. For some goods, therefore, buyers will find it worthwhile to travel long distances to the specialists who provide them, while for other goods they will not be willing

---

[3] Angie Debo, *Prairie City: The Story of an American Community* (New York: A. A. Knopf, 1944), chaps. 1–4, tells a very similar story. The book is a fictionalized account of the growth of a small town in the Oklahoma territory from the very first days of the run. The author's careful research into the facts upon which she bases her account is outlined in the preface.

to travel as far. The distance individuals are willing to go for a particular good is called its *range*. Either because the gains from specialization are not very great or because transport costs per unit are high, some goods have a very short range, and hence are provided by a relatively large number of sellers who are fairly close to one another. Other goods have a very long range and are provided by a relatively small number of sellers with a greater distance between them. If we draw a line enclosing those customers of an establishment who are farthest from it, we will surround a space called the *market area* of the firm. Sellers of some commodities have larger market areas, while others have smaller ones. Market areas are small and the number of sellers large whenever an activity has one or more of the following characteristics: (*a*) savings from specialization are small (often implying small capital requirements); (*b*) transport costs per unit per mile are relatively high; (*c*) the commodity involved is difficult to store at home and must be purchased frequently. Over time, entrepreneurs will set up shops between the existing ones until eventually there will be just as many of each specialist as there are individuals who can raise their incomes by specializing. The market area of each specialist will then be as small as transport costs and specialization economies permit. This is, of course, an advantage to customers, since travel distances will be relatively short; but transport costs will not yet be as small as they should be, for the specialists are not yet optimally located, as we shall now explain.

Thus far we have discussed why there are specialists in nonagricultural activities in an argricultural area, why there are more of one kind of specialist than another, and hence why the average distance between customers and sellers will differ for different services. We have not explained, however, why sellers will locate together to form villages and towns. Nor have we explained which sellers will locate in any particular village.

Suppose there is a general store and farmers must visit it frequently. Obviously, if a blacksmith is located next to the store, a farmer requiring the smithy's services will be able to combine that trip with a trip to the store that had to be made anyway, thereby lowering his transport costs. The blacksmith located near the general store therefore has a competitive advantage over one that is not so located, and eventually the blacksmiths who stay in business will each be an easy distance from a general store. (This argument is symmetrical. The likelihood of the general store surviving competition is raised by the presence of the blacksmith. Historically, the juxtaposition of a general store, a grist mill, and the county seat assured a long and healthy life for a village.) What is true of the blacksmith is true of other specialists as well. Hence the general store becomes a focus around which other activities group. But the same activities will not group about each store, for reasons we have already explained. The market area of a general store is small, since among the large variety of goods it purveys, many must be purchased frequently. Hence from the very beginning there will be many general stores in any newly opened area. (Indeed, many of the wagons that rushed into the Oklahoma territory at the first pistol shot were equipped to function as general stores the instant they unhooked from their teams.) The smithy, however, is less frequently visited and people come to him from longer distances. Hence there will be fewer blacksmith shops than general stores. Shoemakers will appear even less frequently, but when they do appear they will also be in close proximity to a general store and perhaps a blacksmith because proximity still offers a saving in transport costs to the consumer. Obviously, then, towns and villages of different sizes are going to spring up in a region. In different countries and at different times, the functions performed in them will differ, but the largest cities will be larger because more different activities are performed in them. Located within them will be those activities which have the very largest market areas. In the United States in the late nineteenth century, these included such firms as the food wholesalers, marble works, silversmiths, and coffee shops, as well as all the more common businesses. Furthermore, many providers of the more common activities, such as retail groceries, will be larger and more numerous in the larger settlements, since visitors from the hinterland as well as from their immediate market area will occasionally shop in them. The smaller settlements will have only the more common functions. Finally, there may even be isolated general stores with no more than a church steeple and some barn roofs visible to the horizon.

A town, therefore, cannot be understood solely in terms of its own characteristics. The functions performed in any town are in part explained by those performed in the neighboring towns and villages. All the towns, villages, and cities taken together form a complete system, each with its place in the hierarchy of urban places serving a region. Furthermore, the towns in a region can be understood only when that region is viewed as a subsystem of an interdependent system of regions. Thus, in a real sense all the urban places in the United States together form a system of places, usually called "central places," interrelated by the interdependence of the economic functions undertaken within them.

A system of cities and a transport network generally develop at the same time, for they are interdependent elements. The number of central places and their spacing thus depend, in part, upon the prevailing transport technology at the time of settlement. As we shall soon see in detail, technological changes in transport drastically alter the system of settlements over time. Transport costs are hardly ever the same in every direction from any particular location. Before the advent of the railroad, where there were waterways and flat lands, as in the river valleys, transport was made easier and cheaper. One merchant could be many miles farther from a farmer than another, but if he and the farmer were located on the same waterway, he might be the preferred seller. Since transport by boat was cheaper than by wagon, locating along a waterway stretched out a seller's market area along that waterway. Hence those settlements that were at ports (inland or ocean) contained larger and more numerous firms and moved up the hierarchy of cities. The railroads and the highway system, when they came into being, had similar effects on the settlements located along them.

Since cities and transport must develop concurrently, with the transport system sometimes running ahead in anticipation of cities to come and with cities sometimes appearing in anticipation of extensions of the transport system, it is not very useful to ask which came first in a particular instance, or in general. Similarly, growing cities and growing agriculture go hand in hand in a newly settled region, and it is not very constructive to ask whether or not, in general, the farmers preceded the merchants in time or vice versa. Many cities started as isolated forts (Pittsburgh), fur-trading posts (St. Louis), or religious outposts (San Diego) in the wilderness far from any farm. It is also true that land developers who clustered in the wilderness towns advanced the growth of their regions by manning real estate offices, by advertising, by lobbying for transport improvements in the territorial legislatures and at the head offices of the railroads. The railroads, too, often brought agriculture into their market areas. But many cities, grandly designed and planted in the wilderness, remained unfulfilled dreams forever, or languished for decades until the agricultural frontier finally advanced to their locations. Sometimes the skill of an entrepreneur was decisive in making a city successful, while its competitor a short distance away grew not at all. However, with rare exceptions, in the eighteenth and nineteenth centuries, sustained urban growth had to be preceded by a successful agriculture. (Most of the exceptions were based at the outset on nearby timber or mineral deposits or on exceptionally good fishing.) Even the port city of Baltimore was barely more than a plantation landing dock until the 1760s, when a wheat-producing hinterland emerged.

We can conclude this discussion of the network of commercial centers serving agriculture in a newly settled region by pointing out the difficulty this view of urban growth poses for defining just what a city is. Commercial centers of the kind we have described here are usually referred to simply as *central places* by geographers. The juxtaposition of commerical and artisan activities, as we have described it, makes no reference whatever to any political boundaries which may be established. In this definition, the neighborhood shopping center and the residents that use it within any political jurisdiction called a city are no different in kind from the small towns surrounding that city. Once political jurisdictions are created, however, they can and will affect the distribution of functions among the central places, for city governments have the power to affect the most profitable location of an activity. Differences in zoning, property tax rates, and the provision of water, waste disposal, and fire and police protection will affect profits and, therefore, location decisions differently in different settlements. Perhaps most significantly, cities control transport routes through the layout of streets and differences in street sizes.

Industrialization and the City

A factory is a building in which material enters at one end (or at the top); is pushed, beaten, and struck upon; and emerges at the other end (or at the bottom) to be loaded on a truck or railroad car and moved somewhere else. That is, some stuff has to be assembled from one or more places, manipulated in one or more ways, and then shipped out again to one or more places. The art in locating a factory, then, is to locate the assembly point so that it minimizes the cost of the product at the market. For a particular product, cost at the market will differ between any two assembly locations because (*a*) one location may be nearer the source of the inputs, and/or nearer to the market; and/or (*b*) the things that have to be bought at the factory site (labor, fuel, land, and taxes) are cheaper at one site than at the other—or, more precisely, because of the sum consequence of these two sets of factors. Since a factory may employ thousands of workers who in turn must be served by hundreds of merchants and artisans, where factories locate affects the size of settlements in the system. The factory affects not only the size of the city, but the kinds of jobs, the amount of tax revenue, and the quality of air and water in it. We must, therefore, have some understanding of why manufacturing establishments locate where they do if we are to understand the economy of the city and the quality of life of urban residents.

Much can be learned from a very simple example. Consider the problem confronting an entrepreneur who wants to set up a plant at a location which makes it possible for him to sell bottled soda at the lowest possible price. There are three major components to a bottle of soda pop bought at a supermarket: syrup, water, and a bottle. The potential bottler knows of two cities in which the bottles as well as such inputs as heat, land, taxes, and water are all available at the same price. In city *A*, there is a plant which produces syrup, but there are also a large number of bottlers serving the city. In city *B*, while there are no syrup producers, there are also no bottlers, and hence the entrepreneur decides to sell bottled soda in city *B*. Where now should the bottler locate his plant? If he locates in city *A*, he will have easy access to syrup, but he will have to ship the bottled soda to city *B*. If he locates in city *B*, he will have to pay to have the syrup transported to his bottling plant. Since there is a direct road connecting the two cities, he can also locate somewhere along that road (line *AB* in Figures 15.1 through 15.6). As he considers roadside sites increasingly closer to city *B*, he is implicitly weighing the effect on his costs of transporting the syrup needed for a bottle of soda one mile farther while transporting the bottles of soda one mile less. Of course, it is going to prove cheaper to move the syrup than the bottled soda because less weight and less volume are involved, and therefore the bottler is going to locate at his market, but it is instructive to analyze the problem in more detail.

To see the possible solutions schematically, look first at Figure 15.1. The cost of shipping the syrup in a bottle of soda one mile is the slope of line

FIGURE 15.1

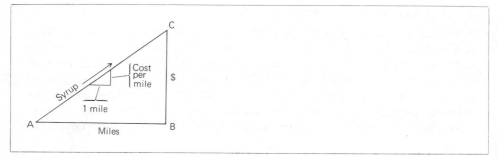

AC, and the cost of shipping a bottle to any point along *AB* can be read off line *AC*. If the entrepreneur locates at city *B*, the cost of shipping the syrup all the way to *B* will be *BC*. Figure 15.2 shows that if the firm locates at *A*, the cost of moving the bottled soda one mile is the slope of *BD*, and the cost of shipping all the way from *A* to *B* can be read at *D*. By superimposing these two diagrams (Figure 15.3), we get line *CD*, which is the cost of delivering a bottle of soda at *B* from any point along *AB*. The slope of the line *CD* reflects the cost saving, if any, of moving the plant one mile along *AB*. In Figure 15.3, the line *CD* has been drawn parallel to *AB*, implying that it is as costly to move a bottle of soda as it is to move only the syrup in it. If the firm were to locate at point *E*, for example, the cost would be *F*, the same as the cost associated with locating at *A* or *B* or indeed any point in between. Profits will thus be the same in the city or in the countryside adjacent to the transport route. By way of contrast, look at Figure 15.4. In this case, the smaller volume which makes the cost of shipping the concentrate much less than that of shipping the bottled soda is taken into account, so that the cost at *B* (which is *BC*) is much less than the cost at *A* (which is *AD*). Since point *C* is the lowest (i.e., cheapest) point on line *CD*, the most profitable location is at the market (*B*). It is no longer profitable to locate in the countryside or in city *A*. Figure 15.5 takes into account that the cost of shipping a product an additional mile decreases as mileage increases (e.g., a truck uses less gas once it reaches and maintains a

FIGURE 15.2

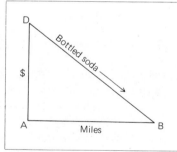

FIGURE 15.3

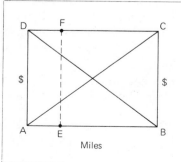

FIGURE 15.4

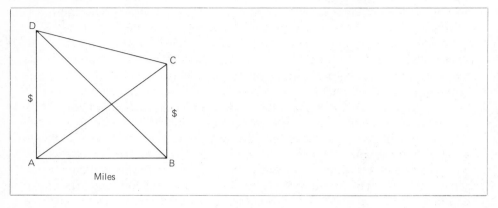

FIGURE 15.5

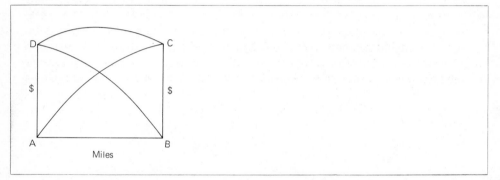

constant speed). If transport costs for each additional mile are the same for both syrup and bottles (as in Figure 15.3), then it is obvious that it is most profitable to locate in either city, but once again, it is not profitable to locate in the countryside.

Transportation costs can be thought of as the sum of two components. One component is the cost of moving a unit of the good one mile when it is already on the ultimate transport carrier. These are called "line-haul costs," and they are the costs we have been discussing thus far. There is also a cost associated with loading the product on the carrier—the costs, for example, that a railroad must charge for loading the product on a freight car, assembling the train, and then removing the product from the train at its destination. These costs are called "terminal costs," and they differ for different products and for different carriers. Suppose, for example, that terminal costs at *B* were higher than at *A*. Then we would have the situation shown in Figure 15.6. Since *C* is obviously the lowest-cost point, the firm should locate at the market.

These simple examples illustrate some of the ways in which transport costs exert pressure on firms to locate their plants where other economic activity

FIGURE 15.6

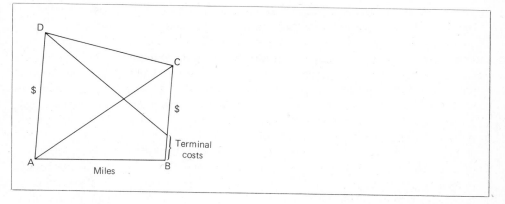

is already concentrated. The sources of both raw materials and semifabricated inputs as well as the markets for most producers will be in cities, and it is to these cities that the producers will be drawn by terminal costs, by differences in transport rates per ton-mile for different commodities, and by the tendency for the rates per ton-mile to fall as distance increases.

Transport costs are not the sole factor tending to produce manufacturing agglomerations. A second set of factors, somewhat different from transport costs but closely related to them, are economies of scale. Economies of scale exist when, as more of all inputs are used, output expands more than proportionally. Many activities exhibit such scale economies over some range of output, and that fact has considerable significance for the location of economic activity. Much manufacturing, public utilities, communications, and some services, such as insurance, banking, and advertising, are especially affected by scale economies.

It is important to distinguish among the many levels at which economies of scale can be manifested. They may accrue to the plant, the firm, the industry, or all firms in all industries in a city. Scale economies at the plant level arise from several sources. First, as output expands, the advantages of the specialization of labor (including specialization among the managers) can be captured. Second, there are technical sources of scale economies. As particular kinds of equipment become larger, their ability to produce output increases more rapidly than the raw materials required. The ability to heat or generate steam power or exert weight increases as the volume of the machine increases, while the raw material required to construct the machine increases only with the square of the sides. (And, of course, one workman may operate many a larger machine as readily as a small one.) Think of a boiler, whose output of steam depends upon its volume, or of a metal stamp, whose energy output depends upon its mass and the distance from drop to anvil. There also may be economies in marketing and finance, though these are also available to large firms with several small plants. Larger and hence better-known plants or firms may be more easily able to sell shares of stock and because of their larger inflow of cash may be able to borrow at more favorable rates. Finally, the larger plant or firm may achieve considerable economies in buying and selling. It is no more costly for a salesman to write a large order than a small one. Buying in carload lots generates economies to sellers, some of which will be passed on to the buyer. Therefore, shipping in larger lots in turn will yield economies, some of which can be passed on to the buyer. (The larger plant, of course, may also have monopoly power which can yield increased profits not based on cost savings at all.) Finally, as sales expand, inventories need not increase proportionately, and savings on storage and interest charges may be generated. There are, however, important diseconomies of scale in marketing which accrue to the single large plant. As output and sales expand, other things being equal, the market area must get larger, raising transport costs. The extra transport costs may eat up the economies of scale, making smaller dispersed plants more profitable than a single large plant. On the other hand, innovations which over time yield reductions in transport costs, *ceteris paribus*, will expand the market area of a single plant and increase the possibilities for greater centralization of productive activity.

The single large plant may make for a large city around it. Its several hundred workers, plus the hundreds of workers servicing its workers, plus the workers servicing those workers, and so on, plus the workers' families, could come to several thousand people. However, historically, large plants have been associated with small as well as large cities, while medium-sized cities tend to be associated with medium-sized plants highly concentrated in a single industry.

The process which generates towns dominated by a single industry seems to be something like the following: A large plant has many different kinds of activities going on within it. A large steel works at the beginning of the twentieth century contained several open-hearth and Bessemer converters at its heart, but also rolled rails, hoops, sheets, bars, and drawing wire. The mill also had a personnel recruitment and training department; purchasing, marketing, warehousing, and shipping departments; a research and development group; a typing pool; printing, carpentry, and machine shops; and perhaps a cafeteria, restaurant, drugstore, realtor, and bank. There are two key points to be made about the great diversity of activities that may take place in a factory. First, each of these activities is *not* subject to economies of scale at the same rate. Some, like the recruitment and training departments, exhaust their scale economies at relatively low levels of output. Other activities, like rolling bars and drawing wire, experience scale economies up to very high output levels; nevertheless, they peak at a level of output at which a complex of open-hearth furnaces has great economies of scale yet to exploit. Hence, as a great steel plant expands its output, it exhausts the scale economies available to it in successive activities and eventually, therefore, benefits from decentralizing. Thus, if recruitment and training exhaust their scale economies at 25 new workers a month, a plant that hires 100 new workers a month would prefer to get its workers from four technical training schools each operating at optimal scale, rather than to train the workers itself. Using its funds and personnel for training purposes involves it in activities in which it has no competitive advantage, and it would be more profitable for the competitive market to provide trained workers at the lowest feasible price, freeing the firm to devote its resources to those processes for which unit costs are still falling and the firm still has a comparative advantage. The firm will want to know what the schools are teaching and how competent their personnel are, and such knowledge is facilitated if the schools and the plant are in close proximity. What is true of training is true on a larger scale for bar-rolling and wire-drawing facilities. In short, as output expands in a plant, activities that went on within it are split off and come to stand alone, very often not only as separate establishments but as separate firms. Scale economies in a single open hearth, for example, are so great that a hearth can serve several rolling mills. These new facilities locate close at hand. This practice is obviously accelerated if two or more steel works locate in the same city because they get their raw materials from the same general location and share common market areas. The firms that specialize in training, rolling bars, and drawing wire can then draw from the several works. Furthermore the appearance of highly competitive firms specializing in training puddlers and other steel men, in furnace cleaning, and so on may attract other steel works to the city. The outcome is a steel town—a town in which the scale economies open to an industry are fully taken advantage of. What is true for steel is true for other industries—ship building, breweries, electrical machinery, textiles, boots and shoes, automobile assembly, and so on.

The process just described is called "vertical disintegration," and it is a substitute for a single large integrated plant because the savings realized by locating together—that is, localization economies—may in some instances be at least as great as within-plant scale economies. Where localization economies are exploited, average plant size will be smaller than where the plant performs all its functions within its own confines. Typically, also, where localization economies are exploited, the city will be relatively large, while when the plant is very large, the city in which it is located will be relatively small. This is most easily seen from the other side of the coin. Where there are a large number of producers in a single industry in a city, any plant can specialize and be relatively small. In a small city or an isolated location, the plant must do a great many things internally, for there is no input market on which it can draw, and hence it must be relatively large. Where markets are very large and dense, however, all plants can be much larger than otherwise, since the cost of transporting a given quantity of goods will be smaller. Very large plants are therefore located not only in small cities but in the very large ones.

The process of vertical disintegration with its accompanying localization economies is probably especially important in the early stages of an industry's growth. Since new industries often require new kinds and qualities of materials and equipment and their demands are too specialized and too uncertain to be met by producers of related products, they must produce these items themselves. Similarly, specialized labor will be trained by the new industry, and it must engage in wholesaling and retailing its output. It is only when the industry becomes established and output becomes sufficiently high and steady that vertical disintegration can be expected to occur.

However, once specialists appear, as vertical disintegration gets underway, they may find that their skills equip them to serve quite different industries. (See Chapter 12.) Thus, the first machine-making shops in the United States appeared in the textile firms of Lowell, Massachusetts and Manchester, New Hampshire in the 1820s. When railroads were introduced, these machine shops added the production of locomotives. By 1845, the Lowell Machine Shop was spun off from the textile mill. The great Baldwin Locomotive Works grew out of a shop devoted to textile-printing machinery. Turret-lathe, milling-machine, and precision-grinder producers grew out of firms originally meeting the requirements of gun or sewing-machine producers. Over time, these machine-producing firms became less specialized in their output, but more specialized in the processes they employed. The requirements of the different industries generated similar problems with similar solutions of which these firms were aware. Around these machine producers entirely new industries came to be grouped. Thus, vertical disintegration within an industry led, on more than one occasion, to many different industries locating together to obtain economies of scale from specialized producers who serviced them all. Such economies are called "urbanization economies." Less directly, the cafeteria, banking, printing, and real estate operations that have to be performed by large isolated plants are also best performed by specialists near a plant concentrating on other activities. The second key point, then, about the diverse activities that must be performed in the large isolated plant is that they give rise to a third kind of scale economy available in cities. If a manufacturing plant is located in the downtown area of a city, specialists performing the functions it requires which are so different from its primary tasks will abound. The transport terminals, such as ports and train stations, developed to service one industry or a small group of industries, which act as a lodestone to other industries, are the most important example of a facility offering urbanization economies.

Transport costs and agglomeration economies are two factors which affect the location of manufacturing activities, and in general they tend to push manufacturing establishments toward urban as opposed to rural locations. There is a third class of factors, however, which affect industrial location in a somewhat ambiguous way. The prices of land, labor, water, borrowed funds, and public services (taxes) vary between the city and hinterland, and these too affect the location decision. Cities, by definition, have a greater number of people and activities per acre than do rural areas. This increase in the demand for land relative to its supply raises its price per acre, even for a parcel which happens to be vacant. Vacant land within cities is scarce, however, so that assembling the large parcels necessary for modern factories often requires buying and then razing existing structures, which can be very expensive in money and time. For this reason, large horizontal plants may find it profitable to forego the advantages of urban locations. In general, however, compromise is possible, with heavily land-using plants locating at the edge of existing cities, thereby stretching the city out in an economic, if not a political sense. The trend toward the suburbanization of factories became very pronounced in the 1920s, was retarded by the Great Depression and World War II, and has accelerated since that time.

In general, labor costs per hour are higher in cities than in rural areas. There are many reasons for this. Perhaps the most important is that city workers must be compensated for the high costs associated with journeying to work. Rural areas also are less likely to be unionized (the costs of forming unions among dispersed workers are high) and are more likely to have under-employed secondary workers (farm wives and farmers taking industrial jobs in the winter who are willing to sacrifice some income for proximity to their place of primary employment). Skilled labor, however, is less expensive in the cities, since it is in greater supply because it benefits from the choice of employers which competition for its services provides. Manufacturing activities that can use predominantly unskilled workers and can operate seasonally, such as cotton textiles, hosiery, wood furniture, and meat slaughtering, have found rural areas the most profitable places in which to locate.

Clean water used to be available nearly everywhere. Streams into which manufacturing wastes could be dumped with impunity also used to be common. Now both are scarce resources affecting the location of such heavy users of clean water as the steel and chemical industries. Although it is too early to say, the need for usable water may lead to some dispersion of heavy industry into rural areas.

Tax rates are almost always higher in urban areas, but public services are also uniformly better in these areas. Since most municipal services are subject to scale economies, the cost per unit of government services may be less in most cities. But because governments finance their activities from general taxes, particularly property taxes, rather than from user charges, manufacturers must buy the whole bundle of available municipal services and not just the ones they need. A manufacturer not requiring some urban services may, therefore, also prefer a rural area.

The location of any particular manufacturing establishment, then, is the outcome of balancing a wide variety of factors. The place from which most of its inputs come and the place in which it sells most of its output are important constraints on its location. The nature of the inputs and outputs are also important. If a large part of the raw material does not find its way into the final product—as when coal is burned up, or ore is refined, or wheat is separated from chaff—then the manufacturer will be pulled toward its raw materials. Transport rates are also important if transport costs are higher for the final product than for the raw material because the former is more bulky or needs more careful handling then the latter, as is so often the case. In such a situation the manufacturer will be pulled toward its market. On the other hand, agglomeration economies or differences in factor prices may take the firm away from that location at which transport costs are at a minimum. Furthermore, all the factors affecting the optimal location for manufacturers change over time, so that while any building is virtually immobile, the distribution of manufacturing as a whole is constantly undergoing change.

Despite the large number of significant factors at work, the net outcome of the interaction of benefits and costs on the distribution of manufacturing between cities and rural areas is quite unambiguous. They have operated to stretch the city out in space, but they have also put most manufacturing into the cities. Indeed, as we shall soon see, American cities have come to be so large in land area and have absorbed such a large part of the population, that the rural–urban distinction is no longer economically meaningful. Even a large part of agriculture now takes place within cities, economically defined.

SOME EXPECTATIONS ABOUT THE HISTORICAL RECORD SUGGESTED BY THE THEORY

On the basis of the model outlined above, one would expect the size and spacing of cities to change over time as the three underlying forces which shape them change. As large land areas are brought under cultivation and as market areas change because innovations alter scale economies in production and the costs of transportation, the system of cities should be transformed.

As the lines of settlement moved from the East and West Coasts toward the Rockies, and from the southeast toward the southwest, new lands opened to mass settlement in large, relatively discrete blocks. In each block a new hierarchy of towns and villages emerged. These new subsystems were hooked in turn to the preexisting system at a few key points at the periphery of the older areas of settlement. These key nodes were thus expanded and gained in size relative to other, perhaps once-larger cities. Thus, the relatively large cities of 1790 (New York, Philadelphia, Boston, Baltimore, and Charleston) grew initially as part of the Western European system of cities, bound by law to trade with the mother country. New York began its rise to the top of the seaboard hierarchy toward the end of the colonial period because it hooked most readily into the richest inland area of settlement, the Hudson and Mohawk River Valleys. Albany, favored by its location near the junction of those two once-lovely rivers, acquired a favored position in this inland hierarchy. As the line of settlement moved westward (and as alternate transport routes came to dominate the waterway systems), Albany declined in relative importance. In the westward movement in the South, Lexington, Kentucky grew rapidly, only to be displaced by Louisville in the shift from land to river transport made possible by the steamboat. Agriculture finally spread west along the Ohio and south along the Mississippi in sufficient depth to turn New Orleans from a sleepy, malaria-ridden swamp town into a booming, vibrant, malaria-ridden city. And so it went, with the spread of settlements continually restructuring the hierarchy of commercial cities. That hierarchy received a new shock and was further reorganized with the coming of the urban factories, especially after 1860. However, before turning to that story, it is necessary to explain how technological changes in production and transportation affected the network of commercial centers.

In general, the trend of technological change has been to expand the level of output at which economies of scale are exhausted for commercial (as well as manufacturing) activities. As a consequence, the market areas of commercial activities have tended to become larger. This process has been abetted by the continuous filling in of the transport network and by the continuous improvement in the means of transport. Since individuals and goods could travel ever-greater distances in the same amount of time, some smaller settlements became redundant and disappeared. In general, the major rail lines were located close to the major water routes, and the major highways were then located close to the major railroads because it was cheapest to lay the rails and highways in the flat lands of the river basins. There were many places, however, where the new transport system diverged from its predecessor. Rail depots, in particular, appeared where there were no ports or landings, and sometimes no town at all. At these latter points new towns often arose. Some of these new towns and the older settlements which acquired railroad stations displaced old river landings in importance. More villages disappeared in this process. By 1900, the number of commercial settlements in the United States was probably declining and this decline was accelerated when the automobile once more restructured the hierarchy. The underlying factors affecting the system of cities did not change, however; only the force of their impact changed as the hierarchy was extended across the country, thinned in its number of levels, and was ever more tightly integrated by the technological advance of production and transportation.

Income and Population Effects

Rising income per capita and rising population are two additional dominant trends in American economic history which have affected urbanization. The importance of rising per capita income is that as income rises, a smaller proportion of it is spent on agricultural products. That fact, plus the rapid advance of technology in the agricultural sector, due in no small measure to the production of agricultural equipment in the cities, has meant that first the proportion and then the absolute number of workers on farms has declined, necessitating the movement of vast numbers of people from the rural areas to the cities, even though the cities have also reached out to embrace former farm lands. Rural–urban migration, plus the population growth due to immigration from abroad and the excess of births over deaths in the cities, provided the labor force without which urban expansion would have been literally impossible.

Effects of Manufacturing

The effects of the factory on the system of cities were many. In some cases the factories brought entirely new cities into existence, but most often large-scale manufacturing added to the labor demand in preexisting commercial centers, often drastically increasing the size of those cities as in-plant scale and localization economies were exploited. (National Cash Register in Dayton and General Electric in Schenectady are spectacular examples.)

A second and perhaps more important way in which manufacturing has affected the network of cities is through its effects on the various regions of the country and hence upon the several subsystems of the network. Some of these differential effects and their causes can be illustrated by considering the changes which have occurred over time in the location of the iron and steel industries.

When the iron industry began to expand in the United States in the 1830s after the adoption of the blast furnace, it took roughly 3 tons of anthracite coal to produce a single ton of pig iron, and it was obviously cheapest to locate the furnaces in the coal fields. Over time, several things happened. It was learned that turning the coal to coke would reduce the amount of coal required per ton of iron. Better grades of iron ore were discovered, and less impurities meant that less coal was needed. These factors made for less dependence upon coal, and thus the furnaces could be profitably located near some markets as well as at the coal sites. At the same time, in order to reduce the use of fuel, integrated iron works, consisting of furnaces, forges, and mills in which the iron could be kept continuously hot from ore to finished product, came into being. For this whole process perhaps 5 tons of coal were needed per ton of bar iron, and 10 tons of coal per ton of iron and steel finished goods. Coal clearly was of overwhelming importance for locating these integrated works and those firms for which iron and steel were the primary inputs. Technological change continued, however. The Bessemer and open-hearth furnaces drastically reduced fuel requirements for steel, which replaced iron as the primary ferrous metal. By the 1930s, 2 tons of fuel were required per ton of finished steel, and the industry was free to locate near either its ore sites or its markets. The effect was a shift away from Pittsburgh toward Chicago and Cleveland. Buffalo, Philadelphia, and Baltimore (Sparrows Point) also became feasible as sites to serve the eastern seaboard and the export markets, especially as Nova Scotia and Venezuelan ore deposits were opened to commercial exploitation. Further, scrap steel was for a long time a growing input into steel production, and scrap steel is available in the large urban markets. The pull toward markets became overwhelming. Because it could use relatively large quantities of scrap steel, and because it was sheltered from competition by high transmontane shipping costs from Chicago, even the West Coast, devoid of both high-quality ore and coal, has been able to develop a small steel industry. The pull of markets has not meant total elimination of steel capacity at the coal sites, however, in part because they are important markets. Other manufacturers needing steel were drawn to the coal sites by their own need for cheap fuel. Also, the presence of steel producers in part creates its own market, as heavy steel users are drawn to the furnaces and mills to save transport costs on their own major input.

A continuing series of technological innovations has reduced the amount of raw materials required per unit of output.[4] One consequence of this trend has been that manufacturing has decentralized and moved toward its markets, as steel has done. Furthermore, as in the case of steel on the West Coast, several regional markets have now grown large enough to support manufacturing activities subject to substantial scale economies (automobile assembly is a

4 See Chapter 7.

good example), further abetting the national decentralization of manufacturing and its drift toward its market. These decentralizing plants, while large, need not be as large as the largest in the industry, partly because, again like West Coast steel, they are sheltered by high transport costs from competition with the mammoth producers. For this reason, the factory has become more common in the smaller cities. The decline in raw-material requirements plus the substantial fall in transport costs have also made manufacturing more "footloose." That is, the profits of many manufacturers are now largely unaffected by location. The footloose firms have been free to choose their sites for their amenties. Factories can be located profitably where people are eager to live because of the availability of open space, recreational facilities, and pleasant weather. Indeed, workers will accept a lower money wage to be in such places. Since warm weather is preferred over cold, these footloose firms are locating to the advantage of those in the South and West.

The movement of manufacturing to the South and West has been further encouraged by the tendency for petroleum and natural gas to replace coal as the dominant organic fuel. That, plus the growth of the petrochemicals industry per se (including synthetic fibers) are additional major forces spreading the growth of cities into the South.

Manufacturing, then, has been a continuing factor causing differential rates of growth among the various regions and hence the various subsystems of the hierarchy of cities.

Effects of the Service Industries

By 1920, the growth of the service sector had become as important for the cities as the growth of manufacturing. The service industries include wholesale and retail trade, artisan activities, and real estate—the commercial activities that were the primary central-place activities brought into existence in the newly settled regions by the territorial advance of agriculture. Today their growth flows from the rate of natural increase of population in the cities and the growth of per capita income, but their locations are still dominated by accessibility to population; hence, they have moved from the city centers outward with the movement of residences within the cities. Their spacing continues to be determined by the interaction of scale economies in production and transport costs. The locations of some other rapidly growing areas of the service sector—the primary schools and junior colleges, for example—are determined by the same forces, although political considerations also enter. Other service industries must make their location decisions on a basis like that of manufacturing. Scale economies which accrue from expanding the size of a single production facility have been important in the concentrated location pattern of the communications industry. Some parts of the service sector—for example, insurance and finance and the complex of federal government activities in Washington, D.C.—benefit from localization economies. Key among these advantages is the availability of a pool of skilled labor. A rapidly expanding Defense Department in the early 1960s could quickly acquire qualified procurement personnel already approved by the Civil Service

Commission from the declining Agency for International Development. Others, such as the advertising–printing–television complexes of New York and Los Angeles, benefit substantially from urbanization economies. The primary resource of the rapidly growing outdoor recreation industries are natural amenities like warm weather and open space. The recreation industries have added to the growth of some large cities, but they also have promoted the growth of the smaller towns which are attractive precisely because they have remained far down in the hierarchy of commercial centers.

THE GROWTH OF AMERICAN CITIES

Figure 15.7 is a striking portrayal of the process of city growth in the United States between 1790 and 1950. The chart was constructed in the following way: In each of five years (1790, 1840, 1880, 1920, 1950), the cities were ranked by population size from the largest to the smallest. Each city's population was then plotted against its rank (i.e., in 1950, New York held rank 1, Chicago rank 2, etc.). This chart and Table 15.1 reveal the persistently staggering increase in the number of cities (from 24 to over 4000), and the phenomenal growth in size of the largest cities (from slightly under 100,000 people to somewhat under 10 million). It also shows that the relationship between size and rank was not disturbed by rapid growth, since the lines are

FIGURE 15.7
City size and rank in selected years, 1790–1950, logarithmic scale

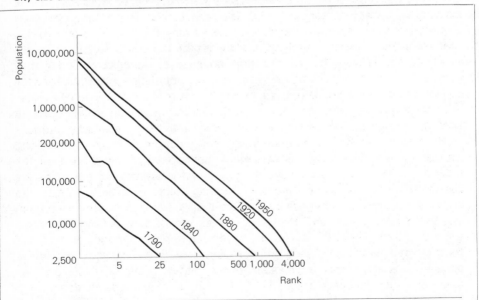

SOURCE: Adapted from C. H. Madden, "On Some Indications of Stability in the Growth of Cities in the United States," *Economic Development and Cultural Change*, vol. 4 (April 1956), p. 239.

nearly parallel. In any year, if we take the rank of any city and multiply it by its population, the result is a good approximation to the size of the largest city in that year. (This works better in the later years than it does in the earlier ones.) Though the system of cities grew from 24 urban places in 1790 to more than 4000 in 1950 (and the percentage of total population in cities grew from 5 to 60 percent), a regular relationship (linear in the logarithms) between a city's population and its rank in the hierarchy was maintained. This regularity

TABLE 15.1
Urban growth in the United States, 1790–1960,
old census definition (2500 or more)

Year	Number of Cities	Urban Population		
		Population (thousands)	Growth per Decade (percent)	Percent of Total Population
1790	24	202		5.1
			59.9	
1800	33	322		6.1
			63.0	
1810	46	525		7.2
			31.9	
1820	61	693		7.2
			62.6	
1830	90	1,127		8.8
			63.7	
1840	131	1,845		10.8
			92.1	
1850	236	3,544		15.3
			75.4	
1860	392	6,216		19.8
			59.3	
1870	663	9,902		25.7
			42.7	
1880	939	14,130		28.2
			56.5	
1890	1,348	22,106		35.1
			36.4	
1900	1,737	30,160		39.7
			39.3	
1910	2,262	41,999		45.7
			29.0	
1920	2,722	54,158		51.2
			27.3	
1930	3,165	68,955		56.2
			7.9	
1940	3,464	74,424		56.5
			20.6	
1950	4,054	89,749		59.6
			25.4	
1960	4,966	112,532		63.0

SOURCE: U.S. Bureau of the Census, *Census of Population: 1960*, vol. 1, *Characteristics of the Population* (Washington: U.S. Government Printing Office, 1961), Part A, pp. 1–14, 1–15, Table 8.

is in many ways quite surprising. The nation has not only created great metropolises which dwarf the cities of 1790, but it has continued to spawn colonial-sized cities. Indeed, cities have emerged in like proportion in every size class. There is no tendency toward a greater concentration of large cities, as might have reasonably been expected, though it is true that the cities cluster into great metropolitan areas and that there have been significant changes in the ranks of particular cities. (Since 1880, only New York among the nation's major cities has retained its rank over the entire period.) Overall, however, there is a persistent regularity which is consistent with the idea that the cities are locked in a single continuously evolving, ever-expanding system.

Figure 15.7 is based on a census definition of cities. Most of the areas designated as cities in this way are so defined by political considerations (they are areas that hold city charters from their respective states) and by population (they contain 2500 persons or more), although a few unincorporated places of large, dense population concentrations are also classified as cities. The definition does *not* refer to the network of central places described in the theoretical overview, since the large cities have many central places within them and there are many smaller centers in the rural areas. Nevertheless the character of central places as a system expanding over time in an orderly way comes through clearly.

The space between the lines of Figure 15.7 provides a visual impression of the rate of increase of the urban population during the intervening years. Table 15.1 shows that a very rapid growth of the cities occurred between 1820 and 1890. The most rapid growth of the cities was in the 1840s, but relative to the nation as a whole cities grew most rapidly in the 1880s. After 1890, the rate of urban growth as measured by the Census Bureau slowed considerably.

Both the chart and table somewhat exaggerate the decline in the growth rate of cities because of the way cities are defined. Cities have always tended to outgrow their political boundaries, and in the nineteenth century, cities grew in part by annexing land about them which was not within their corporate limits but was, nevertheless, an integral part of their economies. Something of a classic of that kind of movement occurred in 1898 when New York City, already the largest city, annexed Brooklyn, which at that time was the fourth largest city in the nation. However, while annexation is still continuing, especially in the West and Southwest, it has not occurred quite so regularly in the twentieth century. As a result the economic and political boundaries of cities have become increasingly out of joint.[5] Figure 15.8 illustrates how cities as economic units have grown in area. In black are all those areas from which workers commuted daily to the central cities (the large solid black areas) to work in 1960. The unpopulated parts of the remainder are shaded.

---

[5] Even in the decade from 1950 to 1960, annexation was a major source of city growth. In the absence of annexation, cities, politically defined, would have grown by a mere 1.5 percent during that decade. The inclusion of annexed areas raises the cities' growth rate to 10.7 percent [Leo F. Schnore, *The Urban Scene* (New York: Free Press, 1965), p.120].

FIGURE 15.8
The metropolitanized areas of the United States in 1960

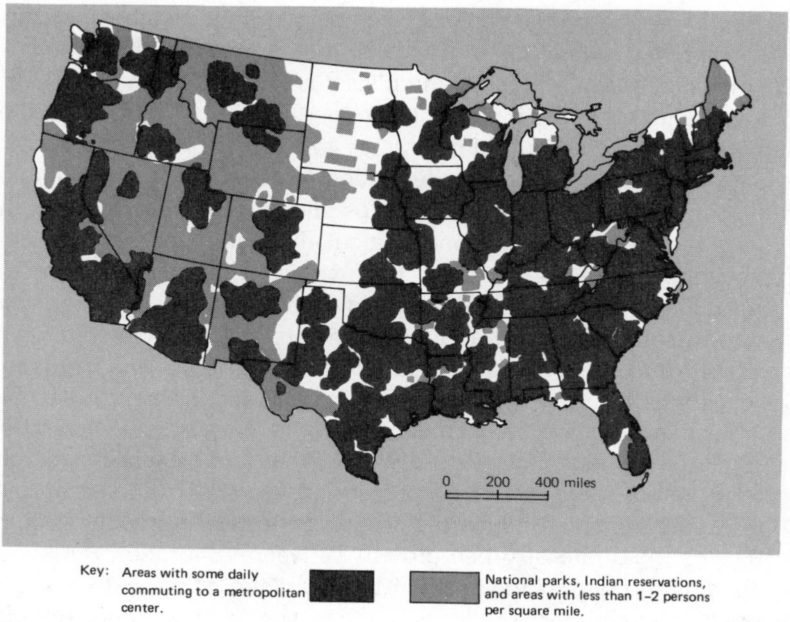

Key: Areas with some daily commuting to a metropolitan center.   National parks, Indian reservations, and areas with less than 1–2 persons per square mile.

SOURCE: Brian J. L. Berry with Peter G. Goheen and Harold Goldstein, *Metropolitan Area Definition: A Re-evaluation of Concept and Statistical Practice* (rev.), Bureau of the Census Working Paper no. 28(Washington: U.S. Government Printing Office, 1969), p. 23, Figure 13.

Thus, only the white areas lay beyond the zones of metropolitan influence in 1960.[6] If we had defined a city, as is reasonable for many purposes, as the area in which people both work and live, then 87 percent of the population would have lived in urban areas in 1960. Based on that figure, city growth between 1920 and 1960 was .04 percent per year less than in the period 1840–1880. The map also suggests that the urbanization of the United States is now virtually complete. The process is now almost entirely of historical interest.

The relatively rapid growth of the cities between 1790 and 1840 was due primarily to the development of urban commercial settlements, while the growth which occurred between 1840 and 1890 coincides with the period when the United States became an industrial power and when commercial centers were established west of the Mississippi. Some manufacturing in factories or factory-like circumstances took place in the colonies almost from the beginning—flour and lumber milling, beer brewing, and whisky distilling, for example. Somewhat later, as the nation's trade grew, further agricultural

[6] This figure is based upon the Bureau of the Budget definition of a metropolitan area in 1960—that is, a city with a population of over 50,000.

processing was added—tanning and tobacco processing particularly—while the needs of shipping were also met in manufacturing plants—ship building, barrels and casks and other cooperage, and printing and publishing. Consumer goods and goods needed by the construction industry have also been manufactured in significant quantities since early in the nineteenth century—furniture, carriages, glass, nails, paint, and plaster are examples. In the 1830s, however, manufacturing activity began to expand rapidly. Textiles led the way, locating not in the cities but in new areas where there was cheap water power—especially along the Merrimac River and in the suburbs of Baltimore and Philadelphia, the ports near the mountains and its water power. Thus in one important sense, industrialization—particularly manufacturing in New England—preceded the rapid growth of the cities. (Cities did grow more rapidly from 1830 to 1840 than they had earlier, but not spectacularly so.) By the 1840s, the iron industry was being transformed from scattered local collieries and forges to massive plants feeding and being fed by the railroads. In symbiotic association, the iron industry, the railroads, and the metal-fabricating industries crept westward over the next few decades. When their work was done, the industrial heartland of the Northeast had been forged, the great megalopolis from New York to Chicago had taken shape, and urbanization and industrialization had become closely intertwined processes. While it is clear that the rapid rate of urban growth between 1840 and 1890, and especially the rapid growth of the cities in the heartland of the nation, were intimately intertwined with industrialization, the quantitative interconnections have not yet been thoroughly studied. Some very crude idea of the magnitudes involved can be gleaned from Table 15.2, which relates population growth to the growth of manufacturing employment in the cities perched atop the urban hierarchy in 1890. If, as seems a reasonable first approximation, each job in manufacturing supported one nonmanufacturing job in the older cities and two jobs in the newer cities, and if four out of every ten persons were in the labor force, then the direct and indirect effects of manufacturing growth in these cities account for more growth in population than actually took place.

While the trend in urban growth has been persistently upward, averaging about 10.5 percent in the period before 1870 and somewhat less (10.3 percent) thereafter, the growth rate has varied considerably from decade to decade. As Figure 15.9 indicates, urban growth rates exhibit a long cycle of some 15–25 years' duration. Such a cycle has been observed in many kinds of demographic variables—population growth, labor-force growth, growth in the number of households, birth and death rates, immigration, and internal migration. No completely satisfactory explanation of these long cycles exists. Indeed, there is considerable doubt that they are truly cycles in the sense of self-generating swings. The way this irregular process of demographic change has affected urban growth has, however, been explained. Migration from rural to urban areas and immigration from abroad were essential elements in the growth of cities. Cities would not have reached anything like their current size and importance simply by virtue of the excess of births over deaths within their confines. One view of the process of urban growth is described below.

TABLE 15.2

Population and manufacturing labor force compared, 1860–1890, selected cities in the United States (thousands of persons)

City	Population 1860	Population 1890	Manufacturing Labor Force 1860	Manufacturing Labor Force 1890	Absolute Increase Manufacturing Labor Force 1860	Absolute Increase Population 1890
New York	1175.0	2507.0	106.0	477.0	371	1332.0
Philadelphia	565.5	1047.0	99.0	260.0	161	482.0
Chicago	112.0	1100.0	5.0	210.0	205	9.880
St. Louis	161.0	452.0	9.0	94.0	85	291.0
Boston	178.0	448.5	19.0	91.0	72	270.5
Baltimore	212.0	434.0	17.0	84.0	67	222.0
Pittsburgh	78.0	344.0	9.0	56.0	47	266.0
San Francisco	57.0	299.0	1.5	48.5	47	242.0
Cleveland	43.0	261.0	35.0	51.0	16	218.0
Detroit	46.0	206.0	2.0	38.0	36	160.0

SOURCES: A. R. Pred, *The Spatial Dynamics of U.S. Urban–Industrial Growth, 1800–1914* (Cambridge, Mass.: M.I.T. Press, 1966), p. 20; and U.S. census data.

FIGURE 15.9

Decade rate of urban growth, United States, 1790–1960 (old census definition)

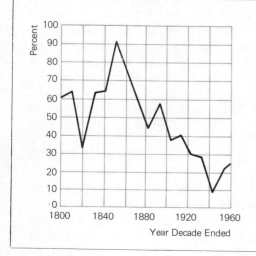

Consider first the period before World War II, when a typical upswing may have occurred as follows : Assume that an increase in the demand for nonfarm labor, a rise in wages, and a fall in unemployment occurred. Increased opportunities would trigger a flow of labor from the farms and from abroad to the cities. Cities in every size class in virtually every region would grow, and new cities would come into being (as their populations reached 2500) as a direct response to this flow of labor. The increased spending power generated by these new urban workers would set up a secondary boom in the cities. Residential construction and the transfer of real estate would boom. Roads, water supply, and sewer systems would be expanded. Electricity and telephone sales, retail and wholesale trade would benefit. Manufacturing of consumer goods would also expand and the boom would lengthen, but eventually it would terminate. After 15 to 25 years, another great increase in demand would be initiated, probably through exploitation of some innovation of widespread consequence such as the automobile, and the process would begin anew.

In the period since World War II, things have been a little different because of the curtailment of immigration and the depletion of the farm labor force. An upswing in the demand for labor was met, therefore, by young and secondary workers. The rapid occupational upgrading of young workers and their rise in income lowered the marriage age, accelerated household formation, and raised the birth rate. The secondary effects were similar, however, as a secondary urban development boom was triggered in nearly all regions and in cities of all sizes. The most recent such boom, the only one of this variety, terminated in the mid-1950s.

Wave after wave of city building booms have now virtually urbanized the nation. Except for national parks, Indian reservations, the large stretches in the West with fewer than two persons per square mile, and a small pocket in central Appalachia, nearly all workers live within daily commuting distance of the center of a metropolitan area. The vast majority of the population has been collected in a small proportion of the nation's land area, rather than being evenly dispersed across it. Urbanization has not been due primarily to national or even local government policies ; rather, it has been a necessary concomitant of economic growth. City growth has been the result of many thousands of entrepreneurs independently choosing where to locate their businesses and millions upon millions of heads of households choosing where to locate their residences.

Economic growth has produced the cities, but the existence of cities has also had feedbacks affecting the rate and structure of national growth. Urbanites have had lower birth rates than farm folk, and hence, urbanization has affected the rate of population growth, the age distribution of the population, and the labor-force participation rate—all of which have altered demand and supply conditions for individual products and for the aggregate of economic activity. By and large, these demographic effects tend to lower the aggregate rate of growth of income, but the effect on the rate of growth of income per capita is less certain.

Cities have also had feedback effects which have accelerated the growth of the economy, other than those like the urban building booms which we have already mentioned. The proximity of entrepreneurs to one another undoubtedly speeded the rate at which innovations were initially adopted, for example, and then diffused throughout the economy. The shift in the structure of output toward services is also, at least in part, a consequence of urban growth. The city makes restaurants a virtual necessity for lunch. Laundries and dry-cleaning establishments are more necessary because people interact in cities so much more than in rural areas, and such interaction somehow demands a fresh-scrubbed look, while the great demand makes scale economies possible so that these activities are shifted from the household at reasonable cost. Further examples of such feedback effects could be provided endlessly.

SUMMARY

The burden of this chapter has been to explore the interconnections between economic growth and urban growth. The exploration has yielded the following fundamental result: City growth and national economic growth proceeded together because cities constitute the most efficient way to organize economic activity in space. Indeed the city is so efficient that it has embraced within it almost all of the economic units of the country. Urban growth is not without its costs, however, and much will be said of them in a subsequent chapter.

SUGGESTED READING

Alonso, W. "Location Theory." In *Regional Development and Planning: A Reader,* edited by J. Friedmann and W. Alonso. Cambridge, Mass.: M.I.T. Press, 1964.

Berry, Brian J. L. *Geography of Market Centers and Retail Distribution.* Englewood Cliffs, N.J.: Prentice-Hall, 1967.

Easterlin, Richard A. *Population, Labor Force, and Long Swings in Economic Growth.* New York: National Bureau of Economic Research, 1968.

Florence, P. S. *Investment, Location and Size of Plant.* Cambridge, England: Cambridge University Press, 1948.

Glaab, C. N., and T. Brown. *A History of Urban America.* New York: Macmillan, 1967.

Isard, W. *Location and Space Economy.* Cambridge, Mass.: M.I.T. Press, 1956.

Isard, W. "Some Location Factors in the Iron and Steel Industry Since the Early Nineteenth Century." *Journal of Political Economy,* vol. 56 (June 1948).

Kain, J. F. "The Distribution and Movement of Jobs and Industry." In *The Metropolitan Enigma,* edited by J. Q. Wilson. Cambridge, Mass.: Harvard University Press, 1968.

Pred, A. R. *The Spatial Dynamics of U.S. Urban–Industrial Growth, 1800–1914.* Cambridge, Mass.: M.I.T. Press, 1966.

Smolensky. Eugene (with D. Ratajczak). "The Conception of Cities," *Explorations in Entrepreneurial History* (Winter 1965).

Stigler, G. "The Division of Labor Is Limited by the Extent of the Market." *Journal of Political Economy,* vol. 59 (June 1951).

Tunnard, C., and H. H. Reed. *American Skyline.* New York: New American Library, 1956.

Wade, R. *The Urban Frontier.* Cambridge, Mass.: Harvard University Press, 1959.

part V
ORGANIZATION FOR ECONOMIC LIFE

16
THE MANAGEMENT OF URBAN AGGLOMERATION

Cities are both a consequence and a cause of national economic growth. They are also both cause and consequence of some of our most pressing and persistent socioeconomic problems, and it is that melancholy aspect of the city which will be emphasized in this chapter.[1]

America's urban economic problems stem, in large part, from the failure of the market system to put a price on certain goods. The nature of this source of market failure and the political processes which deal with it are discussed first. Since the severity of this market failure reflects the spatial distribution of particular groups and activities, a fair amount of attention is then given over to a discussion of the ecology of the city. The chapter concludes by using the concept of market failure and a simple model of the urban ecology to examine three urban problems in their historical context.

EXTERNALITIES IN THE CITY

Cities increase physical output per unit of input, but their existence contributes nevertheless to economic inefficiency, paradoxical as that may sound. In a market economy, in most circumstances, if each person does what he considers best for himself, society's interest is also fully served. However, if an action taken by one person affects the welfare of another without at the same time appropriately affecting money prices, pursuit of self-interest may fail fully to advance the social good. For example, if I live in a city and do not own a fire extinguisher, it is more likely that the neighboring houses will burn down. Suppose that I would buy a fire extinguisher if its price were $10 less, and that collectively my neighbors would place a value (to them) of $10 on my owning that extinguisher. In that case my neighbors and I as a group would buy that extinguisher, and be glad of it, if only we could get together to

[1] For the brighter side, see Chapter 15.

arrange the transaction. However, there may be no market in which such transactions are arranged. If that is so, the fire extinguisher will not be purchased, and my neighbors and I will be less well off than we could be.

Externalities, as these kinds of circumstances are called, cause the market system to fail in the sense that some desirable activities will be terminated too soon and some socially undesirable activities will not be stopped soon enough. In our example, too few extinguishers will be bought in the special sense that there is a group of people able and willing to buy an additional one, but no mechanism to get that transaction consummated exists.

Markets fail to appear when the costs of forming them exceed their benefits. Consider some of the difficulties an entrepreneur would experience if he tried to form a market by collecting a fee from each of the effected neighbors and using the receipts to provide me with an extinguisher and to compensate himself for his time. First, the appropriate fee must be determined. Ideally every person should pay an amount equal to what he believes will be the money value to him of my extinguisher. It is to the advantage of each person, however, to assert that he would get no benefit, for if his neighbors protect themselves from the fire hazard, they will inevitably protect him also. Furthermore, tenants who previously were willing to buy fire extinguishers may now find it to their advantage to say that they are unwilling to do so. Every tenant thus becomes a player in a game, each with his own strategy. The game may or may not eventually produce a fee schedule which will be appropriate for each contributor and sufficient to cover the costs of the extinguisher and the entrepreneur's time, but if the number of people involved is very large, the costs of coming to an agreement are likely to be prohibitive. Left to the market alone, therefore, the consequence may well be a greater than necessary risk of fire for everyone in the neighborhood.

Where markets fail it is possible for political intervention to improve the situation. The simplest and cheapest way to solve the problem may be for the government to require that everyone own a fire extinguisher, even though that policy would be coercive and inequitable. An alternative approach is for the government either to levy a tax on those who do not own fire extinguishers or to subsidize their purchase. Another option is to make tenants who do not own fire extinguishers liable for the damages that occur to others through private litigation in the courts. There are other possibilities too, of course, one of which is to rely on municipal fire departments. All we can say is that, left to the market alone, there is a greater risk of loss from fire than need be, and that political intervention may improve the situation. Government action is not necessarily desirable, however.

Invoking the power of the state may not improve things simply because government officials, like everyone else, make mistakes. Moreover, political solutions to market failure may lead to a less than satisfactory outcome because of inherent conceptual problems.

If a task falls to the government because of some market failure, then the causes of that failure are also going to complicate decision making for the hard-working bureaucrat. To get public or congressional support, the official must show that the benefits of his program outweigh the costs. By their very nature, however, benefits will be difficult to perceive while the costs, in the form of taxes, will be painfully obvious. To get out of this inhibiting situation, the decision maker will of course try to make the benefits tangible. However, he will have great difficulty putting a dollar value on them precisely because there are externalities involved for which there is no market price. What is the value of a hydroelectric dam? If it is all in the electricity it generates and if benefits exceed costs, building that dam is a perfectly appropriate task for the private sector. If benefits do not exceed costs, then it should not be built by either the private sector or the government. If, however, the sale of generated electricity would not cover costs, but pleasure is produced by the beautiful view and the quiet uncongested open space the dam affords, and if the value of these amenities plus the value of the electricity exceeds the costs, then the dam should be built. It will be built, it seems safe to say, only if the government intervenes. However, how is the value of such an intangible benefit to be measured and meaningfully conveyed to the taxpayers? Such difficulties are likely to result in too few dams.

Even if benefits and costs can be appropriately measured, they will not be the same for all persons, and some problems may remain. Suppose two solutions for a problem have the same net benefits. Which one should be adopted? Suppose the decision is to be made by majority vote, and to keep things simple, assume that there are three voters. Denote the voters as 1, 2, and 3 and the three solutions as A, B, and C. In Table 16.1 the preferences of each voter are listed in order. If A were to be put up against B, A would be selected. If A were now put up against C, the latter would be chosen and that would resolve the issue. Implementing C, however, would be quite arbitrary, for if B were not put up against C, B would win. There is no genuine majority.

Even if there were a genuine majority (e.g., if 3 had the preferences illustrated in Table 16.2), then relying on majority voting would continue to raise a significant problem. As portrayed in Table 16.2, there is a clear majority in favor of option B: These voters would choose B, no matter in what order the pairs of choices were voted upon. Suppose, however, that voter 1 preferred A to B by a wide margin, voter 3 was nearly indifferent between B and A, and voter 2 was really unenthusiastic about any choice, but only mildly preferred even B to A. In this circumstance, if voter 1 were willing to make a

TABLE 16.1

	Voter		
	1	2	3
First choice	A	B	C
Second choice	B	C	A
Third choice	C	A	B

TABLE 16.2

	Voter		
	1	2	3
First choice	A	B	B
Second choice	B	C	A
Third choice	C	A	C

small money payment to 3 which would cause him to vote for A over B, the gain in satisfaction to voter 1 would far exceed the loss in utility to individual 2. Majority rule without any way to bargain would generate an inefficient outcome. In economic markets, intensity of feeling is routinely expressed by the willingness of some individuals to pay more than others for something in order to have their way. Direct cash payments to buy votes is, however, a punishable offense in most circumstances. The political process attacks this problem through a barter arrangement euphemistically called *log-rolling*. Obviously, however, log-rolling as a register of the intensity with which individuals want things is a poor substitute for an economic market. Furthermore, if 1 and 3 find it convenient to form a permanent bloc, then they will have the power to do great harm to voter 2. In an extreme case they can choose only those government actions from which they receive all the benefits, forcing voter 2 to pay at least one third of the cost. If coalitions are constantly shifting, a more equitable result is likely, but it may very well result in uneconomic pressure toward continuous government expansion in order to produce trading opportunities.

When people are densely collected together, externalities productive of economic inefficiency are more likely to appear than when people are widely scattered. If I live in the countryside one half acre from my nearest neighbor, my neighbor's fire is less likely to become my fire. In the city, where my neighbor and I may share a common cardboard wall, the fact that he smokes in bed becomes a hazard to my safety. In the city, therefore, there needs to be political intervention in essentially economic activities which would not be required if everyone lived at the center of a 160-acre farm. Making that intervention efficient is, however, fraught with difficulties.

To counterbalance the emphasis of the discussion thus far, it must be pointed out that externalities may raise as well as lower welfare. In the city, my neighbor's beautiful roses become my beautiful view. The result is still inefficient, however. Since I enjoy my neighbor's roses free of charge, it is likely that he grows too few of them. If I were to pay him $10 because that is the value I put on the lovely view, he might be encouraged to enhance the beauty of his garden even further. For efficiency, political intervention may once again be required because the appropriate market does not exist.

The interrelationship between urban growth and social welfare is more complicated than the interrelationship between urban growth and economic growth as captured in measures like gross national product per capita. A very large part of urban history reflects the efforts of the cities to expand those activities that yield desirable externalities and to curtail those that yield undesirable ones. The remainder of this chapter is concerned with a few of the manifestations of unpleasant externalities, a few of their causes, and some of the political responses to them.

THE ECOLOGY OF THE URBAN POPULATION

Density Gradients

The hierarchy of central places that pervades the nation and its regions emanates from and structures the cities.[2] Each city has a hierarchy of central places within it which are oriented around one large nucleus which is its central business district (CBD). In the CBD are those activities with very small market areas. More importantly, the CBD also houses large department stores, specialty shops, specialists in personal and business services, banks, offices of large business firms, and the offices of the municipal government, all of which draw their patrons from the whole of the city and perhaps from its suburbs as well. Nearly everyone must patronize these establishments from time to time, and many find their way there each day to work. Access to the central business district, then, is essential, and easy access commands a price. As the distance from the center increases, the quantity of land grows: That is a fact of geometry. Since there is more land the same distance from the center, rent per unit of land would fall with distance from the center even if individuals were indifferent to being close to or far from it. Individuals are not indifferent, however, and therefore land rents rise precipitously from the periphery to the center. Since rents are higher, builders will use land more sparingly the closer they are to the center. Hence, density will fall from the center of the city to the periphery for nearly every land use. Nearly all cities, then, are characterized by a "density gradient" as pictured in Figure 16.1. This is one empirical regularity which we observe within cities, and it contributes significantly to some urban problems—notably housing congestion near the city and the daily traffic jams between 7:00 and 9:00 in the morning and between 4:00 and 6:00 in the afternoon. It is also associated with other social problems, as we shall soon see.

Zones, Sectors, and Clusters

A density gradient for population, manufacturing, retailing, and wholesaling enterprises and a similar gradient for land rent are not the only empirical regularities which characterize cities. Although most American cities developed without rigid social traditions, without explicit plans,[3] and without legal

---

[2] For a discussion of the hierarchy of central places, see Chapter 15.
[3] Nearly all cities grew initially according to some street plan and with some allowance for open space. The original plans for New Haven, Philadelphia, and beautiful Savannah are still discernible, but those plans do not affect the argument being made here.

FIGURE 16.1
Typical density gradients

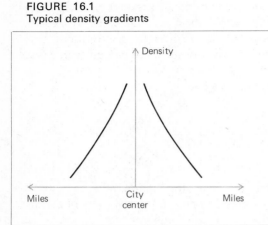

segregation, most of them have come to be divided into economic sectors, family status zones, and ethnic ghettos. One schematic representation seems to describe the layout of a surprising number of urban centers in the United States (and, indeed, throughout the world) for a long time. In that idealized representation of the ecology of the city, economic status, stage of the life cycle, and ethnicity seem to describe well the differentiation among residential sections of the city (see Figure 16.2). To consider an explicit alternative, the contemporary American city might now be a concrete square divided into neighborhoods within which the same people lived and worked. Such neighborhoods would contain individuals of all income classes and all races, and their common characteristic would be the occupation and industry in which the household heads were employed. Such neighborhoods characterized cities in earlier times, and some cities and some parts of the city in the United States in the colonial period, but it does not describe the American city today. Instead, the American city is a core area of concentrated businesses around which residential areas have grown in something like concentric zones. Each zone has a fairly homogeneous population with respect to family status or age. The unmarried, childless families, and parents whose children have set up their own households, reside in the zone nearest the center, while the larger families are in the less densely populated, more open areas further from the city's core. The area immediately surrounding the core is usually relatively old, many of its structures are dilapidated, and it generally has been invaded by a sprinkling of light manufacturing and wholesaling activities which could not be accommodated within the core. This zone, the zone of blight or transition, in which land is relatively expensive because of accessibility to the center, houses not the wealthy but the poor. To provide accommodations which the poor can afford on this high-rent land requires high density. It is in this zone, where living space per person is least, that we expect to find the worst of the urban slums. Surrounding this zone is another zone in which land has slightly less value and population is somewhat less dense; here are

FIGURE 16.2
A generalized view of the ecology of the city

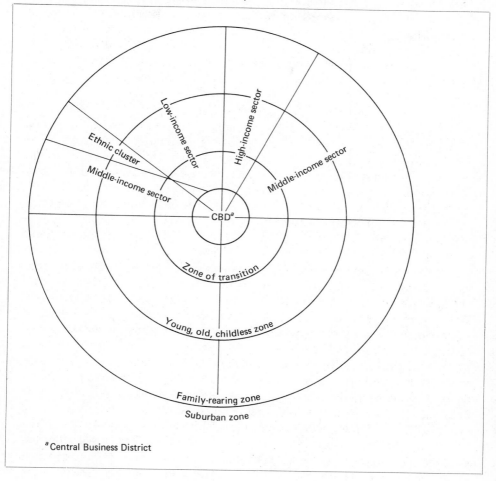

Low-income sector

High-income sector

Ethnic cluster

Middle-income sector

Middle-income sector

CBD[a]

Zone of transition

Young, old, childless zone

Family-rearing zone

Suburban zone

[a] Central Business District

found lower middle-class workers raising families. Beyond, where land is even cheaper and population can be even less dense, is a large middle-income zone of single-family houses and white-collar workers with children young enough to be living at home. Still further out are the suburbs, where land is even cheaper per acre and lot sizes are larger, and the middle- and upper-income groups can exercise their tastes for large lawns and open space for the price of a long and harrowing daily journey to work. That the poor occupy expensive inner-city land while the affluent must expend enormous effort to get to work each day is an extraordinary testament to either the love of open space or the power of the American matriarchy.

Cutting across the concentric zones are sectors which radiate out from the center of the city. These sectors are bounded by fairly sharp edges, some of which are formed by wooded ridges, pleasant creek valleys, and clean beachfronts. Other edges are formed by the spokes of the transport network: the railroad lines, the express highways, and the larger streets running from the center to the periphery. Within each sector, as we move out from the center, what we observe will be affected by the fact that we are crossing successive concentric zones. In each zone income will rise as we move from the center to the periphery. Across zones, at the same distance from the city center, however, income will vary substantially. High-income, highly educated families will stretch out along the edges characterized by amenities. Low-income, less educated families will be strung out along the public mass transit routes. Thus, near the center of the city, in some zones, incomes will be on the average very high, higher than at the periphery of other zones. The affluent, therefore, are found at every distance from the city center, although not in some zones. The very poor, however, are found only near the city center and in particular zones. The lower-income groups, but not the poorest, will be found at almost every distance from the city center, too, but, once again, they are collected in particular zones.

Ethnicity, a third factor which affects the ecology of the city, is the grouping of individuals into ethnic concentrations. In the United States at least, groups which share the same country of origin, the same language, religion, or color have clustered in particular sections of the city. Each ethnic cluster is itself divided into zones and sectors which further differentiate its members by family status and income. Language barriers, common interests, religious affiliation, and a sense of alienation in a new country led to the emergence of immigrant enclaves with each immigrant wave of the nineteenth century. The immigrants arrived from particular countries in a relatively short period, and they collected near those with similar backgrounds. Often one generation developed a cluster within a city and then, almost as a bloc, relocated farther from the city center as their incomes rose, their old neighborhoods being occupied by a different, more recent group of immigrants. The aged and the less successful remained behind and, in a sense, formed the core area of the inner-city ghettos. Eventually, large elements of each ethnic group dispersed, but some residue was left behind. Blacks, migrating from the South to the North during and in the decade after World War I and in the 1940s and 1950s, have followed residential patterns similar to those of the European immigrants. There is little evidence thus far, however, that the pattern of dispersal followed by earlier immigrants will be followed by blacks. The twentieth century has seen increasing segregation of the black American, especially in the South, although there is some slim evidence of recent dispersal in the cities of the Northeast.

Of course, this schematic portrayal of the ecology of the cities is accurate only in broad detail. The definitiveness of the zones, sectors, and ethnic clusters varies substantially from city to city. In some cities of the Southwest, the pattern seems not to be observable at all, but very recent research suggests that Figure 16.2 remains broadly descriptive of the ecology of the American city even in the 1960s.

One factor which tends to drive the city away from any neat representation is growth itself. As the city's population grows, within each zone and sector there is increased density—that is, a large part of population growth is absorbed within some initial set of zones, sectors, and clusters. However, some growth spills out across the older boundaries. Each specialized zone widens, moves outward, and encroaches upon its outer neighbor. In the process, the edges may become nearly as large as the zones and sectors themselves. These edges are composed of heterogeneous populations, differing in race, age, and income. However, over time, populations in a neighborhood tend once again to become more homogeneous in taste, life style, education, and income. Of particular interest in this process is the pattern of movement of ethnic clusters. Starting out as low-income populations within the zone of blight, these clusters expand in space as incomes rise. However, apparently they do not proceed along the sector in which they were spawned. Across the edge is a sector higher in income and social status in which there is a highly upwardly mobile population which is moving rapidly outward from the city center. It is into that the void created by that sector that the ethnic clusters seem to expand. At the cluster's moving edge is its high-income population; thus, as it enters a neighborhood in the higher-income sector, it tends to place within that sector higher-income individuals than those who are left behind. Lower-income individuals in that ethnic group then follow after some time. The movement of these ethnic groups creates a sector with a new orientation toward the city center (as in Figure 16.2).

URBAN TENSIONS AND NATIONAL PROBLEMS

The residents of the city, then, are not distributed about in random fashion. There is an order which, when sketched as in Figure 16.2, provides graphic representation of the class and caste structure of the society. The city is not itself a cause of such distinctions, but it is within the city that class differences manifest themselves most virulently.

The Neighborhood as a Community

The homogeneous neighborhoods where people of like tastes, incomes, and hence expenditure patterns congregate at the end of the workday serve to offset some of the tensions of urban life. In an impersonal environment of continual interaction among people brought together by necessity, the neighborhood furnishes an identity with a community, and that sense of identity serves many useful psychological and social purposes. It makes feasible those community centers like Hull House which ameliorated the traumatic change between rural European and urban American life styles for many immigrants. It makes possible the specialized food suppliers (the Turkish coffeehouse, the kosher butcher shop, the soul-food grocery) which provide some continuity of tradition for the immigrant. It nourishes the Polish–American clubs, the Spanish-language newspapers, the Jewish burial societies, and the like, which not only give the alien a sense of belonging but which provide the conduits by which the older immigrants can transmit their experiences to the new, thereby facilitating their adaptation to an often hostile environment. It forms the basis for political representation of the special interests congregated in the various wards of the city. Finally, it serves to shield long-settled and acculturated Americans from that which is alien to them and thereby serves their needs in the very same, though somewhat less obvious, ways. The white, Protestant suburbs are not usually called "ghettos," but often that is in fact what they are.

The homogeneous neighborhoods produced by the interplay of zone, sector, and cluster thus have a social value, but they also serve to mass individuals who are very much alike and to place them so that they confront quite different social groups across permeable boundaries. It has not been uncommon throughout our history for conflict to flash across neighborhood edges; indeed, it would be surprising if the edges had always been peaceful fences making for good neighbors.

Growing populations create the most serious conflict situations, but conflict is also inevitable over the placement and nature of public facilities. Elementary schools and playgrounds, fire stations and libraries, and even bus transportation, can be planned to meet the needs of different neighborhoods. They may not be responsive to such requirements, but they can be. High schools, subway systems, hospitals, and other facilities which at optimum size must draw on a larger population than that of a neighborhood are, however, an inherent source of conflict. One facility must cater to widely different and conflicting demands, which it may not be able to reconcile by segregation. For example, it may not be possible to draw the boundaries around congressional districts containing several hundred thousand persons without totally submerging the interests of some neighborhoods. Where segregation is neither feasible nor desirable, the burden of reconciliation falls on the politicans, often crushing them.

When the population of a city is rapidly growing, conflict is exacerbated. Some of the growth is absorbed through increased density. When growth is especially rapid, the increased density can lead to deteriorated, overcrowded housing, overcrowded schools, inadequate refuse collection, and terrible congestion of the transport system as the expansion of municipal services inevitably lags behind population growth. Some growth is also accommodated by the expansion of the zones, sectors, and clusters. The cities spread into former farm lands without sewers, transport, schools, and other urban services. The city often grows out of its political boundaries altogether, swelling neighboring towns and producing urban sprawl. The higher-income families now reside outside the city, but they flow into it each day to work. The city must provide these daily commuters with access routes, fire and police protection, emergency health service, clean water, and the like; but since they rely on a property tax, they may be deprived of a growth in the tax base commensurate with the growth in the need for these municipal services. Urban sprawl thus creates a fiscal crisis for the cities.

A more immediate and violent problem may be produced by residential movement across old boundaries. The wealthy suburbanites on their two-acre estates may be scandalized by the invasion of quarter-acre, $40,000 houses into their immediate environment, and the apparently insatiable demand of their new neighbors for additional schools. Skilled manual workers shoulder their way into middle-class neighborhoods, and perhaps there is even the ultimate horror of blacks buying their way into white areas. The democratic proclivities of the market, which fails to segregate dollars by the class or color of their holders, have strained the social and political structure again and again.

The Evolution of Urban Form

Population growth was distributed among the zones, sectors, and clusters so as to generate first a steepening and then a flattening of the density gradients of most cities during the last half of the nineteenth century. The precise outcome was structured by a host of developments. There were important innovations in residential construction, in intraurban transportation, in communication, in health and sanitary measures, in fire control, and in administrative techniques. There was the massive flow of migrants to the city from the farms of America and of Europe. There was also the spectacular rise in income.

In 1850 it was possible to walk the length and breadth of even the largest American city in a day. An important advance in residential construction, the balloon frame, had already had some effect in spreading out the city, however. In Chicago in 1833, Augustine Taylor had built St. Mary's Roman Catholic Church in a new way. In place of massive 16-inch square beams fitted together with great care by master carpenters and an enormous gang of laborers, he had built a lightweight balloon frame of thin plates and 2 × 4 studs, on which he hung the walls with nails. (Nails had begun a dramatic fall in price after 1817.) The single-family wooden house became a considerably cheaper structure that could be made easily by a do-it-yourself householder and his son. With this new technique, cities like San Francisco and Chicago could rise from tent cities to substantial permanent settlements in less than a year. Older cities could stretch at their peripheries at a considerably lower cost than before, and they did so. However, spatial extension was limited by transport costs, since low-income families could not afford a horse and carriage. The horse-drawn, free-rolling omnibus, which had become popular during the 1820s, was some help, but the major innovation was the horse-drawn, rail-guided car, which Stephenson had invented in the 1830s, but which began to be widely adopted, like the balloon frame, in the 1850s. (Less important, but not unimportant, was the intercity steam railroad which served as a kind of commuter rail line.) As the horse-drawn trolley spread the city out linearly along its tracks, a complementary series of innovations raised densities near their approach to the city center. Although they had made their appearance earlier, New York's tenements began to mushroom along the tracks in the 1850s and 1860s. A single tenement housed perhaps 500 people in 100 rooms, many without windows, without plumbing or heating, and with perhaps a dozen privies all in the basement. (It is sobering to note that contemporaries thought these tenements a substantial improvement in the housing conditions of the poor.) In Boston, Newark, Chicago, and St. Louis, the balloon-frame wood house reached up three or four stories in long lines of densely packed fire traps. In Philadelphia and Baltimore, a new machine-made pressed brick was used to expand the production of row houses with their dense occupancy.

In the 40 years (1850–1890) in which it dominated intraurban transport, the horse-drawn trolley perhaps doubled the radius of the city, while the density at the center increased. The innovation that was eventually to reduce central density was made operational by Ewan Sprague in Richmond, Virginia in 1887. Sprague electrified the trolley, and his invention spread incredibly rapidly throughout the country. In a decade or two, it increased the radius of the city fourfold. Furthermore, electrification was adapted to other transport modes. New York City had an elevated steam railroad in 1870, but resistance to this noisy, dirty, spark-throwing horror stopped its expansion. Electrified, new elevated lines were added in New York and other cities. The electric train also nourished the subway, and Boston had completed the first link in its system by 1897.

Construction techniques were also advancing in manufacturing, warehousing, retailing, and hotel and office structures. Cast iron construction capable of greater heights and larger open spaces unbroken by columns appeared in warehouses in the 1840s, and spread to other commercial buildings. In New York City in 1848, James Bogardus showed that iron frames and brick walls could be substituted for all load-bearing masonry walls. The saving from eliminating massive masonry walls in the lower stories reduced the cost of taller structures dramatically. The Otis elevator, invented in 1853, improved subsequently, and widely adopted in the 1880s, made circulation within tall buildings feasible. Finally, in 1884, William Jenney hooked the brick curtain wall to the steel frame and opened the age of the skyscraper. When one adds to these other changes which occurred between 1860 and 1910—advances in bridge-building techniques, asphalt paving, water and sewage filtration processes, the incandescent light, and the telephone—the panoply of technical change which impinged upon the city in the last third of the nineteenth century and which made it feasible for the city to absorb 20 million people can still only be dimly comprehended.[4] The result of these innovations was not merely their effect on the population, size, and hence density of the city. This interplay of technology and population growth also structured the ecology of the city. The city had been an area of segregated land uses even before the Civil War, but the patterning became more distinct. There had been a central business district, but it now was enlarged dramatically in area and height. There had long been some separation of places of work from places of residence, but that separation was now a dominant characteristic of the city. The poor and

[4] It has recently been asserted that the rate of technological change in the provision of urban services is inherently slow and that is one reason that the cities are in such great difficulty today. See W. J. Baumol, "Macroeconomics of Unbalanced Growth: The Anatomy of Urban Crises," *American Economic Review*, vol. 57 (June 1967), pp. 415–427. The argument is weak on many scores, but the most relevant historical response is the comment by C. S. Bell, "The Economics of Unbalanced Growth: Comment," *American Economic Review*, vol. 58, Part II (September 1968), pp. 877–884

rich, young and old, white and black had been segregated, but the edges became more distinct than before.

The last of these developments deserves, perhaps, a bit more comment. As the city spread in space over this period, probably only the top half of the income distribution could afford the outward move. The newly built areas also were, without any predesigned government policy, fairly rigidly segregated by income class. This was so due to the decisions of the developers, who built densely and with monotonous uniformity of architectural style along and about the trolley lines. They guessed that people like to live with people like themselves and will pay a premium if the opportunity to do so is guaranteed by the builder's choice of lot size and house size and style. In the jargon of economists, the builders were internalizing positive externalities in consumption without the aid of government. In the interstices farms remained, but there were also some more expensive houses, custom built on large lots for the carriage riders. The presence of a particular kind of church could also assure ethnic enclaves. It was thus that the zones, sectors, and clusters came to be fully articulated.

Social-Overhead Capital and the Political Boss System

The city between 1865 and 1910 was a place of prodigious investment. Investment in residential construction, in trolleys and rails, electric power stations, street lighting, road construction, street paving and bridge building, sewer systems, and sanitation vehicles was not only awesome in quantity but often had the special quality of producing substantial external benefits.

The value of a man's house depends upon the value of the land it rests upon and the characteristics of the house. The value of the structure depends primarily upon its size, its state of repair, and its design. These are all under the control of the buyer. He can—within limits, of course—alter the design and fix the maintenance level and even the size which he believes is in accord with demand so as to maximize the return on his investment. Or, if his tastes are not common ones, he may forego some market return when he sells his house in the future for the satisfaction of having the kind of house he wants in the present. What is important is that the owner has primary control over the value of his residence, a situation which contrasts sharply with his lack of control over the value of his land.

Urban land values depend, in part, upon accessibility to the city center, as mentioned previously. Accessibility to the city center is not something the home owner can control after he has purchased his house, for it depends primarily on where the new transport routes are put. If tracks for a horse-drawn trolley had been put down in the middle of the street on which you lived in the 1870s, the effect on your house's value would have been uncertain. Its value as a residence would have gone down, but its value for commercial purposes would have risen, and the extent to which it rose would have varied inversely with its distance from the nearest central place—that is, cluster of shops. There is no doubt, however, about the effects of the trolley on land values one, two, three, or four blocks away. Those property values would have risen because access to the city center was made easier with no serious increase in noise or dirt. Owners of property near to but a little away from the trolley lines, then, would get a capital gain out of the appearance of the trolley.

Access is not the only determinant of urban land value. If the house next to yours were a rundown shack or a butcher shop, or if this were the nineteenth century and you were a white, Protestant, second-generation American and the resident next door were Irish or Polish or Italian-born, the value of your house would be less than it would have been otherwise. Still in the nine-teenth century, if your street had a first-class sewer below ground level, were illuminated with electric street lights, were paved with asphalt, or were near but not too near an elementary school, then the value of your land would be higher than otherwise.

There can be only a few trolley routes in a city. Not everyone wanted to live on a street with tracks down the middle and constant reminders that a horse recently passed by. Street lights could not be electrified all at once, and not everyone wanted them enough to pay the tax assessment for them anyway. The same was true of other civic improvements. That is, demand differed for each improvement in different parts of the city in any time period. On the supply side, there were also constraints on the number of facilities or the speed with which they could be put in place. Laying rails, especially rails level with the street, and buying horses and drays were expensive. Businessmen would have found it most advantageous to know how many trolley lines there were to be, and where and when they would appear, before they decided to invest. Residential builders could have operated with greater confidence if the city had assured them that land use in their vicinity would be controlled in a favorable way. By early in the twentieth century, therefore, cities were pre-paring zoning ordinances.

Given demand and supply considerations, then, there will be a restricted number of trolley lines and suppliers of public utilities and zoned residential neighborhoods, and the services provided will not be equally distributed, at least for a long time, throughout the city. By deciding who will provide facilities and where they will be provided, the city is affecting whose land values will rise and who will make profitable investments. City officials thus control something of value, and it is not surprising that a market for the city's beneficent powers developed in the nineteenth century. The buyers were the industrialists and land owners, and the sellers the leaders of the parties in power.

How did the market operate? The profits from a trolley line were the excess of the fare each rider paid less the cost per rider, multiplied by the number of riders. Cities generally had control of the fare, and hence some control over profits. They also controlled the transport routes, and hence had some control over the number of riders on any line and profits. Control was exercised through the issuance of franchises which specified, among other things, the fare, the quality of service, the route, and the length of life of the franchise. If the franchises were auctioned off to the highest bidder and there were competition among bidders, the price of a franchise, given the location and fare, to the highest bidder would then have earned only normal profits on that trolley line, and the city treasury would have been enriched accordingly. But if the franchise were allotted by the party in power, then its price could be less than what the highest bidder would have paid, and consequently the buyer would be willing to pay something, perhaps even the difference, to the party in the form of a "kickback." Such kickbacks were rife in the nineteenth century, and they enriched the Tweeds of New York, the Crumps of Memphis, the McManes of Philadelphia, and the Pendergasts of Kansas City, at the expense of the city treasury. Of course, this was illegal and from time to time the boss paid with a jail sentence. Boss Tweed, the leader of Tammany Hall in New York City and the personification of bossism, died in prison. It should be added, however, that he died a wealthy man, and an old man, and that his stay in prison had been fairly short.

It was not necessary, however, for the party to violate the law to enrich itself and its leaders. It has already been indicated that where the public facilities were put created windfall capital gains for property owners who did not expect to be near a trolley line when they purchased their houses, and were not, in fact, too close to it. To an owner of a trolley company, however, or a party official, where a trolley line was put did not come as a surprise. Inside information could make it possible to buy land cheaply before the improvement and later sell it dearly. It was legal. As George Washington Plunkitt, the lovable state senator from New York City, could say upon his retirement, "There's an honest graft, and I'm an example of how it works. I might sum up the whole thing by saying 'I seen my opportunities and I took 'em.'"[5]

Such practices may have built up the city faster and more efficiently than would have been possible otherwise. The fare that could be charged on a trolley line was after all limited by the elasticity of the demand for trolley rides. At higher fares, fewer people would ride the trolley, and they would ride less frequently. Since that was the case, it is possible that for some trolley lines which were built there was no fare at which a profit would have been made on the operation of the line alone. If, however, the owners could also capture some part of the rise in real estate value along their route, the investment might be profitable. Owners or investors, knowing this, might have invested in a line only on the condition that it be located where they could first buy up land in the vicinity. Where that was true, it was socially desirable to have such a system. The kickback to the bosses can thus be viewed as a payment for creating a socially useful market.

This last argument, however, clearly did not apply generally, if ever. The bosses sold city jobs. Since individuals were willing to pay for these jobs, it must have been true that city wages were higher than would have been necessary to get the number and quality of workers they hired. Cities also sold the right to do street work to particular paving companies. Since the companies were willing to pay a kickback, it must be that the price charged the city for

[5] William L. Riorden, *Plunkitt of Tammany Hall* (New York: Dutton, 1963), p. 3.

this work was higher than necessary. No useful social purpose was best served by such practices.

The reaction against the bosses was almost immediate, and by the 1880s was a partly coordinated, full-fledged movement. The reformers were a blend of journalists, academicians, church leaders, do-gooders, and businessmen. By and large the reform movement was elitist, anti-immigrant, and unable to do more than periodically interrupt boss rule in a particular city. However, some of its demands soon were seen to be in the best interests of the parties, as well as of good government. Reformers wanted a strong mayor in the interests of efficiency. To that end they worked for city charters that would bar the states from the daily conduct of the cities' business. They strove also for a shift of power from the city councils to the mayor. These were not demands which a party boss found it difficult to support. Nor did the bosses object to the introduction of licenses to undertake those businesses which dealt in the health and safety of consumers. Indeed, licenses are franchises, and the bosses were eager to define businesses as crucial to health and safety, since it meant more franchises to sell. Zoning laws were likewise desirable for one reason to the good government movement and for another reason to the bosses. In other areas, the parties found it politically expedient to accede to demands which they would rather have frustrated if they could. Civil service classification and examinations for city workers were one example. In the end a trend slowly emerged. To resolve the difficult issues over which important and powerful business interests contended, the regulatory functions were given over to skilled technicians who devised a set of explicit, publicly pronounced rules by which to make decisions. To do otherwise was to risk powerful political enemies and to divide the business community into unpredictable factions. The social services and welfare agencies, which redistributed income among groups which were highly stable over time, were turned over to a well-entrenched bureaucracy, insulated from politics by the civil service and from the other groups by an impenetrable wall of rules and a bewildering and paralyzing multiplicity of overlapping responsibilities. Another potentially explosive issue for the parties was thus defused. What the party kept for itself was taxation and assessment, where individual concessions, each of small consequence to the city but of great import to any single individual or business, could be bargained over without a significant response from the mass of voters. Such favors could achieve individual commitments of time and money to the party. Bossism thus evolved into party politics more like that at the national level.

The conflicts between the boss-dominated political machine and the reformers in the early period, and the dominant versus the minority party in the later period reflected the ecology of the city. The inner-city wards were the strongholds of the bosses and are the basic source of strength of the dominant party to this day. The key exceptions are the "blue-stocking districts"—that is, the innermost parts of the high-income sectors. The dominant party's strength radiated out toward the periphery through the low-income sectors. The minority party dominated the outer ring in the city and the suburbs and the high-income sectors. The middle ring voted and still votes most frequently with the dominant party, but also contained the voters who on occasion could swing the election to the minority party.

The ecology of voting has had significant consequences. In nearly every state it has made it difficult for the political parties to mediate the inevitable conflicts between city and suburb, and the city and rural areas, since different parties speak for each group. Early in the nineteenth century, for example, annexation was a way for the ruling propertied classes to keep political control, but that became less and less feasible as the rate of growth of the immigrant population swelled. It remains true, however, that the city's dominant party tends to abhor annexation, while the city's minority party favors it. The suburbs increasingly resisted annexation once it became clear that they would thus be put under the rule of the party they loathed. Since within the city, the only real party competition was over the middle-class ring, it was there that the parties vied to place the best public services. Services were also maintained in the high-income sectors in order to maintain the tax base of the city. The inner core received the dregs from the public purse, but the party contributed directly through charity and patronage just enough to keep the inner-ward citizens coming to the polls in sufficient numbers. To the problems of low income were therefore added poor services, which accelerated the deterioration of the inner ring. Gradually, as the inner zone came to be inhabited by people who perceived that their stay would not be transient, and as the development of welfare programs created readily perceivable uses for political power, the inner city developed political consciousness and an organization which is just now bearing fruit.

Health and Safety

Fire and health are two urban problems which technological and managerial innovations have confronted with some success. Despite their general unhealthiness and their generally higher death rates throughout the nineteenth century, cities have grown. The higher death rate was due to such infectious diseases as tuberculosis and hence to a large extent can be attributed to greater population density. It is probable that an index of the healthiness of the cities' residents would have been inverse to the density gradient throughout history. It is certainly the case now, and logic suggests that it was always so, even if the data are not available to fully substantiate this conjecture.

First of all, higher density makes for more serious sanitation problems. For most of the nineteenth century, privies or outhouses were the universal method of human waste disposal. On the farm this was not a serious problem, but in the dense city it was a source of continuous disagreeableness and not infrequent disaster. In the better neighborhoods in the first half of the century, the privies emptied into open sewers which ran down the crowns or sides of the city streets. These sewers might have been flushed out periodically, but, then, they might not have been. In other areas, the night soil was collected and placed with the rubbish to be picked up by the cartman. Hogs were turned loose in the streets to root among the trash, add to the excrement, and endanger the children.

Housing quality was, of course, variable, and slums appeared early. In 1800, houses were packed so close together in one stretch of Broad Street in New York City that there was no room for privies at all, and eventually the city could see no alternative but simply buying up the area and tearing down the structures. Water was drawn from wells in both the city and the country, and efforts were made to separate the privy from the nearest well. In the city, however, the seepage of excrement, garbage, and offal into the water polluted the wells a short distance away. The effect was to spread typhoid through the city water system.

Since the early cities were ports, they were subject to additional health hazards. The immigrants, even the earliest ones, traveled in considerable filth. They inevitably carried sickness with them, particularly typhus and tuberculosis. Sailors brought with them the exotic diseases of the tropics, which roared through the cities in repeated epidemics. Yellow fever struck down nearly 10 percent of Philadelphia's population in 1793, and by 1795 had passed through Baltimore, New Haven, Norfolk, and New York. It struck Philadelphia again in 1798; New York was revisited with particular virulence in 1805. Yellow fever did not disappear from the northern cities until 1825. These epidemics promoted the first serious health-improvement measures. Philadelphia responded with the first municipal water system. The Schuylkill River was tapped for drinking water and wells were liberally drilled throughout the city so that the streets could be regularly flushed out (and so that fires could be more effectively fought). These measures seemed to have an immediate payoff when Philadelphia avoided the epidemic of 1805.

There were other epidemics as well. Cholera, for example, struck the country in 1832, 1849, and 1866. Malaria was widespread, especially in the South. Consumption was a major endemic source of death which spread continuously through the dense urban areas. Doctors and hospitals were of little assistance and perhaps of great harm. The reputation of hospitals was so poor that they received only the indigent, transient, and moribund. Drugs were often adulterated and, in any event, were of variable potency. Overdoses were probably common for this reason, as doctors tried to compensate for adulteration which sometimes had not occurred.

The healthiness of the cities probably deteriorated throughout the first half of the nineteenth century. There were reasons to expect improving conditions, however. The newer cities were smaller, and often they were not ports. Drainage was better, and health conditions were probably better than in the old cities. Nevertheless, where growth was rapid, sanitation levels deteriorated. It was not until the 1850s that the health situation began to improve, largely because of improved sanitary conditions. In the mid-1840s, municipalities began to insure that the drinking water was relatively clean. In the 1850s, closed sewers were being built rapidly, although as late as 1860, only one third of New York City sewage was moving through them. Water closets were replacing the privy. Hospitals began to improve. Nurses were being substituted for convicts as hospital labor. Sanitation was dramatically improved in the hospitals. Surgery was moving out of the wards and into sanitary surgical rooms.

In New York City, the death rate rose from 21 per 1000 in 1810 to 29 per 1000 in 1826 to 40 per 1000 in 1845–1855, but was back to 30 per 1000 by about 1860. Perhaps more revealing is the death rate of children under 5. Until 1835, that figure had remained about one third of all deaths. Shortly thereafter, the death rate of young children began to rise, reaching a peak at 56 percent of all deaths in the City of New York between 1850 and 1860. (Of course, the proportion of children under 5 years of age also rose some during this period, but not enough to explain the terrible rate of deaths.) In Chicago, in one especially bad year, for example, the death rate of children less than 1 year old hit 70 percent. In part, this was undoubtedly due to the sale of swill milk, which was gotten from city cows who were fed on distillery wastes. The cows themselves lived less than a year, developed numerous diseases, and when they died were butchered and sold to the poor. As late as 1890, Jacob Riis was attributing a part of the high death rate among slum children in New York City to the drinking of swill milk. More importantly, perhaps, before pasteurization milk was a carrier of bacterial diseases of all sorts.

By 1880, evidence was accumulating that urban health was at last improving rapidly. The census of that year notes that the urban death rate was at least one and a half times the rural death rate, but it adds:

> In this country, as elsewhere, the death rate in the cities is larger than in the rural districts, but how much larger we cannot state positively from the data at our command. As compared with the rural districts, the cities have been for the last twenty years gaining most in healthiness, owing to the fact that systematic sanitary work has been carried on in them to a much greater extent than in the small towns and villages. The larger mortality of cities is mainly due to the excess of deaths in the earlier years of life.[6]

Great advances had been made in medicine by 1880. Doctors had begun to realize the danger of infection and had begun the use of antiseptics. The germ theory had been proposed and was beginning to be widely accepted. It provided a rationale for those who had been arguing from the beginning for improved sanitation, although the pragmatic view that dirt caused disease and therefore to eliminate dirt was to reduce disease had been widely accepted before. Sterile procedures began to eliminate postoperative infections. By 1900, nursing had become a respected profession and the care of patients was greatly improved. Cleanliness, in the hospitals at least, became a passion. Conditions were so improved over the era when hospitals were for the poor and the stranger only, that private and denominational hospitals were being erected. It finally became certain that there was some advantage in being treated by the medical profession for a disease. Nevertheless, the major sources of the lower death rates were undoubtedly the improvements in sewage treatment, water supply, and diet that came with higher income.

---

[6] U.S. Bureau of the Census, *Census of Population: 1880*, vol. 12, *Mortality and Vital Statistics* (Washington: U.S. Government Printing Office, 1883), Part II, p. xxii.

While health in the urban areas was improving rapidly, rural health probably was not. In those states for which data are available, the urban death rate was running about 21 per 1000 and the rural death rate about 15 per 1000 in 1890. By 1900, the death rate in the urban areas was a little under 19 per 1000 and it was just over 15 per 1000 in the rural areas. While the rural areas were still healthier than the cities, the difference was no longer as great and was chiefly the result of the high death rate in cities due to infectious diseases among the children under 5. At some point in the twentieth century, health standards in the cities rose above those of the countryside. The availability of modern sanitation equipment, the greater numbers of doctors and hospitals relative to population, higher incomes, and the development of innoculation against epidemic-type diseases reduced the death rate in the cities despite their continuing high density levels.

To summarize, then, there was a dramatic improvement in health, particularly in the cities, during the last half of the nineteenth century. Improvement in sanitation and diet was probably more important than advances in medicine because the major gains came from reducing mortality due to the infectious diseases, but by the end of the period medical improvements were also of substantial importance.[7] Since infectious diseases are inherently more destructive in densely packed settlements, their control raised health levels in the city more rapidly than in the countryside.

Crime was a serious urban problem by the end of the seventeenth century, but fire was the major threat to safety during the eighteenth and nineteenth centuries. The magnitude of the threat was established early—Jamestown was destroyed in January 1608. Boston had eight major fires between 1653 and 1763, and the pattern of serious conflagrations in the young cities persisted until late in the nineteenth century. The great Chicago fire of 1871 destroyed some 15,000 houses, but the last great conflagration was probably the Seattle blaze of 1889 (apart, of course, from the fire that attended the San Francisco earthquake). The development of municipal fire departments to implement the succession of improvements in the reporting of fires, in getting equipment to them, and in fighting them, combined with the development of municipal water systems and the use of nonflammable materials in heating systems and in household exteriors finally reduced fire to an individual as opposed to a municipal disaster.

Immigration

Beginning late in the 1840s, immigration from abroad changed both quantitatively and qualitatively. During the first four decades of the nineteenth century, immigrant growth was less than 5 percent of the growth of the white population. For most of the next 70 years, although the number of immigrants fluctuated in long waves, immigration consistently accounted for more than 25

---

[7] We know more about health improvement in England than in the United States, and it is from that evidence that this conclusion was inferred. See T. McKeown and R. G. Brown, "Medical Evidence Related to English Population Changes in the 18th Century," *Population Studies*, vol. 9 (1955–1956), pp. 119–141; and T. McKeown and R. G. Record, "The Decline of Mortality in England and Wales During the 19th Century," *Population Studies*, vol. 16 (1962), pp. 94–122.

percent of population growth. The increased numbers were a continuing source of consternation to many "natives," but religion was a source of even greater enmity. The reaction to the Irish Catholics was swift, widespread, and ugly. By the mid-1870s, however, the Irish had won for themselves a special place in urban political life, and the crisis, if not the hostility, passed. Beginning in the 1880s, however, the onset of a flood of Italian and Polish Catholics, Orthodox Slavs, and Russian Jews reestablished explicit ethnic conflict. The temperature of the discourse is best revealed, perhaps, by some quotations from a leading liberal. The following are all from housing reformer Jacob Riis. Of the Italians:

> In the slums he is welcomed as a tenant who "makes less trouble" than the contentious Irishman or the order loving Germans, that is to say: is content to live in a pig sty and submit to robbery at the hands of the rent collector without murmur. . . . like the Chinese, the Italian is a born gambler. His soul is in the game from the moment the cards are on the table, and very frequently the knife is in it too before the game is ended.[8]

Of the Jews:

> Thrift is the watchword of Jewtown, as of its people the world over. . . . Money is their God. Life is of little value compared with even the leanest bank account.[9]

Of the Chinese:

> It is not altogether by chance the Chinaman has chosen the laundry as his distinctive field. He is by nature as clean as the cat, which he resembles in his traits of cruel cunning and savage fury when aroused.[10]

The hate-mongers were saved from mass boredom after immigration was virtually terminated during the 1920s by the substitute flow of rural blacks to the cities. Blacks did not urbanize as fast as whites during the nineteenth century despite a steady flow off the farms and to the North after emancipation. From World War I forward, however, black urbanization proceeded more quickly than white, so that by 1950 as large a percentage of blacks as of whites lived in the cities. Between 1910 and 1960, blacks changed from 73 percent rural to 73 percent urban. The rate of flow during the 1940s was especially extraordinary. In that decade, the urban black population grew nearly twice as fast as the native white urban population. Most of this higher growth rate reflected rural–urban migration, since the rural black population declined by 30 percent during the same decade.

The majority of rural–urban moves occurred within the South, usually within the same county, but there was also a substantial interregional flow. The trend north, west, and to Florida and the Gulf Coast set in just after the Civil War. Along channels that ran from Tallahassee to New York City, from New Orleans to Chicago, and from Houston to Los Angeles, the blacks fled the boll weevil, the mechanization of cotton picking, and racial injustice. Though pushed by adversity, they were also drawn by hopes of greater economic opportunity.

---

[8] Jacob Riis, *How the Other Half Lives* (New York: Scribner, 1920), pp. 48, 52.
[9] *Ibid.*, pp. 106, 107.
[10] *Ibid.*, p. 97.

The migrants were on the average younger than the black population that remained behind (although they were also disproportionately from among the old) ; nevertheless, they arrived in the city with below-average education and occupational skills. This vast flow put greater strains on the assimilative power of the cities than did the flow of foreign-born immigrants. The immigrants of the 1880s and thereafter were much more likely to settle in the cities than were the earlier immigrants, but they probably did not come to the cities in any greater proportions than did native whites at that time. They augmented a flow of natives responding to the burgeoning demand emanating from the urban industrial and service sectors. The cities were where the opportunities were then. Furthermore, the immigrants distributed themselves throughout the urban hierarchy.

The timing of black immigration and its distribution by city size has been less fortuitous. The deterioration of their position in the southern farm economy pushed the blacks into the cities even during the Great Depression, albeit at a reduced rate, and for reasons yet unexplained the blacks congregated in the very largest of the cities, at the end of the channels in which they found themselves.

> Fifty-eight percent of Negroes born in the South Atlantic division and now living else-where, live in the four northeastern SMSA's greater than a million (Buffalo, New York, Philadelphia, and Pittsburgh). Similarly, about 40 percent of the Negro lifetime migrants from the East South Central division have moved to the five East North Central SMSA's greater than a million (Chicago, Detroit, Cincinnati, Cleveland and Milwaukee). Finally, about 36 percent of the same group from the West South Central division live in the four Pacific SMSA's greater than a million (Los Angeles, San Diego, San Francisco and Seattle).[11]

The inflow of blacks into the big cities coincided in time, therefore, with the outward flow of manufacturing from the city center. Not only did the under-educated migrant face a market in which demand for unskilled workers was growing ever more slowly, but unskilled jobs were locating in places that housing segregation and mass transit routes made inaccessible.

The urban explosions that began in Watts in 1965 may be rooted in this historic process, but the connection is by no means direct. Even though half the adult nonwhite urban population of the big northern cities originated in the South, it is not from that group that the rioters have come. On the contrary, they are young and, to an overwhelming extent, long-time residents of their cities.

Even though black urbanites constitute the most immobile of all groups, they are nevertheless on the move, and it is the better-educated urbanite who is moving—migrating from city to city in search of the equality and the opportunity that is his right.

---

[11] J. F. Kain and J. J. Persky, "The North's Stake in Southern Rural Poverty," in The President's National Advisory Commission on Rural Poverty, *Rural Poverty in the United States* (Washington : U.S. Government Printing Office, 1968), p. 292. SMSA's are Standard Metropolitan Statistical Areas—that is, cities and their suburbs.

A FINAL NOTE: URBAN PROBLEMS
IN HISTORICAL PERSPECTIVE

There has not been (and probably can never be) space enough to situate every kind of urban problem in its historical perspective. We have not even touched upon such important aberrations as crime, environmental pollution, labor strife, congestion, and fiscal difficulties. Nor has it been feasible to consider any problem in great detail. Particularly sketchy has been the treatment of urban housing and urban poverty. Two additional points, however, must be made even in this brief chapter. First, it must be pointed out that some urban problems are, for all practical purposes, unsolvable. Second, it must be emphasized that American intellectuals have tended to extol the virtues of rural life and to denigrate urban life, while other people have probably held a more balanced view.

Success or failure in meeting some problems can be measured meaningfully against an absolute standard. In most circumstances, for example, rising life expectancy can be taken as an indication that physical health is improving. Even more partial measures, in most instances, can be reasonably interpreted as signaling an improvement. For example, if the incidence of tuberculosis is showing a marked decline, it may usually be said that health is improving, since such a decline frequently comes from a benign source. In dealing with other problems, however, there is no meaningful absolute standard against which progress may be measured. Poverty and housing are two such issues.

Consider poverty as an example. In the United States today poverty is generally defined as an income of $3600 or less for a family of four. Thus, it would seem that if a smaller number of families have that income in one period than was the case in all preceding periods, progress had been made toward eliminating the poverty problem. Experience, however, suggests that future generations will consider the progress to have been illusory. The reason lies in the subjective criteria by which a poverty line must be chosen. In what sense is $3600 an appropriate cutoff line for defining poverty? It is appropriate only in the sense that it seems reasonable to reasonable men at this point in time. At any earlier time, the definition would have struck nearly anyone as absurd. For example, by the current definition nearly 60 percent of all families were poor in the extraordinarily prosperous year of 1929.[12] Poverty, then, is a concept relative to time and place, and as time passes the income level below which people are considered to be impoverished can be expected to rise.

For the proportion of urbanites who are poor to decline over some long period probably requires that income rises very fast on the average and simultaneously becomes more equitably distributed. If the income of those at the bottom end of the distribution were to rise relative to the national average very quickly, reasonable men might feel that poverty was declining. This may have happened once in our history (between 1940 and 1944). If the more usual case prevails, with income at the bottom end of the distribution rising at

---

[12] Eugene Smolensky, "The Past and Present Poor," in *The Concept of Poverty*, First Report of the Task Force on Economic Growth and Opportunity (Washington: Chamber of Commerce of the United States, 1965). p. 46.

about the national average, then from time to time the poverty line will probably be readjusted upward to capture the rise in average income. For this reason, urban poverty will always be with us and in unchanging proportions, even though by some fixed standard the quality of life of the poor will have risen substantially.

Some problems, then, are always going to plague the city, while others will gradually be reduced in importance. Some few may pass away entirely, and from time to time completely new problems will arise.

As different problems rise, crest, and perhaps recede, one seems almost always to take on overriding importance and to become the focal point of policy discussion. Since World War II, for example, virtually every urban problem has been discussed primarily with reference to the drive of black Americans for equality. While everyone will admit that crime, blight, poverty, suburbanization, and the quality of public education would be serious problems even if there were no blacks, contemporary discussion emphasizes the connection between blacks and each of these. In the period from 1850 through the 1920s, industrialization, bossism, urban corruption and reform, slums, and poverty were attributed to the immigrant. Earlier urban problems, such as epidemic diseases, were attributed primarily to the innate depravity of the lower classes. The tendency to attribute urban problems to an uneven distribution of sin among classes of people and to search out the sinful who bear God's brand has repeatedly misdirected policy, prolonged the life of solvable problems, and confused the attack on those problems which are innately insoluble.

> The American city has been thought by American intellectuals to be: too big, too noisy, too dusty, too full of immigrants, too full of Jews, too full of Irishmen, Italians, Poles, too industrial, too pushing, too mobile, too fast, too artificial, destructive of conversation, destructive of communication, too greedy, too capitalistic, too full of automobiles, too scientific, insufficiently poetic, too lacking in manners, too mechanical, destructive of family, tribal and patriotic feeling.[13]

Yet it is in the city that not only the vast majority of Americans, but also nearly every American intellectual has chosen to live. One can only conclude that the discussion of the American city has been childish. The city has its hateful aspects. It is inefficient. Its scale is inhuman. Most of its architecture is monotonous. It is violent. Most hateful of all, it magnifies and irritates every blemish in the American character. But it is the best way we know of to organize space. Having chosen to pile ourselves upon one another in the cities, we cannot dwell only upon the costs of that choice. Certainly we cannot afford the puerile fantasy that we can have all the city's benefits and none of its costs.

We must, of course, struggle on to increase the benefits and lower the costs of urban life, but the benefits cannot exceed the costs by much. American capital seems to earn a return of about 10 percent per year. The city represents a form of capital, and its benefits are not likely to exceed its costs by more than this same 10 percent. We must strive for more, but it is stupid to be bitter when we fail to get more from our cities than from any of our other artifacts.

[13] Morton White and Lucia White, *The Intellectual Versus the City* (New York: New American Library, 1964), p. 222.

RETROSPECT AND PROSPECT

The distinction between urban and rural is no longer significant, for the urbanization of the United States is virtually complete. The meaningful distinction now is between the central city and its periphery. It is the centripetal force operating within cities rather than the centrifugal energy working within the nation that will now be crucial.

As in the past, technology will be a major determinant of urban form and it will pick out which cities will grow and which will stagnate. While it is futile to try to guess the long-term nature and direction of technological change, it seems fairly certain that recent trends will be perpetuated into the foreseeable future. Transport will continue to fall relative to production costs and communication will continue to substitute for transportation. Cities will therefore become less and less densely populated at their centers. Central places within metropolitanized areas will grow in number and size while central places between them will perish. Cities in the South and West will grow relative to those in the North and East. Transport systems indifferent to land and water will continue to proliferate, and the port cities will continue to grow more slowly than the inland centers. Romantic enthusiasm will continue its drift away from the glorification of the rural life toward nostalgic romanticizing about life in the old compact city. Futuristic dreams of a technology that will restore the dense city will be omnipresent, but they will be rejected in the marketplace. The sprawling metropolis will threaten the existing political system. The struggle, already under way, to find a means to govern in the face of a multitude of overlapping political jurisdictions will continue. Success will be limited. Poverty, housing, and crime will continue to be pressing urban problems, but the racial crisis will eventually pass. Technological change will ameliorate the problem of environmental pollution, but because assigning the cost of eliminating this externality is conceptually intractable, it will remain with us.

To conclude, then, it may be said that despite the end to urbanization, the interplay between the city and economic growth and between the city and particular socioeconomic problems will continue to make history.

SUGGESTED READING

Bator, F. *The Question of Government Spending*. New York: Crowell Collier & Macmillan, 1960.

Buchanan, James M. *The Public Finances*. Homewood, Ill.: Irwin, 1970, chap. 35.

Glaab, C. N., and T. Brown. *A History of Urban America*. New York: Macmillan, 1967.

Hoover, E. M. "The Evolving Form and Organization of the Metropolis." In *Issues in Urban Economics*, edited by H. S. Perloff and L. Wingo, Jr. Baltimore: Johns Hopkins, 1968.

Lowi, Theodore J. *At the Pleasure of the Mayor: Patronage and Power in New York City 1898–1958*. New York: Free Press, 1967.

Taeuber, K. E., and A. F. Taeuber, *Negroes in Cities*. Chicago: Aldine, 1965.

Tunnard, C., and H. H. Reed. *American Skyline*. New York: New American Library, 1956.

Warner, Sam B., Jr., *Streetcar Suburbs*. Cambridge, Mass.: Harvard University Press, 1962.

17
GOVERNMENT AND THE AMERICAN ECONOMY

Throughout American history, governments—federal, state, and local—have played a role in economic activity. The earlier chapters of this book have examined this role at many points, but our objective in this chapter is to provide a systematic survey of the government's relation to the economy. Specifically, we seek to explain (*a*) what factors have determined the different proportions, or mix, of government and private activity in the various sectors of the economy, and the changes in those proportions over time; (*b*) what factors have determined changes over time in the aggregate level of government activity relative to the total volume of economic activity in the United States; and (*c*) what objectively have been the effects of government activity upon both the rate of growth of income and output, and the changing pattern of income distribution in the economy. Of necessity, our discussion of these questions will be tentative, and more often than not it must be confined to suggesting necessary research, which in most instances has not yet been done.

The analysis in this chapter differs from existing studies of the role of government in attempting to provide a theoretical framework for government participation. This framework is developed in the following section and is then applied to the American historical experience.

THE THEORETICAL FRAMEWORK

The basic postulates of economic theory which underlie this entire book are extended in this chapter in an effort to explain the structure of economic organization and the political structures and policies which affect it. We assume a fundamental institutional environment and a particular pattern of preferences on the part of the population. Within these constraints the motivational force guiding the evolving political structure and the changing public–private mix of economic organization is taken to be the existence of potential economic gains perceived by individuals or groups—gains not currently being received by them but capable of being captured through some change in the institutional arrangements. We shall take into account also (as factors exogenous to our model) changes in the fundamental institutional environment or in people's basic preferences. Our objective is to specify what kinds of institutional arrangements will evolve in a market economy existing in a democracy in which economic decisions may also be made through a political process.

Sources of Institutional Innovation

The potential economic gains leading to institutional innovation are of three sorts: (*a*) gains that can be had from economies of scale, (*b*) gains deriving from overcoming market failure or reducing market imperfections, and (*c*) gains from income redistribution through the coercive powers of government. The first two of these involve also an increase in society's income and do not necessarily require any redistribution of income (although in fact some redistribution usually takes place). In the third case, the redistribution may be accomplished either by government or by a voluntary organization which has received tacit or explicit governmental sanction (trade unions and the American Medical Association are typical examples). Since the government is the source of all legal coercion, voluntary institutional arrangements to redistribute income must involve some restriction in supply which can be legally enforced only by government sanction.

We can see from this discussion that some institutional arrangements are purely voluntary. The corporation, for example, which was a quasigovernmental organization in colonial times, is viewed as a purely voluntary organization (although with well-defined rights sanctioned by law) and a major type of institutional arrangement to achieve economies of scale. The reduction of market imperfections may be accomplished either by the innovation of voluntary organizations or by an appeal to government. For example, where a wide difference in prices prevails between two markets because of lack of information or uncertainty, it may pay an individual to gather and sell information to encourage the arbitrage of such differences. On the other hand, when there is widespread piracy, brigandage, or theft, it may pay an individual or group to induce government to expand its military or police force to protect private property rights, so that the gains of the transactions can accrue to the individuals directly involved instead of to interlopers. In the case of a dam for hydroelectric power which would reduce flood damage downstream (and therefore benefit downstream property owners), the builder might appropriate a share of the downstream benefits by prior purchase of some of the downstream property (voluntary organization), or he might appeal to government to impose a tax on downstream beneficiaries and to reduce his own taxes proportionately (a government solution). These last two are examples of *externalities*—that is, of benefits (or costs) which accrue to others than the parties directly participating in a transaction and which may be internalized by a regrouping of property rights or by institutional innovations.

We can now be more specific about the forces making for market failure or imperfections. In our history general breakdowns in the market system have occurred in the form of depressions or recessions characterized by more or less prolonged periods of underemployment of society's economic resources. (Any market system operating on the basis of the individual decisions of consumers and investors is susceptible to such fluctuations in income and employment.) Imperfections in individual markets, however, stem from what may be called "transaction costs." These are the organizational costs of operating any economic system. The more efficient the system, the lower these costs will be. The efficiency of the system may be impaired if some of the benefits or costs in a transaction accrue to parties other than those directly participating. Such benefits or costs, being external to the enterprise, will not be taken into account in private decision making. In the above illustration, the return on the income from power sales alone may be too low to pay a power company to construct a dam, but the total return to society, computed by taking into account both the income from power and the benefits to downstream property owners, may be very high. The latter benefits are externalities if the project is financed by the power company, but they may be internalized if the downstream owners are made or allowed to participate in the cost of construction and operation. The costs of acquiring information and of bearing uncertainty with respect to the outcome of an action also may be considered as transaction costs. One assumption of economic theory has been that perfect knowledge was available in markets without the use of any resources to acquire it. In fact, information is costly, and the degree to which all possible prices are known is a function of the expenditure on information. While the cost of transmitting information enters into this transaction cost, its major component stems from uncertainty. Since the provision of a market for information or the creation of institutions to reduce or protect against uncertainty (such as insurance companies or futures markets) will reduce transaction costs, many organizational innovations result from the effort to reduce these costs.

Given the perception of profitable opportunities, individuals and groups will develop organizational forms (or institute legal changes) which will realize economies of scale, overcome market failure, or reduce transaction costs. Whether voluntary organization or an appeal to government will be chosen to accomplish these goals will depend on the relative benefits and costs of the necessary organization. Under either alternative, the cost of reaching agreement varies directly with the number of individuals who must agree: The larger the number involved, the greater the costs, unless an existing organization can be expanded or redirected.

But an additional cost is incurred in undertaking economic activities through the agency of government: Once having achieved agreement by recourse to government, the economic unit is subject to the coercive power of government in making subsequent decisions. For example, if I agree to the passage of a zoning ordinance, my subsequent uses of my property are restricted; if I wish to use it for purposes prohibited by the ordinance, I can no longer do so. In short, people who agree to put themselves within the framework of governmental laws are bound to abide by the decisions made by government (barring emigration or revolution as possible alternative courses of action). The decision rule in the United States typically permits a bare majority to decide policies which may adversely affect the well-being of an entire group. Yet small minorities with a strong interest of a particular sort are frequently able to enact policies against the preferences of a majority which does not feel very strongly on the issue. We shall explore this matter in detail later in this chapter. The benefits that accrue from the forming of organizations will of course reflect the degree to which they reduce market imperfections and the degree of effectiveness with which voluntary or governmental organization can do so. Government has significant advantages over voluntary organization as a result of its coercive power (a) to collect taxes, (b) to spend money, (c) to enact regulatory legislation, and (d) to appropriate property under certain circumstances with compensation to the private owners (eminent domain).

Whenever income redistribution occurs, either as the intended result of a new institutional arrangement or as a side effect, we should expect opposing interest groups to develop. As potential losses are larger and more concentrated, effective political opposition becomes more likely and the outcome becomes more uncertain. We have no body of political theory which can predict the course and final issue of such struggles. We can uncover some of the factors that induce individuals or groups to attempt new institutional arrangements, and in retrospect we can observe the result, but we cannot make many valid predictive statements. The following considerations, however, are relevant:

1. Since the costs of organization usually vary directly with the numbers of people involved, the organization of a large segment of society to redistribute income in its own favor is very expensive.

2. Since a legislative enactment to redistribute income in favor of a segment of society will benefit members of that segment whether or not they have been involved in achieving the passage of that legislation, it is to the individual's advantage not to incur the costs of involvement. (This is the dilemma of the "free rider." If all individuals act as free riders, they will all lose, but if only some become involved, they will bear the costs, while all will benefit.) Therefore, the most effective organizations in redistributing income are (a) those involving small numbers in which each individual perceives the relation between costs and benefits, or (b) those in which members gain additional benefits from which outsiders can be excluded. It follows that producer groups have been more effectively organized to redistribute income (as by tariff legislation) than have consumer groups, and that organizations that offer their members exclusive benefits not open to outsiders (such as trade unions and the American Medical Association) have been more effective than those which did not offer such exclusive advantages.

3. The political process in the United States involves the election of agents (representatives, senators, etc.) who actually enact the legislation. The interest of the agent is to maintain himself in office (i.e., to receive the approval of 51 percent of the voting electorate at election time). This means that under conditions of uncertainty about the behavior of the electorate he must cater

to many and conflicting interest groups. Under these circumstances, a "passionate minority" whose vote he will lose completely if he does not support measures to redistribute income in their favor will be effective against an unorganized majority whose members are more deeply involved by a variety of other issues. The history of farm legislation in the United States is but one of the many examples of this effect.

4. The potential benefits of redistribution will vary directly with the coercive ability of the government to appropriate wealth and income. An increase in the general taxing power of the government, an extension of its regulatory powers, or the enactment of a zoning ordinance—all such changes raise the potential benefits of redistributive efforts since they increase the benefits which can be received by a group undertaking such activity.

Disequilibrium

The dynamic forces which introduce disequilibrium into the system may occur as a result of changes in the basic rules of the game—for example, property rights or political franchise, as well as people's attitudes toward them—or as a result of forces "endogenous" to the system. We shall devote considerable attention in this essay to describing the formation of these rules of the game in the constitution of the United States and their subsequent modification by constitutional amendment and by the changing interpretations put on the constitution by the Supreme Court.

In our present state of theoretical knowledge we cannot incorporate changes in these rules into our theoretical model, even though we realize that our failure to do so weakens our analysis. Within the structure disequilibrium occurs from (a) changes in the size of markets, (b) technological innovations, and (c) a breakdown in the market system. Each of these factors deserves consideration.

1. Transaction costs are by nature "fixed costs"; that is, the cost of acquiring information is independent of the extent to which it is used. For a small number of transactions it may not be worthwhile to incur these costs, but as the number of users and the extent of use increase, the cost per user or per unit of use falls to a point at which it can be incurred. As long as the volume of mortgage business in the West was small, for example, it did not pay eastern lenders to send out agents to gather the information needed to deal in those mortgages. However, as the volume of western business grew, it became profitable to take advantage of the higher western mortgage rates and effect the arbitrage of this market. The cost of sending the agent was independent of the number of mortgages to be purchased. Other costs of institutional arrangements may grow with the volume of transactions but at a much slower rate. A functional relationship of this sort characterizes the organizational costs of insurance to cover risk and of police protection to private property.

2. Technological change has produced many cases of falling unit costs with increasing scale of output; more complex organizational forms have developed to permit realization of these scale effects. Another evident result

of technological change has been a sharp decline in the cost of information. The introduction of more efficient transport and communication media—from the fore-and-aft rig on sailing ships to the computer—has led to a succession of changes in institutional forms. Many of these innovations in communication possess the attributes of public goods—that one person's consumption in no way impairs consumption by another (television is the most celebrated and discussed illustration)—and this situation leads to the new problem of how to exclude nonparticipants.

New goods and services with public-goods characteristics are but one aspect of the more pervasive growth of externalities. The synonymous term "neighborhood effects" perhaps tells more about the indirect way by which technological change has led to such consequences. Technological change has produced, along with economies of scale, the factory system and the agglomeration of economic activity in the urban industrial complexes of today. The massing of people in vast metropolitan districts, together with their propinquity to productive activity, have led to neighborhood effects on a scale unimaginable in an agrarian society. Air and water pollution and traffic congestion are but three of the more obvious consequences of this development. The demographic revolution and the population growth of the past two centuries are essential parts of this phenomenon. Some neighborhood effects can be internalized by voluntary organization, but together they have been a major influence in the reorganization and redefinition of property rights through government intervention in the twentieth century.

3. A breakdown in the market system of any substantial duration, producing prolonged unemployment, may lead to a concerted effort to invoke the power of government in an effort to stimulate the economy. Indeed, prolonged unemployment frequently leads to political pressure to change the basic mode of organization in the direction of a planned economy. However, in the United States the direction of governmental activity has been to shore up the operation of the market economy.

Level of Government Activity

When we shift from the first question asked in this essay, that of the public–private mix in any sector, to the second question, pertaining to the aggregate level of government in economic activity, we must ask some additional questions. Specifically, we are concerned with the changes over time in the character of the demand for goods and services in the society, and whether the kinds of goods and services in growing demand are those which can be provided better by the public sector than by voluntary or collective action. In a society of growing incomes we may say that those goods that have a high income elasticity of demand—that is, those that will claim a growing share of people's purchases as their income rises—will influence the aggregate pattern of governmental activity. If these happen to be the kinds of goods and services that government can produce, or can play a role in producing, more effectively than can the private sector, a growth in the aggregate level of government will result, as we shall see when we discuss the twentieth century. The most important illustrations of this tendency are military and defense expenditures, which fit the category of public goods discussed above.[1] Such goods will fall in the governmental sector because it is to each individual's self-interest to avoid paying for such a good and to enjoy a free ride in its consumption.

The Results of Government Action

The third general question proposed by this essay, that of the consequences of governmental action, has been little studied to date. It is a surprising feature of economic history that while innumerable assertions have been made about the way in which governmental activity has influenced the growth of the economy or has redistributed income, few systematic studies have employed economic analysis and sophisticated econometric techniques to test these assertions. The tools are readily available. The impact of government upon economic growth can be studied by the techniques of benefit-cost analysis that have been systematically developed by economists over the past several decades. Essentially, the procedure requires an estimate of the social—as contrasted to the private—returns of a particular investment, and a comparison of these with social costs, to derive a ratio of benefits to costs and a net rate of return upon that investment.

The difference between this technique and a simple measure of the private profitability of economic activity lies in the value of the returns not measured by the marketplace. That is, where gains or losses accrue to other than the individual producers, investors, or sellers, we must attempt to measure the total returns to society as contrasted with the returns to the individual investor. The procedure usually is carried out by measuring the external effects of a particular investment—the benefits or costs to groups in the society other than those who would be concerned in a private transaction—and adding the result to the latter's measurement of the private (internal) benefits and costs.

When we turn to look at the influence of government on the distribution of income, the standard tools used by the economist in measuring what has happened to the distribution of income to different groups will enable us to assess consequences of governmental policy. However, as noted earlier and in Chapter 2, little such work has yet been systematically done; all we shall be able to do in this chapter is to point out directions for research and perhaps suggest the probable outcome of investigations which could be undertaken.

GOVERNMENT AND THE ECONOMY IN THE EIGHTEENTH CENTURY

This chapter is concerned primarily with the role of government in the America of the nineteenth and twentieth centuries; yet the heritage of our colonial beginnings played an important part in forming some of the institutions which have evolved and in the public–private mix in effect at the time of the Revolution and thereafter.

---

[1] In fact, if the government sector is dominated by public goods subject to increasing returns and the private sector is characterized by "constant returns," then even with identical demand functions in each sector, the public sector will increase relative to the private sector.

The Colonial Period and the Revolution

Before the American colonies were settled by the English in the early seventeenth century, the intermixture of government in economic activity had typically been characterized as mercantilist; moreover, the pattern of land ownership still contained many elements of a feudal society. Both of these aspects were carried over into early colonial America. Perhaps the most striking evidence of this fact occurred in the early years of the Virginia Company, when an attempt was made to recreate a structure of land ownership and property rights derived from late feudal society. As would be expected (from the free-rider dilemma), the communal ownership of land and communal division of work and proceeds left the settlers with no motivation to work; a gradual shift to a system of freeholds therefore took place in the first 20 years following the dissolution of the Virginia Company. The same pattern was repeated throughout the colonies. The existence of an unlimited supply of land meant that any restrictions on a settler's rights to the land could be avoided simply by migration.

Property rights to the land became established very early in the American colonies as the basic organizational concept for American farming. Since colonial America was primarily an agricultural society, a large part of it was composed of self-sufficient farms largely developed under these property rights. Since the externalities described above were not associated with agriculture, powerful governments and other complex institutional forms were not required. However, in the areas in which an export trade grew up, the situation was quite different. There the whole structure of British and colonial mercantile enterprise rested on the government's ability to reduce the risks deriving from ignorance of remote markets and the danger of piracy on the high seas.

There is still controversy over the aims of British imperial policy. Was it deliberately oriented toward redistributing income from the colonies to Britain, or was its aim simply to redistribute income from the rest of the world to the British Empire including the colonies? The Navigation Acts—which may stand for all the acts designed to integrate the economy of the American colonies with that of the rest of the British Empire—established specific requirements with respect to the structure of external trade and prohibitions against the production by colonists of certain kinds of commodities for this trade. Specifically, the major export items of tobacco and rice were enumerated —that is, it was required that they be shipped to Britain before they could be re-exported to other countries. Similarly, the major imports that the colonies received from other countries had to be shipped via Britain. Certain commodities which the British considered important to their economy, such as naval stores and (in the eighteenth century) indigo, were subsidized by the government in order to encourage their production in the colonies. Other commodities, like molasses from the West Indies, were taxed to provide a favored market for the British or British colonial product.

No overall assessment exists of the consequences of the British navigation policy on the growth of the American colonies or the redistribution of income in them. Until 1763, the characteristics of this imperial program were not a matter of serious disagreement with the mother country. But in the years 1763–1775 they became a critical issue. The immediate sources of friction emerged after the lengthy and expensive war between the French and English which lasted from 1755 to 1763. With its termination, the British imposed a number of taxes upon the American colonies which are a familiar part of American history. In the 12 years that followed, the controversy over these policies grew in vehemence.

What were the real consequences of these policies? Did they, as many colonists (as well as later historians) felt, slow down the colonies' rate of growth? Recent tentative studies suggest that the consequences were not nearly as serious as such views would indicate. It is true that a significant burden upon the colonists resulted from the enumeration of tobacco and other commodities. Imports were also more costly because they had to come through Britain. But it is equally true that the colonists received very substantial benefits in the form of protection from the Indians by British military forces and against piracy and privateering on the high seas by the British navy. Tentative assessments suggest that the overall burden on the colonists may not have been very great, but that there may have been significant burdens upon small but influential groups in the colonies. Further study will be required to see whether in fact there is a significant relationship between the burden upon particular groups and their political views, as for example in the case of the New England merchants, whose attitude toward independence was a major factor in the coming of the Revolution.

The Constitutional Period

The extraordinary era in American history inaugurated by the achievement of national status has implications not only for the growth of the American economy but for any study of economic growth concerned with the public–private mix and its effect on economic development. The Americans emerged from the war independent and in a position to develop for themselves a set of rules which would set their course for the future. The era of confederation and the subsequent decade of the 1790s represent a most interesting area for scholarly study; yet, surprisingly enough, no analytical studies have been made of the implications and the consequences of the institutions and organizational forms of government that evolved.

The newly independent nation in the 1780s faced two sets of problems. There were short-run problems inherited from the war; the other, longer-run problems required the creation of a viable set of institutional arrangements to permit society to achieve economic expansion. The solution to the short-run problems significantly influenced the resolution of the long-run ones. The immediate problems included the repayment of the substantial debts incurred by both the state and national governments in the war, the relationship between the several states and the Confederation with respect to the control and disposition of the public domain, the development of a monetary system, and many similar practical matters. Efforts at resolving these problems were only partially successful under the Articles of Confederation. The lack of taxing power of the central government inevitably gave the states a dominant hand in the matters of debt assumption ; the states also developed independent commercial policies with foreign countries resulting in a hodgepodge of different tariffs and tonnage duties deleterious to commerce and trade.

Yet the Articles of Confederation did produce some substantial results. Perhaps the most striking was the enactment of three land ordinances between 1784 and 1787. The first of these made it clear that the federal government was taking charge of the disposition of the public domain. The second laid out the rectangular survey system described in Chapter 4 ; the third developed basic provisions for the sale of public land to private individuals which, while modified many times by subsequent acts, governed the transfer of this vast supply of land and resources into private hands during the rest of the eighteenth and nineteenth centuries.

When Daniel Shays, former captain in the Revolutionary War, led a group of discontented Massachusetts farmers in revolt against the burdens of taxation, it became clear how fragile was the structure of law and order in the new society. Shays' Rebellion pointed up the need for unified policies among the states, which heretofore had gone their several ways with respect to entry fees, tonnage duties, tariffs, etc. The constitutional convention gathered in Philadelphia in 1787 produced a document whose provisions have remained as the basic set of ground rules undergirding the development of the American society and economy. The most important economic achievement of the constitution was the establishment of the central government's authority to levy taxes. In the short run this made it possible for the federal government to redeem its debts from the Revolutionary War and to assume debts that had been incurred by the states. In the longer run it created a system of public credit which became an important base for establishing a capital market. The constitution also assigned to the federal government the exclusive right to coin money, to engage in foreign affairs, to levy tariffs, and to negotiate treaties. Interstate commerce became subject to federal authority, a constitutional provision which strongly influenced the shape of future economic activity. The constitution prohibited states from enacting any law impairing the obligation of contract and created a supreme federal court to adjudicate disputes over jurisdiction and conflicts between laws. It gave to the Congress the power to develop a postal system, a common standard of weights and measures, and a patent system which provided further reinforcement for the rights of private property and enabled an inventor to capture some of the gains from his invention.

The Federalist program of the 1790s continued the enactment of basic measures, primarily under the leadership of Alexander Hamilton. Hamilton's *Report on Public Credit* paved the way for the assumption of state debts and the issuance of bonds to pay off debtors. Hamilton was also instrumental in promoting the creation of the first Bank of the United States to develop an efficient and stable monetary system. While his *Report on Manufactures* had less immediate effect, it contained an insightful analysis of the economy.

This view of the constitutional period has been colored by the classic work of Charles Beard, in particular his *Economic Interpretation of the Constitution*, published in 1911. Beard's argument was that the constitution was created by a group of delegates to the constitutional convention who had a direct financial interest in promoting their cause and that these creditors, merchants, manufacturers, and shippers, in the face of the threats of the propertyless class, created the constitution to protect the rights of private property. Beard's thesis, which is consistent with a Marxist interpretation of history, suffers from a fundamental and fatal defect. The issues of the time were not those between a propertied bourgeoisie and a landless proletariat, as Beard supposed. Rather, they were between the disparate interests of propertied groups, who wished to devise a set of rules specifying the rights and obligations of private property, particularly in situations involving conflicting uses. (See Chapter 4 on resource appropriation.) Beard's thesis required that all property owners have a common interest, or at least that they be willing to submerge any differences in the face of their basic conflict with the propertyless. In fact, all the issues involved in the creation of the constitution and the subsequent enactments of the Federalists concerned the ways that rights of ownership in private property might be clarified and strengthened consistently with the goal of creating maximum economic opportunity. Madison's celebrated *Federalist Paper* no. 10, in which he warned of the dangers of factions, has frequently been cited as supporting Beard's and the Marxian view; in fact, however, Madison's position simply recognizes the ability of a "passionate minority" (or majority) in an unregulated democracy to work its will to redistribute income in its favor. Madison viewed the constitution as establishing a bulwark against such redistributive arrangements through a system of checks and balances which raised the costs of such efforts.

Since no general analytical account of this period exists, we must await further research, but at least some tentative conclusions can be stated at this point. Clearly, the major achievement of the era was the constitution itself, followed by the enactment of the Federalist program which provided a framework within which property rights could be as precisely defined as possible, thus reducing transaction costs in many respects. Uncertainty was reduced by the enforcement of contract. An incentive to increased productivity was supplied by patent and copyright laws and their guarantee that the returns to intellectual property should accrue to the innovator. (Although Eli Whitney was later to record that they were far from effective.) Bankruptcy laws further insured that private property rights would be stipulated and enforced. A militia at home and a navy at sea protected property rights by reducing loss via internal disorder and piracy. In short, the whole structure of the institutions and the legal enactments of this period was designed to encourage the growth of the private sector by reducing transaction costs, with the supplemental result of shifting the private–public mix in favor of the former.

THE NINETEENTH CENTURY

The public–private mix in the nineteenth century underwent substantial transformation. At the beginning of the era, government intervention was widespread, particularly at the state level, as has been documented in studies by Oscar and Mary Handlin and Louis Hartz. These authors, as well as Carter Goodrich and his students, have amply demonstrated that the government at both the state and local levels did participate in a wide variety of economic activities, subsidizing some types, providing bounties for others, and restricting still others. By and large, the activities in which the state intervened were characterized by a high degree of uncertainty, and government participation served to redistribute risks more widely than would have been possible under private ownership. It should be emphasized that economic activity was always overwhelmingly private ; nevertheless, the American economic scene exhibited many carry-overs from mercantilist society, and the philosophy of tne period was that the state could and should intervene in a wide variety of areas to reduce uncertainties and to undertake projects which were considered "too risky to be undertaken by the private entrepreneur."

The Public–Private Mix

The changes in the basic institutional environment which occurred in the constitutional era played a major role in shifting the public–private mix in favor of the private sector. Voting qualifications were left in the hands of the several states, which not only restricted the franchise by property qualifications but also excluded major groups from voting privileges. The whole structure of checks and balances, the indirect representation of senators, the tripartite division of powers, as well as the reservation of power by the states, made any governmental efforts to redistribute income—at least from the rich to the poor—very costly. The specification and enforcement of property rights reduced transaction costs, thereby tipping the balance of advantage toward voluntary—and away from governmental—forms of organization.

In addition, several basic economic forces were pushing in the same direction. First, the size of the market underwent radical expansion. At the beginning of the century, except for those in international trade, markets were predominantly local, and most economic units either were self-sufficient or produced for local consumption. As markets grew in volume during the century, a natural consequence was a marked fall in transaction costs, since these are subject to economies of scale. This trend was particularly evident in the development of national and international markets for major agricultural commodities such as cotton and wheat. Falling transaction costs, favoring voluntary rather than governmental activity, were a major source of the shift toward private entrepreneurial activity.

A second source of organizational change lay in the new technologies of the nineteenth century. Larger-scale production with fixed, power-driven equipment permitted economies but required substantial capital. The result was the introduction of the corporation, its spread, and its eventual domination of most manufacturing and transportation enterprises in nineteenth-century America. Representing the classic form of voluntary organization, the corporation began in charitable and philanthropic projects and a variety of semipublic economic activities. In these roles it was endowed by the government with special privileges which gave it in essence a degree of monopoly power.

Corporations were direct creations of government, each one requiring special legislative enactment by the state ; and the early corporation was often in a position to capture most of the gains from an activity, since the formality of the chartering procedure made entry difficult. But with the growth of markets and economies of scale in production, the corporation became more and more an acknowledged form of private enterprise, and the state's function shifted from special chartering of individual corporations to passage of general incorporation laws which were adopted by the various states in the mid-nineteenth century.

In addition to scale effects, another consequence of technological change in the nineteenth century was the lowering of the costs of information. The development of steam railroads, the telegraph, the telephone, and (at the end of the century) the internal combustion engine, each led to a sharp fall in the cost of information. The fall in transaction costs and the increasing scale of economic activities raised the rate of return on voluntary solutions without comparably changing the benefits and costs of governmental alternatives. The unique advantages of government—that is, coercive power and an already-existing organizational structure—were no longer essential to realize these gains, while the great disadvantages of government organization—the costs of being bound by government decisions—continued.

The forces described above in general led to a public–private mix increasingly favoring the private sector over the nineteenth century. But other factors were pulling in the opposite direction. In the early part of the century, the primitive state of the private capital market in contrast to the relatively well-developed structure of state government made government flotation of state bonds for transport development preferable to private financing. As the capital market improved and investors discovered that even state governments defaulted on bonds in the early 1840s, this form of government participation declined. Nevertheless, in transportation policy new bases of government activity emerged. The most significant of these were the problems involved in ex-cluding nonparticipants from receiving benefits from the development of a certain kind of activity—particularly transportation. The development of rail-roads represents a classic case in which groups other than the producer of the service inevitably received benefits. The railroad could not charge each customer a different rate based upon the net saving he received from the railroad as compared to his next best alternative. Nor could it recover the benefits from rising land values and urban growth along its right-of-way. Thus it provided external benefits to customers and outsiders as well. If the benefits for which it could charge—that is, the private rate of return—were insufficient to induce a railroad company to build, a case could be made for government support to railroad construction.

Another area in which government expanded its activities was associated with its police power. The first such extension in the early nineteenth century was aimed at eliminating the Barbary pirates, and certainly was not contro-versial. Far more in dispute was the wisdom of the wars with the American Indians, which were lengthy and (relative to total government expenditures) very costly. Conceived in narrow economic terms, the army did gradually prevent the Indian from interfering in the great rolling surge of westward settlement. In another context, however, the results were the reservation system for the Indian and a century of costs associated with his alienation from American society, with the resultant adverse consequences for his welfare still evident today.

A third area in which the public–private mix favored the public sector was the growing investment in education. Americans became convinced in the nineteenth century that society stood to gain from an educated population and that since these gains were not completely capturable by individuals, public education should be subsidized or carried on by the state. The growth of the educational system was perhaps the most significant force in the shift toward public investment of all the types of economic activities evident in the nineteenth century.

Efforts by groups to redistribute income directly in their favor were sporadic during the past century and were concentrated among producers' groups. Certainly the most spectacular and most successful efforts were those by manufacturing groups to impose high protective tariffs. Later in the nineteenth century, a movement among farmers which began with the more limited objectives of creating producer and consumer cooperatives or banding together for social purposes gradually led to the large-scale intervention of farmers in politics. In this period, these groups made unsuccessful efforts to change income distribution by controlling price deflation or by capturing some of the gains of lower transportation costs which accrued in unequal measure to various users of the railroad.

The factors controlling nineteenth-century decisions about the public–private mix operated at three levels of government activity—local, state, and federal, and the relative significance of these levels changed markedly during the period. As markets shifted from local to state to national, the scope of political activity and its potential gains moved in the same direction. Thus, when farmers tried to regulate rates at a state level, they were told by the Supreme Court that since the railroad was in interstate commerce it could not be controlled at the state level (*Wabash, St. Louis and Pacific Railroad* v. *Illinois*, 1886). The Supreme Court's decision on this point hastened the change in the political center of gravity from the local or state capitals to Washington.

Areas of Government Activity

Major areas of governmental activity in the nineteenth century were investment in transport and education, disposal of the public domain, and efforts by producer groups to redistribute income. We shall examine each of these in turn.

The most substantial government investment in this century went into transportation. Two major obstacles to private development dictated the need for governmental intervention in this area. The first, already cited, was the problem of externalities in cases in which private costs exceeded private revenues unless some government action increased the latter. The second concerned the lack of a national capital market in the United States. Raising the relatively huge sums needed for the building of transport facilities posed serious difficulties, and the uncertainty resulting from lack of information made the purchase of bonds risky in the eyes of possible investors. The backing of government, with its guaranteed resources of tax revenues, made the prospect far more alluring. The state, therefore, became an important organizer of capital for transport service.

The first means of transport in whose construction government participated in the nineteenth century were the turnpikes. Organized as a corporate activity, the turnpike was typically a mixture of private and public endeavor. In New England and the Middle Atlantic states (except Pennsylvania), where the capital market was better developed, the turnpike, which usually involved an initial capital requirement of less than $100,000, was typically privately financed. But elsewhere in the United States, the states participated on a more substantial scale. In Pennsylvania, by 1822, approximately $2 million of state funds had been invested out of $6 million in total turnpike investment. In the western states most of the investment was made by governments.

We do not know the magnitude of the state investment in the turnpikes, but it was certainly nothing like the aggregate level of investment that surged into canals in the decades following the completion of the Erie Canal in 1825 and its successful operation. Unlike turnpikes, canals typically involved millions of dollars of initial investment. It is not surprising, given the character of the capital market, that the states played a dominant role in this area and by the time of the Civil War had invested approximately $102 million in canal construction.

While the turnpikes were built with a mixture of public and private funds and the canals (with the exception of the coal canals) were typically built with public funds, the railroad was predominantly privately financed. By the time it emerged, the capital market had developed to a degree that made private financing more feasible (i.e., bonds could be marketed at an interest rate that appeared profitable to the railroad promoter). Having said this, however, one should recognize that railroad subsidies were substantial not only at the federal and the state levels but even at the local level—and at each for a different reason. The incentive for local investment was provided by feverish competition between areas to capture the gains of cheaper transport facilities; in fact, therefore, it became at this level a scramble to redistribute the proceeds of the innovation. At the state level, the variety of supports for the railroad included provision of credit and loans to railroads, as well as substantial land grants. In Texas alone, approximately 27 million acres were granted to railroads for construction. The federal government in its turn granted an array of benefits including a drawback upon duties on imported railroad iron, which freed railroads from paying duty on this significant capital cost. Federal land grants for the building of transcontinental railroads ultimately involved approximately 131 million acres of land. (The Northern Pacific alone received 44 million acres.) Congress also provided direct financial aid to six railroads, loaning a total of more than $64 million for construction of through lines to the Pacific.

One area which became a predominantly public activity in the nineteenth century was education. Whereas in 1840, less than half of the total investment in education was public, by 1900, almost 80 percent of the expenditure was from public funds, with only elementary and higher education remaining as major areas of private investment. Table 17.1 shows the transformation that occurred.

The public land policy of the government did not represent investment by government. Quite the reverse; it was a source of revenue to the federal government throughout the nineteenth century, although a very erratic one and less remunerative than the tariff which accounted for most of government revenue. Public land policy, however, did represent a way by which a substantial asset, initially government owned, was transferred to the private sector. Its details and course through the nineteenth century are surveyed in Chapter 4. The consequences of this activity have been lost sight of in controversy over the alleged imperfections of the distribution system; but in terms of our concern about the public–private mix, it represented a vast shift of assets from the public to the private sector over approximately a century, surely an unparalled transformation.

The history of the tariff in the United States in the nineteenth century began with a small revenue tariff which gradually became more and more protectionist, the case presenting the prototype of a producer group effectively channeling resources in its favor. Daniel Webster's celebrated shift from opposition to the tariff of 1824 (when Massachusetts was still predominantly a mercantile state engaged in international trade) to support for the high tariff of 1828 (by which time manufacturers had come to play a more important role in state activity) was symptomatic of the transformation of the United States by the political process from a low-tariff to a high-tariff country. The result was to provide an umbrella under whose shelter domestic prices could be initially

TABLE 17.1
Expenditures for formal education (millions of current dollars)[a]

Fiscal Years	Public[b]	Total[c]	Ratio, Public to Total
1840	n.a.	9.2	—
1850	7.6	16.2	.47
1860	19.9	34.7	.57
1870	61.7	95.4	.65
1880	81.5	106.4	.77
1890	147.4	187.3	.79
1900	229.6	289.6	.79

[a] Includes public and private elementary, secondary, and higher educational institutions as well as commercial schools, special schools for the blind, and so on. Reform schools, orphanages, and like institutions are excluded.
[b] For 1850–1870, defined as all public sources of funds, including receipts from permanent school funds for common schools; 1880–1900 includes all public-school expenditures.
[c] Total for years 1840–1870 is income; thereafter, expenditures.

SOURCE: Albert Fishlow, "Levels of Nineteenth Century Investment in Education," *Journal of Economic History*, vol. 26 (December 1966), p. 420.

higher than they would have been without the tariff. As a consequence, income was redistributed from consumers to the producer groups and their employees, who were protected by the tariff. The tariff rose and fell with the interplay of sectional interests throughout the antebellum decades, but with the Civil War it became definitely protectionist and remained so throughout the rest of the century.

On the other hand, the efforts by farmers to improve their lot by a redistribution of income cannot be considered a nineteenth-century success, although it may well have paved the way for the results of the twentieth century. The first concerted effort by farmers took place after the Civil War. Because of their wide spatial distribution, the costs of organization were extremely high. Only a change in these costs could make it worthwhile for farmers to pool their efforts. Part of the necessary change came about because farmers were organized for other than political reasons, and this organizational apparatus lent itself to political uses. The Grange, originally conceived as a social club, was rapidly transformed into a political unit. Other farm groups were organized initially to protect against cattle rustlers or sheepmen, and for a variety of other immediate local private ends; once organized, it was only natural that they turn their attention to the greater political causes of the period.

If the costs of organization for the farmer had gradually fallen as a consequence both of the growth of national markets and the resultant fall in information costs (as well as the immediate factors described above), the benefits that he received had also radically changed. The farmer now saw his position as a relatively declining one in American society. Farm income stagnated during the 1870s; farm population as a percentage of total population and farm income as a percentage of total income were both declining. The farmer felt that he had a moral right to reap some of the benefits of lower transportation and storage costs that came about with the development of railroads and grain elevators. The Greenback, Granger, and Populist attempts to redistribute income fell into two categories. First, farmers felt that inflation induced by an increase in the supply of money (by the issuance of greenbacks and later by development of a bimetallic standard of gold and silver) would not only improve the lot of debtors but would also raise farm prices more rapidly than other prices and therefore improve farmers' terms of trade. Second, farmers wished to appropriate some of the gains of falling transportation and storage costs through legislation to regulate railroad rates and grain elevator rates. As noted above, the interstate commerce clause of the constitution precluded the seeking of redress at the state level and ultimately lifted the farmers' sights toward action at the federal level. The establishment of the Interstate Commerce Commission in 1887 was due to the efforts of all groups interested in transportation, including the farmers. However, it shortly became apparent to the railroads that the ICC offered an effective mechanism to cartellize the industry. While private efforts to regulate railroad rates had been short lived, the ICC proved to be a more effective instrument to accomplish this objective. This early success by railroads was a prelude to the further use of regulatory bodies in their own interests by those regulated at the federal level. The employment of government to eliminate competition and otherwise create monopoly conditions has become widespread in the twentieth century. At the state level, life insurance companies early dominated many of the relevant regulatory bodies for the same purpose.

The Level of Government Spending in the Nineteenth Century

We do not have complete figures on state and local expenditure in the nineteenth century which would permit detailed examination of the trend of government spending. As a percentage of national income, the government sector was small throughout the entire century. Table 17.2 summarizes the general trend of federal government expenditures in the period. It should be observed that activities associated with military endeavor—whether directly related to the army and the navy, or indirectly related in the form of veterans' compensation bonuses—formed a very substantial part of federal government expenditures in the nineteenth century. There can be little doubt that state and local government activities were more significant than those of the federal government for the development of the American economy during this era, particularly since educational investment was almost wholly within their purview.

TABLE 17.2
Expenditures of the federal government in the nineteenth century,
at ten-year intervals (thousands of dollars)

Year	Total[a]	Department of the Army (formerly War Department)	Department of the Navy	Interest on the Public Debt	Other[a]	
					Total	Veterans' Compensation and Pensions[b]
1900	520,861	134,775	55,953	40,160	289,973	140,877
1890	318,041	44,583	22,006	36,099	215,352	106,937
1880	267,643	38,117	13,537	95,758	120,231	56,777
1870	309,654	57,656	21,780	129,235	100,982	28,340
1865[c]	1,297,555	1,031,323	122,613	77,398	66,221	16,339
1860	63,131	16,410	11,515	3,177	32,029	1,103
1850	39,543	9,400	7,905	3,782	18,456	1,870
1840	24,318	7,097	6,114	175	10,932	2,604
1830	15,143	4,767	3,239	1,914	5,223	1,363
1820	18,261	2,630	4,388	5,126	6,116	3,208
1810	8,157	2,294	1,654	2,845	1,363	84
1800	10,786	2,561	3,449	3,375	1,402	64
1789–1791	4,269	633	1	2,349	1,286	176

[a] Includes tax refunds paid and capital transfers for wholly owned government corporations; thereafter, excludes them.
[b] Includes compensation for service-connected injuries and deaths as well as pension for nonservice-connected disabilities and deaths.
[c] Peak in nineteenth century.

SOURCE: U.S. Bureau of the Census, *Historical Statistics of the United States, 1789–1945* (Washington: U.S. Government Printing Office, 1949), pp. 718–719.

The Consequences of Government Policy
in the Nineteenth Century

What effects did governmental policy have upon the economic growth of the American economy in the nineteenth century? Certainly the most significant were the creation and elaboration of a set of rules which established property rights and reduced those areas of uncertainty associated with ambivalent property rights. A variety of decisions by the Supreme Court removed earlier constitutional ambiguities and gradually created a set of established principles with respect to property rights which strengthened the enforcement of contracts and the protection of intellectual as well as real property.

A more controversial issue which has pervaded the discussion of nineteenth-century policy relates to land policy. (See Chapter 4 for a more detailed treatment.) It has been widely argued by historians that the land policy of the United States hindered the growth of the economy and created inequality in the distribution of income. Both contemporaries and subsequent historians have contended that the policy encouraged speculation and discouraged actual farming, yet it is hard in retrospect to conceive of a land policy that would have encouraged a higher rate of economic growth. If the land had been held back for sale at higher prices, the farming of good land would have been delayed with adverse effects upon the growth of the economy; the actual program of selling land at a low price or giving it away served to put it into private hands and into production rapidly. There certainly were some shortcomings to the public land policy, however. Granting free land under the Homestead Act encouraged some inefficiency by attracting to agriculture people who might have been more productive in other employment. And until the Graduation Act of 1854, which reduced the minimum price on unsold land, some land was left idle which would have been put in production at a lower sale price. But in both these cases, the social cost was small. The unit of 160 acres set by the Homestead Act became increasingly inappropriate as arable land gave way to extensive grazing land in the arid West, where efficient use required a much larger tract. Ultimately, this situation led to gradual consolidation, but in the short run it produced malutilization and (in the celebrated fights between homesteaders and cattlemen) bitter conflicts as well.

The granting of 131 million acres of land to aid in the construction of trans-continental railroads has been equally controversial. The argument of opponents has been that this was simply a gift to a railroad monopoly and was not necessary to obtain construction. Proponents, on the other hand, argue that the private rate of return was too low to induce the railroads to build a transcontinental line at that time, whereas the returns to society were very high. When railroads were given part of the land along the right-of-way, they argue, the private rates were raised, since the value of these adjoining lands rose as the cheap transport created by the railroad became available.

Recently, a number of research efforts have been undertaken to attempt to answer this question. In his study of the Union Pacific Railroad, Robert W. Fogel concluded that the social rate of return on capital used in building the railroad was at least 29 percent, and that the private rate was 11.6 percent. A more comprehensive and conclusive study recently made by Lloyd Mercer shows a private rate of return of 12.9 percent, plus 1.2 percent for the proceeds of the federal land grant, and a social rate of return of 28.6 percent. The high social rate implies that the railroad should have been built; however, the private rate of 12.9 percent was probably equal to or above the opportunity costs of capital in other investments of equivalent risk. A decisive answer requires, of course, some clear notion of such actual opportunity costs.

Less information is available about the rate of return to investment in public education in the nineteenth century. The general impression is that it was probably high. Most economists today believe that the complementarity between physical and human capital in a complex industrial society requires substantial investment in elementary and technical education. These notions are reinforced by estimates of the returns on investment in human capital in the twentieth century. We are left to speculate about the nineteenth century; certainly much indirect evidence points to a high return and an important role for public education in the economic welfare of American society.

Overall, government investment probably did not play a major role in nineteenth-century economic growth. It was a very small share of total investment in that period. Some of it was wisely distributed and some was not. Even if the overall social rate of return on government investment was twice the market rate of return on private investment, it would still have made a relatively small contribution to the overall growth of the economy. Even in educational investment, in the absence of government activity, private expenditures would have been much larger. Education for those who could afford it would, however, probably have increased inequality in income distribution over several generations.

Our emphasis so far in evaluating the consequences of governmental policy has been upon economic growth. What were the effects on distribution of income? On land policy, no comprehensive study exists. Large speculators may have fared better than small speculators, since they undoubtedly had access to better information. Probably the major consequence of giving away land under the Homestead Act was a redistribution of income in favor of the homesteader and against taxpayers, both rich and poor, whose burdens might have been reduced had the land been sold. We are equally unsure about the redistributive effects of the land grants to railroads. Clearly, these provided a source of revenue for railroads; the railroads then raised the incomes of settlers in their areas—both those who bought the railroad lands and those on the sections along the lines retained and distributed by the government. Educational investment, as noted above, redistributed income in favor of lower-income groups, since the private educational investment which would probably have been undertaken in the absence of public facilities, would inevitably have favored those who could have afforded it.

Finally, a general effect of the fiscal operations of the federal government in nineteenth-century America was to redistribute income among the various regions of the country. The regions provided tax revenues, and those which were the major beneficiaries of governmental expenditure changed markedly during the century. The chief source of federal revenues was the tariff, which was collected in the major maritime states (particularly New York and the New England states) and rested on all consumers of the commodities upon which a tariff was imposed. Land sales, the other major source of revenues before the Homestead Act, tended to drain income from the newly settled regions in the South, including Washington, D.C., which made that region a major recipient of tax revenues. About 40 percent of the federal budget went for military purposes. The garrisoning of soldiers to fight Indians transferred revenues to the Rocky Mountain states. After 1860, the New England states also received large net transfer payments in the form of veterans' pensions and interest on the public debt accruing from the Civil War.

THE TWENTIETH CENTURY

In the twentieth century, the public–private mix of activities in the American economy has undergone dramatic transformation. Even the aggregate percentage of government participation in total economic activity (roughly 25 percent today) understates the role of government, since in does not take into account the increased regulatory authority that government has assumed.

Causes of the Change

The sources of the disequilibrium which led to the relative rise of government participation have been alluded to in earlier sections of this chapter. Twentieth-century war and depression are commonly charged with joint responsibility for the changing role of government in this period. As we shall see, they indeed played a dominant part in the transformation, but the story is more complicated.

First of all, the nineteenth-century institutional environment has been altered to change the costs and benefits of governmental institutional arrangements. Property qualifications for voting have been eliminated, and the franchise had been widened to include women and a more effective participation by blacks. While extending the franchise to women does not appear to have significantly affected public policy, the effective extension of the franchise to a low-income minority group can be expected to have significant impact upon redistribution policies. Decisions of the Supreme Court—particularly the liberal construction placed on the interstate commerce clause—encouraged government institutional arrangements; and in recent years, the Court's doctrine of "one man–one vote" has had revolutionary implications for the makeup of elected bodies—effects which are still being experienced. The extension of government taxing power with the personal and corporate income tax further raised the potential for governmental activities.

In addition to the widening of the scope of government by legal change, economic forces were moving in the same direction. Among these we may specify four.

1. Neighborhood effects—externalities associated with growth of an urban industrialized society—have been a major influence upon government activities. The growth of population and the characteristics of technology which have produced vast urban industrial complexes have introduced external effects into every phase of our society. Economic activities are now affecting the lives of "third parties" on a scale unknown in earlier centuries. Some of these external effects can be (and have been) ameliorated through voluntary organization. But it is only necessary to consider the noise of jets overhead, air pollution threatening health, water pollution destroying amenities for recreation, and traffic congestion throttling mobility, to realize the urgent need for governmental controls. Whether at the local level through zoning ordinances, or at state and national levels, undesirable external effects resulting from modern technology in an urban industrial society are a major source of the demand for more governmental activity.

2. The growth in demand for public goods—in particular the increase in military spending—has been a major factor in government expenditure. Spending on defense and military activity has ranged between a third and a half of the total government budget. A century marked by war has inevitably led to steep escalation in governmental activity.

3. In the introductory section, we pointed out the possibility of massive market failure as well as specific and limited market imperfections in our society. The depressions of the nineteenth century were of shorter duration and had less impact on employment than the massive breakdown of the system in the 1930s. This was an unprecedented phenomenon which persisted throughout an entire decade. The result was to undermine people's confidence in a market economy's ability to resolve its problems on its own. As a result, the Depression years were marked by urgent government activity aimed at increasing employment and bolstering the market economy. This participation by government has endured in the form of regulatory legislation intended to improve the economy's performance in specific markets and monetary and fiscal policies designed to overcome general market failure and produce a full-employment economy.

4. Changes in the composition of the electorate—particularly the relative rise of groups directly concerned with redistributing income—have been marked in the twentieth century. In the nineteenth century, it was predominantly producer groups that were in the position to attempt to redistribute income in their own favor, usually at the expense of consumers. The dominance of producer groups continued because of the relative advantage which a small well-knit group has in the costs of organization, compared to other groups. This advantage persisted into the twentieth century, resulting in more direct efforts to redistribute income through the electoral process. In a democratic society the voter is in a position to undertake direct redistribution of income. Yet not until the 1960s was any serious attempt made directly to redistribute income as an explicit measure of social welfare. The proposed negative income tax which has become a subject of controversy in recent years is a new aspect of the effort to use the electoral process for income redistribution.

The Expansion of Government

All of these factors have tended to change the public–private mix in favor of government. Searching for the origins of this change, we naturally look at the two world wars of the twentieth century and at the Great Depression which lay between them. But in fact we must go back much farther. The beginnings of the change could be seen at the end of the nineteenth century with the creation of the Interstate Commerce Commission mentioned above, and with the enactment of measures such as the Sherman Anti-Trust Act (1890) to set limits on business monopoly. Indeed, the end of the nineteenth and the early part of the twentieth centuries were enlivened by the activities of a host of reform groups disillusioned by the failure of a market economy to produce the welfare results they considered important. The so-called muckrakers, the Progressives, and the conservationists of that period were forthright in their vocal and written attacks on the performance of the private economy. The Progressives of the 1900s and 1910s sponsored further legislation to continue and extend government regulation.

A more drastic change in the role of government in the economy came with World War I. Government had increased its participation in the economy during previous wars, particularly the Civil War. But World War I required an unprecedented effort to reallocate resources to military purposes. In 1917 the federal government took over the operations of the nation's railroads; it also played a significant role in ocean transportation by organizing the Emergency Fleet Corporation for the construction of merchant ships. Through the War Industries Board, it exerted a direct influence in many areas of American industry. However, with the return of peace in 1919 most of these activities, including the railroads, reverted to private hands, and the government reduced its role in the economy to pre-World War I levels.

The 1920s in general were marked by a decline in governmental participation. The one difference was perhaps in the agricultural sector, where the persistence of low agricultural prices and a continuous effort by farmers to improve their lot led to sustained efforts to redistribute income through a series of agricultural bills designed to supply some form of price-support program in agriculture. Several such bills passed Congress; they were vetoed by two Presidents. It was not until the Depression that these efforts resulted in a price-support program for agriculture.

The Depression was heralded by the climactic boom and collapse of the stock market in 1928–1929, but not until 1930 did unemployment of a shocking magnitude appear. From then until 1933, the general course of the economy was downward. By March 1933, when Franklin D. Roosevelt was inaugurated, the American economy was in the grip of massive market failure— cumulative failure on equal a scale so unprecedented that no one had any clue as to what economic policies could reverse it. Under President Hoover, between 1930 and 1932, efforts had been made. The Reconstruction Finance Corporation earmarked $1.5 billion as loans to businesses in an attempt to tide them over the bad times. An additional $500 million went to the Federal Farm Board to stabilize prices, and the Hawley–Smoot Tariff Act was passed in the hope of improving domestic industry by cutting down foreign competition. None of these devices appeared to have any significant effect in checking the downward spiral. When Franklin Roosevelt entered office, the economy seemed near total collapse. Banks had been failing at a catastrophic rate, and the new administration's first act was to declare a "bank holiday." All banks were closed until they could be audited. When the sound banks reopened, they received encouragement as well as support from the government.

The new President's efforts to bring about recovery took a variety of forms. In an effort to raise prices and isolate the country from the downward movement of world prices, the gold standard was abandoned and the dollar price of gold raised from $20 to $35 an ounce. The National Recovery Act permitted industries to reach agreement about basic measures and even to collude for the purpose of raising prices in order to provide businessmen with greater incentive to produce. At the same time the Agricultural Adjustment Act was passed, designed to limit production by farmers so that farm prices, too, would rise. None of these measures appears to have changed effectively the course of the Depression. Accordingly, Roosevelt's third endeavor was directed at "priming the pump." In modern terms, this policy would be called "deficit financing"—a system whereby the government spends more than it collects in tax receipts. In 1936 and 1937, while Roosevelt was experimenting with deficit financing, John Maynard Keynes was providing an economic theory that could underlie such policies.

The efforts of the Roosevelt administration to achieve recovery comprised one facet of increased government participation in economic activity. Another major facet was reform. The basic assumption that a market economy could provide maximum welfare for its citizens had been fundamentally shaken by the collapse in 1929. Under Roosevelt, the philosophy was formed that government could improve upon the operation of an economy by far-reaching and fundamental legislative activity, especially a variety of social security programs. The projects based on this philosophy included old-age insurance, unemployment insurance, and workmen's compensation. In the initial stage, these insurance schemes produced some redistribution of income, since the insured had not contributed to the fund over a long enough period to pay for what they received back in benefits. The philosophy behind these acts was novel. It was based on the notion that society must provide for such groups either by private philanthropy or by other means. Governmental action appeared the most efficient means of accomplishing the result.

A second area of participation by government was in the issue and sale of securities and in banking. The stock-market crash of 1929 and the bank failures of the mid-1920s and early 1930s led to the Banking Act of 1933 which divorced investment banking from commercial banking. The Securities and Exchange Commission, to regulate the stock market, and the Federal Deposit Insurance Corporation, to insure bank accounts, were created; and the Banking Act of 1935 was passed to increase the authority of the Federal Reserve banks in monetary affairs.

At the same time that government was increasing the regulation of business, it was also providing a series of acts to encourage the expansion of trade unions. The Norris–La Guardia Act freed trade unions from the threat of injunction, and Section 7A of the National Industrial Recovery Act (which had enabled trade unions to organize and bargain collectively) was expanded into a separate piece of legislation entitled the National Labor Relations Act in 1935. This act became the Magna Charta for organized labor and underlay a great deal of the rapid expansion in trade-union activities that occurred in the second half of that decade.

Another area of government action in the 1930s took federal funds into a variety of water-resource programs, referred to in Chapter 4. The Tennessee Valley Authority was by far the most ambitious of these projects. Designed as an integrated program for multiple-purpose development of the entire Tennessee Valley, it created a set of dams, waterways, and power complexes for flood control, power, and recreation. In the Pacific Northwest, Grand Coulee Dam provided power as a by-product of its larger goal to irrigate a million acres of the Columbia Basin. The underlying assumption was that the gains to society from such activities—that is, the social benefits—were greater than the private benefits and that therefore they were justified although not privately profitable.

By the end of the 1930s, the federal government had taken on a new role in the economy. It had assumed an obligation to undertake a variety of activities and to intervene in a variety of ways totally alien to its earlier role. With the outbreak of World War II, government participation grew by leaps and bounds. The creation of overall price-control programs and rationing gave the government during the war years a degree of authority over economic activity which it had lacked in previous wars. Price control was reinstituted during the Korean War (1951). Since World War II, the philosophy of reform through governmental participation that gained adherents during the Roosevelt era has continued to exert a major influence on federal policies. With the Employment Act of 1946, the government assumed responsibility for underwriting a full-employment economy through monetary and fiscal policies. The Employment Act not only created the Council of Economic Advisers to the President, whose purpose it is to advise him upon economic policy, but assigned to the federal government the responsibility for preventing massive market failure such as characterized the 1930s.

Our description so far has emphasized the role of federal government in economic activity because its phenomenal increase during both world wars and the Depression overshadows the activities of lower levels of government. The greater participation by state and local government since World War II has come about mostly because of the dramatic increase in expenditures on education, public welfare, and highways. These have been largely state (and to some extent local) activities, in which, however, the federal government has directly or indirectly induced much expansion by the system of matching funds. Full exploration of the changing public–private mix at the various levels of government since World War II is beyond the scope of this chapter. It is alluded to here to suggest the continuing change in the federal–state mix in the direction of greater state and local expenditures.

The Level of Government Expenditures

To what has so far been said about the public—private mix, we need only add that the areas in which the government has increased its participation most abruptly are those whose products are in relatively increasing demand by society. This is particularly true of military expenditures and allied activities such as veterans' payments, bonuses, and hospitalization. This major public good has accounted for a vast share of overall governmental expenditure during the period from 1902 to 1962, as shown in Table 17.3.

Such defense expenditures have typically demanded well over half of the federal government's budget since World War II and have claimed as much as a third to a half of overall federal, state, and local government expenditures, as shown in Table 17.3. Of the other major increases in governmental expenditure, the second is education; the phenomenal rise in the demand for this service on the part of American society is mirrored by its growth between

TABLE 17.3
Federal, state, and local government expenditure,
by function, 1902–1962 (millions of dollars)

Year	Total Expenditure	National Defense	Education	Highways	Public Welfare	Stabilization of Farm Prices and Income
1902	1,660	165	258	175	41	—
1913	3.215	250	582	419	57	—
1922	9,297	875	1,713	1,296	128	—
1927	11,220	616	2,243	1,819	161	—
1932	12,437	721	2,325	1,766	445	—
1934	12,807	553	2,005	1,829	979	382
1936	16,758	932	2,365	1,945	997	602
1938	17,675	1,041	2,653	2,150	1,233	326
1940	20,417	1,590	2,827	2,177	1,314	694
1942	45,576	26,555	2,696	1,765	1,285	929
1944	109,947	85,503	2,805	1,215	1,150	1,532
1946	79,707	50,461	3,711	1,680	1,435	2,012
1948	55,081	16,075	7,721	3,071	2,144	592
1950	70,334	18,355	9,647	3,872	2,904	2,712
1952	99,847	48,187	9,598	4,714	2,830	638
1953	110,054	53,583	10,117	5,053	2,956	2,271
1954	111,332	49,265	11,196	5,586	3,103	3,963
1955	110,717	43,472	12,710	6,520	3,210	3,892
1956	115,796	42,680	14,161	7,035	3,185	4,926
1957	125,463	45,803	15,098	7,931	3,453	4,980
1958	134,931	46,127	16,836	8,702	3,866	4,339
1959	145,748	48,389	18,119	9,726	4,193	5,858
1960	151,288	47,464	19,404	9,565	4,462	4,862
1961	164,875	49,387	21,214	9,995	4,779	7,331
1962	176,240	53,225	22,814	10,508	5,147	7,910

SOURCES

1902–1957: U.S. Bureau of the Census, *Historical Statistics of the United States, Colonial Times to 1957* (Washington: U. S. Government Publishing Office, 1960), Series Y-412–445, p. 723.
1958–1962: U.S. Bureau of the Census, *Historical Statistics of the United States, Continuation to 1962 and Revisions* (Washington: U.S. Government Printing Office, 1965), p. 99.

the two years noted. Since education has typically been viewed as providing social benefits surpassing those that accrue to the individual student, it has continuously received governmental subsidization and therefore has grown at a relatively rapid rate. The scope of expenditures on highways has followed the rapid development of the automobile and truck as a principal means of transportation.

The rising claim of public welfare on the governmental budget is a modern phenomenon dating in significant form only from the Depression. In attempting to aid indigent groups in society who are unable to support themselves, these measures resort to one type or another of direct income redistribution. The last item included in Table 17.3 is the farm price stabilization program, which also has grown to significant size since the Depression, reflecting the success of the farmer as a "passionate minority" in his attempts to have the government restrict supply so that the price of basic agricultural commodities would not fall to a low level.

As noted above, military expenditures are the dominant source of the increase in the total level of government expenditures, and these together with the farm stabilization measures have been carried on at the federal level. Education, highways, and welfare assistance have been predominantly supported at state and local levels. These account for the marked resurgence of state and local expenditure relative to federal spending since World War II.

Consequences of Government Activity

The consequences of government activity both for the rate of growth of the American economy and for the distribution of income are hotly debated to this day. Unfortunately, the warmth of the debate has not been paralleled by any comparable fervor to search out and analyze the issues themselves in order to provide an objective appraisal. Clearly, such a task is long overdue: In a society in which government has undertaken such a significant role, it would pay the citizens to know how well it is performing. Few helpful appraisals exist today of even the effect of government's regulatory activities on individual public projects. We are left with no choice but to raise issues rather than to provide any clear evaluation of the extent to which the government's performance has changed the rate of growth or redistributed income in American society.

In recent decades, the most controversial issue has been the effect of the New Deal. Did the New Deal get the American economy out of the Depression? Did it redistribute income in favor of that one third of a nation which Roosevelt in the 1930s saw to be "ill-housed, ill-clothed, ill-fed"? We can offer only some tentative appraisals at this point.

Take the first issue: Did the federal government's activities lead to significant recovery? Clearly what ultimately produced recovery from the Depression was the advent of World War II. Even as late as 1941, substantial unemployment still existed in American society. Unemployment exceeded 15 percent of the labor force in 1940 and 10 percent of the labor force by the beginning of 1941. Given the state of knowledge in the 1930s about the forces making for business cycles and about appropriate fiscal policy, this is not surprising. In only two years during the 1930s did the operations of government at all its levels—federal, state, and local combined—have a net influence upon aggregate demand significantly more expansionary than they had had in 1929. The two exceptional years were those in which bonus payments to veterans were ordered by Congress—in 1931 and 1936—over the objections of the Hoover and Roosevelt administrations. While federal fiscal policies were somewhat more expansionary (in part as a result of the bonuses just alluded to), they were countered by deflationary state and local policies which canceled them out. At all levels of government, taxes had increased and more money was being collected than spent; thus the direct opposite of an expansionary fiscal policy was achieved.

Another objective of New Deal policy was a redistribution of income in favor of low-income groups. This policy, too, appears to have had at best very limited success, since the share of disposable income going to the lowest 20 percent of consumer units was 4.1 percent in 1935 and rose to only 5 percent in 1947. This figure appears to have fluctuated fairly steadily between 4 and 5 percent from the end of the 1920s until the present. The federal government's efforts to redistribute income included (a) the encouragement of trade unions, (b) the enactment of minimum wage legislation, and (c) direct income transfers. The National Labor Relations Act did promote union growth, and the Fair Labor Standards Act established minimum wages for workers. The price-support program for agriculture, as well as low-cost housing, the rural electrification program, and the Farm Security Administration were designed to provide a subsidy to low-income groups, but none of these achieved the success that had been visualized. In retrospect this is not surprising because only measures such as subsidized housing or social welfare programs could unequivocally and directly redistribute income to the lowest-income groups. It is not at all clear that trade unions lead to redistribution of income in favor of these groups. It is even more doubtful that minimum wage laws have raised their income. Indeed, the logic of economic theory would suggest just the reverse—that they increase unemployment among the least skilled workers and so increase poverty.

Today, government at every level plays a major role in economic activity. Does it promote growth or inhibit it? Does it redistribute income toward the rich or toward the poor? Our forefathers argued about this in colonial times with as much heat as we do and with not much more light. The difference is that today government is such a large share of total economic activity that we cannot afford such ignorance, and we do have the tools at hand to narrow the limits of the controversy.

SUGGESTED READING

Baumol, William J. *Welfare Economics and the Theory of the State.* Cambridge, Mass.: Harvard University Press, 1952.

Brown, E. Cary. "Fiscal Policy in the 'Thirties: A Reappraisal." *American Economic Review,* vol. 46 no. 5 (1956), pp. 857–879.

Buchanan, James M., and Gordon Tullock. *The Calculus of Consent.* Ann Arbor: University of Michigan Press, 1962.

Chandler, Lester V. *America's Greatest Depression, 1929–1941.* New York: Harper & Row, 1970.

Davis, Lance E., and Douglass C. North. *Institutional Change and American Economic Growth.* New York: Cambridge University Press, 1971.

Davis, Lance E., and Douglass C. North. "Institutional Change and Economic Growth: A First Step Towards a Theory of Institutional Innovation." *Journal of Economic History,* vol. 30 (March 1970).

Demsetz, H. "Towards a Theory of Property Rights." *American Economic Review, Proceedings* (May 1967).

Downs, Anthony. *An Economic Theory of Democracy.* New York: Harper & Row, 1957.

Economic Report of the President Together with the Annual Report of the Council of Economic Advisers. Washington: U.S. Government Printing Office, various dates.

Friedman, Milton, and Anna J. Schwartz. *The Great Contraction: 1929–1933.* Princeton: Princeton University Press, 1963.

Goodrich, Carter. *Government Promotion of American Canals and Railroads, 1800–1890.* New York: Columbia University Press, 1960.

Goodrich, Carter. "Internal Improvements Reconsidered." *Journal of Economic History,* vol. 30 no. 2 (June 1970).

Goodrich, Carter (ed.). *The Government and the Economy.* New York and Indianapolis: Bobbs-Merrill, 1967.

Handlin, Oscar. *Commonwealth: A Study of the Role of Government in the American Economy: Massachusetts, 1774–1861.* Cambridge, Mass.: Harvard University Press, 1969.

Hartz, Louis. *The Founding of New Societies.* New York: Harcourt Brace Jovanovich, 1964.

Hartz, Louis. *The Liberal Tradition in America: An Interpretation of American Political Thought since the Revolution.* New York: Harcourt Brace Jovanovich, 1955.

Heath, Milton Sidney. *Constructive Liberalism: The Role of the State in Economic Development in Georgia to 1840.* Cambridge, Mass.: Harvard University Press, 1954.

McAvoy, Paul W. *The Economic Effects of Regulation; The Truck-line Railroad Cartels and the ICC before 1900.* Cambridge, Mass.: M.I.T. Press, 1965.

Olson, Mancur. *The Logic of Collective Action.* Cambridge, Mass.: Harvard University Press, 1965.

Trescott, Paul B. "The United States Government and National Income, 1790–1860." In *Trends in the American Economy in the Nineteenth Century,* edited by William N. Parker. Studies in Income and Wealth, vol. 24. New York: National Bureau of Economic Research 1960.

INDEX

* Throughout the index the symbol (*) refers to a table or figure source note.

71 72 73 74 7 6 5 4 3 2 1

WESTMAR COLLEGE LIBRARY

| 0 | 200 | 400 |
Miles

ALASKA

HAWAII

| 0 | 400 |
Miles

| 0 | 200 |
Miles